EXPLORING ENTREPRENEURSHIP

2nd Edition

Richard Blundel, Nigel Lockett & Catherine Wang

Los Angeles | London | New Delhi
Singapore | Washington DC | Melbourne

Los Angeles | London | New Delhi
Singapore | Washington DC | Melbourne

SAGE Publications Ltd
1 Oliver's Yard
55 City Road
London EC1Y 1SP

SAGE Publications Inc.
2455 Teller Road
Thousand Oaks, California 91320

SAGE Publications India Pvt Ltd
B 1/I 1 Mohan Cooperative Industrial Area
Mathura Road
New Delhi 110 044

SAGE Publications Asia-Pacific Pte Ltd
3 Church Street
#10-04 Samsung Hub
Singapore 049483

Editor: Matthew Waters
Development Editor: Christofere Fila
Editorial assistant: Jasleen Kaur
Production editor: Sarah Cooke
Marketing manager: Alison Borg
Cover design: Francis Kenney
Typeset by: C&M Digitals (P) Ltd, Chennai, India
Printed in the UK

First published 2011
This second edition published 2018

Cover image: The Morph Wheel is the world's first foldable wheelchair wheel. The original patented design for a folding wheel was created by Duncan Fitzsimons in 2007. It has won multiple design awards and has been developed with generous support from the Royal College of Art and the James Dyson Foundation.

Library of Congress Control Number: 2017936381

British Library Cataloguing in Publication data

A catalogue record for this book is available from the British Library

ISBN 978-1-47394-806-8
ISBN 978-1-47394-807-5 (pbk)

At SAGE we take sustainability seriously. Most of our products are printed in the UK using FSC papers and boards. When we print overseas we ensure sustainable papers are used as measured by the PREPS grading system. We undertake an annual audit to monitor our sustainability.

CONTENTS

LIST OF CASES

LIST OF RESEARCHER PROFILES

LIST OF STUDENT FOCUS CASES

LIST OF FIGURES

LIST OF TABLES

PREFACE

We have written this book to help you to explore entrepreneurship in all its complexity and variety. Our approach is based on the view that some subjects, such as medicine, engineering, and entrepreneurship, are particularly well-suited to experience-based learning. The basic idea is that people can learn a lot more if they are able to connect the research evidence and the theory to some kind of direct personal experience. The nature of this 'experience' depends a great deal on what you are studying. For example, a medical student spends time working in different parts of a hospital, while an engineering student might design a new product or test some materials in a laboratory. Providing practical experience is more difficult for entrepreneurship students, but it is possible to re-create some aspects of a 'real-life' experience using new venture exercises, business plan competitions, and computer simulations. In this book, we provide support for all three types of activity. However, experience-based learning is about more than just having an experience. Some of the most important learning happens when practical activity is combined with well-structured reflection. With this in mind, we have designed the book around three related aims:

1. to help you gain essential practical skills and underpinning knowledge, and reflect on the challenges involved in creating an entrepreneurial venture, either individually or as part of a team;

2. to help you develop a deeper understanding of entrepreneurship, as you make connections between your experiences, relevant theoretical concepts, research findings, and the experiences of others;

3. to encourage you to take part in a broader debate about entrepreneurship in the twenty-first century, examining contrasting perspectives on entrepreneurship across a wide range of ventures.

In summary, this book offers a fresh, wide-ranging, and up-to-date approach to entrepreneurship, combining practical relevance with critical reflection. We also hope that it will help you to experience something of the excitement, uncertainty, passion, and sheer hard work that is involved in creating a successful entrepreneurial venture.

WHO ARE WE WRITING FOR?

We have written this book with three kinds of reader in mind. First, we are writing for **undergraduate and postgraduate students** taking courses or modules in Entrepreneurship and/or New Venture Creation, who are looking to develop a combination of practical skills, knowledge, and understanding. We have assumed that most of you will already have some background in business and management subjects such as marketing, finance, and operations. However, we have provided additional support for anyone with more limited business and management knowledge including concise explanations of key terms and suggested readings. Second, we hope that **current, early stage or potential entrepreneurs** will find it useful as they deal with the challenges of creating their own commercial or social ventures, or as they consider this option. Our approach is designed to help you reflect on questions that are rarely addressed in 'recipe book' guides to setting up a business. Third, we hope that our book will be a useful resource for **people working with social and commercial entrepreneurs** (e.g. in regional development, micro-finance, or enterprise support organisations), and for anyone who is looking for an accessible review of contemporary entrepreneurship in its various forms.

WHAT DOES THE BOOK COVER?

Exploring Entrepreneurship covers practical issues related to the creation of an entrepreneurial venture, together with reviews of related research evidence and more theoretical discussion about entrepreneurship. We also make considerable use of case-based examples, so that you can learn from the experiences of real entrepreneurs as they struggle to create and to develop their ventures. It is worth noting two distinctive features of this book. Firstly, it provides detailed coverage of many different types of entrepreneurship. You will find examples of commercial, primarily profit-oriented ventures and what are often termed 'social' enterprises, where the primary aim is to address a social or environmental challenge, rather than simply to secure a profit. In contrast to most other texts, it also addresses 'anti-social' forms of entrepreneurship, with examples that range from the unethical and environmentally destructive behaviour of legitimate firms to the shady world of organised crime. The argument behind these decisions is simple: entrepreneurial activity is clearly a very powerful force in the world. We think it is important for entrepreneurship students to consider seriously how that power is exercised.

HOW IS THE BOOK STRUCTURED?

The book opens with two scene-setting chapters, which are well worth reading before you proceed any further. Chapter 1 introduces the essential terminology, outlines our approach, and offers useful advice on exploring the subject in the remaining chapters. Chapter 2 looks at the wide variety of entrepreneurial activity that you're likely to encounter, highlights key similarities and differences, and explains why they are important to your understanding of entrepreneurship. The remainder of the book is divided into two distinct but inter-related parts:

Part One (Chapters 3–9) tackles the main practical activities involved in creating and building a new entrepreneurial venture. These chapters have a standardised structure, making them easy to navigate. Each chapter includes a number of cases (including video cases), practical activities and discussion topics, an annotated guide to further reading and a bibliography. You will also have a number of useful resources, including a glossary of all the highlighted key terms, on the Online Resources. These chapters can be used in various ways, so depending on your interests you can:

- Read through them in order as a concise, stand-alone introduction to entrepreneurship practices, with a particular focus on the process of creating a new venture;

- Treat them as a practical, structured guide that will help you to complete a new venture creation exercise, business plan competition, or entrepreneurship simulation activity;

- Use them as a resource to compare with, or benchmark against, your own approach to creating and building a new venture.

Part Two (Chapters 10–15) explores entrepreneurship from several different perspectives. Each chapter draws on some of the latest research evidence, along with the voices of entrepreneurs, researchers, and policy-makers. These chapters can also be used in different ways:

- A concise, stand-alone overview of contemporary entrepreneurship research and policy-making, with recommendations for further reading;
- A complement to the Part One chapters, enabling students, prospective entrepreneurs, and others to make connections between their practical experience, the experience of others, and relevant research evidence and to help you reflect on your experience.

Chapter 16 concludes the book, with a series of reflections on entrepreneurial learning and a summary of the main themes covered in Part One and Part Two.

WHAT'S NEW IN THE SECOND EDITION?

For the Second Edition of *Exploring Entrepreneurship* we expanded our authoring team. Richard Blundel and Nigel Lockett are joined by Catherine Wang, who brings additional insights and specialist knowledge in key areas, including entrepreneurial learning, ethnic minority entrepreneurship, social entrepreneurship, and international entrepreneurship. We have made a number of changes based on our own experience in using the book, invaluable feedback on the First Edition from many students and tutors that have used the book in a wide range of institutions, and detailed recommendations of six expert reviewers. Here, we summarise the main changes, particularly for the benefit of anyone who was familiar with the previous edition:

For students and other readers: we have added new chapters and features to broaden the scope of the text and to make it more useful and easier to navigate:

- new Chapter 2 – 'Varieties of entrepreneurship' to provide a concise and accessible overview of the field;
- new Chapter 16 – 'Reflections: entrepreneurial learning' to summarise the different approaches to learning;
- new case studies, including more international examples, new challenge video cases, 'Student focus' cases and additional researcher profiles;
- new 'Recommended readings' feature in each chapter, which introduce more advanced material for those wishing to pursue a particular theme in greater depth (e.g. as the basis for a coursework project or dissertation); we have also made these carefully selected articles freely available to view and download via the Online Resources;
- expanded Online Resources, including new web-based exercises.

For lecturers / course tutors: we have produced a number of new and enhanced resources, all of which are available by registering on the Online Resources, including:

- additional mini-cases with questions, suitable for seminars or short assignments;
- suggested answers to all of the case study questions featured in the textbook;
- new reveal videos for challenge video cases;
- improved Powerpoint slides for each chapter;

- revised testbank with solutions;
- new lecturer guide and author presentation, including practical suggestions on running new venture creation activities and simulations.

WHICH ASPECTS ARE GIVEN LESS EMPHASIS?

Exploring Entrepreneurship has an ambitious agenda, but clearly it is not possible to deal with *every* aspect of entrepreneurship in a single textbook, nor can we cover all of our chosen themes in equal depth. The main focus of Chapters 3–9 is on the challenge of *creating* a new venture, up to the point where it has secured the support it needs to become established. We do not concentrate on management issues in small *established* businesses (i.e. small business management). Rather than providing general introductions to the main business functions (e.g. marketing, human resource management, and strategy), we consider how these areas of activity need to be adapted in order to address the challenges of new venture creation. For example, Chapter 5 reviews emerging practices in entrepreneurial marketing and Chapter 8 evaluates different options for financing a new venture.

Entrepreneurship is an extremely complex, varied, and powerful social phenomenon, and it is well worth exploring in some depth. The best way to embark on such an exploration is to combine your own practical experience with the experiences of others, reinforced by research findings and critical reflection. For students, this often means completing a challenging new venture creation exercise, while also keeping a diary (or log book), and reading about entrepreneurship. This is not an easy combination to achieve. In our experience, students often focus on their new venture creation activity, leaving insufficient time for reading and reflection. It is difficult to balance all three areas, but doing so can lead to some very rewarding, and possibly 'life-changing' personal insights. We encourage you to make the most of this opportunity to explore entrepreneurship and wish you well on the journey.

Richard Blundel, Nigel Lockett and Catherine Wang

ACKNOWLEDGEMENTS

We would like to take this opportunity to thank the many colleagues, friends, and relatives who have helped us to produce this Second Edition of *Exploring Entrepreneurship*. It is difficult to identify everyone, but we would like to express particular thanks to the following: members of our publisher's international panel of expert reviewers, who provided informed and constructive feedback on the draft chapters, and numerous colleagues who kindly shared their insights and experiences as we developed particular sections of the manuscript. We are particularly grateful to Haider Ali at The Open University for his continuing contribution to the mini-cases and test bank on our Online Resources, and to the editorial, production and marketing teams at Sage, including Matthew Waters, Christofere Fila, Gemma Shields, Sarah Cooke, and Alison Borg, for their help in creating this new edition. Thanks to all the entrepreneurs interviewed for the challenge cases and case studies in Part One; Bruce Macfarlane, for sharing his considerable experience as a business angel and venture capitalist; other entrepreneurs and practitioners who contributed to our Part Two cases; the entrepreneurship scholars who were interviewed for the 'researcher profiles' cases: Per Davidsson, Sarah Jack, Othmar Lehner, Helle Neergaard, David Rae, Mary Rose, Ute Stephan, and Friederike Welter; and other researchers whose work features prominently in various Part Two cases and illustrations. Thanks to current students at the University of Lancaster, Brunel University, and The Open University, and to our many former students for their contribution over the years; we wish you well in your different ventures and hope you can keep us updated on progress. Lastly, to Beverley, Fay, Sandy, Mhairi and Georgie (NL), Tina, Freya, and Robbie (RB), Mohammed and Sara (CW), thanks for your unfailing support, encouragement and inspiration.

PUBLISHER'S ACKNOWLEDGEMENTS

Every effort has been made to trace and contact copyright holders but this has not been possible in every case. If notified, the publisher will undertake to rectify any errors or omissions at the earliest opportunity.

HOW TO USE THIS BOOK

Look out for the following features, which will help you to navigate and make the most of *Exploring Entrepreneurship*.

- **Learning outcomes** are listed in bullet point format at the start of each chapter to help you to focus your learning.

- **Case studies** illustrate issues raised in the chapter and provide material that can be used in practical activities, discussions and research. The narratives are often based on the lives of 'real world' entrepreneurs and their entrepreneurial ventures. The Part One chapters include a number of challenge video cases, which can be viewed on the Online Resources. Each Part Two chapter includes a 'Student focus' case and a 'Researcher profile', which are designed to help you understand the links between entrepreneurship research and practice.

- **Chapter summaries** are short 'bullet point' lists at the end of each chapter that highlight key themes and findings. You can also use them, in conjunction with the Learning outcomes summaries and the multiple choice questions on the Online Resources, to evaluate your knowledge and understanding.

- **Practical activities** are a variety of exercises that can be used by individuals and in team-based settings. The Part One activities are designed to improve your understanding of key issues and to provide practical experiences related to the venture creation process. Part Two activities provide opportunities to apply research methods and findings in a more practical way.

- **Discussion topics** at the end of each chapter encourage you to reflect on the techniques, practices, arguments, and evidence presented in the chapter. They can be used for individual study and as a basis for group discussions.

- **Recommended readings** are concise summaries of articles that you can use to get a deeper understanding of the topics covered in each chapter. Each of these recommended readings is freely available to view or download via the Online Resources.

- **References** is a full listing of the sources cited in the chapter and is presented in standard Harvard format. You can use these references, along with the Recommended readings, as a starting point for further study (e.g. when preparing an essay, project or dissertation).

HOW TO USE THE ONLINE RESOURCES

To support this text, there is a wide range of web-based content for lecturers and students at **https://study.sagepub.com/blundel**

FOR STUDENTS

- **Pre-reading guide.** Suggestions for background reading cover the functional areas addressed in Part One, to help those new to the subject.

- **Additional case studies.** In addition to the many case studies included in the text, extra case studies with questions provide the opportunity to apply what you have learned and analyse real-life examples.

- **Additional study materials.** You will find reference in the text to additional detail online of a particular topic. This coverage gives you a deeper understanding of interesting aspects of Entrepreneurship.

- **Flashcard glossary.** Glossary terms presented in an interactive flashcard format to help revise key terms and concepts.

- **Learning objectives.** Learning objectives from the book help you evaluate your knowledge and understanding of each chapter.

- **New venture creation checklists.** Checklists which cover the main tasks of developing a new venture provide a useful reference.

- **Revision tips.** Advice is provided on how to prepare for a new venture creation assignment and a reflective essay assignment.

- **Self-test questions.** Each chapter is accompanied by ten self-test questions that you can complete online. These self-marking questions include instant feedback on your answers and cross-references back to the textbook to assist with your independent study.

- **Challenge videos.** These showcase real-life entrepreneurs and freezes a moment in time when they need to make an important decision about their businesses. A few options are set out for the reader to then discuss in a group or consider individually.

FOR LECTURERS

- **PowerPoint® slides.** A suite of fully customisable PowerPoint® slides have been included for use in lecture presentations to save preparation time. Downloadable by chapter and picking out the key points from each topic, these also make a useful class handout.

- **Reveal videos for Challenge cases**. Access is provided to the Reveal videos of the entrepreneur explaining their decisions for the Challenge cases in Part One to help incorporate these video cases into your teaching.

1

INTRODUCTION

The heart of entrepreneurship is never about what we have. It's about what we do.

Jessica Jackley, co-founder of Kiva

If you've got an idea, start today. There's no better time than now to get going.

Kevin Strystrøm, co-founder of Instagram

LEARNING OUTCOMES

After reading this chapter you should be able to:

- Appreciate the economic, social and environmental significance of enterprise and entrepreneurship in the twenty-first century.

- Identify different interpretations of the terms, 'entrepreneur', 'entrepreneurship', and 'enterprise', including 'social' and 'commercial' forms, and adopt suitable working definitions.

- Understand the distinctive approach to studying entrepreneurship that has been adopted in this textbook, the purpose of its two-part structure, and how to make use of various components, including case studies, in order to connect entrepreneurial thinking, practice, and reflection.

- Explore entrepreneurship in greater depth in the remaining chapters by engaging with entrepreneurial practice, with a particular focus on new venture creation (Part One), and by critically reviewing different research perspectives (Part Two).

1.1 INTRODUCTION: ENTREPRENEURSHIP IN THE TWENTY-FIRST CENTURY

Welcome to *Exploring Entrepreneurship*. This short opening chapter will provide you with a general introduction to entrepreneurship, an outline of our approach to the subject and some essential tools and guidance for exploring the subject further. Exploring Entrepreneurship is concerned with the real world of entrepreneurial policy and practice. Though there is an enormous amount of variety in our subject, there are also some common patterns to discover, and many useful lessons to be drawn from the research evidence.

The rest of the chapter is organised as follows. In Section 1.2, we consider the scope of entrepreneurship as a field of study, and how to define some of its core terms (i.e. 'entrepreneur', 'entrepreneurial', 'entrepreneurship', and 'enterprise'). Section 1.3 takes a closer look at the rich variety of ways in which entrepreneurial activity takes place, and includes some discussion of the differences between commercial and social entrepreneurship. In Section 1.4, we introduce our distinctive approach to studying entrepreneurship, which builds on a combination of practical experience (both direct and indirect), critical reflection and drawing on a variety of perspectives.

1.2 SCOPING AND DEFINING ENTREPRENEURSHIP

1.2.1 The 'slippery concept'

So, what is it that you are studying? It might be reasonable to expect a textbook to be mapping out the scope of the field at this point, and providing its readers with some clear, unambiguous definitions of the key terms. Unfortunately, things are not that simple. Many years ago, the economist Edith Penrose commented that, 'Enterprise, or "entrepreneurship" as it is sometimes called, is a slippery concept, not easy to work into formal economic analysis, because it is so closely associated with the temperament or personal qualities of individuals' (Penrose [1959] 2009: 33). Today, entrepreneurship researchers, policy-makers, and practitioners are still struggling with this slippery concept, and there is a continuing lack of agreement over the meaning of these terms. So how should we approach the terminology? Clearly, it would be easier if we provided you with one universally accepted definition, but that would also be very misleading. The best approach is to recognise that people may use the same words, yet understand them differently. This is not a major problem because, as we shall discover, the range of interpretations is quite limited. However, it is important to be aware of these differences as you read about entrepreneurship, or listen to people talking about the subject. If you are not sure how they are using terms like 'entrepreneur', 'entrepreneurial', 'entrepreneurship', or 'enterprise', try to check their understanding. If you are still not sure about the definition that is being used, bear this in mind when you interpret their comments.

1.2.2 Key terms: 'entrepreneur', 'entrepreneurship', and 'enterprise'

In this section we review some of the key terminology and provide working definitions of three key terms: 'entrepreneurship', 'entrepreneur', and 'enterprise'. Additional explanations of these and other key terms can be found in the **Glossary** at the end of the book (see p. **442**).

These three words derive from the same linguistic source, the French transitive verb '*entreprendre*' (meaning literally to begin, tackle, or undertake something) and the associated noun, '*entreprise*' (meaning a company or business). The Irish-born writer Richard Cantillon described the entrepreneur as someone who specialises in taking on a financial risk in his celebrated, *Essai sur la Nature du Commerce en Général*, first published (posthumously) in 1755. Other eighteenth-century figures, such as English philosopher and political economist, John Stuart Mill experimented with alternatives such as, 'undertaker' (see Chapter 12), but over time it was the original French word 'entrepreneur' that became firmly established in the English language.

Given their widespread use in twenty-first-century politics, economics, and popular culture, the terms 'entrepreneur', 'entrepreneurship', and 'enterprise' are surprisingly ill-defined, and you can sometimes find people using the same word to mean entirely different things! Since our book is called *Exploring Entrepreneurship*, we are keen for you to keep an open mind on their precise meaning and scope for the time being. However, it also seems reasonable to offer you some working definitions as a starting-point for your studies. Then, as you discover more about entrepreneurship in the remaining chapters, you can develop a more fully rounded understanding of each term.

'Entrepreneur'

The term 'entrepreneur' has a variety of meanings. For example, in North America, it is often used to describe anyone who establishes their own business, whatever its size. But does it make sense to use the same word to describe a 30-year-old billionaire who has set up five Internet businesses and the 70-year-old, the semi-retired owner of a small picture-framing business, or a 40-year-old who sets up a community-based enterprise to provide work opportunities for homeless people? Some people argue that the term 'entrepreneur' should be more tightly defined. For example, they would only use it to describe people like the Internet tycoon, and opt for alternatives such as 'small business owner' for everyone else. The main counter-argument is that, while there may be considerable differences between them, there are also some common features that are worthy of more detailed examination.

The Organisation for Economic Cooperation and Development (OECD) and Eurostat have considered this issue at length. They operate an 'Entrepreneurship Indicators Programme' (EIP) in order to collect better statistics on entrepreneurial activity in OECD member states and around the world. Their definition of the term 'entrepreneur', which builds on previous reviews of the entrepreneurship research literature, covers people engaged in a wide range of entrepreneurial activities, including those who set up a new business:

> **Entrepreneurs** are those persons (business owners) who seek to generate value, through the creation or expansion of economic activity, by identifying and exploiting new products, processes or markets.

We will adopt this OECD wording as our working definition, but how do we resolve the problem of distinguishing between different *types* of entrepreneur? The most common solution is to insert adjectives based on the sort of activity that is taking place. For example, our Internet tycoon might be described as a **'serial'** (i.e. repeat) entrepreneur, while the picture-framer as a **'lifestyle'** entrepreneur, and the founder of the community-based enterprise is a **'social'** entrepreneur.

'Entrepreneurship'

The OECD and Eurostat's EIP team have also agreed on the following definition of the term 'entrepreneurship', which we can adopt as a starting point:

> **Entrepreneurship** is the phenomenon associated with entrepreneurial activity, which is the enterprising human action in pursuit of the generation of value, through the creation or expansion of economic activity, by identifying and

exploiting new products, processes or markets. In this sense, entrepreneurship is a phenomenon that manifests itself throughout the economy and in many different forms with many different outcomes, not always related to the creation of financial wealth; for example, they may be related to increasing employment, tackling inequalities or environmental issues. (OECD, 2016: 12–13)

This definition describes entrepreneurship as a phenomenon that is 'associated with' entrepreneurial activity. It recognises that, while the activities of individual entrepreneurs clearly play a central role, the entrepreneurship process extends beyond the individual, to teams, organisations, social networks, and institutions (e.g. rules and regulations, cultural norms). But what does it mean to describe a particular activity, or set of activities, as 'entrepreneurial'? While founding a small firm or social enterprise might in itself be described as an entrepreneurial act, the owners and managers often settle into a relatively stable routine and may even actively resist opportunities for further growth. The OECD-Eurostat definition recognises this distinction between entrepreneurial activity, which it sees as generating additional value by expanding economic activity, and the ongoing management of an existing firm. It is also interesting to note how the OECD-Eurostat definition acknowledges different **outcomes** of entrepreneurial activity, other than simply the generation of financial wealth. This is important because it recognises the role that both social enterprises and commercial ventures can play in creating 'social' value, either by contributing to social well-being or by reducing our negative impacts on the natural world.

'Enterprise'

This term is often found in discussions alongside entrepreneurs, entrepreneurial activity, and entrepreneurship. Though this English word is clearly derived from the same French source, a great deal of time and effort has been spent in attempts to differentiate it from the others. Another complication arises because the meaning of the word 'enterprise' differs depending on whether it is being used as a noun or an adjective. As a noun, the word is normally refers to a particular business venture. For example, farmers talk about each of the commercial activities that they engage in, such as raising sheep, growing wheat, or running a farm shop, as separate 'enterprises'. It is also used in the term 'free enterprise', to describe a liberal market economy with low levels of government intervention and in the term 'enterprise culture', first promoted by economists and politicians in the United States and the United Kingdom in the late twentieth century, and which has since extended its influence around the world (Della-Guista and King 2008; Burrows 2015) (Chapter 10). We also refer to individuals as 'enterprising', in the sense of being adventurous, dynamic, taking the initiative, and making their mark on the world. This meaning of enterprise does not necessarily mean that someone is engaged in 'entrepreneurial activity' as previously defined. For example, you might describe a polar explorer, a performance artist, or a human rights campaigner as 'enterprising' in this wider sense. To avoid confusion, we are going to restrict our use of the expression 'enterprise' to the following working definitions:

> ***Enterprise*** *is an alternative term for a business or firm, as in the widely used term 'small and medium-sized enterprise' (SME). They include 'social enterprises', which are trading organisations that serve a primary social purpose, and which can take a variety of legal forms, including cooperative, a limited company, and a community interest company.*

The enterprise culture *is a political project designed to encourage an increase in entrepreneurial activity and a corresponding decrease in the role of the state in regulating and intervening in the economy.*

1.2.3 The range and scope of entrepreneurial activity

Throughout this textbook, you will encounter different varieties of entrepreneurship, a topic that we address in more detail in Chapter 2. It is important to recognise that there is more than one way of acting entrepreneurially. As a consequence, the world of entrepreneurship is not exclusive: it is open to a very wide range of people. There are three main sources of variety: the way entrepreneurial activity is organised, the context in which it takes place, and the goals that it pursues:

- **Where is it taking place?** Entrepreneurial activity can take place in many different settings. For example, it might be a niche food business, such as The Kids Food Company, The Herbivorous Butcher and SuperJam (Case 3.3); an international fair trade business marketing artisan products from Kenya and Uganda (Zuri Design) or organic cotton sportswear (Gossypium) (Case 5.2); a technology-based venture, such as the telecommunications company Comtact (Case 8.4); or a social enterprise like The Big Issue, Belu Water, Divine Chocolates or Fifteen Foundation (Case 9.4). You can also find entrepreneurial activity taking place in established organisations, including large corporations, government agencies and charities. This is usually described as 'intrapreneurship' or 'corporate entrepreneurship'. Wherever it takes place, it will be possible to find some common entrepreneurial features. However, as we will see in Chapter 2, the context is also likely to exert a powerful influence on the kind of activity that occurs, the potential for growing it into a successful venture, and in terms of its economic, social, and environmental impact.

- **How is it organised?**: Entrepreneurial activity can be organised in a variety of ways, each of which has its own advantages and disadvantages. For example, by forming a limited company you can raise finance for your commercial venture by persuading shareholders to invest, though this may also mean 'giving away' some degree of control. Many small start-up ventures begin as unincorporated businesses; in other words, they do not have a separate legal identity from that of the individual founder. This might avoid some of the paperwork involved in creating a limited company, but it does mean that the founder is personally liable for all of the debts of the business and would need to repay its creditors (i.e. those it owes money) in the event of its failure. As they become established, start-ups are often converted into limited companies, though many smaller businesses remain unincorporated for the whole of their existence. Social enterprises can also be set up in a variety of ways, ranging from small unincorporated organisations operating locally, to more formal legal structures, such as 'Community Interest Companies' (CICs).

- **What is it seeking to achieve?** Entrepreneurial activity can be inspired by the pursuit of some radically different goals. For example, a team of university scientists may be motivated by the opportunity to launch an innovative pharmaceutical product. If the product is successful, it may save or improve the quality of many lives. In addition, the commercialisation of their intellectual property may also provide the scientists with considerable personal wealth. In contrast, a group of social entrepreneurs may be motivated by the prospect of using an innovative technology to help empower young disabled people; having decided to adopt a not-for-profit legal form, the founders will have no prospect of creating personal fortunes from their idea, even if it subsequently grows into a large and very successful organisation. At the other extreme, there are countless examples of entrepreneurial activity in the world of organised crime, whether it be protection rackets, drugs smuggling operations, Internet pornography, or prostitution. Here, the primary motivation is likely to be financial gain, with some secondary goals such as maintaining influence among powerful local figures (e.g. politicians, police forces) and possibly some attempt at securing community support.

Having discussed some of the key terms and mapped out the scope of the field, it is time to consider how to learn more about entrepreneurship. In the next section, we introduce the distinctive approach adopted in this book.

1.3 EXPLORING ENTREPRENEURSHIP: OUR APPROACH

1.3.1 Introducing the two part approach

In Part One of this text, we are focusing on the process of developing a new venture, from the initial generation of an idea/opportunity to the stage when it is converted into a fully worked out venture proposal that can be presented to potential investors, financiers, or sponsors. In Part Two, we look at some of the broader questions about what entrepreneurship is, how it works, and what it can achieve. So why are we taking this approach? We begin by considering the new venture creation activity, which forms the basis for Part One. All new ventures have to go through a process in which a 'raw' idea is refined into a coherent proposal. There is a lot of work to be done, and a lot to learn, in order to maximise the chances that a venture:

- responds to an attractive market opportunity or real social/environmental need;
- has the potential to add greater economic and/or social value compared to existing offerings and rival proposals;
- can be achieved operationally in a cost-effective way;
- is based around a realistic business model that is capable of attracting the financing required to achieve its growth targets;
- is being delivered by a capable and credible entrepreneurial team, with access to any necessary external expertise.

Creating a new entrepreneurial venture, even for the purposes of an exercise, is a very demanding task. One of the main challenges is to handle, and to integrate effectively, information and resources from several different fields (e.g. marketing, operations, human resources, accounting, and finance). You may have some experience of integrating in other courses (e.g. when analysing a strategic management case study). However, a new venture creation exercise presents you with a much more open-ended challenge. In most cases, you begin with a blank sheet of paper. Your task is to identify a need/opportunity in the outside world and to assemble a working solution in the form of a comprehensive venture proposal that can be defended in front of an audience of potential investors. Your venture proposal will typically be developed by a team of students, and written up as a business plan, possibly combined with a face-to-face presentation or a poster session. You can also complete the exercise working on your own. This will involve more work, but at least there is less scope for argument.

1.3.2 Part One: can you 'learn' to be entrepreneurial?

Part One of this book is focused on the practice of entrepreneurship. The focus on practice reflects our belief that entrepreneurship is something you can learn about, through direct personal experience and from the experiences of others. Some people argue, often in very forceful terms, that entrepreneurs are 'born' not 'made'. As entrepreneurship educators, you would not be surprised to hear that we take a different view – to quote the words of a popular management writer:

> *Most of what you hear about entrepreneurship is all wrong. It's not magic; it's not mysterious; and it has nothing to do with genes. It's a discipline and, like any discipline, it can be learned. (Drucker 1982: 143)*

Peter Drucker is surely correct in arguing against a simple genetic link to entrepreneurial success. However, your prospects of embarking on an entrepreneurial career will be affected to some extent by the place and time you are born, as well as by the people who surround you in your early years. It is also true that you will never become a successful entrepreneur simply by reading a book, or taking part in a new venture creation exercise. Governments around the world are also asking how universities and other organisations can promote enterprise skills and mindsets in the next generation (Jones et al. 2013; QAA 2012; Rae et al. 2012; Wilson 2012). In the past, entrepreneurship education was often divided into two distinct categories:

- 'For' entrepreneurship: this was seen as a primarily practical focus, where the aim was to develop entrepreneurial skills and mindsets;
- 'About' entrepreneurship: this was developing an understanding of entrepreneurship as a social phenomenon.

Though this is a useful distinction, our experience is that entrepreneurial learning can be deeper and more creative if the two aspects are integrated to some degree (Wang and Chugh 2014). It is widely accepted that a combination of practical exercises, study, and critical reflection can be a good way to open up your thinking about entrepreneurship. To develop entrepreneurial skills, a combination of entrepreneurial learning styles can be used, such as learning from experience, learning from peers, role models, and mentors, learning by doing, and formal learning in schools, colleges, and universities. We will discuss these learning styles in Chapter 16.

And where might those thoughts lead you in a few years' time? Over the years, we have heard from many former students who have gone on to set up their own commercial and social enterprises, and from others who are either working in 'entrepreneurial' roles within existing organisations, or are engaging with entrepreneurs as suppliers, customers, policy-makers, financiers, or consultants. In the closing case, we catch up with three recent graduates in order to find out about their experiences (Case 16.3).

1.3.3 Part One: chapter structure and contents

The Part One chapters draw on examples of successful ventures, and feature the voices of real entrepreneurs, talking about their experiences. Chapters 3–9 have a standard format. Each chapter begins with an introduction which includes a short opening case, which sets the scene for the chapter. This is followed by two further mini-cases, which explore the main chapter themes in more depth. Explanatory text and useful frameworks help draw the key learning points from each case and set these in the context of the chapter. At the end of each chapter, there is a case, which draws on an interview with an entrepreneur.

Learning from each chapter is also supported by a video case where we 'freeze' the action at a critical moment, allowing you to consider the choices open to the entrepreneurs at an important stage of their enterprise's development. These are available on **⑤SAGE edge™**. Watch the opening video case, featuring *Emma Sheldon*, to see how the business challenge cases work. Emma explains her challenge and then reveals her decision.

Each Part One chapter builds on the previous one to take you, as a prospective entrepreneur, from an initial vision – which might be little more than a rough outline of an idea – all the way to the founding of a living, breathing venture that can make a real difference to the world. In Chapter 3, we start with an overview of the challenge of turning an entrepreneurial vision into a coherent new venture plan and how it can be expressed as an opportunity business model. Subsequent chapters explore various aspects of that challenge: Chapter 4 – identifying and shaping entrepreneurial opportunities; Chapter 5 – providing leadership for the venture and creating effective teams and networks; Chapter 6 – analysing markets and industries and finding ways to enter them; Chapter 7 – designing and managing the operational side of the venture; Chapter 8 – financial forecasting and planning; Chapter 9 – raising finance. In other words, everything you are likely to need in order to begin the process of exploiting an entrepreneurial opportunity. Opportunity business models will provide you with a structured way of doing this. Put simply, opportunity business models are about the proposition, people, place, process, and profit of the new venture or the system of what the venture is about, where it will operate, who will make it happen, how they will do it and all importantly why. That means not just the financial return but the alignment of the venture to wider values as expressed by the entrepreneur, their enterprise, and the society at large (Table 1.1).

One of the main themes running through the Part One chapters is around entrepreneurial thinking, by which we mean the distinctive set of thought processes that drive entrepreneurial processes. You will discover how 'real-world' entrepreneurs think their way through practical challenges, often displaying a combination of creativity, determination and resilience along the way. We will also examine how this kind of thinking is

TABLE 1.1 Chapters 3–9: structure and dimensions

Chapter	Title	Opportunity business model dimension	System dimension
3	Visions: creating new ventures	Proposition	What
4	Opportunities: nurturing creativity and innovation	Proposition	What
5	People: leading teams and networks	People	Who
6	Markets: understanding customers and competitors	Place	Where
7	Operations: implementing technologies, processes and controls	Process	How

influenced by particular factors, notably the entrepreneur's attributes, previous experiences, social networks, and personal values. The reference to 'values' might sound surprising, but throughout Part One we will see how values are at the centre of entrepreneurial activity in the twenty-first century. Of course, financial returns are still essential for any entrepreneurial venture, but there is an increasing interest in creating enterprises with a strong social or environmental purpose – and there is strong evidence to show that people are taking these initiatives in order to live out their own values, something that can be more difficult to do when you are working in a large organisation.

In summary, Part One provides you with an opportunity to develop your own entrepreneurial skills and ways of thinking. We take you through the process of new venture creation in seven 'easy' stages, but it's important to recognise that things are much more complex in a real-world setting, because each of these sets of tasks is inter-connected. It is also imperative to recognise that you are not working through a 'one-off' process, but rather embarking on a continuous cycle of learning, which is as much about yourself as it is about your new enterprise (Figure 1.1). Entrepreneurship cannot be reduced to a straightforward linear process, or a series of predictable steps that can be reproduced in any situation – like replicating a formula. It is more like a learning cycle (Mumford 1997; Cope and Watts 2000; Corbett 2005), which accelerates rapidly as soon as you begin to engage in any kind of entrepreneurial activity. This might also go some way to explaining why successful entrepreneurs can become serial entrepreneurs (e.g. Cases 4.4, 7.4, and 16.1).

Books need to be structured in some kind of logical sequence. However, real life – including the practice of entrepreneurship – is not so straightforward. So though we have to

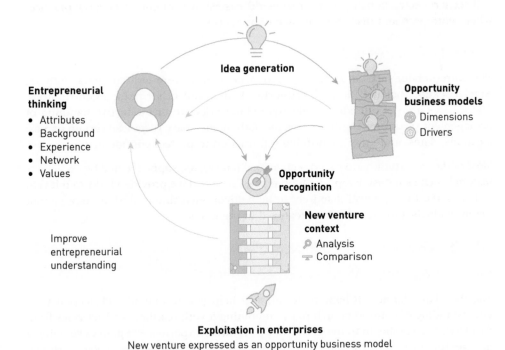

FIGURE 1.1 Our approach to entrepreneurial learning.

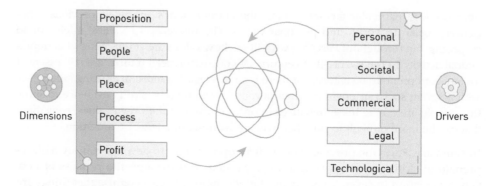

FIGURE 1.2 An atomic metaphor for entrepreneurship.

structure our exploration of entrepreneurship in a linear way, the reality (or 'lived experience') of the entrepreneur is rather different. Entrepreneurial practice involves all of the activities we will discuss in the Part One chapters. Each of these activities influences the others (e.g. marketing decisions affect financing, and vice versa), and they continue to circle around an opportunity that is itself in motion, continuing to evolve as you move towards the creation of your venture. In other words, entrepreneurship is not so much a simple linear process as a series of dynamic, inter-related activities, closer to the traditional image of electrons (dimensions) orbiting a nucleus (vision) that are constantly being buffeted by external forces (drivers) (Figure 1.2).

Our atomic metaphor may still sound rather abstract and remote from reality but you will see it reflected in many of the 'real-world' case studies of entrepreneurial practice, where entrepreneurs discuss their own experiences.

A note about the featured cases

The entrepreneur cases in *Exploring Entrepreneurship* were written by the authors, Nigel Lockett, Richard Blundel, Catherine Wang, and other named contributors. These cases are not intended to illustrate either effective or ineffective handling of management situations. In some cases the authors may have disguised certain names, locations, dates, and other identifying information to protect confidentiality.

Most of the case studies are based on personal interviews, supplemented by secondary material such as industry reports. Where possible, we have provided links to relevant websites and to other useful sources to help anyone wishing to find out more about the individuals and organisations featured in the cases.

1.4 RESEARCHING ENTREPRENEURSHIP

1.4.1 Part Two: new insights and perspectives

The Part Two chapters (Chapters 10–16) will help you to extend and deepen your understanding of entrepreneurship. By combining it with readings and activities from Part One, you can begin to integrate your own direct experience (e.g. in developing a new venture proposal), the indirect experiences of 'real-world' entrepreneurs that you read about in the case studies, and an extensive body of academic research that has

TABLE 1.2 Chapters 10–16: perspectives on entrepreneurship

Chapter	Title
10	Research matters: an overview
11	Individual perspectives: beyond the 'heroic' entrepreneur
12	Social perspectives: understanding people and places
13	Economic perspectives: influences and impacts
14	Historical perspectives: the 'long view'
15	Political perspectives: from policy to practice
16	Reflection: Entrepreneurial learning

examined many different aspects of the subject. Individual entrepreneurs often know a great deal about the specifics of their own enterprises and can also have a really sophisticated understanding of their own industry sector. However, their approach may not be as effective in another context. As Chapter 2 demonstrates, there is a wide variety of forms of entrepreneurial practice around the world, so there is a great deal to gain by broadening your perspective. You can use entrepreneurship research to gain these additional insights. Chapter 10 provides an overview of the field and shows why 'research matters' to the worlds of policy and practice. The remaining chapters focus on a different area of entrepreneurship research, explaining the approaches that researchers have adopted, highlighting key findings and drawing out the practical implications. Each Part Two chapter includes a 'Student Focus' case, which illustrates how entrepreneurship students have made use of research in their studies, and a 'Researcher profile', where we have interviewed leading entrepreneurship researchers about their work. The structure of Part Two is summarised in Table 1.2. Chapter 10 provides a more detailed introduction to the approach adopted.

1.5 SUMMARY

- Entrepreneurial activity is a complex and powerful phenomenon. It has positive and negative impacts on economies, societies, and the natural environment. For these reasons, it is well worth exploring entrepreneurship in greater depth, whether you are an existing or prospective entrepreneur, someone who engages with entrepreneurs, or simply someone who is interested in how the world works.

- Entrepreneurship is a slippery concept. The four core terms, 'entrepreneur', 'entrepreneurial', 'entrepreneurship', and 'enterprise' are each open to different interpretations. In order to avoid confusion it is important to: (a) recognise the different meanings that other people attribute to these terms; (b) make your own definitions and assumptions clear.

- This textbook adopts a distinctive approach to studying entrepreneurship. It encourages readers to develop their own capacity for entrepreneurial learning and critical reflection. The two-part structure, and features such as the new venture creation activity, critical incident cases, and further reading guides, provide opportunities for you to integrate learning: (a) from your own experience; (b) from real-world entrepreneurs; and (c) from leading entrepreneurship researchers.

Practical activities

1. How entrepreneurial do you think you are?

Complete the questionnaire at one of the websites listed on the Online Resources, or one recommended by your tutor, and obtain the results of the assessment.

- Do the findings reflect your own assessment of your entrepreneurial abilities and/or potential, and that of your friends and family? Do you think you can increase your capacity to act entrepreneurially by studying the subject in this way? Did these results affect your view?

- What do the entrepreneurs say? Conduct a quick online search for written accounts in which entrepreneurs talk about their experiences. Select one account and find out about the person's motivations and how these have influenced the kinds of ventures they have created. You can use the following questions as a guide, but feel free to adapt them, or to add your own questions: (a) Why did you want to become an entrepreneur? (b) What kind of activities are you engaged in? (c) Who else is involved in the venture? (d) What are your ambitions for the future? (e) What lessons have you learned along the way? Summarise your findings in the form of a 1,000 word report or a short presentation.

2. What's happening in your area?

Conduct a web search of your city, town or region to identify: (a) five successful entrepreneurial ventures, including a mix of social and commercial enterprises; (b) five organisations encouraging or supporting entrepreneurship and enterprise-related activities, including commercial, public sector, and voluntary sector providers. Prepare a table, with summary information on each organisation, including their history and objectives.

Discussion topics

1. Why am I studying entrepreneurship?

Based on previous experience, we guess that you are probably starting this exploration of entrepreneurship with one, or possibly several, of the following thoughts in your mind:

- I already consider myself to be an entrepreneur, but think it might be useful to fill some gaps in my experience or to 'test out' a venture concept;

- I definitely want to set up my own business but feel the need to gain some relevant skills and get some ideas for potential ventures;

- I am wondering if I have 'what it takes' to be an entrepreneur, and want to find out in a 'safe' environment;

- I want to know how entrepreneurship links into other subjects, such as strategy and economics (e.g. how it relates to economic growth and competitive advantage);

- I am mainly interested in the social and cultural aspects of entrepreneurship (e.g. the role of gender, ethnicity, and family background);

- I am basically critical of entrepreneurship, and see it doing lasting damage to societies and the natural environment;

- To be honest, my main reason for selecting this course was: (a) someone recommended it; (b) it fits my timetable; or (c) there is no exam!

Spend a few minutes thinking through your reasons for studying entrepreneurship, then discuss with others. Is there a common pattern? Do you think your initial motivation might change as you study the subject further? Keep a record of this discussion, and refer back to it once you have completed your course and/or this book.

2. What does it take to be an entrepreneur?

This chapter has highlighted the many different qualities that have been associated with 'being an entrepreneur', and the wide variety of activities that have been defined as 'entrepreneurial'. Prepare three lists stating what you consider to be the minimum requirements needed in order for someone to:

- Be a prospective entrepreneur?
- Act entrepreneurially?
- Become a successful entrepreneur?

After completing your three lists, compare them and see if there are any differences. How did you identify these requirements? Retain your list and review it again, when you have completed most of the book and/or your course of study.

Recommended reading

These readings address important topics in entrepreneurial practice and are recommended for anyone wanting to build on the material covered in this chapter. Recommended readings have been selected from leading Sage journals and are freely available for readers of this textbook to download via the Online Resources.

Zulfiqar, S., Sohail, K., and Qureshi, M. S. (2016) 'Sam's Cake Factory: a delectable journey of a woman entrepreneur'. *Asian Journal of Management Cases*, 13, 2: 67–81.

This article is a case study that reflects on the life of a woman entrepreneur, Sumaira Waseem, who had set up an online cake business by the name of Sam's Cake Factory. Sam's Cake Factory was a start-up, which was only four years old but had become the preferred choice among the consumers looking for customised fondant cakes in the city of Karachi, Pakistan. The case describes the entrepreneurial journey embarked upon by Sumaira who, through her passion, resilience, and creativity, turned a home-based small business into a full-fledged growing enterprise. The case further examines the vision Sumaira had of expanding her business and taking it to the next level.

Imas, J. M., Wilson, N., and Weston, A. (2012) 'Barefoot entrepreneurs'. *Organization*, 19, 5: 563–85.

The authors of this article explore what they describe as 'barefoot' entrepreneur[ing], meaning the entrepreneurial practices and narratives of individuals who live primarily in marginal, poor, and excluded places and contexts. By sharing the stories of barefoot entrepreneurs in deprived areas of Chile, Argentina, Zimbabwe, and Ghana, they challenge us to reconsider our existing ideas about entrepreneurship and how it should be explored.

References

Allen, P. (2007) *Your Ethical Business: How to Plan, Start and Succeed in a Company with a Conscience*. London: ngo.media.

Bannatyne, D. (2007) *Anyone Can Do It: My Story*. London: Orion.

Branson, R. (1999) *Losing My Virginity: The Autobiography*. London: Virgin Books.

Branson, R. (2008) *Business Stripped Bare: Adventures of a Global Entrepreneur*. London: Virgin Books.

Burrows, R. (ed.) (2015) *Deciphering the Enterprise Culture: Entrepreneurship, Petty Capitalism and the Restructuring of Britain* (new edn). Abingdon: Routledge.

Caan, J. (2009) *The Real Deal: My Story from Brick Lane to 'Dragons' Den'*. London: Virgin.

Casson, M., Yeung, B., Basu, A., and Wadeson, N. (2008) *The Oxford Handbook of Entrepreneurship*. Oxford: Oxford University Press.

Cope, J. and Watts, G. (2000) 'Learning by doing – An exploration of experience, critical incidents and reflection in entrepreneurial learning'. *International Journal of Entrepreneurial Behaviour and Research* 6, 3: 104–24.

Corbett, A. (2005) 'Experiential learning within the process of opportunity identification and exploitation'. *Entrepreneurship: Theory and Practice* 29, 4: 473–91.

Della-Guista, M. and King, Z. (2008) 'Enterprise culture'. In M. Casson et al. (eds.) op. cit. (629–47).

Drucker, P. (1982) *The Changing World of the Executive*. New York: Times Books.

Dyson, J. (2003) *Against the Odds: An Autobiography*. New York: Texere.

Grimson, L. and Mitchell, A. (2008) *Making It: Women Entrepreneurs Reveal Their Secrets of Success*. London: Capstone.

Imas, J. M., Wilson, N., and Weston, A. (2012) 'Barefoot entrepreneurs'. *Organization*, 19, 5: 563–85.

Jones P., Jones A., Skinner H., and Packham, G. (2013) 'Embedding enterprise: a business school undergraduate course with an enterprise focus'. *Industry & Higher Education*, 27, 3: 205–15.

Kirby, D. (2004) 'Entrepreneurship education: can business schools meet the challenge?' *Journal of Education and Training*, 46, 8/9: 510–19.

Levie, J. (1999) 'Entrepreneurship education in Higher Education in England: a survey'. London: Department for Education and Employment.

Mumford, A. (1997) *Action Learning at Work*. London: Gower.

OECD (2016) *Entrepreneurship at a Glance 2016*. Paris: OECD Publishing.

Penrose, E.T. ([1959] 2009) *The Theory of the Growth of the Firm* (4th edn). Oxford: Oxford University Press.

Preedy, S. and Jones, P. (2017) 'Student-led enterprise groups and entrepreneurial learning: A UK perspective'. *Industry and Higher Education* [online first].

QAA (2012) *Enterprise and Entrepreneurship Education: Guidance for UK Higher Education Providers*. London: The Quality Assurance Agency for Higher Education.

Rae D., Martin L., Antcliff V., and Hannon, P. (2012) 'Enterprise and entrepreneurship in English higher education: 2010 and beyond'. *Journal of Small Business and Enterprise Development*, 19, 3: 380–401.

Swedberg, R. (ed.) (2000) *Entrepreneurship: The Social Science View*. Oxford: Oxford University Press.

Tracey, P., Philips, N., and Haugh, H. (2005) 'Beyond philanthropy: community enterprise as a basis for corporate citizenship'. *Journal of Business Ethics*, 58, 4: 327–44.

Wang, C. L. and Chugh, H. (2014) 'Entrepreneurial learning: past research and future challenges'. *International Journal of Management Reviews*, 16, 1: 24–61.

Whitford, D. (2010) 'Can you learn to be an entrepreneur?' *Fortune* (22 March).

Wilson, T. (2012) *A Review of Business–University Collaboration*. London: Department for Business, Innovation and Skills.

2

VARIETIES OF ENTREPRENEURSHIP

While the total supply of entrepreneurs varies among societies, the productive contribution of the society's entrepreneurial activities varies much more because of their allocation between productive activities such as innovation and largely unproductive activities such as rent seeking or organized crime.

William J. Baumol, economist

Life-fulfilling work is never about the money – when you feel true passion for something, you instinctively find ways to nurture it.

Eileen Fisher, entrepreneur

LEARNING OUTCOMES

After reading this chapter you should be able to:

- Recognise a wide variety of ways in which entrepreneurial activity is organised, the many different contexts in which it takes place, and the range of goals to which it is directed.
- Identify links between different types of entrepreneur, and approaches to entrepreneurship, and Part One chapter themes (e.g. marketing, operations and finance).
- Appreciate how research can add to our understanding of entrepreneurial activity in a range of different contexts.
- Consider the practical implications whether you are thinking about, or have already embarked on, an entrepreneurial career.

2.1 INTRODUCTION

This chapter examines some of the varied ways in which entrepreneurship is practised around the world. In the Part Two chapters, we will be taking a more detailed look at the *causes* and *consequences* of these differences, but for the moment we will focus on the main *types* that you are likely to encounter in the course of your studies and note some of the ways in which they differ from one another. We will also consider the practical implications of these differences and how they link to topics addressed in the Part One chapters, from shaping a vision for your venture (Chapter 3), to finding the right people (Chapter 5), or organising your marketing (Chapter 6), operations (Chapter 7) and financing (Chapter 9).

One of the potential benefits of an entrepreneurial career is that you can, within limits, make some choices about the kind of venture you are creating. This chapter might also help you to start thinking about the choices that are open to you, whether it is about deciding on the kind of opportunity you want to pursue (Chapter 4), or the kind of organisation you would like to create. Eileen Fisher, the entrepreneur who is quoted at the beginning of this chapter, established her premium clothing brand in the United States in 1984 with just $350 in start-up funding (Close 2015). This successful multi-million dollar business has a distinctive social mission, which reflects the values of its founder:

'For the last 30 years, we've been united in our efforts to support the environment, human rights and initiatives for women and girls – and we believe that this work is becoming more and more important. Our pledge in 2017 is to expand our activism and outreach, to lend our voices, to help empower and protect. WE PROMISE TO: Do all we can to empower women and girls – we believe the future depends on it; Double down our efforts to support human rights and the fair treatment of all people; Protect our limited natural resources, fight climate change and help shift the fashion industry toward sustainability; Respect and honor differences in gender, age, race, ethnicity, sexual orientation and political views. Now more than ever we believe it's time to reach out, speak up and stand together.' (Eileen Fisher 2017)

We begin by taking a look at some of the different types of entrepreneur that you are likely to encounter (Section 2.2), before considering some practical examples of entrepreneurial variety in greater detail. In Section 2.3 we examine national and cultural differences, with a particular focus on immigrant and ethnic minority entrepreneurship. Section 2.4 looks at the differences between what is termed 'replicative' and 'innovative' entrepreneurship, and includes a special feature on the resurgence of entrepreneurial activity in modern China. Section 2.5 concludes our review with an introduction to social entrepreneurship.

2.2 DIFFERENT TYPES OF ENTREPRENEUR

There are many different types of entrepreneur and the terminology can sometimes be confusing. We have selected nine of the more common categories to review in this section.

Corporate entrepreneur / intrapreneur

These terms are both used to describe someone who acts entrepreneurially inside an existing organisation, which may range from a medium-sized firm to a large corporation, government agency, or charity. The constraint of operating from within an organisational hierarchy, rather than being free to act independently, is the key feature that distinguishes corporate entrepreneurs / intrapreneurs from other entrepreneurs. Some organisations actively encourage corporate entrepreneurship / intrapreneurship as a way of promoting innovation and adaptability. There are strong parallels between this role and that of 'product champion', which is a term sometimes used by innovation researchers.

E-preneur

This term has been derived from the wider use of the letter 'e' to refer to 'electronic' (as in 'email' and 'e-commerce'). It is used to refer to the growing number of people who run businesses that depend entirely on the Internet. With the proliferation of Internet-based businesses, it now represents a very broad category, and could include anyone from the owner of a large online retailing empire to a self-employed person using an online shopping platform (such as eBay.com or Etsy.com) to sell specialist products from home.

Ecopreneur

This term has become popular as a way of describing entrepreneurs who establish ventures, or introduce new initiatives with the aim of tackling specific environmental problems. In practice, this can mean a wide variety of activities, ranging from a small, community-based enterprise selling organic fresh produce to a large commercial business operating in a low-carbon industry sector, such as the manufacture or installation of solar photovoltaic (PV) panels.

Lifestyle entrepreneur

This term is normally used to describe a person who has set up a small business in order to pursue a personal interest such as a craft (e.g. a pottery studio) or a sporting activity (e.g. horse-riding holidays). It is sometimes seen as a negative term, with the same kind of implied criticism as for 'hobby' farmers. The term refers to the idea that this type of entrepreneur prioritises quality of life over other common motivations for running a business. They might want to achieve a reasonable level of income from the venture, but are not actively pursuing purely commercial goals such as growing it into a much larger business, or securing large (or short-term) financial returns.

Portfolio entrepreneur

This term refers to someone who operates several different ventures at the same time. There are different types of portfolio entrepreneur. They can range from extremely wealthy owners of multiple businesses to much less prosperous people, often based in remote rural areas, who engage in several different small enterprises in order to reduce risks and to maintain an income when local markets, or economic conditions more generally, are depressed or uncertain (note the distinction between this term and the 'serial entrepreneur').

Rural entrepreneur

This term refers to people who create or operate businesses in the countryside. It is sometimes used in a more restricted way to focus on the traditional rural industries, such as agriculture, forestry, food manufacturing, and rural crafts. However, the term is also used to refer to those running a variety of businesses that happen to be located in a rural area. It can also be difficult to define the geographic boundaries of rural businesses (e.g. does it include an entrepreneur whose business is located in a village that is on the fringes of a large city, or someone based in a remote rural location who spends much of their time doing business internationally?).

Serial entrepreneur

This term refers to someone who sets up several different ventures over a period of time, often reinvesting profits from the sale of an existing business in order to finance a new one, sometimes in an entirely different field of activity. This pattern may reflect the entrepreneur's preference for creating new ventures rather than managing larger established businesses (note the distinction between this term and the 'portfolio entrepreneur').

Social entrepreneur

This term is normally used to identify the founder(s) of a social venture, or someone who initiates a larger programme of social change. The distinctive feature of this type of entrepreneurship is that the primary purpose is to address social or environmental problems rather than simply to achieve commercial goals. This suggests a number of differences, including the values involved, how people understand concepts such as entrepreneurial 'opportunity', and the way that organisations are run. There has been a lot of interest in social entrepreneurship in recent years and this has generated many competing definitions, which we will revisit in Section 2.4 and in subsequent chapters.

Technology entrepreneur

This term typically describes a person who has founded a new venture in order to develop some form of advanced technology, most commonly in industry sectors such as information and communications technology (ICT), biotechnology, nanotechnology, and other applied sciences. This kind of entrepreneurial activity is often very fast-moving, as a result of new scientific discoveries and often intensive international competition, and is also associated with technological innovation. Governments around the world see technology-based entrepreneurship as an important source of economic growth as well as offering possible solutions to major societal challenges. Technology entrepreneurship is examined in more detail in Section 2.4 and remains a strong theme throughout the book – look out for the 'Innovation focus' features in the Part One chapters.

It can be helpful to identify particular categories of entrepreneur, and you can probably see how each has a few distinctive features. However, when you start to investigate particular entrepreneurs it is also important to recognise that people may not necessarily fit neatly into one of these categories. In practice, the definitions are blurred and often overlap. For example, someone might be based in the countryside (rural entrepreneur) but running several web-based businesses (technology and portfolio entrepreneur). You may also come across some more informal, and generally less helpful, variants such as 'kidpreneur' (for very young business founders) and the problematic term, 'mompreneur' (Krueger 2015).

So how do you begin to decide what kind of entrepreneur you would like to be – or whether this is really the direction you want your career to take? In **Case 2.1**, we follow James as he considers the options.

CASE 2.1

 ◀ Decisions: James's challenge video

In this challenge video case, James is reviewing his options for employment or new venture creation following his MBA: (a) apply for corporate positions; (b) create a new luxury tourism venture; or (c) relaunch property development business. Watch the video and decide which option you think James will choose. You might find it useful to discuss the case with friends or colleagues before deciding. Please note that lecturers can have access to the reveal video, which reveals the actual decision taken by the entrepreneur.

Source: This video case is primarily based on an interview with James by Nigel Lockett.

In addition to the different types of entrepreneur discussed above, there are also different ways of categorising entrepreneurship. In the following sections, we discuss three of these types: immigrant and ethnic minority entrepreneurship (Section 2.3), replicative and innovative entrepreneurship (Section 2.4), and social entrepreneurship (Section 2.5). In reality, there are many more types that we will continue to explore in the Part One and Part Two chapters. For example, there is a great deal of interest in gender and the experiences of women as entrepreneurs, a theme that was illustrated by the Eileen Fisher brand in the opening section of this chapter and that we will revisit in later chapters.

2.3 IMMIGRANT AND ETHNIC MINORITY ENTREPRENEURSHIP

Peter Vandor and Nikolaus Franke (2016) asked an interesting question: what do Arianna Huffington (*The Huffington Post* (now *HuffPost*), Thrive Global), Elon Musk (Tesla, SpaceX), and Sergey Brin (Google) have in common? They then pointed out that, apart from being successful entrepreneurs, they share one distinct characteristic: extensive cross-cultural experience. Arianna Huffington grew up in Greece, studied in Cambridge, the UK, and moved to the USA in her thirties. Elon Musk was born in South Africa, and studied in Canada and the USA before pursuing his entrepreneurial career in Internet and renewable energy. At the age of six, Sergey Brin emigrated from the former Soviet Union to the USA, where he studied mathematics and computer science before becoming an Internet entrepreneur. These immigrant entrepreneurs represent an interesting phenomenon – 'the most entrepreneurial group in the U.S. wasn't born in the U.S.' (Bluestein 2015). Over 25% of new businesses in the USA are set up by immigrants although they account for only about 13% of the population (Bluestein 2015). In the high-tech sectors, about 25% of the high-tech firms in Silicon Valley in the 1980s and 1990s were founded or being run by immigrants (Saxenian 2002). Extending this study, Wadhwa et al. (2007) analysed firms in the rest of the country and other industries in 1995–2005 and found a similar percentage of immigrant-founded firms. Indeed, it is evidence that the rates of business ownership are higher among immigrant entrepreneurs than natives in many developed countries, including the USA, the UK, Canada, and Australia (Bluestein 2015).

Entrepreneurship scholars are interested in to what extent immigrant and ethnic minority entrepreneurship is distinctive from mainstream entrepreneurship and why it is distinctive (Deakins et al. 2003). Wang and Altinay (2012) summarised two main schools of thought on this issue. One school of thought looks at immigrant and ethnic minority entrepreneurship from the culturalist perspective, and argues that ethnic minority entrepreneurs and their businesses are intrinsically intertwined in their family and co-ethnic networks in which individual behaviour, social relations and economic transactions are shaped by the cultural heritage (Aldrich and Waldinger 1990). For example, Wang and Altinay (2012) found that Chinese and Turkish ethnic minority small businesses' entrepreneurial orientation (i.e. proactiveness in the market, risk-taking, and innovativeness) is positively associated with their access to co-ethnic products and suppliers of utilities and facilities. This means that being embedded in their own ethnic community brings about new opportunities for ethnic minority enterprises. Moreover, ethnic minority entrepreneurs manifest a 'self-help' ethos and culture, that provides an impetus for them to start up own businesses (Werbner 1994; Basu 2004).

Another school of thought looks at immigrant and ethnic minority entrepreneurship from the structuralist perspective (Mulholland 1997; Ram and Jones 1998; Virdee 2006). Scholars in this camp argue that ethnic minorities start up their own businesses not because the unique advantage associated with their ethos, culture or embeddedness in the ethnic community, but because self-employment is one of the most effective strategies for ethnic minority individuals to pursue upward socio-economic mobility (Glazer and Moynihan 1963; Modood 1997). Self-employment may be the only alternative for ethnic minority people who are disadvantaged in the mainstream labour market due to structural barriers (such as racial exclusion and discrimination) and blocked mobility arising from skill deficiency (Zhou 2004). In other words, self-employment is 'more a confirmation of subordinate status than an escape from it' (McEvoy et al. 1982: 10). In this case, self-employment is not necessarily a manifestation of entrepreneurial spirit, as owners of many small businesses (such as takeaways or corner shops) show little ambition for or potential of business growth. Therefore, it is worth noting that immigrant and ethnic minority entrepreneurship is not all about the glory of fast-growing enterprises typically associated with immigrant entrepreneurs in the high-tech sectors in the Silicon Valley; it is also about the struggle of micro or small business owners who work hard for a living.

The culturalist and structuralist perspectives together help to understand the motivations of immigrant and ethnic minority entrepreneurship. Structural barriers in the socio-economic context form a 'push' factor, and ethno-cultural resources are a 'pull' factor (Jones et al. 1985). Consequently, scholars argue that it is the two factors together that give rise to immigrant and ethnic minority entrepreneurship: the ethno-cultural resources provide the means for entrepreneurship, and the labour market disadvantage provides the motive (Waldinger et al. 1990).

2.4 REPLICATIVE AND INNOVATIVE ENTREPRENEURSHIP

We talked about entrepreneurs, such as Sergey Brin and Elon Musk, but we also mentioned entrepreneurs who set up businesses such as takeaways, corner shops, dry cleaners and grocery shops. There are vast differences between their motives of, and approaches to, entrepreneurship. Indeed, there are many faces of entrepreneurship, and not all entrepreneurship is the same. William Baumol (2010) particularly distinguishes two types of entrepreneurs who engage in different entrepreneurial activity in an economy: innovative entrepreneurs who create something new, such as a new technology, a new product, or a new business model) and commercialise it in the marketplace; replicative entrepreneurs who set up businesses mimicking tried-and-proved business models to sell existing products to existing markets. Figure 2.1 illustrates these differences: the team that designed and marketed the Brompton folding bike provides a good example of innovative entrepreneurship, while the owner-manager who runs The Corner Deli could be described as a replicative entrepreneur.

FIGURE 2.1 Distinguishing replicative and innovative entrepreneurship

Innovative and replicative entrepreneurs possess different characteristics and personal traits (see Chapter 11) as well as cognitive and learning styles (see Chapter 16). Joseph Schumpeter wrote extensively about innovative entrepreneurs. He described innovative entrepreneurs as 'creative destructors' – those who act as destabilising influences in an economy, and their creation – a new technology, a new product, or a new business model triggering 'creative destruction' that disrupts the existing economic or industrial structure and creates a new industry or a new industrial structure through innovation (Schumpeter 1942). Amazon is an example of innovative entrepreneurship, and has transformed the book publishing and retailing industry.

In its early days, Amazon revolutionised the distribution and retailing of books from traditional physical bookstores to online retailing. As a result, many small bookstores and even large ones closed. Borders Group was one among many victims of this industry disruption. In 2010, Borders ran over 500 superstores in the USA, and employed over 1000 staff across its UK bookstores before they went into administration towards the end of December 2010. Amazon also introduced a number of new initiatives and business models to transform the way in which books are published. According to figures provided by Forbes (Mitra 2008), in traditional book publishing, retailers take about 50% of the retail price of a book, followed by agents that take 15–20%, and book publishers that take up to 20%. Authors only get less than 10% of the retail price of a book. One of Amazon's initiatives was to cut out the middlemen (publishers and agents) and directly engage with authors. To achieve this, it acquired BookSurge, a print-on-demand company (later to be known as CreateSpace), and Mobipocket.com, an e-book software company in 2005. In the same year, it launched the e-book reader Kindle. By cutting out the middlemen, Amazon increased its retailer's share from 50% to 65% of book revenues, and offering 35% to authors (Mitra 2008).

In contrast, replicative entrepreneurship is aligned with Israel Kirzner's theory of entrepreneurship: entrepreneurs have flashes of insights that enable them to spot opportunities in the market (Kirzner 1973) – opportunities of arbitrage to profit from price discrepancies in the market tending toward eradicating such discrepancies (von

Mises 1949). In other words, replicative entrepreneurs act as efficient coordinators of resource usage in an industry or an economy, rather than creative destructors in innovative entrepreneurship.

Replicative entrepreneurship makes up a large segment of the economy and serves a growing population. A main contribution of replicative entrepreneurship is job creation, primarily through self-employment, such as in the case of China (Kelley et al. 2016) (Case 2.2).

CASE 2.2

Chinese entrepreneurship

China took over from the USA to become the world's largest economy in size in 2014, according to the International Monetary Fund. This phenomenal growth was achieved in just three decades since China's economic reform in 1978. From the early 1980s to the mid-1990s, China's growth was largely attributed to rural industries – the township and village enterprises; it is only since the late 1990s that  China's self-employed private entrepreneurs have been the key drivers of growth (Yueh 2008). The rise of private entrepreneurship was brought about by the restructuring of state-owned enterprises in the mid-1990s. The guaranteed lifetime employment system broke down, and there were massive layoffs by the state-owned enterprises. This, among many other institutional and cultural changes, made state-owned enterprises less attractive as a career choice, and kick-started private entrepreneurship in China.

Today, China has become a very entrepreneurial country. The Global Entrepreneurship Monitor's (GEM) 2015/2016 Global Report (Kelley et al. 2016) ranked China very favourably among the 60 nations surveyed by the GEM, in the areas of entrepreneurial intentions, total early-stage entrepreneurial activity, women entrepreneurship, job creations by entrepreneurial firms, and high status given to entrepreneurs.

However, China is not yet an innovative economy. According to the Global Competitiveness Report 2015–2016 (Schwab 2016), China remains in the league of efficiency-drive economies. The growth of Chinese economy has been largely fuelled by investment, low wages, and urbanisation until recently (Schwab 2016). In this institutional context, China's private entrepreneurship primarily engages in replicative activities – competing on costs, rather than innovation. Even high-tech firms are mostly just copycats of firms in the Silicon Valley: Baidu was a replica of Google, and Tencent a copy of Yahoo!

Some call this 'catch-up entrepreneurship' (or replicative entrepreneurship), as opposed to frontier entrepreneurship (or innovative entrepreneurship) (Huang 2010). This viewpoint coincides with the GEM findings: a main contribution of China's

(Continued)

(Continued)

entrepreneurship is job creation. Indeed, China ranks fifth out of 60 countries surveyed by the GEM, in terms of job creation. Catch-up entrepreneurship thrives in China, within the constraints of its institutional environment – a stable political system that delivers basic infrastructure.

To give a flavour of China's replicative entrepreneurship, we look at the entrepreneurial journeys of two Chinese entrepreneurs, Mr Zhang and Ms Li, who both set up their own technology-based firms in the mid-1990s in Beijing.

MR ZHANG AND SPINALFIXTURE

Mr Zhang is a retiree entrepreneur. Following an early retirement from a state-owned aerospace organisation with secure pension and benefits, Mr Zhang set up SpinalFixture in 1996 in Beijing. SpinalFixture focused on adapting foreign bone fixture technology to the requirements of Chinese patients. Since its start-up, SpinalFixture pursued organic growth through self-finance. In early 2000s, facing increasing market pressure due to price-based competition, SpinalFixture focused on increasing efficiency and capacity. To achieve this, it moved into a large rural site in 2005, and transformed its ad-hoc workshop-style management to a formal, functional management structure to achieve efficiency and standardisation. However, since 2009 SpinalFixture faced intensified domestic competition in the low-end market and international competition in the high-end market, and the Founder realised that the opportunity lay in the mid-range domestic market. However, SpinalFixture needed to improve its research and development (R&D) capability, develop an entrepreneurial mindset and break down 'organisational silos' caused by functional management in order to create an innovative culture. The Founder wanted to transform SpinalFixture into an employee-owned organisation with effective reward systems for innovation.

MS LI AND LIVERPHARMA

Ms Li is what we call a returnee entrepreneur. She was a doctor in a state-owned hospital in China, before her departure to pursue a Master of Public Administration in the US. On her return to China, she was dissatisfied by the control in state-owned hospitals, and decided to quit her secure medical profession to set up LiverPharma with the help of her husband, a renowned doctor specialising in Hepatitis B. Unlike SpinalFixture, LiverPharma could not pursue organic growth due to high R&D investment (about 50% of sales annually) required for developing its technology. This was exacerbated by the lack of external finance due to the immature capital market, and the lack of government support for private enterprises in China. Consequently, LiverPharma in parallel developed over-the-counter skincare products through licensing-in technology from a state-owned hospital; its revenue was re-invested in the research and development (R&D) of Hepatitis B. Compared with its peers, LiverPharma had strong R&D capability and a culture that respected learning.

MR ZHANG AND MS LI'S LEARNING JOURNEYS

Their prior knowledge, skills, and experience accumulated over decades of working in state-owned organisations were instrumental to the identification of their business opportunities. For example, Mr Zhang said:

I have expertise in designing aerospace products using titanium, the same material for bone fixtures [...] However, I didn't have medical knowledge, so I informally learnt medical knowledge from experts, and combined such knowledge with my engineering knowledge of aerospace design with titanium accumulated over the past 30 years.

Their social networks, including family members, close social groups (e.g. friends and ex-colleagues), and wider expert communities, provided much needed information, advice and support. For example, Mr Zhang and Ms Li recalled:

After I took early retirement, I talked to the Head of a [state-owned] hospital, who is a friend of mine. He told me that there was a good opportunity to develop bone fixtures. [Mr Zhang]

He [the co-founder] travels a lot, giving lectures and seminars, attending conferences, and training people and doctors [...] He could always find new information from Internet, books, or other sources [...] He is my teacher providing us information. [Ms Li]

Finally, both Mr Zhang and Ms Li spent years pondering over their business ideas, and preparing themselves for the right moment to start their own businesses. Ms Li provided a good example of how she and her co-founder worked secretly on their own project while being employed by a state-owned hospital:

I presented a paper on Hepatitis at a US conference [in 1983], and it was very well received [...] During the coffee break, someone [a leading international expert] approached me and asked me to carry on with my research... He also invited me to collaborate with him on his [Hepatitis] technology [...] I promised to work on it. However, when I got back to work, the Head of the Hospital did not allow me to work on it. I was furious and hurt, shouting at him and also banging the table [...] Later on, I informally and secretly worked with a colleague on the project.

Both Mr Zhang and Ms Li's entrepreneurial experiences entail a great deal of learning within China's institutional constrains. Their experience may not be shared by the new generations of entrepreneurs, who have shown more creative flare and readiness to compete head-on with the world's biggest high-tech names, such as Apple and Samsung (Thompson 2016).

QUESTIONS

1. How did the entrepreneurs above prepare themselves for setting up new ventures?
2. What factors were influential to the identification of entrepreneurial opportunities?
3. How did China's institutional environment shape the entrepreneurs' learning experience?

The case was written by Catherine Wang. It contains an extract from a case study written by Wang et al. (2014). The entrepreneurs are anonymised for confidentiality purpose.

Both innovative and replicative entrepreneurship are important to an economy, despite having different approaches to economic value creation. In Case 2.2, we can see how Mr Zhang's business idea was based on adapting foreign products and technology for Chinese patients – an example of replicative entrepreneurship. Similarly, Ms Li's business idea was to develop a Hepatitis B diagnosis and treatment for Chinese patients. Although it required a higher level of R&D investment compared with that of Mr Zhang's idea, the business was not a radical departure from existing technology.

2.5 SOCIAL ENTREPRENEURSHIP

Social entrepreneurship has really struck a chord with many entrepreneurs who are keen to combine their passion for a social mission with an image of business discipline, innovation and determination in their ventures (Dees 1998; Short et al. 2009; Stephan et al. 2015). The phenomenon of social entrepreneurship has received much attention over the past two decades, but its practice can be traced back to much earlier social initiatives. Among the many renowned social reformers and innovators of the nineteenth and twentieth centuries, Florence Nightingale (1820–1910) is often mentioned as an example of what we would now term a 'social entrepreneur'. She not only revolutionised nursing and pioneered new ways of presenting medical statistics, but also set up the first professional nursing school and transformed the way hospitals were built. Another example is John Muir (1838–1914), a conservationist who helped to establish the US National Park System and founded the Sierra Club, one of the first large-scale environmental conservation organisations in the world.

In more recent times, social entrepreneurship has become a vehicle for both government agencies and private foundations, such as Ashoka, Schwab and the Skoll Foundation, to support social initiatives and develop programmes to solve social problems, especially in disadvantaged or under-represented communities (Noruzi et al. 2010). The Ashoka Foundation was founded by Bill Drayton, an American entrepreneur, first in India in 1980. It now operates globally. Bill Drayton's belief is that 'the most powerful force for good in the world is a social entrepreneur: a person driven by an innovative idea that can help correct an entrenched global problem. The world's leading social entrepreneurs pursue system-changing solutions that permanently alter existing patterns of activity' (Ashoka 2016). Today, the Ashoka Foundation is a leading international organisation that identifies, empowers, trains, and connects social entrepreneurs, as well as investing in promising social enterprises for good causes. Arianna Huffington, the Founder of *The Huffington Post*, reminds us of the true spirit of social entrepreneurship as exemplified in Ashoka: 'Bill Drayton emphasised to us [that] empathy is increasingly becoming our primary resource for dealing with the exponential rate of change the world is going through' (Ashoka 2016).

In the UK, the rise of social entrepreneurship led to the creation of the Community Interest Company (or the 'CIC') in 2005. The CIC is a dedicated legal form for social enterprises. Stephen Lloyd, a former senior partner at Bates Wells Braithwaite, a London-based law firm, is credited with the creation of the CIC legal framework; he is described as 'the father of CICs' (BWB 2016). As of 2016, 11,922 social enterprises were formally registered as CICs, and over 2,700 new CICs were set up in 2015–2016 (Regulator of Community Interest Companies 2016). It is worth mentioning that many more companies are run as social enterprises driven by social missions, but are not registered as CICs. According to BMG Research (2013) based on 2012 BIS Small Business Survey, there were 70,000 social enterprises in the UK employing about a million people and contributing £18.5 billion to the UK economy.

Social entrepreneurship is particularly attractive among women and ethnic minority communities. According to a five-year study of social enterprises in the UK, women and ethnic minority people are more likely to set up social enterprises (Khan 2008). About 38% of social enterprises have a woman CEO, compared with 19% of SMEs and 3% of FTSE 100 companies (Robert Half 2013). Social enterprises are twice as likely as mainstream SMEs to be led by an ethnic minority entrepreneur (Villeneuve-Smith and Chung 2013). Women and ethnic minority people, because of their background and experiences, are more likely to have empathy on social problems, and to be more motivated to find solutions to the problems.

As can be seen from these examples, the practice of social entrepreneurship is long-standing, and the social enterprise sector has made a considerable impact on both the economy and the society that we live in. Social entrepreneurship practice has inspired academic research, but many issues remain to be clarified. For example, social entrepreneurship remains a contested concept (Choi and Majumdar 2014). It has many competing definitions and no unifying conceptual work (e.g. Mair and Martí 2006; Certo and Miller 2008; Short et al. 2009; Hill et al. 2010). In fact, some scholars even question whether a universal definition is possible (Choi and Majumdar 2014). As a result, Choi and Majumdar (2014) argue that social entrepreneurship should be considered as a cluster concept – a conglomerate of several sub-concepts, namely social value creation, the social entrepreneur, the social enterprise, market orientation, and social innovation.

In reality, social entrepreneurship covers a wide range of practices – from corporate social entrepreneurship (Austin et al. 2006) to innovative activity with social intent in the for-profit sector or the non-profit sector (Dees 1998; Gras and Mendoza-Abarca 2013). If you are interested in finding out more about this increasingly popular type of entrepreneurial activity, Ridley-Duff and Bull (2015) is an accessible text, which reveals how social enterprises in different sectors engage in social and economic value creation.

Social enterprises face a variety of challenges. In contrast to charitable organisations that primarily rely on donations and grants, they need to maintain their core social mission while also building a profitable business model. Otherwise they would not be able to generate sufficient income to maintain their organisation or to invest in its future development (Dees and Anderson 2003; Certo and Miller 2008; Choi and Majumdar 2014). This combination of economic and social value creation is sometimes described as the 'double bottom line' of social enterprises. In those social enterprises that have a high concern for the environment, it extends to include a third objective – environmental sustainability and the 'triple bottom line' (Elkington 1997). Social enterprises' success often depends upon their ability to satisfy the three-pronged fork of profitability, environmental quality, and social justice (Elkington 1997). Case 2.3, which reports on the performance of Community Interest Companies (CICs), a legal form that was created for social enterprises operating in the UK, summarises several key challenges and opportunities for social enterprises.

CASE 2.3

Social enterprises: ten years on

Community Interest Companies (CICs, pronounced 'kicks') are a legal form for social enterprises in the United Kingdom and by 2016 there were more than 12,000 CICs on the register of the Regulator of Community Interest Companies. The CICs sector saw phenomenal growth in the UK since it was created in 2005. This extract from a report for the regulator illustrates how social enterprises have contributed to both economic and social value creation. However, while celebrating the diversity and prosperity of the sector, the report also identifies several key challenges, as well as opportunities for the future.

Honing business models for growth. The past ten years have seen many social enterprises well established in their communities. Their challenge is how to scale up their businesses, especially given the resource constraints in the sector and the nature of personalised products and services highly tailored to the community needs. Social franchising has been brought to the table as a cost-effective way of growing a social enterprise and maintaining a personal touch. Social enterprises that are geared up towards growth would benefit from hands-on support on business models and development.

Leveraging resources for the grassroots. Many social enterprises operate on a very small scale, due to the nature of niche products or services and resource constraints, especially the difficulty of accessing finance. Resource bricolage enables grassroots social enterprises to cross the 'valley of death'. In addition, the misperception of social enterprises as wishy-washy do-gooders remains among parts of the private and public sectors. Some social entrepreneurs feel that they have to work that much harder to establish themselves in a commercial world.

Consolidating reputation and impacts. Social enterprises need to balance the dual demands – doing good and doing well financially. There is a risk that commercially successful social enterprises may drift away from their social missions. Firmly steering the social mission at the very core of a successful business is key to cementing the reputation of social enterprises. There are also opportunities for successful social enterprises to take the lead in consolidating impacts that are fragmented at the grassroots level.

Disseminating best practices. There is scope for successful CICs to disseminate their business models and practices among the wider community – nationally and internationally, especially in developing countries that are in need of guidance on CICs. Opportunities are there for influential CICs to engage and lobby various stakeholders in both public and private sectors, to shape policy, practice and research, to attract talents into the sector, and to create a stronger impact of the sector.

Social enterprises' pursuit of a social mission with a business-like discipline has inspired both private and public sectors. Public sector organisations have embraced the public–private partnership model to inject entrepreneurial energy. Private sector organisations have become increasingly committed to social responsibility. The B-Corporations initiative is a testament of this. The next ten years should see CICs build on their success into a new era of growth.

QUESTIONS

1. What are the main obstacles facing these community-based social enterprises?

2. What kinds of solutions are identified in this extract?

3. What other legal forms are used by social enterprises (you could conduct a quick web search to find two or three examples from other countries)?

Note: the text of this case is based on material originally published in the *CICs Annual Report 2015–2016* by the Regulator of Community Interest Companies (Wang 2016).

We hope that the examples discussed in this chapter have given you at least a flavour of the many 'faces' of entrepreneurship that you are likely to encounter during your studies. We have also tried to highlight a few of the many ways that entrepreneurial practice can vary in different situations, as well as identifying some common themes.

Entrepreneurship research has flourished in the past three decades, resulting in a rich body of knowledge that we will be exploring in greater detail in later chapters. By way of introduction, Case 2.4 illustrates Professor Sarah Jack's research on entrepreneurship in different contexts. You will find a series of these 'Researcher Profile' cases in Part Two of *Exploring Entrepreneurship*. Each chapter showcases the work of a leading entrepreneurship researcher, with a short biography followed by an informal discussion.

CASE 2.4 RESEARCHER PROFILE

SARAH JACK: EXAMINING ENTREPRENEURSHIP IN DIFFERENT CONTEXTS

Sarah Jack is both a Professor of Innovative and Sustainable Business Development at Stockholm School of Economics and a Professor of Entrepreneurship at Lancaster University. Previously, she worked at the University of Aberdeen where she gained her PhD. Her specific interests are in understanding the relationship between entrepreneurship and social context. She co-edited, *Entrepreneurial Process and Social Networks: A Dynamic Perspective* (Fayolle et al. 2016), which takes the view that entrepreneurship is a social process and creating a firm requires the mobilisation of social networks and use of social capital. She has been involved in various research projects, the most recent being a 'Horizon 2020' collaboration with partners from across Europe titled, 'Social Innovation in Marginalised Rural Areas', led by Professor Maria Nijnik of The James Hutton Institute, Aberdeen (SIMRA 2017).

In this interview, Sarah discusses her research interests around the relationship between entrepreneurial activity and the varied contexts in which it is located.

(Continued)

(Continued)

Why did you want to research in this area?

I have always been curious about how entrepreneurs operate in reality. When I embarked on my doctoral studies, I was given the opportunity to choose my topic. I found the link between entrepreneurs and social context fascinating. I grew up in the northern periphery of Scotland where my interests in the relevance of social relationships was formed.

When I started my doctoral studies, it became clear little was known about entrepreneurship in rural areas. At the same time, there was a growing interest in trying to understand the impact of social context. Influenced by the work of Elizabeth Bott, Jeremy Boissevain, Mark Granovetter, Howard Aldrich, Bengt Johannisson, and Alistair Anderson, among others, I saw this as a real opportunity. I was very fortunate in working with Alistair Anderson. He encouraged me to explore my interests. Following the completion of my doctoral thesis, I continue to engage with these areas. My interests have also extended to include social innovation, social skills (Jack et al. 2017), social entrepreneurship (Steiner et al. 2008), and social incubation (Soetanto and Jack, 2013, 2016). I have always had an interest in entrepreneurship education and social context (Anderson and Jack 1999; Jack and Anderson 2008; Dodd et al. 2013;

Lockett et al. 2017). More recently, I have been looking at entrepreneurship in the contexts of family business (Konopaski et al. 2015; Discua Cruz et al. 2012) and in Spain (Gil et al. 2016) and Finland (Leppäaho and Jack 2016), entrepreneurship in the contexts of Belarus (Ivy et al. 2014) and Alaska (Ivy et al. 2015), and the Syrian refugee crisis (Alkhaled et al. 2017).

How did you decide on your main research questions?

My approach has always been context matters and that to understand entrepreneurship, we should look at it the context in which it takes place. What really interests me in all this is how context shapes entrepreneurship, the interplay between entrepreneurship and social context, and how entrepreneurship may actually shape context. Entrepreneurship is a contextual event and so the ideas of embeddedness, social capital, social bonds, and social networks play meaningful roles in the entrepreneurial process. Entrepreneurship is both shaped and influenced by context, and it is therefore critical to look at entrepreneurial matters in their context. I also believe that understanding the role of relationships and how those that exist between entrepreneurs and the communities with whom they engage can influence practice and outcomes, is important (McKeever et al. 2015). Entrepreneurship sustains communities over time and vice versa. This links back to my roots and growing up in a rural community where entrepreneurship and enterprise activity were very critical for survival. So, I suppose my research questions are developed through a real desire to extend understanding and contribute to the knowledge gaps which seem to exist in entrepreneurship research and their implications for policy, theory, and practice.

What methods did you use?

My approach has always been qualitative. For my doctoral thesis, I drew on ethnographic techniques to understand the situations entrepreneurs encounter. I focus on 'why' and 'how' questions and enjoy working with rich data and interrogating it, working through the patterns and themes to the analysis to arrive at understanding.

What were your key findings?

A key finding is that entrepreneurship is a social process with economic outcomes. I like to interrogate theoretical perspectives within the context of entrepreneurship, Granovetter's ideas about strong and weak ties being one example. I enjoy unpicking processes to show the realities entrepreneurs face. Ivy et al. (2014) looks at an emerging economy and the situations entrepreneurs face. It especially raises questions about the applicability of applying Western-style concepts to other parts of the world.

Were there any particular challenges in conducting these studies?

The type of work I do is challenging; you end up with lots of rich data to analyse and interpret to extend understanding. You have to present it in a way which takes the reader on the journey with you. This is critical but also difficult. I like to put as much data forward as I can. Final presentations can look so neat and structured and really hide the messiness (and joy) of working with qualitative data.

Where do you think research in this area needs to develop in future?

Current work excites me. I see entrepreneurship as offering a mechanism to deal with some critical global challenges we face. How we move forward and use knowledge to make a difference to the lives of people across the world is critical. Entrepreneurship exists in many different ways and that is why we need to look at it in the context in which it takes place. Only by doing so, can we really generate a better appreciation of how and why it happens in the way it does. More ethnographic work could help and looking at how social context and entrepreneurship come together to build and sustain different forms of communities across the world is interesting. Challenging a lot of the perspectives that have been developed and which we currently work with, is critical to enhancing how we view and understand entrepreneurship.

2.6 SUMMARY

- Entrepreneurial activity can be found in organisations of various kinds (e.g. a small entrepreneurial team founding a technology-based start-up venture, a social entrepreneur developing a new social enterprise, or a group of intrapreneurs developing new ventures within the boundaries of a large corporation).
- Entrepreneurial activity can also take place in different places and spaces (e.g. a remote rural community, a university science park, or a suburban garden shed). There are also differences in the kinds of entrepreneurship found in different countries and regions.

- Entrepreneurs display a variety of motivations and their ventures are directed towards economic, social, and personal goals (e.g. launching an innovative pharmaceutical product, empowering young disabled people, creating a personal fortune for the founder).

- Entrepreneurs may engage in one or more types of entrepreneurship. For example, a technology entrepreneur is likely to engage in innovative entrepreneurship, but this activity might also be described as 'social entrepreneurship' if the primary aim is to address a social problem.

- It is important to recognise both the *sources* of variety in entrepreneurship and the *consequences* of pursuing different types of entrepreneurial activity. Understanding these differences can be equally valuable, whether you are a researcher, a practitioner (e.g. a consultant or financier), or a prospective entrepreneur.

Practical activities

1   Conduct a web search to find your own examples of at least *five* of the nine types of entrepreneur summarised in Section 2.2 and prepare short summaries. How far to your examples match the descriptions given in the chapter? Did you find any overlapping categories?

2   Refer back to the Chapter 1 activity 'What does it take to be an entrepreneur?'.

Select *one* type of entrepreneur and try to identify any additional requirements. For example, if you selected a 'technology entrepreneur' you might refer to technical expertise (or at least a capacity to understand and work with the relevant specialists).

Discussion topics

1   Rates of business ownership are higher among immigrant entrepreneurs and much higher than those of natives in many developed countries, including the USA, UK, Canada, and Australia (Bluestein 2015) (Section 2.3). How can we explain these differences?

2   Do you think it is more important for a government to promote *innovative* entrepreneurship or *replicative* entrepreneurship (Baumol 2010) (Section 2.4)? Give reasons for your answer.

3   We have categorised 'social entrepreneurship' as one type of entrepreneurship, alongside 'rural entrepreneurship' for example. Do you think this is appropriate, or is social entrepreneurship fundamentally different from the other types we have considered in this chapter?

Recommended reading

These readings address two important topics in entrepreneurship research and are recommended for anyone wanting to build on the material covered in this chapter. Recommended readings have been selected from leading Sage journals and are freely available for readers of this textbook to download via the Online Resources.

Swan, C. D. and Morgan, D. (2016) 'Who wants to be an eco-entrepreneur?: identifying entrepreneurial types and practices in ecotourism businesses'. *The International Journal of Entrepreneurship and Innovation*, **17, 2: 120–32.**

Within the small-business sector of ecotourism, entrepreneurs must balance competing goals pertaining to business objectives, lifestyle aspirations and, most importantly, sustainable environmental practices. This study reports how ecotourism *eco-entrepreneurs* perceive and manage these goals, consistent with concerns and motivations, based on semi-structured interviews of small business operators. The findings show that eco-entrepreneurs' social and sustainable characteristics are critical to overcome financially challenging and complex operating environments while also delivering a desired lifestyle. As a business strategy, eco-entrepreneurs were found to deliberately maintain small, low-impact ecotourism operations consistent with identified *eco*-values.

Tlaiss, H. A. (2013) 'Entrepreneurial motivations of women: evidence from the United Arab Emirates'. *International Small Business Journal*, **33, 5: 562–81.**

This article explores the entrepreneurial motivations of women entrepreneurs in the United Arab Emirates. It analyses the impact of macro social forces and cultural values on the motivation for entrepreneurship and explores how post-materialism, legitimation and dissatisfaction theories may explain these motives. In-depth semi-structured interviews were conducted with local women entrepreneurs and analysed using an interpretive approach. The results illustrate how Emirati women entrepreneurs navigate the patriarchy of their society, socio-economic realities, and structural and attitudinal organisational barriers to construct and negotiate their entrepreneurial motivations.

References

Aldrich, H. E. and Waldinger, R. (1990) 'Ethnicity and entrepreneurship'. *Annual Review of Sociology,* 16: 111–35.

Alkhaled, S., Jack, S. L. and Kreuger, N. (2017) 'Entrepreneurship-as-survival: Syrian Women Refugees in Jordan'. *Babson College Entrepreneurship Conference*, University of Oklahoma, Norman, OK, 7–10 June.

Anderson, A. R. and Jack, S. L. (1999) 'Entrepreneurship education within the enterprise culture: producing reflective practitioners'. *International Journal of Entrepreneurial Behaviour and Research* (Special Issue), 5, 3: 110–25.

Ashoka (2016) *Ashoka website*. Available at https://www.ashoka.org/ (accessed 30 November 2016).

Austin, J., Stevenson, H., and Wei-Skillern, J. (2006) 'Social and commercial entrepreneurship: same, different, or both?' *Entrepreneurship Theory and Practice*, 30, 1: 1–22.

Basu, A. (2004) 'Entrepreneurial aspirations among family business owners: an analysis of ethnic business owners in the UK'. *International Journal of Entrepreneurial Behaviour and Research*, 10(1/2): 12–33.

Baumol, W. J. (1996) 'Entrepreneurship: productive, unproductive, and destructive'. *Journal of Business Venturing*, 11, 1: 3–22.

Baumol, W. J. (2010) *The Microtheory of Entrepreneurship*. Princeton University Press.

Bluestein, A. (2015) 'The most entrepreneurial group in America wasn't born in America'. *Inc. Magazine*. February. Available at http://www.inc.com/magazine/201612/leigh-buchanan/state-of-entrepreneurship-2017.html (accessed 30 November 2016).

BMG Research (2013) *Social Enterprise: Market Trends Based upon BIS Small Business Survey 2012*. Cabinet Office. Available at www.gov.uk/government/uploads/system/uploads/attachment_data/file/205291/Social_Enterprises_Market_Trends_-_report_v1.pdf (accessed 30 November 2016).

Bradshaw, D. (2014) 'The rise of China's entrepreneurial spirit'. *The Financial Times*. Available at http://www.ft.com/cms/s/2/962a905a-70a3-11e4-9129-00144feabdc0.html#axzz45EHrmVqU (accessed 24 December 2016).

BWB (2016) *Remembering Stephen Lloyd*. Bates Wells Braithwaite. Available http://www.bwbllp.com/in-memory-of-stephen-lloyd (accessed 30 November 2016).

Carter, B. (2014) 'Is China's economy really the largest in the world?' *BBC News*, 16 December 2014, Available at http://www.bbc.co.uk/news/magazine-30483762 (accessed 24 December 2016).

Certo, S. T. and Miller, T. (2008) 'Social entrepreneurship: key issues and concepts'. *Business Horizons*, 51, 4: 267–71.

Choi, N. and Majumdar, S. (2014) 'Social entrepreneurship as an essentially contested concept: opening a new avenue for systematic future research'. *Journal of Business Venturing*, 29, 3: 363–76.

Close, K. (2015) 'Fashion Designer Eileen Fisher's $210 Million Fortune Built On Simple Basics'. *Forbes*, 28 May.

Deakins, D., Ram, M., and Smallbone, D. (2003) 'Addressing the business support needs of ethnic minority firms in the UK'. *Environment and Planning C: Government and Policy*, 21, 6: 843–59.

Dees, J. G. (1998) *The Meaning of Social Entrepreneurship*. Available at http://www.redalmarza.cl/ing/pdf/TheMeaningofsocialEntrepreneurship.pdf (accessed 24 December 2016).

Dees, J. G. and Anderson, B. B. (2003) 'For-profit social ventures'. *International Journal of Entrepreneurship Education* (Special Issue on Social Entrepreneurship), 2: 1–26.

Dees, J. G. and Elias, J. (1998) 'The challenges of combining social and commercial enterprise'. *Business Ethics Quarterly*, 8, 1: 165–78.

Discua Cruz, A., Hamilton, E., and Jack, S. L. (2012) 'Understanding entrepreneurial cultures in family businesses: a study of family business groups in Honduras'. *Journal of Family Business Strategy*, 3, 3: 147–61.

Dodd, S., Jack, S. L., and Anderson, A. R. (2013) 'From admiration to abhorrence: the contentious appeal of entrepreneurship across Europe'. *Entrepreneurship and Regional Development*, 24, 1–2: 69–89.

Elkington, J. (1997) *Cannibals with Forks: The Triple Bottom Line of 21st Century Business*. Oxford: Capstone.

Fayolle, A., Jack, S. L., Lamine, W., and Chabaud, D. (2016) *Entrepreneurial Process and Social Networks: A Dynamic Perspective*. Cheltenham: Edward Elgar.

Eileen Fisher (2017) 'We have a history of living the values that have shaped us'. Available at: http://www.eileenfisher.com/values (accessed 25 January 2017).

Font, J. and Méndez, M. (2013) *Surveying Ethnic Minorities and Immigrant Populations: Methodological Challenges and Research Strategies*. Amsterdam: Amsterdam University Press.

Gil, A., Zozimo, R., San Román, E., and Jack, S. L. (2016) 'At the crossroads: management and business history in entrepreneurship research'. *Journal of Evolutionary Studies in Business*, 2, 1: 156–200.

Glazer, N. and Moynihan, D. P. (1963) *Beyond the Melting Pot*. Cambridge, MA: MIT Press.

Gras, D. and Mendoza-Abarca, K. I. (2014) 'Risky business?: the survival implications of exploiting commercial opportunities by nonprofits'. *Journal of Business Venturing*, 29, 3: 392–404.

Hamilton, E. E, Discua Cruz, A. F., and Jack, S. L. (2016) 'Re-framing the status of narrative in family business research: towards an understanding of families in business'. *Journal of Family Business Strategy*. Forthcoming.

Hill, T. L., Kothari, T. H., and Shea, M. (2010) 'Patterns of meaning in the social entrepreneurship literature: a research platform'. *Journal of Social Entrepreneurship*, 1, 1: 5–31.

Huang, Y. (2010) 'Entrepreneurship in China'. *The World Financial Review*. Available at http://www.worldfinancialreview.com/?p=2782 (accessed 24 December 2016).

Ivy, J., Jack, S. L., and Larty, J. (2014) 'Entrepreneurship and the conditions for building networks in an emerging economy: the case of Belarus'. *74th Annual Meeting of the Academy of Management*, Philadelphia, PA, 1–5 August.

Ivy, J., Larty, J., and Jack, S. L. (2015) 'Searching for relevance: NGO-donor relationships in a geographically isolated community'. *Journal of Management Inquiry*, 24, 3: 280–99.

Jack, S. L. and Anderson, A. R. (2008) 'Role typologies for enterprising education: the professional artisan?' *Journal of Small Business and Enterprise Development*, 5, 2: 259–73.

Jack, S. L., Lamine, W., Fayolle, A., and Mian, S. (2017) 'The social skill sets of entrepreneurs'. *Journal of Small Business Management*. Forthcoming.

Jones, T. P., McEvoy, D., and Barrett, G. (1985) *Small Business Initiative: Ethnic Minority Business Component*. Swindon: Economic and Social Research Council.

Kelley, D., Singer, S., and Herrington, M. (2016) *Global Entrepreneurship Monitor, 2015/2016 Global Report*. Available at http://gemconsortium.org/report/49480 (accessed 24 December 2016).

Khan, U. (2008) Entrepreneurship higher amongst ethnic minorities. *The Daily Telegraph*, 9 July. Available at http://www.telegraph.co.uk/news/uknews/2276141/Entrepreneurship-higher-amongst-ethnic-minorities.html (accessed 30 November 2016).

Kirzner, I. M. (1973) *Competition and Entrepreneurship*. Chicago, IL: University of Chicago Press.

Konopaski, M., Jack, S. L., and Hamilton, E. (2015) 'How family business members learn about continuity'. *Academy of Management Learning and Education*, 14, 3: 347–64.

Krueger, M. J. (2015) 'Care and capitalist crisis in anglophone digital landscapes: the case of the mompreneur'. Doctoral dissertation. Washington DC: University of Washington.

Kubski, J. and Skodova, M. (2013) 'Why are more women leading social businesses?'. *The Guardian*, 23 Oct. Available at https://www.theguardian.com/ social-enterprise-network/women-in-leadership-blog/2013/oct/23/why-more-women-leading-social-business (accessed 30 November 2016).

Leppäaho, T. and Jack, S. L. (2016) 'Imprinting, embeddeness and social network ties in the internationalization of small- and medium-sized family enterprises'. Presented at the Babson College Entrepreneurship Conference, Bodo, Norway, June.

Lockett, N., Middleton, K., Padilla-Meléndez, A., Quesada Pallares, C., and Jack, S. L. (2017) '"Lost in Space": the role of social networking in university-based entrepreneurial learning'. *Industry and Higher Education*. Forthcoming

Mair, J. and Martí, I. (2006) 'Social entrepreneurship research: a source of explanation, prediction and delight'. *Journal of World Business*, 41, 1: 36–44.

McEvoy, D., Jones, T. P., Cater J., and Aldrich, H. (1982) 'Asian immigrant businesses in British cities'. Paper presented to the British Association for the Advancement of Science, Annual Meeting, September.

McKeever, E., Anderson, A. R., and Jack, S. L. (2015) 'Entrepreneurship and mutuality: social capital in processes and practices'. *Entrepreneurship and Regional Development*, 26, 5–6: 453–77.

McKeever, E., Jack, S. L., and Anderson, A. R. (2015) 'Embedded entrepreneurship in the creative re-construction of place', *Journal of Business Venturing*, 30, 1: 50–65.

Mitra, S. (2008) 'How Amazon could change publishing'. Forbes, 16 May. Available at http://www.forbes.com/2008/05/16/mitra-amazon-books-tech-enter-cx_sm_0516mitra.html (accessed 23 December 2016).

Modood, T. (1997) 'Employment'. In Modood, T., Berthoud, R., Lakey, J., Nazroo, J., Smith, P., Virdee, S., and Beishon, S. (eds), *Ethnic Minorities in Britain: Diversity and Disadvantage*. London: Policy Studies Institute.

Mulholland, K. (1997) 'The family enterprise and business strategies'. *Work, Employment and Society*, 11, 4: 685–711.

Noruzi, M. R., Westover, J. H., and Rahimi, G. R. (2010) 'An exploration of social entrepreneurship in the entrepreneurship era'. *Asian Social Science*, 6, 6: 3–10.

Ram, M. and Jones, T. (1998) *Ethnic Minorities in Business*. London: Small Business Research Trust, The Open University.

Regulator of Community Interest Companies (2016) *Annual Report 2015/2016*. Regulator of Community Interest Companies.

Ridley-Duff, R. and Bull, M. (2015) *Understanding Social Enterprise: Theory and Practice* (2nd edn). London: Sage Publications.

Robert Half (2013) 'FTSE 100 CEO Tracker'. Available at www.roberthalf.co.uk/id/ PR-03593/FTSE-100-Companies-UK-Press-Release (accessed 30 November 2016).

Saxenian, A. (2002) 'Silicon Valley's new immigrant high-growth entrepreneurs'. *Economic Development Quarterly*, 16, 1: 20–31.

Schumpeter, J. A. (1942) *Capitalism, Socialism and Democracy*. New York: Harper & Row.

Schwab, K. (ed.) (2016) *The Global Competitiveness Report 2016–17*. Geneva: World Economic Forum.

Short, J. C., Moss, T. W. and Lumpkin, G. T. (2009) 'Research in social entrepreneurship: past contributions and future opportunities'. *Strategic Entrepreneurship Journal*, 3, 2: 161–94.

SIMRA (2017) 'Social Innovation in Marginalised Rural Areas (SIMRA)' [Horizon 2020 project]. Available at http://www.simra-h2020.eu/ (accessed 14 January 2017).

Soetanto, D. and Jack, S. L. (2013) 'Business incubators and the networks of technology based firms'. *Journal of Technology Transfer*, 38, 4: 476–86.

Soetanto, D. and Jack, S. L (2016) 'The impact of university-based incubation support on the innovation strategy of academic spin-offs'. *Technovation*, 50–51: 25–40.

Steiner, A., Jack, S. L., and Farmer, J. (2008) 'Social entrepreneurship in a rural context: an ideaological state'. *Journal of Rural Enterprise and Management*, 4, 1: 20–39.

Stephan, U., Uhlaner, L. M., and Stride, C. (2015) 'Institutions and social entrepreneurship: the role of institutional voids, institutional support, and institutional configurations'. *Journal of International Business Studies*, 46, 3: 308–31.

Thompson, C. (2016) 'China is no longer a nation of tech copycats'. *Wired.co.uk*, 20 March. Available at http://www.wired.co.uk/magazine/archive/2016/04/features/china-tech-copycat-yy-meituan-xinchejian-zepp-labs (accessed 24 December 2016).

Vandor, P. and Franke, N. (2016) 'Why are immigrants more entrepreneurial?' *Harvard Business Review*, 27 October. Available at https://hbr.org/2016/10/why-are-immigrants-more-entrepreneurial (accessed 30 November 2016).

Villeneuve-Smith, F. and Chung, C. (2013) *The People's Business: State of Social Enterprise Survey 2013*. London: Social Enterprise UK. Available at http://www.socialenterprise.org.uk/uploads/files/2013/07/the_peoples_business.pdf (accessed 30 November 2016).

Virdee, S. (2006) 'Race, employment and social change: a critique of current orthodoxies'. *Ethnic and Racial Studies*, 29, 4: 605–28.

von Mises, L. (1949) *Human Action: A Treatise on Economics*. New Haven, CT: Yale University Press.

Wadhwa, V., Saxenian, A., Rissing, B., and Gere, G. (2007) *America's New Immigrant Entrepreneurs*. Durham, NC: Duke University.

Waldinger, R. D., Aldrich, H., and Ward, R. (1990) *Ethnic Entrepreneurs: Immigrant Business in Industrial Societies*. Sage Publications, Thousand Oaks, CA.

Wang, C. L. (2016) 'Social enterprises: ten years on'. *CICs Annual Report 2015–2016*. London: The Office of the Regulator of Community Interest Companies (CICs).

Wang, C. L. and Altinay, L. (2012) 'Social embeddedness, entrepreneurial orientation and firm growth in ethnic minority small businesses in the United Kingdom'. *The International Small Business Journal*, 30, 1: 3–23.

Wang, C. L., Rafiq, M., Li, X., and Zheng, Y. (2014) 'Entrepreneurial preparedness: an exploratory case study of Chinese private enterprises'. *International Journal of Entrepreneurial Behavior & Research*, 20, 4: 351–74.

Werbner, P. (1994) 'Renewing an industrial past: British Pakistani entrepreneurship in Manchester'. In J. M. Brown and R. Foot (eds), *Migration: The Asian Experience*. New York, NY, St Martin's Press, 104–30.

Worstall, T. (2014) 'China's now the world number one economy and it doesn't matter a darn'. *Forbes*, 7 Dec. Available at http://www.forbes.com/sites/timworstall/2014/12/07/chinas-now-the-world-number-one-economy-and-it-doesnt-matter-a-darn/#1ef255d75cb4 (accessed on 24 December 2016).

Yueh, L. (2008) *China's Entrepreneurs*. University of Oxford, Department of Economics, Discussion Paper No. 324. Available at http://www.economics.ox.ac.uk/Research/wp/pdf/paper324.pdf) and forthcoming in World Development (accessed on 24 December 2016).

Zhou, M. (2004) 'Revisiting ethnic entrepreneurship: convergencies, controversies, and conceptual advancements'. *The International Migration Review*, 38, 3: 1040–74.

PART I
ENTREPRENEURSHIP IN PRACTICE

3

VISIONS: CREATING NEW VENTURES

Vision without action is a daydream. Action without vision is a nightmare.

Japanese proverb

To be a successful entrepreneur one needs a vision of greatness for one's work. If we dream extravagantly we will be inspired to forge a reality beyond the straight jacket of practicalities.

Sir Ernest Hall, musician and serial entrepreneur

LEARNING OUTCOMES

After reading this chapter you should be able to:

- Appreciate the role played by entrepreneurial vision in creating a new venture.
- Distinguish between three distinct approaches to shaping an entrepreneurial vision: (a) the emerging vision; (b) the traditional business plan; (c) the entrepreneurial 'opportunity business model' (OBM).
- Understand how the entrepreneurial 'opportunity business model' (OBM) can be used to establish the outlines of a venture and to communicate your vision to others.
- Identify the dimensions and drivers that underpin an entrepreneurial opportunity, and relate these to the context you intend to operate in.
- Recognise how the challenge of shaping a vision relates to the themes addressed in other Part One chapters.
- Apply these concepts and techniques in order to create your own entrepreneurial venture.

3.1 INTRODUCTION

3.1.1 Visions, opportunities, and the entrepreneurial process

This chapter examines the way that entrepreneurs shape and realise their visions. One of the key skills of successful entrepreneurs is being able to identify relevant drivers and to recognise the **entrepreneurial opportunities** that they make possible.

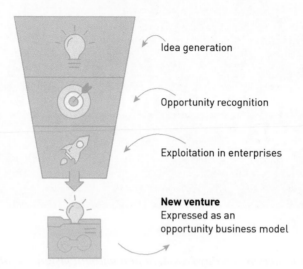

FIGURE 3.1 Simplified illustration of the entrepreneurial process.

The **entrepreneurial process** that takes us from idea generation and opportunity recognition to the point where an opportunity is exploited, or converted into a real venture. Figure 3.1 is a simplified illustration of this process, which comprises three distinct but closely related activities. Initially, it will involve you in generating new business ideas (i.e. creativity and **innovation**) and recognising opportunities that have the potential for exploitation (i.e. evaluation and selection). In practice, there is often a lot of interplay between these activities, which we explore further in Chapter 4. Meanwhile, as a result of these interactions, entrepreneurs are likely to narrow down their options, refine their ideas, and organise their resources until they are in a position to engage in the third set of activities, exploiting an opportunity. The end result may be a new commercial (*classic entrepreneurship*) or social venture (*social entrepreneurship*). It could also take the form of a corporate venture (*intrapreneurship*) that operates within an existing organisation.

In this chapter, we concentrate on the first two activities in the entrepreneurial process and look at how you translate your vision into something more tangible. There are broadly three approaches to shaping a vision (emergent visions, traditional business plans, and business models). We discuss the alternatives and introduce the opportunity business model (OBM) as a technique that can help you with this task. Understanding the dimensions and drivers for a business idea will allow you (and others) to decide whether you have got a genuine entrepreneurial opportunity that can be exploited.

3.1.2 Entrepreneurial learning

The entrepreneurial process of idea generation, opportunity recognition, and exploitation in enterprises is part of a larger cycle of **entrepreneurial learning**, which we introduced in Chapter 1 (Figure 3.2). The framework is reproduced here to show how the opportunity business models fit into the process, as a way of helping entrepreneurs to get a clearer vision of their new ventures. As the linked features

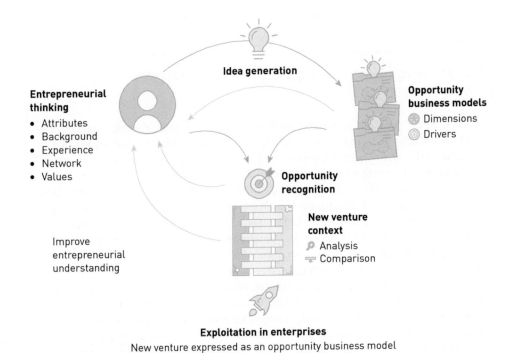

Idea generation

Entrepreneurial thinking
- Attributes
- Background
- Experience
- Network
- Values

Opportunity business models
- Dimensions
- Drivers

Opportunity recognition

New venture context
- Analysis
- Comparison

Improve entrepreneurial understanding

Exploitation in enterprises
New venture expressed as an opportunity business model

FIGURE 3.2 Entrepreneurial learning and opportunity business models.

of Figure 3.2 suggest, this is certainly not a one-off event. Entrepreneurial learning takes place in a continuous cycle, with people learning more about themselves as well as about their new ventures.

Case 3.1 illustrates how two successful entrepreneurs, Karen Darby and Juliet Davenport, were able to articulate personal visions in ways that engaged key audiences. In doing so, they created two highly successful enterprises, SimplySwitch and Good Energy. In both instances, a change in legislation was an initial driver, creating an environment in which these new ventures could flourish. Karen had several years' experience of running a telemarketing company and was herself frustrated by the process of changing electricity supplier. Industry deregulation was the driver for change, but Karen also had the crucial insight that helping people switch supplier could be a real entrepreneurial opportunity. She also recognised that she was able to bring together the resources required to exploit this opportunity, even though this meant selling an equity share to an investor in order to finance the venture (Chapter 9). Karen's ability to present a convincing vision for her new venture was a critical factor in gaining this investment. So how do you create this kind of vision? Just think for a moment. How would you go about persuading a potential investor to take an interest in your own venture, even though it was not yet trading? Why should other people risk their money on what may be little more than your bright idea? As you begin to shape your vision it is worth keeping these potential investors in mind. Step into their shoes from time to time and ask yourself whether 'that idea' is still of any interest.

CASE 3.1

Electrifying ideas: deregulation lights up new opportunities

In 1989, the UK government passed the Electricity Act that was, over the course of the next two decades, to transform a monopoly into a dynamic market supplying electricity to commercial and domestic consumers (http://www.legislation.gov.uk). The intention was to allow customers to purchase their electricity from a range of competing providers, albeit still distributed over the national grid, thereby increasing competitive forces and reducing prices. Intuitively we think of large corporations like E.ON (http://www.eon.com) and Scottish Power (http://www.scottishpower.com) competing in such a large established market rather than smaller providers, let alone new ones. In this case we will explore how individuals created a vision for their new ventures, which were only made possible by the legal driver of deregulation.

The first, **Karen Darby** gained extensive experience in telemarketing by running her own call centre business, Decisions Group, for seven years before selling her shares in 1990 (https://www.linkedin.com/in/karen-darby-a22394a). She drew on this experience, when deregulation came along, to help consumers understand the promotions being offered by electricity providers. Telesales is all about selling products over the phone but Karen realised that in such a congested marketplace consumers needed advice not promotions. In other words, 'People don't like the idea of being sold to' (Sunday Times 2004). Her vision was to establish a service company that provided consumers with independent advice on which provider offered the best deal for them. In this way, **SimplySwitch** was born (http://www.simplyswitch.com). Karen's first challenge was to share the vision of her new venture plan with potential investors. She was able to secure £125,000 investment in return for a 35% equity stake and launched SimplySwitch in 2003. In 2006 it was sold for £22 million (€29 million) (Guardian 2007a).

Ethical point Karen now describes herself as a social entrepreneur and believes that a business can both make money and have a social purpose (YouTube 2012a). Karen had a clear vision of how she could help consumers and use her experience and skills to develop a new venture in a new market. Interestingly, this intermediary business model has been widely adopted across many sectors and is often underpinned by the Internet. There have been a number of successful comparison websites with Money Super Market (http://www.moneysupermarket.com) being one of the better-known examples. But what opportunities were there for new ventures actually to generate electricity and supply it, over the national grid, directly to consumers? Surely this was only the preserve of large corporations.

Juliet Davenport faced a particularly difficult challenge. Her vision also involved people changing electricity provider, but she also wanted them to switch to 'green energy'. It was responding to both to the legal driver of deregulation and the societal driver of climate change. In 2002, Juliet became chief executive of an existing renewable energy company, which then began to offer shares to customers, enabling the company to buy a wind farm in Cornwall. The new company, which was re-branded as **Good Energy** (http://www.goodenergy.co.uk), now provides more than 50,000 domestic and business customers with electricity generated by 100% renewable sources. Good Energy employs over 250 people and has an annual turnover of over £58 million (€76 million). How did it achieve this breakthrough in such a short period of time? In part, it was because Juliet had a clear vision, saving 1 million tonnes of carbon a year, which she could communicate to investors, independent generators, and customers. The vision is based on a shared set of values, which are closely linked to fighting climate change by 'home grown energy'. As Juliet once described it. 'Local generators delivering [energy] to local customers' (YouTube 2010). As a result, many Good Energy customers are also shareholders in the company. The vision is also being spread through a growing community of over 800 independent renewable electricity generators and over 75,000 feed-in tariff generation customers across the UK. In 2016, customer numbers increased by 36% to 240,000, revenues increased by 45% to £46 million and profits increased by 164% to £1.4 million (YouTube 2016).

Ethical point There is still much debate about what 'green power' really is and it is sometimes difficult for consumers to compare green credentials. In the UK, the Green Energy Supply Certification Scheme has emerged to respond to these concerns (http://www.greenenergyscheme.org). How do we know which companies really are green? Good Energy is independently accredited as an Ethical Company (http://www.ethical-company-organisation.org).

POINTS TO CONSIDER

1. Deregulation is a good example of a legal driver that is beyond the control of a single enterprise. What other industries have been changed by regulation and deregulation? Try to identify a new venture that has emerged to exploit these opportunities.

2. Environmental concerns are driving many product innovations, such as EcoButton (https://www.ecobutton.com) and Nest Labs (https://nest.com/uk/thermostat/). What entrepreneurial opportunities can you identify that respond to this societal driver?

3. What particular challenges did Karen and Juliet face as they created their visions and translated them into new ventures?

Sources: Sunday Times 2004; Guardian 2007a; YouTube 2010, 2012a, 2016.

This chapter is organised as follows. In Section 3.2 we discuss three approaches to shaping the vision for a new venture: emergent visions, traditional business plans, and business models. Section 3.3 is a more detailed examination of the opportunity business model with examples showing how it can be applied in practice. Section 3.4 shows how the challenge of shaping any entrepreneurial opportunity is addressed in more detail in the remaining Part One chapters. The chapter concludes by considering Steve and Julie Pankhurst development of Friends Reunited as one of the first commercially successful online social networking communities (Case 3.4 *Steve Pankhurst: with a little help from our friends*) and introduces two video cases on $SAGE edge™ *Visions: Jonathan's challenge* (Case 3.5b) and *Visions: Rana's challenge* (Case 3.5a) to test your understanding of this chapter.

3.2 SHAPING THE VISION: THREE APPROACHES

3.2.1 The importance of vision

Having a vision is the key to your entrepreneurial new venture. Without it there is no driving force or sense of direction. However, your vision needs to be backed up otherwise it is pure fantasy. Entrepreneurs and entrepreneurial organisations may convince themselves they have a winning idea but ultimately it is the customer or market that will decide. For example, when they launched their new venture in 1998, the three founders of Boo.com where convinced they had found the solution to the selling branded fashions over the Internet. They also convinced venture capitalists to invest over $135 million (€125 million) in their idea. However, in less than two years the money was spent and the business closed. Failed visions are not the sole preserve of individual entrepreneurs; large corporations can also make mistakes. For example, the idea for handheld personal digital assistant devices (PDAs) was introduced by Apple Computers in 1993, with the launch of the Newton MessagePad. In hindsight, we can see this was the right idea but at the wrong time (i.e. the technology and the market was not sufficiently advanced). Some radical innovations never find their 'right time' while others, including the PDA, relaunch successfully at a later date. It can be difficult to differentiate between crazy ideas that have no future and others that might appear crazy, but which could be the next 'big thing'. Thomas John Watson, president of International Business Machines (IBM), was once famously misquoted to the effect that, 'I think there is a world market for maybe five computers.' Watson may not have made this comment, but at the time (1943), there was a general assumption that the demand for computers was limited; today's huge market for personal computers, let alone carrying powerful smartphones around in our pockets, would have been unimaginable to early industry leaders like Watson. The entrepreneur's initial task is to convert a personal vision into a coherent proposition, and then to articulate (i.e. communicate) it in ways that will attract interest and gain credibility with investors, customers, suppliers, and others (e.g. regulators). This is not an easy task and it often requires considerable persistence in order to succeed. For example, James Dyson's original idea for a bagless vacuum cleaner was rejected by several leading manufacturers. In the end, he decided to set up his own venture and launched what was to become a highly successful range of products.

→ **PERSPECTIVES** See Section 12.4 for further information.

3.2.2 Introducing the three approaches

One of the main challenges facing any individual or group seeking to create a new venture is to recognise which of their various business ideas can be converted into a real entrepreneurial opportunity. We should not underestimate the scale or difficulty of this task. There are broadly three approaches that you can adopt to shape your ideas for a new venture:

1. Following an emergent vision.

2. Drafting a traditional business plan.

3. Developing an opportunity business model.

In this section, we consider each of these options in some detail, then present an argument for adopting the third option, the entrepreneurial business model, as the most effective way of shaping your vision. In practice, as entrepreneurs you may make use of more than one of these approaches, depending on their circumstances. Though we focus attention on the opportunity business model (OBM) we also highlight the strengths of the other approaches. Our basic aim is to provide a good balance between the flexibility offered by emergent visions and the logical structure of the traditional business plan.

3.2.3 Following an emergent vision

Many entrepreneurs begin by following their vision without the assistance of a formal business plan. In other words, they adopt a highly intuitive approach, with key strategic decisions often relying heavily on the entrepreneur's 'gut feeling' and previous industry and market experience. There are many advantages to such an approach, including its flexibility. Even when more formal approaches are adopted, there is no substitute for being close to the market and drawing on your previous experience of a particular product or industry sector. One of the major disadvantages of the emergent approach is that it can be difficult to explain your vision to other people, including potential financiers and partners. These informal approaches are currently attracting a lot of attention from **entrepreneurship** researchers, who analyse them using labels such as '**effectuation**' and '**bricolage**' (Section 12.4). Indeed, effectuation theory is attractive with the five constructs of (i) bird in the hand, (ii) affordable loss, (iii) crazy quilt, (iv) make lemonade, and (v) pilot in the plane (Sarasvathy 2009). See ⑤SAGE edge™ for video interview with *Emma Sheldon* discussing her business in terms of effectuation theory. They may be appropriate for some kinds of venture, including those that are less growth-oriented and more locally based. Emergent visions can also be effective during the early phases of a venture's development. However, in some situations, including technology-based ventures, this approach is likely to lack the rigour that is required to secure funding and to gain legitimacy (e.g. securing approval from industry regulators). Consider it from the perspective of a business angel or venture capitalist. What is the minimum level of detail and analysis that you would expect an entrepreneur to provide before you agreed to part with a very large sum of money, to be invested in an unproven idea?

→ **PERSPECTIVES** See Sections 12.3 and 12.4 for further information.

3.2.4 Drafting a traditional business plan

One response to the need for clear articulation of a new venture is to produce a traditional formal business plan. You may already be familiar with the idea of a business plan as they are often created as part of a school or student enterprise activity (i.e. the 'business plan competition'). Banks and investors also require some form of business plan in support of requests for business loans or investment. Business plans for start-up ventures are documents that set out the goals of the venture and how they will be achieved. A typical business plan contains the following sections:

- **Executive summary** Outlines the key features of the venture and may highlight relevant points such as funding required, growth potential, and returns for investors.

- **The business opportunity** Sets out what the venture aims to provide, why there is a demand, and who is involved in the process (e.g. customers, suppliers, partners).

- **Management team** Provides information on key people, often in the form of biographies that highlight relevant skills, knowledge, and experience.

- **Marketing and promotional strategy** Analyses potential market and competition, summarises marketing mix, and explains how products and services will be promoted.
- **Operational strategy** Sets out practical aspects of the venture including key processes, information systems, assets (e.g. premises, technologies), and controls.
- **Financial forecasts** Provide a quantified summary of the other sections, including projected cash flows, profit and loss accounts, and balance sheets.

There are a wide variety of software programs and other services to help you produce your business plan. These include commercial products and others provided at no cost by banks and enterprise development organisations. Accountants also offer support to clients who wish to produce business plans or to calculate their financial projections. There are many step-by-step guides to writing a business plan, including Tiffany et al. (2012), Mullins (2013), and Finch (2006). The Online Resources provide links to several of these products. We have also included a simple business plan template that can be downloaded and adapted to meet your needs.

> **online resources** 'Business Plans for Start-Up Ventures'

The main limitation of business plans as a way of gaining an understanding of new ventures is that they do not reflect the way that people shape their entrepreneurial visions. Business plans are formal written documents, with a linear structure, in which various aspects of your venture (e.g. marketing, operations) are divided into separate sections. However, when you are thinking through the practicalities of a new venture your mind will often be working in a much more flexible, creative, iterative and holistic way. For example, you might be thinking about the ways that marketing and operational aspects of the venture are inter-related. If you are drafting a formal business plan, it is important to ensure that it reinforces rather than limits your thinking. When it comes to convincing other people that your venture is worthwhile, it is essential that you and your team need to have a real, in-depth understanding of your vision. In addition, you need to be able to communicate your vision clearly, concisely and with enthusiasm. You can see how this works in practice in the popular television series *Dragons' Den*, where budding entrepreneurs who are seeking finance for their ventures are asked to make short presentations to a panel of investors (i.e. this is sometimes termed an 'elevator pitch'). The applicants face some very tough questioning, which often results in one or all of the investors deciding that they are 'out' (i.e. that they are no longer interested in the venture). Of course, the initial pitch is just the start of the process and any investor would need a lot more information before a contract was signed. However, investors are busy people. They often reject a proposal on the basis of that initial pitch. The key lesson is that unless you and your team are *personally* convincing, your audience is unlikely to invest more time in reading your business plan. Business plans certainly have an important role to play, but in the next sub-section we consider a more dynamic alternative that could help you to shape and articulate your vision more effectively.

3.2.5 Developing a business model

The concept of the business model emerged around 2000 as a way of understanding and comparing the plethora of new business ideas that developed around the Internet. The concept has since been refined and applied to other kinds of entrepreneurial venture. It offers two important advantages over the other approaches discussed in this section. Firstly, it provides you with a clear and concise way to communicate an entrepreneurial opportunity to potential investors and other interested parties. Secondly, in the process of constructing a business model, you can improve your own understanding of the underlying concept, enabling you to refine it further and build a more convincing case. Back in the early 2000s, investors were struggling to make sense of thousands of business plans claiming that their venture was uniquely positioned to exploit the boundless commercial opportunities of the web. The dot-com boom popularised terms such as 'first mover advantage' and 'burn rate' (i.e. the speed at which a venture drains cash flow) (Wolfe 1999; Lewis 2001). It also saw some dramatic failures, including WebVan and Boo.com. In this dynamic and turbulent world, business models offered a way of reaching a shared understanding of the dimensions and drivers of an entrepreneurial opportunity. By identifying these key components, and their underlying assumptions, business models allowed analysts to make comparisons and to identify ideas that were unique or particularly robust. It also became possible to track how business models were changing over time, enabling investors to categorise models and to identify new trends.

A business model can be seen as a working version of the traditional business plan. In essence, it shows how a venture is going to be able to generate revenues and to make a profit from its operations. The model identifies key components and functions of the business, and shows how these relate to its financial performance. Table 3.1 lists some more detailed definitions from the business and management field and Ovans (2015) provides a useful summary of business model articles published in the *Harvard Business Review*. Business models have now become something of a buzzword, but their effectiveness depends largely on how well they are applied. Poorly thought-out business models contributed to the downfall of many dotcoms in the last two decades, and even the most carefully constructed business model is not an automatic guarantee of success.

TABLE 3.1 Defining business models

'An architecture for the product, service and information flows, including a description of the various business actors and their roles; and a description of the potential benefits for the various business actors; and description of the sources of revenues.' (Timmers 2000: 32)

'A distinct system of suppliers, distributors, commerce services providers, and customers that use the Internet for their primary business communications and transactions.' (Tapscott et al. 2000: 19)

'Business models describe, as a system, how the pieces fit together.' (Magretta 2002: 87)

'The system of components, linkages and associated dynamics, which make commercial advantage of the Internet.' (Afuah and Tucci 2001: 6)

'A plan or diagram that is used to describe a business idea. How an enterprise competes, uses its resources, structures its relationships, interfaces with customers and creates value and generates profit.' (Barringer and Ireland 2012: 142)

'Every business model needs quantitatively to address five key elements': (i) revenue model, (ii) gross margin model, iii) operating model, iv) working capital model and (v) investment model. (Mullins 2013: 258)

'A business model describes the rationale of how an organisation creates, delivers and captures value.' (Osterwalder and Pigneur 2010: 14)

The business models concept has been refined in various ways. For example, more recent contributions pay greater attention to the role of competition. In one of the earliest contributions, Hamel (2000) created a framework comprising four major components: core strategy, strategic resources, customer interface, and value network, which can be linked to customer benefits and company boundaries. These components were also underpinned by four factors: efficiency, uniqueness, fit, and profits boosters. Osterwalder and Pigneur (2004) reviewed the literature and proposed another business model classification consisting of four main areas of activity:

- infrastructure management (capabilities, partnerships, and value configuration);
- product innovation (offering and value proposition);
- customer relationship (customer, channel, and relationship);
- financial aspects (cost, profit, and revenue).

Though much of the early work on business models was concerned with new business ideas in the digital economy, the concept has also proved to be highly relevant to understanding new entrepreneurial opportunities in other fields (Chesbrough and Rosenbloom 2002; Hitt et al. 2002; Morris et al. 2005). More recently, the *Business Model Canvas* (Osterwalder and Pigneur 2010; Osterwalder et al. 2014) has emerged as a popular way of exploring and expressing a new venture. The concept of business models emerged around 2000 in response to the proliferation of new Internet-based ventures. Influential sources include Timmers (2000), Amit and Zott (2001), Weill and Vitale (2001), and Currie (2004). The business models literature has generated several useful frameworks, with Professor Gary Hamel becoming a particularly well-respected author in the field: Hamel (2000). By the late 2000s, the original models had been further developed and adapted by authors interested in new venture creation. Recent applications of the concept include Zott and Amit (2007) and Barringer and Ireland (2012). However, Osterwalder and Pigneur's (2010) *Business Model Canvas* has become the most widely adopted framework with many online resources – https://strategyzer.com. See also *Value Proposition Design* (Osterwalder et al. 2014). There are also many online resources available, including an open educational resource on managing the digital economy by Professor Michael Rappa (http://digitalenterprise.org) and a blog about innovative business models by Alexander Osterwalder (http://www.businessmodelalchemist.com).

These help introduce the concept of the entrepreneurial business models, which describes both the key dimensions and the key drivers that enable new business ideas to be exploited in entrepreneurial ventures. In the remaining sections of this chapter, and throughout Part One of this book, we will be refining this newer application of the business model concept in order to evaluate, select, and pursue entrepreneurial opportunities.

Before considering how opportunity business models can be applied, it may be useful to consider following case (Case 3.2). It shows how a strong vision, if correctly presented, can be used to penetrate established, highly competitive markets in order to bring about positive social change. Sales of bottled water in Western Europe continue to grow at an alarming pace, in spite of the fact that tap water is usually safe to drink. Meanwhile, there are still chronic shortages of clean drinking water in some parts of the developing world. The case shows how two social entrepreneurs shaped their visions to challenge this imbalance in novel ways.

CASE 3.2

Water, water everywhere: but not a drop to drink

In the last 30 years sales of bottled water have grown to more than 1.3 billion litres in the UK and to over 9 billion litres in the USA. By 2017, this will mean global consumption of bottled water could exceed 300 billion litres. This is of little comfort to the 663 million people in the world who don't have access to safe drinking water (WaterAid 2016). Of course, there are many governments and NGOs trying to address this imbalance but what can we, as individuals, do about it?

Let us look at one individual who has a vision to change this imbalance by exploiting the market for bottled water rather than fighting against it. **Duncan Goose**, founder of Global Ethics and **One Water** (http://www.one difference.org), set up a new venture, in 2005, to sell ethical bottled water and donate 100% of its profits to installing a specialised water pumping systems called PlayPump (http://www.playpumps.org). He recognised the potential: 'The water market is an absolutely huge market in the UK, worth £1.5 billion' (Guardian 2007b). At one level Duncan's vision is simple: use all the profits from selling water, to people who can afford it, to provide clean water for people who cannot. Clearly, there needs to be more to it than that. In his younger days, Duncan travelled the world; in fact, he was inspired by Ted Simon's motorcycle journey in the 1970s, detailed in his book *Jupiter's Travels* (1979). Duncan is in good company: actors Ewan McGregor and Charley Boorman were also inspired by reading *Jupiter's Travels*. As you can imagine, Duncan has his own adventures, including surviving Hurricane Mike, which destroyed many communities in Honduras in 1998. Duncan recalled, 'What really struck me was to make a difference we did not need a lot of money, just a little money spent in the right way' (Sunday Times 2008).

He and his friends identified access to clean drinking water as a major global issue and set about doing something about it (YouTube 2008). One Water was conceived and launched in 2005, just at the same time as Bob Geldof's Live 8 appeal was launched (http://www.live8live.com). Having created a vision and shared it with organisers of Live 8, he faced the challenge of promoting and supplying it to individual consumers. Can you imagine how you would go about persuading retailers and supermarkets, which have shelves full of numerous brands of bottled water, to de-list one and put yours it its place? Indeed, it was very hard work for Duncan, but when Total (http://www.total.co.uk) became the first national stockist in 2006, others started to follow. In their first year, One Water donated £70,000 to charities working in Africa and India. By 2015, this had exceeded £12m in just 10 years

(Continued)

(Continued)

and transformed over 3 million lives. Then One Difference started expanding its product range to include One Eggs and One Kitchen Foil. Interestingly, Duncan has recruited other people to promote his vision, including actors David Tennant and Rebecca Lacey. Duncan Goose, is not alone in using the sales of water to fund humanitarian projects, **Kate Alcott** created **FRANK Water** (http://www.frankwater.com) in 2005 in order to generate funds for clean water projects in India. Kate had suffered from dysentery caused by drinking dirty water in India. Frank Water not only supplies bottled water but also water coolers to offices. Kate had a clear vision of how each purchase connected to providing clean water in India: 'Every bottled cooler you take on provides an initial 10,000 litres of safe drinking water to Frank Water Projects. Every refill provides a further 1,000 litres.' By 2016, FRANK Water had funded safe drinking water and sanitation for more than 300,000 people. Do not underestimate how difficult it is to enter a high competitive market, such as bottled water. Even large companies with significant resources can get it wrong. In 2004 Coca-Cola, one of the largest drinks companies in the world, withdrew its bottled water brand, Dasani, from the UK after spending a reported £10 million on launching it (TimesOnline 2004). Perhaps this really does put Duncan's and Kate's achievement into perspective. **Ethical point** Duncan earns a salary £6,000 a year from One Water and Kate draws no salary from Frank Water (Sunday Times 2007b).

QUESTIONS

1.   The societal driver for both One Water and Frank Water was providing clean water in developing countries. What other ways can you think of to achieve this?

2.   Look at the websites for both enterprises and see how strongly their vision is presented. If you had to buy a bottle of water from either which would you choose and why?

3.   Duncan and Kate use others to promote their vision, such as One Ambassadors and FRANK Champions. How important do you think this is and how successful has each been?

Sources: TimesOnline 2004; Guardian 2007b; Sunday Times 2007b, 2008; YouTube 2008; WaterAid 2016.

Case 3.2 provides two examples of turning a vision into a coherent and compelling proposal for a new venture. Duncan Goose and Kate Alcott had clear visions to help others by selling bottled water. Each of them achieved their vision in different ways, but what they had in common was an ability to shape their vision effectively. They recognised an entrepreneurial opportunity and obtained the resources to turn their ideas into a reality. Both were motivated by more than personal financial gain, which may also have been a factor contributing to their success. Their achievement was to make consumers see a connection between purchasing bottled water in one part of the world and providing clean water in another, where it was most needed. This connection between value proposition and driver is an important element of the entrepreneurial process. Throughout Part One there are many other examples of entrepreneurs who have been successful in converting their ideas into reality. In the next section, we begin to apply the opportunity business model as a way of shaping your entrepreneurial vision.

3.3 APPLYING THE OPPORTUNITY BUSINESS MODEL

3.3.1 Introducing the dimensions and drivers

The opportunity business model is a description of the key dimensions (Proposition, People, Place, Process, Profit) and drivers (Personal, Societal, Commercial, Legal, Technological) that underpin any new business idea and enable it to be exploited in an enterprise (Figure 3.3). Expressing your vision as an opportunity business model can be an effective way of accelerating your entrepreneurial learning and of developing opportunities into viable entrepreneurial ventures.

In this section, we provide some working definitions of these dimensions and drivers and show how they can be applied in practice. However, before proceeding further it may be helpful to explain why we are adopting this language. Many students on business management courses will have encountered two popular strategic analysis tools, which address a similar set of factors:

- **SWOT (Strengths, Weakness, Opportunities, and Threats) analysis** is used to make connections between external and (environmental) internal (organisational) factors.

- **PEST (Political, Economic, Social, and Technological) analysis** is used to identify different elements in the macro-environment. There are also a number of variations, each with their own acronym, for example, PESTLE (Political, Economic, Sociological, Technological, Legal, and Environmental); PESTER (Political, Economic Social, Technological, Environmental, and Regulatory) and STEEP (Social, Technological, Economic, Environmental, and Political).

Though these are tried and tested strategic analysis tools, they work most effectively when applied to existing organisations, industries, and markets. It can be difficult to adapt these tools, and to adjust your own approach, in order to analyse

Dimensions

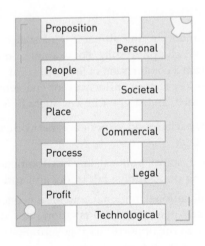

Drivers

FIGURE 3.3 The opportunity business model.

entrepreneurial opportunities, and to relate the findings to the practical challenges of creating a new venture. For these reasons, and given the increasing attention being paid to entrepreneurial business models, we will adopt the language of dimensions and drivers throughout Part One (Section 1.3). This recognises the need not just to clearly express the components or elements (*Dimensions*) of your business idea but also the important factors (*Drivers*) which underpin its success.

3.3.2 Dimensions: the core components of an idea

Dimensions are a way of expressing the different components or elements of the business idea. They help support analysis, structure discussion, and enable comparison. The five opportunity business model dimensions express the key components, elements, or building blocks of the business idea:

- **Proposition** What is the core value proposition, as perceived by the customer, of the opportunity? This could be expressed as a mission statement but needs to be clear and concise. Indeed, can this value proposition be expressed in just seven words?

- **People** Who are the leader, management team, and network of advisors, customers, suppliers, and stakeholders? How does social capital and networking support the business opportunity?

- **Place** Where is the market? Who are the customers and competitors? This could involve analysis of market and industry to identify segments and gaps.

- **Process** How is the enterprise structured? What are the key processes and relationships? How will these be enabled and supported? What role does information technology play?

- **Profit** Why do it? What are the real returns? Financials, gross profit, net profit, forecasts, KPIs, and capital required. Is there a social return? This might also include a consideration of the ownership structure and exit strategy.

3.3.3 Drivers: the factors underpinning an opportunity

Drivers are the factors underpinning an entrepreneurial opportunity. Often, one or more driver will apply to each opportunity. For example, an idea for a new road safety product might emerge from a combination of Societal, Legal, and Technological drivers. The four drivers express key factors, influences, or enablers that provide the foundations of a new business idea, and suggest how it might be exploited in an enterprise:

- **Personal** Attributes, background, experience, network, and values. Deep industry and market knowledge.

- **Societal** Wider global, social, political, and environmental factors, such as climate change, energy, aging populations, fair trade, and anti-social behaviour.

- **Commercial** Global, national, regional, and local economic and financial factors, such as currency exchange rates, local taxation rates, and the price of oil. What might be the impact on the opportunity if governments introduced a greenhouse gas emission trading scheme?

- **Legal** Legislation, rules, and regulatory requirements, typically set by governments and consortiam, such as data protection law and trade associations.

- **Technological** New and emerging technologies such as 3G mobile communication networks, public broadband, online social networks, and nanotechnology.

Drivers differ from dimensions in two ways. Firstly, not all drivers apply to every opportunity business model. By considering the most relevant drivers, you can focus more directly on the factors that enable a specific entrepreneurial opportunity. Secondly, it is important to recognise that drivers, except for Personal, are usually beyond the direct influence of individual entrepreneurs. Societal, Commercial, and Regulatory drivers are almost always outside your direct control. Technological drivers, such as broadband Internet, are also effectively a 'given'. An exception would be where a technology-driven venture develops a proprietary technology that they can protect with patents, or introduces a radical innovation that changes the 'rules of the game'. One way of visualising drivers in action is to imagine yourself as a surfer, selecting and then riding a series of powerful waves. Like the surfer, your success will depend on a number of factors, including judgement, persistence, and balance. For similar reasons, any attempt to challenge a driver directly (i.e. to stand up against a wave) is almost certain to end in failure. Consider the failed attempts of photographic film manufacturers to respond to the emergence of digital photography.

→ **PERSPECTIVES** See Section 11.3 for further information.

3.3.4 Applying the opportunity business model

We have argued that the opportunity business model is particularly effective when creating new entrepreneurial ventures. However, in order to illustrate how the model is applied, we have selected two existing organisations, one of which will be familiar to most readers and the other certainly less so. Initially, we explore each element of Apple Computer's digital music business, focusing on its 'iTunes store' business model before considering a very different new venture – The Cambridge Satchel Company.

Apple's history spans more than four decades, making it an 'old hand' in the highly competitive world of technology. It is also widely recognised as one of the world's most innovative companies (Economist 2007). But what is particularly striking is Apple's expansion since the late 1990s, from its original business in personal computers and operating systems into the emerging field of digital multimedia products and services. How can we make sense of the company's wide range of product and service offerings in this new business, and the drivers that underpin them?

Firstly, we need to consider the *dimensions* of each offering, in this case the online music store **iTunes**, which was launched by Apple in 2003:

- **Proposition** The core value proposition is to provide access online to music and videos, which can be purchased at a relatively low price. These can be downloaded to either an Apple Mac or Windows PC and then transferred to an iPod, the company's portable media player.

- **People** Apple is clearly at the centre of this service but requires relationships with the record companies who own the copyright for the music or video. This would not have been a simple task and would have required much negotiation. Apple's strong brand and high level of customer loyalty would have played a key role in this. Why didn't the record companies simply produce their own online music download service?

- **Place** The Internet has provided consumers with access to seemingly unlimited content. The music industry is a competitive market and perhaps surprisingly, Apple as a new entrant was able to achieve a dominant position in online music sales. Why was Apple able to achieve this?

- **Process** The use of the iTunes store requires an Apple Mac or Windows PC to run the iTunes software through which music files could be downloaded, stored, and copyright protected in a proprietary encrypted file format. Interestingly, this meant that Apple had to develop an application for Microsoft Windows. What might have been the consequences if Apple had not done this?

- **Profit** In this model, a percentage of the sales revenue is shared with the record companies and subsequently the artist. What might be the split between the three parties?

Secondly, we need to consider the *drivers* that underpin the 'iTunes store' business model:

- **Personal** Perhaps the charismatic late CEO, Steve Jobs, was another driver. He had in-depth industry knowledge, extensive networks, and a reputation for delivering successful innovation to the market.

- **Societal** While the growth of the Internet, on which iTunes store depends, is having a profound effect on society, it is not in itself a driver for this business model. What are your expectations of access to music in the future?

- **Commercial** Since the late 1990s the growth of illegal sharing of music files over the Internet has been seen as a major financial threat to the music industry's revenues. The iTunes store represented a much needed legitimate alternative to the industry. Clearly, the industry wanted a commercial solution which could gain the loyalty of artists and consumers alike. Why might this be so important?

- **Legal** In spite of a plethora of copyright law, the sharing of music files continues to pose a threat to the music industry. How many people do you know who still share music files and what would need to change to stop them doing it?

- **Technological** The widespread availability of a near ubiquitous electronic communications platform, the Internet, is a prerequisite to the iTunes store's business model and is clearly outside the control of Apple Computers. However, the company has developed proprietary applications and a file format which gave them a competitive advantage by protecting their intellectual property. How might the growth of 3G mobile networks affect Apple's iTunes service?

Business models usually extend well beyond the boundaries of the organisation, and in the case of Apple we can see how the introduction of the iPhone introduced a new set of external partners, telecommunications providers in each of the countries served. These include AT&T in the United States, T-Mobile in Germany, and O2 in the UK. With more than 10 billion songs downloaded (Apple 2010), the success of iTunes store is beyond question. But even the most successful business models need to evolve in response to a rapidly changing world. How might Apples 'iTunes store' model develop in the future? For example, what is the significance of offering videos, movies, TV shows, games, and free radio podcasts? And what are the likely long-term effects on the entertainment industry?

Representing Apple Computer's digital multimedia product and service offerings as an opportunity business model can help us to better understand the entrepreneurial opportunity. In addition, it can support a discussion about what is unique about the model when compared to its competitors. For example, Samsung is a leading manufacturer of mobile telephones. The company also provides a range of products and services that exploit the convergence of the Internet and communications industries. How could Samsung compete with, and differentiate its offerings from, those of Apple? One of the strengths of the opportunity business model is that it provides an analytical framework for this kind of thinking.

Now let us consider the opportunity business of a very different type pf company – **The Cambridge Satchel Company** (http://www.cambridgesatchel.com) founded by Julie Deane, OBE, in 2008.

Firstly, we need to consider the *dimensions*:

- **Proposition** Julie's company is all about manufacturing very high-quality, designer, leather satchels in the UK. But can we express that as a proposition in just seven words? *Produce high-quality, designer, British leather satchels.* Can you do better than this?

- **People** Julie and Freda, her mother, a growing management team, no doubt lots of advisers, and a growing network of designers. Who else might be involved?

- **Place** Three shops in the UK, two in London. Paperchase as national stockist and international stockist. But perhaps more interesting, a growing online business, including massive growth in markets like China.

- **Process** The satchel company has to be good at designing and manufacturing leather satchels and marketing and protecting its brand.

- **Profit** The company started in 2008 with just £600 (€800). Interestingly, it raised £12 million (€16 million) by selling equity to a leading venture capital company in Europe.

Secondly, we need to consider the most important drivers that underpin the Cambridge Satchel business model. What are the factors outside of Julie's control which are driving the extraordinary growth of this company?

- **Personal** Julie founded the business with her mother, Freya Thomas, in 2008. She had previously worked as an accountant and had the 'great determination and passion' to start a successful company to pay for her children's school fees (YouTube 2012b).

- **Societal** According to the International Monetary Fund, China took over from the USA to become the world's largest economy in size in 2014 and with that has emerged a growing middle class who want to demonstrate their wealth by buying consumer goods. One way to demonstrate this new wealth is by buying designer consumer goods. Julie knows this. She says, 'Customers from China come when they visit London. They know the brand and they seek out the stores – I know the demand is there' (Independent 2014).

- **Commercial** Britain really is cool. The Olympic Games in 2012, the opening ceremony with The Queen and James Bond, even Mr. Bean – all of these are contributing to a perceived value of British products (YouTube 2012c). But what are these brand values? Perhaps quality, trustworthiness, heritage, fashionable, and even fun.

It's important to remember that Julie has done very little to create *Cool Britannia* and certainly nothing to create China as the emerging economic powerhouse in the world. But her company has benefited from these drivers.

Having looked at an established Apple and Cambridge Satchel, our next case examines how the opportunity business model drivers operate in an entrepreneurial start-up venture. Case 3.3 traces the way that a societal driver, in this instance the trend towards safer and healthier food, has spawned a seemingly endless array of entrepreneurial opportunities.

CASE 3.3

Food for thought: a simple driver with infinite responses

We all need to eat. However, the desire for safe, healthy, nutritious, and tasty foods goes far beyond this simple human need. There is a great deal of interest in the food and drinks we consume. This interest is often expressed in the form of fashions and trends that can generate new entrepreneurial opportunities. The four entrepreneurs that make up this case illustrate a variety of responses to the basic requirement for food. They also demonstrate the creativity, focus, and determination that are required to be successful in such a competitive market.

1. KIDDYLICIOUS

Sally Preston founded her highly successful business, The Kids Food Company, in 2009 (http://www.kiddylicious.co.uk). Sally's entrepreneurial journey started in 2001, while bringing up two young children, she became aware of a gap in the market for quality, frozen baby food and used her previous experience as a food scientist, with Marks & Spencer, to develop a range of new products under the name **Babylicious**. From day one, Sally had a big vision for Babylicious in multiple retailers and she was determined 'to convince the supermarkets that, although frozen, her range of baby food should be displayed where mothers expect to find it.' (Startups 2013). Her first large customer was Waitrose, a large UK supermarket chain, with an order for eight varieties of meals to be stocked in 27 stores. Babylicious has subsequently been sold by Asda, Tesco, and Sainsbury's, having had annual sales around £4 million in 2006 (Bridge 2010). Clearly, Sally was able to share her vision for healthy and nutritious baby food with many other parents and build a successful venture around this simple premise. However, while the premise might have seemed simple, putting it into practice was an altogether more complex matter. Consumers demand that food is safe, particularly where children are concerned, and Sally's expertise was also critical in winning the confidence of consumers and investors alike. She recalled that as a trained food technologist, 'I knew how to insure my food complied with all the criteria for traceability, health and safety' (Sunday Times 2007a). Sally founded The Kids Food Company in 2009 and includes both Babylicious and Kiddylicious brands (https://www.linkedin.com/in/sally-preston-381437).

2. THE HERBIVOROUS BUTCHER

Aubry and Kale Walch, brother and sister and both committed vegans, started their Minneapolis (Minnesota) based business in 2106 after Aubry's seemingly throwaway remark, 'Let's open a vegan butcher shop!' (http://www.theherbivorousbutcher.com).

The key to their success might be the combination of innovative 'meat-free meats' products and use of social media (@TheHerbivorousB, https://www.facebook.com/theherbivorous-butcher; https://www.instagram.com/theherbivorousb/) to promote themselves within Minneapolis and beyond (BBC 2016; Huffington Post 2016). Within just one month of starting the business Aubry and Kale had attracted huge media attention with over 50 articles in the US and internationally. The BBC even produced 39 second video highlighting, 'The first vegan butcher shop in America has opened in Minneapolis. Each meat-free meat is made from non-GMO wheat with added seasonings and sauces' (BBC 2016).

3. SUPERJAM

Fraser Doherty, who learned to make jam from his grandmother, was only 14 years old when he set up his company, SuperJam, selling to church fetes and farmers markets in Scotland (http://www.superjam.co.uk). But surely there were already enough choices of jam – how could Fraser's jam be different from all those familiar, well-established brands? Basically, **SuperJam** had no added sugar, being sweetened by grape juice rather than sugar. It also contained *superfoods*, such as blueberries. In just four years, Fraser developed a venture from this initial vision. He got the opportunity to pitch his idea to Waitrose when he attended a 'meet the buyer' day. His SuperJam was subsequently launched in the UK by Waitrose and is now sold in a number of leading stores. In 2008 Fraser was producing about 400,000 jars a year (Times 2007) and by 2010 'the jam boy' was reporting on his weekly blog that almost 1 million jars had been sold. Meanwhile, he was continuing to develop export markets, Denmark 2014, and to introduce new product lines, such as SuperTea. Fraser also speaks and writes about his experiences as an entrepreneur (http://www.fraserdoherty.com).

QUESTIONS

1. Food is something all of the above entrepreneurs have in common, but what particular aspect of food distinguishes each of them? Is this factor a personal 'driver' in their business model?

2. Look at the websites for each company and consider who the most likely customers are. How could they be grouped and described?

3. How did the entrepreneurs' background, experience, or training influence the choice of market?

Sources: BBC 2016; Huffington Post 2016; Times 2007; Bridge 2010; Times 2008; Startups 2013; Sunday Times 2007a.

3.3.5 Exploring the context

The three entrepreneurs highlighted in the *Food for thought* case (Case 3.3) are compelling examples of how to create a new venture from a strong vision that is underpinned by a driver. Sally Preston and Fraser Doherty each developed an enterprise to exploit an entrepreneurial opportunity, and each of them has managed to build a business in a highly competitive market. When you read a case study, you have the benefit of hindsight. In other words, we already know what happened. By contrast, the three entrepreneurs had to make decisions without any advance

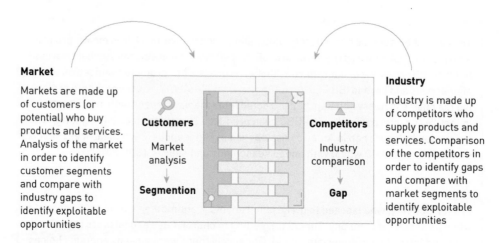

Market

Markets are made up of customers (or potential) who buy products and services. Analysis of the market in order to identify customer segments and compare with industry gaps to identify exploitable opportunities

Customers
|
Market analysis
↓
Segmention

Competitors
|
Industry comparison
↓
Gap

Industry

Industry is made up of competitors who supply products and services. Comparison of the competitors in order to identify gaps and compare with market segments to identify exploitable opportunities

FIGURE 3.4 The entrepreneurial opportunity context.

knowledge of the likely outcome. As you explore the context for your own venture, there are a number of questions to consider, such as:

- Can this market accommodate another player?
- What type of customers want our product or service?
- Is there a gap that existing firms are not exploiting?

Once you have expressed your idea in the form of an opportunity business model, the next step is to explore the market and industry (i.e. the context) in which the enterprise will operate (Figure 3.4). We consider these questions in more detail in Chapter 7, as part of a review of entrepreneurial marketing. In this section, we introduce the main features of the context and relate them to the opportunity business model. Figure 3.4 provides a simplified summary of the opportunity context. It indicates how markets consist of customers (or potential customers) in need of products and services, while industry sectors consist of competitors (or potential competitors) offering products and services. One of the critical requirements in exploiting any new business idea is to gain an understanding of your customers. When you are creating a new venture, analysing the market and the sector can reveal a market segment that is currently under-served by existing firms. This represents the gap in which your venture is going to operate.

This is only the beginning of the process. As you refine your idea, continued analysis of customers and competitors can help you to maintain your focus. This will enable you to serve your customer segment in ways that satisfy their changing needs while also differentiating your venture from the competition.

3.4 SHAPING THE VISION: A CONTINUING CHALLENGE

In this chapter, we have considered the role of vision in the context of new venture creation. We have also looked at the complex relationship between emerging visions and more formal approaches to planning a business. We introduced the concept of opportunity business models as a technique for analysing entrepreneurial opportunities by identifying the key dimensions and drivers that underpin them. The next case in this chapter (Case 3.4), considers the extraordinary entrepreneurial journey of *Steve Pankhurst: with a little help from our friends*, one of the founders of Friends Reunited. It takes us through the process of idea generation (seven worth exploring) to recognising a real business opportunity (from an unlooked for source) and its exploitation as a new venture (acquired for £120 million just five years later). In addition, there are two video cases available on **SAGE edge** (Case 3.5a *Visions: Jonathan's Challenge* and Case 3.5b *Visions: Rana's Challenge*). Each video case is based on an interview with an entrepreneur facing a challenge related to this chapter. Watch each video and decide which option you think the entrepreneur will choose. You might find it useful to discuss the case with friends or colleagues before deciding. Please note that lecturers can have access to the video which reveals the actual decision taken by the entrepreneur.

Each of the remaining Part One chapters builds on the previous one to take you from the entrepreneurial vision, as discussed in this chapter, to the creation of a new entrepreneurial venture. They should also help you to work through the dimensions and drivers of the opportunity business model in greater detail and highlight ways in which the different components of the model interact.

3.5 SUMMARY

- The entrepreneurial process can be represented as three linked activities: (1) generating new business ideas; (2) recognising opportunities; (3) exploitation in enterprises.

- The entrepreneurial learning cycle provides a useful practical framework for developing entrepreneurial thinking.

- Entrepreneurs can adopt three broad approaches to shaping an entrepreneurial vision: (a) the emerging vision; (b) the traditional business plan; (c) the 'opportunity business model' (OBM).

- The opportunity business model is a useful approach that can be used both to shape an entrepreneurial opportunity and to articulate it more clearly to potential investors, partners, and other interested parties.

- When expressing an entrepreneurial opportunity as a business model, it is essential to consider the context in which you are operating. This requires research to analyse the characteristics of potential suppliers, customers, and competitors.

CASE 3.4

Steve Pankhurst: with a little help from our friends

In 2000, **Steve** and **Julie Pankhurst** simply had a good idea, which after many trials and tribulations, emerged as one of the first commercially successful online social networking communities: **Friends Reunited**. In just five years they took what in hindsight might look like a 'sure-fire' winner from concept through exploitation to an eventual sale for £120 million (€155 million). Very few entrepreneurs achieve this level

(Continued)

(Continued)

of financial wealth, and even fewer do so over such a short period of time. However, similar principles and skills can be reapplied in other kinds of venture, including social enterprises. Since the sale of Friends Reunited, Steve and Julie have established the Happy Charitable Trust to support good causes.

INFORMATION TECHNOLOGY RULES

Despite having a degree in Mathematics from Imperial College London, Steve Pankhurst did not like computers. Despite this, his first job was as an IT software analyst and software programmer. He quickly gained experience in various industry sectors, including defence, financial pensions, building, and construction, before setting up his own business. Steve recalled, 'I was a programmer moving to analyst, got bored with working for people. I suppose I always had in my mind to work for myself. I met Jason Porter in 1992 and left to do contracting, so we basically set up a little freelance company.' They mostly worked for small companies on marketing systems and procurement systems 'Our company name was VCS which stood for Visual Computing Solutions but the real unofficial name was "very crap software", and in 1992 we started working for a company providing pension solutions for insurance companies.' This was in response to government legislation to regulate the selling of pensions. Steve remembers, 'It turned out to be seven years' work, nearly full time.'

In 2000, Steve and Jason stopped working full time for the pension solutions company and set up the Happy Group. 'Fortunately, we were kept on with a bit of consultancy and he [the owner] invested in us ... he actually put in seed capital ... if you think back to 1999/2000 all these Internet companies came up with an idea. People, VCs and banks, were throwing millions at them. We had many ideas, anybody could come to us with an idea and we literally had a pipeline list of 20. People would come to us because they knew we could do it. Some of the ideas were just embarrassingly bad ... a lot of people thought they could just make money from advertising ... this was madness. We'd got £50,000 in the bank to buy servers and to get us going ... our philosophy was we would spend a maximum of £7,000 ... the minute we went over £7,000 and it wasn't making any money or wasn't working we'd drop it.' There were more ideas than the seven that could be developed, for example, a singles dating website didn't succeed. However, their Happy party bags idea was 'doing well, but that took a lot of money ... it is nothing more than a glorified mail order catalogue. So, there is a lot of buying stock, a lot of manual work ... it also made us realise that we didn't want to do that bit because you had to deal with orders; you had to deal with deliveries, with complaints.'

YET ANOTHER IDEA

Julie Pankhurst was also a software programmer before becoming pregnant and taking a break in her career. Steve recalled, 'She had the school reunion idea and really it was going to be a project for her while she was on maternity leave to learn the new technology that I had learned. It never happened of course because being a mum takes up a lot of time ... Julie had this nagging idea ... she wanted to track down old friends ... I actually thought it was rubbish because I hated looking back ... I hated school.' Julie kept the pressure on for the reunion website idea to be developed. Steve recalls a critical point, 'I remember it well, she said *I have found the site. My site!* It turned out to be an American version of her idea but not quite. So, that was the changing point for me ... I did a search around and there were a couple of very, very basic sites in Britain. It made me think, *Hang on a minute! If it is working in America your idea should work over here.*'

'Friends Reunited was very much a backburner project. It was easy to write for me. It took me about a week in my spare time ... the original version was awful ... there was nothing to it.' It was difficult to identify how the website could generate any revenue from advertising or subscriptions. Steve recalled, 'We always thought that model [subscription] may work but we weren't sure. We thought, *We need to get 100,000 people on there to make it critical mass so that people have a reason to pay.* But we didn't know how to get there.'

FROM A SMALL TRICKLE

Steve remembered, 'I just put it live June 2000 ... within a day or so someone registered ... within a week ten people had. Julie used to get a few email responses and asked me to do changes, like a message board ... so it became this little hobby. For the first six months it was nothing more than a hobby but the concept was beginning to take shape ... then someone emailed us and said, *What a great idea, I have just found someone I haven't seen for 30 years.* That was quite a key point. It made me realise I can put a little bit more time and effort into it and Julie kept on coming up with the ideas ... Julie was passionate about it.' But, there was still the challenge of increasing the number of users: 'I would find lots of people looking for other people on message boards. I would send a personalised email to them saying, *You are looking for someone? Come to Friends Reunited and see if you can find them* ... I got it up to about 70 people registering a day through just hard grafting. Just a bit of time every day.'

Then suddenly, 'The Friends Reunited server just died. I looked into it and we had been 'website of the day' on the Steve Wright show on Radio 2. Every time we rebooted the server died ... what the hell is happening? It felt like everybody in the world was trying to connect to our tiny little server ... you could see hundreds of people trying to access the site. We bought another server ... Jason worked through the night and got it going.' Steve recalled, 'Well that was January 2001. By February we realised we really could be on to something. We started to get a few local papers contacting us.' But, having built up the number of users, how could they generate revenue to fund the website? Steve remembers, 'We decided to charge £5 to send emails. So you can use the site, find people. The WOW factor was, 'My God. There is that person.' It seemed harsh to us and to people. But why not £5 a year?'

But why £5? 'We bought two drinks in a pub and didn't get any change out of a fiver! At the same time we took what was a very good calculated risk. We resigned from our consultancy jobs because we thought, *Right. We have really got to go for this.*'

'The first day one person paid. The second day three people paid. The next day five people paid. Then it went ten, 50, and honestly the amount of money! If I showed you the stats it's scary. We made, I don't know, £2,000 the first month, £10,000 the second, £50,000 the third, £200,000 the fourth, £600,000 the fifth, a million pounds

(Continued)

(Continued)

the sixth. It really went like that. It was all a bit of a blur. Within a month we were being called in to do local radio shows. Which is scary as hell. The local press as well, so it was growing … We were contacted by a PR [public relations] company … they put a plan together and we never really implemented it because events took over … then we were contacted by the *Guardian*. Within a month we had been in *The Times*, *The Sun*, BBC 6 o'clock news.'

All this publicity increased the number of users. Steve recalled, 'It was strange how everything was. It was 24 hour days, 7 days a week. The biggest mistake we made was we didn't delegate. But the problem was it was happening so fast … Within two months of my first radio interview, I could do six radio interviews just like that. It almost came natural. Julie was doing the same; we were getting invited to do this, that and the other. We were answering 3,000 emails a day… we used to do shifts all day long. We had this screen which showed how many registrations that day and how much money. You hit the refresh button and as you refresh every few seconds the money would go up by £50 and then £100 and the registrations were up by 200 every five seconds and Julie and I would just sit there sometimes and say *Oh my … God what have we created?* This is brilliant but scary.'

But how long could it continue? 'In 2001, we had two or three customer services people … It was just bizarre. You just open the paper and there was a whole page feature on me and Julie and our life and how we had created this thing. But the stress levels were just unbelievable. We were working non-stop, eating badly and drinking to get through the evening. Never going out. Going to sleep worrying.'

'In 2002 we sat down and we thought, *For the next year, we will just go with it. We will do it properly. We are going to recruit ten people.* We recruited a proper customer service manager and a couple of developers.' Steve remembers another key moment, 'We were still growing and I came up with a new idea for Genes Reunited. This was all about building your own family tree and sharing it. My idea came from my cousin who was doing a massive family tree and he put it on the Internet. Somebody, a distant relative from Canada, had also been doing it. So we had done a whole year of hard grafting in 2002. It got better because we had employed people.'

NO SHORTAGE OF SUITORS

Serious offers to buy the company started to come in. But Steve recounts how this caused problems, 'It distracts you for months while due diligence takes place. So by the end of 2003, we did it all officially. Got in contact with all the interested parties and it took days and days of presenting it. We were making £3 million profit a year and we had ten million registered users with a lot of them coming back.' In spite of this, no suitor made a serious offer.

Then, Michael Murphy joined the company as the Chief Executive. Steve recalled, 'Michael is brilliant, he is a real networker. He is really down to earth … he knew all the VCs. His desk was clear and he got other people to do everything. He is brilliant at just getting things done.'

By 2005, 'Profits were £7 million … they put feelers out and suddenly it was leaked … We had about four/five serious offers and figures that we never ever dreamed about … ITV felt right.' Friends Reunited was sold to ITV in December 2005 for £120 million.

HAPPY?

After the sale of Friends Reunited, Steve remembers deciding to set up a charitable trust, 'Yes, we call it the Happy Foundation ... We build schools abroad, we are on our fourth now. It is the best thing I do. We get a pile of requests for money, although it is quite hard because you have to reject 99 out of 100 of them. Julie went to see the one in Ghana and had an amazing experience. We visited the one in Peru last year, which was an amazing experience for our children to see the slums and we are just about to start one in Vietnam.'

AND INTO THE SUNSET ...

On 19 January 2016, Steve Pankhurst announced 'the sunset of an era' in an email to Friends Reunited users stating 'it is with a heavy heart, that we have decided to close the service down'. Steve also took the opportunity to promote a new service called Liife (www.liife.com). 'Liife is all about capturing key moments in your life – both the past and the present. And then sharing them with just the important people who actually took part in those moments.'

Source: This case is primarily based on an interview with Steve Pankhurst and was written by Nigel Lockett.

CASE 3.5A

Visions: Jonathan's challenge video

In this video case, **Jonathan** explores the visions for launching his educational publishing company for teachers in three ways: (a) print and mail order service; (b) online service; and (c) local sales agents. Watch the video and decide which option you think Jonathan will choose. You might find it useful to discuss the case with friends or colleagues before deciding. Please note that lecturers can have access to the video which reveals the actual decision taken by the entrepreneur.

Source: This video case is primarily based on an interview with Jonathan by Nigel Lockett.

CASE 3.5B

Visions: Rana's challenge video

In this video case, **Rana** explores the visions for growing her successful online racking business in three ways: (a) open a retail store; (b) introduce new products to existing customers; and (c) develop new product range for new customers. Watch the video and decide which option you think Rana will choose. You might find it useful to discuss the case with friends or colleagues before deciding. Please note that lecturers can have access to the video which reveals the actual decision taken by the entrepreneur.

Source: This video case is primarily based on an interview with Rana by Nigel Lockett.

Practical activities

1. **Innovation challenge** Individually or working in small groups, select any two new or emerging technologies from the list of technological drivers below. Develop a new business idea which uses both technologies and prepare a 10-minute presentation detailing your new business idea using the opportunity business model (Figure 3.3). If you are working in groups, give your presentations and follow with a discussion, identifying the strongest ideas and noting any significant weaknesses.

Ten technological drivers	
Broadband wireless in public spaces	Online social networks
Digital multimedia	Radio frequency identification devices
3D printing	Visualisation
Cloud business applications	Building-integrated photovoltaics
Micro-fuel cells	Multi-touch interfaces

Further details on these emerging technologies and other examples of opportunity business model drivers can be found on the Online Resource page.

- **Online resources 'Emerging technologies and other drivers.'** Please visit https://uk.sagepub.com/blundel-lockett-wang for further information.

2. **Business plan** What should be in a business plan? Find three examples of business plans and compare them in order to identify the similarities and differences. Visit the website of a major international bank and see what advice they give for producing business plans?

3. **Entrepreneur's perspective** Arrange to interview an entrepreneur. Ask them how they came up with the idea for their business. Did they mention their own skills and experience or other people? How much of this is down to luck or being in the *right place at the right time*? What was planned and what emerged? How often do they formally review the venture plan and make changes to the business? Dhaliwal (2008, 2016) captured several entrepreneurial stories from both Asian and young entrepreneurs.

Discussion topics

1. Using opportunity business models carry out a comparison of a successful and an unsuccessful new business idea. Develop criteria for evaluating new business ideas which would be useful for selecting entrepreneurial opportunities.

2. Why does the fashion industry have so many small innovative firms yet the automotive industry is dominated by large international corporations?

3. Compare the drivers for the Sony MiniDisc (https://en.wikipedia.org/wiki/MiniDisc) in the 1990s and the Apple iPod (http://www.apple.com/itunes) in the early 2000s. Can you account for their different levels of success?

Recommended reading

We have also provided links and resources related to business plans on the Online Resources page. There is also a wide literature on business models, which are increasingly being seen as strategic analysis and venture generation tools.

Foss, N. J. and Saebi, T. (2016) 'Fifteen years of research on business model innovation: how far have we come, and where should we go?'. *Journal of Management*, **43, 1: 200–27.**

This article takes stock of 15 years of business model research and identifies important avenues for future research and shows how complexity theory, innovation, and other streams of literature can help overcome research gaps.

Zott, C. and Amit, R. (2013) 'The business model: a theoretically anchored robust construct for strategic analysis.' *Strategic Organization*, **11, 4: 403–11.**

This article establishes that the theoretical and empirical advancements in business model research provide solid conceptual and empirical foundations on which scholars can build in order to explore a range of important, yet unanswered research questions.

Jones, C., Penaluna, A., Matlay, H., and Penaluna, K. (2013) 'The student business plan: useful or not?' *Industry and Higher Education*, **27, 6: 491–8.**

This article offers a critical discussion of the role of the business plan in current enterprise educational practice and provides insights into emerging alternative practices in the field of enterprise education.

Bridge, B. and Hegarty, C. (2012) 'An alternative to business plan based advice for start-ups?' *Industry and Higher Education*, **26, 6: 443–52.**

This article compares the pros and cons of different approaches and suggests that an exploration approach is often more natural, logical and effective than the business plan based alternative.

References

Amit, R. and Zott, C. (2001) 'Value creation in eBusiness'. *Strategic Management Journal*, 22, 6/7: 493–520.

Apple (2010) '10 billion song countdown'. Available at http://www.apple.com/itunes/10-billion-song-countdown (accessed 27 May 2010).

Barringer, B. and Ireland, D. (2012) *Entrepreneurship: Successfully Launching New Ventures* (4th edn). Harlow: Pearson Education.

BBC (2016) 'First US vegan 'butcher' shop open in Minneapolis' http://www.bbc.co.uk/news/world-us-canada-35413486 (accessed 1 February 2016).

Bridge, R. (2010) *My Big Idea: 30 Successful Entrepreneurs Reveal How They Found Inspiration*. London: Kogan Page.

Chesbrough, H. and Rosenbloom, R. S. (2002) 'The role of business model in capturing value from innovation: evidence from Xerox corporation's technology spin-off companies'. *Industrial and Corporate Change*, 11, 3: 65–73.

Currie, W. (ed.) (2004) *Value Creation from e-Business Models*. Oxford: Butterworth-Heinemann.

Dhaliwal, S. (2008) *Making a Fortune: Learning from the Asian Phenomenon*. Chichester: Capstone.

Dhaliwal, S. (2016) *The Millennial Millionaire: How Young Entrepreneurs Turn Dreams into Business*. London: Palgrave Macmillan.

Economist (2007) 'Lessons from Apple: what other companies can learn from California's master of innovation'. *The Economist* (7 June).

Finch, B. (2006) *How to Write a Business Plan*. London: Kogan Page.

Guardian (2007a) 'There is no point having a load of money unless you enjoy it'. 12 October.

Guardian (2007b) 'Springs and roundabouts'. 22 March.

Guardian (2009) 'We must tackle these false claims for domestic green power tariffs'. 9 February.

Hamel, G. (2000) *Leading the Revolution: How to Thrive in Turbulent Times by Making Innovation a Way of Life*. Boston, MA: Harvard Business School Press.

Hitt, M., Ireland, D., Camp, M., and Sexton, D. (2002) *Strategic Entrepreneurship: Creating a New Mindset*. Oxford: Blackwell.

Huffington Post (2016) 'The first vegan butcher shop in the U.S. is opening in Minneapolis'. 13 January.

Independent (2014) 'Moneybags: humble British satchel conquers the world'. *The Independent*, 24 January.

Lewis, M. (2001) *The New New Thing: A Silicon Valley Story*. London: Penguin.

Margretta, J. (2002) 'Why business models matter'. *Harvard Business Review*, May: 86–92.

Morris, M., Schindehutte, M., and Allen, J. (2005) 'The entrepreneur's business model: toward a unified perspective'. *Journal of Business Research*, 58, 6: 726–35.

Mullins, J. (2013) *The New Business Road Test: What Entrepreneurs and Executives Should Do before Writing a Business Plan* (4th edn). Harlow: FT Prentice Hall.

Osterwalder, A. and Pigneur, Y. (2004) 'An ontology for e-business models'. In W. Currie (ed.) op. cit. (65–97).

Osterwalder, A. and Pigneur, Y. (2010) *Business Model Generation: A Handbook for Visionaries, Game Changers, and Challengers*. Chichester: Wiley.

Osterwalder, A., Pigneur, Y., Bernarda, G., and Smith, A. (2014) *Value Proposition Design: How to Create Products and Services Customers Want*. Chichester: Wiley.

Ovans, A. (2015) What Is a Business Model? *Harvard Business Review* 23 January 2015.

Sarasvathy, S. D. (2009) *Effectuation: Elements of Entrepreneurial Expertise*. Northampton, MA: Edward Elgar.

Startups (2013) 'Babylicious: Sally Preston'. Available at http://www.startups.co.uk (accessed 30 May 2017).

Sunday Times (2004) 'How I made it: Karen Darby, founder of Simply Switch'. 22 August 2004.

Sunday Times (2007a) 'Best of times, worst of times: Sally Preston'. 18 November 2007.

Sunday Times (2007b) 'Do the right-on thing'. 1 April 2007.

Sunday Times (2008) 'How I made it: Duncan Goose, founder of One Water'. 7 December 2018.

Tapscott, D., Ticoll, D., and Lowe, A. (2000) *Digital Capital: Harnessing the Power of the Business Web*. London: Nicholas Brealey.

Tiffany, P., Peterson, S., and Barrow, C. (2012) *Business Plans for Dummies* (3rd edn). Chichester: Wiley.

Times (2007) 'Teenager's homemade jam to earn him pots of money'. *The Times*, 21 February.

Times (2008) 'How I made it: Perween Warsi, founder of chilled meals company S&A Foods'. *The Times*, 3 August.

TimesOnline (2004) 'Coca-Cola halts European Dasani launch'. TimesOnline, 24 March.

Timmers, P. (2000) *Electronic Commerce: Strategies and Models for Business to Business Trading*. Chichester: Wiley.

WaterAid (2016) 'the-crisis'. Available at http://www.wateraid.org (accessed 30 May 2017).

Weill, P. and Vitale, M. (2001) *Place to Space: Migrating to eBusiness Models*. Boston, MA: Harvard Business School Press.

Wolfe, M. (1999) *Burn Rate: How I Survived the Gold Rush Years on the Internet*. New York: Touchstone.

YouTube (2008) http://www.youtube.com/watch?v=oWAG_vGzdtU (accessed 6 January 2017). *One Water: Duncan Goose on ABC Western Australia Part one*.

YouTube (2009) http://www.youtube.com/watch?v=4MK9aGXJz3Y (accessed 6 January 2017). *The Entrepreneurial Exchange Conference 2009 – Karen Darby*.

YouTube (2010) https://www.youtube.com/watch?v=dn41RpIMYgo (accessed 6 January 2017). *Juliet Davenport, Good Energy CEO and Founder.mov*.

YouTube (2012a) https://www.youtube.com/watch?v=KbvP4zlgMBA (accessed 6 January 2017). *Own a Business, Make a Difference: Karen Darby at TEDxSquareMile*.

YouTube (2012b) https://www.youtube.com/watch?v=MM4HvXaYTPY (accessed 6 January 2017). *Our Story – The Cambridge Satchel Company*.

YouTube (2012c) https://youtu.be/4As0e4de-rI (accessed 6 January 2017). *The Complete London 2012 Opening Ceremony | London 2012 Olympic Games*.

YouTube (2016) https://youtu.be/0GI4ErWw4JY (accessed 6 January 2017). *Juliet Davenport, Good Energy CEO and Founder.mov*.

Zott, C. and Amit, R. (2007) 'Business model design and the performance of entrepreneurial firms'. *Organization Science*, 18, 2: 181–99.

4

OPPORTUNITIES: NURTURING CREATIVITY AND INNOVATION

The entrepreneur believes he [or she] is right, while everyone else is wrong. Thus, the essence of entrepreneurship is being different – being different because one has a different perception of the situation.

Mark Casson, economist

Nobody talks of entrepreneurship as survival, but that's exactly what it is and what nurtures creative thinking.

Anita Roddick, entrepreneur and founder of The Body Shop

LEARNING OUTCOMES

After reading this chapter you should be able to:

- Distinguish the different ways that opportunities are recognised, evaluated, and developed into viable business propositions.
- Appreciate the role and significance of creativity when creating and pursuing entrepreneurial opportunities.
- Appreciate the role and significance of innovation, including its complex relationship with creativity and entrepreneurship.
- Apply the principles and techniques identified in this chapter to pursue your own entrepreneurial opportunities in creative and innovative ways.

4.1 INTRODUCTION

In this chapter, we explore the concept of opportunity, the entrepreneurial opportunity in particular, and try to locate it within the broader **entrepreneurial process**. In doing so, we also examine the closely related roles of creativity and innovation as someone's 'bright idea' is evaluated, refined, and developed into a living, breathing entrepreneurial venture.

Opportunities are a familiar feature of everyday life, and we have all had the experience creating, exploiting and, in some cases, missing them. Sometimes the opportunity

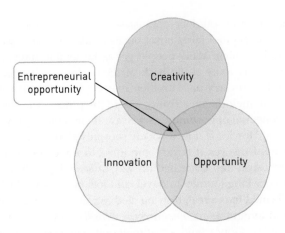

FIGURE 4.1 Opportunity, creativity, and innovation.

may be quite insignificant (e.g. the chance to meet a visitor for lunch), while other opportunities may have longer-lasting consequences (e.g. an offer to work abroad). Entrepreneurial opportunities are a particular type of opportunity, which could lead you to create a self-sustaining venture. The process is complex, and is closely related to two other important themes: creativity and innovation. The combination of creativity, innovation, and opportunity recognition can also result in unpredictable, and often surprising, outcomes (Figure 4.1).

Many successful ventures have developed from what would once have looked like an extremely unlikely or unpromising idea. For example, each of the following innovations has appeared in the last 20 years:

- **Products** camera phones, patio heaters, hybrid vehicles.
- **Services** social networking websites, speed-dating, 'free-cycling' unwanted products.

At the same time, there have been some spectacular failures, including the Sinclair C5 (a small battery-powered vehicle), the WebVan (an online grocery delivery service), and Boo.com (an online fashion clothing service). The relationships between opportunity, creativity, and innovation have been the subject of considerable debate among entrepreneurship researchers. Some of these arguments may seem very distant from the 'down to earth' world of the entrepreneur creating a new venture. However, as we shall see, they do have some important practical implications. Here are a few examples, indicating the kinds of questions we are considering in this chapter:

- Where do entrepreneurial opportunities come from?
- Why do entrepreneurs see potential opportunities differently?
- What is the importance of creativity in identifying and developing opportunities?
- How do you nurture creativity in this phase of an entrepreneurial venture?
- Why is invention not the same as innovation?
- What do entrepreneurs contribute to the innovation process?
- How do you communicate entrepreneurial opportunities effectively?

The opening case illustrates how David and Clare Hieatt, the founders of Howies, became convinced that they had identified a real opportunity. They began by identifying a promising target market: outdoor enthusiasts, rather like themselves. They linked these potential customers to a fairly novel business idea: retailing well-designed, high-performance ethical clothing. Many people get as far as this stage, but go no further; they file their 'pet' ideas away at the back of their minds, or perhaps jot them down in a notebook, and then carry on with their existing lives. The Hieatts were different; they decided to make their dream a reality, and in the process they created what can be termed an entrepreneurial opportunity. As we saw, their venture proved to be extremely successful, such that Howies is now a widely recognised, premium international brand with a bright future. However, it is very important to remember that *none of this was clear at the outset*. David and Clare had no way of knowing if their idea would really 'fly'. There was a very long journey to travel, and lots of work to do, before those early ideas were transformed into a real, thriving clothing business. For many other budding entrepreneurs (and intrapreneurs, i.e. **entrepreneurship** in larger firms), the story has a very different ending. Opportunities that might once have seemed very attractive turn out to be disappointing or elusive. Seemingly brilliant business ideas and bright, shiny technological inventions often fail to deliver or struggle into life only to collapse when confronted by the harsh, competitive realities of the markets and finances.

CASE 4.1

A long way from home: from sheep to shop

The fashion industry is full of specialist retailers with each purporting to offer a unique range of clothes that will appeal to a unique group of customers. But how do such niches emerge in what seems like an already crowded market? In New Zealand, merino sheep graze on upland pastures throughout the year and 'ethical wool' from their fleeces is used in high-performance textiles prized by many specialist active outdoor and sports clothing companies throughout the world. The Zque trademark, developed by the New Zealand Merino Company, provides a traceable value chain, which includes an accreditation programme that ensures environmental, social, and economic sustainability, animal welfare, and traceability (http://www.nzmerino.co.nz). While home-grown New Zealand companies, such as Ground Effect (http://www.groundeffect.co.nz), use merino-based fabrics, the market for merino is worldwide.

Just like the mainstream fashion industry, the active outdoor and sports clothing industry is highly competitive. Many small companies have emerged to meet the needs of customers in this increasing global niche sector. One such company is Howies, which was founded June 1995 by **David** and **Clare Hieatt** in the living room of their London flat (Wikipedia 2016). Initially, they designed just four T-shirts and launched them in a mountain biking magazine – the T-shirts cost £30. The orders came in and the company was in business. During the next decade **Howies** developed into a leading designer of simple, functional, long-lasting clothes made with a concern for the environment their customers enjoyed so much in mind. In February 2007, after over a decade of independent ownership, the US footwear company Timberland (http://www.timberland.com) acquired Howies (BBC 2007). By 2012, the management team purchased the company. Let us consider the first two of the three critical stages of Howies story: the decision to start the company (opportunity recognition); the expansion and the move to Cardigan

Bay, in Wales (growth); and the sale to Timberland (acquisition). We will also see that cutting through these are the founders' personal ethical values. In 2011, Timberland merged with VF Corporation (http://www.vfc.com) and Howies was sold to its own management in 2012.

Opportunity recognition The identification of the mountain biking sector was a key factor starting the company. The founders and early staff members were passionate about biking, snowboarding, and skateboarding. They knew what their potential customers wanted: something unusual and something different. Initially, Howies sold through shops, with 45 selling their product by the end of 1999, but in 2000 they realised this business model wasn't sustainable; the decision to move into mail order, that is selling from a printed catalogue, was made and the first catalogue was produced.

Growth Space is nearly always an issue for growing firms, and Howies was no different. The company moved to commercial premises in Wales and secured a grant from the then Welsh Development Agency in 2003. Previously, the company was funded by the founders and conventional banking. Howies continued to grow by producing ethically sourced, specialist clothing for outdoor enthusiasts. The mail-order catalogue sales were increasing and were supported by e-commerce sales and the company considered moving back into retail by selling through Selfridges in London and even opening their own shops. By the end of 2005 sales were just over £2 million. Clothes were still promoted as ethically produced, both in terms of manufacturing and the textiles used, including hemp, bamboo, organic cotton (http://www.soilassocation.org), and the Zque-accredited merino wool from New Zealand. The company even moved to the ethical bank Triodos (http://www.triodos.com).

The real challenge is recognising, of all the things you could do, which are the ones worth investing your time and money in. It is also worth noting that, once an opportunity is recognised and exploited in an enterprise, it has to be constantly reassessed.

Acquisition In early 2007 Howies was acquired by Timberland, the large US-based outdoor clothing company (http://www.timberland.com). The founders of Howies could see that in order for the company to grow to meet ever-increasing demand more working capital was required. The amount of money involved was beyond the reach of conventional funding, such as secured loans. This would either mean raising venture capital or finding a partner with similar values. David and Clare Hieatt felt that for Howies to maintain its values there was only one option. At the time of the acquisition Jeffrey Swartz, President and CEO of Timberland, said: 'We are excited and inspired by the brand potential we see in Howies and are pleased to welcome them to the Timberland family. We look to invest in like-minded brands that are focused on innovation, authenticity and integrity, and Howies encompasses all of these core values' (BBC 2007).

Interestingly, David and Clare Hieatt went on to found Hiut Denim, a new venture focused on manufacturing jeans from organic and salvage denim in 2011 (http://hiut denim.co.uk).

Ethical point In addition to promoting environmental sustainable material such as merino wool, hemp, bamboo, and organic cotton, the company uses only 100% renewable electricity from Good Energy (http://www.good-energy.co.uk) for its London store and in 2005 moved to ethical bank Triodos (http://www.triodos.com).

(Continued)

(Continued)

POINTS TO CONSIDER

1. With hindsight it is often easy to see the various stages of a company's develop-
    ment. But is it possible for the entrepreneurs who run growing companies to see
    these at the time?

2. Why would a company, like Timberland, decide to buy a smaller company rather
    than just develop competing products and brands? Perhaps it is hard for larger
    companies to be entrepreneurial, or does opportunity recognition become more
    difficult?

3. The founders of Howies wanted to express their ethical values through their
    business. Was that important to their customers? Provided sales were growing
    and the company was profitable, did it really matter?

Sources: BBC 2007; Wikipedia 2016.

The chapter is organised as follows. In Section 4.2, we explore the concept and
sources of entrepreneurial opportunities; in Section 4.3, we consider what creativity
means in this context, and how you might make yourself more creative; in Section 4.4,
we discuss the relationship between innovation and entrepreneurship; in Section 4.5
we consider how these come together in realising the entrepreneurial opportunity.
Three cases are used to illustrate the concepts and ideas in action: In Section 4.3, the
5-A-DAY case highlights the link between creativity and innovation; in Section 4.4,
the *Passion for chocolate* case illustrates how innovation provides entrepreneurial
opportunities; at the end of Section 4.5, in the *Deirdre Bounds: seeing eye to eye* case,
we have the chance to meet a successful entrepreneur. The chapter concludes with
a video case **⑤SAGE** edge™ based on *Opportunities: Achille's challenge* (Case 4.5) to
test your understanding of this chapter.

4.2 EXPLORING ENTREPRENEURIAL OPPORTUNITY

4.2.1 A world of opportunity?

The world seems to offer limitless opportunities for the prospective entrepreneur. Yet
only a small proportion of these opportunities are converted into new ventures, and
fewer still become successful and sustainable businesses. For example, the transat-
lantic skies are crowded with airlines competing for business class passengers. How
did Richards Branson's Virgin Atlantic (http://www.virginatlantic.com) emerge and,
despite having no track record in aviation, become an established business? At the
turn of the new century, the growth of the Internet was creating opportunities for an
ever-increasing number of search engines. How did two young technologists manage
to develop a new service, Google (http://www.google.com), which now dominates
the Internet – and not just in its original form of searching for content but also as a
vehicle for generating online adverting revenues and supplying online applications,
such as Google Docs? The world is also full of opportunities for social entrepreneurs
(Bornstein 2007; Bornstein and Davis 2010; Young Foundation 2007). For example,
consider Andrea Coleman who created an innovative new venture called 'Riders for
Health'. Andrea realised that one way to improve healthcare in rural Africa was to

provide health workers with access to reliable transportation. However, it also reflected her long-standing passion for motorbikes (http://www.ridersintl.org). So how do you turn your interesting ideas into real entrepreneurial opportunities that are capable of supporting an entrepreneurial venture?

If you are a student embarking on a new venture creation exercise, one of your initial challenges is to make some kind of sense of what looks like an infinite number of tempting possibilities. We often see student teams almost paralysed by the amount of information that is 'out there'. So how do you decide which opportunity to pursue? In practice, the opportunities open to any particular entrepreneur, or **entrepreneurial team**, are much more limited than they might at first appear. In this section, we take a closer look at entrepreneurial opportunity and try to understand how it works in practice. Our starting point is the rather abstract question: 'Are entrepreneurial opportunities objective or subjective phenomena?' In other words, are they out there in the world waiting to be discovered (objective) or are they in people's minds (subjective)? Bear with us, and you will see why your opportunities are, like those of any entrepreneur, much thinner on the ground than you might at first imagine. With these limitations in mind, we can then consider the best technique for identifying, evaluating, and developing specific opportunities into viable business propositions.

4.2.2 The nature of opportunity: exploiting 'concrete knowledge'

Why do entrepreneurial opportunities exist in the first place? The simple answer is: 'because people know different things about the world'. Some kinds of knowledge are readily accessible to all. Everyone 'knows' what day of the week it is or why it gets dark at night. However, there are other kinds, sometimes termed 'concrete' (or 'local') knowledge, that are only accessible to particular individuals and groups:

> *The concrete knowledge which guides the action of any group of people never exists as a consistent and coherent body. It only exists in the dispersed, incomplete and inconsistent form in which it appears in many individual minds ... (Hayek 1955: 29–30)*

From this perspective, entrepreneurial opportunities arise because some people have access to potentially valuable concrete knowledge, which is not available to others (Section 11.3). Here are a few practical examples:

- Due to knowing so much about her local property market, Natalia is able to spot the development potential of an old warehouse that is being put up for auction.

- As Robert has developed an extensive network of suppliers in a specialist area of automobile engineering, he is able to secure first-tier supplier contacts with leading manufacturers.

- With experience in both child healthcare and opto-electronics, members of a university research team are able to develop a new surgical procedure.

  → **PERSPECTIVES** See Section 11.3 for further information.

Of course, it is not enough to have access to the knowledge. Entrepreneurs need a combination of alertness and vision if they are to identify and exploit opportunities before they become apparent to the rest of us (Kirzner 1973). This idea is also the basis for the old saying, 'Once you can see a bandwagon, it is already too late to jump on it.' Indeed, Foss et al (2008: 88) argue that entrepreneurship is a 'creative team act ... which is creatively superior to individual entrepreneurship' and that entrepreneurship research should focus also on the exploitation of opportunities through group as well as individual action. So, it is not only the resources an entrepreneur can access that are important but also their concrete knowledge, entrepreneurial team, and, above all, opportunity recognition. This entrepreneurial process is not a single act of an individual but a virtuous and ongoing cycle carried out by an entrepreneurial team in order to recognise, evaluate, and exploit opportunities based on this knowledge (Zahra et al. 2008).

4.2.3 Sources of opportunity: where to start looking

Though we will never be able to spot *every* possible opportunity, clearly it would help if we had a better understanding of the main sources. When you start to speak to successful entrepreneurs or read *their* own accounts of their successful ventures it becomes increasingly apparent that the sources of entrepreneurial opportunity are immensely personal. That is, they experience or perceive something which other people do not. Hundreds of thousands of people have flown across the Atlantic, but it was Richard Branson who experienced a service he was unhappy with and perceived that it could be done differently. This impulse for action, he describes as getting up 'from behind your desk' and seeing for yourself where ideas and people lead to innovation; 'the distinction between innovation and day-to-day delivery is barely noticeable and unimportant' (Branson 2008: 216). Millions of T-shirts are sold everyday, but it was David and Clare Hieatt, the founders of Howies (see Case 4.1) who saw the opportunity to produce ethically sourced and manufactured clothing for outdoor pursuits enthusiasts like themselves. When Geetie Singh opened her first organic gastro pub, the Duke of Cambridge (http://www.dukeorganic.co.uk) in London, it was only after working for many years in the restaurant business and becoming personally disillusioned by the lack of sustainability that she found the determination to change things herself. How many other people have sat in a restaurant and had similar thoughts but done nothing? So, we can see that the source of the opportunity is external – a bad flight or an indifferent meal – but its perception is internal (within the entrepreneur). Instead of just complaining they seem compelled to do something about it.

Take the example of Wangari Maathai who founded the Green Belt Movement in Kenya (http://www.greenbeltmovement.org) as an environmental **social enterprise** focused on the planting of trees, conservation, and women's rights. In 2004, Wangari became the first African woman and environmentalist to receive the Nobel Peace Prize for her contribution to sustainable development, democracy, and peace. On receiving the prize, she stated, 'If we conserved our resources better, fighting over them would not then occur ... so, protecting the global environment is directly related to securing peace ... those of us who understand the complex concept of the environment have the burden to act. We must not tire, we must not give up, we must persist.' Clearly, Wangari has a big vision but started in a simple way by focusing on planting trees, particularly indigenous and fruit trees, on farms with women groups as the main implementers. So, the source of opportunities may be close at hand and can lead to unexpected consequences.

So, where do we start looking? If we reflect on the previous examples the answer has to be within us. We need to experience life, in all its richness, but use our perception to seek out these opportunities – looking for new products, services, markets, suppliers, customers, technologies, and ways of organising. The drivers that underpin these opportunities, such as climate change and demographics, are all around us, but we have to perceive them in order to see the sources of opportunity. The UK entrepreneur and former panel member of BBC's *Dragons' Den*, Duncan Bannatyne, is clear that you find opportunities by solving problems, copying, or innovation: 'Ideas for new businesses broadly fall into three categories – those that solve a problem, those that copy another business and those spawned by genuine innovation'; (Bannatyne 2008: 38) and of these the last is the most rare.

In the next two sections, we 'complicate' the question of opportunity in two ways. Firstly, we ask what role creativity has to play in the formation of an entrepreneurial venture, and in the pursuit of entrepreneurial opportunities in particular (Section 4.3). Secondly, we look at the relationship between entrepreneurial opportunity, creativity, and innovation (Section 4.4). It is important to stress, at the outset, that in order to help to explain entrepreneurship we appear to be describing entrepreneurship as a linear process, but do not be deceived. While a single opportunity may form the basis for a new venture, entrepreneurs are constantly pursuing new opportunities (products, markets, suppliers, and ways of organising) and reinventing existing ones.

4.3 CREATIVITY IN ENTREPRENEURIAL VENTURES

Creativity is found in many areas of life, including poetry, music, painting, and the performing arts. Many new entrepreneurial ventures are also intrinsically creative, in that they bring to the world something that is somehow new and original. However, **entrepreneurial activity** is not always particularly creative. For example, some successful new ventures simply imitate, or make minor adaptations to, an existing product or service, with the originality coming from other sources, such as using a different supplier, or selling into a new market (Section 7.1). Creativity is a familiar concept, but its meaning can be quite difficult to pin down. A dictionary definition suggests that creativity is the 'power or faculty; ability to create', that is 'involving the use of the imagination or original ideas to create something [new]' (Oxford English Dictionary). Creativity can be studied at many different levels (Henry 2006: ix). It is often explained by looking at cognitive (i.e. thinking) processes within individuals (Section 11.3). However, creativity is also influenced by social factors, such as the interactions between people in an entrepreneurial team (Section 5.2), or the cultures of organisations and geographic regions (Section 12.3).

In *Back to Methuselah*, the Irish playwright, George Bernard Shaw (1921), writes:

- Some people see things that are and ask 'why?'

- I dream of things that never were and ask, 'why not?'

    → **PERSPECTIVES** See Sections 11.3 and 12.3 for further information.

We are all creative in our own way and to varying degrees: decorating our homes, making music, writing a poem, or even just compiling a text message. We all have an innate sense of individual creativity, but what role does it play in the creation of new ventures? Creativity in this phase of the entrepreneurial process is mainly concerned with the ability of entrepreneurs, managers, and firms to generate or invent new business ideas. These ideas might be related to new products, processes, services, or markets, with the first two often being referred to as inventions. However, for many reasons the vast majority of these new business ideas will not be developed beyond this conceptual stage.

Of those that can be protected, a few will become formalised in a patent, and of these less than 5% will be commercialised. We can clearly see that the attrition rate is very high, but without creativity we have no innovation and without innovation no entrepreneurial opportunities. The economist Joseph Schumpeter recognised the role of the entrepreneur in finding these 'new combinations' that enable new ventures to form (Section 11.3). He argued that entrepreneurial activity drives a cycle of '**creative destruction**' in which established organisations can become undermined by new entrants if they fail to maintain their innovative drive. Innovation researchers have built on these ideas in order to explore how creativity operates in the context of innovation and entrepreneurship:

> *The making and communicating of meaningful new connections to help us think of many possibilities; to help us think and experience in varied ways and using different points of view; to help us think of new and unusual possibilities; and to guide us in generating and selecting alternatives. (Tidd et al. 2005: 174)*

→ **PERSPECTIVES** See Section 11.3 for further information.

Creative ideas have to be both new and appropriate (Henry 2001). But, what does appropriate mean for entrepreneurial opportunities? Of course, being creative is another matter and this will depend on individual characteristics, including ability, mental skill, relevant experience, intrinsic motivation, and the context. Put more simply, creativity is about generating and articulating new ideas, new things, new processes, or new markets. This could be achieved using a range of techniques or even happen by chance – simply being in the right place at the right time with the right idea.

We have seen that creativity is important, but what is the relationship with new venture creation and how do enterprise continue to be creative? The *5-A-DAY* case (Case 4.2) shows how one firm, Innocent Smoothies, responded creatively to the increasing need and desire for people to eat healthily but in a convenient and exciting way. Health experts and governments recognised the need to do something about this; however, we will see how one company emerged to respond to this societal health driver, while large existing companies did not. This can also be seen as an example of Schumpeter's 'creative destruction' in action.

CASE 4.2

5-a-day: squeezing the most from the entrepreneurial opportunities

Everywhere we look there is an expert ready to tell us what we can and can't eat, what is good for us and what isn't (http://www.nhs.uk/livewell/5aday). Sometimes it all seems a bit too much! But there is one message that remains consistent – eating more fruit and vegetables is vital for good health. According to research, the average person is eating considerably less than the recommended five pieces of fruit and vegetables a day (5-A-DAY). This is even lower among young people. So how are entrepreneurs responding creatively to the opportunities that are emerging from this health imperative?

The last two decades has seen a huge growth in the fresh fruit-based drinks market (smoothies) in the UK. This trend has largely been led by small entrepreneurial firms, such as

Innocent Drinks founded by **Richard Reed, Adam Balon**, and **Jon Wright** also in 1999 (http://www.innocentdrinks.co.uk). Not surprisingly, the company has a strong 'look after your health' ethos for their products, but additionally Innocent Drinks has strong ethical values expressed through its commitment to sustainable packaging, carbon footprint reduction, and the Innocent Foundation, which supports building sustainable agricultural communities mostly in countries where Innocent Drinks sources its fruit (http://www.innocentfoundation.org). Clearly, these entrepreneurial individuals had the creativity to invent new drinks based on their own personal values; and they also identified a growing consumer need or demand they addressed by forming a company. By 2008 Innocent Drinks supplied the majority of the £280 million smoothies sector in the UK just before Coca-Cola Company acquired a minority shareholding in 2009. The smoothies sector was the fastest growing segment of the £1 billion pure fruit juice market in 2008 (Mintel 2008). This entrepreneurial opportunity was successfully exploited not by an existing incumbent, such as Tropicana (http://www.tropicana.co.uk), part of PepsiCo (http://www.pepsico.com) since 1998, or Del Monte (http://www.delmonte.com), but by a new venture.

Creativity It is potentially quite revealing if we look more closely at Innocent Drinks. The company seems to have maintained its creativity throughout its short history. The product range is increasing from simply smoothies (based on fruit) to drinks including live probiotic yoghurt, foods rich in specific nutrients, and, more recently, portions of vegetables. The company now even produces pure orange juice – seemingly, in direct competition to the large corporates. Interestingly the company also appears to be creative in the way it sources its packaging, claiming that all smoothie bottles are made from 100% recycled plastic, thus showing them to be a resource-efficient business (Innocent 2016).

Ethical point Innocent Drinks contributes to the Innocent Foundation charity and from 2103 to 2018 will contribute a minimum of £950,000. In 2015, total income was £1,009,000 (Innocent Foundation 2015).

QUESTION

1. Why was the smoothies market sector exploited by small entrepreneurial firms rather than the larger existing fruit juice suppliers? What was the role of creativity?

2. How would you describe the business model of Innocent Drinks and how does it differ from that of Del Monte? What are the drivers (imperatives) for this entrepreneurial opportunity?

3. What strategy would you recommend for an existing fruit juice supplier wishing to enter the smoothies market sector?

Sources: Mintel 2008; Innocent 2016; Innocent Foundation 2015.

The *5-A-DAY* case also serves as a reminder of how difficult it is for incumbent firms to innovate and exploit entrepreneurial opportunities. In some cases, even when large firms successfully innovate, the entrepreneurial managers involved have to operate outside the normal management structures until recognition is achieved; for example, the development of IBM's e-business services and Shell's renewable energy divisions (Hamel 2000). From this, we can see that the recognition and subsequent exploitation of entrepreneurial opportunities in enterprises is vital.

4.4 INNOVATION AND ENTREPRENEURSHIP

4.4.1 What is innovation?

Creativity may be required to identify the new business ideas but how do you select between competing ideas and subsequently develop your chosen idea to the point of exploitation in a new entrepreneurial venture? That is the role of innovation.

Innovation is popularly defined as 'the introduction of novelties; the alteration of what is established by the introduction of new elements or forms'. In commercial terms, it's described as 'the action of introducing a new product into the market; a product newly brought to the market' and the action or process of innovating as making 'changes in something established, especially introducing a new methods, ideas or products' (Oxford English Dictionary).

Innovation, as defined by Porter (1990), 'can be manifested in a new product design, a new production process, a new marketing approach, or a new way of conduct-ing training' and linked to companies achieving competitive advantage. Porter also argues that much of innovation is 'mundane and incremental, depending more on an accumulation of small insights and advances than on a single, major technological breakthrough'. Drucker ([1985] 2007: 17) goes further to link innovation to entre-preneurship as the 'specific tool of entrepreneurs, the means by which they exploit change as an opportunity for a different business or service'. This definition reflects our interest in the role that innovation can play in an entrepreneurial venture. We discuss the broader implications of entrepreneurship, innovation, and economic development in Chapters 11 and 14.

> → **PERSPECTIVES** See Sections 11.4 and 14.3 for further information.

In the context of entrepreneurship, innovation is best thought of as the way in which new business ideas – be they new products, processes, services, or markets – are recognised and developed as potential entrepreneurial opportunities. Clearly it is not a new phenomenon but one that is at the root of human, societal, and economic development. It differs from inventions or new business ideas in one key respect: the attempt to put them into practice, implemented, and, in the view of some, to be commercially exploited (Fagerberg et al. 2005; Parsons and Rose 2009). More recently what has become increasingly important is the ability of firms to consciously, deliberately, and continuously innovate (Christensen 1997; Hamel 2000; Christensen and Raynor 2003; Christensen et al. 2004). It could be argued that is it not the innovation itself that results in an entrepreneurial opportunity but the way in which it is utilised to provide new products, processes, services, and markets, which result in added value to the customer or competitive advantage in markets.

Government and industry alike stress the importance of innovation to both the econ-omy and society. The UK Government Innovation Report (DTI 2003), which defined innovation as the successful exploitation of new ideas, stated:

> *Innovation matters because it can deliver better products and services, new, cleaner and more efficient production processes and improved business models ... for the economy as a whole innovation is the key to higher productivity and greater prosperity for all.*

TABLE 4.1 Types of innovation

Type	Changes in	Examples
Product	Product/service offered	Apple's iPod (product) and iTunes (service)
Process	How they are created and delivered	Dell's built-to-order manufacturing process
Position	The way they are introduced to market	Amazon's online store
Paradigm	Underlying business models	eBay's online marketplace
Incremental	Small improvements to product/service	Increased hard disk storage capacity
Radical	New product/service	Digital cameras vs photographic film
Component	Improvement to a part of product/service	Increase in LCD display definition and clarity
System	Improvement affecting all product/service	Introduction of plasma displays
Product	New product	Apple's iPod
Service	New service	Apple's iTunes

Source: Developed from Francis and Bessant (2005).

What types of innovation have been identified? Francis and Bessant (2005) proposed the 4Ps of innovation product, process, position, and paradigm, with characteristic ranges from incremental vs radical, component vs system to product vs service (Table 4.1). This can be a useful framework to map out ideas for new ventures, and to help identify the type or types of innovation that you may be using.

The concept of innovation has become a powerful metaphor for both entrepreneurs and large firms alike. For example, Hewlett Packard, the international information technology, imaging, and printer provider (http://www.hp.com), reinvented its image by moving from 'Hewlett Packard' to 'HP Invent' in order to signify its renewed focus on innovation exploitation. Like many large companies, such as SAP (SAP Labs) and Alcatel-Lucent (Bell Laboratories), it has its own research facilities located in HP Labs across the world (http://www.hpl.hp.com). Indeed, one way to determine how innovative a firm is could be to measure the number of new products and services are developed in-house or even what percentage of current sales or profit come from products launched in the last five years. 3M (http://www.3m.com) endeavours to serve its global customers and communities with innovative products and services. In its Annual Report 2014 the company highlighted investing in innovation as one of three strategic levers and invested $1.4 billion in research and development (3M 2014: 2).

Innovations are not solely based on new technologies. Social innovation involves the introduction of new social practices, activities, or ways of organising. Examples of social innovation that have been influential in recent years include:

- **Car sharing schemes**, where people find a work colleague who lives locally and share the commuting journey, reducing costs and carbon emissions.
- **Book clubs**, where readers meet up on a regular basis to share their ideas about a book they have been reading.
- **Raves**, where people come together for large, all-night dance parties that are often organised in unusual, and occasionally illegal, locations.

Social innovation is now seen as an important way to tackle economic, social, and environmental challenges. This is creating many new opportunities for entrepreneurs to make a difference by turning new ideas into a reality:

> The results of social innovation are all around us. Self-help health groups and self-build housing; telephone help lines and telethon fundraising; neighbourhood nurseries and neighbourhood wardens; Wikipedia and the Open University; complementary medicine, holistic health and hospices; microcredit and consumer cooperatives; charity shops and the fair-trade movement; zero carbon housing schemes and community wind farms; restorative justice and community courts. All are examples of social innovation – new ideas that work to meet pressing unmet needs and improve peoples' lives. (Young Foundation 2007: 7)

Technologies often have a role to play in a social innovation, but they are not necessarily the primary source of the innovation. Therefore, what are the sources of innovation? Drucker ([1985] 2007) mentions eight sources for innovation opportunity as part of what he called 'purposeful innovation' (Table 4.2).

TABLE 4.2 Sources of innovation

Source	Example
Internal	
1. The unexpected	i) Success
	ii) Failure
	iii) Outside event
2. Incongruities	i) Incongruous economic realities
	ii) Between reality and the assumptions about it
	iii) Between perceived and actual customer value and expectations
	iv) Within the rhythm or logic of a process
3. Process need	
4. Industry and market structures	i) Automobile story
	ii) Opportunity
	iii) When industry structure changes
External	
5. Demographics	i) Demographics
6. Changes in perception, meaning, and mood	i) Glass is half full
	ii) Problem of timing
7. New knowledge	i) Characteristics of knowledge-based innovation (convergences)
	ii) What knowledge-based innovation requires
	iii) Unique risks (shakeout and receptivity gamble)
Additional	
8. Bright idea	

Source: Developed from Drucker ([1985] 2007).

In the case of social innovation, the key to identifying the best ideas is for innovators to get out into the world and in direct contact with people, to ask good questions, and to find out for themselves what needs to be done:

> *Some of the best innovators spot needs which are not being adequately met by the market or the state. They are often good at talking and listening, digging below the surface to understand peoples' needs and dislocations, dissatisfactions and 'blockages'. (Young Foundation 2007: 22)*

Innovation can be a source of entrepreneurial opportunity in all kinds of organisations, large and small, and in the private, public, and voluntary sectors. However, there are significant differences in the ways that organisations manage the process. For example, in the case of Apple's iPhone and iTunes products (http://www.apple.com), new technologies were developed and exploited within a single firm. By contrast, some large firms choose to obtain their innovations from third parties. Examples include Timberland's acquisition of Howies (Case 4.1) and the Coca-Cola Company's 2009 purchase of a minority share of Innocent Drinks. There are also many collaborative, network-based, approaches to innovation in which organisations and individuals work together to develop new ideas (e.g. Seely Brown and Hagel 2006; Conway and Steward 2009) (Section 6.3).

Having outlined some essential features of innovation, we now need to consider how to harness creativity and innovation effectively in order to generate new business ideas. There are a number of important questions to address. For example, how do we identify which ideas have the potential to be genuinely entrepreneurial opportunities? Here, one of the main criteria is whether the resulting venture is going to be 'sustainable'. For some entrepreneurs, this may mean little more than it being financially viable (i.e. in terms of cash flow, profits and capital growth), and therefore capable of providing a return on the initial investment. However, there are also issues related to social and environmental sustainability (e.g. will it provide safe and secure employment opportunities?, will it reduce or minimise environmental impacts?). Today, entrepreneurs need to consider all three elements of sustainability as part of the innovation process. For example, many large businesses are responding to environmental challenges, such as global warming, with innovative technologies. For example, car manufacturers are designing smaller vehicles with electric engines, such as the Nissan Leaf (http://www.nissan-global.com), while some new ventures are being created to market vehicles powered by electricity, such as Tesla Motors founded in 2003 by Elon Musk (https://www.tesla.com). There appears to be no shortage of innovation but how do entrepreneurs or entrepreneurial companies decide which ideas are worth developing? What is the role of risk in these decisions?

4.4.2 Linking innovation and creativity

People sometimes find it difficult to make a clear distinction between creativity and innovation (Conway and Steward 2009: 8–10). We tend to think of innovation as beginning with a dramatic burst of creativity, which gives rise to new ideas and inventions (Section 12.3). However, many questions remain. For example:

- How is a creative ideas developed into a fully-fledged innovation?
- Why do so many ideas fail to get beyond the drawing board?
- Can we identify a distinctively 'entrepreneurial' role in this process?

TABLE 4.3 Creativity, innovation, and the entrepreneurial role

Creativity	Entrepreneurial role	Innovation
Generating new ideas	Translating ideas into practice	Realisation of new ideas
After 10 years working in the fashion industry, including some work with an organic cotton supplier, Katherine has the idea of developing a more environmentally-friendly approach to dry cleaning. It could have remained no more than an idea but, by chance, she meets a materials scientist and the pair manage to develop a new cleaning technology. Katherine's idea has now become an invention, but they are not sure how it should be commercialised.	The inventors realise that they need someone else in their team who is capable of championing the idea. They develop a relationship with an experienced technology entrepreneur who has an interest in the natural environment. The entrepreneur helps to evaluate and refine the concept, secure the intellectual property rights, research the market, develop a business model, and build links with suppliers, regulators and other important contacts.	The dry cleaning venture is launched with five directly managed outlets in major cities. The business expands in the home country using a franchising model, and the technology is subsequently licensed for use in other countries. The new venture faces competition from powerful incumbent businesses, prompting a number of operational and strategic changes. However, over a period of time, the venture grows and the technology is widely disseminated.

Source: Fictional illustration drafted by the authors.

One way of addressing these questions is to picture the entrepreneurial role as a kind of bridge between creativity and innovation. Entrepreneurs translate ideas and inventions into practice, modifying them where necessary and rejecting those that are either technically weak or lacking in credibility. In some cases, the same people manage to occupy the role of the idea generator or inventor and that of the entrepreneur. However, there are also many examples in which the roles are taken by several members of an entrepreneurial team (Section 7.2). Table 4.3 is a simplified illustration, distinguishing between these roles, and suggesting one of the ways that they might be combined.

From much of the media coverage of new inventions, it might seem that the key lesson is to focus your attention on the most creative new ideas and those with the greatest potential for innovation. However, there is no guarantee that such a combination will end in success. The example cited in Chapter 3, the Apple Newton (https://en.wikipedia.org/wiki/MessagePad), a digital personal organiser launched in 1993 met both of these criteria, being highly innovative and displaying a great deal of creativity on the part of its designers. Despite this, the Newton was replaced within one year by a series of alternative products (i.e. MemoPads), which were themselves withdrawn after a few years. In this case, there was a happy ending. A decade later, the company launched a new kind of digital organiser, the Apple iPhone; unlike its predecessors, this innovative product has proved to be highly successful.

At this point, some readers may be wondering if there is any chance of identifying an entrepreneurial opportunity that can support a new venture. However, it may be reassuring to know that many highly creative and innovative ideas emerge from what might be described as 'everyday experiences'. As in the case of social innovations (Section 4.4.1), think about the contact you have with other people, perhaps waiting in a queue in a shop or overcoming a difficulty at work. Also, while watching the news or reading a paper, consider events in their wide context: are there any trends?

4.4.3 Entrepreneurs and innovation

Having considered the sources of creativity and innovation and the relationship between them, we need to identify the role of the entrepreneur in this process. It is often thought that entrepreneurs are the agents, who help to convert an invention into an innovation and then exploit this innovation in an enterprise. In terms of Majaro, they can certainly help to shift things towards the top-left corner (Figure 4.2). Innovation generally means taking the idea to market and, in many cases, building a new organisation around it that is capable of operationalising it. Sometimes, the role of inventor and entrepreneur are combined in one individual. James Dyson is a well-known example, but this is not the norm (http://www.dyson.co.uk) (Case 10.4). Some inventors can become highly influential people without necessarily creating a company to exploit their inventions. Examples include Tim Berners-Lee, the inventor of the World Wide Web, and Linus Torvalds, who helped to develop the Linux operating system (http://www.linux.org). Perhaps more commonly, entrepreneurs and inventors form teams in order to combine their distinctive strengths. For example, Jenny is an engineering design graduate who has invented a simple movement-sensing device, which operates through conventional electrical wiring. One evening Jenny meets Maryam at a friend's party. Maryam is a graduate in marketing with a few years' experience in an international management consultancy and has contacts in a venture capital firm that specialises in new technologies. Together they are able to raise the funds, from family and friends, to develop five demonstrators, which they lend to a local security firm who specialise in large buildings, such as hospitals. The device enables them to monitor movement patterns in the hospital centrally and reduce the number of security staff at night as well as providing a better service to the hospital. Armed with letters of support from both the security firm and the hospital, Maryam and Jenny are able to develop a business plan and raise venture capital funding to start their business.

Chocolate is a favourite treat for many people, but it is also widely available in many different forms, and the industry is well established with a number of large confectionery companies. How can you create an innovation based on such a familiar product? And how can a passion for chocolate provide the basis for a real business opportunity? In the following case, we examine the relationship between creativity, innovation, and entrepreneurial opportunity (Case 4.3).

CASE 4.3

Passion for chocolate: new business opportunities from a long-standing love affair

The ever-increasing love affair with chocolate dates back centuries and takes many forms. Today, the industry is dominated by large companies, such as Mars, Cadbury (Mondelēz International), and Nestlé (ICCO 2016), yet supports a range of more specialist chocolate confectioners, such as Green & Black's, now owned by Mondelēz International (http://www.greenandblacks.com), Thorntons (http://www.thorntons.co.uk), and **Hotel Chocolat** (http://www.hotelchocolat.co.uk). In such a well-established and crowded

(Continued)

(Continued)

market it might seem difficult to create a new way of exploiting our passion for choco-late. Hotel Chocolat (formerly ChocExpress) was founded in 1993 as a catalogue-based company in the UK (Barber 2010).

- **Creativity Angus Thirlwell** and **Peter Harris** had the idea that some people might prefer to buy and receive delivery of chocolates from the comfort of their own homes. More than that, they might want also to buy specialised chocolates that they could not buy easily from retail shops.

- **Innovation** Sourcing and selecting the best chocolates made from premium wholesome ingredients from specialised chocolatiers from across Europe and offering these as a mail-order service was an innovative idea.

Entrepreneurial opportunity Not only was the idea creative and innovative, but cus-tomers loved it and kept coming back for more. Over the last 15 years the business has grown significantly yet still retained the founders' ethical principles based on a fair price to cocoa bean growers. Interestingly, Hotel Chocolat has continued to look cre-atively for entrepreneurial opportunities; it now has over 75 stores in the UK and 3 stores in Copenhagen. The company also owns a cocoa plantation in St Lucia and has created an innovative chocolate tasting club. The Chocolate Tasting Club (http://www.  hotelchocolat.com/uk/tasting-club) offers monthly deliveries of new chocolate selec-tions, which customers then score, creating a loyal customer base passionate about chocolate. Hotel Chocolat is a good example of creativity being applied to business idea generation (i.e. the tasting club), opportunity recognition (i.e. being used to support its existing catalogue-based sales), and exploitation in an enterprise (i.e. developing a complementary brand and new income stream within the main business operation).

    Ethical point Hotel Chocolat has developed what they call an Engaged Ethics approach in cocoa plantations in St Lucia and Ghana (Hotel Chocolat 2016).

QUESTIONS

1. Considering how competitive the chocolate market is, why do you think Hotel Chocolat have been able to become established and expand their channels to market?

2. Compare Hotel Chocolat (http://www.hotelchocolat.co.uk) with other catalogue-based companies in the UK, such as Healthspan (http://www.healthspan.co.uk) and I Want One of Those (http://www.iwantoneofthose.com). What are the simi-larities and differences?

3. What other markets would you recommend Hotel Chocolat to consider developing and why? Who are likely to be their main competitors?

Sources: Barber 2010; Hotel Chocolat 2016; ICCO 2016.

4.5 REALISING ENTREPRENEURIAL OPPORTUNITY

We can see from the examples in this chapter that in the context of entrepreneurship, the process of innovation is the generation of new business ideas, through creativity (*idea generation*) and the subsequent selection and development (*opportunity recognition*) of those with the potential for *exploitation in enterprises*. It is through this entrepreneurial process that entrepreneurs and entrepreneurial managers exploit entrepreneurial opportunities in existing businesses, new ventures, or social enterprises (*enterprises*) in order to add value to the customer or gain competitive advantage in markets (Figure 4.2).

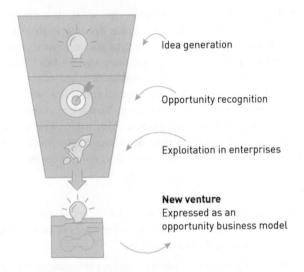

Idea generation

Opportunity recognition

Exploitation in enterprises

New venture
Expressed as an
opportunity business model

FIGURE 4.2 The entrepreneurial process.

As we warned at the beginning of this chapter, the entrepreneurial process diagram indicates the relationship between creativity, innovation, and the entrepreneurial process, but it is highly simplified and does not reflect the holistic and circular nature of entrepreneurship. Exploiting entrepreneurial opportunities is not a single one-off action but a continuous process of reflection and change. How conscious are entrepreneurs of their engagement in such a process? They often describe their success as being based much more on an intrinsic 'gut feel' rather than the result of a deliberate process. Perhaps this should not be too surprising given the intrinsically people- and team-focused nature of entrepreneurship.

But in all this focus on processes it is important that we remember the importance of serendipity, chance, or just old-fashioned good luck. When asked, entrepreneurs will often recall a lucky incident or break. For example, Duncan Bannatyne describes in his autobiography how the impetus to start the chain of health clubs came about by accident (Bannatyne 2007: 202). Similarly, the late Anita Roddick, founder of Body Shop (http://www.thebodyshop.co.uk), describes how the decision to open a shop was partly born out of her decision not to go back to the 'gruelling business of running a restaurant' (Roddick 2005: 36).

The best collections for innovation and entrepreneurship research are the *Oxford Handbook of Innovation*, edited by Fagerberg et al. (2005); the *Oxford Handbook of*

Entrepreneurship, edited by Casson et al. (2008); the *Oxford Handbook of Innovation Management*, edited by Dodgson et al. (2015); and the *Oxford Handbook of Creativity, Innovation, and Entrepreneurship*, edited by Zhou et al. (2015).

In this chapter, we have seen how innovations can be in products, processes, services, or markets and their exploitation achieved in a wide range of enterprises. And while, quite rightly, this chapter highlighted new technology as a potential source of creativity and innovation, it also considered broader sources of innovation and examples of exploitation in new ventures, existing businesses, and social enterprises. We have defined both creativity and innovation and considered their relationship with the entrepreneurial process.

The next case in this chapter (Case 4.4) provides us with a chance to share the entrepreneurial journey in *Deirdre Bounds: seeing eye to eye*. Deirdre Bounds's own experiences of travelling and her commitment to social justice proved strong personal drivers to founding the ethical travel company she sold in 2006 for £14 million. In addition, there is a video case available on **$SAGE edge**™ (Case 4.5 *Opportunties: Achille's challenge*). This video case is based on an interview with an entrepreneur, Achille, facing a challenge related to this chapter. Watch the video and decide which option you think the entrepreneur will choose. You might find it useful to discuss the case with friends or colleagues before deciding. Please note that lecturers can have access to the video that reveals the actual decision taken by the entrepreneur.

4.6 SUMMARY

- Creativity, innovation, and opportunity are at the heart of entrepreneurial opportunities. Understand the nature of creativity and sources of innovation that become concrete knowledge and real opportunities.

- In the entrepreneurial process, creativity involves the generation of new business ideas, which through the process of innovation are developed into entrepreneurial opportunities that can be exploited in enterprises.

- Innovations can be in products, processes, services, or markets. Social innovations involve changes in everyday practices and are often designed to satisfy unmet needs.

- Entrepreneurs draw on various sources of innovation, both within and beyond the organisation. Some innovations, including many social innovations, emerge as a result of direct personal experiences.

- **Entrepreneurial creativity** can be developed through a combination of individual factors, related to psychology and cognition, and social factors, such as the membership of your venture team.

CASE 4.4

Deirdre Bounds: seeing eye to eye

Deirdre Bounds' success in business seems to spring from her boundless energy, enthusiasm, and keen sense of social justice. In 1996, she launched what was to become a highly successful ethical travel company (**i-to-i**), which she sold just ten years later for £14 million. However, far from slowing Deirdre down, the sale of the company has fuelled other social, ethical, and charitable activities. She has also developed her profile as a motivational speaker, mentor, and published her first personal development book, *Fulfilled*, in 2009.

BREEDING GROUND FOR SOCIAL JUSTICE

Deirdre went to a comprehensive school in Liverpool before studying for a degree in Sociology and Business Studies in Leeds. Having gained an ordinary degree she left, rather than staying to complete her honours. She recalled that she thought, 'I can't bear academia any more ... it was the boredom of study. It was the futility of it ... also I didn't quite fit in with the whole middle class university crowd and I felt very much like I was on the outside looking in ... Now, if I went to university I would look at it as a place to really expand my mind. I understand the value of education.' Deirdre is the youngest of five children: 'My sister is the eldest. She went first. She is now a teacher. She was kind of a role model for me because all I wanted to do really was get out of Prescott ... it was just a dead end, no work place ... My family are Irish and they didn't belong there.'

However, Deirdre didn't recall being particularly entrepreneurial, 'I am a worker but I was never a young entrepreneur. I didn't have great enterprising ideas. I wanted to earn money. I knew the value of money and I suppose I came from a background of lack of money. Just get out and get a job and the way to get a decent job is to get a good education.' However, she also recalled, 'I am a decision-maker, once it is made it takes time to get there. When I was 11, I had a really miserable time at primary school. I had no friends and there were a couple of bullying girl twins and I will never forget they made my life a misery ... I thought, *Right you are moving now Deirdre and this is your time to make a big mark in this school Get into the top band of the comprehensive school. Just make sure that you do that.* I remember making that decision ... I became a bit of a leader in the school.'

Looking back, Deirdre remembers struggling to achieve what she wanted, 'I only started my business when I was 29 and before then I had no entrepreneurial skills whatsoever. At the age of 27, I had no money. I was a bit of a floater, doing nothing ... I was a lost soul. I had ten years where life wasn't kind of going my way and I was a bit rudderless. Really, I didn't know what I was doing ... I look back now and I think again that lack of direction took me off to Japan as an English teacher.'

THE IMPACT OF TRAVELLING

Deirdre's decision to travel played an important part in helping her find an entrepreneurial opportunity: 'I went to Japan and I met some great people there ... I travelled around, went to Australia ... I would take a palm coated mini bus to the bus station at six o'clock in the morning ... the wind howled up the Sydney High Street and I remember standing there, I was 27, I thought, *Is this what my life is, touting for back packers?* ... but then I was able to turn it around. I made the decision to *do the best that I can.*' She soon continued her travels, 'I worked for a school over in Greece ... the head teacher ran a massive school. I said, *How do you do it?* She said, *I am not just interested in success, I am interested in successful people and it is just a game.*' Inspired, Deirdre returned to the UK and became a youth worker and stand-up comedian. She recalled, 'People told me I am quite funny and again I just made these decisions ... I couldn't really work for

(Continued)

(Continued)

anybody ... the best training, for going into very scary situations in business and doing public speaking, was my stand up comedy. Unbelievable, nothing can be as bad as being booed off stage by 300 people! I couldn't work for anyone else, I was too much of a maverick.'

All these experiences had an impact on Deirdre: 'I became kind of fearless after that because I really pushed out and tried different things ... there were lots of young kids at the youth club saying, *How did you travel?* ... I looked around and I thought, *These kids are never going to get a chance to take one of these gap year* things. It was very expensive and it was the domain of the middle class children ... I thought, *Well why the hell not?!*'

THROUGH HER OWN EYES

Deirdre recognised a problem and had an innovative solution. She recalled, 'I know it changed people's lives because I know it changed mine ... how are they [these kids] going to get this opportunity when there is no avenue for them?' Deirdre went to Leeds Education Department and asked if she could put on a course, 'How to teach English as a foreign language' ... 'I looked at her and she looked at me and I tried to keep my face straight because I thought I can't believe what I have just said and she said okay ... I put the courses on in about 13 schools in Leeds and then decided to put it on at the weekends. Then people started to ask, *Can you get me work placements abroad?* Now I'd become a tour operator!'

Deirdre contacted different schools around the world asking if they wanted English teachers: 'I knew this was a bottomless pit of people waiting for native English speakers. I had been there and so I saw the problem. The proposition to these school owners was too good ... All they had to do was to provide them with a place to live and a job. I went to India, Sri Lanka and Russia.' However, Deirdre faced her first big challenge – having generated interest she received a visit from a school in St Petersburg: 'They wanted to see my school and I was still in the bedsit in Leeds. By then you become unstoppable, if you really want something. I thought, *Well, okay, you want to come and see my school? Fine* ... I said, *Yes* ... I contacted the head teacher of a college in Leeds and said, *I have got these Russians can I borrow your office for a few hours?* It doesn't matter how you are going to do it as long as you commit to it and then you will find a way ... Somebody somewhere knows that and has connections to do what you want to do.'

Deirdre began to see the value in her network of contacts. She recalled, 'I see things, I am a very big thinker, I am not a details person ... you know I could see this could become a global phenomenon. Now what did I know about opening businesses across the world? Nothing. But there is always somebody who does. You have a good lawyer or you talk to somebody who has done it, and then you just keep moving towards what you see in your mind's eye.'

A GLOBAL BUSINESS WITH SOUL

Deirdre recalls, 'I think back now; *i-to-i* is the largest trainer of English as a foreign language [TEFL] teachers in the world; we teach 17,000 people a year. It is the biggest gap year company; it sends about 7,000 abroad to do volunteer projects around the world and I look back and I think, *Yes all these people are "inch by inch" making the world a bit of a better place* ... It was the value of the company. Honestly, I think *i-to-i* is a great company. It was a very profitable company because it was a very niche company. We were the leaders of the pack. We were not the dedicated followers of fashion. That is what I took delight in.'

The company was very personal to Deirdre: 'Every fibre of me went into that company and that is why it was a success. You know, that is the top and bottom of it. Yes, it was the right place at the right time and a bit of luck ... At the end of the day, even when I had a great team around me, I had to have the mental stamina to keep the global juggernaut going.' But how did she go about building a 'great' team? 'I had no idea of recruitment policy ... I just learned recruitment processes and wrote a decent job spec and 50% of the time it worked and 50% of the time it didn't. I created a team through the pain of recruiting really bad people. In the end, I realised what I was not good at. I really had to practise a lot of patience and tolerance with some. Staff are very, very challenging because you can't control it. You can't control people. People will do what they like, when they like, how they like. Now I understand the importance of vision, translating that to the team, having strategic direction ... one day to the next. How are we going to get buy in [commitment] from the team? How are we going to deliver this? How are we going to get this from general management books? ... I got approached by someone who wanted to join, so he came in as a project development person and then I made him MD.' Just ten years later Deirdre sold the company for £14 million.

PERSONAL DEVELOPMENT AND BEYOND

Deirdre's undoubted business success did not come easily and she remembers, 'The rocky years were between from about 18 to 27 and then I found it ... quite phenomenal success.' But she also recognises her strengths: 'I have got a talent I have some sort of innate talent ... I think there are a couple of types of entrepreneurs. There are entrepreneurs who are brilliant dealmakers; they smell a deal ... I am not that sort of entrepreneur. I am the creator of the concepts and I get things off the ground and I see problems and I see great solutions.'

Interestingly, Deirdre was not deterred by her limited financial experience: 'The importance of just watching your bank balances go up and that was about as much of finance as I knew. I didn't know anything about spreadsheets. I can't use Excel. I am just about at the level now where I can read a balance sheet and read a profit and loss. My mathematics is dreadful. Did that stop me? *No!*'

In 2015, Deirdre launched GoCambio, a travel and language exchange site (https://www.gocambio.com) described by Lonely Planet as a 'ground-breaking barter system for exchanging language lessons in return for free accommodation has already spread to 114 different countries' (Lonely Planet 2015).

Sources: This case is primarily based on an interview with Deirdre Bounds and was written by Nigel Lockett.

CASE 4.5

 ◀ Opportunties: Achille's challenge video

In this video case, **Achille** explains three new business opportunities: (a) voucher management solution, (b) multi-retailer loyalty app, and (c) smart shelf solution. Watch the video and decide which option you think Achille will choose. You might find it useful to discuss the case with friends or colleagues before deciding. Please note that lecturers can have access to the video that reveals the actual decision taken by the entrepreneur.

Source: This video case is primarily based on an interview with Achille by Nigel Lockett.

Practical activities

1. **Creativity** We know that being creative is important for entrepreneurship. Think about creative people you know personally or have read about. What common behaviours do they exhibit? They might be optimistic, positive, passionate, determined, focused, problem solvers, imaginative, but which of these are important to creativity? Imagine you had a sack containing five random objects – say, a teddy bear, blank CD-RW, toothbrush, bag of sawdust, and a pair of old shoes. Pick any one of these, and see how many business ideas you can think of in five minutes. Get someone else to do this with the same object and compare your results. Which ideas are the same, which ones are already businesses, and which do you both agree are the best ideas worth exploring further?

2. **Autobiography** Read an autobiography of a successful business person and prepare a short five-minute presentation exploring three successes and one failure. Try to highlight some of the key characteristics of the person you think have contributed to their success. Are these characteristics unique, or could they be learned or copied? What have they learned from failure? Try to compare these with other people's reviews of different autobiographies. What are the differences and similarities?

3. **Disruptive technologies** Analyse the most recent edition of the *Economist's Technology Quarterly Review* (http://www.economist.com/technology-quarterly/) in order to identify disruptive technologies, *innovations*, that could create new products, services, or markets. Consider how long it might take for these to come to market? Research which existing companies are best placed to take advantage of these and investigate their websites and annual reports to see if these disruptive technologies are mentioned.

Discussion topics

1. Discuss what characteristics creative people have and see if you can agree which are the three most relevant characteristics of creativity for entrepreneurship.

2. 3M (http://www.3m.com) are seen as an innovative technology company. How can we make such a judgement? Who might be their biggest competitor and how innovative are they?

3. Is acquisition by a large firm the most likely fate for successful business ideas exploited in new ventures? Compare Howies (http://www.howies.co.uk), and WebEx (http://www.webex.com) with Dyson (http://www.dyson.co.uk), and Dell (http://www.dell.com).

Recommended reading

These readings address important topics in entrepreneurship research and are recommended for anyone wanting to build on the material covered in this chapter. Recommended readings have been selected from leading Sage journals and are freely available for readers of this textbook to download via the Online Resources.

Love, J. H. and Roper, S. (2015) 'SME innovation, exporting and growth: a review of existing evidence'. *International Small Business Journal*, **33, 1: 28–48.**

This article summarises and synthesises the evidence on SME innovation, exporting and growth, paying particular attention to ecosystem enablers, and for the interplay between innovation and exporting in SME growth.

Martin, L. and Wilson, N. (2014) 'Opportunity, discovery and creativity: a critical realist perspective'. *International Small Business Journal*, **34, 3: 261–75.**

This article draws on the philosophy of critical realism to reflect upon issues concerning discovery processes and opportunity development. It concludes with conceptual and practical comment on the importance of ontological theorising for entrepreneurship.

Wynarczyk, P., Piperopoulos, P. and McAdam, M. (2013) 'Open innovation in small and medium-sized enterprises: an overview'. *International Small Business Journal*, **31, 3: 240–55.**

This article considers open innovation model and reviews a special issue, which offers a critical contribution to this gap with four articles that explore differing aspects of open innovation within smaller firms.

References

3M (2014) *3M Annual Report 2014*. St Paul, MN: 3M.

Bannatyne, D. (2007) *Anyone Can Do It: My Story*. London: Orion Publishing Group.

Bannatyne, D. (2008) *Wake Up and Change Your Life*. London: Orion Publishing Group.

Barber M. (2010) 'Building a brand: Hotel Chocolat', *Growing Business Magazine*, 17 February.

BBC (2007) 'Timberland buys "green" company', 13 February.

Bornstein, D. (2007) *How to Change the World: Social Entrepreneurs and the Power of New Ideas* (2nd edn) New York: Oxford University Press.

Bornstein, D. and Davis, S. (2010) *Social Entrepreneurship What Everyone Needs to Know*. New York: Oxford University Press.

Branson, R. (2008) *Business Stripped Bare: Adventures of a Global Entrepreneur*. London: Virgin Books.

Casson, M., Yeung, B., Basu, A., and Wadeson, N. (2008) *Oxford Handbook of Entrepreneurship*. Oxford: Oxford University Press.

Christensen, C. (1997) *The Innovator's Dilemma: When New Technologies Cause Great Firms to Fail*. Boston, MA: Harvard Business School Press.

Christensen, C. and Raynor, M. (2003) *The Innovator's Solution: Creating and Sustaining Successful Growth*. Boston, MA: Harvard Business School Press.

Christensen, C., Roth, E., and Scott, A. (2004) *Seeing What's Next: Using Theories of Innovation to Predict Industry Change*. Boston, MA: Harvard Business School Press.

Conway, S. and Steward, F. (2009) *Managing and Shaping Innovation*. Oxford: Oxford University Press.

Dodgson, M., Gann, D. M., and Phillips, N. (2015) *Oxford Handbook of Innovation Management*. Oxford: Oxford University Press.

Drucker, P. ([1985] 2007) *Innovation and Entrepreneurship*. Oxford: Butterworth-Heinemann.

DTI (2003) *Innovation Report: Competing in the Global Economy: The Innovation Challenge*. London: HMSO.

Fagerberg, J., Mowery, D., and Nelson, R. (2005) *Oxford Handbook of Innovation*. Oxford: Oxford University Press.

Foss, N., Klein, P. G., Kor, Y. K., and Mahoney, J. T. (2008) 'Entrepreneurship, subjectivism, and the resource-based view: toward a new systhesis'. *Strategic Entrepreneurship Journal*, 2: 73–94.

Francis, D. and Bessant, J. (2005) 'Targeting innovation and implications for capability development.' *Technovation*, 25, 3: 171–83.

Hamel, G. (2000) *Leading the Revolution: How to Thrive in Turbulent Times by Making Innovation a Way of Life*. Boston, MA: Harvard Business School Press.

Hayek, F.A. (1955) *The Counter-Revolution of Science*. New York: The Free Press.

Henry, J. (2001) *Creativity and Perception in Management*. London: Sage Publications.

Henry, J. (ed.) (2006) *Creative Management and Development* (3rd edn). London: Sage.

Hotel Chocolat (2016) http://www.hotelchocolat.com/uk/help/our-ethical-policy (accessed 1 February 2016).

ICCO (2016) International Cocoa Organization http://www.icco.org/about-cocoa/chocolate-industry.html (accessed 1 February 2016).

Innocent (2016) http://www.innocentdrinks.co.uk/us/being-sustainable/packaging (accessed 1 February 2016).

Innocent Foundation (2015) http://www.innocentfoundation.org/about-us/finances (accessed 6 January 2017).

Kirzner, I. (1973) *Competition and Entrepreneurship*. Chicago, IL: University of Chicago Press.

Lonely Planet (2015) http://www.lonelyplanet.com/news/2015/09/18/gocambio-a-unique-travel-experience-that-wont-cost-the-earth/ (accessed 6 January 2017).

Majaro, S. (1988) *The Creativity Gap: Managing Ideas for Profit*. London: Longman.

Mintel (2008) 'Smoothies – UK – October 2008'. Mintel International Group, London.

Parsons, M. and Rose, M. (2009) 'Innovation, entrepreneurship and networks: a dance of two questions'. In P. Fernández Pérez, and M. Rose, (eds) *Innovation and Entrepreneurial Networks in Europe*. London: Routledge (41–60).

Porter, M. (1990) *The Competitive Advantage of Nations*. Chichester: Jossey Bass.

Roddick, A. (2005) *Business as Unusual: My Entrepreneurial Journey – Profits with Principles*. London: Anita Roddick Books.

Seely Brown, J. and Hagel, J. (2006) 'Creation nets: getting the most from open innovation'. *The McKinsey Quarterly*, 2: 41–51.

Tidd, J. and Bessant, J. (2013) *Managing Innovation: Integrating Technological, Market and Organizational Change* (5th edn). Chichester: John Wiley & Sons.

Tidd, J., Bessant, J., and Pavitt. K. (2005) *Managing Innovation: Integrating Technological, Market and Organizational Change*. Chichester: John Wiley & Sons.

Wikipedia (2016) Howies https://en.wikipedia.org/wiki/Howies (accessed 1 February 2016).

Young Foundation (2007) *Social Innovation: What It Is, Why It Matters and How It Can Be Accelerated*. Oxford: Skoll Centre for Social Entrepreneurship.

Zahra, S. A., Rawhouser, H. N., Bhawe, N., Neubaum, D. O., and Hayton, J. C. (2008) 'Globalization of social entrepreneurship'. *Strategic Entrepreneurship Journal* 2, 2: 117–31.

Zhou, J., Shalley, C. and Hitt, M. A. (2015) *Oxford Handbook of Creativity, Innovation Entrepreneurship*. Oxford: Oxford University Press.

5

PEOPLE: LEADING TEAMS AND NETWORKS

Never doubt that a small group of thoughtful, committed people can change the world. Indeed, it is the only thing that ever has.

Margaret Mead, cultural anthropologist

As a leader, you need courage born of integrity in order to be capable of powerful leadership. To achieve this courage, you must search your heart, and make sure your conscience is clear and your behaviour is beyond reproach.

Konosuke Matsushita, Japanese industrialist and founder of Panasonic

LEARNING OUTCOMES

After reading this chapter you should be able to:

- Appreciate how entrepreneurial leadership, teams, and networks can contribute to the success or failure of a venture, and to its overall performance.
- Identify significant features of a successful entrepreneurial team.
- Understand the processes influencing the development of an entrepreneurial team during the creation of a new venture.
- Identify significant features of an effective entrepreneurial network.
- Understand the processes influencing the development of an entrepreneurial network during the creation of a new venture.
- Apply relevant principles and techniques in order to create your own entrepreneurial leadership, teams and networks.

5.1 INTRODUCTION

In Chapter 1, we noted some of the typical psychological characteristics and behaviours associated with entrepreneurs, and began to consider whether it took a particular kind of person to establish a new commercial or social venture. We also saw that much of the discussion about entrepreneurship, both in the academic literature and more widely in our culture, has emphasised the role played by particular individuals. The entrepreneur is often presented as the hero of the story, an exceptional individual who has single-handedly founded a new business empire, transformed an entire industry, or pioneered a radical social change. For example, consider the following extracts:

> **Muhammad Yunus** is to economic development what Nelson Mandela is to world peace – a revered figure whose Grameen Bank has helped millions of Bangladeshis out of rural poverty by lending them small amounts of money, or microfinance, to set up their own businesses. It has 8 million borrowers, 97% of whom are women, and since 1982 has issued more than $6bn. (Benjamin 2009)

> While he **[Tony Hawk]** was still in high school, he used his winnings to buy a house in Carlsbad, and a few years later, he started his first company (Birdhouse) even though the skateboard industry was tanking at the time ... at 41, Hawk rules an empire. He is the worlds highest-paid action sports athlete ... there are Tony Hawk skateboards, bicycles, clothes, shoes, a bestselling autobiography, Jam exhibition tour and a video game series that's a phenomenon unto itself, with worldwide sales topping $1.6 billion since 1999. (Cohn 2009)

→ **PERSPECTIVES** See Section 12.1 for further information.

Of course, there may be some truth behind this myth of the heroic lone entrepreneur, but we must be careful not to fall into the trap of oversimplification. We can see from the opening case (Case 5.1) that there is good cause for caution when considering the entrepreneurial activities that can be attributed to the actions of one individual. Clearly, both Trevor Rowley (Postoptics) and Jamie Murray-Wells (Glasses Direct) are both entrepreneurial individuals and could easily be portrayed as hero figures, but on closer examination we can see the danger of oversimplification. In both cases, each built an internal management team (entrepreneurial team) and deliberately developed a number of external professional or supplier networks (entrepreneurial networks). The truth behind this myth is that they are entrepreneurs, but a significant part of their undoubted success can be directly attributed to their leadership skills and ability to create internal teams and external networks.

The evidence to support this observation comes from beyond this opening case. Firstly, there is plenty of empirical evidence to suggest that most new ventures are established by what is sometimes termed the solo entrepreneur, who subsequently becomes the owner-manager of a business. Secondly, some important and influential approaches to studying entrepreneurship, most notably those based on economic principles, continue to focus our attention on the decision-making behaviour of individuals (Casson 1982). However, it is also the case that several people, working closely together as a team, establish new commercial businesses and social sector organisations, for example, the founding of Facebook (http://www.facebook.com) in 2004 by Mark Zuckerberg, Eduardo Saverin, Dustin Moskovitz, and Chris Hughes; and also Innocent Drinks (http://www.innocentdrinks.co.uk) in 1999 by Richard Reed, Adam Balon, and Jon Wright. Some teams may be led by a prominent individual, while others consist of more equal partners. In any event, it is unlikely that the team will include someone who has specialised in human resource management (HRM). Many entrepreneurs lack experience in managing people, so this crucial role is typically covered by a non-specialist during the start-up phase. Furthermore, the performance of entrepreneurial ventures – whether solo or team-based – is also dependent on external sources of skill, knowledge, and experience of another group of people, existing beyond the immediate venture, but who become involved, either directly or indirectly, in its progress. To gain a rounded understanding of entrepreneurship, we need to consider these sets of relationships and how they can be managed effectively.

CASE 5.1

I can see clearly now: optical illusions or optical solutions?

The deregulation of the UK healthcare sector over the last two decades has resulted in significant changes to the way that individuals accessed and paid for services. These changes were most noticeable in community-based services, such as general practice and dentistry. Optometry, the care and treatment of the eyes, was no exception. The testing, treatment, and supply of related services experienced increasing competition between both existing providers and new entrants giving rise to fertile grounds for entrepreneurship. It was in this turbulent environment that Trevor Rowley and Jamie Murray-Wells founded their own companies, Postoptics and Glasses Direct respectively.

By 2008, **Trevor Rowley's Postoptics** had ten years' of experience and had become the UK's largest online supplier of contact lenses and solutions and operated out of purpose-built facilities in York. In 2007, the company was chosen by Boots, the UK's largest retail chemist, to handle its own mail-order contact lenses web presence, and Trevor was recognised for his pioneering work with a Future Entrepreneur of the Year award by *Enterprise* magazine. He stated, 'Boots offers one of the most well-known and trusted brands on the high street. We are delighted to be working in partnership with Boots Opticians on this venture, it is a credit to the whole team at Postoptics that our normal working practices have met the stringent demands required by Boots' (Optometry 2007).

Clearly, Trevor Rowley was an entrepreneurial leader in an emerging market. After all he had taken his mail-order dotcom start-up and integrated it with a specialist call centre to build one of the country's fastest-growing small firms: expanding at between 20% and 30% per year. In fact, at its peak it held about 90% of the online contact lens and solutions market. But, did Trevor get there on this own?

Postoptics had not only to build its internal team from scratch but also an external network of opticians and suppliers. The law required that customers needed a recent prescription in order to buy lenses and, after some initial reluctance to collaborate, Postoptics built a network of over 200 opticians. However, Trevor acknowledges that it was his specialist call centre team that provided the company with a unique competence and stated, 'We have a very low churn rate and we aren't wasting all that time recruiting and training people who then leave ... there's more to it than sitting at a screen reading a script.' Early on in the company's development he decided to appoint a HR manager to lead the development of the call centre. Instead of relying on learning on the job, the company introduced a programme of training and development, which empowered call centre staff. More specifically, this included an induction programme, regular staff appraisals, and reviews of customer feedback. This resulted in an unprecedented staff turnover rate of less than 1%. And, in a sector that was so highly regulated, reputation was everything. Trevor stated, 'Reputation is critical ... satisfied customers are the best and cheapest form of advertising. And for satisfied customers you need good service' (Sunday Times 2004).

In 2014, Trevor Rowley continued to run Viewpoint (http://www.viewpoint.co.uk), an optician's business, and Optix (http://www.optix.co.uk), providing software systems for opticians, with sales in excess of £1.5 million and year on year growth of 30% (York Press 2014).

Jamie Murray-Wells faced similar growth issues to Trevor when he decided to start his own business, **Glasses Direct** (http://www.glassesdirect.co.uk), selling glasses directly to consumers. After being horrified at the price of his first pair of glasses on the high street, he put his degree studies on hold and set about finding a glasses laboratory willing to supply him. He launched his business in 2004 and was soon receiving orders for cut-price prescription glasses over the Internet. By 2009 he had built the largest online glasses company in the UK, selling a pair every three minutes. But to build his business so quickly was the work of more than one person. Glasses Direct consisted of a team of people committed to quality of service. The first team member was finance manager, Deirdre Walker, quickly followed by office manager, Amy Kent, and several customer service advisors to handle the growing number of sales calls. In 2005, Glasses Direct was featured in the *Sunday Times*, the *Express*, the *Mirror*, and the *Daily Mail* all on the same day. As sales continued to grow, so did the team. Next to join were two clinical advisors who helped to increase the reputation in the industry and to enhance quality standards for the online business. Just as Trevor had done with Postoptics, Jamie established an external network of dispensing opticians to support his customers. The company continued to grow rapidly, recruited a fulfilment team to run its new warehouse, and Jamie won the Shell LiveWIRE Young Entrepreneur of the Year and the NatWest Young Entrepreneur of the Year for 2005. In 2006, David Magliano joined the team, and the company secured its third round of venture capital funding, launched new services, and received its first shipment of glasses from China. Jamie also won Isambard Kingdom Brunel Young Entrepreneur of the Year. In 2007, a multi-million pound venture investment from Index Ventures and Highland Capital Partners was secured and an experienced senior team was recruited. In the following year, Kevin Cornils, former MD of match.com and buy.at, joined the senior management team (PNE 2008; Glasses Direct 2010). In 2015, Jamie was appointed an OBE. In 2016, MyOptique, which included Glasses Direct, was bought by Essilor itself valued on the Paris stock exchange at £21 billion (Telegraph 2016).

POINTS TO CONSIDER

1. What are the similarities and differences between Trevor Rowley (Postoptics) and Jamie Murray-Wells (Glasses Direct)? Consider their personalities, professional backgrounds, and experience.

2. It would appear that Trevor Rowley focused on developing his own internal team, whereas Jamie Murray-Wells seemed to recruit in expertise. Is this true? What influence did raising investment have on their respective human resources strategies?

3. Both companies developed external networks of optometry professionals. Why was this important to their development?

Sources: Glasses Direct 2010; Optometry 2007; PNE 2008; Sunday Times 2004; Telegraph 2016; York Press 2014.

In this chapter, we begin by considering what it takes to create a successful entrepreneurial team (Section 5.2). This includes the factors to consider when putting a new team together, and the major challenges of keeping a team working effectively as the venture progresses. While some of the issues may be familiar from previous studies of management teams in existing organisations, we pay particular attention to the issues confronting teams, which are formed as part of the process of creating an innovative, growth-oriented venture (Section 5.3). In the second part of the chapter (Section 5.4), we turn our attention to the entrepreneurial network, the wider cast of actors who operate beyond the boundaries of the venture, but who are drawn upon in various ways. We ask how they are formed, why they are so important, and what can be done to ensure that they provide the kind of support that is needed in order to establish a successful venture. We conclude with some thoughts about the links between individuals, teams, and networks, including the kind of tensions that arise when people try to balance the need to collaborate against their personal ambitions. At the end of Section 5.6, in the *Victoria Tomlinson: network, network, network* case, we consider the importance of networks for one successful entrepreneur. The chapter concludes with video case ⓢSAGE edge" based on *People: Claire's challenge* (Case 5.5) to test your understanding of this chapter.

5.2 CREATING ENTREPRENEURIAL TEAMS

5.2.1 What is an entrepreneurial team?

New ventures are often based around people working together as members of an entrepreneurial team. There is still considerable disagreement over the definition of this term (Birley and Stockley 2000: 289–90; Cooney 2005: 229–30). Given the focus of this text, we will define the team as comprising two or more people who are actively collaborating in the founding of a venture in which they have a direct financial and/or personal stake. Practical examples of such teams include:

- six members of a family who relocate to a new country and establish a chain of restaurants;
- four university-based scientists who convert their discovery in the field of medical genetics into a spin-off venture;
- three university friends who decide to turn their shared passion for snowboarding into an Internet retailing business;
- a professional couple, who quit their jobs, re-mortgage their house, and use the capital to set up a regional organization to help homeless children.

This pragmatic approach to teams recognises that we are social beings and intrinsically familiar with working in small groups based on cohesion and continuity (Lewthwaite 2006). Not surprisingly, there are variations in the size and composition of start-up ventures according to the type of product or service being developed. For example, software development appears to have a higher number of single founders than the electronics sector, probable explanations including the range of skills that are needed (i.e. in software development, these skills are commonly found in an individual person, but not in the case of electronics-based ventures) and the amount of capital investment required in the initial stages (Cooper 1998).

In the remaining parts of this section we consider two key issues that arise when you try to create an effective entrepreneurial team from scratch: firstly, *team composition* (i.e. who is going to be in the team); and secondly, *team roles* (i.e. what part are they going to play in the team?). As you read these sections, try to link the ideas discussed to your personal experiences of being in a team, perhaps as a student involved in a group coursework assignment, an employee working on a collaborative project, or a member of a sports team competing against your rivals. It would also be useful to contrast issues applicable to entrepreneurial ventures with those covered on specialist HRM modules, where the focus is more likely to be on large, established organisations. Though some of the issues discussed are specific to entrepreneurial ventures, you should also find some common features in these approaches to dealing with people and organisations. It might also be useful to reflect on what experience and ability many new entrepreneurs have of creating and managing teams. The skills needed to generate new business ideas and recognise which are **entrepreneurial opportunities** might be different from the skills needed to build and motivate the new venture team. Understanding the importance of team composition could be the first step towards achieving this.

5.2.2 Team composition

In some situations, your capacity to select team members may be limited. For example, in the family-based restaurant venture it could be difficult to exclude a close relative, even though that individual might not appear to be the ideal candidate. However, there are usually opportunities during the course of the venture creation process for the founding entrepreneurs to make modifications to their core team. In the case of the medical genetics spin-off venture, the initial team comprised the four university scientists, who had been directly involved in the preceding research programme. The scientists might realise that they lacked certain skills and therefore look for additional team members who had a useful role to play, such as people with experience in intellectual property rights (IPR), finance, and marketing. In self-selected student teams, you often begin by selecting your friends, or at least people you already know, but if you find that there is scope to review team composition, it is well worth making the extra effort. Establishing a new venture is a challenging enough activity without the additional problems that are bound to arise if a team is either unbalanced or in some other way incomplete.

A recent review of the research on management teams has proposed a distinction between the factors influencing entrepreneurial teams during the initial phase of venture creation and those that only become relevant once the venture is becoming established. Future research needs to be clearer about the variables and avoid confusing those that are relevant to venture creation with those that are relevant to venture growth or indeed to mature organisations (Vyakarnam and Handelberg 2005: 246). While agreeing with the general proposition that some factors may become more or less influential as a venture develops, we would suggest that other factors, such as social integration and commitment to task, only become relevant once a firm is growing.

Though it may be relatively straightforward to list a set of issues concerning team composition, our experience suggests that it is much more complex and demanding to apply the underlying principles in practice. In order to help us think through some of these issues in a more concrete way, consider the following worked example.

Creating an entrepreneurial team: a worked example

SquishSquash – organic children's drinks

Imagine that you have just decided to create a new venture that will manufacture and market a range of organic soft drinks for babies and young children. Your venture is going to operate under the brand name, *SquishSquash*, which you see as capturing the essential characteristics of the product (i.e. enjoyable and natural). You get hold of a blank sheet of paper and begin to list the key requirements for the members of your ideal entrepreneurial team. One way to begin your search would be to identify people who could match your requirements in each of three important areas, namely (i) skills, knowledge, and experience; (ii) tangible and intangible resources; and (iii) shared vision, values, and motivation.

Skills, knowledge, and experience

Many ventures demand a wider range of skills, knowledge, and experience than are typically found in a single person, however gifted. New ventures often encounter problems because the solo entrepreneur of the entrepreneurial team is lacking these in one or more of their key areas of activity. In the organic drinks case, your team is going to be involved in both manufacturing and marketing the product. Though there are some degree courses that combine these fields, it is likely that you will need at least one person with a specialised background in the sourcing and processing of fresh produce, including the relevant food hygiene and food safety regulations (an essential requirement!). In addition, you will need someone with the skills required to develop the brand identity, to research the market, and to approach the retail buyers.

Tangible and intangible resources

Tangible resources include a variety of physical assets that are necessary for the venture. Financial capital is perhaps the most obvious tangible resource that founding team members need to bring. Some members of the team may be able to substitute their share of the initial capital for what is sometimes called sweat capital (i.e. when a person contributes their hard work and time rather than their own money). However, someone is going to have to be able to supply initial finance in order to purchase equipment, buy or lease manufacturing plant, warehousing, etc. (see Chapter 9, 'Finances: raising capital for new ventures'). Intangible resources include a number of things that may be more difficult to specify, but which can be crucially important. For the new organic drinks venture, it will be essential to establish a trustworthy reputation among customers, suppliers, and other external agencies (e.g. food standards regulators). These can be among the most valuable resources to acquire. For example, your food production and marketing people will need to establish their credibility when approaching farmers and major multiple retailers (see Chapter 6, 'Markets: understanding customers and competitors', and Chapter 7, 'Operations: implementing technologies, processes and controls').

Shared vision, values, and motivation

It is difficult to overemphasise the importance of these three factors. Firstly, establishing a shared *vision* for the venture requires that members of the team start out with an essentially similar set of ideas about what they want to create. We saw in Chapter 3 ('Visions') how difficult it can be to create the new venture plan. While there are bound to be differences at the level of the details, everyone in the team needs to be in agreement about the overall aims and the strategic priorities. Returning to the worked example, this means that your team members are able to agree about the kind of product they want to produce, the way they intend to produce it, and the market at which it is targeted. Given the many uncertainties surrounding venture creation, the team will also need to be flexible, adapting the vision where necessary. However, unless there is some degree of consensus in the early stages, it will be difficult to move forward. Fundamental agreements over issues such as the product specification (e.g. Should all the ingredients be organic? Should the fruit be locally sourced? Should preference be given to fair trade produce?) or the target market (e.g. Should it be exclusively for children? Should it be a premium brand?) could be very damaging. In addition, you will find it even harder to convince external audiences, such as prospective financiers, that you are a credible team that is capable of delivering on the investment.

Secondly, members of the team need to begin with a broadly similar set of *values* regarding the proposed venture. In this context, the term 'values' refers to moral principles and standards of behaviour regarding the kind of venture you want to establish and your general approach to the task. Differences over key values for the *SquishSquash* venture might revolve around the importance attached to children's health versus more general environmental concerns, or the desire to change consumer behaviour for the better, versus the need to achieve commercial success. People may also have different standards of behaviour in the way they conduct business dealings, such as negotiating with suppliers or selling to customers. For some, it may be good business practice, to use misleading language in order to get a better price, or to secure a sale; for others such behaviour would be a necessary evil that they would try to avoid, or something entirely unacceptable, that could cause them to abandon the venture. By the time you reach adulthood, these personal values and associated standards tend to be quite firmly established. However, differences in values between team members might only become apparent as the venture develops, particularly in situations where people have not previously worked together. In these cases, it would be worthwhile for team members to discuss their values openly at an early stage.

Thirdly, we need to consider the *motivation* of individual team members. There are two relevant aspects to motivation: the *source* of the motivation (i.e. what are the factors driving this person to take part in the venture?); and its *strength* (i.e. how strongly is the person driven to contribute to the success of the venture?). For example, for Martha (age 23, single) one of the founders of the venture, the primary motivation may be to take control of her life, abandon a boring, poorly paid job and hopefully to become a millionaire in the process. Another member of the founding team, Tariq (age 55, married) may be motivated by the chance to create a healthier food product for his grandchildren, while a third, Jan (age 38, divorced), who is already a successful entrepreneur, may see it as a great opportunity to have some fun with a new venture, and perhaps in the process to rediscover the excitement of earlier times, something that was missing from her life as the owner of several well-established businesses.

Source: This is a fictionalised case written by Richard Blundel.

→ **PERSPECTIVES** See Section 12.3 for further information.

As you can see from the worked example, there is a close relationship between vision, values, and motivation. As a consequence, all three need to be addressed as part of the process of building a new venture team. It is a common experience that entrepreneurial teams become so focused on the *task* (i.e. creating their venture) that they lose sight of essential aspects of the *process* (i.e. how they work together in order to achieve the task). We return to these three factors in Section 5.3 when we consider how to manage a growing entrepreneurial team. We have suggested that personal values of team members tend to be quite firmly established and resistant to change. People can also have fairly fixed ideas about the aims and future direction of a venture. However, there is some scope for modifying a person's values and also for inspiring them towards a new vision for the venture. The source and strength of someone's personal motivation can also vary over time, sometimes in response to external factors (e.g. if the venture is received particularly well by potential investors and other audiences) and factors closer to home (e.g. there is conflict within the team, and/or major changes in the personal circumstances of a team member). We have already seen that entrepreneurship is not a one-off process but a continuous cycle of learning about yourself, your **enterprise**, and the new venture team.

5.2.3 Team roles

Having considered the basic composition of the new venture team, we can turn to the kinds of roles that team members will play. When considering how an entrepreneurial team might divide up the work, we can draw on a popular approach that was first applied to conventional management teams. The research underlying this approach suggests that team performance can be enhanced by ensuring that you have a well-balanced team. In practice, solo entrepreneurs and members of small start-up ventures have to take on many more roles than their counterparts in larger or more established organisations. However, where there is scope to make modifications to an entrepreneurial team, it may be possible to apply some of these lessons. There are many approaches to understanding team roles, ranging from Lewthwaite's suggested roles of (i) expert, (ii) functional, and (iii) supporting (2006) to Belbin's eight roles originating from a series of experiments involving industrial managers who were attending short courses (1981, 1993, 2010a, 2010b). In the latter, researchers compared the performance of different teams competing against one another in a series of business games. By measuring psychological and behavioural characteristics of individuals and by experimenting with teams comprising different mixes of people, they were able to isolate eight distinct team roles (Table 5.1).

The researchers found that the higher-performing teams contained what they described as a balanced combination of these roles, whereas the unbalanced teams tended to perform less well and to display signs of dysfunction. While it is healthy to have some cognitive conflict, such as a constructive task-oriented argument over how to approach some aspect of the venture, it is not helpful to have affective conflict, where the disagreement is focused on individuals and based on personal disaffection (Amason and Sapienza 1997). The notion of a balance between roles suggests that there are several distinct communication tasks to be achieved if an entrepreneurial team is to operate effectively. For example, the Chair's role is concerned primarily with coordinating the intense flow of messages between team members, while the Innovator is synthesising new ideas from a more diverse range of sources, which may extend far beyond the team's boundaries. The Monitor-Evaluator is primarily engaged with cognitive, task-related messages, trying to ensure that the team meets its targets, while the Team Worker is more concerned with the exchange of affective (i.e. emotional), process-related messages, trying to hold the team together and to ensure that everyone is well-motivated.

As the original researchers recognised, it is not easy to form ideal teams in real-world organisations. The task is complicated by a number of practical constraints. For example, you may need to include an individual in your team because she has some essential area of technical expertise, irrespective of any team roles that she might be able to fulfil. Similarly, someone may be an ideal Chair for a team that is lacking this role, yet meet none of the other requirements discussed in the previous section. In a new venture situation, teams are often simply too small to be balanced. A person's ability to fulfil a team role may also be constrained by other obstacles, such as differences in status, cultural factors, or lack of time to devote to the task. In short, teams are always something of a compromise. Rather than aiming for perfection, it is more realistic to aim for a reasonable spread of team roles with the expectation that some of the imbalances can be offset by team members remaining flexible, and being willing to adopt alternative roles in order to cover the gaps. If we take these important limitations into account, two key conclusions about team roles remain applicable to entrepreneurial situations. Firstly, there needs to be some degree of balance in a team: what is needed is not well-balanced individuals but individuals who balance well with one another. In that way, human frailties can be underpinned and strengths used to full advantage (Belbin 1981: 75). Secondly, and perhaps more importantly in this context, team-building should be seen as an *art*, something that can be practised and improved upon (Belbin 1993: 87–95). We develop the theme of team-building in the next section.

TABLE 5.1 The concept of team roles: a communication perspective

Team role	Primary contribution	Implied communication task
Chair	Organizes, co-ordinates, and seeks to retain teams focus and involvement.	Monitors and co-ordinates messages between team members.
Team Leader	Initiates, provides leadership, and drives team towards achieving task.	Generates persuasive bilateral and multilateral messages directed at team members.
Innovator	Creates novel ideas and solutions in support of the task.	Synthesises messages from diverse internal and external information sources.
Monitor-Evaluator	Provides objective assessments of performance in relation to stated purpose.	Analyses primarily cognitive task-related messages within the team.
Team Worker	Encourages other members, fosters team morale, and reduces negative emotions.	Assesses and generates primarily affective, process-related messages within the team.
Completer	Maintains a check on outcomes in relation to project milestones and deadlines.	Analyses primarily cognitive task-related messages within the team.
Implementer	Carries out much of the practical work required to achieve stated purpose.	Receives bilateral messages (i.e. instructions) and avoids distraction from other internal exchanges.
Resource-Investigator	Establishes external contacts to secure resources in support of stated purpose.	Engages in bilateral exchanges of persuasive messages beyond the boundaries of the team.

Sources: Belbin (1993; 2010b); Blundel et al. (2013: 358).

5.3 MANAGING THE GROWING TEAM

5.3.1 Forming, storming, and norming: creating the team

You may already have encountered Tuckman's (1965) widely reported model of team dynamics. This suggests that the developing team passes through several distinct stages of development: forming, storming, norming, and adjourning (Table 5.2). Though each stage sounds plausible, critics have argued that an ideal-typical model of this kind is unlikely to represent the variety of processes taking place in real organisations. For example, if a venture team comprised people with shared motivation, vision, and values (Section 5.2.3), it might make a rapid transition from forming directly to performing. By contrast, if membership of a venture team introduced pre-existing conflicts (e.g. the team included two former work colleagues involved in a long-standing dispute), it might become stuck permanently at the storming stage. One useful way of reapplying the basic Tuckman model is to consider the patterns of communication associated with the different stages whenever they occur (Blundel and Ippolito 2008: 363). The examples given in Table 5.2 indicate why it is such a challenging exercise to keep communicating effectively in the fast-changing world of a new venture team. At some points, it may involve intense exchanges between many participants, while at other times it becomes dominated by bilateral exchanges.

The main lesson to take away from the work of Tuckman and from related research on group dynamics is that it is going to require a great deal of skill to manage the dramatic transitions that are bound to take place during the life of an entrepreneurial team. In particular, it is important to recognise the need for different patterns of communication as the venture develops, and to make the necessary adjustments in order to ensure that they occur (Hackman et al. 2000).

TABLE 5.2 Applying the Tuckman model to a new venture

Stage	Outline of activity in a new venture	Typical communication patterns within the entrepreneurial team
Forming	Individuals meet, initial attempts at team composition, establishing aims of venture (i.e. task) and ways of working (i.e. process).	Fairly open and multilateral exchanges as people seek an initial indication of each others capabilities and potential roles.
Storming	Disagreements emerge over both task and process issues; some internal conflict and hostility.	Strong bilateral, persuasive communication as members exchange arguments.
Norming	Efforts to resolve differences; venture team reaches agreement over task and process issues.	Greater attention to feedback as team leaders confirm consent and establish roles.
Performing	Team concentrates on achieving its common purpose, while maintaining process dimension.	Bilateral exchanges between team members engaged in delegated roles, with some multilateral communication to ensure activities are co-ordinated.
Adjourning	Focus on completion of task and dissolution of the team.	Combination of intensified multilateral exchanges and some unilateral direction as task is pulled together.

Sources: Tuckman (1965); Blundel et al. (2013: 357).

5.3.2 Team development: from venture creation to venture growth

Having created (forming, storming, norming) the founding entrepreneurial team, which has seen the new venture through the initial start-up phase, it would seem logical that a performing phase would develop. Indeed for the venture to continue, any issues arising from the forming, storming, norming phases will need to have been resolved. Again it is important to reiterate that the entrepreneurial team will be operating within a highly dynamic environment, and its development is unlikely to be linear and progress sequentially through each phase.

We have already acknowledged that entrepreneurs can, all too often, concentrate on creating a vision for their new venture rather than building entrepreneurial teams. In the *Better by design* case (Case 5.2), we will be able to see examples of entrepreneurial leaders who succeeded in overcoming this trap. Both Helen Scanlan (Zuri Design) and Abigail and Thomas Petit (Gossypium) approached this challenge in different ways but both built entrepreneurial teams that shared their vision and the entrepreneurial networks required to bring it into reality.

CASE 5.2

Better by design: creating teams and network, not just products

When **Helen Scanlan** founded **Zuri Design** (http://www.zuridesign.com) in 2004, she was driven by a passion for producing African, fair trade, and handcrafted products in order to make a positive and long-term impact on the lives of some of Africa's poorest people. But Helen also gathered an early committed team around her. Firstly, Kathleen Scanlan, Overseas Manager, joined on a voluntary basis to help in all aspects of the business including working on market stalls, sourcing products, stock control in Africa, and running exhibition stands. She has since gone on to develop the Zuri Network. Secondly, Julie Scanlan who designed the company's website, managed busy Christmas market stalls, and took part in triathlons to fundraise for the new venture. Additionally, the company readily acknowledges the help received from friends and family.

Interestingly, Helen and her entrepreneurial team were aware of the importance of building a network of producers (Zuri Network), which met their strict ethical and quality standards. Each producer had their own individual story; for example, Zakala Creations, in Kenya, was based in a refurbished workshop and fitted with Internet access. In 2011, the Zuri Foundation, a UK based charity, was established and by 2015, Zuri Design orders had created work for more than 200 men and woman in Kenya and Uganda, worked with over ten workshops, financed the start-up and development of a bead making workshop in Kibera Slum (Zuri Design 2017).

Many entrepreneurial teams start much closer to home. Before husband and wife team **Abigail** and **Thomas Petit** started their new venture, **Gossypium** (http://www.gossypium.co.uk) in 2000, they visited the cotton fields of Kutch, in western India, in order to find cotton that wouldn't harm the environment or exploit Indian farmers. This led directly to the formation of Agrocel (http://www.agrocel.co.in) whose mission is to

(Continued)

(Continued)

'build a strong and loyal customer base for Agrocel's Pure & Fair brand of cotton as well as for other value-added agri-products so that a long-term, trusting and tangible relationship is developed between the farmer who nurtures nature and the customer who cares about how cotton is grown and how products are made' (Agrocel 2017).

Based on the south coast of England, Gossypium is now a leading brand in fair trade certified organic cotton hand-crafted yogawear. In her children's book, *The Eye of the Needle*, Abigail tells the story behind Gossypium and introduces the complexities of both the textiles industry and cotton farming. It raises issues of child labour (Petit 2005). For Gossypium, fair trade means responsibility, sustainability, transparency, agriculture, and textile processing – 'At Gossypium, we are passionate about crafting all our products in an ethical and sustainable manner' (Gossypium 2017). In 2016, Gossypium obtained the best rating and topped the table of the ethical consumer (http://www.ethicalconsumer.org) sportswear guide.

Ethical point Not only did Helen Scanlan (Zuri Design) and Abigail and Thomas Petit (Gossypium) form entrepreneurial teams, they were instrumental in forming entrepreneurial networks, consisting of suppliers, based around their ethical values. In 2012, Helen also founded a charity, Zuri Foundation, to work with grassroots organisations in the slums within Kenya to empower youth.

QUESTIONS

1. Why would Helen Scanlan decide to build an entrepreneurial team so early on in Zuri Designs development? What Belbin roles did Helen, Kathleen and Julie play?

2. What might be the advantages and disadvantages of family-based entrepreneurial teams, like the one created by Abigail and Thomas Petit?

3. Is it significant that both Zuri Design and Gossypium placed so much importance on building their external supplier networks? Was it simply because of their ethical value?

Sources: Petit 2005; Agrocel 2017; Gossypium 2017; Zuri Design 2017.

The *Better by design* case illustrates the importance of personal linkages in creating entrepreneurial teams. Both Zuri Design and Gossypium required strong internal teams to support their extended enterprises and to guarantee their ethical values were maintained. But in addition, both enterprises relied on networks that extend beyond the boundaries of the venture team. We develop this theme in the following section, by examining the role of external networks in new venture creation (Section 5.4).

There is an extensive literature on management teams, but inevitably it is mainly related to the operation of teams in large, established organisations. We have already referred to some of the classic team studies, including Belbin's (1981, 1993, 2010a, 2010b) research on team roles and Tuckman's (1965) early work on team development. Blundel et al. (2013) include a chapter summarising some of this research, and commenting on communication issues that may influence the effectiveness of a team. Birley and Stockley (2000) provide a useful overview of research on entrepreneurial teams. The networks literature is vast, and can be difficult to navigate. Useful reviews of the field include Nohria (1992), Ebers (1999), which concentrates on the formation of networks, and

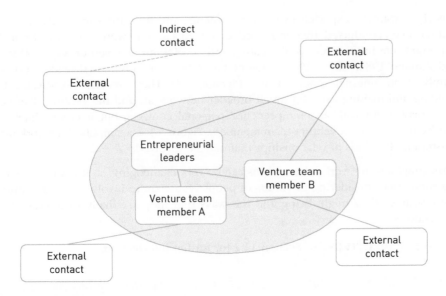

FIGURE 5.1 Entrepreneurial leaders, teams, and networks

Penrose (1996), which examines the link between networking and the growth of firms. The entrepreneurial networks literature includes pioneering work that emphasised the role of personal networking, including Birley (1985), Dubini and Aldrich (1991), and Johannisson and Monsted (1997). Research that has questioned the role of networking for many small firms, such as Curran et al. (1993), and studies of networking in particular sectors, such as Brown and Butler (1995), Johannisson (1998), and Jones (2001). Chell and Baines (2000) and Johannisson (2000) provide interesting overviews, plus their own insights into entrepreneurial networks and networking. There are also 'how to' guides for small business owners, including Barlow (2015) and Wellington (2017).

We have seen in this section how an entrepreneurial leader can create and develop entrepreneurial teams. In this section we consider how entrepreneurial networks can play a critical role in new venture creation. Entrepreneurial leaders build teams and networks with the latter coming directly from their own contacts (primary networks) and also from their team's contacts (secondary networks), see Figure 5.1.

5.4 CREATING ENTREPRENEURIAL NETWORKS

5.4.1 What is an entrepreneurial network?

Whether you are acting as a solo entrepreneur or as part of an entrepreneurial team, it is always necessary to make use of existing personal contacts, and to form new ones, in order to secure the services of individuals and organisations that are not directly involved in the new venture. This developing pattern of connections with the outside world is often described as an **entrepreneurial network**. These networks take many different forms, but are likely to include several of the following types of role:

- suppliers of raw materials, products and services;
- regulatory agencies;
- distributors and retailers;
- customers and end-consumers.

It is clear from the experiences of entrepreneurs, and from the substantial research that has been conducted, that entrepreneurial teams and networks play an extremely important role in the process of creating and developing new ventures (e.g. Aldrich and Zimmer 1986, Birley 1985, Johannisson 2000). Entrepreneurial leaders do not simply create internal venture teams (Section 5.3). They are also responsible for building and making use of a much broader network around the venture. The network may begin with an entrepreneurs' personal contacts, but it is also likely to involve those of other venture team members. Figure 5.1 is a simplified network map illustrating the kinds of relationships that may be involved.

Managing these network relationships can be very challenging, so it is worth spending some time considering the kinds of people you want to involve in your venture, the resources they might bring and the ways that they are likely to interact with one another.

→ **PERSPECTIVES** See Section 13.2 for further information.

5.4.2 Creating ventures: the role of personal contact networks

The role of networks in *creating* new ventures is now identified as an important area of **entrepreneurial activity,** and has been the subject of many research studies (e.g. Larson and Starr 1993; Johannisson 1998). One of the early findings was that entrepreneurs rely largely on *informal* sources in their personal contact network (PCN) to mobilise resources before the formation of a venture (Birley 1985: 113). The unique connections between people in the PCN play an important communication role, enabling the entrepreneur to identify opportunities that are not evident to others. At the heart of this network, there are normally a small number of strong ties that provide the entrepreneur with a shelter from the opportunism and uncertainty of the market. For example, one study found that most business owners report between three and ten strong ties, primarily business associates plus a few close friends and family members (Aldrich et al. 1989). The time and energy that entrepreneurs invest in these pre-organisational networks appears to be converted into future benefits for their emerging firms. This includes human capital, in the form of relevant experiences, skills and knowledge, and social capital (i.e. being known and trusted by others). Trust facilitates access to resources, through collaboration, and helps to overcome institutional barriers to entrepreneurial activity (e.g. local political resistance to a proposed development). However, the extensive personal ties used by entrepreneurs often lead to a blurring of business and social life, with mixed consequences. For example, reliance on particular individuals can sometimes lead to sudden, unpredictable, and potentially disruptive structural changes. Furthermore, while all start-up businesses make some entrepreneurial use of their personal networks, most small firms settle down into an established and fairly limited pattern of interactions. By contrast, entrepreneurs continuously develop their networks, with the more or less explicit aim of expanding existing ventures or establishing new ones. To achieve this, they maintain a broader latent network, parts of which are activated when required (Ramachandran and Ramnarayan 1993).

5.5 MANAGING NETWORK RELATIONSHIPS

What happens to the entrepreneurial network as the venture develops? Researchers have found that entrepreneurs are active in managing the complex pattern relationships that make up their network. What appears to happen is that the actions of solo entrepreneurs and entrepreneurial teams create a favourable organising context around the venture, in which it becomes relatively easier to deal with uncertainties and to exploit emerging opportunities (Johannisson 2000: 379). In other words, your network becomes an extension of the venture, providing you have additional resources, support, and sources of information. We can simplify the complicated processes involved in entrepreneurial networking into three broad tasks that entrepreneurs need to pursue in order to develop successful ventures: creating new ties; developing existing ties; and reviewing existing ties, pruning them where necessary in order to re-focus resources (Larson and Starr 1993):

- **Creating new ties** This is the task that most people associate with the typical entrepreneur. We can imagine the kind of people who are very confident in social situations, whether it is a business meeting, an international conference, a local sports event, or simply waiting for a flight in an airport lounge. Their networking abilities are displayed in various ways, including: the ease with which they establish friendly relationships with other people; how they are able to discover a great deal about a person in a very short time; a capacity to promote their own infectious enthusiasm for a venture, so that the other person also becomes interested; ensuring that contact details are exchanged (e.g. swapping business cards or email addresses); and, most importantly, following up on any promising contacts. This kind of networking, in order to create new ties, is often seen as a purely individual activity. However, it is also apparent that entrepreneurs create new ties with the help of other members of their core team, who may act as brokers or intermediaries. For example, you have a major design problem with a new product. Another team member introduces you to her brother-in-law, who has a background in product engineering. She acted as the broker. You can then establish a new relationship, and hopefully get some useful advice!

- **Developing existing ties** We have seen that entrepreneurial networks tend to be very extensive, with lots of weak ties that could become more important in the future. Entrepreneurs need to have a capacity to develop these existing ties, which may have remained dormant (or latent) for some time. Developing these ties involves people becoming closer through increasing trust and involvement; this is a process that we have all experienced, in our personal friendships and relationships. In an entrepreneurial setting, you might be renewing contact with an old school friend, now working in a finance house, to provide advice or support for the venture; converting an informal contact made while on holiday into a potential client; or building a much closer relationship with a supplier, which may lead to a formal alliance or merger. In network terms, this process tends to result in weak ties becoming stronger ones, and the related flows along the ties becoming richer in content (i.e. in technical language, multiplex), possibly containing a mixture of information, advice, economic transactions, and friendship. For example, you are running a charity fundraising auction and have been asked to provide a football signed by your national team. You have no personal contacts in the national team but your uncle coaches a local junior club. He offers to speak to the club president who is a friend of the national team coach. In just three steps you can obtain your signed football.

- **Reviewing and pruning existing ties** Networking takes time, effort, and resources. Even the most energetic entrepreneur has a finite capacity to create, maintain, and develop network relationships. Furthermore, there must be a trade-off between the costs involved in additional networking and the alternative uses to which that energy can be applied. As a result, the third networking activity involves a process of reviewing the current pattern of relationships and making any necessary adjustments. In some cases, where there does not appear to be much more to gain from a particular tie, the entrepreneur may decide to either limit or even abandon the relationship.

We are all familiar with social networking via the Internet, with sites such as Facebook attracting millions of users worldwide. Case 5.3 looks at how these technologies can be used to support entrepreneurial networks.

CASE 5.3

Beyond Facebook: creating online entrepreneurial networks

The extraordinary growth of online social networking websites, such as Facebook (http://www.facebook.com) and LinkedIn (http://www.linkedin.com) took many by surprise, not least the existing Internet companies who were slow to develop their own response. In Chapter 3, we hear the story of Steve and Julie Pankhurst, who simply had a wish to contact old friends. After many trials and tribulations, this idea emerged as one of the first commercially successful online social networking communities: Friends Reunited (Case 3.4). Facebook and Friends Reunited are exemplars of entrepreneurs creating a new venture around the demand for social networking. But can the web be used to promote *entrepreneurial* networking? In this case, we look at three contrasting examples of new ventures that have attempted to meet this need:

THE BEAT SUITE

When **Steve Bainbridge** started **The Beat Suite** (http://www.beatsuite.com) in 2003, he recognised the potential of using online creative communities to build a royalty-free music library. The concept seems simple: The Beat Suite provides companies in the creative multimedia, broadcast, and computer games industry online access to high-quality music and sounds to incorporate into their own productions. 'We spend lots of time making sure that our website is in full working order and that every feature is as simple as possible to use – meaning that you get the most convenient online digital music downloading. We have developed a music licensing structure that we feel is fair, convenient and affordable to the various users of production music.' Steve and his entrepreneurial team had a background as music producers, DJs, and composers, which meant that they understood the needs of both the producers and consumers of music and sounds. Music composers submit music tracks to the online music library for producers to access and include in their creative projects. Thus, The Beat Suite acts as a platform that unites the creative networks of composers and producers (Beat Suite 2017).

MADVENTURE

John Lawler faced just such a challenge when he wanted to create **Madventure** (http://www.madventurer.com). His vision was to create 'the number one provider of sustainable and ethical projects and challenging adventures worldwide'. What was important to John was to work with local communities in developing countries in order to enable adventurous travellers to have 'life-changing experiences through cultural integration, challenge, education and adventure'. It was John's personal experience as a gap-year student in 1998 that inspired the original idea. He stated, 'Through responsible travel, volunteering and development we all have the opportunity to give back to the fantastic regions we travel to. In our own small way by visiting some of these places and spending time with people, whether it is rural Ghana or mountainous Peru, we can learn so much more than just watching [celebrities on television]. So this year, make it happen and step out of your comfort zone. Take a gap and don't look back.' (ifwecanyoucan 2010). John gained funding from three organisations that support new enterprises: the Princes Trust (http://www.princes-trust.org.uk), Shell LiveWire (http://www.shell-livewire.org), and PNE (http://www.pne.org) to start his venture. He recalled, 'They also taught me how to write a business plan which was needed not only to get these funds but also to put my idea down on paper, which helped in terms of seeing what my vision might look like [...] to be a successful entrepreneur you need to ignore all the people who are negative – everything is achievable!' (ifwecanyoucan 2010). By 2017, Madventure was a social enterprise dedicated to empowering global communities through sustainable service, transformative learning, and adventurous exploration (Madventure 2017).

Ethical point John Lawler, of Madventure, formed the MAD Foundation in 2010 to advance education and aid in the relief in poverty. By 2015, the MAD Foundation was operating in Ghana, South Africa, Kenya, Tanzania, and Fiji with a combined income of £100,000 (MAD Foundation 2015).

QUESTIONS

1. The Beat Suite succeeded in uniting networks of composers and producers on a transaction platform, which allowed both content and payment to be processed online. Can you think of other examples of this business model?

2. Both examples in this case use the Internet to support online networking. What are the limitations to this approach when building entrepreneurial networks?

3. The Internet is a powerful global communication platform. How could it be used to support internal entrepreneurial teams and external entrepreneurial networks in the future?

Sources: Beat Suite 2017; ifwecanyoucan 2010; MAD Foundation 2015; Madventure 2017.

5.6 TOP DOG OR TEAM PLAYER? THE PARADOX OF COLLABORATION

This chapter has emphasised the importance of effective collaboration with other people, both within a core entrepreneurial team and in a wider entrepreneurial network. But you may be wondering, where does that leave the *competitive* nature of entrepreneurship and, in particular, the view of the entrepreneur as an exceptional *individual*, the top dog who stands out because they have outperformed (or out-manoeuvred) any potential rivals? As we noted in the introduction, it is difficult to establish a successful new venture without the active collaboration of other people. Teams and networks need to be created and developed, since the tasks require a degree of trust and reciprocity between all the people involved. However, it would be naive to imagine that either team-working or networking is going to be free from individual rivalries and power struggles. Among those who are attracted to setting up new entrepreneurial ventures, there are likely to be many people with lively person-alities, big personal ambitions, strongly held views about the best way to achieve a particular task, and a very strong competitive drive. If an entrepreneurial team includes two or more people with these characteristics, the combination can be explosive! In extreme cases, it may lead to the failure of a venture, as team meetings descend into continual arguments and internal competition between individuals causes the team to fragment. However, if team members are able to *channel* their energies towards the venture, rather than the satisfaction of their own personal needs, the result can be dramatically different.

As tutors, we have many student venture teams who struggle with precisely this kind of situation. Sometimes the team members simply fail to manage their internal rivalries. Despite our best efforts as external counsellors, the arguments continue and the clash of those with the biggest egos results in the break up of the team. Even if the team survives, it is unlikely to produce a high-quality venture proposal; and prospective investors are unlikely to be impressed if the team presentation is delivered by two opposing camps!

It has been said that there is no limit to what you can achieve if you don't care who gets the credit. For entrepreneurs, a willingness to share credit lies along the 'critical path' to success, simply because the more credit they share, the more people typically will want to help them (Bornstein 2004: 235).

Importantly, this willingness to share the praise and recognition for achieving some-thing grows out of a person's basic motivation. If an entrepreneur's true intention is simply to make change happen, then sharing credit will come naturally. However, if the true intention is to be *recognised* as having made a change happen, sharing credit may run against the grain. (Bornstein 2004: 235; emphasis in original).

And finally, remember that entrepreneurship is about motivating other people, or as Victoria Tomlinson (Case 5.4) puts it:

> *I have learned how to motivate other people and that is a huge thrill. For a recent campaign, we had such a short time frame for the clients because they were strug-gling to get there before the end of the year … I said just give me the contract and we will make it happen and we had to go out and get partners involved in this … suddenly they were all delivering. So we managed to deliver it in that time scale.*

In addition, there is a video case available on §SAGE edge" (Case 5.5 *People: Claire's challenge*). This video case is based on an interview with an entrepreneur, Claire, fac-ing a challenge in her outsourced HR company which is related to this chapter. Watch the video and decide which option you think the entrepreneur will choose. You might find it useful to discuss the case with friends or colleagues before deciding. Please note that lecturers can have access to the video which reveals the actual decision taken by the entrepreneur.

5.7 SUMMARY

- Entrepreneurship cannot be explained through the actions of individuals alone; we also need to consider the collaborative activity that takes place in entrepreneurial teams and networks.

- Entrepreneurial teams can be defined as two or more people who are actively collaborating in the founding of a venture in which they have a direct financial and/or personal stake.

- There are several factors to consider regarding the composition of an entrepreneurial team, which can be summarised under the three headings: skills, knowledge, and experience; tangible and intangible resources; shared vision, values, and motivation.

- If they are to be effective, teams need to be reasonably balanced and members need to be flexible enough to ensure that a number of different roles are addressed.

- Building and developing an entrepreneurial team is an art rather than a science, and it requires practise to deal with the dramatic changes that are bound to take place as the venture develops.

- Entrepreneurial networks can be defined as enduring patterns of connections between entrepreneurs and other actors, which provide an organising context for activity.

- The personal contact networks (PCNs) of entrepreneurs play an important role in the creation of ventures.

- Entrepreneurial networking activity can be broken down into three broad tasks: creating new ties; developing existing ties; reviewing and pruning existing ties.

- There is an unresolved tension between the collaborative aspects of entrepreneurial teamworking and networking and the competitive nature of entrepreneurship that emphasises the competitiveness of individuals seeking to be top dog.

CASE 5.4

Victoria Tomlinson: network, network, network

At the beginning of June 2004, **Victoria Tomlinson** knew she had reached a crossroads in her public relations (PR) company's development. Fifteen years previously, Victoria had taken the decision to leave the corporate world to set up her own PR company **(Northern Lights PR)** when her then employer, Arthur Young, merged to form Ernst & Young. After years of developing her business, the team, and an impressive client base, she faced the loss of her biggest customer. Was this an opportunity to downsize, change the way the company worked or simply sell it?

BIOGRAPHY

Victoria's early life provided constant challenges. Her father was a test pilot in the Royal Air Force and she moved schools frequently – the most being five schools in

(Continued)

(Continued)

two years. She recalled, 'I learned a lot from this, particularly how to make friendships. I was very shy and realised that the trick was to be interested in other people rather than myself.' Her academic career was not outstanding and she chose some subjects for the wrong reasons, taking A-levels in Pure Maths, Applied Maths, Physics, and Geography to 'prove I was brainy'. She moved again after A-levels, joining her family abroad when her father took a two-year contract in Saudi Arabia. She remembers it as 'a great experience'. On her return she completed an HND in Business Studies and immediately got a job with Plessey Aerospace. 'They recruited one person from our course each year,' she said, 'and it meant I was lucky enough to go in as a graduate trainee with the same terms and conditions as the proper graduates.' After two years she took voluntary redundancy as manufacturing was hit in the late 1970s.

Victoria then considered a number of careers, including Marks & Spencer's management training programme. However, as a woman she could only join if she went in on the HR [Human Resources] side. She wanted store management, so turned it down. She also applied for a job on another Plessey site, still on the contracts side, which had been advertised at £10,000. She was offered the job, but only at £4,000. The manager said she would already be the highest paid female on site and this was as high as they could go. She turned this job down also.

Throughout this period, Victoria also had to deal with having Crohn's disease, an inflammatory disease of the intestines. She joined a peer-support group and soon became involved in the early days of the National Association for Colitis and Crohn's Disease (NACC).

EARLY YEARS IN PUBLIC RELATIONS

Victoria soon found a job with Bradbury Wilkinson, which became De La Rue, selling banknotes around the world. While she was abroad, NACC gave Victoria their public relations brief to handle on a voluntary basis. Victoria recalled she had no experience: 'I knew nothing about PR so asked a number of friends and contacts if they would teach me how to go about this. They taught me about strategies, target audiences and how to design PR campaigns. We did this in the evenings after work and in return I'd cook them supper as thanks.'

After six years at Bradbury Wilkinson, an opportunity came up at Arthur Young to join their start-up marketing and PR team – with the new legislation in 1986, accountants and lawyers were able to promote themselves. Victoria remembers the fast-moving environment. 'Suddenly professional firms were recruiting marketing/PR teams. I went in as part of that start up marketing to one of the divisions and within months was handling half the firm's PR. We split the firm into markets and I took on the international banking group and international insurance group among others.'

The culture at Arthur Young was a far cry from Victoria's experience in manufacturing, 'It [manufacturing] was a negative atmosphere, everything was no, with managers and the trades unions playing bluff and double bluff with each other over pay negotiations. There were strikes and nobody respected or trusted each other. When I went to Arthur Young, suddenly people said, Yes, try it. Do something creative. It was entrepreneurial.'

Victoria was promoted again and into new areas. The firm had launched a major culture change initiative, and she was concerned that the focus was only on fee-earning professionals. She came out of a presentation fuming that the people she saw as the grafters were being ignored in plans and training. She walked into the Managing Partners office to ask what was to be done about it.

Perhaps, not surprisingly Victoria was asked to sort it out. She recalled, 'I had a division of nearly 100 people and was given the task of managing culture change for the whole London office of about 1,500 people and was on the management team.' This also provided another chance for learning on the job. 'I needed new skills for this job,' she added, 'as it was a big management task. I asked if I could buy some internal management consultancy time to help me in the role.'

The whole professional services sector was changing, and in 1989 Arthur Young decided to merge with Ernst and Whinney to form one of the Big Four, the four largest international accountancy and professional services firms, including PricewaterhouseCoopers (PwC), Deloitte Touche Tohmatsu (Deloitte), and KPMG. It was time for a change for Victoria as well.

VICTORIA'S NEW VENTURE

In the same year that Ernst & Young was formed, Victoria decided to leave the company, got married and headed north to Yorkshire. She had been thinking of starting her own business for some time, but had struggled to find the great idea. She recalled, 'I'd spotted the opportunities for recycling very early on, but when I rang a number of paper mills to see what they would pay per tonne, it was peanuts. I couldn't see how to make money from it.'

Once Victoria had moved to Yorkshire it all became urgent. She added 'My husband was concerned I'd be bored and I wanted to show I could sort out my new life. The one thing I had was PR skills which I felt could be packaged with my strong business background. I rang the *Yorkshire Post* to see what they felt about PR agencies in the region and it seemed there was an opportunity'. She got going quickly, finding a serviced office with a manned phone number and had cards printed. She wrote to everyone she knew in London who had connections in Yorkshire and asked for introductions. She also joined half a dozen networks and attended numerous events.

Victoria also combined starting her business with raising two children.

Unusually for the PR sector, the company built a loyal client base, focusing on business to business, education, and public sector, including a large government organisation. Naturally, Victoria built her team to support this important client.

The company became recognised for providing both good PR services and partnerships based on mutual trust. Networking became fundamental to their way of doing business – both attracting new clients and helping existing clients with contacts and support. Victoria recalled, 'We help clients and contacts all the time, introducing people who might have mutual business interests. You want to help them but actually it is always repaid in droves. Whatever you give out it comes back ten times over. I think some of this is instinctive – you meet someone and think I know just the person who could help you and so that new network starts.'

Victoria's business background was core to the way they did PR, both in terms of designing campaigns and the client relationship. She recalls one large client who was spending too much money with her company. 'We raised the subject with the client and outlined how they should restructure the PR in-house. It was to our short-term disadvantage but we created a life-long relationship. Clients trust you, come back again and recommend you. A huge number of our clients also become friends.'

(Continued)

(Continued)

REACHING FOR THE STARS

Today, Victoria's company, Northern Lights PR, succesfully works to understand her clients' business goals and then delivers the skills, tools, content, and campaigns needed to communicate with their customers. Northern Lights, with offices in the UK and the UAE, has become trusted to deliver B2B communications for clients from professional services to third sector firms by providing pioneering multi-channel communications campaigns that fuse traditional PR and media relations with the latest digital and social media marketing technologies (http://www.northernlightspr.com). Victoria is an expert woman, contributing to the BBC Academy, on social media, business, and education. She is a speaker on strategic social media for business and has trained business leaders in social media, both individually and as management teams. She is author of a number of ebooks on social media (http://www.northernlightspr.com/downloads/).

Source: This case is primarily based on an interview with Victoria Tomlinson and was written by Nigel Lockett.

CASE 5.5

 ◄ People: Claire's challenge video

In this video case, **Claire** explains three ways she can respond to increased demand from her customers: (a) taking on a semi-skilled HR assistant, (b) hiring another HR manager, and (c) restructure her company. Watch the video and decide which option you think Claire will choose. You might find it useful to discuss the case with friends or colleagues before deciding. Please note that lecturers can have access to the video that reveals the actual decision taken by the entrepreneur.

Source: This video case is primarily based on an interview with Claire by Nigel Lockett.

Practical activities

1. **Team formation audit** Use the guidance in Section 5.2 to identify the requirements of an effective team. You can either base this activity on your own proposed venture, or use one of the following scenarios:

    (a) You and your partner are 21 years old and both of you have recently graduated with degrees in Fine Art. You have an idea for a new business, based on the use of traditional painting techniques and specialist software that could produce real high-quality customised paintings based on digital images. Your target market consists of top commercial art galleries and large corporations who buy original art.

    (b) You are an environmental scientist with a technological **innovation** that could help families to reduce their reliance on fossil fuels. You want your idea to have the maximum impact on society, and to be widely available to people, irrespective of their income. You have the support of a wealthy donor, but need some additional expertise in order to establish this social venture.

2. **Network audit** Use the guidance in Section 5.4 to identify the requirements for an effective network. You can either base this activity on your own proposed venture, or use one of the scenarios from Activity 1 above. Prepare a network map, indicating the main external contacts for your venture (NB: Figure 5.1 can be used as a model for your map, but you may wish to adapt the presentation format in order to fit your own information). Highlight the connections that you consider to be the most important and note the likely content of the flows between these actors and your venture.

Discussion topics

1. Teams and team-working

   (a) Would it be better to create a new venture with a group of close friends, who you have known for many years, or with a group of people you know less well?

   (b) What are the most important factors you would consider when deciding who to include in your team?

   (c) Why have you chosen these factors?

   (d) What do you see as the four biggest challenges in keeping an entrepreneurial team? In what ways (if any) do they differ from those faced by management teams in established organisations? How would you respond to the challenges you have identified?

2. Networks and networking

   (a) Why might there be a difference between the accounts of famous entrepreneurs, which tend to emphasise their individual achievements, and the evidence on networking and collaboration? Can these contrasting views of entrepreneurship be reconciled?

   (b) How do you think the networking behaviour of entrepreneurs differs from that of other small business owners? What effect are such differences likely to have on the ventures that they create?

   (c) Review your own personal contact network, or that of another student/student team prepared as part of the network audit (Activity 2 above). Try to identify another way of connecting members of your PCN in order to create a different commercial or social venture to the one you have already identified. What does this exercise tell you about the role of entrepreneurial networks and networking?

Recommended reading

These readings address important topics in entrepreneurship research and are recommended for anyone wanting to build on the material covered in this chapter. Recommended readings have been selected from leading Sage journals and are freely available for readers of this textbook to download via the Online Resources.

Piva, E. and Rossi-Lamastra, C. (2016) 'Should I sell my shares to an external buyer? The role of the entrepreneurial team in entrepreneurial exit'. *International Small Business Journal.*

This quantitative research paper advances the debate on entrepreneurial exit by shedding new light on the role of the entrepreneurial team in the exit process.

Debrulle, J., Maes, J., and Sels, L. (2013) 'Start-up absorptive capacity: does the owner's human and social capital matter?' *International Small Business Journal*, **32, 7: 777–801.**

This article explores how a business owner's human and social capital in Flemish start-up affects absorptive capacity under different environmental conditions. It concludes that owners' start-up experience and bridging social capital are positively and significantly related to the new venture's ability to acquire, assimilate and exploit external information.

Soetanto, D. P. and Jack, S. L. (2011) 'Networks and networking activities of innovative firms in incubators: an exploratory study'. *International Journal of Entrepreneurship and Innovation*, **12, 2: 127–36.**

This paper systematically examines how firms in incubators develop their networks and what types of networks they might aim to build. It concludes that the networking support provided by incubators needs to be customised to the actual needs of the incubating firms.

Jack, S., Moult, S., Anderson, A. R., and Dodd, D. (2010) 'An entrepreneurial network evolving: patterns of change'. *International Small Business Journal*, **28, 4: 315–37.**

This case study article considers the development of a network for new entrepreneurs first established by a local enterprise support agency in north-east Scotland. It shows how network structure shifts from calculative to affective ties and demonstrate the importance of social ties for the operation of a network.

References

Agrocel (2017) http://www.agrocel.co.in/new/agri_mission.html (accessed 6 January 2017).

Aldrich, H. E. and Zimmer, C. (1986) 'Entrepreneurship through social networks'. In D. Sexton and R. Smilor (eds), *The Art and Science of Entrepreneurship*. New York: Ballinger (3–23).

Aldrich, H., Reese, P., Dubini, P., Rosen, B., and Woodward, B. (1989) 'Women on the verge of a breakthrough: networking between entrepreneurs in the United States and Italy'. *Entrepreneurship and Regional Development*, 1: 339–56.

Amason, A. C. and Sapienza, H. J. (1997) 'The effects of top management team size and interaction norms on cognitive and affective conflict'. *Journal of Management*, 23, 4: 495–516.

Barlow, J. (2015) *Managing People: Five Golden Rules for the Small Business*. CreateSpace Independent Publishing Platform.

Beat Suite (2017) http://www.beatsuite.com (accessed 6 January 2017).

Belbin, R. M. (1981) *Management Teams: Why They Succeed or Fail*. Oxford: Butterworth-Heinemann.

Belbin, R. M. (1993) *Team Roles at Work*. Oxford: Butterworth-Heinemann.

Belbin, R. M. (2010a) *Management Teams: Why They Succeed or Fail* (3rd edn). Oxford: Routledge.

Belbin, R. M. (2010b) *Team Roles at Work* (2nd edn). Oxford: Routledge.

Benjamin, A. (2009) 'Money well lent'. *The Guardian*, 3 June.

Birley, S. (1985) 'The role of networks in the entrepreneurial process'. *Journal of Business Venturing*, 1: 107–17.

Birley, S. and Stockley, S. (2000) 'Entrepreneurial teams and venture growth'. In D. L. Sexton and H. Landström (eds), *The Blackwell Handbook of Entrepreneurship*. Oxford: Blackwell (287–307).

Blundel, R. K. and Ippolito, K. (2008) *Effective Organisational Communication: Perspectives, Principles and Practices* (3rd edn). Harlow: FT Prentice Hall.

Bornstein, D. (2004) *How to Change the World: Social Entrepreneurs and the Power of New Ideas*. Oxford: Oxford University Press.

Brown, B. and Butler, J. E. (1995) 'Competitors as allies: a study of entrepreneurial networks in the US wine industry'. *Journal of Small Business Management*, 33, 3: 57–66.

Casson, M. (1982) *The Entrepreneur: An Economic Theory*. Oxford: Martin Robertson.

Chell, E. and Baines, S. (2000) 'Networking, entrepreneurship and microbusiness behaviour'. *Entrepreneurship and Regional Development*, 12, 3: 195–215.

Cohn, G. (2009) 'Tony Hawk carves a new niche'. *Entrepreneur Magazine*, October.

Cooney, T. (2005) 'Editorial: what is an entrepreneurial team?' *International Small Business Journal*, 23, 3: 226–35.

Cooper, S. Y. (1998) 'Entrepreneurship and the location of high technology small firms: implications for regional development'. In R. P. Oakey (ed.), *New Technology-Based Firms in the 1990s*. London: Paul Chapman (245–67).

Curran, J., Jarvis, R., Blackburn, R. A., and Black, S. (1993) 'Networks and small firms: constructs, methodological strategies and some findings'. *International Small Business Journal*, 11, 2: 13–25.

Dubini, P. and Aldrich, H. (1991) 'Personal and extended networks are central to the entrepreneurial process'. *Journal of Business Venturing*, 6: 305–13.

Ebers, M. (ed.) (1999) *The Formation of Inter-organizational Networks*. Oxford: Oxford University Press.

Glasses Direct (2010) http://www.glassesdirect.co.uk/about/story/ (accessed 3 May 2010).

Gossypium (2017) http://www.gossypium.co.uk/pages/about-us (accessed 6 January 2017).

Hackman, J. R., Wageman, R., Ruddy, T. M., and Ray, C. L. (2000) 'Team effectiveness in theory and practice'. In C. L. Cooper and E. A. Locke (eds), *Industrial and Organizational Psychology: Linking Theory with Practice*. Oxford: Blackwell (109–29).

ifwecanyoucan (2010) http://www.ifwecanyoucan.co.uk/Entrepreneurs/John-Lawler (accessed 3 May 2010).

Johannisson, B. (1998) 'Personal networks in emerging knowledge-based firms: spatial and functional patterns'. *Entrepreneurship and Regional Development*, 10, 4: 297–312.

Johannisson, B. (2000) 'Networking and venture growth'. In D. L. Sexton and H. Landström (eds), *The Blackwell Handbook of Entrepreneurship*. Oxford: Blackwell (368–86).

Johannisson, B. and Monsted, M. (1997) 'Contextualizing entrepreneurial networking'. *International Studies of Management and Organization*, 27, 3 (Fall): 109–36.

Jones, C. (2001) 'Co-evolution of entrepreneurial careers, institutional rules and competitive dynamics in American film, 1895–1920'. *Organization Studies*, 22, 6: 911–44.

Larson, A. and Starr, J. A. (1993) 'A network model of organization formation'. *Entrepreneurship Theory and Practice*, 4: 5–15.

Lewthwaite, J. (2006) *Managing People for the First Time: Gaining Commitment and Improving Performance*. London: Thorogood Publishing.

MAD Foundation (2015) MAD *Foundation Limited Reports and Accounts for the Year Ending 30 September 2014*. UK Charity Commission (https://www.gov.uk/government/organisations/charity-commission).

Madventure (2017) http://www.madventurer.com/about/the-mad-story.html (accessed 6 January 2017).

Nohria, N. (1992) 'Is a network perspective a useful way of studying organizations?' In N. Nohria and R. G. Eccles (eds) op. cit. (1–22).

Nohria, N. and Eccles, R. G. (eds) (1992) *Networks and Organisation: Structure, Form and Action*. Boston MA: Harvard Business School Press.

Oakey, R. P. (1995) *High Technology New Firms: Variable Barriers to Growth*. London: Paul Chapman.

Optometry (2007) 'Boots chooses Postoptics for its lenses by mail offer'. 12 October.

Penrose, E. T. (1996) 'Growth of the firm and networking'. In M. Warner (ed.), *International Encyclopaedia of Business and Management*. London: International Thompson Business Press (1716–24).

Petit, A. (2005) *The Eye of the Needle*. Lewes: Gossypium.

PNE (2008) Jamie Murray-Wells, Glasses Direct, http://www.pne.org/casestudies (accessed 3 May 2010).

Ramachandran, K. and Ramnarayan, S. (1993) 'Entrepreneurial orientation and networking: some Indian evidence'. *Journal of Business Venturing*, 8, 65: 513–24.

Sunday Times (2004) 'Opticians focus on HR pays dividends'. 14 March.

Telegraph (2016) 'Glasses Direct and Sunglasses Shop owner sold to eyewear giant Essilor'. http://www.telegraph.co.uk (accessed 30 May 2017).

Tuckman, B. W. (1965) 'Developmental sequences in small groups'. *Psychological Bulletin*, 63: 384–99.

Vyakarnam, S. and Handelberg, J. (2005) 'Four themes of the impact of management teams on organizational performance'. *International Small Business Journal*, 23, 3: 236–56.

Wellington, P (2017) *Effective People Management* (2nd edn). London: Kogan Page.

York Press (2014) 'Trevor Rowley, managing director of Optix software and Viewpoint Opticians'. http://www.yorkpress.co.uk (accessed 30 May 2017).

Zuri Design (2017) http://zuridesign.com/our-story/ (accessed 6 January 2017).

6

MARKETS: UNDERSTANDING CUSTOMERS AND COMPETITORS

A customer is the most important visitor on our premises. He is not dependent on us; we are dependent on him. He is not an interruption in our work; he is the purpose of it. He is not an outsider in our business; he is part of it.

Mahatma Gandhi, spiritual leader and political activist

In web 2.0 culture, person-to-person connection is key.

John Grant, marketing practitioner and author

LEARNING OUTCOMES

After reading this chapter you should be able to:

- Recognise the principal opportunities and challenges faced by entrepreneurs attempting to market a new venture.
- Identify the main features of entrepreneurial marketing and how it relates to mainstream marketing approaches.
- Appreciate how entrepreneurial marketing practices can contribute to the task of creating and establishing a new venture.
- Understand how mainstream marketing approaches might be incorporated for analysis and decision-making in an entrepreneurial setting.
- Appreciate how marketing practices connect with themes discussed in other chapters, including leadership, teams, networks, operations, and accounts.
- Apply relevant principles and techniques in order to market your own venture.

6.1 INTRODUCTION

Marketing is a fundamental issue for any enterprise, but for new ventures it can be particularly challenging. The topics addressed by marketing specialists are wide ranging, and include understanding customer behaviour, product pricing, promotional strategies, public relations, relationship marketing, marketing planning, and evaluation. During the twentieth century, marketing became a specialised management function, a profession with its own codes of practice and a field of academic research. Despite this, many entrepreneurs get their products to market without any formal training in the subject. So what can we learn from these successes, and from the many less successful marketing efforts? This chapter concentrates on the best ways to apply marketing techniques in an entrepreneurial setting, with a particular focus on creating new ventures. Before beginning our review, it is worth thinking how entrepreneurial marketing might differ from mainstream (or 'regular') marketing approaches. The most obvious differences are in the way the process is managed, and in the skills, or competencies, that are required:

> *The management of regular marketing can be characterised by a careful plan-ning process which is informed by market research to guide the selection of target markets and the composition of a marketing mix with which to position products competitively within the marketplace. Consequently, the competencies which it requires include planning, rigour and familiarity with statistics and figures. In contrast, [...] the management of entrepreneurial marketing is characterised by intuition, informality and speed of decision making, all of which require different competencies. (Collinson and Shaw 2001: 763)*

The difference between marketing in a corporate setting and an entrepreneurial one is highlighted by the experience of people who have moved out of a large organisation in order to establish their own venture. For example, the realities of this transition struck one senior marketing manager a few months after she left her job in a famous name retailer. She was attending her first trade show as an independent entrepreneur, and the most immediate difference was the lack of resources: there was nobody to arrange her travel, book her room, or pay her expenses. Perhaps more significant was the experience of walking into the show without the backing of an established brand. In the past, she could gain easy access to business contacts because of the organisation that employed her. Now, she had to rely solely on her personal credibility and skills in persuasive communication. Entrepreneurial marketing involves a distinctive set of techniques and practical competencies that you need to develop, both within your **entrepreneurial team** and through your network relationships, in order for a new venture to thrive.

The language of '**markets**' and '**industries**' is sometimes used interchangeably, which can lead to confusion. It is therefore worth clarifying the distinct meanings attached to each of these terms, and how they can be related to one another:

- **Markets** are made up of customers and potential customers, which are sometimes divided up into segments, comprising product and customers that share common characteristics. Marketers often distinguish between 'business to consumer' (B2C) and 'business to business' (B2B) markets. For example, in the market for furniture, you might identify B2C segments for contemporary design or second-hand 'retro' products, and B2B segments for hotel or office furniture. The main focus here is on commercial markets, but many of the practices discussed are also applicable to social markets. For example, in some countries there are social markets in healthcare and education, with end-users being able to exercise a degree of choice between alternative publicly funded and social sector providers.

- **Industries** (and industry sectors) are made up of competitors offering products or services to these customers. For example, the furniture manufacturing industry is made up of several fairly distinct sectors. Some firms specialise in the manufacture of particular product categories, such as beds, while others serve particular mar-kets, such as flat-pack furniture for home assembly. The terminology of industries and industry sectors is commonly used to refer to commercial enterprises, but can also be applied to **social enterprises**. Many of these organisations operate in competition – and sometimes in collaboration – with their public and private sector counterparts. For example, there are many social enterprises operating in competitive markets such as sports and leisure, healthcare, housing, and waste disposal.

There are two further introductory points, which are particularly relevant to entrepreneurs in search of new opportunities. Firstly, there are many situations in which one market, or market segment, can be served by more than one industry or industry sector. For example, the market for long-distance transportation of goods is served by the aviation, shipping, and railway industries. These overlaps may seem fairly obvious, and they are certainly not new. What has changed in recent years is the increased blurring of boundaries between different industries and markets. This has been driven by a combination of technological **innovation**, notably the spread of the Internet, and other political, legal, and socio-economic changes. Perhaps the most striking example is the evolution of the mobile phone market. In the 1980s, the first products provided little more than telephone communication without a landline. Since then, the increasing functionality of phones has required the integration of several previously separate industries, including: telecommunications, computing, photography, entertainment, retailing, and advertising. As industries converge, there is often scope for entrepreneurs to broker these 'new combinations'. Secondly, as the mobile phone example illustrates, markets and industries are rarely static. The resulting changes are often another major source of **entrepreneurial opportunity**. For example, if the existing (or 'incumbent') firms in an industry fail to keep pace with the changing demands of their markets, there is scope for entrepreneurial rivals, or potential new entrants to intervene; this is the kind of situation outlined in the opening case, where Made.com is posing a direct challenge to existing players in the furniture industry (Case 6.1). Another example would be the launch of a new technological product, such as the Apple iPad (http://www.apple.com/ipad), or the provision of innovative services such as micro-credit and skills training for women in a remote rural community (Case 11.1). Each of these provides a powerful example of entrepreneurial marketing in action.

→ **PERSPECTIVES** See Sections 10.1 and 11.1 for further information.

CASE 6.1

More than selling sofas? Made.com

Made.com (http://www.made.com) was launched in 2010 by a 28-year-old entrepreneur **Ning Li**, and a small team based in Notting Hill Gate, London. The start-up raised £2.5 million and had the backing of prominent entrepreneurs, including Brent Hoberman and Marc Simoncini, John Hunt and Profounders Capital, a London-based venture capital fund (http://www.profounderscapital.com). Ning Li was born in Foshan, a city in China's main furniture manufacturing region, and co-founded a related venture in France, called Myfab.com (Butcher 2010). His original vision for the new company, as outlined in his website profile, reflects a personal frustration with existing products and with the underlying structure of the furniture industry:

(Continued)

(Continued)

We think the high street and expensive designer brands give consumers a raw deal. That's because everyone along the way takes a cut, from agents to landlords. And you – our discerning customer – pay for that cut. So we're making a stand: taking on the high street to offer you original furniture design at affordable prices. (Made.com 2017)

The profiles of the design team suggest that the company is developing a distinctive culture. They also indicate the particular combination of design talent and specialist knowledge that has been assembled to pursue this vision (Made.com 2017):

- EMILY HUMPHREY: Vintage, characterful, bold
- FUTHARK DESIGN: Nordic, functional, sleek
- IAN ARCHER: Timeless, dynamic, beautiful
- JAMES PATTERSON: Simple, honest, enduring
- PTOLEMY MANN: Colourful, architectural, graphic
- ROSIE COOK: Abstract, simple, playful
- AARON PROBYN: Subtle, smooth, effortless
- BODIL BJERKVIK BLAIN: Sophisticated, exaggerated, approachable
- CATE & NELSON: Bold, straightforward, detailed

The Made.com venture reflected broader socio-economic trends towards 'co-creation' and 'mass customization'. Through the use of Internet technologies, the company is able to connect up previously separated ordering, design, manufacturing, and delivery functions in real time, enabling customers to become directly involved in the process:

> *Once registered on the website, customers are given the option of tracking the progress of their furniture from the point of ordering, through the various production stages, and as it travels to its final destination. At its launch, the company was working with 20 manufacturers. While most were located in the Far East, there were some UK-based firms, 'mostly in the upholstery area' (Butcher 2010).*

The business model for Made.com is based on web-enabled interaction between a wide variety of people, including customers, designers, manufacturers, and distributors. It has been designed to encourage active participation in the design and production process, while also minimising costs. The effect has been described as a transition from retailing to 'me-tailing', with the consumer taking increasing control (Hoffman and Sang 2010: 2). This can create an attractive proposition for customers, while also reducing production costs:

> The website showcases furniture designs and holds public votes, with the most popular designs going into production. Anyone who voted receives a discount in return for their participation in the selection process. Orders are then placed direct with a manufacturer for mass production in container quantities. In theory, there is no unsold inventory and no wastage as the factory only manufactures the exact number of items ordered. (Wray 2010)

The furniture industry is a long-established one, with a complex pattern of larger and smaller firms involved in design, manufacture, and marketing. It has been through many transitions, including the growth in markets for inexpensive, self-assembly furniture during the late twentieth century, led by large international companies such as IKEA, and more recent efforts to bring contemporary designer furniture to a wider market, some of which have proved unsuccessful. Currently, around 80% of the UK's furniture market is sourced from China (Butcher 2010). Made. com has a truly radical ambition, not simply to offer new products to a market, but to alter the structure and practices of an industry.

POINTS TO CONSIDER

1. What are the main differences between the marketing approach adopted by Made. com and that of a conventional 'High Street' furniture retailer?
2. Why do you think Ning Li decided to step down as the Chief Executive?
3. Can mainstream marketing concepts, such as the 4Ps, be applied to this kind of enterprise?

Sources: Butcher 2010; Hoffman and Sang 2010; Made.com 2010, 2017; Telegraph 2016; Wray 2010.

The rest of the chapter is organised as follows. In Section 6.2, we introduce entrepreneurial marketing and outline some of the ways it differs from mainstream marketing approaches. Section 6.3 takes a closer look at some of the more widely used entrepreneurial marketing practices, and how they might help in creating and establishing a new venture. In Section 6.4, we revisit some mainstream approaches and see how they might be used in order to analyse markets and make strategic decisions. In Section 6.5, we review the practical implications of engaging in entrepreneurial marketing, including the implications for leading your entrepreneurial team, building your social networks, and managing other functional areas of your venture, including operations and accounts. In the *Mark Robinson: strategy mapping business* case (Case 6.4), we consider the importance of finding the right market for a new venture. The chapter concludes with video case **◆SAGE** edge™ based on *Markets: Becky's Challenge* (Case 6.5) to test your understanding of this chapter.

6.2 HOW DO YOU MARKET AN ENTREPRENEURIAL VENTURE?

6.2.1 Distinctive challenges and opportunities

As we saw in the opening case (Case 6.1), new entrepreneurial ventures face a different set of marketing opportunities and challenges, as compared to their larger and better-established counterparts. The challenges, which we explore further in the next two sections of this chapter, include: lack of resources, lack of legitimacy, and powerful incumbents. However, the founders of entrepreneurial ventures are also well placed to exploit opportunities, due to their inherent flexibility, closeness to customers, and capacity to form new networks. In addition, they are usually seeking to create something that is new, either with respect to the product itself, or the market that is to be served.

Though much of the research on entrepreneurial marketing has looked at commercial ventures, it appears that social enterprises experience a similar set of challenges and opportunities (Shaw 2004; Martin and Thompson 2010). This prompts two questions. Firstly, are mainstream marketing approaches capable of meeting the needs of entrepreneurial ventures? (Section 6.2.2.) Secondly, are alternative – and more effective – options available? (Section 6.2.3.)

6.2.2 Mainstream marketing approaches

During the twentieth century, particular approaches to marketing were developed to meet the requirements of large corporations selling branded consumer goods, including food, household and leisure products in large volumes. The essential tools and techniques of 'fast moving consumer goods' (FMCGs) marketing include marketing research, **market segmentation**, product positioning, and brand management (e.g. Perreault et al. 2014). Marketers made use of developments in psychology and the social sciences to develop new ways of analysing and exploiting different consumer preferences and behaviours. They applied this knowledge in marketing research, which was used to refine product offerings and advertising messages. Many aspects of the marketing function were quantified and systematised. For example, the effectiveness of mass media advertising was evaluated through the statistical analysis of survey data, with respondents being asked questions that measure 'prompted' and 'unprompted' recall of particular campaign messages. Marketing professionals continue to make use of these mainstream approaches, and we revisit several of them later in this chapter (Section 5.4), to see how they might be applied more effectively in an entrepreneurial setting. However, the dominance of this kind of marketing is increasingly challenged by alternative approaches. These changes in marketing practice are affecting organisations of all kinds, but here we are mainly concerned with the implications for those engaged in **entrepreneurial activity**. The nature and scale of the change is summed up in the following comment on the future of branding, and how it has to move away from practices that were designed for twentieth-century FMCG markets:

> Brands were constructed for ugly industrialised manufacturing businesses (including farming, unfortunately) by adding attractive cultural images, personalities and descriptions. A factory-made fruit pie would become a Mr Kipling home-baked style fruit pie. This was a process of communication; an advertising message delivered through mass media. The audience was the passive receiver of this. I say 'was' because many, including myself, have been arguing for over a decade that (except in selected 'image category' preserves such as the perfume market) this model is all but dead. The main reason is growing consumer literacy, marketing resistance and cynicism. People don't trust many companies. Put the two together and you can guess the result. (Grant 2008: 5)

Recent marketing textbooks ranging from introductory to more advanced include Dibb and Simkin (2013), Palmer (2012), and Baines and Fill (2014). Scott (2016) and Kitchen and Ivanescu (2015) provide up-to-date coverage of social media, including viral marketing and the use of blogs. Bjerke and Hultman (2004) addresses entrepreneurial marketing. Martin and Thompson (2010) includes a chapter on marketing for social enterprises. Blundel et al. (2013) is a general introduction to organisational communication, including its role in marketing and public relations.

We can now consider these more recent marketing approaches in greater detail, again with a focus on their potential application in entrepreneurial settings.

6.2.3 New marketing approaches: customer engagement

John Grant was the co-founder of the innovative St Luke's advertising agency (http://www.stlukes.co.uk), and a leading figure in the 'New Marketing' movement. Interestingly, St Luke's promoted its own ethical approach by supporting Cool Earth and being carbon neutral (St Luke's 2017). John Grant describes the new marketing approaches as being based on active customer engagement. This often means that customers become directly involved in the production process:

> *You work together to create ideas, communities, events and lifestyles. It's not a patronising, 'the customer is king' view; it's a new openness, porosity and creative dialogue that can impact product development, retailing experiences and the service – for instance reader reviews on Amazon.com – quite apart from activities which actively engage people – like Nike's Run London. (Grant 2008: 5)*

The new approach extends beyond branding and into other areas of marketing, including customer relations management (CRM) and direct marketing. One of the common themes is the widespread and innovative use of new communications technologies, including social media.

The argument is that, as consumers, we have become more visually literate and have access to much more diverse sources of advertising and other communications. With so many sources of information (e.g. price comparison sites, online reviews, specialist interest blogs), we are much less open to be influenced by/more alienated from the mass market brands. This has created many opportunities for new enterprises. One of the early lessons of marketing effectively in this new arena was demonstrated by *Friends Reunited* (Case 3.4); the secret was to imitate traditional, and therefore familiar, models of social interaction:

> *One of the first successful social networks online was Friends Reunited. This didn't seem like joining some weird virtual community. Why? Because it was 'just like a school reunion' (only much better, you could browse what others had been up to and so on). (Grant 2008: 233)*

As the author notes, Facebook worked on a similar principle, taking a face-to-face model that was already well established at universities in the United States, and reinterpreting it as an online community. Other techniques include viral marketing, a form of persuasive communication in which the users of a service are encouraged to forward electronic messages (e.g. emails, texts, or tweets) around their personal contact network. Recent examples include, 'One Difference' (Case 2.2), which used Facebook and YouTube to promote World Water Day 2010 and managed to recruit 250,000 fans.

This is essentially an electronic extension of traditional 'word-of-mouth' promotion, but with much greater scope and potential. People have always talked to their immediate circle of friends about favourite bands, clothes, or clubs. Viral marketing enables these interactions to extend beyond your immediate circle of friends, reaching people who would not have been connected in previous times (Scott 2015). 'Buzz' marketing is a similar reworking of a traditional technique. In the past, you might be offered a free or reduced price product (e.g. a meal) in the hope that you would encourage your friends to try it. With electronic media, it is possible to coordinate this kind of promotion more tightly, and to encourage the viral spread of promotional messages. While 'word-of-mouth' continues to operate, it has also changed as a result of the new communications technologies and the way they are being used for promotional purposes. Proponents of the new marketing argue that innovations of this kind can make it easier for less well-resourced initiatives, including new commercial ventures and social enterprises, to have an impact in marketing terms:

> One difficulty is that the projects with the most ambitious objectives tend to be those with the least means, for instance because they are start-ups. However, with web 2.0, word-of-mouth and community there is a much more level playing field for good ideas. (Grant 2008: 13)

While this might sound like good news for the independent entrepreneur, it is becoming less of an advantage as larger and more established organisations begin to learn the lessons of the new marketing, often by acquiring some of the small, entrepreneurial pioneers. So, can entrepreneurial marketing provide a new venture with the kind of advantage it needs to survive and thrive in a competitive marketplace? The next section summarises some of the more popular entrepreneurial marketing techniques and introduces the distinctive way of thinking about marketing that is often found in successful ventures.

6.3 EXPLORING ENTREPRENEURIAL MARKETING

6.3.1 Techniques and philosophy

As we have noted, entrepreneurial ventures face a number of challenges, including a lack of resources, lack of legitimacy, and powerful incumbents (Section 6.2.2). Many new ventures fail, at least in part, because they are unable to address these challenges, while others find it difficult to expand beyond their initial market niche. Entrepreneurial marketing techniques enable new ventures to grow in more innovative ways (Bjerke and Hultman 2004: 146–51). To do so, they play on the inherent strengths of a new venture. Though these might vary depending on circumstances, they typically include flexibility, closeness to an initial customer base, and capacity to use the personal contact networks of the founders; for example, *Victoria Tomlinson* (Case 5.4). As a consequence, entrepreneurial marketing tends to be based around more informal, personal, and strongly interactive marketing techniques. For example, in the early stages, 'marketing communications' – though this term is unlikely to be used – relies much more on the quality of your personal relationships than it does on a nicely designed advert or brand identity. If the venture is entirely new, the first task for the founding team is to establish their personal credibility with particular audiences. If a product or service is not yet fully defined, the only way of judging a venture is through the knowledge, experience, motivation, and character of the people involved. Therefore, marketing yourself becomes a necessary starting-point, if you are to gain access to potential customers, as well as to the most suitable partners and investors. From these initial contacts, the next step is to refine your social networks in order to serve a number of essential functions. In an entrepreneurial setting, networks are likely to be the main source of market intelligence and one of the most important channels for promotional activity, particularly in the initial stages. Then, as the venture becomes operational, relationships with customers are an increasingly important element. As Bjerke and Hultman (2004: 159) observe, one of the key points to recognise is that 'customer value is subjective'. Given that perceptions of value emerge wherever customers are based, it is essential to remain closely engaged with them throughout the process – an approach to marketing that can be described as the 'co-creation of customer value' (Bjerke and Hultman 2004: 158–85). This close engagement can be very difficult to achieve in practice, particularly when a process extends beyond the control of the venture team to involve other partners. The difference between deliberate and emergent strategy has long been acknowledged as a distinguishing feature of entrepreneurial marketing (Mintzberg and Waters 1982, 1985). Consider, for example, how customer value is generated in the case of Made.com (Case 6.1). The company is coordinating a much wider network or 'value constellation' (Normann and Ramirez 1994), which involves external partners, including the furniture manufacturers and delivery companies. Table 6.1 summarises these marketing techniques and provides some illustrations of how they are applied in practice.

Entrepreneurial marketing is not limited to smaller organisations, as suggested in some marketing texts. Larger organisations can also use entrepreneurial marketing techniques (Hills and Hultman 2006: 225). However, as research on corporate **entrepreneurship** (or 'intrapreneurship') has shown, there are inevitable tensions in such organisations, between the requirements for formalised planning and a desire to encourage more flexible and emergent approaches. Social enterprises may also face some distinctive marketing challenges.

online resources 'Social enterprises: a different language?'

In previous chapters, we have discussed the importance of creating a vision and of pursuing entrepreneurial opportunities (Sections 3.1 and 4.2). The entrepreneurial marketing techniques outlined in this chapter show how the founders of new ventures are able to make this happen as they gain a deeper understanding of their customer. We can illustrate how these ideas can be applied in practice through a

TABLE 6.1 Entrepreneurial marketing techniques

Technique	Practical example
Establishing personal credibility	Tim Lockett (Case 7.4), Neil Meredith (Case 9.4)
Building and refining social networks	Victoria Tomlinson (Case 5.4), Steve Pankhurst (Case 3.4)
Co-creation of customer value	Mark Robinson (Case 6.4), Deirdre Bounds (Case 4.4)
Co-ordinating value constellation	Jonathan Hick (Case 16.1)

fictionalised account of Michèle Bertrand, a fashion buyer working for a leading women's clothing retailer, located in central Paris.

'Maison des Peaux' (episode 1): entrepreneurial marketing

In her role as a fashion buyer, Michèle Bertrand spends a lot of time talking to existing customers, attending trade shows, and visiting competitors' stores. She notices that an increasing number of her younger customers are customising their mobile phones according to the clothes they most like to wear, and in some cases to match a specific outfit. Michèle approaches her manager and suggests that they should consider developing a range of mobile phone 'skins' to complement the next season's range. As a fashion house, they will be able to offer a unique product that cannot be readily imitated by rival firms. Her manager seems unconvinced by the idea, and tells her to focus on her work. Disappointed by this negative reaction, Michèle talks to several friends, including an industrial designer whose work she respects. Their response is completely different. Jaime, the designer, offers to produce designs for three skins, which he thinks will be popular. Michèle asks five close friends to her apartment one evening and invites them to bring two people they think would be interested in these designer skins. The evening is a great success and Michèle decides to develop a range of ten skins targeted at fashion-conscious women and designed to match the summer season's key themes.

Michèle finds a local manufacturer who is prepared to produce her designs in small quantities. She also asks her partner, a web designer, to create a simple website and logo for 'Maison des Peaux'. As a trial promotion, she gives the 15 people who attended the initial evening three skins each. Each night after work she checks for orders and posts them to the customers. In just five weeks she has sold nearly all of her initial stock. Michèle notices that one customer ordered only one design and bought ten skins at a time. Quite naturally, she assumes it was the design the customer likes. Michèle is getting positive feedback from her customers but decides to conduct some informal market research. She emails all her customers a link to a simple online survey that includes a 'free text' field. Michèle is surprised by the responses. Nearly all of the customers reply and say that they learned about 'Maison des Peaux' from someone who had already purchased a skin. Interestingly, the customer who bought ten skins at a time is more interested in the material than the design. He runs a specialist eco-store, which only sells ethical and biodegradable products. By sheer chance one of Michèle's skins was made of ethically sourced latex, rather than plastic. Her customers also confirm that while there were plenty of companies in France selling skins, she has no direct competitors.

Michèle has been using Facebook for a few years to keep in touch with her friends and work colleagues. Encouraged by the response to her online survey she decides to set up a Facebook group for 'Maison des Peaux'. She is surprised that all her customers join and this attracts even more members to the group as news spreads from member to member. Michèle also starts to Twitter and blog about herself and designer skins.

The story of 'Maison des Peaux' is continued in the next two chapters. Having seen promising results from her initial marketing activities, we follow Michèle's efforts to ensure that her new online venture will also work operationally (Section 7.2). In the next section, we take a fresh look at some familiar approaches to marketing to see how they might be redeployed in an entrepreneurial setting.

6.4 MARKETING IN A NEW VENTURE CONTEXT

6.4.1 Using 'mainstream' marketing tools

We began this chapter by highlighting the distinctive challenges and opportunities associated with entrepreneurial marketing. Mainstream marketing concepts were discussed briefly, and we then developed the argument for adopting a more emergent entrepreneurial marketing approach, with several illustrations of its application in practice. However, taking an entrepreneurial marketing approach does not necessarily mean that you have to abandon mainstream marketing altogether. Rather, it is a question of learning from both approaches, and of applying mainstream tools and techniques in ways that meet the needs of an entrepreneurial and new venture context (Hills and Hultman 2006: 223). In this section we discuss a series of marketing-related tasks, highlighting key issues that arise in entrepreneurial settings, and particularly during the launch phase of a new venture. These are summarised in Figure 6.1 as three distinct but closely related areas of activity. The idea is to show how you can combine different tools and techniques in order to: (a) better understand your marketplace; (b) define and articulate their product more clearly; and (c) convince both yourself and other people that you have got the essential foundations for a successful venture.

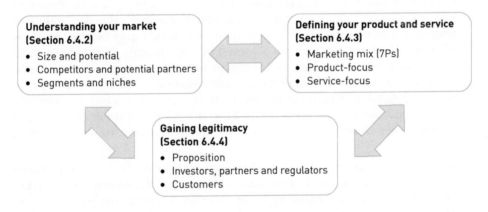

Understanding your market (Section 6.4.2)
- Size and potential
- Competitors and potential partners
- Segments and niches

Defining your product and service (Section 6.4.3)
- Marketing mix (7Ps)
- Product-focus
- Service-focus

Gaining legitimacy (Section 6.4.4)
- Proposition
- Investors, partners and regulators
- Customers

FIGURE 6.1 Marketing in a new venture context.

Source: The authors.

6.4.2 Understanding your market

Developing a better understanding of your intended market is an essential and ongoing task, which contributes to the related tasks of refining the product and gaining legitimacy. Mainstream marketing techniques have a role to play, but they need to be complemented by approaches that are better-suited to an entrepreneurial context. Key challenges include a lack of resources and, in the case of innovation-led ventures, new and largely unknown markets.

- **Establishing market size and potential** Calculating the size of a market can be difficult, but it is usually possible to get some idea of its scale, and of recent market trends. One approach is to assemble relevant secondary data sources, and use it as the basis for your own calculations. You can also make use of your own experiences and observations (e.g. spending time experiencing the product or service you are intending to provide), and in talking informally to people involved in the market. The market forecasts may later prove to be incorrect. Despite this, they remain important because they can influence potential investors and others to support the venture. Some markets are intrinsically more attractive than others. They might be larger, faster growing, have greater potential, or be more robust to changes in external conditions (e.g. recessions, changes in fashion or technology). Against this, markets with more opportunities are also likely to attract stronger competition. Therefore, entrepreneurs face a difficult trade-off between entering a new growth market and waiting until it has developed and become more stable.

- **Competitors and partners** There are a wide variety of techniques for analysing industry competitors. These range from the more strategic, such as Michael Porter's well-known 'Five Forces' model (Porter 1985), which provides a high-level overview, to much more detailed analysis of the product offerings of potential rivals. For the more detailed analysis, you may be drawing on local sources, such as telephone directories and published sets of accounts. As we saw with markets, there is also considerable scope for more conducting of informal research. The opening case study of Made.com (Case 6.1), illustrated how 'co-creation' can lead not just to increased customer value (i.e. adding to what was already offered), but something new, which goes beyond previous offerings. However, this was not achieved by the company alone, but through a 'value constellation' (Bjerke and Hultman 2004: 164), comprising consumers, independent designers, manufacturers, and distributors, all of whom are connected using Internet-based technologies. Many ventures succeed with the help of strong partners, while many others have struggled as a result of a partner's incompetence or bad behaviour. As a consequence, it is worth investing time in this area.

- **Market segments and niches** In addition to estimating the size and potential of a market, you also need to consider which part of the market you intend to target. In mainstream marketing, segmentation is a tried and tested process of dividing any market into groups of customers or segments by some differentiating characteristic, such as size, location, or behaviour. For example, the lunchtime sandwich market could be segmented by dietary requirements, such as meat, vegetarian, dairy free, or nut free. In principle, there should be homogeneity (i.e. similarities) within segments and heterogeneity (i.e. differences) between them. They should also be measurable, identifiable, accessible, and large enough to be profitable. This is not an easy task and it requires effort, research, and fine-tuning. There are two main ways of segmenting a market, either based on a particular characteristic or on actual and potential customer needs (Table 6.2).

online resources 'Understanding your market: additional examples and practical applications'.

Entrepreneurs who engage closely with customers can be particularly good at segmenting on the basis of customer need, as they can develop an intuitive understanding. For example, the company Anything Left-Handed (http://www. anythingleft-handed.co.uk) has concentrated on this needs-based segment for more than 40 years, providing a wide range of products and services for a needs-based segment. It is a family business, run by two left-handed people, which also hosts a forum and publishes newsletters for its members. A capacity to understand your customers' needs better than anyone else – in some cases better than they do – can become a powerful source of competitive advantage. In effect, these ventures are creating a distinctive market niche, which is difficult for other organisations to enter. The process can take some time, and the effect is not always obvious to outsiders. For example, the chief executive of Vickers Laboratories (http://www.viclabs.co.uk) explained the company's success over 30 years in the following terms:

> *We're almost invisible! We have become embedded in our customers' supply chains and add value to their service offering, which makes it counter-productive to move from us. [...] Our markets are deliberately diverse and we are constantly looking for new business that is difficult! Why? Well, we are really a solutions company. Not chemical ones – we solve problems and that draws on our knowledge. (Lockett 2010)*

In the next case (Case 6.2), we see how this process operated for an unusual company that has developed a niche in supplying an emerging market for wholefood, organic, and ethically sourced foods. We will see how understanding the needs of small independent retailers is the key to Suma's success, perhaps achieved, in no small part, due to their own innovative cooperative structure, which attracted staff with experience of and similar values to the market sector they served.

TABLE 6.2 Characteristics-based and needs-based segmentation

Characteristics-based:

- Geography: Neighbourhood, province, state, country, region.
- Population density: City, rural, or urban.
- Climate: Continental, dry, temperate, tropical.
- Demography: Age, education, ethnicity, family structure, gender, income, nationality, occupation.
- Psychographic: Activities, lifestyle, interests, or opinions.
- Behaviouralistic: Behaviour towards the product or service.

Needs-based:

- Personal: Based on individual's needs or preferences. For example, mobile phone providers try to bundle services together differently to appeal to the call, text or data needs of different user groups. In 2006, Orange launched four plans characterised by animals: Dolphin, Canary, Racoon and Panther.
- Organizational: Based on the needs of a company or organization. For example, Igloo Thermo Logistics (Case 7.1) emerging in an unstructured third-party temperature controlled distribution sector to provide added value services (www.igloo-thermo.com).

CASE 6.2

In the niche: how Suma got to know its customers

The publication of Rachel Carson's book, *Silent Spring*, was one of several early steps in the growth of the environmental movement. Carson, a respected marine biologist, drew attention to the potential environmental consequences of the world's growing reliance on industrialised forms of agriculture, and specifically to the artificial pesticide, DDT. In one of the more frequently quoted passages, she warned her readers that. 'Over increasingly large areas of the United States, spring now comes unheralded by the return of the birds, and the early mornings are strangely silent, where once they were filled with the beauty of birdsong' (Carson 1962: 189). The origins of the organic movement can be traced back further in time, with influential books such as Eve Balfour's *The Living Soil* (Balfour [1943] 2006). The movement was led by social ventures, such as Rudolf Steiner's 'biodynamic' approach at Demeter (http://www.demeter.net) and the Soil Association (http://www.soilassociation.org), which worked with farmers, growers, and others to encourage a different approach to agricultural production.

The market for organic food began to grow in Europe during the last quarter of the twentieth century as consumers became more interested in purchasing food that was produced without using artificial fertilisers, herbicides, or pesticides. Demand was fuelled by a combination of health and environmental concerns. The work of accreditation bodies, including Demeter, the Soil Association, Debio (http://www.debio.no), and KRAV (http://www.krav.se), facilitated the growth of the market. On the distribution side, a number of entrepreneurial individuals became involved, and helped to expand the niche. The following account describes how **Reg Tayler** founded **Suma**, the pioneering wholefoods and organic wholesaler:

> Reg had already gained some experience of wholefoods in London, and when he moved to Leeds he opened a retail shop, Plain Grain. In August 1975, at a meeting attended by all the wholefood shops in the north of England, he proposed they set up a wholefoods wholesaling cooperative in order to supply each other. Reg and friends set up in the back kitchen of a house in Victoria Road, Leeds, from where they sold cereal flakes, dried fruits and brown rice. They soon needed more room, and so rented a lock-up garage nearby – this is where the name 'Suma' was first used for the growing business. At the time, Reg was working as a delivery driver for Jonathan Silver, taking clothes to his chain of menswear shops around the north of England. Reg delivered the wholefood orders in between the 'official' deliveries for his boss, who knew what was going on but turned a blind eye even so. Within a year they needed proper premises, and in 1976 acquired a tiny two-storey warehouse in Wharf Street, Leeds. Lots of stairs had made the warehouse unsuitable for storing food, and there's even one particular story of a time when several tonnes of fruit were carried upstairs, resulting in a horrible creaking noise as the ceiling started to collapse! Luckily the day was saved thanks to a little ingenuity and several large pieces of wood used as makeshift 'props'. A retail shop called Beano was established round the corner and soon became an independent cooperative, separate from the wholesaling side of the enterprise. In 1977, Reg sold the Suma business to the then seven employees, who became the founder members of Triangle Wholefoods Collective, trading as Suma (Suma 2010). In 1978 Suma moved into a much larger three-storey warehouse

across the road. It seemed huge – the entire stock fitted into one half of the ground floor. However, rapid expansion of the wholefood market meant that by 1986 the whole place was bursting at the seams and Suma moved to a larger warehouse. There followed 15 years of steady growth, both of turnover and of the cooperative. Alongside the growth in size there was a corresponding increase in the complexity and sophistication of the business, and the structure of the co-op went through many modifications to manage this change. In 2001, Suma moved to 8,000 m² purpose-built premises in Elland, where currently around 150 are employed. (Suma 2010, 2017)

Suma was awarded Specialist Wholesaler of the Year in 2009 and Employer of the Year in 2016 (http://www.thegrocer.co.uk). The company continues to specialise in vegetarian, fairly traded, organic, ethical, and wholefood products. Its 'own brand' range of food and household products is sourced ethically and with the environment in mind. Suma has a policy of working with other regional cooperatives, rather than competing to be the largest national distributor. Its status as an employee-owned cooperative also reflects the organisation's core values. Cooperative members and employees receive the same net hourly rate of pay, no matter what their job or responsibilities, and they encourage people to work in different areas of the business, which helps them get closer to their customers:

We find that splitting up difficult jobs and doing them with a team is often better than relying on one expert. When people work in more than one part of a business, they understand the 'bigger picture' better. Many Suma customers have experienced this greater understanding. (Suma 2010)

Suma's employees embrace the distinctive ethos of the product range and work to see these values realised. Close relationships with customers enable niche suppliers to build trusted brands that can be difficult for the competitors to overcome. As the organic niche has grown, larger manufacturers have attempted to enter, though most have found it difficult. One strategy has been for corporations to acquire niche companies (e.g. Seeds of Change, acquired by Mars in 1995, and Cadbury's 2005 acquisition of Green and Black's), in order to gain access and experience of its supply chain.

Ethical point Suma has an Ethical Policy, which sets the standards for products, working practices, employment and environment. Practical examples of this policy include: 100% renewable electricity for warehousing and office facilities; reducing environmental impact in product packaging; offsetting CO_2 emissions by tree planting.

QUESTIONS

1. Answer one of the following: (a) What factors have influenced the growth of the organic food market? (b) How has the market segment supplied by Suma changed over time?

2. Suma is an example of an organisation with a good understanding of its niche, and of the customers it serves. Can you identify and compare two other examples?

3. How can values-based niche organisations survive the growth of their market, and increasing interest from larger and more powerful competitors?

Sources: Balfour 1943; Carson 1962; Suma 2010, 2017. Case compiled by the authors with grateful acknowledgement to Bob Cannell, Suma.

6.4.3 Defining your product and service

Having identified the market gap, how can we define the products and services to be offered? The marketing mix is a traditional, but still popular framework that can be used to consider the market positioning of products and services. Though it is primarily a mainstream marketing approach (e.g. Perreault et al. 2014), the marketing mix can be applied effectively to new entrepreneurial ventures. The mix consists of four elements: (1) Product; (2) Price; (3) Place; (4) Promotion. This original list has been extended into '7Ps' in order to make it more relevant to the marketing of services, and their distinctive characteristics such as intangibility. The three additional elements are: (5) People: (6) Processes; (7) Physical Evidence. Each of these elements is considered briefly in Table 6.3.

TABLE 6.3 Elements of the marketing mix

Product-focused (4Ps)
• **Product:** Specifications of the goods or services and how these relate to the consumer's needs. This should include some feedback mechanism to determine customer satisfaction. Consider the product life cycle including service and warranty.
What are the practical benefits offered customers and to what extent do these constitute a unique selling proposition (USP)?
• **Price:** Process of setting the price for a product or service that will generate a return. This may vary depending on the customer or segment. Consider discounting policy.
What pricing strategy (or combination of strategies) can the entrepreneur adopt: cost-based, customer-based, or competitor-based?
• **Place:** How the product or service is delivered to the customer. This will include the routes or channels to market. For example, retail, direct sales, wholesale, mail order, and online. Place also considers the customer segments to be addressed.
What is the entrepreneur's route to market? What are the entry barriers? Is direct marketing or licensing feasible? Can a multi-channel approach be taken?
• **Promotion:** Including advertising, sales promotion, public relations, personal selling, and branding. What is the entrepreneurial marketing mix?
What can the entrepreneur afford? How innovative is the promotional strategy in terms of publicity and PR and social media?

Service-focused (in addition to the '4Ps')
• **People:** Everyone who comes into contact with the customer and can affect the overall experience of your product or service. Even those outside your control, such as retailers.
What social capital does the entrepreneur possess? Can they sell and negotiate? Can they network?
• **Processes:** Systems and procedures that can impact on the customer experience, for example, information systems, telephones, online ordering, and debt collection reminders.
Can the service be delivered virtually? What is the scope for process innovation?
• **Physical evidence:** One of the main challenges of marketing a service or a product with a service element is providing a potential customer with enough reassurance that the stated service will be delivered. This is particularly important for industries like financial services and information systems. Offering free trials or testimonials from existing customers can help. A good reference customer can be invaluable. It might be worth discounting to gain reference customers for new ventures.
What is the product/service mix? Has sufficient attention been applied to design, styling, and packaging?

6.4.4 Gaining legitimacy

There is convincing evidence that efforts to gain legitimacy make a real difference to the initial survival rates of new ventures (e.g. Delmar and Shane 2007). Legitimacy is a broad term which refers here to the way a venture is perceived by other people and organisations. The core requirement is that you can establish mutual trust between yourselves and those you need to do business with; this is likely to include customers, suppliers, partners, and other influential actors such as industry regulators. Since trust is often built up over time, based on past experience, much will depend on your track record (if any) in related fields. Your personal credibility is also important, especially in situations where you have no track record (e.g. when moving into a new sphere of activity). This is a persuasive communication challenge. In the absence of proof, can you convince people that you and your team are capable of delivering on your claims? Establishing legitimacy can be particularly difficult for innovating organisations, or industry pioneers, compared to new ventures that are mainly imitative, reproducing well-established practices (Aldrich and Fiol 1994: 650). In the early stages, the key tasks are to articulate (i.e. explain) your venture idea in a clear and convincing way, and to ensure that you understand your customers:

- **Articulating the proposition** Demonstrating that your market is growing and robust will increase your confidence and that of investors and lenders. It is also essential to show how your venture relates to that market opportunity. The opportunity business model (Section 3.2) could be a useful vehicle for explaining your venture idea in a clear, concise, and convincing way. Setting out the drivers of your opportunity business model provides a relatively straightforward way of summarising the market opportunity, while the dimensions can be used to outline the key components of the venture itself. It is often helpful to illustrate an abstract idea using a diagram. You may also be able to make use of samples, prototypes, or video clips in order to make your product more tangible. It is also important to ensure that you have built a credible team (Section 5.2).

  online resources 'Practical advice on pitching a new venture idea'.

- **Understanding your customers** It is important to develop your knowledge of the buying process and the various people that are likely to be involved. This understanding can both inform decisions on the marketing mix, and help in establishing trust and legitimacy. When you are developing a new product or service, it is easy to become overenthusiastic and make unrealistic or oversimplified assumptions about your potential customers. It is always worth just pausing for a moment to consider who is making the buying decision. Even in a 'Business to Consumer' (B2C) market, where you are selling directly to the end-user or consumer, other people may influence or control the final decision. For example, while parents and relatives may be the main purchasers of toys, advertisers target the influencers and end-consumers (i.e. children). Similarly, if you were marketing an alarm for use by elderly people in difficulty, the main influencer is likely to be a younger relative (e.g. a son or daughter), since they are more likely to recognise the need for such a device. The differences may be quite subtle and difficult to identify. The situation can be more complicated in 'Business to Business' (B2B) markets. Here, it is very important to recognise the different roles and levels of power being exercised by the various actors in the buying process, each with different roles. Consider the following examples. Firstly, imagine that you have just launched an innovative bandage that reduces post-operative complications for patients convalescing at home.

The bandage is given to patients as part of the overall charge for their treatment. The patients' general practitioners (GPs) have much to gain from the new product because it reduces the overall cost of care and improves patient well-being. Here, there is little to gain by promoting the product directly to patients. The customer is likely to be a GP's surgery, the general practitioners are the main influencers, and the patient is the consumer or ultimate user. Secondly, imagine that you have just developed a new software application that can be run on an organisation's intranet, enabling staff to monitor their energy consumption in real-time. A typical purchasing team might include the sustainability manager, who is keen to do anything that can help to reduce the organisation's carbon footprint (i.e. an 'advocate' role). However, any decision regarding software has to be approved by the information systems manager, who could reject the proposal on technical grounds (i.e. a 'gatekeeper' role). In addition, you will probably need to persuade another senior manager, the budget holder, that there is a convincing business case for the investment (i.e. a 'strategic decision' role).

6.4.5 Bringing it all together: taking a dynamic perspective

Markets change over time. In the traditional markets of the pre-industrial world (e.g. food, craft products), the process of change was often quite slow, though trading conditions could be transformed by unexpected events such as floods, droughts, or conflicts. In many of today's markets (e.g. consumer electronics, fashion, media), the pace of change is much faster, with rapid changes in technologies and consumer preferences. As a result, market gaps can open up, and close down, within a very short space of time. Gaps emerge when existing products and services fail to offer customers what they want. This can result directly from customer demand (i.e. 'pull' factors), or when new products and services create new demand (i.e. 'push' factors). The actions of entrepreneurial individuals and organisations can also create gaps, which encourage further waves of innovation and opportunity. As we noted in the opening section (Section 6.1), it can be difficult for established organisations to adapt quickly to these kinds of market dynamics, opening up new opportunities for nimble and creative entrepreneurial ventures. So the real challenge for entrepreneurs is not only identifying the market segment most in need of their product or service but also in finding the gaps in demand that are not being served by their competitors. This can only be achieved by fully appreciating both your customers and competitors. This means really understanding your customers' needs and your competitors' capabilities, product and service offerings and intentions. The next case (Case 6.3) illustrates how an entrepreneur was able to create a gap in a fast-moving market that was already dominated by some powerful incumbent firms.

CASE 6.3

Finding new customers for GPS: the 'Buddi' story

Vehicle-based satellite navigation (satnav) has become a huge global market, with European sales exceeding €1.5 billion (£1.2 billion) (Reuters 2010). Competition has intensified, with satnav companies such as Garmin (http://www.garmin.com) and TomTom (http://www.tomtom.com), becoming household names. By using Global

Positioning Systems (GPS), satnav devices determine the geographic location of a vehicle by linking to a central database via mobile cellular, radio, or satellite technologies. The position can be displayed on a map in real-time or recorded to identify movements or routes. GPS systems are used in a variety of other B2B and B2C markets, including surveying, agriculture, yachting, mountaineering, and tourism.

So how can an entrepreneur find new market opportunities in a field dominated by such strong industry competition? The story of **Sara Murray** and '**buddi**' illustrates how it can be achieved. Sara traces the source of her idea for a new GPS-based tracking product to an incident when her daughter went missing in a large supermarket – the child had gone in search of one of the small trolleys; Sara called the security staff and fortunately her daughter was rediscovered after a few minutes. Though the incident ended happily, it seems that this personal experience remained with Sara. It was reinforced a few years' later when they went on a skiing holiday and her daughter was attending ski school:

> When I used to go on holiday with my daughter, I took to leaving a scrap of paper in her pocket with my number on, just in case. I knew there must be a safer and better way. I found nothing on the internet so I had to invent it myself. (Sara Murray, quoted in Burn-Callander 2008)

Having realised that there must be a better solution to keeping track of children, Sara's initial plan was to find a suitable technology, such as an existing GPS device that could be used or adapted for this market. Having searched the Internet, she located a company in California that appeared to have a suitable product, but she was unable to source it:

> 'I went to try to buy one. They said it wasn't in stock. It's going to be a while'. Then they admitted it wasn't available in Europe. Ms Murray even offered to be their European distribution agent, but the device was set up only to work in US metropolitan areas. 'I decided to make one myself,' she says. 'I knew the difficult thing would be building the hardware, because I had never done it before'. (Sara Murray, quoted in Waller 2009)

Creating your own electronic device might seem a daunting task, but Sara was already a serial entrepreneur with considerable experience in creating online businesses. She also had some personal capital to invest and a number of high-level contacts who could provide access to the relevant financial and technical expertise. Sara was a graduate of Oxford University, with a first degree in physiology, psychology, and philosophy. After gaining experience in management consultancy and a traditional investment bank, she started her own marketing consultancy in 1992, specialising in the pharmaceutical sector. Seven years later, she created another venture, which provided instant comparisons between insurance company quotations. She later sold the company, which was then re-branded as 'Confused.com' (http://www.confused.com). Now, having been introduced to two engineers, her next challenge was to develop a product that was both technically sound and able to meet the needs of potential users:

> 'I was completely consumer-orientated. I said, this is what I would like it to do for my child. They were completely technology-orientated. There was a gap,' she admits. 'Most technology companies build technology and look at where they can sell it.' (Sara Murray, quoted in Waller 2009)

(Continued)

(Continued)

The resulting product was branded as the 'buddi' (http://www.buddi.co.uk). It comprises a compact device based on GPS technology. The device, which could be at £10 per week, is linked to a website that enables registered users to track the person wearing it via Google Maps (Buddi 2017). It incorporates a 'panic button' which is linked to a call centre. This facility can be used to contact named individuals and to provide access to emergency services. Though still addressing its original target market, there are other emerging applications. For example, the 'buddi' system is now being used by home-based carers of people suffering with Alzheimer's disease (i.e. dementia), lone workers who may be vulnerable to attack (e.g. social workers making home visits), and even dog owners. These new segments cut across B2C (consumer) and B2B (business) markets, and have the potential to create both social and economic value. For example, by enabling Alzheimer's sufferers to remain at home, you could both enhance an individual's quality of life and reduce the cost of residential care. In her spare time, Sara is a keen sailor and skier. She is also a member of the advisory board of Seedcamp, an initiative that provides mentoring and micro seed funding to the next generation of young entrepreneurs (http://www.seedcamp.com). In 2009, 'Entrepreneur of the Year' (http://www.nationalbusinessawards.co.uk). In 2012, she was appointed an OBE or services to entrepreneurship and innovation.

Meanwhile, GPS technologies continue to develop at a rapid pace, creating new market opportunities and encouraging new entrants into the sector. Hundreds of specialist applications (apps) have become available to take advantage of the increased functionality of mobile phones, including Apple's iPhone.

QUESTIONS

1. In what ways does Sara Murray story illustrate the techniques of successful entrepreneurial marketing?

2. What lessons can you draw from the way that Sara used her background, experience and contacts to establish legitimacy for her 'Buddi' concept?

3. How can a relatively new organisation such as Sara's keep close to its customers in such a dynamic and fast-changing market?

Sources: Buddi 2017; Burn-Callander 2008; Waller 2009; Reuters 2010.

The online resources page includes a number of checklists designed to help you to identify (or envisage), and to assess potential opportunities. There are also a number of short exercises that will help you identify concrete, practical ways so that your venture can be launched effectively, taking into account the specific characteristics of the market that you are trying to enter.

online resources 'Marketing checklists and practical exercises'.

The *Mark Robinson: strategy mapping business* case (Case 6.4) examines the interconnected relationship between customers, markets and industry sectors. The case shows how Mark identified and pursued a niche market segment, containing customers whose needs were not well served. In addition, there is a video case available on ⓈSAGE edge™

(Case 6.5 *Markets: Becky's Challenge*). This video case is based on an interview with an entrepreneur, Becky, facing a challenge in her creative agency, specialising in the student marketing, which is related to this chapter. Watch the video and decide which option you think Becky will choose. You might find it useful to discuss the case with friends or colleagues before deciding. Please note that lecturers can have access to the video which reveals the actual decision taken by the entrepreneur.

6.5 SUMMARY

- People in entrepreneurial settings, including entrepreneurs attempting to market a new venture, face a number of distinct challenges including lack of resources, lack of legitimacy, and powerful incumbents. However, they are also well-placed to exploit opportunities, due to their inherent flexibility, closeness to customers, and capacity to form new networks.

- Marketing practices are now moving away from the industrialised, mass market approaches that developed during the twentieth century, and organisations of all kinds are experimenting with new marketing approaches, including the use of social media.

- Entrepreneurial marketing comprises a number of techniques and practices, based on an opportunity-oriented approach to marketing. These approaches tend to emphasise direct engagement with customers, who sometimes become co-producers of a product or service.

- Several mainstream entrepreneurial marketing techniques can also be modified in order support the creation of new entrepreneurial ventures. These include market segmentation, market positioning, and the 7Ps of the extended marketing mix.

- Strategic analysis has a role to play, but it is important to recognise that there are a number of ways of acting strategically, some of which are more likely to be effective in an entrepreneurial setting.

- Effective entrepreneurial marketing requires a strong commitment from the entire team, with core principles such as customer engagement being communicated throughout the venture, including operational and financial areas, as well as its external networks.

CASE 6.4

Mark Robinson: strategy mapping business

By the end of January 2007, experienced manager **Mark Robinson** had helped his nephew's environmental management company, EnviroManage in London, achieve a good market share. He also became convinced there was an opportunity for the company (**Escendency**) to provide a generic strategy mapping application and had even developed a software prototype. But the board weren't convinced. Mark was excited about the opportunity for the new application and needed to prepare a new venture plan for presentation at the board meeting in two weeks.

(Continued)

(Continued)

BIOGRAPHY

Mark graduated with a degree in chemistry from the University of York in 1985, just as the first computer chips were being produced by the then fledgling semiconductor industry in Silicon Glen, Scotland. Within just five years in this rapidly expanding industry, he was promoted to departmental manager responsible for 35 highly skilled engineers designing and making microprocessors for some of the world's leading technology companies. It was not long before he was headhunted into international sales by an American company based in Silicon Valley, California. Mark adopted a completely different lifestyle: 'flying about on aeroplanes to visit the US and customers or potential customers in Europe'. After 15 years travelling the world, he was able to bring his own personal vision of opening a high-technology factory in the north-west of England into reality. In 2000, having brought a US and a UK corporation together with the UK government, he made it happen. The operation quickly became really big: 'We went from zero to $25 million in the first year.' However, following changes to the senior management structure, Mark decided to leave the company and look for a new challenge.

ENVIROMANAGE

During the late 1990s governments around the world were increasingly expecting companies to comply with international environmental management standards, such as ISO14000. In 1998 Mark's nephew decided to set up a new venture, EnviroManage, to provide environmental consulting services to companies keen to meet these new standards. It soon became apparent that EnviroManage's customers needed a software application to help them manage their environmental practices, and EnviroManage rapidly developed into a software and consultancy company. Within the context of an expanding market opportunity, Mark was soon invited to help his nephew develop the company's sales to large companies. Not surprisingly, given Mark's previous experiences, he quickly won new business with international corporations like GlaxoSmithKline, Vodafone, Orange, and even UK government departments.

EnviroManage rapidly become a well respected market leader in the environmental management sector. Mark had an unusual position in the company. He was not a director. However, being an experienced manager and the uncle of the founder and managing director gave him significant influence within the company. While EnviroManage used the Internet to support its environmental management application, it had a traditional sales model of a large initial licence fee for the use of the software and a small annual charge for maintenance and support.

APPLICATION SERVICE PROVISION

The Internet has provided numerous entrepreneurial opportunities and many new business models emerged. Some business models, such as online retailing (http://www.amazon.com) and online marketplaces (http://www.ebay.com), have flourished. One of these new sectors is *cloud computing* – consisting of software developers providing access to applications over the Internet, such as simple hosted email (http://www.hotmail.com) and highly complex hosted enterprise applications (http://www.

sap.com). Cloud computing offers software as a service (SaaS), also known as hosted applications, on-demand applications and web-based applications.

One such cloud computing service, which became particularly well-known, was Salesforce.com (http://www.salesforce.com), founded in 1999 by Marc Benioff. In less than ten years, Salesforce.com became one of the largest providers and specialised in providing its customers with sophisticated customer relationship management (CRM) applications. CRM applications were used to support sales and marketing activities, including telesales, e-commerce, sales data analysis, and marketing campaigns. Organisations used these web-based applications rather than just buying the software and installing it on their own computer networks as it took less time, resources, expertise, and money. Cloud computing reduced costs by hosting and managing software applications centrally and providing access to remote users via web browsers or thin clients. The costs were shared across many organisations, and service providers rented access to these applications, typically between 10% and 20% of the equivalent purchase price. Perhaps unexpectedly, early adopters were large companies rather than small- to medium-sized enterprises.

UNDERLYING CONCEPTS AND FUNDAMENTAL TRUTHS

Mark had spent much of his working life selling services to chief executives of large international corporations around the world. He had always been interested in the underlying concepts behind a particular issue, opportunity, or problem. 'I have a passion for physics, I have always been that way, I like to look for the underlying concepts and fundamental truths ... If you can understand the general concepts you can deal with complexity.' He felt that while EnviroManage customers appreciated having an excellent environmental management application they had many other complex issues to deal with. After some time working in his nephew's company, Mark persuaded them to explore the development of a more generic management application, which could map an organisation's strategy onto individual objectives and action plan that could be monitored over time.

Mark's previous experience as a manager in a high-pressure industry had taught him that motivating individual people was the key to getting things done on time and on budget. Therefore, instead of making the office or factory the unit of analysis, he proposed that it was the individual who contributed to achieving these objectives that were central to any successful performance management system. Mark's belief was that it was 'all about people ... the smallest atom in the unit needed to be a person not a factory'.

The board of directors consisted mainly of people with a vision to provide environmental management to make the world a greener place. However, after much persuasion and some disagreement within the board, Mark was allowed to build a software prototype of his strategy mapping application. The project used the latest web-based technologies and was designed to be delivered as a service over the Internet paid for on a subscription – in other words, rented not purchased. Perhaps not surprisingly, the prototype project attracted the interest of some of the best programmers in the company. Mark recalled that, 'The two development engineers tended to have a crowd of people around them looking over their shoulders and seeing what they were doing ... Everyone wanted to get involved.'

(Continued)

(Continued)

Mark and his development team built a software prototype, which captured his vision of linking an organisation's highest level mission to actions undertaken by individuals working towards achieving their objectives. This involved establishing a hierarchy of information and linking many objectives to the organisation's mission. Mark's vision behind the prototype was for it to:

> Become the world standard for the realisation of the strategy of any organisation, partnership or community. By realisation we mean the creation, planning and agreement of your continuously improving strategy, making it real and visible to all those involved, so that they can view what they need online at anytime via their individually configured dashboards. Using the power and economics of the web to deliver software-as-a-service business model means that there is no software or hardware to buy. One low-cost subscription covers all the people and includes system hosting, support, maintenance, help, backups, and all future enhancements.

THE BOARD REACTION

Having successfully built the prototype, Mark went back to EnviroManage's board and presented the business plan for taking the new strategy mapping application to market. Some directors had previously expressed concerns about diversifying away from environmental management and even after seeing the prototype did not change their views. Mark believed that some of the directors had never actually met customers and talked to them about their real needs. Some directors viewed the prototype as a cuckoo in the nest, taking resources away from the core activity of environmental management. Furthermore, between authorising the building of the prototype and presenting the business plan, the company had 'overreached themselves a little bit ... They had won some fairly large contracts' and overheads had grown but 'it became apparent that it [winning large contracts] was not going to happen every month and we needed to cut back'.

By January 2007, the whole climate had changed. The board suggested that Mark might want to develop a new venture plan for a spin-out company taking the strategy mapping application to market under a licensing agreement with EnviroManage. This would involve taking key developers with him and agreeing which markets could be developed. 'Rather than make people redundant, I got the opportunity to take this prototype off their hands and take some of their staff with me.'

> They wanted to restrict me to the public sector for the first few years so that we weren't treading on each other's toes ... The public sector is a massive market in the UK.

GOING TO MARKET

Mark successfully persuaded the board to release the prototype strategy mapping application and he formed Escendency to take the new service to market. In 2010, after several years of providing strategy mapping to a wide range of sectors, from councils to corporates, Mark discovered a segment of the market, special schools, which had specific needs that were not being met by other providers. In other words, a gap in the market to which he had a unique solution. Mark recognised that these entrepreneurial opportunities don't come along every day and quickly developed a specialist offer called – *OnwardsandUpwards* (http://onwardsandupwards.com). Special schools are typically for children and young people who have severe and complex learning difficulties and they need to be able to track the progress of each pupil in both academic and non-academic areas.

> *The OnwardsandUpwards unified system solves this problem and tracks the progress of any individual pupil, any cohort and, indeed, your whole school. You can select from our vast library and/or add your own iCan statements to match your curriculum and track pupils from early years through to young adulthood.*

Mark is rapidly developing a market leading position for providing cloud-based mapping systems tailored to the need of special schools.

Source: This case is primarily based on an interview with Mark Robinson and was written by Nigel Lockett.

CASE 6.5

Markets: Becky's challenge video

In this video case, **Becky** explains the three potential growth areas for her creative agency specialising in student marketing: (a) work with more students' unions, (b) broaden the university client base, and (c) work with brands wanting to reach students. Watch the video and decide which option you think Becky will choose. You might find it useful to discuss the case with friends or colleagues before deciding. Please note that lecturers can have access to the video that reveals the actual decision taken by the entrepreneur.

Source: This video case is primarily based on an interview with Becky by Nigel Lockett.

Practical activities

1. **New product launch: the branding challenge** You are responsible for developing a branding strategy to use when launching an entrepreneurial venture based around an innovative product or service. First, select your venture (e.g. it could be one of the following: health food retailer; running shoes; music and arts venue; advice service for young people). Next, outline how you might build a brand image, using: (a) mainstream FMCG-style marketing approaches as introduced in Section 6.2.2; (b) new marketing approaches, as outlined in Section 6.2.3. Highlight the main differences between the two approaches.

2. **Understanding customer types** The founders of a new venture have developed an educational software application that allows dyslexic students to develop a personal online dictionary of words and phrases they use. These are displayed as a list of predicted words based on the letters being typed. The software application supports multiple word processing packages and the company also produce a free

Apple iPhone application. To use the service, students must be at a school that has purchased a licence and installed the software: (a) Who are the customers? (b) Who are the consumers? (c) Who else may be involved in the buying decision? (d) What marketing strategy would you suggest for the software company?

3. **From segmentation to practice** For each of the following markets, try to identify THREE possible segments based on relevant characteristics and THREE segments based on customer needs. Refer to Section 6.4.2 for guidance. In each case, select the segment that you consider to be most attractive for a new venture. Draft a 300-word outline of the proposed ventures, including your ideas for marketing them effectively: (1) outdoor clothing; (2) mail order cycles and cycling accessories; (3) fresh growing herbs sold to retailers; (4) laboratory equipment.

Discussion topics

1. **Finding the gaps** What approach would you adopt in order to identify unmet customer needs in *one* of the following areas: home delivered groceries; night clubs; care for the elderly; fairly traded clothing? Would this process also help you in satisfying those needs?

2. **Customer perceptions** Identify *five* ways in which the founders of a new service-based venture (e.g. restaurant, sports centre, office cleaning company, opticians, or design consultancy) could get a better understanding of customer perceptions. Which of these would you expect to be: (a) quickest; (b) cheapest; (c) most insightful; (d) least insightful?

3. **Entrepreneurs and the new marketing** Many of the larger and more established organisations are now adopting 'new' marketing approaches. What can entrepreneurs do to ensure that their marketing efforts remain competitive?

Recommended reading

These readings address important topics in entrepreneurship research and are recommended for anyone wanting to build on the material covered in this chapter. Recommended readings have been selected from leading Sage journals and are freely available for readers of this textbook to download via the Online Resources.

Fillis, I., Lehman, K., and Miles, M. P. (2016) 'The Museum of Old and New Art: leveraging entrepreneurial marketing to create a unique arts and vacation venture'. *Journal of Vacation Marketing.*

In this article, entrepreneurial marketing is used to understand new venture creation in the vacation tourism sector through a case study of private art museum in Tasmania that has become a tourist destination of major international significance.

Carvalho, L. and Williams, B. (2014) 'Let the cork fly: creativity and innovation in a family business'. *International Journal of Entrepreneurship and Innovation.* **15, 2: 127–33.**

This case study explores the growth and internationalisation of a traditional cork company situated in the remote south of Portugal. This case illustrates how a brand can be developed for international growth and expansion by a small family business.

Lam, W. and Harker M.J. (2013) 'Marketing and entrepreneurship: an integrated view from the entrepreneur's perspective'. *International Small Business Journal*, 33, 3: 321–48.

This article explores the role and significance of marketing in the entrepreneurial process by an 11-year longitudinal study of the interrelationship between marketing and entrepreneurship at different stages of the business life cycle.

Jones, R. and Rowley, J. (2011) 'Entrepreneurial marketing in small businesses: a conceptual exploration'. *International Small Business Journal*, 29, 1: 25–36.

This article draws on the earlier research in entrepreneurial orientation, market orientation, innovation orientation and customer orientation literatures to propose a conceptual model for entrepreneurial marketing in relation to customer engagement, innovation and entrepreneurial approaches to marketing.

References

Aldrich, H. and Fiol, M. (1994) 'Fools rush in?: the institutional context of industry creation'. *Academy of Management Review*, 19, 4: 645–70.

Baines, P. and Fill, C. (2014) *Marketing* (3rd edn). Oxford: Oxford University Press.

Balfour, E. ([1943] 2006) *The living soil*. London: The Soil Association.

Bjerke, B. and Hultman, C.M. (2004) *Entrepreneurial Marketing: The Growth of Small Firms in the New Economic Era*. Cheltenham: Edward Elgar.

Blundel, R.K., Ippolito, K., and Donnarumma, D. (2013) *Effective Organisational Communication: Perspectives, Principles and Practices* (4th edn). Harlow: Pearson.

Buddi (2017) https://www.buddi.co.uk (accessed 6 January 2017).

Burn-Callander, R. (2008) 'Tracking device firm snares £4m in its first year'. *Real Business*, 23 June. Available at: http://www.realbusiness.co.uk/business_woman (accessed 20 March 2010).

Butcher, M. (2010) 'Made.com raises £2.5m to assault designer furniture industry'. *Tech Crunch Europe*, 21 March 2010. http://eu.techcrunch.com (accessed 5 January 2017).

Carson, R. (1962) *Silent Spring*. Boston, MA: Houghton Mifflin.

Collinson, E. and Shaw, E. (2001) 'Entrepreneurial marketing: a historical perspective on development and practice'. *Management Decision*, 39, 9: 761–6.

Delmar, F. and Shane, S. (2007) 'Legitimating first: organizing activities and the survival of new ventures'. *Journal of Business Venturing* 19, 3: 385–410.

Dibb, S. and Simkin, L. (2013) *Marketing Essentials* (2nd edn). London: Cengage.

Grant, J. (2008) *The Green Marketing Manifesto*. Chichester: Wiley.

Hills, G. E. and Hultman, C. M. (2006) 'Entrepreneurial marketing'. In S. Lagrosen and G. Svensson (eds) *Marketing: Broadening the Horizons*. Lund: Studentlitteratur.

Hoffman, J. L. and Sang, R. V. (2010) 'The "me-tail" revolution'. *Outlook: the Journal of High-performance Business*, 1: 1–6 (February), Accenture.

Kitchen and Ivanescu (2015) *Profitable Social Media Marketing: How To Grow Your Business Using Facebook, Twitter, Instagram, LinkedIn And More* (2nd edn). CreateSpace Independent Publishing Platform.

Lockett, N. (2010) 'New Year's resolution: time to get closer to your customers?' http://www.nigellockett.com/?p=102 (accessed 6 January 2017).

Made.com (2010) 'About us: beautiful furniture doesn't have to cost the earth'. http://www.made.com/about-us (accessed 3 May 2010).

Made.com (2017) 'Our Designers'. http://www.made.com/designers/ (accessed 5 January 2017).

Martin, F. and Thompson, M. (2010) *Social Enterprise: Developing Sustainable Businesses*. Basingstoke: Palgrave.

Mintzberg, H. and Waters, J. A. (1982) 'Tracking strategy in an entrepreneurial firm'. *Academy of Management Journal*, 25, 3: 465–99.

Mintzberg, H. and Waters, J. A. (1985) 'Of strategies, deliberate and emergent'. *Strategic Management Journal*, 6, 3: 257–72.

Mintzberg, H., Ahlstrand, B. and Lampel, J.B. (2009) *Strategy Safari: The Complete Guide Through the Wilds of Strategic Management* (2nd edn). Harlow: FT Prentice Hall.

Normann, R. and Ramirez, R. (1994) *Designing Interactive Strategy: From Value Chain to Value Constellation*. Chichester: Wiley.

Palmer, A. (2012) *Introduction to Marketing: Theory and Practice* (3rd edition). Oxford: Oxford University Press.

Perreault, W. D., Cannon, J. P., and McCarthy, E. J. (2014) *Essentials of marketing: a marketing and strategy planning approach* (14th edn). Columbus OH: McGraw-Hill.

Porter, M. (1985) *Competitive Advantage*. New York: The Free Press.

Reuters (2010) 'Satnav 2009 unit sales down 12 pct in main-Europe' at http://www.reuters.com (accessed 3 May 2010).

Scott, D. M. (2015) *The New Rules of Marketing and PR: How to Use News Releases, Blogs, Podcasting, Viral Marketing and Online Media to Reach Buyers Directly* (5th edn). Hoboken NJ: Wiley.

Shaw, E. (2004) 'Marketing in the social enterprise context: is it entrepreneurial?' *Qualitative Market Research: An International Journal*, 7, 3: 194–205.

St Luke's (2017) http://stlukes.co.uk/who-we-are/green-stuff/ (accessed 6 January 2017).

Suma (2010) 'A brief history'. Suma Wholefoods. Available at http://www.suma.coop (accessed 22 March 2010).

Suma (2017) 'http://www.suma.coop/about/ (accessed 6 January 2017).

Telegraph (2016) 'Made.com founder steps down as chief executive as furniture retailer approaches £100m in sales'. Telegraph, 22 November 2016.

Waller, M. (2009) 'Sara Murray: the woman behind buddi, the personal tracking device'. *The Times*, 3 June 2009. Available at http://www.timesonline.co.uk (accessed 20 March 2010).

Wernerfelt, B. (1984) 'A resource-based view of the firm'. *Strategic Management Journal*, 5: 171–80.

Wray, R. (2010) 'Made.com aims to halve designer furniture prices'. *The Guardian*, 22 March 2010.

7

OPERATIONS: IMPLEMENTING TECHNOLOGIES, PROCESSES AND CONTROLS

In thinking, keep to the simple. In conflict, be fair and generous. In governing, don't try to control. In work, do what you enjoy.

Lao Tzu, ancient Chinese philosopher

No institution can possibly survive if it needs geniuses … to manage it. It must be organized in such a way as to be able to get along under a leadership composed of average human beings.

Peter Drucker, professor of management and author

LEARNING OUTCOMES

After reading this chapter you should be able to:

- Appreciate the importance of managing operations, technologies, and controls.
- Understand the key elements of information systems.
- Appreciate the opportunities for gaining competitive advantage from internal systems, customer relationship management, and the extended enterprise.
- Understand the role of controls.
- Appreciate the importance of electronic communication platforms and the opportunities for gaining competitive advantage.

7.1 INTRODUCTION

Throughout this book we have considered many challenging and exciting aspects of **entrepreneurship**. But what do the, seemingly ordinary, tasks of managing operations, technologies and controls have to do with **innovation** and entrepreneurship? The answer is simple, 'the Devil is in the details', a favourite saying of German art historian Aby Warburg (1866–1929). When considering your new venture it is important to distinguish between the processes that simply have to be done to a minimum standard from those that could provide you with a real competitive advantage. When considering your new venture think about the things you will have do better than your competitors in order to win new customers, for example, if you were opening a new café in a poplar area of town. Of course, you would have to be in attractive premises that meet legislation for food hygiene standards but how would you be distinctive from and better than your competitors? It might be service, location, decor, or product quality. But, how do you achieve higher service levels than your competitors? Perhaps your staff are better trained, better motivated, or more knowledgeable. So the key is to think about the processes in your new venture that make you different to competitors. We will consider the former shortly, but in the opening *Defrosting investors: from hot dragons to chilled food* case (Case 7.1) we can clearly see that for Igloo to be successful it has to offer a high quality of service. Not just in terms of delivery but also in terms of consistency of temperature controlled delivery. This can only be achieved by attention to detail. Seemingly mundane procedures become of vital importance to success and gaining a competitive advantage. For Igloo, this means investing in accredited quality systems audited by the British Retail Consortium and the technologies and information systems to monitor this. This means that all Igloo's vehicles are equipped with temperature monitors and in-cab printers, along with remote location and temperature tracing through a satellite telemetry system (Igloo 2017a). Much innovation is mundane, incremental, and depends more on the accumulation of small insights (Porter 1990).

This chapter acknowledges that many entrepreneurs are successful, at least in part, because of their ability to manage their enterprise's operations, the technologies they use, and to introduce the necessary controls required, adding value not cost. We cannot attempt, in this chapter, to cover all the operational, technological, and control issues faced by new ventures. However, we will focus on three cross-cutting themes, which are increasingly becoming sources of competitive advantage, namely, information systems, controls, and electronic communication platforms. Some of these rely on the Internet, not just to interact with customers but also strategic partners, suppliers, and service providers.

CASE 7.1

Defrosting investors: from hot dragons to chilled food

In 2007, when **Anthony Coates-Smith** and **Alistair Turner**, who had been trading for just over two years, decided to pitch for investment on the BBC's *Dragons' Den* (Series 4: Episode 1 http://www.bbc.co.uk/dragonsden/), little did they realise that their business, **Igloo Thermo Logistics** (http://www.igloo-thermo.com), would receive an investment of £160,000 for 22.5% of the equity from Richard Farleigh and Duncan Bannatyne (thisis-money 2008). The company's purpose was to deliver chilled and frozen foods from its own distribution centres. Not surprisingly, interest in the company grew after their appearance on television. Anthony commented, 'It sent our sales into orbit. We have doubled our capacity and we are still fully booked' and they recognised that existing suppliers' service levels could be improved, as 'most were not customer focused' (Telegraph 2007).

By the end of 2016, Igloo was providing a range of refrigerated delivery services for consignments of all sizes, from parcels to pallets, from locations throughout the UK in its own fleet of temperature-controlled vehicles transports chilled and frozen products. It claimed that, *'For the last 10 years Igloo has committed itself to delivering an exceptional refrigerated delivery service. With an ever increasing list of satisfied clients our expanding delivery network is growing from strength to strength'* (Igloo 2017a).

But in order for Igloo to provide such well regarded service, they needed to carefully manage distribution, warehousing, vehicles, and the systems that integrate them.

Distribution Igloo offered services ranging from transporting a single case from A to B to long-term service requiring a tailored solution. Their temperature-controlled distribution service operated on a daily basis throughout the UK and regularly to key European destinations. They provided complete temperature assurance, visibility, and high-quality service.

Warehousing Igloo used large pallet storage facilities for chilled, frozen, ambient, and temperate goods at both their Watford, Leeds, Glasgow depots. These were secure managed sites protected by remote monitored CCTV systems linked to red care alarm monitoring. Temperature compliance alerts are linked to auto-diallers that alert staff to any storage facility developing temperature compliance issues. Warehouse personnel were trained in safe operating and temperature control procedures. They picked over of 70,000 items a week.

Vehicles Igloo operated a fleet of over 50 vehicles ranging in size from refrigerated Smart cars to refrigerated 18 ton HGVs. These vehicles offered dual temperature compartments operating temperature ranges between +25 °C and −25 °C. All the vehicles were equipped with temperature monitors and in-cab printers, as well as remote location and temperature tracing through a satellite telemetry system.

In addition to transporting food, Igloo provided a national pharmaceutical courier service with a modern fleet of temperature controlled vehicles and MHRA accredited facilities. Through increasing scale and continued investment in the latest technologies for efficient healthcare transport throughout the UK. They stated,

> *'Igloo ensures temperature integrity throughout the supply chain, from point of collection & goods-in to pharmaceutical storage to final delivery. All of our modern vehicles are equipped with heat & cool refrigeration equipment. Dual evaporators independently control the temperature of the front & rear compartments of the vehicle hold. For MHRA compliance our vehicles and storage facilities are temperature mapped on a regular basis and installed with monitoring equipment to provide temperature readings throughout the day'.* (Igloo 2017b).

In 2011, Anthony Coates-Smith had left the company leaving Alistair Turner as the CEO.

POINTS TO CONSIDER

1. How did Igloo Thermo Logistics track its distribution fleet?

2. What role did information systems play in the company's success?

3. Anthony and Alistair making their Dragon's Den pitch (http://www.bbc.co.uk/programmes/b00795b7). What did they do well? What could they have improved? How did the 'dragons' behave?

Sources: Igloo 2017a, 2017b; Telegraph 2007; thisismoney 2008.

This chapter is divided into four sections. The next section briefly reviews the basics of operations management. Section 7.3 considers the increasing importance and availability of information systems to support new venture development. Section 7.4 introduces how controls can be used to add value to products and services. Finally, in section 7.5 the significance of emerging electronic communication platforms for gaining competitive advantage is highlighted. New ventures are supported by processes and in many cases it is these processes that provide competitive advantage. In *Tim Lockett: using technology to gain competitive advantage* case (Case 7.4), we consider the importance of information systems in gaining a marketing leading position. The chapter concludes with video case $SAGE edge™ based on *Operations: Jonathan's Challenge* (Case 7.5) to test your understanding of this chapter.

7.2 BASICS OF OPERATIONS MANAGEMENT

Managing operations is concerned with the production of goods and services. It involves ensuring that processes are efficient, use as few resources as possible, and are effective in meeting customer requirements. It can be described in terms of converting inputs (materials, labour, and energy) into outputs (goods and services). However, to be competitive an enterprise needs to add value, as perceived by its customers, by the processes. Any venture will have a wide range of processes that cover everything from legal 'terms and conditions' for customers to 'employment contracts' with staff. Your new venture will have to perform these to a certain minimum standard just to compete in your marketplace. The discipline of operations management has developed over a long period with many of the core processes being well understood (Greasley 2013; Slack et al. 2015, 2016). These explore the subject in some detail, including design, planning, control, quality, and challenges. Operations and Process Management: Principles and Practice for Strategic Impact (Slack et al. 2015) takes a more strategic view of operations. Business information systems and e-business systems are constantly changing. The core principles are well covered by Chaffey (2014) and Bocij et al. (2014). Social media and digital technologies are attracting increased interest (Chaffey and Ellis-Chadwick (2015), Kitchen and Ivanescu (2015) and Scott (2015)).

Let us again consider the example of 'Maison des Peaux', Michèle Bertrand's new venture, introduced in the previous chapter on Markets (Section 6.3).

7.2.1 'Maison des Peaux' (episode 2): building processes

Michèle's new venture for supplying designer skins for mobile phones is beginning to grow. Fortunately, her employer, a French women's clothing retailer, agrees for her to move to a part-time contract. She now has 30 designs, which she wants to launch in time for the Paris fashion week. Michèle is still running her business, 'Maison des Peaux', from her flat, and her partner continues to develop the functionality on the website. She now has three manufacturers supplying about 10 designs each. But, as the orders continue to grow, so does the amount of information she is collecting. Michèle decides to use a contact management system which can be linked to her website in the future. This is a big step for her but because her partner is a web designer he is able to implement the system.

Michèle can just about cope with running her growing business but is finding it difficult to get the manufacturers to deliver on time and at the right quality. But,

Michèle is particularly worried about the one using the ethically sourced latex as recent deliveries have been late. Fortunately, she now has computer records of all orders by each supplier and plans to visit them to discuss future plans. The owner of the specialist eco-store is still her largest customer and wants to have an exclusive design. He is also slow to pay for the goods and this combined with larger amounts of stock is beginning to cause her cashflow problems. Her most reliable manufacturer, which by coincidence is located in Michèle's home town, is interested in helping her to develop her business and if she will provide ethically sourced latex has agreed to manufacturer this range.

Michèle's meeting with her most reliable manufacturer went very well. They recognised the market opportunity for 'Maison des Peaux' and offered to provide funding in return for a 30% share in the company. They also want to manufacture or source all the products in return for taking full responsibility for stock. This would enable Michèle to run the business full time, employ an assistant, and open a small shop in a fashionable area of Paris. Michèle knows the manufacturer and is still friends with the daughter, Aimée who is also a regular customer. Aimée is a journalist for the regional newspaper, and Michèle asks her to take over writing the blogs and tweets for Maison des Peaux so that she can focus on setting up the shop and dealing with the designers.

Setting up the shop is taking much more time than Michèle thought it would. She hadn't appreciated all the legal and planning requirements and even finding the right location at the right price has been slow. At last she finds a shop she can afford. Even though it is very small, she knows it is in the right part of the fashion district and very close to the new Apple and Samsung retail stores. These are yet to open, but a close friend has been involved in negotiating these tenancies on behalf of the property developer.

With a big feature in a national fashion magazine coming out in a month, Michèle just has to recruit the shop assistant and chase the contractors to finish the shop refurbishment. She knows that the article will mention the ethical sourcing of the latex and decides to visit the plantation and arrange for photographs. Michèle has a 'gut feeling' this will be important and also decides to check that all the latex she uses is accredited as ethical. Aimée starts to write blogs and tweets about the trip and build a special section on the website.

Just like any entrepreneur, Michèle is managing a varying number of processes at any one time. These depend on the venture's stage of development, external factors, and of course the market. At times it can feel like you are just dealing with the most pressing matter rather than following a strategy. Just like jugglers keeping a number of plates spinning but continually switching their attention to the one that most needs input.

The cases in this chapter are used to highlight the reality that many different enterprises use multiple processes, which span managing operations, technologies, and controls. We have already seen how Igloo (Case 7.1) used sophisticated systems to monitor temperature and track vehicle locations and were experimenting with RFID (http://www.rfidjournal.com) to provide sealed individual consignment tracking. The next section considers how enterprises innovatively use information systems to manage their operations and develop channels to market, specifically the use of internal systems, **customer relationship management,** and the **extended enterprise**.

Case 7.2, *A Stitch in time*, highlights these for two manufacturing companies. The third section considers quality control, accreditation, and legislation. Case 7.3, *Entrepreneurial explosion*, moves beyond considering selling products to selling carbon offsetting services and the role the control can play. Not surprisingly, the ability to reassure customers that controls are transparent and auditable becomes vital. The final section considers the opportunity for gaining competitive advantage from new and emerging electronic communication platforms, such as the Internet. The final case, *Tim Lockett: using technology to gain competitive advantage* (Case 7.4), highlights one entrepreneur's challenge in doing just this.

In the next section we consider the importance of information systems to new venture creation.

7.3 INFORMATION SYSTEMS

Even in the 'simplest' of ventures managing information will be a key process. What information will be important to your new venture? Think about the information you need and you generate. What information do you need to run your enterprise, provide customers, or meet the requirements of regulation? In this section we will consider three main aspects of information: (i) internal systems, (ii) customer relationship management, and (iii) the extended enterprise, Figure 7.1. We will discuss the strategic opportunity of emerging electronic communication platforms, such as the Internet, in the final section (7.5) at the end of this chapter.

All information systems should be adequately protected from viruses and hacking. Disaster recovery procedures should be put in place and routinely tested and validated.

7.3.1 Internal systems

In the next chapter, we will look at the role of information systems in accounting and, more particularly, integrated systems that link general, purchase, and sales ledgers with sales order and purchase order processing. In this section, we will take a more general view of the internal information systems used by enterprises.

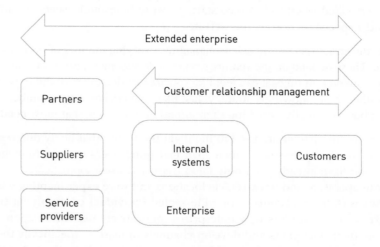

FIGURE 7.1 Relationship between information systems.

It is increasingly difficult to imagine any new venture that does not require some form of information system to support its internal systems. Even something as essential as managing contacts, be they customers or suppliers, is increasingly complex. We have seen, in Chapter 5, how important networking is to new venture creation. As our contact lists expand, both in terms of size and individual contact information, we need to be able to store and retrieve information quickly. It is possible to manage this reasonably well at a personal level with smart mobile phones and entry-level contact management software, such as Microsoft Outlook. The synchronisation of devices helps to extend this functionality further. But this will become increasingly difficult to do as your venture expands. More sophisticated contact management applications have emerged to meet this demand, for example, Act! (https://www.act.com) and Goldmine (http://www.goldmine.com). Contact management systems need to include the ability to create and manage contact lists, the interactions with the enterprise (appointments, events, and communications), support analysis, and generate and manage tasks. Remember to back up this information regularly. You might be able to rebuild your personal contact list but doing this for an expanding new venture is another matter all together! Of course, social media platforms, such as Facebook, Twitter and LinkedIn, are playing an important role in managing contacts and promoting products and services.

Many of the administrative functions of an enterprise can be supported by office automation systems. These help to create, collect, store, manipulate, and analyse office information. All office functions can be improved from typing to filing and from faxing to telephoning. The creation, manipulation, and sharing of documents and spreadsheets can easily be enhanced. There are an increasing number of office productivity tools available, for example, the popular Microsoft Office (https://products.office.com), free open-source Apache OpenOffice (http://www.openoffice.org), and Google's free online document tools (https://docs.google.com).

The need for more specialised information systems will depend largely on the type of enterprise. For example:

- **Manufacturing companies** Manufacturing resource planning (MRP II), including production scheduling, bill of materials, inventory management, material requirements planning, and cost management.
- **Design and manufacturing companies** Computer aided design (CAD), including 2D and 3D modelling. Computer-aided manufacturing (CAM) to control machine tools.
- **Creative media companies** Multimedia applications for creating and editing music, images, film and animation.
- **Publishing companies** Desktop publishing software (DTP) for designing and printing promotional material.

7.3.2 Customer relationship management

A critical aspect of any enterprise is its relationship with customers, which sits within the broader discipline of relationship marketing. Relationship marketing is defined as 'proactively creating, developing and maintaining committed, interactive and profitable exchanges with selected customers (partners) over time' (Harker 1999). This is based on the premise that it is far cheaper to retain an existing customer than it is to win a new one, the economic case for developing such long-term relationships is clear.

Reichheld (2001) noted there is a very strong correlation between the loyalty of an organisation's customers and its profitability. Customer relationship management (CRM) has emerged as a collective that encompasses the activities required to achieve this. It is defined as the business process that 'addresses all aspects of identifying customers, creating knowledge, building customer relationships and shaping their perceptions of the organization and its products' (Srivastava et al. 1999). Key characteristics of CRM include (Ryals and Knox 2001):

- Adoption of a strong and explicit customer orientation;
- Comprehensive collection and storage of integrated customer information;
- Use of dedicated data analysis software;
- Segmentation of customers by their anticipated life-time value;
- Re-engineering of business processes to deliver customer value;
- Profiling of customers to enable tailored delivery of products and services;
- A strong focus on managing customer, as opposed to product portfolios.

Clearly, implementing a system that can accommodate these characteristics will require a software application that integrates technology, processes, and activities around the customer. It is imperative that any application helps you build strong relationships with customers, add value, and satisfy their needs. In particular, it should help you to:

- Manage the sales process to potential customers (prospects);
- Improve your service to existing customers;
- Make better informed sales and marketing decisions;
- Integrate with your other information systems.

It is about having a 'single view' of a customer across all your channels to market and all your points of contact with them. Think about the information your new venture will generate by interacting with customers. How important will this be to your success? How will you capture, manage, and analyse this information? Compare your intentions with your competitors. Consider the different channels to market and what challenges these will present if you are to have a 'single view' of your customers.

Not surprisingly, a wide range of software applications have emerged to meet this need. The more popular integrated business accounting software packages will include basic CRM functionality, for example Quickbooks (https://www.quickbooks.co.uk) and Sage (http://www.sage.co.uk). Specialist applications are also available, including Microsoft's Dynamics (https://www.microsoft.com/en-us/dynamics365), NetSuite CRM (http://www.netsuite.com/portal/products/crm.shtml) and Salesforce.com (http://www.salesforce.com). These CRM applications should provide a wide range of functionality, including, marketing automation, sales force automation, customer service, customer support, and reporting. We will discuss online social networking, online sales, and e-commerce in more detail in section 7.5.

7.3.3 The extended enterprise

Even the largest corporation does not exist in a vacuum and has to interact with suppliers, partners, and customers. But, for so many new ventures this interaction is at the core of its activities. Any new venture has to extend itself to interact with external organisations. In fact, successful enterprises, out of sheer necessity, can become particularly good at it! In the following case, *'Best foot forward'* (Case 7.2), we see how. David Price's Foot Shop Ltd group developed its online customer ordering facilities several steps further. Not only had it developed multiple catalogue mail order operations, it used information systems extensively to achieve this. Describing itself as a 'multi-channel marketing' company, the group had a 'single view' of the customer across postal, telephone, and online ordering systems.

Your new venture will also interact with suppliers, partners, service providers, and above all customers. How can you configure and manage these relationships in order to gain competitive advantage? Redesigning or reconfiguring the supply chain is an important source of innovation. It seems somewhat obvious to us now, but when Jeff Bezos launched Amazon.com in 1994 the key element of his new venture was to replace high street retailers in the book supply chain and when Michel Dell founded Dell, in 1984, he removed the need for computer resellers.

CASE 7.2

Best foot forward: the networked model for entrepreneurship

David Price, who bought Somerset-based **Cosyfeet** (http://www.cosyfeet.com) in 1990, took a different approach to using information systems to develop his business, which operates through multiple marketing channels: retail, mail order, telephone and online (YouTube 2017). The specialist footwear company became part of David's Foot Shop Ltd group (Foot Shop 2017), which employed over 90 people and sought to develop long-term relationships with suppliers. Other specialist companies in the group also included Walktall (http://www.walktall.co.uk – shoes in large sizes). In 2013, Cosyfeet celebrated 30 years in business (BFA 2013).

David used information systems to transform his traditional shoe-making business from a conventional mail order company to one that embraced web technology throughout its marketing, sales and distribution. His confidence in the company's systems was high, 'Yes, we're very good at footwear – we're world leaders at what we do – but actually if we came in to work tomorrow and all our footwear factories had burned to the ground, our core systems and skills would allow us to set up selling virtually any product. So I believe what we're really good at are systems, marketing and transactional websites; which means we are always looking for business opportunities where we can use our knowledge of systems. From my perspective, it has to be niche and the Internet has to be in there somewhere. The old adage that the shoemaker should stick to his last is also very appropriate for us – until now we have stuck to our comfort zone (footwear) but we've started to move into new areas, such as clothing'. David added, 'We're always benchmarking ourselves against other companies and we've come to realise that we're very good at what we do' (Sanderson 2010).

POINTS TO CONSIDER

1. Why does David Price describe his company as a 'multi-channel marketing' business?
2. What is the role of information systems in Cosyfeet?

Sources: BFA 2013, Foot Shop 2017; Sanderson 2010; YouTube 2017.

However, other entrepreneurs have also used information systems to achieve competitive advantage. For example:

- Alastair Mitchell and Andy McLoughlin: Hurdle, providing secure online workspaces (http://www.huddle.net)
- Ben Black: My Family Care, online booking of carers (http://www.myfamilycare.co.uk)
- Bradley McLoughlin: Trading4u, managing online auctions (http://www.trading4u.com)
- Cabrelli and Miles Latham: Affixxius Productions, producing alternative corporate videos (http://www.affixxius.com)
- Henry Bennett: Island Wall Entertainment, developing mobile applications (http://www.islandwall.com)
- Holly Tucker and Sophie Cornish: Notonthehightstreet.com, selling unusual products online (http://www.notonthehightstreet.com)
- Lisa and Jonathan Wilkinson: t-mac Technologies, providing energy management services (http://www.t-mac.co.uk)
- Sara Murray: buddi, offering tracking services (http://www.buddi.co.uk)

7.4 CONTROLS

For many enterprises, existing information systems, particularly accounting applications, will provide the necessary control mechanisms. However, it is worth exploring two areas where additional controls might be appropriate, namely quality control and accreditation.

7.4.1 Quality control

Quality control can simply be the process by which enterprises manage the production of products and delivery of services to an appropriate standard. Provided customers are happy with the standard achieved then no action is required. However, many organisations are required, by law or an external partner, to demonstrate quality control procedures are in operation and are audited by an independent body. The International Organization for Standardization provides a number of international standards across a wide range of markets and industries, known collectively as ISO standards (http://www.iso.org). These ISO standards specify the requirements for products, services, processes, materials, and systems and for assessment, managerial, and organisational practices, for example, ISO 9001 is a quality policy that sets out the organisation's working practices and monitors these for any non-conformances that result in corrective actions. Good quality policies are linked to satisfying customers' needs.

But why would a new venture be interested in informal quality systems if they are not required to use them? The rigour required, for operating formal quality systems, can be of competitive advantage to new ventures because it encourages all staff to focus on the processes required to meet customer needs. Even if formal ISO accreditation is not sought, the discipline of recording non-conformances instils a focus on quality that can identify areas for improvement or corrective action.

When considering your new venture, think about the ways in which quality can be controlled and in particular how you could use it to gain competitive advantage.

Do not underestimate the knowledge and expertise required to develop and implement quality control systems but also the possibility that existing enterprises may have entrenched processes that add cost not value. Remember that it is how the customer perceives this value not the enterprise.

7.4.2 Accreditation

In addition to accreditation to ISO quality standards, there are numerous accreditation systems that can impact of a new venture's success. National and international schemes can apply equally to large and small organisations. Accreditation may be voluntary and developed by a trade association in support of its members, by an independent standard body or in response to legislation and applies to all organisations. For example, the provision of care in people's own homes is regulated under the UK's 'Domiciliary Care Agencies Regulations 2002'. In California, the Department of Social Services regulates 'Residential Care Facilities for the Elderly' by setting out the standards required and monitoring procedure. It is imperative to be fully aware of legislation and how to comply.

However, accreditation under voluntary codes can be a source of competitive advantage. Launched in 1993, Investors in People standard is overseen by the UK Commission for Employment and Skills. It is promoted as a highly versatile framework, which 'helps organisations transform their business performance ... by focusing all our advice and assessment around meeting your organisation's needs. The first thing we do is find out what your performance targets or key priorities are. These then become central to all our work, so we support your business plan and maximise the value you gain from working with us'. (https://www.investorsinpeople.com)

Rabbit Contracting was founded in 2002 specialising in epoxy and polyurethane coating and screed systems (http://www.rabbitcontracting.co.uk). By 2009, it employed six people and operated across the UK on a national basis, particularly in the manufacturing, food processing, and medical sectors. Managing director, Adrian Breeds stated, 'The significant benefits of our engagement with Investors in People have much more than justified our investment. We would definitely recommend it to other small companies in a similar position. We only wish we had known about it five years earlier.' He agreed that, 'without the Investors in People programme Rabbit Contracting would not have still been in business'. The benefits to Rabbit Contracting were (IIP 2010):

- Directors had to establish a vision for the enterprise;
- Directors were better skilled for recruitment and development;
- Performance improved. Turnover increased 39% year-on-year and profitability by 25%;
- Increased quality and repeat customers;
- More completely satisfied customers;
- Returns from investment training and development activities.

In the following case, '*Entrepreneurial explosion*' (Case 7.3), we can see how a market has emerged in response to concerns over climate change and in particular production of carbon dioxide. Competitors are vying to provide carbon footprint calculations and verified offsetting schemes. But, what can the organisations gain from voluntarily joining such schemes?

CASE 7.3

Entrepreneurial explosion: carbon offset fuels new standards

There has been a dramatic increase in awareness of the issue of climate change. Individuals, companies, organisations, and governments have responded in various ways. The need to do something to help reduce greenhouse gas emissions has resulted in an increasing number of schemes that allow for the offsetting of carbon dioxide produced by human activities. There are two markets for this carbon offsetting. The first operates for large companies, governments, or entities to buy carbon offsets so that they can comply with the limits they are allowed to emit. The second and much smaller voluntary market enables individuals and companies to offset their greenhouse gas emissions from transportation, energy, and other sources. These schemes offer the chance to offset against specific schemes funded by the payments. Typically, these might be renewable energy generation (wind farms, solar power, hydroelectric schemes, and biofuel plants), reforestation, and reduction schemes that replace high carbon producing activities with less harmful ones.

Many innovative and entrepreneurial companies have emerged to exploit this opportunity; for example, Clear and Carbon Footprint. But how do such companies persuade potential customers that the calculation of their emissions is accurate (their carbon footprint) and the schemes provided will genuinely offset these emissions? Clearly, there is a need for both trust and simplicity, which can only come from robust transparency systems. Consumers need to feel confident in the management, monitoring, and control of schemes and easy access to validated information. The Quality Assurance Standard emerged in 2009, with UK government support, to ensure that organisations could easily identify carbon offsets which had been thoroughly and independently audited to the highest standards available (qascarbonneutral 2014).

The first company to qualify for the scheme was **Clear**, founded in 2007, run by **Dr Bruce Elliott** and **Ben Hedley**. They tried to differentiate themselves by only offsetting using Certified Emission Reductions (CERs) which have been issued every time the United Nations prevents one tonne of carbon dioxide equivalent being emitted through carbon projects registered with the Clean Development Mechanism (CDM) (Clear 2017).

Also, **Carbon Footprint** Ltd, founded by **John** and **Wendy Buckley** in 2005, focused on businesses looking for carbon management consultancy services. They help these clients to reduce energy consumption and emissions and offset unavoidable emissions through internationally recognised carbon offsetting schemes. John Buckley obtained a degree in Engineering and MSc before working 14 years as a scientist. Wendy Buckley had a PhD in Physics and a background in sustainable energy development (Carbon Footprint 2017). Customers of Carbon Footprint services included New Forest District Council, IKEA and TSL Education.

In addition, the **CarbonNeutral Company**, founded by **Sue Welland** and **Dan Morrell** in 1997 and one of the oldest providers, was not part of the government scheme, choosing instead to be a founding member of the International Carbon Reduction and Offset Alliance (http://www.icroa.org). By 2017, it working with over 300 businesses in over 35 countries. Customers of the CarbonNeutral Company included ASOS, Microsoft, Scandinavian Airlines, TUI and UPS (CarbonNeutral 2017a).

Its schemes include:

- Francisco Morazán Wind Power: Delivering energy access to communities while supporting the achievement of national renewable energy targets.

- India Improved Cookstoves: Efficient cookstoves bring improved health and financial security to 245,000 households in India.

- Kanungu Run-of-River Hydro: Generating renewable power to enhance rural energy access and reduce carbon.

- Uganda Community Reforestation: Working with 6,000 farmers to improve financial security and build sustainable livelihoods through community-based tree planting programmes.

(CarbonNeutral 2017b).

POINTS TO CONSIDER

1. What was the role of the government Quality Assurance Scheme for Carbon Offsetting? Why did the CarbonNeutral Company not join the scheme?

2. How do Carbon Footprint, Clear, and the CarbonNeutral Company differentiate themselves from each other?

3. Why would an organisation want to voluntarily offset and how could they use this to gain a competitive advantage?

Sources: Carbon Footprint 2017; CarbonNeutral 2017a, 2017b; Clear 2017; qascarbonneutral 2014.

The above case highlights how regulation emerged as the market for carbon offsetting developed. However, convincing potential customers of the added value of voluntarily offsetting goes beyond regulation to understanding their underlying needs. In the next section we will consider how emerging electronic communication platforms provide opportunities for innovation.

7.5 ELECTRONIC COMMUNICATION PLATFORMS

New technologies are constantly emerging and having an impact on markets and industries – creating opportunities. One particularly significant group of emerging technologies is electronic communication platforms, for example the Internet and 4G mobile networks. The Internet has changed the landscape in many sectors and in many ways. Of course, retailing has changed to accommodate online sales (e-commerce).

So, it is clear that Internet changes the marketing environment by introducing a new channel or route to market: e-commerce. This is not just the preserve of large companies but can also provide significant opportunities for new ventures and small businesses. For the latter, the Internet is viewed as an important and growing new channel (Lockett and Doherty 2008). However, the Internet, and increasingly 4G mobile networks, is changing not just the channels to market but also the way businesses process and collaborate (often referred to as e-business). Information systems' functionality and capabilities have changed profoundly and dramatically as a result of these new electronic communication platforms.

Your new venture may, directly or indirectly, use the Internet for marketing to customer, communicating with suppliers, processing information, or working with key partners. Increasingly, internal information system development is moving to an external development and provision model (outsourcing), driven by the need for lower costs, faster implementation, easier-to-use applications, and effective use of scarce resources (Peppard and Ward 2016). The emergence of hosted e-business enterprise applications is a prime example of a profound change deriving directly from the availability of low cost, ubiquitous electronic communication networks, such as the Internet. E-business is defined as 'the use of electronic communication networks to transact, process and collaborate in business markets' (Lockett and Brown 2005: 22). These hosted applications provide functionality ranging from email to contact management and from sales order entry to financial ledgers with report generators.

Telecommunication, technology, and service companies have emerged or evolved to provide a range of web services and hosted applications designed to exploit existing communication infrastructures. Typically, this is known as *Cloud Computing*. This fundamental change in the relationship between user, hardware, and software presents opportunities for new business models for service provision. Typically these hosted applications are offered on a rental or fee basis, rather than the traditional purchase model. The fee normally includes the use of the software and the provision of the processing and storage platforms, but not the provision of the electronic communication networks. One provider, which became particularly well-known, was Salesforce.com (http://www.salesforce.com), founded in 1999 by Marc Benioff. In less than 10 years, Salesforce.com became one of the largest providers and specialised in providing its customers with sophisticated customer relationship management (CRM) applications. CRM applications were used to support sales and marketing activities, including telesales, e-commerce, sales data analysis, and marketing campaigns.

The provision of hosted enterprise applications is increasing, particularly in the US, and the potential for hosted services is strong. The Internet has provided numerous **entrepreneurial opportunities**, and many new business models have emerged. Some business models, such as online retailing (http://www.amazon.com) and online marketplaces (https://www.alibaba.com; http://www.ebay.com), have flourished. One of these new sectors consisted of software developers providing access to applications over the Internet, from simple hosted email (http://www.gmail.com) to highly complex hosted enterprise applications (http://www.sap.com). Organisations use these web-based applications rather than just buying the software and installing it on their own computer networks as it takes less time, expertise, and resources. Cloud computing reduces costs by hosting and managing software applications centrally and providing access to remote users via web browsers or thin clients. The costs are shared across many organisations, and ASPs rent access to these applications at typically between 10% and 20% of the equivalent purchase price. In Chapter 6, we heard from Mark Robinson (Case 6.4) who built a software prototype of his strategy mapping application. The project used the latest web-based technologies designed to be delivered as a service over the Internet and paid for on a subscription basis.

So, electronic communication platforms are increasingly changing the way enterprises transact and process. However, they also provide a platform for emerging collaborative and interactive online networking services. These include social media technologies for blogging, forums and tweets, which support the growth of online social networks, such as Facebook (http://www.facebook.com) and LinkedIn (http://www.linkedin. com). In Chapter 3, we heard from Steve Pankhurst who co-founded Friends Reunited (http://www.friendsreunited.co.uk), arguably the first commercially successful online social networking community (Case 3.4). We see how in just five years they took what may in hindsight seem to us like a 'sure-fire' winner from concept through exploitation to eventual sale for £120 million.

Using social media platforms in order to increase your 'digital footprint' will be an important element in your online strategy. How can blogging, online social networks and tweeting help our new venture?

This chapter provides insights into the opportunities for gaining competitive advantage through managing operations, technologies, and controls. The *Tim Lockett: using technology to gain competitive advantage* case (Case 7.4) examines the role of Internet technologies can play in supporting business growth and gaining advantage. The case shows how Tim responded to opportunity to buy back his old company and use information systems to gain a marketing leading position in his industry. In addition, there is a video case available on **$SAGE edge** (Case 7.5 *Operations: Jonathan's Challenge*). This video case is based on an interview with an entrepreneur, Jonathan, keen to expand his business, which supplies waste and recycling containers. Watch the video and decide which option you think Jonathan will choose. You might find it useful to discuss the case with friends or colleagues before deciding. Please note that lecturers can have access to the video which reveals the actual decision taken by the entrepreneur.

7.6 SUMMARY

- Managing operations, technologies, and controls are important to running any enterprise but can also provide opportunities for gaining competitive advantage.

- Information systems play a vital role in many new ventures by developing internal systems, customer relationship management, and the extended enterprise.

- Customer relationship management provides an opportunity to achieve a 'single view' of a customer and effectively support multi-channels to markets.

- Controls can support quality and accreditations systems, which in turn can deliver a recognised service standard and provide opportunities for gaining competitive advantage.

- Electronic communication platforms are increasingly important to new ventures, not only in supporting transactions and processes but also collaboration, such as online social networks.

CASE 7.4

Tim Lockett: using technology to gain competitive advantage

In 2005, **Tim Lockett** was the managing director of his own healthcare distribution business (**Deliver Net**). In fact, it was his third business. He and his brother had set up their first business in 1998 but they lost control of it after an unsuccessful joint venture with a large medical company. Tim felt that with nearly 20 years' experience in the UK community care sector he knew the market and industry extremely well. He had developed strong relationships with key suppliers and contracts with national care home groups. His business strategy was simple: use new technology to provide the most efficient and cost-effective service possible. His customers seemed to agree, sales were growing, and Tim felt he could put his past behind him. But rumours had started that the old company had lost a big contract and was in difficulties. Should he try to buy it or simply walk away?

BIOGRAPHY

Apart from the first two years of his working life, Tim has always worked for himself. He reflected, 'I was probably inspired by my father, who when he left the army in the early seventies started a family business running care homes. I was, either consciously or subconsciously, influenced by the idea that if you work hard you can achieve goals that you wouldn't necessarily achieve in a normal working environment. I have always wanted to be my own boss.' Tim's working life started after he graduated from university with a business studies qualification. Then in his early twenties he became a management trainee for a big timber importer. Tim recalled, 'I did that for about a year and decided that I wanted to see the world. So, I backpacked for two years through Australia and America.' On his return to the UK, he took up another management trainee role this time in Campbell's, the food company, and quickly became a successful area sales representative. Tim's working life then took a sudden change of direction. He recalled, 'About a year later my brother came up with the idea of starting our own healthcare distribution business. I did think long and hard about the decision because I could see a good career path for me in Campbell's.'

Tim and his brother launched their healthcare distribution business in 1988. Tim recalled, 'We started from scratch! By the mid-1990s we had a turnover of over £5 million, were making profits and making mistakes! It was about then we were approached by one of our suppliers, a large and successful medical company, with a view of setting up a joint venture company. Their objective was to develop the first truly national distributor to the community care sector. We were offered a 50/50 partnership. They contributed a small equipment division plus a significant capital injection and we put in all of our business to form the new company. We saw it as a way of taking the business forward five years in one single step.'

Tim's role was critical to the company. He stated, 'I was the sales director concentrating on generating new business ... going out there developing relationships with customers ... I am a great believer in not closing doors. You can lose a customer through no fault of your own. It could just be a change of personnel and somebody wants to make their own mark and so see the need to change suppliers. But as long as you exit with dignity then that leaves the door open in the future.'

But the joint venture didn't develop as planned. As Tim, recalled, 'Unfortunately, these things don't always work out and although we doubled the size of the business, we realised that we had set up a joint venture with problems built in. We thought we had done all our due diligence but hadn't understood the business model of their equipment division. We felt like an ocean liner just heading completely in the wrong direction. There were attempts to rectify it but in our first year we lost a significant amount of money. It was almost from that point that I knew the joint venture wasn't going to work.' The large medical company purchased outright control but Tim remained as the sales director for another year.

OUT OF THE FRYING PAN, INTO THE FIRE

Then in his early thirties, Tim found himself out of a job and was not permitted to work in the healthcare distribution sector for 12 months. He recalled, 'I had negotiated a pretty good contract so my exit payment was reasonable. It gave me time to think.' Not surprisingly, after ten years in the one industry, Tim had built up strong relationships with customers and key suppliers. It was not long before he was approached to go back into it. He recalled, 'My first reaction was … *I'm not interested.* But they kept badgering me. So, I thought, "*If I am going to do this I have got to do it differently.*" I didn't just want to duplicate what we had achieved before.'

Tim knew the care home market was changing rapidly. He saw the move from a small 'cottage-type' industry into an industry that was attracting big corporate investment. Tim commented, 'In 1988, a group might consist of three homes and now the biggest group in the country has over 700 homes. But, this change had only really started in the mid-1990s but it was gathering pace in 2000. So, I needed to offer something that was different and although the product range was similar I wanted to offer quality products across key product categories. I identified key strategic suppliers who were willing to work with me to develop their business in the care home market.'

Having developed his product offering Tim turned his attention to the customer. He recalled, 'The other issue was identifying potential customers who were willing to embrace change in order to benefit from a more efficient service to lower costs. I became increasingly convinced that with the right strategic suppliers and an efficient delivery service I could win the business of the larger group customers.' Tim needed to expand quickly and he remembered how he achieved this: 'Through my network. I had been involved with the business over ten years, people that were regional managers had gone on to become directors or even owners of businesses. I realised quite quickly that I knew a lot of key players within the industry and I simply approached them, explained what I was doing. They were intrigued that I was back in the marketplace. I got an opportunity to talk to people and say, "*If you work with me I will deliver you best quality at the lowest achievable price.*" They could understand that.'

BEST IN CLASS

By this time the Internet was beginning to emerge as a real business tool. Tim stated, 'I started to see the Internet as the vehicle that would make a real difference … we were in

(Continued)

(Continued)

a very competitive industry. You could lose business if you were not competitive enough. So price played a big part.' But how could Tim's business be different? 'I thought, "*How do we differentiate ourselves from other distributors?*" We are not going to replace the driver, the vehicle, the person who picks the goods. The logistics and distribution part of this business – I didn't see being particularly different in ten years. So, what part of our business could we streamline? It was the administrative part. The Internet became the focus of our strategy. We more than tripled our sales but halved our administrative costs.'

Then in 2005, rumours started that the old company had lost a big contract. It was clear that they were running into difficulties. Tim recalled this moment, 'My brother had helped me set up the new business and we decided to contact the legal guy we still knew in the large medical company ... within 24 hours we were having a meeting with two main board directors ... in 48 hours we negotiated a stock, assets and goodwill purchase of the old company.'

What about due diligence? Tim and his brother were allowed to walk around the warehouse that evening to view the stock and met the largest customer the following day. Tim knew that it was important to meet this customer. He recalled, 'It was an interesting meeting and it was clear straight away that the service they were getting was appalling ... they were very close to losing the contract. They had just got a new buyer and while I was waiting to see him, this voice said, "*Hello Tim, how are you?*" It was the Managing Director and he remembered me. He had been a manager with another group previously. So, he came over and shook my hand and I knew he would give us a chance to sort it out.'

The scene was set. Tim decided to buy back his old company and rapidly expand the business. Over the next decade Tim's company, Deliver Net, emerged as the market leader (http://www.delivernet.co.uk). His instinct proved right – the business couldn't differentiate itself through changes to logistics and distribution but could use technology to gain competitive advantage.

> We developed online templated order forms that the customer approved and adjusted according to their needs and budget. This formed the basis of our 'best in class' online ordering system, PICS, that we manage so effectively across thousands of customers. This ensures Deliver Net has a differentiating factor, which we truly embrace, ensuring our customers get the greatest value from our service. Following a particularly busy year in 2011, we passed £20m in revenues for the first time ... it was clear that we were then the UK's largest supplier of consumables to the Care Home sector.

Source: This case is primarily based on an interview with Tim Lockett and was written by Nigel Lockett.

CASE 7.5

 ◀ Operations: Jonathan's challenge video

In this video case, **Jonathan** explains the three aspects of operations he needs to consider to expand his business, which supplies waste and recycling containers: (a) continue outsourcing design and manufacturing, (b) bring design in-house, and

(c) bring design and manufacturing in-house. Watch the video and decide which option you think Jonathan will choose. You might find it useful to discuss the case with friends or colleagues before deciding. Please note that lecturers can have access to the video that reveals the actual decision taken by the entrepreneur.

Source: This video case is primarily based on an interview with Jonathan by Nigel Lockett.

Practical activities

1. **Information systems** What information systems will be important for the following enterprises:?

    (a) A manufacturer of sandwiches, which are supplied to over 100 local fuel service stations.

    (b) A team of five IT engineers offering next-day on-site repair or replace services.

    (c) A social enterprise providing home care to over 200 partially sighted individuals within a 60-mile radius.

2. **Controls** You are launching a new venture, which delivers documents in a busy city centre. You will be offering bicycle, motorcycle, and small van one-hour deliveries. You decided that all of these would be promoted as carbon neutral. Find two organisations that provide an accredited service. Approximately how much will it cost?

3. **Electronic communication platforms** Review the service offered by NetLedger (http://www.netsuite.com) in terms of functionality and cost. Investigate three other similar providers of hosted enterprise applications in order to identify any difference. Which do you think would particularly appeal to new ventures and why?

Discussion topics

1. **Information systems** Why should a new venture be consider using a customer relationship management system?

2. **Controls** Which is the most used quality system? How do the standards differ for a product and service company? What does accreditation involve?

3. **Electronic communication platforms** What are the requirements for an effective online social network? Visit Facebook (http://www.facebook.com) and LinkedIn (http://www.linkedin.com) and compare the functionality for setting up and developing online groups. What particular features could be useful for the virtual footprint of a new venture? How can the use of social media support this objective?

Recommended reading

These readings address important topics in entrepreneurship research and are recommended for anyone wanting to build on the material covered in this chapter. Recommended readings have been selected from leading Sage journals and are freely available for readers of this textbook to download via the Online Resources.

Radicic, D., Pugh, G., Hollanders, H., Wintjes, R. and Fairburn, J. (2015) 'The impact of innovation support programs on small and medium enterprises innovation in traditional manufacturing industries: an evaluation for seven European Union regions'. *Environment and Planning C: Government and Policy*, 34, 8: 1425–52.

This article evaluates the effect of innovation support programmes on output innovation by small and medium enterprises in traditional manufacturing industry and concludes that the estimated effects of innovation support programmes are positive, typically increasing the probability of innovation and of its commercial success by around 15%.

Awiagah, R., Kang, J., and Lim, J. I. (2015) 'Factors affecting e-commerce adoption among SMEs in Ghana'. *Information Development*, 32, 4: 815–36.

This article identifies the major determining factors in Ghanaian small and medium-sized enterprises' e-commerce adoption. The results indicate that government support has the greatest direct impact on intentions to use e-commerce. Managerial support and the influence of enabling and regulatory conditions also play a vital role.

Gresty, M. (2013) 'What role do information systems play in the knowledge management activities of SMEs?' *Business Information Review*, 30, 3: 144–51.

This case study article considers information systems application for knowledge management in small to medium-sized enterprises (SMEs. This study, therefore, presents a case study of an SME's use of information systems in its management of knowledge.

Peltier, J. W., Schibrowsky, J. A., and Zhao, Y. (2009) 'Understanding the antecedents to the adoption of CRM technology by small retailers: entrepreneurs vs owner-managers'. *International Small Business Journal*, 27, 3: 307–36.

This article explores CRM adoption by small businesses. The findings show that CRM adopters had higher product class knowledge, a greater risk orientation, saw a stronger relative advantage, perceived higher environmental complexity and hostility, and had a more open business change orientation.

References

BFA (2013) http://britishfootwearassociation.co.uk/brand-of-the-month-cosyfeet/ (accessed 5 January 2017).

Bocij, P., Greasley, A., and Hickie, S. (2014) *Business Information Systems: Technology, Development and Management for the e-Business* (5th edn). Harlow, UK: Financial Times/Prentice Hall.

Carbon Footprint (2017) http://www.carbonfootprint.com/ourteam.html (accessed 3 May 2010).

CarbonNeutral (2017a) http://www.carbonneutral.com/our-clients (accessed 5 January 2017).

CarbonNeutral (2017b) http://www.naturalcapitalpartners.com/projects (accessed 5 January 2017).

Chaffey, D. (2014) *Digital Business and e-Commerce Management* (6th edn). Harlow, UK: Pearson Education.

Chaffey, D. and Ellis-Chadwick, F. (2015) *Digital Marketing: Strategy, Implementation and Practice* (6th edn). Harlow, UK: Pearson Education.

Clear (2017) http://www.clear-offset.com/the-team.php (accessed 5 January 2017).

DEFRA (2012) *Biodiversity Offsetting Pilots: Guidance for Offset Providers*. Department for Environment Food and Rural Affairs, March 2012.

Drucker, P. (1949) *Concept of the Corporation*. New York: John Day Company.

Foot Shop (2017) http://www.footshopltd.co.uk (accessed 6 January 2017).

Greasley, A. (2013) *Operations Management* (3rd edn). Chichester: John Wiley & Sons.

Harker, M. J. (1999) 'Relationship marketing defined? An examination of current relationship marketing definitions'. *Marketing Intelligence and Planning*, 17, 1: 13–20.

Igloo (2017a) http://www.igloothermo.com/about-us (accessed 5 January 2017).

Igloo (2017b) http://www.igloothermo.com/services/pharmaceutical-courier (accessed 5 January 2017).

IIP (2010) 'Case studies – Rabbit Consulting'. http://www.investorsinpeople.co.uk/MediaResearch/CaseStudy (accessed 25 March 2010).

Kitchen and Ivanescu (2015) *Profitable Social Media Marketing: How To Grow Your Business Using Facebook, Twitter, Instagram, LinkedIn and More* (2nd edn). CreateSpace Independent Publishing Platform.

Lockett, N. and Brown, D. (2004) 'The potential of critical e-applications for engaging SMEs in e-business'. *European Journal of Information Systems*, 13, 1: 21–34.

Lockett, N. and Doherty, N. (2008) 'Mind the gap: exploring the links between expectations of relationship marketing and reality of electronic-CRM'. *International Journal of e-Business Management*, 2, 2: 19–34.

Peppard, J. and Ward, J. (2016) *The Strategic Management of Information Systems: Building a Digital Strategy* (4th edn). Chichester: John Wiley & Sons.

Porter, M. (1990) *The Competitive Advantage of Nations*. New York: Free Press.

qascarbonnetutral (2014) https://qascarbonneutral.com/beyond-doubt/ (accessed 6 January 2017).

Reichheld, F. F. (2001) *The Loyalty Effect: The Hidden Force behind Growth, Profits, and Lasting Value*. Boston, MA: Harvard Business School Press.

Ryals, L. and Knox, S. (2001) 'Cross-functional issues in the implementation of relationship marketing through customer relationship management'. *European Management Journal*, 19, 5: 534–42.

Sanderson (2010) *A Comfortable Fit*. Elucid Case Study Cosyfeet Sanderson.

Scott, D. M. (2015) *The New Rules of Marketing and PR: How to Use News Releases, Blogs, Podcasting, Viral Marketing and Online Media to Reach Buyers Directly* (5th edn). Hoboken NJ: Wiley.

Slack, N., Brandon-Jones, A., Johnston, R., and Betts, A. (2015) *Operations and Process Management: Principles and Practice for Strategic Impact* (4th edn) Harlow, UK: Pearson Education.

Slack, N., Brandon-Jones, A., and Johnston, R. (2016) *Operations Management* (8th edn). Harlow, UK: Pearson Education.

Srivastava, R., Shervani, T.A., and Fahey, L. (1999) 'Marketing, business processes and shareholder value: An organisationally embedded view of marketing activities and the discipline of marketing'. *Journal of Marketing*, 63: 168–79.

Telegraph (2007) 'Dragons turn white van men into millionaires'. *The Daily Telegraph*, 26 June.

thisismoney (2008) 'Our story, by the Dragons' Den millionaires'. *This Is Money* 27 August.

Thomases, H. (2010) *Twitter Marketing: An Hour a Day*. Chichester: John Wiley & Sons.

YouTube (2017) https://youtu.be/iy2udsY8C-8 (accessed 6 January 2017). *Behind the scenes at Cosyfeet.*

8

ACCOUNTS: INTERPRETING FINANCIAL PERFORMANCE

Good plans shape good decisions. That's why good planning helps to make elusive dreams come true.

Lester Bittel, professor of management

Annual income twenty pounds, annual expenditure nineteen pounds nineteen and six, result happiness. Annual income twenty pounds, annual expenditure twenty pounds ought and six, result misery.

Wilkins Micawber, fictional character

LEARNING OUTCOMES

After reading this chapter you should be able to:

- Appreciate the importance of effective financial forecasting and planning for a new entrepreneurial venture.
- Understand the key elements of business accounting as they apply to a new venture.
- Prepare basic financial statements, including projected profit and loss accounts, balance sheets, and cash flow statements.
- Appreciate the value of key performance indicators as a way of managing a new venture.
- Recognise the differences between quantitative and qualitative measures of performance, and how these might be relevant to commercial and social enterprises.
- Apply relevant principles and techniques of forecasting and planning in order to understand the overall performance of your own venture.

8.1 INTRODUCTION

Having identified an entrepreneurial opportunity, reviewed the markets, and considered operations we now turn to the vital task of interpreting financial performance. Forecasting and planning are important skills for any entrepreneur to have or to develop.

In order to construct these forecasts, you may need to make use of historical information, market analysis, and some of your own 'gut feelings' about how the venture is going to operate over specified periods (e.g. daily, weekly, monthly, quarterly, or annually). The financial information produced to support a new venture usually relies on a combination of sources. Some figures may be soundly based in accurate data, while others are based on assumptions and your own 'best guess' of the likely outcome. Financial information is important. It provides evidence to support your decisions about the venture and also helps you to justify those decisions when you present them to other people. As the venture proceeds, you can also compare your previous forecasts with actual performance. This allows you (and others) to monitor your performance. Analysis of this kind can also help you to improve the accuracy of future forecasts.

→ **PERSPECTIVES** See Section 11.1 for further information.

Forecasting can be used in many areas of a venture, for example, predicting customer demand for a product can be used in production planning both internally and through your supply chain and in the production of business plans. However, it is important to keep in mind that all ventures are affected, to a greater or lesser extent, by risk and uncertainty. Though good forecasting can help to quantify risk factors and to highlight areas of uncertainty, it cannot be relied on exclusively.

As mentioned in Chapter 3, one response to this need for articulation is to produce a traditional formal business plan. Business plans are a formal statement, with a set of business goals and objectives. They often include detailed market analysis and financial forecasts. They may have to be produced as a requirement of loans and updated regularly. While there are inherent advantages in spending some time writing business plans, they can be time consuming to produce. The key question to ask is: *If I were investing in the business, what is the critical information I would need and how often would I need it?* (That is, *need* rather than want or like.) Remember that any business plan is out of date as soon as it is printed and that in practice we don't run ventures by following business plans but by reacting to changes in our markets and to operational challenges. But they can provide a welcome opportunity to reflect on previous assumptions and actual versus forecasted performance. In fact, banks, lenders, and investors all seem to place considerable importance in them so they must be important. However, they are simply a formal document that states the enterprise's goals and how they will be achieved and often include detailed financial projections and marketing plans.

It can seem difficult to feel any connection between a long document full of positive statements, market analysis, and financial forecasts based on numerous assumptions and your 'gut feel' for an entrepreneurial opportunity you passionately feel is worth exploiting. In the end, it is not the role of this book to provide a step-by-step guide to writing a business plan. If this is what you want you might be better starting with one of the more popular business planning guides, such as *Business Plans for Dummies* (Tiffany et al. 2012) or *How to Write a Business Plan* (Finch 2016).

The first challenge presented by the subject of this chapter, *Accounts: interpreting financial performance*, is using often commercially sensitive information to illustrate the principles of business accounting, forecasting, and planning without revealing the identity of the organisations. This is successfully achieved by integrating four anonymous cases that build on each other. The opening case, *Beyond outdoor clothing for enthusiasts* (Case 8.1), requires us to analyse sales information and explore the relationship between sales, margin, and gross profit. Case 8.2, *Cleaning up in business*, presents a seemingly successful business with good sales, margin, gross profit, and net profit, which faces a cash flow problem. This, all too familiar, problem can be understood by considering the relationship between the profit and loss and balance sheet statements and the importance of managing these. Case 8.3, *A recipe for success*, moves beyond considering trading statements to considering an investment decision. Many enterprises can only trade successfully by purchasing plant and machinery, but this may require money to be borrowed or new investment to be obtained. Understanding the basic elements of return on investment can assist in making these critical decisions. The final case, *Steve Woodford* (Case 8.4), is based on interviews with a social entrepreneur whose main focus was not financial performance but the real impact of his charity's activities. This serves to illustrate that entrepreneurs become successful because they understand the importance of managing both finances and other key performance indicators. The former uses universally acknowledged principles and practices, but the latter will be unique to the industry, market, and enterprise. We have seen in Chapter 6 (Markets) how important marketing and industry analysis is to successful enterprise, and this chapter builds on these by recognising the importance of measuring performance either quantitatively or qualitatively.

We can clearly see, from the opening case, how accurate sales information is important for forecasting the impact of a critical decision. However, whether the company decides to become the exclusive wholesaler for the 'ethical' brand will also be strongly influenced by Naomi's 'gut feel'.

CASE 8.1

Beyond outdoor clothing for enthusiasts

Opened in 2007 in the Scottish Highlands, by 2016, **Kate** and **Andy Field's** specialist outdoor clothing company had grown from a single shop to a national chain of 14 stores, each situated in one of the UK's national parks (http://www.nationalparks.gov.uk). Kate and Andy, who are brother and sister, were passionate about combining top quality branded products with high-quality customer service. All the staff in the stores were experienced and trained outdoor pursuits enthusiasts. They offered expert advice to their customers who often came back for replacement and additional clothing and equipment. They had a well-earned reputation in the industry for providing good service at an affordable price.

In response to customer demands, they launched a website in 2011 to provide an easy way for their existing customers to order products. Two of the company's store managers, one with a background in IT (Anjam) and the other in fashion retailing (Naomi), volunteered to oversee this project. By 2016, online sales had increased significantly and became greater than any individual store. Anjam and Naomi relocated to Scotland to directly manage the online operations and the new warehouse built next to the first store. This warehouse supplied all their stores and dispatched the online orders.

In 2015, Kate and Andy decided to appoint Anjam and Naomi as directors, and at the beginning of 2016 they held their first strategy away day to discuss the future of the

(Continued)

(Continued)

company. They all agreed that the existing 14 stores were well established and not to expand by opening any new stores. However, they needed to find ways of growing sales to help fund the new warehouse and agreed to set a 10% increase in sales for each store and a 20% increase for online sales. The directors realised that their historical success was largely due to building a loyal customer base by providing high levels of customer service in the store.

Total store sales for 2015 could be divided into: waterproof clothing (25%), clothing (30%), footwear (20%), rucksacks (10%), and equipment (15%). For online sales these were: waterproof clothing (30%), clothing (45%), footwear (10%), rucksacks (10%), and equipment (5%). The split between men and women was consistently 60% and 40% respectively for both store and online sales. The profit margin varied depending on the category – with all clothing and rucksacks being 30%, footwear 35%, and equipment 25%. Online margins were 5% less for all categories. For 2015, the total store sales were £2,400,000 and the online sales were £1,200,000. Total store sales had increased by 10% compared to 2014 with no new stores being opened since 2013. However, online sales had increased at 20% for each of the last two years. Based on sales reports from the stores and online, Kate had prepared some sales analysis for 2015 and developed a sales forecast for 2016 for discussion (see below).

KATE AND ANDY'S SALES ANALYSIS

2015	Store	Online	Total	2016	Store	Online	Total
				Sales growth	10.0%	20.0%	13.3%
Sales (Actual)	2,400,000	1,200,000	3,600,000	Sales (Forecast)	2,640,000	1,440.000	4,080,000
Sales by category (2015)	Store	Online	Total	Sales by category (2016)	Store	Online	Total
Waterproof clothing	25.0%	300%	26.7%	Waterproof clothing	25.0%	300%	30.3%
Clothing	30.0%	45.0%	35.0%	Clothing	30.0%	45.0%	400%
Footwear	20.0%	10.0%	16.7%	Footwear	20.0%	10.0%	18.7%
Rucksacks	10.0%	10.0%	10.0%	Rucksacks	10.0%	10.0%	11.3%
Equipment	15.0%	5.0%	11.7%	Equipment	15.0%	5.0%	13.0%
	100.0%	100.0%	100.0%		1000%	100.0%	113.3%
Sales by category (2015)	Store	Online	Total	Sales by category (2016)	Store	Online	Total
Waterproof clothing	600,000	360,000	960,000	Waterproof clothing	660,000	432,000	1,092,000
Clothing	720,000	540,000	1,260,000	Clothing	792,000	648,000	1,440,000
Footwear	460,000	120,000	600,000	Footwear	528,000	144,000	672,000
Rucksacks	240,000	120,000	360,000	Rucksacks	264,000	144,000	408,000
Equipment	360,000	60,000	420,000	Equipment	396,000	72,000	468,000
Total	2,400,000	1,200,000	3,600,000	Total	2,640.000	1,440,000	4,080,000

2015	Store	Online	Total	2016	Store	Online	Total
Margin (2015)	Store	Online	Total	Margin (2016)	Store	Online	Total
Waterproof clothing	30.0%	25.0%	28.1%	Waterproof clothing	30.0%	250%	280%
Clothing	30.0%	25.0%	27.9%	Clothing	30.0%	25.0%	27.8%
Footwear	35.0%	30.0%	34.0%	Footwear	35.0%	30.0%	339%
Rucksacks	30.0%	25.0%	28.3%	Rucksacks	30.0%	25.0%	28.2%
Equipment	25.0%	20.0%	24.3%	Equipment	25.0%	20.0%	24.2%
Total	30.3%	25.3%	28.6%	Total	30.3%	25.3%	29.5%
Growth profit (2015)	Store	Online	Total	Growth profrt (2016)	Store	Online	Total
Waterproof clothing	180,000	90,000	270,000	Waterproof clothing	198,000	108,000	306,600
Clothing	216,000	135,000	351,000	Clothing	237,600	162,000	399,600
Footwear	166,000	36,000	204,000	Footwear	184,800	43,200	228,000
Rucksacks	72,,000	30,000	102,000	Rucksacks	79,200	36,000	115,200
Equipment	90,000	12,000	102,000	Equipment	99,000	14,400	113,400
Total	726,000	303,000	1,029,000	Total	798,600	363,600	1,162,200
Analysis	Store	Online		Analysis	Store	Online	
Proportion of sales	66.7%	33.3%		Proportion of sales	64.7%	35.3%	
Proportion of gross profit	70.6%	29.4%		Proportion of gross profit	68.7%	31.3%	

Note: full spreadsheet is available on the Online Resources page.

Somewhat unexpectedly, Anjam and Naomi reported that the growth of online sales was coming from new customers who had not previously purchased from a store and that their purchasing profile was different from store customers. Naomi explained that the new online customers were purchasing branded clothing, particularly non-waterproof, and that her 'gut feel' was that these were not outdoor enthusiasts but brand conscious consumers with a general interest in outdoor activities. In fact, Naomi had got Anjam to include a temporary chat room feature on the website, which had enabled her to chat with some of these customers during their shopping. Andy, who was responsible for purchasing, said that the new 'ethical' brand, introduced at the end of 20014, was selling very well and accounted for 25% of the clothing sales. Furthermore, Andy informed the board that the overseas manufacturer had approached them to become their exclusive wholesaler in the UK. This would mean supplying other small retailers, something they had never done before. They would get an increase of 5%

(Continued)

(Continued)

margin but had to agree to supply other retailers at 20% discount. It was estimated that this would only represent 25% of the sales. Time was of the essence as the manufacturer had given them two weeks to decide before they would approach another wholesaler.

The directors discussed many options but narrowed these down to two options:

1. Decline the offer to become the exclusive wholesalers for the 'ethical' brand. This would mean them purchasing off the new alternative wholesaler at a reduced margin of less than 20% rather than 27.9% (30% from store sales and 25% from online sales).

2. Accept the exclusive offer. This would mean an increased margin of 35% from store sales and 30% from online sales on 25% of clothing sales but also £105,000 of new sales to smaller retailers at 20% margin.

Both Naomi and Andy were keen to go for option 2. Naomi also suggested launching an additional website under a new trading name only selling the 'ethical' brand and targeting this at more brand conscious consumers. Kate said they should do more analysis to determine the overall impact on margin and gross profit before making a decision. She was concerned about taking on trade debtors. It was agreed to calculate the new margin and meet the following day to make a decision.

POINTS TO CONSIDER

1. Assuming option 2, what will be the margin and gross profit for the clothing category for 2016? (Assuming everything else remains the same.)

2. Assuming option 2, what will be the overall company margin and gross profit for 2016? (Don't forget to include the sales to smaller retailers.)

3. What other information is needed before making this decision? Can it be gathered within the two weeks left before the decision is made?

4. Is Naomi right to develop an additional website under a new trading name? What is the basis for this decision?

5. What could be done to reduce the risk of supplying smaller retailers?

Source: This case was written by Nigel Lockett. It is not based on a real company but draws on the commercial experience of the author.

The chapter is organised as follows: In Section 8.2, we identify the accounting information that is required in any new venture and define some key terms. There is also a brief discussion of taxation rules. Section 8.3 reviews the three most important financial statements, the profit and loss account, balance sheet, and cash flow statement. Section 8.4 considers the importance of key performance indicators, including the role of quantitative and qualitative information. In *Steve Woodford: more than just numbers* (Case 8.4), we consider the importance of both quantitative and qualitative key performance indicators. The chapter concludes with video case ⑤SAGE edge™ based on *Accounts: Lou's Challenge* (Case 8.5) to test your understanding of this chapter.

8.2 ACCOUNTING FOR YOUR VENTURE

8.2.1 Importance of business accounting

As an entrepreneur, it is essential that you have a good grasp of business accounting. While it is not essential to be an accountant or to have formal accounting qualifications, it is imperative that you can understand the figures and be aware of your current financial position. The first element to consider is profit: how is your venture going to make more money than it costs to provide the product and/or service? In order to make sensible business decisions, entrepreneurs need to know about the trading performance of their venture and be able to gauge the impact of any changes on its future performance. Financial decision-making is complex and can be affected by unforeseen changes to markets, or by the actions of customers and competitors. However, you should still try to base your decisions on the best available information, and this can only be obtained by adopting good business accounting practices. Commercial and social ventures also need accurate financial information in order to calculate their tax liabilities (Section 8.2.3), and in most cases there will be a legal requirement to submit their accounting statements. For all of these reasons, good business accounting is not simply a 'nice to have' option, but a 'must have' capability within any entrepreneurial team. In this section, we focus on profit and taxation. Cash flow, another vital area of accounting, is addressed in Section 8.3.3. We have also provided additional information on accounting and on selecting an accountant on the Online Resources page.

> **online resources** 'Gaining an understanding of business accounts and choosing an accountant'.

There are many introductory guides to business accounting and book-keeping, including Drury (2015), Kelly et al. (2016), Sangster and Wood (2015a,b), Tiffany et al. (2012) and Tracy and Barrow (2011). For advice and further readings on business plan preparation, see Chapter 2 and the Online Resources. The professional accounting associations are another useful source of information. These include the Association of Chartered Certified Accountants (ACCA) (http://www.accaglobal.com), Chartered Institute of Management Accountants (CIMA) (http://www.cimaglobal.com), Institute of Chartered Accountants in England and Wales (ICAEW) (http://www.icaew.com), and Institute of Chartered Accountants in Scotland (ICAS) (http://www.icas.org.uk). For introductions to the use of key performance indicators to manage your venture, see Parmenter (2015) and Eckerson (2010).

Most new ventures will make use of business accounting software. The function and relationship between the different accounting ledgers and modules is represented

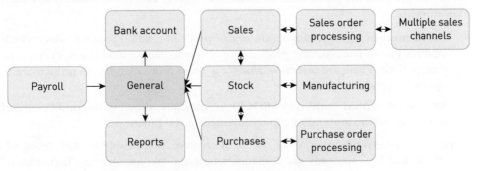

FIGURE 8.1 Simplified relationship between accounting software modules.

in Figure 8.1. At the core of any accounting system will be a sales ledger (with information about customers), purchase ledger (with information about suppliers), and a general or nominal ledger (with summary information about all sales, purchases, assets, and liabilities). It is possible to run a simple business using just these ledgers. However, as a venture grows it will need more complex invoicing and purchasing information, which can be achieved using sales order processing (SOP) and purchase order processing (POP) modules. Some businesses will hold stock and/or manufacture goods for sale, which can be supported by appropriate modules.

Accounting software tends to be country specific, although some providers, such as Oracle and SAP, provide multi-country, multi-language, and multi-currency applications (http://www.oracle.com; http://www.sap.com). In the UK, popular accounting software packages for small to medium-sized enterprises include Sage One (Start & Accounting), Live, 50 and 200 suites (http://www.sage.co.uk) and Intuit's QuickBooks Self-Employed and Small Businesses (Essentials and Plus) (https://www.quickbooks.co.uk). Choosing and implementing the right accounting software package can be difficult, and mistakes can be both costly and time consuming. Selection depends on the size and complexity of the venture. Unless you are using only entry-level or basic accounting software, it is important that you also choose a good value added reseller (VAR), who will help you install the software and configure it to your needs. Your accountants might have useful advice to give you and may even recommend packages and resellers.

8.2.2 Profit measures

You are likely to make use of some or all of the following profit measures:

- **Gross profit** A simple measure of profit obtained from the sale of goods and services; also referred to as sales profit.
- **Net profit** A measure of company performance after deducting operating expenses and interest but not taxes.
- **Operating profit** Gross profit less all operating expenses but not interest and taxes; also referred to as earnings before interest and taxes (EBIT). This can be useful for potential lenders or investors because it indicates the likely trading performance without any borrowings and highly company-specific tax calculations.

There are also a number of ways of calculating profitability. These take the form of ratios that compare the profit measure to another figure. Two of the most widely used indicators are:

- **Profit margin** A comparative indicator of profit in relation to sales value, which enables you to compare the profitability of particular product types, customers, time periods. There are several versions (e.g. gross profit margin, net profit margin, operating profit margin).
- **Return on capital employed (ROCE)** An indicator showing the profits earned in relation to the amount of capital invested in the business.

Some social enterprises may make use of alternative, but closely related, terminology. Profit and loss accounts are sometimes replaced by 'Income and Expenditure' accounts, and the term 'surplus' may be used in place of 'profit'.

8.2.3 Taxation

Having determined your expected and actual profit, it is then important to be aware how tax might affect your venture. Most people accept that we need to pay taxes in order for governments to make the necessary investments in infrastructure and public services. However, even the most responsible taxpayers are unlikely to want to pay more than their 'fair share'. In this section we consider two forms of taxation that you are likely to encounter, Value Added Tax (VAT) and various forms of company tax:

- **Value Added Tax (VAT)** VAT is added to nearly all sales made by VAT-registered businesses at levels set by government. VAT is also known as general sales tax (GST) or just sales tax. Typically, it is levied on sales made within a country or trading zone but not on export sales. The UK standard VAT rate is 20%, the reduced rate is 5%, and the zero rate is 0%. Different rates will apply to products depending on their type; for example, televisions are electrical consumer goods and charged at the standard rate (20%); heating fuel is domestic fuel and power and charged at the reduced rate (5%); fruit and vegetables are food and charged at the zero rate (0%). Rates and product types vary by country: in Finland, the standard rate of VAT was 22%, but rose by one percentage point to 23% in July 2010 and in Sweden, VAT is split into three levels with 25% being the highest rate and applied to most goods and services. An important aspect of VAT is that most VAT-registered companies charge VAT on sales, but they also have VAT added to their purchases from VAT-registered companies. Periodically (often quarterly or monthly), they calculate the net VAT by deducting the VAT charged to them from the VAT they charge to their customers. Normally this results in payments to the government, but for some new businesses and in periods of high investment this can result in payments, or credit against future payments, from the government. It is also important to include VAT in cash flow forecasting. Ultimately, VAT is paid by consumers or non VAT-registered organisations, such as charities and smaller companies with sales below a certain threshold, currently £83,000 in the UK (2016). Certain products are exempt from VAT only when certain individuals buy these products. For example, disabled people buying medical equipment. Each country has its own VAT rules for products and thresholds.

- **Company tax** As a general rule, profitable companies pay company tax, also known as corporation tax in the UK. Any losses retained from previous accounting periods can normally be offset against profits before the company tax due is calculated. Tax is worked out by taking the 'taxable profits' (net profit (see 8.2.2) plus any depreciation charges already deducted, less any capital allowances and retained losses) and applying the relevant company tax rate, say 30%. Calculating company tax can be difficult and most businesses employ a tax advisor, normally a specialist within their accountants. Even if the rate of company tax remains the same, the rules will often change over time. Governments will typically fine companies that make errors, charging interest on outstanding balances. Many small businesses are not registered as companies, preferring instead to operate as sole traders or partnerships. The advantages of being a sole trader include: easier to start up in business, fewer rules and regulations, the owner has full control, and taxes are calculated after any personal tax allowances have been deducted. However, sole traders have unlimited liability for any debts or claims, and often prefer to change status to a limited liability company (limited company) as they grow and expand their workforce. This is an important decision and needs to be researched carefully and should include taking professional advice from an accountant and solicitor.

Government taxation policies are not fixed, and changes in tax rates and related regulations can have a significant effect on businesses. You may also find yourself encountering new forms of taxation as the venture develops. For example, if you start to export products to other countries, you are likely to be charged an import duty. In some cases, high import duties can have a significant impact on profitability. You are also likely to face a variety of local taxes (e.g. rates charged on your premises and charges for waste disposal services). It can be difficult to keep track of tax changes, or to understand what they mean for your own venture. Though many entrepreneurs produce their own accounting information, they often seek professional advice on taxation. Even when the rules and guidance from government seem clear, they can remain open to interpretation. Differences of opinion over the rules can lead to costly disputes and 'test cases' (e.g. the introduction of IR35 in the UK in 2000, and other taxation issues, which are discussed on the Online Resources page).

online resources 'Examples of country specific tax policies: IR35 (UK).'

8.3 FINANCIAL STATEMENTS

8.3.1 Profit and loss

A company's profit and loss statement (sometimes referred to as the 'P&L') indicates the relationship between sales (revenue or turnover), cost of sales, gross profit, operating expenses, interest, tax, and net profit for a specific period (i.e. per month, quarter, or year). This is vital management information for directors, shareholders, and staff and needs to be produced in a timely manner. In other words, quickly enough after a period end so that decisions can be taken to maintain or improve the trading position. There is a standard format for profit and loss statements, which often includes the current and equivalent previous period (Table 8.1).

Typically, profit and loss statements are simplified so that only key information is displayed. Sales information is the total for the company or business unit rather than by customer type or segment. Expenditure is the total for a particular area, such as administration, rather than subdivisions, for example office costs, stationery, and postage. For management purposes, the profit and loss statement should indicate the general trading performance and resultant net profit or loss.

At the simplest level the profit and loss statement will include:

- income – generated by business activities but not interest received;
- cost of sales – cost of purchased good and manufactured goods (including direct manufacturing overheads and wages);
- gross profit – income less cost of goods;
- profit margin (gross profit/income × 100);
- operating expenses – overhead and staff excluding manufacturing wages;
- depreciation;
- operating profit (gross profit less operating expenses);
- interest;
- net profit (gross profit less operating expenses and interest);
- net profit before tax;

- net margin (net profit before tax/income × 100;
- corporation tax;
- net profit after taxes.

The precise structure of profit and loss statements will vary depending on the type of operation. For example, distributors typically invoice for goods delivered and will have stock or inventory, whereas service providers will invoice for staff time and have no stock holding. Stock adds an additional layer of complexity because it must be valued using a consistent method, such as FIFO (first in first out) or average valuation, and must be checked to ensure that physical stock is reconciled with computer stock lists. Manufacturing operations need to account for raw materials, finished goods, and 'work-in-progress' (with the latter including the value of parts used and the estimated staff costs for any partly completed items).

TABLE 8.1 Sample profit and loss statement

PROFIT AND LOSS STATEMENT for the year ended 31 December 2016		
Income	£	£
Sales		6,600,000
Stock at 1 January 2016	700,000	
Purchases	4,900,000	
	5,600,000	
Stock at 31st December 2016	(980,000)	
		4,620,000
Gross Profit		1,980,000
Profit Margin		30.0%
Expenditure		
Establishment expenses	160,000	
Administration	370,000	
Selling and distribution expenses	1,200,000	
Finance charges	20,000	
Total operating expenses		1,750,000
Operating profit		230,000
Net interest	30,000	
		30,000
Net profit before taxation		200,000
Net margin		3.0%
Tax	40,000	
Dividends	10,000	
		50,000
Net profit retained		150,000

Note: Full spreadsheet is available on the Online Resources page.

Depreciation is an important concept, which differentiates profit and loss statements from cash flow statements. Depreciation is simply an allowance based on the value of assets (typically equipment or vehicles), which lose actual value over time. This allowance appears in the profit and loss statement throughout the write-down period but does not appear in the cash flow statement. This is because the asset appears in the cash flow statement when it is purchased – in other words sooner! The asset's actual value is recorded in the balance sheet statement and reduces in proportion to the amount written down. To make matters more complicated, different types of assets can depreciate at different rates and in different ways. Furthermore, depreciation is not taken into consideration when calculating tax. Perhaps yet another reason to seek professional advice.

8.3.2 Balance sheet

A balance sheet statement is a summary of the financial position of the business at a specific date, such as at a month end or the year end. It shows the *balance* between the assets, liabilities, and ownership equity. The difference between assets and liabilities is net worth or net assets or, simply, equity. The net worth must equal assets minus liabilities and ownership equity. That is the 'books must balance'. Let us consider each of these in turn:

Assets The value of the company's 'worth' can be expressed in financial terms – the amount it owns or is owed – which includes:

- cash or 'cash in hand' (petty cash, current bank balance, savings account balance, and any short-term investments);
- debtors (accounts receivable from credit or trade customers);
- stock (value of an inventory valued on a consistent basis).

The most easily obtainable or redeemable assets (the most liquid) are listed first.

The total current assets is the sum of cash, debtors, and stock.

Long-term assets are listed subsequently and include plant and machinery (less depreciation since the previous year end), land, property, investments, which cannot be realised in less that one year. The sum of these is the total long-term assets.

Therefore, total assets is the total current assets plus the long-term assets. It is possible to include other assets, such as goodwill, but this is unusual and linked to 'one-off' events; for example, the purchase of a company at a price above its net worth, with goodwill representing the additional amount paid. This goodwill is then 'written off' through the profit and loss, at a rate agreed with your accountant and tax office. Goodwill cannot be introduced spontaneously to increase the asset position of a company. However, land or buildings might reasonably be 're-valued' to improve the strength of the balance sheet.

Liabilities This is the amount a company owes to other entities and includes:

- creditors (accounts payable to suppliers);
- accrued liabilities (expenses incurred but not paid for – including products, services, and wages);
- tax owed (still due – including company tax and employment-related taxes).

The total current liabilities is the sum of creditors, accrued liabilities, and tax owed.

Long-term liabilities include long-term bonds and mortgages, which are not repayable within one year. The total liabilities is the total current liabilities plus the long-term liabilities.

Owners' equity The owners' equity is the difference between the total assets and total liabilities. The ownership equity includes the share capital and retained profit or loss. The share capital can be a nominal sum, such as £100, or a substantial amount. Since the share capital cannot be withdrawn from the company, it can be used to indicate the level of commitment of the founding shareholders. In a new venture the founding directors are normally shareholders.

The owners' equity provides bankers and investors with an indicator to help determine how much it would be prudent to invest or lend to a company.

The overall balance sheet statement is correct when the total assets = total liabilities + owners' equity (Table 8.2).

8.3.3 Cash flow forecasting

In the last two sections we have seen how the profit and loss statement and the balance sheet can give us a greater understanding of an organisation's financial performance. For the profit and loss statement this is for a particular period, such as monthly or annually, while the balance sheet statement shows the picture at a specific point in time. Both statements provide vital management information, but neither tells us

TABLE 8.2 Sample balance sheet statement

SUMMARY BALANCE SHEET as at 31 December 2016		
	£	£
Fixed assets		
Tangible assets	45,000	
Investments	20,000	
		65,000
Current assets		
Stocks	980,000	
Debtors	1,410,000	
Cash at bank and in hand	110,000	
		2,500,000
Total assets		2,565,000
Creditors: amounts falling due within one year		(2,200,000)
Net current liabilities		300,000
Total assets less current liabilities		365,000
Capital and reserves		
Owners share capital	1.000	
Profit and loss account (including £150,000 for year end 31 Dec 2016)	364,000	
		365,000

Note: Full spreadsheet is available on the Online Resources page.

anything about how much money is flowing in and out of the business. This is the role of the cash flow forecast, a financial statement that predicts the movement of cash into and out of a venture over a specified period (e.g. weekly, monthly, or quarterly). In the early phases of most new ventures, there is usually a *negative cash flow*. Lots of cash is flowing out of the business in order to get it established. You may be spending money on equipment, your initial stock of materials, external advisors, and a variety of one-off purchases that you have to pay for 'up-front' (i.e. at the time of purchase) because suppliers are not yet willing to grant you credit terms. As yet there is no cash flowing back the other way, because until you are ready to trade there will be no cash generated from sales – and even when you are trading, you may have to offer credit to your customers and therefore wait to be paid. As the venture becomes established, your cash flows should begin to balance out. However, the cash flow forecast remains an important tool that can be used to identify periods when you may be short of cash. By anticipating these cash shortages well in advance, you can ensure that you have appropriate sources of funding (e.g. bank loans or overdrafts) in place to avoid a shortfall.

Running out of cash can have a catastrophic impact on any organisation, even if it is in an otherwise healthy state. A venture can be highly profitable yet find itself with insufficient cash to continue trading. New and high-growth ventures are particularly vulnerable to this problem, which is often described as 'over trading'. There are many reasons for over trading to occur, and they can often occur in combination:

- having to pay in advance for large amounts of stock to meet increased customer demand;
- offer extended credit terms to attract new customers;
- customers delaying (or refusing) payment of their invoices;
- suppliers requiring immediate payment due to the venture's limited trading record or lack of accounting statements.

The cash flow forecast is based on a number of key assumptions, which vary depending on the type and the period of the forecast. It is best to develop a simple spreadsheet so that you can vary the assumptions to see how sensitive your projections are to any changes. These include:

- Sales forecast – based on a percentage increase or decrease perhaps due to planned marketing activities or contract proposals submitted. Beware of being too optimistic about sales. It is better to report sales above your forecast than explain why you did not achieve them. Accurate sales forecasting builds confidence in your abilities and enables more positive discussions with bank managers and investors.

- Cost of sales – based on predicted profit margin. This might remain fairly consistent or vary considerably depending of mix of sales. What can be done to increase the sales of higher margin products and services?

- Payments received from customers – based on historical performance and expressed as debtor days, for example 60 days. This is a critical area to manage, particularly for new ventures. Keep a close eye on debtors, take up credit references or use credit reference agencies and be prepared to be persistent and firm. Get to know the staff responsible for payments. You have a right to the money for goods or services you have provided. Remember that any bad debt has to be replaced by the equivalent amount in net profit rather than gross profit or sales. Consider offering prompt or early payment incentives to customers but remember to include extra profit margin to compensate for this.

- Operating expenses – based on previous costs and known or expected changes due to price increases or inflation. Be prepared to negotiate with all suppliers but remember that service levels can be just as important as price.

- Staff costs usually make up the largest proportion of operating expenses for organisations. Controlling these costs is vital in maintaining profitability. Employer and employee tax relating to employment and collected by employers is presented after wages.

- Payments made to suppliers – based on historical performance and expressed as creditor days, for example 30 days. Some of your suppliers may offer you early settlement discounts and, provided you have the funds, could increase your profit margin. Try to be fair and consistent with your payments. If you have problems with payments talk to your suppliers and negotiate a payment schedule but be careful to keep to any agreement.

- Interest – based on amount of borrowing and the interest rate charged by lenders and the prevailing national bank base rate. Think carefully about securing loans using your house as collateral. Signing a 'personal guarantee' could also provide lenders with access to all your assets, including your house. Be sure to consider the risks carefully and consult all those concerned, such as your partner. Sometimes there is no option but to give a personal guarantee.

- VAT – many businesses charge VAT to their customers and are charged VAT by their suppliers. In a profitable company this will tend to result in a net VAT owed to the government. These payments should be included in your cash flow forecast. It is important to recognise this important difference compared with the profit and loss statement. Cash flow forecasts include VAT whereas profit and loss statements do not. Usually, VAT is paid monthly or quarterly. Some enterprises, such as charities or businesses with sales below a certain value, are charged VAT by suppliers but cannot charge it to their customers.

- Tax – based on employment derived tax payments and annual company tax calculations related to declared profits are reported separately. The former is included in operating expenses and paid monthly and the latter after net profit before taxes and paid annually.

The cash flow forecast should be based on the past performance and your assumptions. For shorter periods, say a month, some factors such as inflation and interest based rate changes will have limited impact. However, for longer periods these factors need to be considered very carefully. For each period, in your cash flow forecast, subtract the total cash outflow from the total cash inflow. This will result in either a surplus or deficit for that period. Add this total to the opening cash flow balance for the end of each period to give the projected balance. This enables you to see net amount of cash required, or the net surplus generated (Table 8.3).

The payments received from customers, and made to employees and suppliers, are the lifeblood of any enterprise. Even highly profitable ventures need to manage their sales ledger, purchase ledger, and payroll. In addition to this, it is prudent to establish

TABLE 8.3 Sample cash flow forecast

CASH FLOW FORECAST for 2017		QTR 1	QTR 2	QTR 3	QTR 4
Cash inflows		Jan–Mar	Apr–Jun	Jul–Sep	Oct–Dec
Sales		1,500,000	1,750,000	1,750,000	2,000,000
Purchases		1,030,000	1,200,000	1,250,000	1,400,000
Opening stock at 31 Dec 2016	980,000				
Closing stock		960,000	950,000	970,000	950,000
Gross Profit		450,000	540,000	520,000	580,000
		30%	31%	30%	29%
Net interest		10,000	10,000	15,000	15,000
Total cash inflows		1,690,000	1,810,000	2,115,000	2,115,000
(Assumes all previous period gross sales received in following period)					
Cash outflows					
Expenditure					
Establishment expenses (VAT)		40,000	50,000	50,000	45,000
Administration (VAT)		20,000	20,000	20,000	20,000
Administration wages		90,000	90,000	90,000	90,000
Selling and distribution expenses (VAT)		150,000	145,000	200,000	190,000
Selling and distribution wages		150,000	160,000	180,000	160,000
Finance charges		5,000	5,000	5,000	5,000
Total operating expenses		455,000	470,000	545,000	510,000
Operation profit		(5,000)	70,000	(25,000)	70,000
Tax paid		40,000			
Dividends paid		10,000			
VAT on sales (20%)		300,000	350,000	350,000	400,000
VAT on purchased and expenditure (20%)		248,000	283,000	304,000	331,000
VAT payments		52,000	67,000	46,000	69,000
Tatal cash outflow		1,689,000	1,843,000	1,999,000	2,121,000
(Assumes all Purchases and expenditure paid in same period)					
cash movement		1,000	(33,000)	116,000	(6,000)
Opening cash balance	110,000				
cash balance		111,000	78,000	194,000	188,000

Note: Full spreadsheet is available on the Online Resources page

mechanisms and controls regarding the processing of payments. Over 50% of all small businesses in the UK have been a victim of fraud or online crime (FSB 2009). As your new venture grows, you may need to delegate part of the authorisation of payments to trusted members of staff. Consider what checks and controls you can put in place so that all payments are processed at the appropriate time and made to the right person (Section 8.4). This is particularly important in the case of online payments, which provide additional opportunities for fraud, as the cardholder is not present. If you are unfamiliar with cash flow forecasting, it may be worth taking advice from your accountant. There are also several forecasting software applications available, and some of these can be linked to popular accounting software packages, such as the Sage 50 Forecasting module.

8.3.4 When is a venture profitable?

Having reviewed the main financial statements, we should now be in a position to answer this obvious and seemingly simple question. But how do you establish when a venture has become profitable? For a typical trading business, the simple answer might be: when it is selling goods or services at a higher price than it costs to buy them, less any other related expenditure. In other words, once you are able to calculate a net profit for the venture. However, this calculation indicates the current trading position. In the case of a newly established venture, the fact that you are trading profitably in month 12 does not take account of the month-on-month losses incurred in the previous 11 months. The measure that is used to indicate the point at which a venture moves into profit is known as the *breakeven point*. It can be measured as a point in time, and also in terms of activity (e.g. 'our breakeven sales figure is 10,000 units'). The breakeven point is a very important milestone for new ventures, and it attracts a lot of attention from banks and investors. Achieving breakeven can be satisfying, but as we have seen, it does not guarantee that your cash flow is healthy or that you are getting an adequate return on the capital invested in your business. Lastly, it is worth noting that most entrepreneurs are not simply motivated by profit (Hamilton 2000). Other factors, such as increased personal self-esteem and making a positive social impact, can also be important measures of success (Case 8.4).

Understanding the relationship between the profit and loss and balance sheet statements and the importance of managing cash flow is an important skill. In Case 8.2 *Cleaning up in business* we see how a seemingly successful business with a good level of sales and healthy profit margins can still encounter serious cash flow problems.

CASE 8.2

Cleaning up in business

In 2011, **Ludolf** founded his cleaning supplies company in Brussels, shortly after leaving his sales role at an international chemical manufacturing company. At only 25 years old, he was the youngest sales manager in the company and many of his colleagues were surprised at his decision to leave and set up his own business. The first three years were very difficult. While Ludolf brought with him all this knowledge of cleaning

(Continued)

(Continued)

chemicals and experience of sales, he knew very little about warehousing, distribution, employing people, and running a business. He had to learn quickly, not repeat mistakes twice, and use his intuition on when to trust suppliers and customers. All in all it was a steep learning curve. Ludolf's initial strategy was simple: purchase in bulk from large manufacturers, but sell locally to customers who wanted good quality products and high service levels. He was convinced that if he could deliver the product faster than his competition at the same price then people would use him. This worked for the first four years. By the end of 2014 the company had sales of €500,000 at a margin of 20%, gross profit was €100,000 and net profit before tax was €20,000. This was the first year the company made a net profit. All the profit was retained in the company to offset against €30,000 of accumulated losses from previous years.

Just at the end of 2014, his largest customer, a small group of high-quality hotels that purchased €200,000 and run by Michèle, announced it had been purchased by a large national chain of 50 hotels, which was focused on more discerning business travellers. His contract was at risk. Initially, Ludolf was hopeful as Michèle was to be employed as the buyer for the national hotel chain, itself going through a period of expansion. Michèle had always been honest with him and explained that while the national hotel chain bought some of the products he supplied, they also wanted a cheaper value range and a national delivery service. Their existing supplier had let them down, and Ludolf was given the opportunity to quote for the business. Michèle provided a summary of the products used and a budget based on a margin of 20% for branded products and 15% for the value range.

Ludolf worked hard to analyse the impact this new contract would have on his sales, margin, gross profit, operating costs, and net profit. He produced a forecast for 2015 based on his management accounts for 2014 and the summary from Michèle. With this information, he decided to submit a quotation, which was accepted by the national hotel chain provided that deliveries would start in January. Ludolf managed to speak to his bank manager briefly about the opportunity and estimated that he would need an increase in his overdraft by €25,000 to €65,000. This was agreed in principle provided Ludolf continued to match this with his own capital as equity and produced regular financial statements.

At the end of 2015, after a hectic 12 months of supplying both his existing local independent customers and the national hotel chain, Ludolf faced a number of difficult decisions. Sales to local independent customers had fallen by €100,000, but overall the turnover doubled and resulted in increased margins through greater buyer power. However, the most pressing issue was managing within his overdraft of €65,000 while paying the next month's wages. His bank manager asked to see a cash flow forecast for 2016 before agreeing to increase the overdraft further. She recommended that Ludolf speak to one of the partners of a local accountancy firm. He knew that he had been so busy running the business and had not spent enough time managing his accounts. Ludolf made an appointment to see the accountant and spent the weekend bringing his sales and purchase ledgers up to date. He produced a summary of the profit and loss for 2015 (budget against actual) and projected this forward for 2016. From the profit and loss statement the business looks successful, but he could not seem to stay within the overdraft limit of €65,000 agreed with the bank manager. Ludolf had no more capital of his own to invest in the business so was not optimistic about the bank agreeing to increase the overdraft to nearly €80,000.

QUESTIONS

1. What information should Ludolf prepare for the bank manager?

2. Should Ludolf have taken on the contract with the national hotel chain?

3. Is it important for Ludolf to have local customers? What could Ludolf have done to retain sales to his existing customers?

Sources: This case was written by Nigel Lockett. It is not based on a real company, but draws on the commercial experience of the author.

8.4 KEY PERFORMANCE INDICATORS

In addition to the normal financial statements produced as part of the management or statutory accounts there is other critical information that can give an indication of how well (or not) an organisation is performing. These are known as performance indicators or key performance indicators (KPIs). Typically these indicators have been identified by the organisation as being particularly important in achieving some short-term or long-term organisational goals. Some may be internally focused, such as the number of customer orders dispatched within 24 hours of receiving an order, or externally focused, such as the percentage of completely satisfied customers as measured by an annual survey. To be of real value, KPIs need to be measured and reported on regularly so that necessary decisions and action can be taken. Perhaps not unsurprisingly, many new ventures focus only on financial information and neglect other indicators, which can show how they are performing. The specific KPIs required will depend on the nature of the organisation, its stage of development, and the priorities of the different stakeholders. Establishing the most appropriate indicators can be challenging but is worth getting right. To measure the wrong KPIs will distract the organisation from important areas of concern, but measuring the right ones can increase an organisation's overall performance and give all staff easily understood non-confidential indicators. For example:

- An electrical equipment distributor, who supplies electrical contractors both from trade counters (where the customer collects goods) and by delivering to building sites, might be interested in the following monthly KPIs:
  - number of orders for core product lines completed in full at both trade counters and delivered;
  - number of picking errors for delivered items;
  - number of customer product complaints by supplier;
  - average order value and the number of orders required each week to break even.

- A furniture manufacturer, who makes each item to meet each customer's requirements, which are sold both through independent stores and directly to the customers, might be interested in the following monthly KPIs:

- ○ time taken from receiving order to delivery;
- ○ value of raw materials wasted at each stage of the manufacturing process. Including the cost of labour;
- ○ trends in customer requirements;
- ○ number of existing customers that order again and average time between orders;
- ○ customer complaints.

- An employment agency, supplying accountancy staff to organisations on short-term contracts, might be interested in the following monthly KPIs:
  - ○ number of staff available for immediate employment;
  - ○ average length of contract versus the skill level of the accountancy staff;
  - ○ average length of contract versus type of organisation;
  - ○ number accountancy staff who become employed by the organisation.

The number and type of KPI and frequency of measurement will vary for each organisation and sector but some generic principles apply. Performance management systems should include:

- Planning: By understanding current performance we can identify what is important to be measured and why it could improve performance.
- Measuring: Having identified the indicator we need to periodically measure it and report to decision-makers.
- Reviewing: Is any action required as a result of the KPI and is it still an appropriate indicator? Do we need to revise the KPI?

8.4.1 Quantitative vs qualitative measurement

There is an understandable attraction to relying on rigorously produced quantitative information when making difficult decisions or predictions. We seem to draw some comfort from them. Quantitative data can be easily manipulated and produce useful insights to help explain what is happening and what might reasonably continue to happen based on declared assumptions. There are relatively well-defined techniques, which people have confidence in. Bank managers and other funders rely heavily on quantitative information, which they can easily relate to their own investment or lending criteria. A good knowledge of spreadsheets can be invaluable. However, quantitative measurement has limitations. Some critical decisions can only be made if we understand both what and why something has happened.

Quantitative measurement can be useful in understanding what is happening, for example, analysis of monthly customer sales for the last 12 months. We can identify increasing and decreasing sales by product types and forecast the impact on future sales. However, this may not provide a complete understanding. Why have some products sold well and others not? We might decide to conduct a customer survey to find out more about their buying decisions. Even this might not indicate why, and we may decide to interview customers to understand their behaviour. These insights can be invaluable.

In the following *A recipe for success* case, we move beyond considering trading statements to consider an investment decision and begin to understand the basic elements of return on investment and how qualitative information can assist in making these critical decisions (Case 8.3).

CASE 8.3

A recipe for success

Growing up in the 50-year-old family food manufacturing business, making traditional pasties, served as a 'business apprenticeship' for **Alice**. When her parents wanted to retire in 2011, it seemed only natural for her to take over the running of the business. During 2016, she reflected on her first five years as the owner. Back in 2011, the company made a range of traditional pasties, a pastry case filled with seasoned meat and vegetables, and supplied its own four shops in Cornwall in the south-west of England. The company employed nine people in the factory and office and a further eight people in the shops. As a teenager, Alice worked in the factory during the summer and in the shops at weekends, but she gradually spent more time in the office setting up and running the computer accounting software. In fact, she also helped other local businesses to set up their systems and had recently completed a one-year course in business accounting at a college in London. During this year, Alice noticed the wide variety of fast food outlets, ranging from large international chains to small independent or specialist groups. She spoke to friends and visited the different types to give her some insight into the consumers' buying preferences. She noticed that people liked the predictability and price of the big chains but preferred the atmosphere and personal service of the independent outlets.

During the previous ten years, before Alice took over the business, the turnover had remained fairly constant at about £900,000 per year with the cost of manufacturing, including salaries averaging £500,000. The cost of running the shops had gradually increased from £300,000 to nearly £400,000 per year. This had resulted in net profits falling from a healthy 10% to just over 1%. Fortunately, the company had no borrowings and owned the factory and the three oldest largest shops. Alice's parents had become increasingly reluctant to make any changes to the business, particularly any that affected the people, most of whom had worked for the company for many years.

In 2011, Alice called a meeting of all the staff and explained that changes would need to be made to ensure the future of the company. She was pleasantly surprised by their reaction. Everyone seemed to know that there was a need for change but were also proud of the company's history and the quality of their traditional 'Cornish Pasty'. She was also aware that, even though she was only 25 years old, people looked to her to make the necessary decisions. Alice desperately wanted to make the right choices but decided to spend her first six months running the business just as it had been before and to deliberately work in each section of the business doing as many different jobs as possible. She also visited all the eight businesses she had helped set up accounting software in, ranging from a fashion retailer to a car repair garage. And finally she joined a regional women's business network, which met every month. She was the youngest person in the network but felt welcomed and, more importantly, that there were more experienced people she could discuss her challenges with.

By the start of 2011, Alice was ready to implement her plan for the business. She decided to leave the factory almost unchanged apart from replacing the old and unreliable baking oven at a cost of £200,000. This was the first investment in the factory for over 15 years, and the news was received very well. The factory staff were all too aware of the problems of the old oven. The new oven had twice the output of the previous one and produced a more consistent product finish. Alice also invested another £100,000

(Continued)

(Continued)

in generally improving the interior of the factory, which looked like a historic building from the outside and appeared on the town's tourist literature. The shops fared less well from the new business plan. Alice decided to close the rented shop and sell the oldest and most profitable shop for £600,000. The decision to close the rented shop was relatively easy as it was loss making and the current manager wanted to retire. However, selling the oldest shop was far from popular with the staff and also her parents. In hindsight, Alice recognised this was an important turning point for her. She had to stand up to the pressure from staff and her parents by asserting her authority as the managing director. But why had she made this decision and was it the right one?

The key to understanding this comes from appreciating Alice's strategy. Her vision for the company was built on both the tradition and quality of their 'Cornish Pasty' – what Alice called their 'brand'. She had a two-stage business plan that would take three years and involve closing two shops, selling the oldest shop, investing in the factory, and redeveloping the two largest shops to include a café and hot food takeout facility. To do this the company would need to use all the proceeds from the sale of the shop apart from £100,000, which would be used as a reserve against any losses. The key was to complete the changes to the factory and refurbishment of the shops in the four-month 'low season'. The second part of Alice's strategy was to build the 'brand' value of the business. To help do this she employed a public relations company, owned by Colette, another member of the regional women's network. Alice trusted Colette's judgement and valued her extensive experience working for national corporate clients. Rather than advertising their products to potential local customers, they decided to focus on building the reputation by entering food competitions, promoting in regional newspapers, and developing their website with more about the history, vision, and product. By the end of 2009, Alice wanted to be in a position to expand the business by supplying products to other retail outlets. She identified three potential channels, namely:

1. regional supermarket chain with 20 medium-sized stores;

2. national chain of truck fuel stations, which had recently redeveloped to include facilities to provide hot food to take away;

3. specialist food wholesaler, which delivered to independent cafes in London.

The factory was nearing 70% utilisation and had enough space for another new oven.

Alice had to decide which channels to supply and what the impact on the factory would be. She was very reluctant to borrow money, even to purchase equipment, but she could not supply all the potential new customers without borrowing. To make things more complicated, her most entrepreneurial shop manager had identified a potential new shop for sale at a popular tourist destination nearby and was keen to develop it.

QUESTIONS

1. Alice appears to have made a successfully transformation of the business. Why should she consider expanding the operations by supplying new markets?

2. What additional financial information does she need for each of the three options?

3. What qualitative information would be useful and how could it be obtained?

Sources: This case was written by Nigel Lockett. It is not based on a real company, but draws on the commercial experience of the author.

The *Steve Woodford: more than just numbers* case (Case 8.4) explores the importance of both financial and non-financial reporting in a charity. In addition, there is a video case available on **SAGE** edge™ (Case 8.5 *Accounts: Lou's Challenge*). This video case is based on an interview with an entrepreneur, Lou, wanting to expand her successful café business. Watch the video and decide which option you think Lou will choose. You might find it useful to discuss the case with friends or colleagues before deciding. Please note that lecturers can have access to the video which reveals the actual decision taken by the entrepreneur.

SUMMARY

- Having a good understanding of business accounting is a critical capability if you are creating and running a new venture.

- Financial measures, including gross profit, net profit, and profitability indicators such as profit margins can be used to interpret and to improve your financial performance.

- Tax matters: it is essential to understand the tax implications of your decisions and it can sometimes be worth seeking professional advice.

- Whether you produce your own financial statements or outsource the task to an accountant, a good understanding of profit and loss, balance sheet, and cash flow statements will help you understand your enterprise.

- There are many accounting software packages available. Selecting the right software and the right provider or value added retailer (VAR) are both important.

- Key performance indicators, both quantitative and qualitative, can be used to inform your decision-making.

CASE 8.4

Steve Woodford: more than just numbers

In 2009, **Steve Woodford** knew that the charity he had founded, 25 years previously, to provide support to homeless people, needed to better understand the real impact they were having on 'social exclusion'. As the Chief Executive, he had seen the venture (**Foundation**) grow to employ over 330 staff and a turnover of more than £12 million. However, funding was getting increasingly harder to win. Steve knew they needed to be significantly more competitive. He also knew that they would have to rigorously demonstrate that they provided value for money and the impact they were having on their clients and customers. But how could they actually measure this? Steve also has to prepare for his retirement and handing over to a new Chief Executive.

BIOGRAPHY

Growing up on a farm in rural Suffolk seemed an idyllic way to spend a childhood. However, being the son of a tenant farmer was far from secure, as Steve recalled, 'When I was about six or seven we were forced off the farm.' But his father was nothing if not enterprising, 'He became a teacher and he still grew all the rhubarb for his Suffolk

(Continued)

(Continued)

District Council schools ... I would be employed in the early hours of the morning to go and pick rhubarb or strawberries.' Steve's father had a strong faith and had been a conscientious objector during the Second World War. Perhaps not surprisingly, Steve felt this inspired him and convinced him that he 'wanted to make a difference in the world'.

He decided to go to university and do a social science degree, which included placements with voluntary agencies, local authorities, and social services. Steve recalled one placement in a women's hostel for prostitutes and homeless with mental health problems: 'Being thrust into the centre of Soho [London] it was fascinating and was definitely a watershed for me ... the induction process included spending five days living rough in London with no more than 25p and an emergency telephone number. That is not the sort of induction we would be allowed to do these days!' He remembered the resilience of the people and, 'How much people who have nothing are willing to share ... it is a principle that has stuck with me ever since, that every individual you meet, whatever the circumstances they are in, has almost limitless potential.' Steve finished his degree, working within the probation and prison service in Preston prison and graduated as a probation officer. He worked for three years in the job and recalled, 'A lot of the people I was working with had very few educational opportunities, very disruptive family experiences and there was an injustice about the way that resources were allocated across our society. I wanted to spend my time doing something about creating a better balance, creating more opportunities for individuals who might well have fallen through the net, rather than work for an enforcement agency that tended to "blame" individuals.

'What I actually did was disappear off to the South of France with a young family and a VW camper van!' Steve recalled. 'When I came back I wanted to be involved in something that changed the surroundings of the individuals ... I was still very committed to social justice, supporting people to achieve their potential but I believed that was more achievable by providing housing, jobs and education opportunities by which they could pull themselves up.

In 1978, Steve started running a ten-bed young person's hostel for a voluntary organization in Leeds. He formed two strong partnerships, one was with the council's housing department, to help get people out of the hostel as quickly as possible and into their own accommodation, and the other with the probation office, so that they could work together to deal with crime related issues. Steve remembered, 'This was very formative, in the sense that the whole way that we work now, 25 years later on, is based on this trust ... we still operate around partnerships. You can't do everything yourself, you need other people to be involved in providing the resources that your customers need.'

HOUSING AS A BUILDING BLOCK

'Housing is like a basic building block. Somebody can't have self-esteem or certainly any confidence unless they have got some of their basic needs met ... they need shelter and the chance to make something of themselves. Having said that, my experience has often been that a lot of young people don't necessarily realise what an opportunity that is and will continue to actually make mistakes.' Steve also stressed that, 'One of the things that I have been very keen on, is that people can come back to us. They can fail and come back.'

By 1983, Steve wanted to form a charity to: 'Work out innovative and different ways of trying to solve what was then called "social exclusion". We were looking at homeless people around the city centre who were a nuisance rather than high-level criminals ... it was relatively straightforward to get the commitment from housing, local authority and probation to say, "Well instead of always having these people round a revolving door off into court, or to prison for seven days and out again, why don't we do something more sensible with them?"'

After five years of running the voluntary hostel in Leeds, Steve rejoined the probation service. He recalled, 'I had always vowed I would never go back! ... but a very vision-ary senior person within probation basically brought me into the service because he wanted this to happen on a broader basis.'

By forming a separate charity, Steve was able to get new funding. He developed two roles: 'In those early days, I used to play off being a probation officer, firmly in the statutory sector one day, with being a charity the next. Basically, it worked a treat ... I look back now and it obviously was a business that could deliver added value to key partners as well as impacting on the individuals themselves.'

STEVE'S NEW VENTURE

Recognising that finding innovative ways of solving problems in partnership with others was a new business model that could best be exploited, as a charity or social enterprise, outside of the public sector, was an important moment. Steve recalled, 'The mission in my mind wasn't called ending "social exclusion". It was around creating opportunities for individuals who at that moment had fewer opportunities or who had taken wrong moves in their lives and wanted to get them back on track by collaborating with other organisations.' Steve gave an example: 'The housing department, despite having empty flats, didn't really want to let them out to these guys because they could be a bloody nuisance and upset the neighbours and they would never quite get themselves sorted and they might be drinkers or have other problems. We'd go along to the housing department and say, "Don't worry. Don't give the tenancy directly to them. Give to us." We would sign up the tenancy agreement, we sublet to the individual and gave them the appropriate support to try and help them to make it. If they didn't, we moved them on.'

In 2003, the government introduced a completely new funding mechanism for com-munity services called 'Supporting People'. Steve recalled, 'There was a kind of market before but generally things weren't competitively tendered ... we had always prided ourselves on high-quality service. But we were having to become more competitive by looking at much more rationalisation around overheads, office costs and local manage-ment ... we also had to maintain high level links to strategic networks within the local authorities who were commissioning us. So, we had a complete restructure. Like a lot of organisations our management structure had grown organically, I guess it was somewhat out of hand and we just put a line right through it and established our man-agement for the future. We called this our "future-proofing" and the Board provided an allowance of £250k for shedding staff following a rigorous assessment centre process.'

By 2009 and after 25 years in existence, the charity had grown significantly to an annual turnover in excess of £12 million and employed over 300 highly skilled staff. A healthy surplus of £432,000 was generated in 2009, and there were net assets of

(Continued)

(Continued)

nearly £2 million. At any one time, there were over 3,000 clients being supported a year with 812 supported tenancies. Steve was also increasingly keen to understand the real impact of their activities, not just the financial ones.

PASSING ON THE BATON

In 2012, having established the key performance indictors and annual customer survey for the charity, Steve decided to retired. In 2013, **Maggie Jones** joined as its new Chief Executive. She, knew that the charity needed to better understand the real impact they were having on creating *inclusive communities where everyone matters*'. Maggie gained a degree in Communications Studies before doing a Masters in Applied Social Policy and becoming qualified as a social worker in 1986. She had over 30 years' experience within the statutory and voluntary sectors and immediately before joining Foundation, Maggie was formerly Chief Executive of Children England. Maggie said, "I have worked and volunteered in the charitable sector for over 30 years and continue to be amazed and inspired by the difference dedicated people make in their communities every day. We need to find new and better ways of supporting them because we need their creativity, passion and commitment more than ever."

Just as Steve had done before her, Maggie continued to report financial information, key performance indicators and customer satisfaction each year in order to demonstrate value for money and the impact they were having on clients and customers (see below the information published in 2016).

Summary Income & Expenditure statement for the year ended 31 March 2015

Income	2015 (£000)
Rents & service charges	4,696
Supporting People Income	8,736
Other social housing activties	367
Non social housing activities	502
	14,301
Expenditure	
Governance Costs	135
Other Operating costs	11,557
Interest receivable and other income	30
Actuarial Loss relating to the pension deficit	(41)
	11,692
Revenue Surplus for the Year	77
SUMMARY BALANCE SHEET as at 31 March 2015	
Fixed Assets	720
Current Assets	2,752
Less Current Liabilities	(1,396)
Net current assets	1,356
Net assets	2,076
Funds	(9)
Restricted Income Funds	737
Designated Funds	1,348
General Funds	2,076

Key performance indictors from Impact Report 2015/16

- 816 Customers gained new settled accommodation
- 1,161customers maximised their income
- 561 customers managed their debts better
- 115 of our customers secured paid work
- 263 of our customers took up education and training
- 76% of our customers left the service registered with a dentist
- 97% of our customers left the service registered with a GP
- 590 of our customers were helped to stay safe
- 655 of our customers managed their physical health better
- 24% of our customers left the service currently involved in a club, society or other community activity
- 96% of our customers left the service with a bank or post office account
- 83% of our customers left the service with regular access to the Internet
- 49% of our customers left the service registered to vote
- 41% of our customers left the service using a local library
- 708 customers managed their mental health better
- 557 of our customers were supported to improve the management of their substance misuse
- 474 of our customers complied fully with their statutory court orders
- 16% of our customers who left the service had either been charged with an offence or been in prison within the last six months (a reduction from 42% on entry to our services)
- 84% of our customers had a planned move on from our support and accommodation

Customer Survey 2016

Source: This case is primarily based on an interview with Steve Woodford and was written by Nigel Lockett.

Practical activities

1. **Sales analysis** For each of the different types of company, namely: grocery supermarket, fashion retailer, petrol station, coal merchant, describe between three and six categories of sales they might make. Discuss the likely difference in sales and profit margin. How might VAT be different for each company and category?

2. **Business accounting** For each of the different types of company, namely: (i) mail order catalogue company (selling gifts), (ii) management consultancy, (iii) car gear box manufacturer, and (iv) social landlord providing housing for rent, describe the similarities and differences in the following terms:

    (a) gross profit;

    (b) net profit;

    (c) short-term assets;

    (d) long-term assets.

3. What are the three most popular accounting software packages for small businesses? How much do they cost? What do the systems offer? What training is available?

Discussion topics

1. **Key performance indicators** Any enterprise needs to manage its finances but there might be other non-financial information that could indicate how well a company is doing. How would you set up the following:

    (a) An annual customer satisfaction survey for a management consultancy.

    (b) A system to monitor picking errors in a clothing mail-order company and to calculate the financial cost to the company.

    (c) A 'total quality' measure which includes five different performance measures for a train operating company.

2. **Choosing an accountant** You have decided to start your new office supplies company and need to find an accountant. You produce a shortlist of three. One recommended by your new bank manager, one by a family friend, and one you

meet at a business networking event. You have arranged to see each for one hour before deciding which accountancy firm to appoint. What questions would you ask and how would you differentiate between the answers? What other factors would influence you? Having selected one, what else could you do to reassure yourself?

Recommended reading

These readings address important topics in entrepreneurship research and are recommended for anyone wanting to build on the material covered in this chapter. Recommended readings have been selected from leading Sage journals and are freely available for readers of this textbook to download via the Online Resources.

Esparza-Aguilar, J. L., García-Pérez-de-Lema, D. and Duréndez, A. (2015) 'The effect of accounting information systems on the performance of Mexican micro, small and medium-sized family firms: an exploratory study for the hospitality sector'. *Tourism Economics*, 22, 5: 1104–20.

This study analyses how the implementation of accounting and financial information and management control systems affect the performance of family and non-family micro, small and medium-sized enterprises in the hospitality sector in Mexico.

Brijlal, P., Enow, S., Eslyn, B. H., Isaacs, E. B. H. (2014) 'The use of financial management practices by small, medium and micro enterprises: a perspective from South Africa'. *Industry and Higher Education*, 28, 5: 341–50.

This investigation found that more than half of firms examined use external accounting staff to prepare accounting reports and more than 60% rely on external accounting staff to interpret and use accounting information. A majority of the owners were found to lack interpretation skills and an awareness of how to use information from financial statements.

Barbera, F. and Hasso, T. (2013) 'Do we need to use an accountant? The sales growth and survival benefits to family SMEs'. *Family Business Review*, 26, 3: 271–92.

This article explores the relationship between the usage of an external accountant and family firm sales growth and survival on Australian small and medium-sized family enterprises. In finds that external accountants have a positive impact on sales growth and survival.

References

Drury, C. (2015) *Management and Cost Accounting* (9th edn). Florence, KY: Cengage Learning.

Eckerson, W. W. (2010) *Performance Dashboards: Measuring, Monitoring, and Managing Your Business* (2nd edn). Chichester: John Wiley & Sons.

Finch, B. (2016) *How to Write a Business Plan (Creating Success)* (5th edn). London: Kogan Page Ltd.

FSB (2009) *Inhibiting Enterprise: Fraud and Online Crime against Small Businesses*. London: Federation of Small Businesses.

Hamilton, B. H. (2000) 'Does entrepreneurship pay? An empirical analysis of the returns to self-employment'. *Journal of Political Economy*, 108, 3: 604–30.

Kelly, J., Barrow, P., and Epstein, L. (2016) *Bookkeeping for Dummies* (4th edn). Chichester: John Wiley & Sons.

Parmenter, D. (2015) *Key Performance Indicators: Developing, Implementing, and Using Winning KPIs* (3rd edn). Chichester: John Wiley & Sons.

Sangster, A. and Wood, F. (2015a) *Frank Wood's Business Accounting 1* (13th edn). Harlow: FT Prentice Hall.

Sangster, A. and Wood, F. (2015b) *Frank Wood's Business Accounting 2* (13th edn). Harlow: FT Prentice Hall.

Tiffany, P., Peterson, S., and Barrow, C. (2012) *Business Plans for Dummies* (3rd edn). Chichester: John Wiley & Sons.

Tracy, J. and Barrow, C. (2011) *Understanding Business Accounting for Dummies*. Chichester: John Wiley & Sons.

9

FINANCES: RAISING CAPITAL FOR NEW VENTURES

Pecunia, si uti scis, ancilla est; si nescis, domina – If you can use money, money is your servant; if you can't, money is your master.

Old Roman proverb at a tablet found in Verona

The only function of economic forecasting is to make astrology look respectable.

John Kenneth Galbraith, economist and diplomat

LEARNING OUTCOMES

After reading this chapter you should be able to:

- Appreciate the role of raising capital and securing investment in new venture creation.
- Understand the different types of capital and investment and their sources.
- Understand how to obtain different types of capital and investment.
- Appreciate the need to consider raising capital and securing investment as part of forecasting and planning.

9.1 INTRODUCTION

This chapter considers a fundamental prerequisite to establishing a successful new venture, namely, borrowing capital or raising investment. Without financial resources, a new venture will not be able to obtain the resources and trade to exploit their business idea – no matter how good it is. In this chapter, we will consider the sources of finance, from founders, family and friends, through borrowing from banks to securing equity investments. Each is considered in turn, but this should not be seen as a linear process from one point to another. In reality, borrowing capital and securing investment will vary depending on the type of company, growth rate, historical trading performance, balance sheet, market sector, forecasts, existing shareholders, and the aspirations of the founders and directors. Companies may also have multiple sources of capital and investment at any one time, for example, there may be a limited amount of initial capital from the founding shareholders, a loan from a bank or crowdfunding platform to purchase manufacturing equipment and investment from a business angel. All will have different expectations. The bank will want regular capital and interest payments against a legal contract, whereas the business angel might expect dividends (and contribute to the business strategy), based on distributing retained profit and growth in their original investment when all or part of the company is sold or floated on a stock exchange. Getting this balance right is critical.

→ **PERSPECTIVES** See Section 11.1 for further information.

So, there are broadly three ways of raising finance for your business: (i) founders, friends, and family (bootstrapping), (ii) debt (borrowing), or (iii) equity (raising investment by selling shares). Debt can be obtained by overdrafts, loans, leasing, and invoice discounting. You will pay interest on debt. Raising equity finance from investors will require selling shares in your business to investors who will make a return through dividends and any sale of shares. Selling shares can change the nature of your business and ultimately lead to you losing control. Because returns for shareholders are linked to the financial performance of the company, it can help reduce the cost of finance and bring in outside expertise. However, some entrepreneurs are negative about selling shares to venture capitalists (Delmar 2000). Globally, the amount of money needed to start a business fell from $65,000 in 2006 to $13,000 by 2015 – perhaps 'indicating a willingness to start a business with fewer resources and the capability to do so, thanks to the influence of the Internet' (GEM 2016). Unsurprisingly, the average initial funding requirements varies considerably between global regions with North American ($18,673) and European ($17,221) entrepreneurs requiring the highest amount and Latin American only requiring $2,606 (GEM 2016).

It is also important to remember that the return from a venture could be both financial and social.

The opening case, *'Bruce Macfarlane'* (Case 9.1), gives the perspective of an experienced business angel, venture capitalist, and investment fund manager. It certainly goes some way to dispel the myth that venture capitalists are only focused on maximising their returns. His company has limited investment funds of over £70 million. Bruce stated, 'We get up to 800 business plans a year. From these we back only three or four a year, partly due to just simple resource limitations because this is incredibly labour intensive. Not just the sifting through and the due diligence but after we have invested there is an enormous amount of input and hand-holding that goes on with a growing company. A big issue, as a venture capitalist, is missing the deal that is actually going to blow the lights out. Although we are generalists we do focus very much on companies where we think they can grow faster than the niche they are operating in. So we like growth sectors, such as healthcare, technology and financial services. It all becomes part of the DNA.'

CASE 9.1

Bruce Macfarlane

After a successful career in corporate finance and many years' experience as a business angel, **Bruce Macfarlane** reflects on the first decade of running his hybrid venture capital firm, which manages over £70 million of funds, a portfolio of 20 investments, and a strong syndicate of business angel investors.

HYBRID VENTURE CAPITAL FIRM

'I started in venture as a business angel. Our heritage in this firm is as a group of business angels. What we discovered was, firstly, that the deal flow was completely haphazard: it depended on somebody hearing of something. Secondly, everybody was far too busy to do proper due diligence. We all had day jobs and no time to structure the deals or impose proper legals.' Bruce along with his two founding partners decided there was an opportunity to bring business angels together more professionally.

'Our idea was that we would have an engine room of professionals who would track the deals, sift them, structure them, do the due diligence and the business angels would provide the money. But the business angels would also provide additional resources because they would often make their network of contacts available and help the new ventures get into big companies to sell their products. They could also help with strategic input and valuable mentor type capital.

'Now, we manage £70 million and are growing all the time. Whether you are an angel or a venture capitalist, the truth is that you are backing companies at a fragile stage in their development. You are putting in true equity and have to be prepared to help them as they grow. They almost invariably have gaps on their boards and in the management team and their finance function is often weak. They need advice on how to go international, to grow by direct sales or with resellers. These decisions may be a problem for a large company if they go wrong but for a small company can be absolutely fatal.

'We are very cautious about that larger capital that can wipe out the earlier investors. What it means, in our case, is that we are not going to put money into a business unless we can get it to profitability. That is a very good reason for bringing in other investors alongside you. Once a company is profitable its choices of raising more money are much greater. It is a guiding principle for us. We will often come in where there are already existing business angels. Our team tightens up the documentation and drives the company forward. We have standard documentation and shareholder agreements. We actually have a page of "what we expect from management" and "how we want to operate". This is operating on a basis of complete disclosure on both sides so there are no surprises'.

A LEAP OF FAITH

'The numbers [financials] should tell you how big the market opportunity is and what percentage of it they can realistically win. We have made mistakes: we backed a software business that provided a very clever enterprise solution for mobile phone retailers. The founder had got the software developed very cheaply abroad so the product was priced to sell. What we didn't do properly was assess the market opportunity. The market just wasn't that big. Even if they got 50% it was never going to be that interesting. You have to get a sense of how big the market is. How do you do this? Some entrepreneurs have come from the market and know it inside out; others, who have not come from the market, go out there and talk to the market. I suspect there are few successful entrepreneurs who started out just with the aim of making a stack of money and then came up with an idea. It is far more likely they had some intuitive experience first. I don't think we have ever backed a business where there is no competitor. There is always some sort of competition'.

(Continued)

(Continued)

GETTING A RETURN FOR YOUR MONEY

'Planning the exit at the outset is essential. We have to have a common understanding of where we are going with the business at the time we invest – we sit down with the entrepreneur and agree the timeline, the likely end-buyer and how we can achieve optimal value. The funny thing is that almost all the business plans we see say exit three years down the road but that is usually very optimistic for an early stage business. The average is about five or six years. When we invest in the business we think about exit. In fact, when we write our investment paper, there is a whole section on how we are going to get out and what sort of multiple [return on investment] we can expect to get. Fundamentally, you have to gain the trust of the founder(s). We only succeed and make money if the entrepreneur does. One issue is that the management team is typically diluted as more capital is raised because they do not have the funds to take up their rights. It is essential to keep them incentivised and we ensure that by retaining an option pot for management. Unless it is going to be a really big business you know the entrepreneurs are not going to want to come down much below 10%.'

LOOKING TO THE FUTURE

'Firstly, I think it costs so much less to start a business today than it did even ten years ago. The barriers to starting a business have come down which is tremendously exciting. You can outsource virtually everything and can focus on what is core to your proposition. Secondly, we don't see failure as a serious problem. We actually like people who have tried and it hasn't worked out. An entrepreneur who is self-aware and has learned on from their experiences is by far the most interesting entrepreneur. We are seeing many more talented young people wanting to join small businesses. I think this is very positive. We are seeing this more than ever before and the quality has definitely been going up.'

POINTS TO CONSIDER

1. What are the similarities and differences between business angels and venture capitalists?
2. How has Bruce Macfarlane developed his investment company to include the 'best' elements of business angel and venture capitalist investments?
3. Why would a new venture prefer a trade investor rather than a business angel or a venture capitalist?

Source: This case is mainly based on an interview with Bruce Macfarlane and was written by Nigel Lockett.

There are three further cases in this chapter: The second, *Three of a kind* (Case 9.2), considers sources of early funding for new ventures used by three very different companies: an IT communications provider, a fast food business, and an ethical clothing company. Case 9.3, *The big investment issue*, investigates the growth of alternative investment funds, which explicitly look for both financial and social returns.

The *Professor Neil Meredith: invention, product, and business* case (Case 9.4), draws on an interview with a leading medical academic who became the founder of a rapidly growing international dental implants company. Having successfully grown the venture, he now faces the challenges of leadership for the next stage of growth. The chapter concludes with a video case ⦿SAGE edge™ based on *Finances: Pete's challenge* (Case 9.5) to test your understanding of this chapter.

The next section considers a number of types of capital for new ventures, namely: founders, family, and friends (informal capital), borrowing (formal capital), and equity investment. In the subsequent section three sources of finance (banks, business angels, venture capitalists and crowdfunding) are compared before considering additional capital and investment available to trading businesses (factoring, trade investment, and flotation). The final section looks at the possible returns of enterprise.

9.2 TYPES OF CAPITAL AVAILABLE FOR NEW VENTURE CREATION

9.2.1 Founders, family, and friends

Investment by founders, family, and friends plays a vital and often unrecognised part in new venture creation. A total of $600 billion was invested in 2006 in the 27 countries participating in a GEM study. This compares with less than $40 billion provided by venture capitalists (GEM 2007; 2016). The founders of a business will often try to fund their new venture with their own money, on average representing over 62% in 2006 and 72% in 2015 of the start-up capital needed (GEM 2016). This can be attractive because they believe in the business idea and it can show their commitment to other potential investors. Typically, this initial investment will come from savings and borrowing. The latter might be secure on a property or unsecure on a personal guarantee. Credit cards are an important and often unrecognised source of capital, albeit an expensive one. Balancing multiple credit card debt can be challenging but has the attraction of flexibility and easy access.

Dominic List (see Case 9.2) mentions this as a source of his initial funding. As Bruce Macfarlane (Case 9.1) stated, 'The first place an entrepreneur should go to for finance is friends and family, that is the typical route. He should also see his bank manager. We tend to see businesses when they have already been down that route and are looking for their first £1 or £2 million. We are quite clear that we will invest very early on, often pre-revenue. But we would expect to see the individuals put in some of their own money. We would expect to see them have that kind of commitment to growing the business.'

Having exhausted their personal sources of funding, entrepreneurs will often turn to family and friends (Wingborg and Landström 2000; Ebben and Johnson 2006). This is often referred to as bootstrapping. These informal investors will often settle for lower returns than more formal investors, such as business angels (GEM 2007; 2016). Bruce Macfarlane (see Case 9.1) states, 'The first place an entrepreneur ... should go to for finance is friends and family.' This might even be before any bank is approached for loans. It can certainly help the case of bank lending if funds are available from founders, family, and friends.

Ben Taylor's development of an online tool for nightclubs to promote and sell tickets for their events required his father to secure an application for a £15,000 bank overdraft. Six months later, his father also invested £25,000. Ben's business, Fatsoma (http://www.fatsoma.com), was founded in 2006. In three years it had sales of over £2 million and generated a profit. Having an experienced entrepreneur in the family can be an added bonus and provide useful support and mentoring.

Once this type of very personal capital (founders, family, and friends) is gathered, the new venture may also need to access more formal types of funding by either borrowing capital or raising investments (equity). It is worth noting that family and friends often invest in the person rather than the business idea. And should the business idea be unsuccessful, not only is the investment put at risk but so too are the personal relationships.

There is often an additional source of unrecognised funding for small businesses, which may not be available to new start-ups, namely trade credit. Once a business has a track record, suppliers will look more favourably on providing a trade or credit account.

9.2.2 Borrowing

Banks provide most of the capital borrowed by businesses. They are a vital type of financing for new ventures. As they do not normally take a shareholding or have an equity investment in the business, they require any capital to be repaid and charge interest. This interest might be charged at variable (base rate plus a fixed amount, say 2%) or a fixed rate. A number of variants have emerged in recent years, such as capped rates, which limit the lower and/or higher rates charged. It is important to remember that the bank assesses the risk and their return when calculating rates and each bank will have different policies on this. Banks will normally charge a fee for arranging financing and annually for agreeing overdrafts.

Unsecured borrowing The most used form of unsecured borrowing is credit card debt. Recent US research on new businesses indicates that the majority (65%) of small firm borrowing, typically less than $35,000, is on credit cards (Shane 2009). Credit cards are appealing to small businesses because they are easy to use, can streamline payments, are easier to get than bank borrowing, widely accepted, and an anonymous source of funding, which requires no explanation to the lender. However, credit card debt is more expensive than other formal borrowing – averaging around 15%. In spite of this, they remain popular, with nearly 60% of new businesses using them to fund approximately a third of their debt in their first year (Scott 2009).

An overdraft linked to a current bank account facility remains the most popular method of funding trading activities. It is borrowing at a variable rate with an agreed limit. Typically, this limit is agreed each year, and an arrangement fee is charged. It tends to be used for day-to-day expenses rather than purchasing expensive items of equipment or machinery. Once arranged, it is flexible and there is no penalty for not using it. However, the bank can charge for unauthorised exceeding of the overdraft limit, and in some circumstances, banks may want security from business assets.

Some governments provide loan guarantee schemes for small businesses that meet certain criteria, for example, in the US the Small Business Administration offers SBA Express programmes (http://www.sba.gov) and in the UK the British Business Bank's Enterprise Finance Guarantee scheme (http://british-business-bank.co.uk).

The Enterprise Finance Guarantee (EFG) scheme was a response to the 'credit crunch' in 2009 and by 2017 had supported £2.8bn of finance to more than 26,000 smaller businesses in the UK. Governments intervene because supporting viable small businesses helps to generally increase productivity and job generation. Recent research supports this view by finding that cost-benefit analysis shows that the overall benefits outweigh the cost to the economy and other economic benefits include growth in sales growth, exports, and jobs. Firms that use this scheme are 6% more likely to export, 17% more likely to use new technology, and 24% more likely to use 'cutting edge technology' than similar borrowing firms (Cowling 2010). However, such a scheme can be bureaucratic and time consuming to set up.

Credit cards do not often require the entrepreneur or small business owner to provide security in the form of company assets or personal guarantees. This makes them popular with borrowers but a cause of concern for lenders, even though the interest rates charged may be higher than secured loans. This is a topical area of entrepreneurship research in the United Sates and Europe (e.g. Europe: Hernández-Cánova and Koëter-Kant 2008; Italy: Howorth and Moro 2006; Spain: Jiménez et al. 2006). In 2016, credits cards were the fourth most popular financing choice for US small businesses (behind personal and family, retained profits and bank loans) and provided about 7% of all capital for start-ups (SBA 2016).

Secured borrowing Banks make their money by lending to people and businesses. Tried and tested structures and procedures support this activity, which requires the bank to take a calculated risk against the likelihood of making a net return greater than other forms of investment. This net return is based on the difference between the interest payments they receive against the interest payments they make for accessing funds. The return has also to include deductions for any write-offs for bad loans. Banks reduce these write-offs by carrying out credit checks, developing risk assessment methods, and taking securities against assets.

Obtaining a loan secured against assets tends to be cheaper and easier to obtain than equity finance and you retain control of your business. However, banks like to see a track record in business and may require regular financial information.

Typically, borrowing is secured against property. This might be to purchase the property itself or equipment. It can be helpful to link the security to the item being purchased. If the property being used is a home, it is imperative to consult with anyone affected by this guarantee.

Capital equipment, machinery, and vehicles can also be purchased by specialist loans. These include hire purchase (HP) where you own the asset at the end of the agreement and leasing where you might have the option to purchase the asset at the end of the agreement. HP requires the capital value of the item to be depreciated through the profit and loss account but is not allowable against taxes. Leasing, like rental charges, are deductible in full. For enterprise with stock, whether purchased or manufactured, banks may consider lending and taking these as security.

Banks will seek to have 'first charge' over any assets. This means that in the event of a default, the lender will have legal ownership of the asset, and other secured and unsecured lenders will only receive funds if there is a surplus. In practice, these legal charges are most relevant to property-based securities and in the case of receivership government debts must be cleared first.

9.2.3 Equity

Establishing your business as a limited company allows for the sale of equity (shares) to external investors. This could be used to bring in a new director/shareholder, capital, or a 'private equity' investment firm. Private equity funds are invested, in exchange for a stake in your company, with the investors getting future returns that are dependent on profitability or the growth in value. More often than not they will be looking to invest in growing entrepreneurial businesses. In this instance, the purpose of selling shares is to increase the capital of the firm and possibly bring in new expertise rather than for existing shareholders to make personal gains. There are a number of bodies who can provide this form of investment, such as seed funds, business angels, and venture capitalists.

Case 9.2 brings the different strands of this discussion together in a study of early stage funding and how it worked in practice for three ambitious entrepreneurs.

CASE 9.2

Three of a kind? Sources of early stage funding

Raising the initial capital to start a new venture is one of the first challenges an entrepreneur faces. Dominic List, Amina Ansir, and Penny Jones each had a good business idea and managed to launch them but raised capital by different means.

When **Dominic List** appeared on Channel 4's *Secret Millionaire* programme in October 2009, both he and his successful IT company, **Comtact** (http://www.comtact.co.uk), were exposed to media attention. In the programme he went undercover in Peckham, London, just a few miles from his own flat and saw at first hand the challenges of inner city unemployment. Dominic commented, 'I have been really overwhelmed by the response, I think it has been really great ... it was a great opportunity to highlight those that are doing a really good job in their community and those who represent a really positive image for their communities ... I have also been really happy with the responses and it has been really great to get other people offering their support and assistance to both the people that you have seen on the programme but also for other projects that I might be working on as well' (Channel 4 2009).

When Dominic founded Comtact in 2005 he relied on a combination of credit cards, the remortgaging of his flat, a loan from his father, and the sale of his car. He is an advocate of using family and friends: 'These are the best sources to raise seed capital but [they] also get work done. I had my father's accountant do the accounts for us as a favour.' (Real Business 2009) So he began the business from his own home, using the £100,000 he raised.

Comtact provides converged voice, data, and networking solutions to its corporate customers in order to reduce the telecommunication costs. Perhaps entrepreneurship was in Dominic's blood. His father was a serial entrepreneur starting a range of new ventures, from chip shops and hairdressing to industrial cleaning (Sunday Times 2009). Dominic's advice to new start-ups includes: outsource; work from home or in the car; use a forwarding address; beg or borrow; use non-geographic telephone numbers; use Google Apps; think big (http://www.dominiclist.co.uk). In 2016, Dominic with Comtact joined the top LEAP 100 list of most exciting, fast-growth companies in the UK (http://www.cityam.com/leap-100).

Ethical point Dominic is increasingly involved in social projects, including Fredericks Foundation (http://www.fredericksfoundation.org), Ilderton Foundation (http://www.ildertonfoundation.org.uk), and Peckham Park Youth Project.

Foreign travel was the catalyst for **Amina Ansir** developing her business idea. It was after graduating from college that Amina first decided to run her own business, During a visit to Canada, she was impressed by the various fast food outlets and their use of automation. When one of her relatives visited her from the United States, she shared her vision to create a venture at grassroots level by employing a semi-skilled and skilled workforce. This inspired Amina to investigate the potential for opening a pizza takeaway and delivery business in Islamabad, Pakistan, and she launched Pizza Plus in 2006. She borrowed the money to start her business from family friends (Shell Livewire 2017). Initially, she focused on pizza as her main product but soon expanded to offer a wide variety of pizzas, burgers, parathas, salads, and coffees. Amina launched an online ordering for frozen pizzas to cook in the home and deliveries of food to meetings and conferences. Pizza Plus grew to employ 15 staff.

When, in 2004, **Penny Jones** decided to start the **White T-shirt Company** (http://www.thewhitetshirt.co.uk), she approached a social enterprise, PNE Group, for a start-up loan (PNE Group 2010). She quickly got the money she needed to launch the environmentally friendly White T-shirt Company and after two years secured additional funding from the PNE Group. Penny's business idea was simple yet distinctive, and it helped that she was a former designer and buyer for retailers such as Harrods and Marks & Spencer. The business developed a strong online presence and used the Internet and press coverage to promote the brand. In 2013, three years after her organic yarn supplier closed, Penny relaunched the company with Global Organic Textile Standards certifiction cotton ethically sourced from Turkey, via Ukraine and Denmark before arriving in England (https://www.thewhitetshirt.com/story).

Ethical point Reassuring customers is important (https://www.youtube.com/watch?v=d2XLa5ttHjM).

QUESTIONS

1. What are the five sources of funding mentioned in the cases? What are advantages and risks of borrowing from family and friends?

2. What might be the next sources of capital for each business and why might these be different?

3. If you were starting a new venture, which family members and friends could you approach? What information would you want if a friend asked you for a loan to help set up a new venture?

Sources: Channel 4 2009; Real Business 2009; Sunday Times 2009; PNE Group 2010; Shell Livewire 2017.

9.3 SOURCES OF FINANCE

9.3.1 Banks

Banks are a vital source of formal finance for small businesses and new ventures. In the UK, at the end of 2016, banks provided over £9.6 billion in lending facilities to SMEs of which £4.5 billion was to small businesses. The average loan value approved for smaller businesses was £86,700 while the average for medium-sized businesses was £434,200 (BBA 2016). During the global credit difficulties, inter-bank lending, which provides the liquidity necessary for business lending, was hard for banks to access. Many national governments intervened to help banks borrow money from other institutions, such as the European Investment Bank (http://www.eib.org). Both national and international banks provide finance to business. However, national banks, such as Lloyds TSB (http://www.lloydstsb.com) in the UK, tend to be more visible to entrepreneurs and small business owners than international banks, such as Citibank (http://www.citigroup.com). Some banks operate at both a global and a national level, for example, Barclays (http://group.barclays.com and http://www.bank.barclays.co.uk), HSBC (http://www.hsbc.com and http://www.hsbc.co.uk), and Banco Santander (http://www.santander.com and http://www.santander.co.uk).

Choosing the right bank for you can be difficult because their services can seem very similar. However, banking is a service, albeit a rather important one, and requires that you form a relationship. It is worth investing some time meeting with different banks and asking friends and colleagues for their experiences. Some will also be particularly keen to attract new business customers and provide support and advice beyond just banking, such as insurance.

9.3.2 Business angels

When bank lending and other informal sources are insufficient to finance a rapidly growing venture you may decide that the only way to expand your business further is to sell shares to private equity investors. One of the first types of private equity you might want to consider is business angels. These tend to be wealthy individuals who want to invest their own money in high-growth businesses. They may also be part of a syndicate with other business angels. In addition to money, they often bring with them experience, skills, and contacts. They will tend to look for opportunities in industries and sectors where they feel they have relevant experience. Typically, they will invest between £10,000 and £750,000. Finding the right business angel can be difficult and is just as much about relationships as finance. In the first instance, it is worth approaching regional business groups, such as the Cambridge Network (http://www.cambridgenetwork.co.uk), or larger business angel networks, such as UK Business Angels Association (https://www.ukbusinessangelsassociation.org.uk) or the European Business Angel Network (http://www.eban.org).

Bruce Macfarlane (Case 9.1) stated, 'In a totally rational market, there should be different classes of investor for each stage of a company's development. In the same way, you might argue, there should be different kinds of management at different stages of a company's development. So if it all worked properly business angels would back the entrepreneur at the very early stage, get the business to a position where it needed a few million pounds, hand it over to a venture capital manager (like us) who would develop it further and, finally, we would hand it over to a late-stage development capital firm who would ready it for IPO or trade sale and replace the entrepreneur with professional management. In reality, it doesn't work like that … Business angels sometimes view venture capitalists as red-blooded capitalists who come in and destroy everything. But the advantage of venture capital is that it does bring discipline and an outside perspective.'

Bruce also recalled how difficult and risky investing can be: 'In my early days as a business angel, I backed a business where I ended up losing $100,000 dollars. The founders were healthcare specialists with Harvard MBAs and they [company] had a very good healthcare idea. But their first action was to go to a consulting firm and spend half a million dollars getting advice on the market and a report that wasn't worth anything. There was no money left to get the business going. What you need is a team that have gone out there themselves and worn out their shoe leather in building a proper understanding of their market.'

9.3.3 Venture capitalists

Venture capitalists (VCs) are also a source of private equity capital, but they usually manage larger funds than syndicates of business angels. Venture capital firms usually manage deals of between £250,000 and £2 million (BVCA 2010). They are also more likely to look for an exit through an initial public listing (IPO) or trade sale to a larger company. In the US, the National Venture Capital Association (NVCA) has over 400 member VCs (http://www.nvca.org); the British Private Equity & Venture Capital Association (BVCA) has a membership of over 230 private equity venture capital firms with an accumulated total of approximately £32 billion in funds under management and over 220 professional advisory firms (http://www.bvca.co.uk).

It is important to briefly consider the extent of venture capital funding and the high degree of variation across countries. Firstly, venture capital represented only 6% of new venture funding when compared with informal investment (see Section 9.2.1). Secondly, the relative amount of venture capital invested varies markedly between countries with Ireland (25%), USA (24%), Macedonia (22%), and the Philippines (21%) indicating a closer tie to the start-up community but remains limited in many countries (GEM 2016). In other words, venture capital is an important source of finance, but it is not as important as you might expect.

It is difficult to generalise because every deal is different, but it usually takes between three and eight months to raise funding from VCs. Entrepreneurs can be expected to give at least 20% but sometimes considerably more and the exit is expected within three to seven years (http://www.businesslink.org.uk).

Raising finance is not a one-off event. As Bruce Macfarlane (Case 9.1) stated:

For example, we have backed a new company in the dental implant market, a market where there are some giant companies competing. This company invented a much more efficient implant system. But would the big guys squash them before we got them off the ground? The market as a whole was growing at 15/20% a year and they were all enjoying substantial profits. So why would they bother to squash a tadpole? It was a judgement and we correctly surmised they would not bother. When we invested, the management thought a million pounds would see them through to profitability but that was never going to be the case. We weren't certain how much money would be required. Therefore, to hedge our risk, we invited another venture capital firm to come in with us that had a healthcare background, which would be useful. Every time we go into a business we assume we will have to follow our money. These are growing companies that always require more capital and so if we are putting in a million pounds, we have already mentally worked out we are going to have to put in a further £2 or £3 million. There is no doubt though that, regardless of extensive due diligence, every investment is a leap of faith.

The truth is that when entrepreneurs take professional money they have fundamentally lost their complete freedom of action … It doesn't matter what percentage we own, the shareholder agreement gives us a veto over all important decisions. That is something one has to understand at the outset of going for professional money. However, they will also get powerful support. We backed a digital media company and the founder was very talented, with a background in digital media, who saw the opportunity to grow a 'lead generation' business. They had to get data on people who would be interested in particular products and then they were able to sell those data lists: for example, a cosmetic company which wanted to target women between 25 and 35 for a new skin cream. It is difficult to generate that data because people voluntarily give their information often for something in return. We were very impressed by this entrepreneur, but he didn't have much of a management team. We said we would only invest if we recruited a finance director, which we did. We also found a chairman and chief operating officer for him.

9.3.4 Crowdfunding

Crowdfunding or crowdsourcing a relatively new form of business financing that allows individuals to support new ventures with small contributions and typically online. Globally by 2016, it was estimated that $34 billion was made available through crowdfunding sites. Mostly, this takes the form of equity investment (https://www.crowdcube.com; https://www.crowdfunder.com; https://www.seedrs.com) and loan capital, debt finance or peer-to-peer lending (https://www.fundingcircle.com; https://www.lendingclub.com; https://www.lendingclub.com). Crowdfunding has become prevalent as a source of financing in Greece (19%), Guatemala (18%), the United States (15%), Canada (13%), and Finland (13%) – these entrepreneurs are aware of and savvy about how to connect to platforms and garner attention from individual investors. By contrast, Africa, Asia and Oceania, both at 2%, lag significantly in terms of access to this form of funding (GEM 2016).

The following example from the UK illustrates the innovative nature of the crowdfunding sector – in this case a peer-to-peer lending webiste – ebuildingsociety.com.

Crowdfunding: peer-to-peer lending

Daniel Rajkumar was already an experienced entrepreneur when he founded **Rebuilding Society** in 2012 in response to a perceived need in small business owners wanting transparency, trust, and purpose from financial services, which matched them to a regional online community of lenders with a vested interest in their long-term success. The first deal was agreed in January 2013 and by 2017 ebuildingsociety.com has facilitated over £10m of lending from more than 200 applications. Daniel expressed the value proposition of the site as 'is really an attitude … with the industry reivneting this space … and [we] are here to be the ebay of finance'.

Interestingly, Daniel has a track-record of innovation and is a serial entrepreneur and on the board of several web-based businesses – including Web-Translations, incorporated in 2003. Web-Translations has 'succeeded in assembling a team of the best freelancers in the world and has access to over 25,000 freelance translators, linguists and developers worldwide. Our key asset is our supply base, and our teleworking model means that Web-Translations can scale up to meet the needs of even the most demanding projects.'

Source: https://www.rebuildingsociety.com/about-us/; http://www.web-translations.com/about-us/

9.4 FINANCING AN ONGOING VENTURE

Once you have launched your new venture it is possible to arrange access to the funds tied up with trade customers, a technique called 'factoring' or 'invoice discounting'. Running a high-growth company might also attract the interest of trade investors, either from within the sector or those wishing to enter it. Finally, having successfully established a market position and reputation you and your shareholders might decide to 'exit' by selling the business to a trade investor or by some form of flotation.

9.4.1 Factoring

Factoring and invoice discounting can provide valuable finance to growing companies who trade with other businesses and offer credit accounts. Such companies will raise an invoice for goods or services and give the customer 30 days to pay it. It is not unusual for this period to become extended to an average of over 60 days. This can result in profitable businesses experiencing cash flow difficulties. The two most common methods of accessing these funds are factoring and invoice discounting.

- **Factoring** In this case, the bank agrees to pay a percentage, for example 80%, of approved debts as soon as they receive a copy of the invoice. The balance, in this example 20%, is paid when the customer settles the full invoice. A small percentage or fixed fee is deducted from this payment. You are still responsible for collecting the debt from your customers who are not aware that you have factored the invoice. Factoring agreements normally have a limit to the total amount you can borrow as well as limits on the age of the invoice, such as 90 days.

- **Invoice discounting** This is similar to factoring but is likely to be offered to younger or smaller businesses. It has one important difference: the bank provides the debt collection service and your customer is aware that a third party is involved. This will probably result in a larger service charge. Historically, this type of finance has been seen as a weakness, but many successful companies have used this service so perceptions are changing.

Factoring and invoice discounting can provide a significant and quick boost to cash flow and can be a valuable source of working capital. It can also prove cost effective with modest charges and interest only being charged on the funds used rather than the total available. You might also be able to use this access to funds to negotiate early settlement discounts with your suppliers. With invoice discounting you will need to consider the reaction of your customers. This type of funding can also be available for new start-ups.

9.4.2 Trade investors

Many high-growth companies, particularly in a sector with a history of acquisitions (such as IT and medical), will receive the necessary finance from trade investors, rather than business angels or venture capitalists. Usually, these trade investors will have expert industry knowledge or wish to gain it. The initial investment may be followed by an attempt to acquire the company. These amounts invested or paid tend not to be in the public domain.

Cisco Systems, the large global computer networking company, was founded in 1984 and by 2016 had over 73,400 employees and a turnover of $49 billion. It has a track record of acquiring many smaller high-growth companies with technology it was interested in (http://www.cisco.com). For example, in December 2009, it acquired ScanSafe, a UK Internet security service provider (Cisco 2016) founded by two brothers in 1999, for approximately $183 million. In 2012, the service was renamed Cisco Cloud Web Security. In June 2015, it aquired OpenDNS, which provided advanced threat protection (https://www.opendns.com), for $635 million.

9.4.3 Flotation

Some high-growth companies work through several types of financing until they reach the point where a flotation becomes both desirable and profitable. The instances of successful flotation are few and far between. One mechanism for this is an initial public offering (IPO) or initial public stock offering, where a company offers shares for sale on a public platform, such as the NASDAQ stock market founded in the US (http://www.nasdaqomx.com). This is a complex and costly process involving an underwriting firm to manage it.

Founded in the UK, the Alternative Investment Market (AIM) has allowed over 3,000 companies to become traded since its launch in 1995 (http://www.londonstock exchange.com). It provides an opportunity for smaller and growing companies to raise capital. By 2016, some of the best performing AIM listed shares included Asos (http://www.asos.com), Numis Securities (http://www.numiscorp.com), Mears Group (https://www.mearsgroup.co.uk), Imperial Energy (http://www.imperialenergy.com) and Domino's Pizza (https://www.dominos.co.uk). How there are concerns AIM has not performed well overall (FT 2015).

The flotation of high-growth companies attracts much media attention. But how does the amount of finance raised compare to other forms of investment? During the whole of 2005 in the US, $8.7 billion was raised by the flotation of 965 companies. However, this is less than 3% of the $300 billion of informal funding (founders, families, and friends) used to fund over 3 million companies over the same period (GEM 2007, 2016).

The following example from the recent history of Google illustrates the financing process, from the use of informal sources at the start-up stage (i.e. obtained from the founders, their family, and friends), through venture capital as the enterprise grew rapidly, and finally to flotation (i.e. the 'IPO' or initial public offering).

Financing Google: from start-up to IPO

Google founders **Larry Page** and **Sergey Brin** bought a terabyte of storage at bargain prices and built their own computer housings in Larry's dorm room, which became Google's first data centre. Unable to interest the major portal players of the day, Larry and Sergey decided to make a go of it on their own. All they needed was a little cash to move out of the dorm – and to pay off the credit cards they had maxed out buying their terabyte of memory. So they wrote up a business plan, put their PhD plans on hold, and went looking for an angel investor. Their first visit was with a friend of a faculty member. Andy Bechtolsheim, one of the founders of Sun Microsystems, was used to taking the long view. One look at their demo and he knew Google had potential – a lot of potential. But though his interest had been piqued, he was pressed for time. As Sergey tells it, 'We met him very early one morning on the porch of a Stanford faculty member's home in Palo Alto. We gave him a quick demo. He had to run off somewhere, so he said, "Instead of us discussing all the details, why don't I just write you a check?" It was made out to Google Inc. and was for $100,000.'

The investment created a small dilemma. Since there was no legal entity known as 'Google Inc.,' there was no way to deposit the check. It sat in Larry's desk drawer for a couple of weeks while he and Sergey scrambled to set up a corporation and locate other funders among family, friends, and acquaintances. Ultimately, they brought in a total initial investment of almost $1 million.

On 7 September 1998, more than two years after they began work on their search engine, Google Inc. opened its doors in Menlo Park, California. The door came with a remote control, as it was attached to the garage of a friend who sublet space to the new corporation's staff of three. The office offered several big advantages, including a washer and dryer and a hot tub. It also provided a parking space for the first employee hired by the new company: Craig Silverstein, now Google's director of technology.

Source: Extracts from http://www.google.com/corporate/history.html reported in GEM (2007).

Most of our discussion has concentrated on the financing of commercial ventures. However, social enterprises also require capital in order to achieve their objectives and to expand the scope and scale of their operations. Case 9.3, *The big investment issue: investing for social returns,* looks at how one social enterprise, The Big Issue Foundation, is helping to finance other organisations in order to produce a better return for society and for the environment.

CASE 9.3

The big investment issue: Investing for social returns

Increasingly organisations and governments around the world are recognising the importance of enterprise for bringing about social change. Venture capital funds are beginning to emerge to provide alternative methods for raising capital and making investment. One of the first of these was the **Big Issue Invest**, which is a specialised provider of finance to social enterprises or trading arms of charities that seek to bring about social and environmental transformation (Big Issue Invest 2017). It is part of The Big Issue group of companies. In 2010, Big Issue Invest launched a £10 million Social Enterprise Investment Fund and closed a sebsequent £21 million fund in 2016. They

(Continued)

(Continued)

provided investment from £100,000 to £500,000 in the form of loans, participation loans, and equity to high-impact social enterprises with the potential for scaling-up. It can also arrange larger financing with other social finance institutions. Big Issue Invest also has a loan fund, which provides loans to social enterprises or trading arms of charities that have been trading for three years or more and have a turnover of over £250,000. The Big Issue was founded by **John Bird** in 1991 to help homeless people have the dignity of self-employment through selling.

Campaigns to promote social investments, such as #socialsaturday2016, are increasing and promote successful social enterprises, such as Belu Water, Divine Chocolates, and Fifteen Foundation (http://www.socialsaturday.org.uk).

Belu Water (http://www.belu.org) is the first carbon neutral, bottled water company in the UK. It uses compostable bottles made from corn and invests all surpluses in clean water projects. It supplies leading supermarkets, high-end restaurants, and corporate boardrooms. The CEO, **Reed Paget**, won the *Independent*'s 2008 Social Entrepreneur of the Year award. Belu Water seeks to 'create a sustainable balance between people and the planet' by using all the profits from the sale of bottled water to fund clean water projects and to 'create the most eco-friendly bottled water in the world'. From 2011, all profits went to WaterAid (http://www.wateraid.org/uk) with 2015 generating over £500,000 (from sales of £5.3 millon) and totalling over 1.5 million passed to WaterAid since 2011 (Belu 2017).

Divine Chocolate (http://www.divinechocolate.com/uk/) started in 1998 and was the 'first ever farmer-owned Fairtrade chocolate bar aimed at the mass market was launched onto the UK confectionery market. In an exciting new business model, the cooperative of cocoa farmers in Ghana own shares in the company making the chocolate bar.' From 2015, **Sophi Tranchell**, MBE, Divine Chocolate Ltd's Managing Director, leads a social enterprise, which combines significant operations in the UK and USA and she explained that the new structure 'strengthens the group, making us more resilient and giving us a wider consumer reach, and in doing so gives Divine more power to deliver our mission to fairly and sustainably remunerate smallholder cocoa farmers in West Africa, as well as empowering them to take their future into their own hands' (Divine Chocolate 2017).

Fifteen Foundation (http://www.fifteen.net) was founded by **Jamie Oliver** in 2002 to provide training in the restaurant industry for disadvantaged young people. Fifteen has succeeded in giving young people a transition opportunity to a good career. The Fifteen restaurants serve food of the highest quality made from the best ingredients in the kitchens where the apprentices learn their trade. Fifteen's philosophy is to help young people learn within the work environment, from experts in the field, surrounded by the produce, equipment, and dishes that they will work with. Gradually, their levels of responsibility increase with increasing skill, and their confidence grows despite the setbacks they may have experienced. As Jamie says, 'Now, I've got restaurants in towns and cities all over the UK, so it feels like the time is right to expand the Apprentice Programme out into the regions and across the whole country' (Fifteen Foundation 2017; Jamie Oliver 2017).

Ethical point Interestingly, Big Issue Invest has developed a Social Value Assessment framework to enable investors and corporates to assess their social value and to meet the challenge of developing a 'balanced economy' that will deliver sustainable and equitable economic growth (http://bigissueinvest.com/research/social-value-assessment/).

QUESTIONS

1. Why do social enterprises use alternative funds, like the Big Issue Invest rather than conventional loans?
2. What other social investments are available for social entrepreneurs?
3. Why is there so much interest in social enterprises by governments?
4. Are there any differences in the skills required to be a social entrepreneur rather than an entrepreneur?

Sources: Belu 2010; Big Issue Invest 2017; Fifteen Foundation 2017; Jamie Oliver 2017.

9.5 SECURING A RETURN ON THE INVESTMENT

9.5.1 First things first: what is the investor looking for?

Before considering the return that investors are likely to require, it is worth reminding ourselves what they see as the essential features of a 'good' business idea. The venture capitalist and business angel Bruce Macfarlane (see Case 9.1) has highlighted three key requirements: a strong general proposition, access to experienced people, and an interesting business plan:

* **A strong proposition** 'First of all there is a general proposition. There are plenty of bright ideas out there but it is much easier to have one than to execute it. What makes the difference is somebody's ability to turn that bright idea into a business and deliver it. That is very difficult. In our society, we value people who are very, very clever and we have tended not to value the engineers and the doers. But execution is all important. We need to be sure that the innovative idea also provides a service or product that is needed in the market. We have to understand the market and how they are going to sell to it. What is unattractive is somebody who has a good idea and then just wants money … you need far more than that. It has to be a special idea with insight into a particular market need – are they close enough to the market to appreciate the customer's needs?'

* **Access to experienced people** 'What is very attractive is when someone with a good idea brings in somebody with commercial experience who is going to help them commercialise it. We don't expect a fully fledged team (there are always gaps), but you expect the nucleus to be there.'

* **An interesting business plan** 'We tell people that we want to see a business plan before we meet them. The business plan has got to be sufficiently interesting for us to take it to the next stage. We do not have a template. It is probably true to say a well-written business plan with a clear outline of what the business is all about and where they are going will receive more attention. Someone has to write a coherent, well-thought through business plan with numbers. Of the several hundred we get we then meet about 20%. In the course of a year, we will have whittled down to perhaps 20 plans, on which we are thinking seriously about issuing "heads of terms". I don't think the first formal presentation should be any longer than an hour. The team [company] has to be very concise in an hour and persuade us that it is a compelling proposition. From this very first meeting we'll get a quick sense whether this is something that is worth spending time on.'

In earlier chapters, we have encouraged you to develop an opportunity business model as a way of thinking through and articulating your venture idea clearly and effectively (Section 3.3). However, we also recognised that more formal business plans have a role to play, and one of their primary roles is to support a request for finance. It is important that business plans are written with your audience in mind (Blundel et al. 2013; Mason and Stark 2004). In this case, the challenge is to persuade the potential investor that your venture is attractive, and that your entrepreneurial team is capable of achieving your operational and financial goals.

Making the best case to an investor is difficult and requires you to be able to produce a proposal and be prepared to present this to investors. It will be useful to read some accounts of entrepreneurs who have achieved this and have also become business angels or venture capitalists. These include Duncan Bannatyne (Bannatyne 2006, 2013), James Caan (2008), Yvon Chouinard (2016), Rachel Elnaugh (2008), Peter Jones (2008), Deborah Meaden (2010), Jo Malone (2016), and Theo Paphitis (2009).

9.5.2 The nature of the return to investors

Clearly, entrepreneurs, lenders, and investors all want a return for their effort, finance, and investment. For lenders, this will simply be interest charged on the money borrowed and, for investors, the dividends on shares. But, whereas lenders will want capital repaid over an agreed term, investors will probably be looking for significant capital growth on an equity investment.

However, not all returns are financial. Entrepreneurs could achieve far more personally than money. They may find the challenge of launching a successful business and managing people rewarding as well as enjoy being in control or 'their own boss' as it provides them with an increased quality of life (Hamilton 2000). The aim of most business angels and venture capitalist is not to achieve a personal gain for the founding team but to achieve a return on their investment. Clearly in some cases the interests of the founding team and future investors will be very different. As we saw in Case 9.3, *The big investment issue: investing for social returns*, the returns can be both financial and social. By 2015, there were more than 70,000 social enterprises contributing over £24 billion to the economy. Businesses driven by a social or environmental purpose are attracting talented people from all backgrounds, an indication that non-financial returns can be a powerful incentive (http://www.socialenterprise.org.uk).

The *Professor Neil Meredith: invention, product, and business* case (Case 9.4), highlights how an expert in dental implants exploited his academic knowledge to create a successful medical company, which has grown with founder, venture capital, and trade investment. What has he learned from this experience? Firstly, that 'Venture capitalists are objective business people … what you need to continually do is understand your true value to the business … you need to be very aware of it'.

Secondly, that, 'The invention is 10% of the product and the product is 10% of the business' – Meredith's law of innovation. In addition, there is a video case available (Case 9.5 *Finances: Pete's Challenge*). This video case is based on an interview with an entrepreneur, Pete, looking to fund the development of a new software product. Watch the video and decide which option you think Pete will choose. You might find it useful to discuss the case with friends or colleagues before deciding. Please note that lecturers can have access to the video which reveals the actual decision taken by the entrepreneur.

9.6 SUMMARY

- Raising finance is a critical element of new venture creation.

- Finance for new ventures and growing businesses can come from informal investment from founders, family, and friends. This is often the first source of finance for new entrepreneurs.

- Borrowing can be unsecured or secured. Credit cards form the largest element of unsecured borrowing for small firms. Banks play a critical role in providing finance to new ventures and small businesses.

- Investment can be obtained from selling equity to business angels, venture capitalists and by crowdfunding. This requires detailed business planning and assessment. It can also be used as a mechanism to gain expertise for the company.

- Established businesses can factor their sales invoices to raise working capital.

- Trade investors also make equity investments in attractive high-growth firms.

- The selling of new venture shares on a stock exchanges (flotation) is rare.

- Lenders require interest and capital repayment. Investors seek dividend payments and capital growth.

- Not all returns from enterprise are financial: social outcomes are increasingly evident.

CASE 9.4

Professor Neil Meredith: invention, product, and business

By 2009, Professor **Neil Meredith** had successfully taken his innovative new dental implants venture (**Neoss**) through nearly ten years of continuous growth. As CEO he had personally negotiated through the maze of getting equity investment to fund this high-growth business. Beginning with the founders investment to get early sales, he firstly secured venture capital funding and secondly a strategic investment from a trade investor which helped open up the US market. The company was set for the next stage of development. But was Neil the right person to lead the company? The investors were keen for the restructuring to happen, but Neil had reservations about finding the right person with the right experience who he could work with and the company could afford. A recruitment agency was appointed.

BIOGRAPHY

Neil celebrated his 50th birthday a couple of months ago and remembered his grammar school education in Stockport near Manchester, 'I decided to study dentistry and went to Guys Hospital in 1979 qualifying in 1982. I did a series of hospital jobs in a range of departments. And then, went from Guys Hospital to Glasgow to Kingston. So I rotated around the country quite a lot!' However, in the mid-1980s, Neil decided to go into general practice.

Setting up a new practice in the Isle of Wight was a rare opportunity and Neil recalled, 'It was quite a nice adventure. During that time, I also passed the first part

(Continued)

(Continued)

of the fellowship examinations for the Royal College of Surgeons.' This was unusual, but Neil was particularly interested in restorative dentistry: crowns and bridges. In 1987, he studied for an MSc and then went on to undertake a PhD in bio-mechanics at the Eastman and Imperial College, which he completed in 1992.

It was while working at Imperial College that Neil's interest developed in dental implants. He explained, 'We were talking about dental implants with engineering colleagues. Dental implants are pre titanium screws inserted into bone to which the bone fuses directly. One of the difficulties is knowing how well that osseointegration has worked. The implant may fail to fuse and the patient is completely unaware of it, there is no infection. There is no swelling, pain or discomfort but the implant is mobile. In 1993, we developed a technique called resonance frequency analysis, which was attached a small electronic transducer, similar to a tuning fork, to the implant.' Neil had always had an interest in electronics as a hobby, and his technical understanding proved very useful in this process.

SPINNING OUT IMPLANTS

This interest developed further and Neil moved to Sweden to complete his second PhD, this time looking at resonance frequency analysis. He recalled, 'I came back from Sweden published a number of papers and was coordinator for a European grant of £1.8 million to assess the technical viability of this technique as a clinical diagnostic technique for patients.' By the mid-1990s, Imperial College was encouraging technology transfer, patents were filed, and a spin-off company was formed. Neil soon went to Leeds to become a professor in clinical bio-materials and restorative dentistry. One of the challenges that Neil and his colleagues embraced was that existing dental implant systems were very complex and consisted of up to 3,000 articles. The systems were supplied by six big dental implant companies. Neil recalled, 'You need to be a specialist, not just to place the implant, but to read the catalogues ... we decided it was an appropriate time for the "common sense implant" ... we sat down and designed a dental implant system for interest.' They formed the company, located near Leeds, in 1999 in order to protect the intellectual property (IP) and with £50,000 made prototypes to validate their new system.

FROM PROTOTYPE TO PRODUCTION

It took about 18 months to develop the new dental implant system. The company had no borrowings and no family investment. Early feedback was very positive, and Neil recalled, 'All the clinicians and technicians that saw the system said, "You must do something with it. It is different." It was not crazily different, it was a real evolution. There were some really smart ideas and the combination and design of components resulted in an implant system including instruments and all components of less than one hundred articles but with no clinical restrictions. This meant that the cost of stocking and using the system was lower than the competition and it could be used on all patients.'

However, Neil was concerned not to over-promote the innovation and remembered, 'We just kept it very quiet and I think that it was the right thing to do. Because of the stock as well as development costs and production costs, our intention wasn't to manufacture these articles. There were suppliers around Europe who supplied all the big medical device companies, so there was no need to invest in capital equipment. But there was stock and there was a sales force and setting up the company. Therefore, it needed a significant amount of capital.'

'So I wrote a business plan ... with no financial training. I read widely and sought advice ... without question this was the most challenging part. We talked to over 20 sources of funding before finding our VC [venture capitalist]. Getting that first stage of funding is the most difficult thing I have ever done. The due diligence process is very challenging. Very challenging!' In early 2003, the first stage was secured and the new venture set its sights on international markets from an early point. This was an important decision, as Neil recalled, 'The reason is that the UK was a much smaller market than Europe because of the lack of NHS support and the healthcare structure. The number of implants sold in the UK was approximately 10% of those sold in Germany. We had a very clear plan and recruited very talented people for our German and Australian subsidiaries. Most of the people we recruited have been from other companies... where professional sales people had had very strong relationships with clinical specialists. These companies started to rely on less technically skilled sales people.'

Neil advised, 'One of the things I would say to entrepreneurs is that it is quite difficult to understand the mechanics and mechanisms of funding. It is worth knowing how VC funds work, what their time constraints are, what their interests are, what their motivation is. I would encourage people to ask questions ... talk to some of the people a fund has invested in. Do your own due diligence.'

The first sales were in Germany in 2003 and developed rapidly from there. Neil recalled, 'The company grew rapidly and we moved into different markets. Now, Neoss has subsidiaries in the UK, Germany, Sweden, Italy, Australia, New Zealand and, most recently, in the United States. We have seen year on year growth. Our first year sales were £1 million, second year £2 million, £4 million, £8 million, £12 million and this year was over £14 million. Margins of our product are high at over 70% gross margin. It's obviously an attractive product! It is small and easy to sell – you can put £1,000 worth in a jiffy bag!' The company's success has been driven by product and service innovation, yet this is only a small part of the picture. Neil stated that, 'the invention is 10% of the product and the product is 10% of the business'. He calls this Meredith's law of innovation.

SECURING A TRADE INVESTOR

Even though Neil was pleased with the growth sales and profitability he recognised that the market opportunity, particularly in the US, was far greater and that the company would need more resources to exploit it. The current investors were very happy with the prospect of bringing a new investment but Neil thought there was an opportunity for this to come from a trade investor. Neil arranged a meeting with a large American medical device company. He recalled, 'They brought some of their people over from America including the senior vice president of the business development and we had a very good discussion.' Interestingly, the medical device company had their own venture fund, which they invested in small companies strategically to understand the market. They had been very impressed with Neil's company and he said, 'You need to come forward with a proposal.' By October, they had come back with an offer.

Neil now had to find ways forward. He either increased the investment by the existing venture capitalist firm or brought in a new trade investor. He understood the former but wanted access to the industrial experience and market knowledge of the latter. How

(Continued)

(Continued)

was Neil going to brokerage a deal which kept both parties happy? He knew the existing investors did not want to diminish their influence on the board and recalled, 'Because their agendas are different, their timelines were different, and very often they had views about how it was done ... our current investors were quite rightly anxious about a trade investor. But I thought it was good to have a very prestigious trade investor ... for us to have a strategic affiliation. So I was quite up for it but I hadn't got the experience to give our investors the confidence about negotiations.' A specialist advisor was brought in to help work with all parties and facilitate the deal, and by the end of 2005 the investment came in. However, it was not just about money. Neil recalled, 'This was strategic investment ... we were and continue to be invited to participate in areas of technology development.'

The board expanded to include experienced directors from the venture capital community and a new chairman with a strong medical management background. Neil recognised that his role as CEO had changed and remembered, 'We hadn't really done any research for five years.' Neil had developed strong management skills and gained the trust of the board and investors to lead the company to the next stage of growth. Should he continue to do this or spend more time on product research and development even though his own law – invention is 10% of the product and the product is 10% of the business – suggested otherwise? Perhaps the company could invest in their own R&D capability and Neil could concentrate on the business. He remembered a colleague inviting him to meet with somebody who turned out to be the worldwide chairman of medical devices for one of the world's largest healthcare companies. Neil remembered, 'He had travelled from the US to the UK. We had an excellent discussion and I was deeply impressed with his depth of knowledge and strategic perspective.'

He continued, 'In 2008, we had a very good discussion around the board and every-body felt we should look for a new CEO. We appointed a high-calibre, if rather expensive, recruitment agency. We saw a number of prospective candidates ... I was very open. I believe we can all learn from somebody with more experience.' The investors were keen for the restructuring to happen but Neil had reservations about finding the right person with the right experience, whom he could work with and the company could afford. Everybody was keen to take things forward. Michael J Dormer, previously of Johnson and Johnson's Medical Devices and Diagnostics, who joined the board in 2008.

NEW CHALLENGES

In 2011, Neil had decided to take on a new challenge. This time in academia by taking up professorial positions at the University of Queensland and, in 2015, as Head of Dentistry at the James Cook University in Australia. Michael J. Dormer was appointed CEO. (http://www.neoss.com)

Neoss, the company he co-founded in 2000, continued to expand its international operations with the support of key investors – MMC Ventures (2003), Delta Partners (2003), Medtronic (2006) and Souter Investments (2008). In 2012, Neoss won the Yorkshire Insider International Trade Healthcare Award and in 2014 announced a record 12 months including sales, profits, productivity, research and development. (http://www.mmcventures.com/portfolio/neoss/).

Source: This case is primarily based on an interview with Neil Meredith and was written by Nigel Lockett.

CASE 9.5

Finances: Pete's challenge video

In this video case, **Pete** explains the four options for funding the new software product developed by his technology company: (a) money from existing work, (b) bank loan, (c) angel investor, and (d) crowdfunding. Watch the video and decide which option you think Pete will choose. You might find it useful to discuss the case with friends or colleagues before deciding. Please note that lecturers can have access to the video which reveals the actual decision taken by the entrepreneur.

Source: This video case is primarily based on an interview with Pete by Nigel Lockett.

Practical activities

1. You are approached by a new venture capital fund looking to invest in new technology firms in the emerging area of microgeneration of renewable energy. They have asked you to produce a first-stage assessment framework for them to screen business plans. They expect to receive between 50 and 100 business plans a month and have enough funds for four investments a year.

    (a) List the five most important criteria you would use and how each could be assessed and ranked. Who should do this?

    (b) Who should be on the monthly assessment committee, and how much time can they spend discussing each business plan?

2. Interview an entrepreneur about how they raised the funds to launch their new venture and the current sources of finance:

    (a) Compare types of finance they used before and after the venture was created. Comment on any changes.

    (b) How much planning and forecasting went into determining the amount of finance required to launch the new venture? Were there any differences between the forecast and reality? If so why?

Discussion topics

1. In terms of finding new ventures to invest in, what might be the differences between a venture investment fund and a social investment fund? What additional criteria would you need to use to determine the social impact of a social enterprise looking for investment? How would you calculate the value of these criteria and measure them?

2. Put simply, most of the new jobs created in an economy come from high-growth small businesses. What is the role of governments in funding new venture creation and supporting high-growth firms? Big companies might get grants for relocating in an area of high unemployment. Should public funds also be used to invest in small firms?

Recommended reading

These readings address important topics in entrepreneurship research and are recommended for anyone wanting to build on the material covered in this chapter. Recommended readings have been selected from leading Sage journals and are freely available for readers of this textbook to download via the Online Resources.

Younkin, P. and Kashkooli, K. (2017) 'What problems does crowdfunding solve?' *California Management Review*, 58, 2: 20–43.

This article reviews the types of platform and how should expand. It identifies the range of problems crowdfunding addresses and their performance to date. Crowdfunding succeeds in raising money within and across networks, but efforts to use crowdfunding to educate or to generate recurring revenue are less successful.

Mason, C., Botelho, T. and Zygmunt, J. (2016) 'Why business angels reject investment opportunities: Is it personal?' *International Small Business Journal*.

This article focuses on business angels' decision-making processes and investment criteria when they reject most opportunities. It uses the concept of 'communities-of-practice' as an explanation.

McGuinness, G. and Hogan, T. (2014) 'Bank credit and trade credit: evidence from SMEs over the financial crisis'. *International Small Business Journal*, 34, 4: 412–45.

This article explores the extent to which trade credit acted as a substitute for bank finance in small and medium-sized enterprises, in the aftermath of the financial crisis of 2008. It demonstrates that the reduction in the supply of funds to SMEs was compounded by the contraction of net trade credit within the sector.

Jiang, P., Cai, C.X., Keasey, K., Wright, M. and Zhang, Q. (2014) 'The role of venture capitalists in small and medium-sized enterprise initial public offerings: Evidence from China'. *International Small Business Journal*, 32, 6: 619–43.

This article examines the role of venture capitalists in public firms listed on the Small and Medium Enterprise Board and the Growth Enterprise Board in China. The grandstanding motive is documented for younger VCs which offer higher levels of initial underpricing to enhance their positions in the industry, but no evidence is found to support grandstanding by foreign VCs.

References

Bannatyne, D. (2006) *Anyone Can Do It: My Story*. London: Orion Publishing Group.

Bannatyne, D. (2013) *Riding the Storm*. London: Random House Group.

BBA (2016) *Bank Support for SMEs – 3rd Quarter 2016*. London: British Bankers' Association.

Belu (2017) http://www.belu.org/mission.asp (accessed 4 January 2017).

Big Issue Invest (2017) http://www.bigissueinvest.com (accessed 3 January 2017).

Blundel, R.K., Ippolito, K., and Donnarumma, D. (2013) *Effective Organisational Communication: Perspectives, Principles and Practices* (4th edn). Harlow: Pearson.

BVCA (2010) *A Guide to Private Equity*. British Private Equity & Venture Capital Association (BVCA) publication. http://www.bvca.co.uk (accessed 25 May 2017).

Caan, J. (2008) *The Real Deal: My Story from Brick Lane to Dragons' Den*. London: Virgin Publishing.

Channel 4 (2009) http://www.channel4.com/programmes/the-secret-millionaire/episode-guide/series-6 (accessed 5 January 2017).

Chouinard, Y (2016) *Let My People Go Surfing: The Education of a Reluctant Businessman* (Revised Edition). New York: Penguin Books.

Cisco (2016) Cisco 2016 Annual Report. http://www.cisco.com/c/en/us/about/annual-reports.html (accessed 25 May 2017).

Cowling, M. (2010) *Economic evaluation of the Small Firms Loan Guarantee (SFLG) Scheme*. London: Department of Business, Innovation and Skills.

Delmar, F. (2000) 'The psychology of the entrepreneur'. In S. Carter and D. Jones-Evans (eds) *Enterprise and Small Business*. Harlow: Prentice Hall (132–54).

Divine Chocolate (2017) http://www.divinechocolate.com/uk/about-us/inside-divine (accessed 4 January 2017).

Ebben, J. and Johnson, A. (2006) 'Bootstrapping in small firms: an empirical analysis of change over time'. *Journal of Business Venturing*, 21: 851–65.

Elnaugh, R. (2008) *Business Nightmares: When Entrepreneurs Hit Crisis Point*. Richmond, UK: Crimson Publishing.

Fifteen Foundation (2017) http://www.fifteen.net (accessed 4 January 2017).

FT (2015) *AIM – 20 Years of a Few Winners and Many Losers: Why Has London's Junior Market Performed So Poorly?* 18 June 2015.

GEM (2007) *Global Entrepreneurship Monitor Financing Report 2006*. http://www.gemconsortium.org (accessed 25 May 2017).

GEM (2016) *GEM 2015–2016 Report on Entrepreneurial Financing*. http://gemconsortium.org (accessed 25 May 2017).

Hamilton, B.H. (2000) 'Does entrepreneurship pay? An empirical analysis of the returns to self-employment'. *Journal of Political Economy*, 108, 3: 604–30/

Hernández-Cánova, G. and Koëter-Kant, J. (2008) 'Debt maturity and relationship lending: an analysis of European SMEs'. *International Small Business Journal*, 26, 5: 595–617.

Howorth, C, and Moro, A (2006) 'Trust within entrepreneur bank relationships: insights from Italy'. *Entrepreneurship: Theory and Practice*, 30, 4: 495–517.

Jamie Oliver (2017) http://www.jamieoliver.com/the-fifteen-apprentice-programme/about/story (accessed 4 January 2017).

Jiménez, G., Salas, V., and Saurina, J. (2006) 'Determinants of collateral'. *Journal of Financial Economics*, 81: 255–81.

Jones, P. (2008) *Tycoon*. London: Hodder Paperbacks.

Malone, J. (2016) *Jo Malone: My Story*. London: Simon & Schuster.

Mason, C. and Stark, M. (2004) 'What do investors look for in a business plan? A comparison of the investment criteria of bankers, venture capitalists and business angels'. *International Small Business Journal*, 22, 3: 227–48.

Meaden, D. (2010) *Common Sense Rules: What You Really Need to Know About*. London: Random House Group.

Paphitis, T. (2009) *Enter the Dragon*. London: Orion Publishing Group.

PNE Group (2010) http://www.pne.org/casestudies/ (accessed 3 May 2010).

Real Business (2009) http://realbusiness.co.uk/any-other-business/2009/11/09/dominic-list-how-to-do-business-on-a-budget/ (accessed 5 January 2017).

SBA (2016) https://www.sba.gov/advocacy/frequently-asked-questions-about-small-business (accessed 5 January 2017).

Scott, R. H. (2009) *The Use of Credit Card Debt by New Firms*. Kansas City, MO: Kauffman Foundation.

Shane, S. (2009) *The Illusions of Entrepreneurship: The Costly Myths that Entrepreneurs, Investors, and Policy Makers Live By*. New Haven, CT: Yale University Press.

Shell Livewire (2017) http://www.shell-livewire.com/home/halloffame/pizza_plus/ (accessed 5 January 2017).

Sunday Times (2009) 'How I Made It: Dominic List Founder of Comtact'. *Sunday Times*, 20 September.

Wingborg, J. and Landström, H. (2000) 'Financial bootstrapping in small business: examining small business managers' resource acquisition behaviour'. *Journal of Business Venturing*, 16: 235–54.

PART II

PERSPECTIVES ON ENTREPRENEURSHIP

10

RESEARCH MATTERS: INTRODUCTION AND OVERVIEW

[T]he essence of entrepreneurship is a change of state. And a change of state is a holistic process in which the existing stability disappears. When you try to take it apart, it tends to decompose.

William D. Bygrave, entrepreneurship scholar

There is always a well-known solution to every human problem – neat, plausible, and wrong.

H. L. Mencken, twentieth-century writer

LEARNING OUTCOMES

After reading this chapter you should be able to:

- Recognise the main sources of information about entrepreneurship and distinguish the different types of knowledge created by researchers, journalists, practitioners and others.
- Identify key themes, concepts, challenges and approaches in entrepreneurship research, including connections to two related areas of study – innovation and leadership.
- Explain why high-quality entrepreneurship research is important to various audiences, including policy-makers, practitioners, and the wider community.
- Examine these ideas in greater detail in the remaining Part Two chapters.

10.1 INTRODUCTION

10.1.1 Exploring a wider entrepreneurial landscape

Part One of this textbook concentrates on the practical aspects of creating and building entrepreneurial ventures. In Part Two, we are examining entrepreneurship from the perspective of a researcher, looking in more detail at the underlying factors that drive entrepreneurial activity and its impact on wider world. If you are simply looking to set up your own entrepreneurial business, the material covered in Part One could be

TABLE 10.1 Chapters 10–16: perspectives on entrepreneurship

Chapter	Title
10	Research matters: an overview
11	Individual perspectives: beyond the 'heroic' entrepreneur
12	Social perspectives: understanding people and places
13	Economic perspectives: influences and impacts
14	Historical perspectives: the 'long view'
15	Political perspectives: from policy to practice
16	Reflection: entrepreneurial learning

sufficient, at least for the time being. However, there is a great deal more to learn about entrepreneurship and the wide variety of ways in which it is practised around the world (Chapter 3). In Part Two, we are going to explore this wider entrepreneurial landscape and see how high-quality research can help us to better understand both the varied practices and the underlying processes. Each chapter has a similar format that provides a concise introduction to the leading research perspectives, explains the approaches that researchers have adopted, and highlights some of their more interesting findings. Chapter 16 brings Parts One and Two of the book together by taking a more detailed look at the latest research on entrepreneurial learning (Table 10.1). The world of research may be unfamiliar territory, and although it is now possible to access lots of useful material online, it is also very easy to become lost and disorientated when you are confronted by lots of unfamiliar technical language, conflicting ideas – and by the sheer volume of research publications. Chapter 10 is designed to help you through this maze, so even if you are only focusing on one or two of the research perspectives covered in Part Two, we strongly recommend that you read it first, before starting on the remaining chapters.

10.1.2 Dealing with competing definitions

Chapter 1 provided initial working definitions of the terms entrepreneur, entrepreneurship, and enterprise (Section 1.2.2). Then, in Chapter 2 we introduced the idea that entrepreneurial activity can be found in a wide variety of organisational contexts, at different degrees of intensity, and that is can have wildly contrasting impacts – both positive and negative – on the wider world. This variability has often led to confusion over what constitutes 'entrepreneurship', both in the popular imagination and among academic researchers. Perhaps unsurprisingly, the concept of an individual entrepreneur has also proved difficult to define and, as a consequence, remains open to a variety of interpretations. For many people, influenced by popular media representations of 'celebrity' entrepreneurs, it suggests lavish lifestyles, ostentatious wealth, and political influence. For others, 'entrepreneurs' have entirely negative connotations, including illicit activity, the exploitation of vulnerable people, and environmental degradation.

The variety of ways in which entrepreneurship is practised is broadly to be welcomed. It is, as the old saying goes, 'the spice of life', with entrepreneurial activity of different kinds providing a range of economic and social benefits (e.g. generating wealth and employment, producing useful and desirable products). However, it leaves students of the subject with some major challenges. How do you begin to make sense of a phenomenon that is so complex and varied (Choi and Majumdar 2014; Chowdhury et al. 2015)? It can be tempting to avoid the mental and emotional effort by resorting to myths, metaphors, and stereotypes, which appear to make things simpler (e.g. Clarke et al. 2014; Dodd and Anderson 2007). However, if you want to develop a deeper and more critical understanding of entrepreneurship and the enterprise culture, there are no short-cuts: you just have to accept (and deal with) the inherent variety and complexity. This means making use of knowledge from various sources, including academics, industry specialists, and the entrepreneurs themselves.

10.1.3 Recognising the practical value of entrepreneurship research

Research insights can have important implications for practice, and are often used by policy-makers, business support agencies and practitioners. We will be highlighting these practical applications in several ways:

- **Research in practice:** these case studies trace how findings from earlier work on entrepreneurship have been used by policy-makers and practitioners, and suggest the kind of impact they can have in the 'real world' of entrepreneurship.

- **Researcher profiles:** we have combined background information on leading entrepreneurship researchers with a short interview where the researchers tell us about their reasons for selecting particular topics, the methods they are using, their key findings, and where they see the research area developing in future.

- **Practical implications:** the concluding section of each Part Two chapter is where we look at the way research concepts and findings have been translated into everyday entrepreneurship. We also consider how the latest research is likely to influence future policies and practices.

- **Practical activities:** these tasks provide you with an opportunity to do some research of your own and to experiment with applying research findings to address practical challenges.

The rest of this chapter is structured as follows. In Section 10.2, we begin by looking at the different sources of information available about entrepreneurship and how they can be used to conduct research. Section 10.3 reviews the different types of knowledge that you can use to inform yourself about entrepreneurship. In Section 10.4, we introduce the remaining Part Two chapters by looking at their source disciplines, including economics, psychology, sociology, geography, history, and policy studies. Section 10.5 considers the practical implications of this considerable research effort for policy-makers, practitioners, and citizens.

In the first of our Researcher Profiles, Professor Per Davidsson discusses his work on research methods in the field of entrepreneurship (Case 10.1).

CASE 10.1 RESEARCHER PROFILE

PER DAVIDSSON, ON RESEARCH METHODS IN ENTREPRENEURSHIP

Professor Per Davidsson is Director and Talbot Family Foundation Chair in Entrepreneurship at the Australian Centre for Entrepreneurship Research (ACE) in

(Continued)

(Continued)

the QUT Business School, which is located in Brisbane, the capital of Queensland, Australia. Per studied for his PhD at the Stockholm School of Economics and is one of today's most influential entrepreneurship scholars. He is especially known for his extensive research on start-up and growth of small firms as well as societal well-being and job creation effects of those activities. Apart from many books, book chapters and research reports he has published over 60 peer reviewed articles such as the *Strategic Management Journal, Regional Studies, Journal of Management Studies, Entrepreneurship Theory & Practice, Entrepreneurship and Regional Development*, and *Journal of Business Venturing*, including the most cited articles ever published in the last two journals. He has led several major research programmes and developed large-scale, public data sets in Australia and Sweden. His mentoring, for which he has received the 'Mentor Award' from the Entrepreneurship Division of the Academy of Management, he has more than 25 PhD students to completion and in many cases to international awards and top tier publication. He has also consulted for companies, government departments and agencies, and international organisations. Per was an elected Officer of the Entrepreneurship Division of the Academy of Management for the 2007–12 period and served as its Chair in 2010/11. He is Field Editor of *Journal of Business Venturing* and serves on the editorial boards for several other journals.

In this interview, Per discusses his work on research methods in the field of entrepreneurship. Per has vast experience from working with large, customised data sets from government agencies as well as with large, survey-based panel studies of on-going start-ups. He and his students have also worked with other methodological approaches such as experiments, case studies, participant observation, computer simulation, and analysis of text data. He has written about methods issues in entrepreneurship research in a number of articles and books, most recently in *Researching Entrepreneurship: Conceptualization and Design* (Davidsson 2016).

What interests you about research methods in entrepreneurship?

Almost everything, as you can tell from my recent book (*Researching Entrepreneurship: Conceptualization and Design*). Particularly interesting challenges arise from the fact that entrepreneurship is a process; an experimental, non-linear journey from 'nothing' to 'something' where the focal entity – the new venture – initially only exists as a vague idea that might morph quite a bit along the way. In addition, you can't always tell whether a particular outcome is good or bad; termination may be better than continuation if no long-term success can be reached. This all forces you to think long, hard and creatively about everything from sampling to measurement to interpretation. Entrepreneurship is also a topic that can be approached on many levels of analysis (e.g. individual, [emerging] venture, team, industry, region, nation, etc.), and with many types of data and analysis methods.

Have you ever been surprised by a particular set of research findings?

Often! The most common is the negative surprise that results don't come out as expected, but that can sometimes lead you into a new, important line of inquiry. One of the strongest 'positive' surprises was the incredibly strong relationship we found between firm age and firm size on the one hand, and how firms grow on the other. It turns out that the growth of small and young 'high-growth firms' is almost entirely organic whereas older and larger firms predominantly grow through acquisitions. This was only revealed because we came up with a way to reliably partition these forms of growth in archival data sets. That was in Sweden back in the 1990s; only just recently have I seen the same done in other countries. Separating the forms of growth is important in order to get a correct image of where jobs are created. Acquisitions may reflect important restructuring but the associated growth is not equal to job creation but merely the transfer of jobs from one organisation to the other.

What do you see as the main challenges for entrepreneurship research over the next decade?

Interesting that you should ask – I'm just about to start writing on a book chapter on that topic, which I have promised to deliver by the end of the month. As a maturing field, we face the challenge of matching increased theoretical and methodological sophistication with sustained or increased relevance. It is easy to drift into delving deeper and deeper into smaller and smaller research questions. Or so it seems when you look at individual research articles, because it becomes increasingly impossible for individual researchers and studies to say something fundamentally new about the 'entirety' of broad phenomena such as 'success factors in the start-up process' or 'drivers of growth of young firms'. Therefore, we also need stock-taking of all the individual pieces of the puzzle that individual studies contribute and translation of this into major insights of the kind that matters to entrepreneurs, managers, and policy-makers. On the method side developments make it increasingly difficult to do high-quality survey research due to overload and the fragmented use of communication modes, but on the other hand technological developments lead to the production of entirely new types of data and ways to analyse them.

How do you make a connection between the worlds of research and practice?

The centre I run takes this seriously, and we have been fortunate to have some success on the outreach side. We repeatedly get consulted by various government department and agencies [in Canberra, Australia] and sometimes we have research collaboration with them. We organise events for practitioner audiences. We produce reports that are meant for interested practitioners. We also translate research into brief print and video 'vignettes' that convey research-based insights succinctly in lay language (see Online Resources for links).

(Continued)

(Continued)

What advice would you give to an entrepreneurship student who is navigating the research literature for the first time?

It depends a bit whether it is an undergraduate or a research student. Read my book, *Researching Entrepreneurship* – it's up to date and I've made an effort to make it more readable than most research texts. Read review articles that summarise findings on particular issues. When you start to read regular research articles, don't let jargon or formulae intimidate you; you can get the gist of the article without having to understand every detail in it. Learn about which journals are considered 'high quality' so you don't lean too heavily on questionable research. Try to learn how to assess methodological strengths and weaknesses so you know which results you can trust more and less, respectively. Do NOT just look for results that confirm what you already believe. Instead take findings that challenge your preconceptions seriously – that's how you can learn something new! Take research seriously without necessarily believing every claim you see. If you are going for a career as an entrepreneur, manager or public servant, compare yourself with a pilot or a medical doctor. You would expect them (and their employers) to learn about and apply new research findings throughout their careers, so that they can provide the safest service and best care, right? You can apply the same professional standards to yourself. Make sure your practice is not guided by dated myths or idiosyncratic experiences but by the most updated, systematic knowledge you can find. This would include academic research, although you would have to weigh research-based insights against, for example, industry- and firm-specific knowledge that you gain through reflected practice and experience.

10.2 SOURCES OF INFORMATION

People use many different sources of information to help them engage in, and to better understand, entrepreneurship. As a student, you are also likely to be drawing on a wide selection of sources during your studies in search of ideas, evidence, and inspiration. They are likely to include some or all of the following:

Academic literature (i.e. primarily peer-reviewed research)

- **Articles in peer-reviewed academic journals** such as Entrepreneurship Theory and Practice, Entrepreneurship and Regional Development, The Journal of Business Venturing, The Journal of Social Entrepreneurship and The International Small Business Journal, which are usually available in electronic form.

- **Academic books** are another source of research on entrepreneurship. You can find research monographs and edited books and 'Handbooks' covering particular topics, such as entrepreneurial learning (Rae and Wang 2015; Fayolle 2015; Melin et al. 2014; Neergaard and Ulhøi 2007).

- **Academic textbooks** are not normally sources of original research, but they often present introductions to research concepts and findings, so can be a more accessible way to get into a particular subject area. Some textbooks, including *Exploring Entrepreneurship*, also provide recommendations for further reading and are fully referenced, providing you with a useful entry-point for literature searches. For those with a particular interest in social enterprise, Ridley-Duff and Bull (2015), provides an accessible and up-to-date overview of a rapidly changing field.

'Grey' literature (i.e. research from non-academic sources)

- **Reports and briefings** produced by government agencies, non-governmental organisations (NGOs), and consultancies who may support or collaborate with entrepreneurs. These reports are often also available to view and download on the organisations' websites.

- **Marketing research**: reports related to your proposed venture.

- **Specialist media:** these may include trade publications, which might include reports about entrepreneurial activity in a particular industry sector (e.g. hotels and catering) or market (e.g. computer games).

Other sources

- **Business plan guides** and related practical advice (e.g. law, taxation, employing staff), usually found in popular 'start your own business' books and in brochures or downloads from banks and business support agencies. See the further reading guide for examples.

- **News stories**, analysis, and comment about aspects of entrepreneurship found in newspapers and broadcast media, often available via websites.

- **Documentaries** that feature entrepreneurial activity, which may take the form of films, television programmes, and web-based video clips.

- **Autobiographies or biographies** of entrepreneurs and historical studies of companies and industries, still mostly available in book form (NB short biographies of entrepreneurial founders and short organisational histories can often be found on websites under headings such as 'About Us').

- **Fictionalised accounts** of entrepreneurial activity in novels, films, plays, and television programmes.

- **Advice and personal anecdotes** from people who are directly involved in entrepreneurial activity, such as guest lecturers, relatives, and friends.

- **Your own personal experience** of entrepreneurial activity, perhaps gained during a youth enterprise competition, from setting up your own entrepreneurial venture, or from observing one as an employee or customer.

The kind of knowledge you will find in these sources ranges from the abstract, wide-ranging, and often inconclusive findings produced by academic researchers to the concrete, context-specific, and often very strongly worded advice given by experienced entrepreneurs. Each of these sources can help you to a better understanding of entrepreneurship. Some types of knowledge are going to be more useful than others, depending on your immediate aims. However, in the world of entrepreneurship, it is usually a mistake to ignore either the more 'practical' or the more 'academic' sources entirely. For example, while working on a new venture creation activity (either 'for real' or as part of a business simulation or competition), it certainly makes sense to concentrate on the more 'practical' types of knowledge, such as those found in Part One of this textbook. These activities are usually fairly intense and pressured, so you may think that it is a waste of time to read anything other than a few 'how-to' guides to financial forecasts or marketing plan. Think again! Some of the best new venture ideas we have come across were, at least in part, the product of students pushing themselves beyond the 'safe' territory of the business plan guide. Similarly, when writing a more academically oriented piece of work, such as a dissertation researching an aspect of entrepreneurship or an essay reflecting on your experience while participating in a new venture creation activity, you are likely to focus on academic journal articles, academic books, government reports, and the kind of material that is covered in Part Two of this textbook. These are the best places to locate the concepts, models, and theoretical frameworks that are essential if you are going to structure and make some sense of the empirical evidence (e.g. research findings you have collected for your dissertation or notes from your personal diary that form the raw material of your reflective essay). In these situations, focusing on high-quality academic sources is a sensible option. However, it would be unfortunate if, in an effort to appear suitably 'serious', you were to ignore the less formal sources entirely. The key here is to select and apply the different sources in ways that fit with your basic purpose. Consider the following practical examples (Case 10.2):

CASE 10.2   STUDENT FOCUS

Using research effectively

These short fictionalised accounts, based on real world examples, illustrate how students have made good use of entrepreneurship research to achieve successful outcomes in their studies

CREATING A MORE EXCITING NEW VENTURE PROPOSAL

Three members of the student venture team, 'Smoky Phoenix' gather in one of the university's quieter coffee shops. It is already week five of the enterprise project and everyone is feeling tired and depressed. The team has come up with a few venture ideas, but everyone realises that they are uninspiring – neither innovative, sustainable, or with much in the way of growth potential. 'Yeah, but who cares?' says Jonas, 'all we need is a "pass"'. 'At that moment, Sarah, the last team member rushes in, gets out her tablet and makes some space for it on the crowded table. Everyone glances at the screen, which is full of text. 'What are we looking at?' asks Jonas, as Sarah collapses on the sofa. 'It's the answer to all our problems – look at this ...' she says as she flicks to a series of photos and an extract from a journal article. Sarah has found a description of the world's first capsule hotel:

> 'With rooms made from fibreglass, measuring 90 x 180 x 00 cm, the first capsule hotel was opened in Osaka in 1977 [...]. The capsule hotel is usually located close to major railway stations, designed to service the needs of the businessman (and these are very masculinised spaces) who has missed the last train.' (McNeill 2008: 398)

Jonas frowns and sips his double espresso, 'Nah, I don't get it' he says, 'this is just academic research and we've got much more important things to think about!' Sarah patiently explains her big idea and points out another section, which describes how the idea has been developed:

'The logic of this particular hotel form – so peculiar to Japan – is currently being adapted for use in London. The Yotel company (which emerged out of bringing sushi conveyor belts to the UK) sells the concept of modularised rooms of 10 m², with internal windows, which can be fitted into disused 1950s–80s buildings, or even underground.' (ibid., 398)

By taking this Japanese example and the subsequent applications as inspiration, the Smoky Phoenix team could create its own truly innovative product for a twenty-first century European market. 'How about targeting music festivals and other outdoor events with an alternative to leaky and insecure tents,' she suggests. The other members of the team take a closer look at the article as Sarah continues with her explanation. They also check out the Yotel website (www.yotel.com) to see how the concept has been developed. Having convinced them that the idea is worth exploring – and of the benefits of lateral thinking – Ayisha notes down some details and references from the article while Philip starts a web search on 'capsule hotels'. Jonas takes a quiet look at his phone messages, muttering to himself: 'Yeah, well ... I still think we should have gone with my T-shirts idea.'

GETTING THE FINAL YEAR PROJECT BACK ON TRACK

Katerina is studying at a university in Australia. She's decided that her final year project is going to be in the area of gender and entrepreneurship. Her parents both left teaching careers to set up a small business and her older sister Pernille has recently set up a business at home in Denmark. Katrina's become interested in the idea that there may be differences around the kinds of ventures men and women establish, and they way that they build their businesses. She has spent some time on the library's e-journals collection using search terms like, 'gender entrepreneurship' and 'women entrepreneurs', and now has more than 60 journal articles downloaded as PDFs. There is also a pile of library books on the floor beside her desk, including a couple of textbooks and an old dissertation. She's managed to write a few pages of text, summarising some of these sources, but it's still just a list of facts and ideas – everything seems disconnected. Katerina is feeling confused and a little disappointed with herself – maybe this wasn't a good subject after all. She flicks randomly through the sources and is really not sure what to do next. Eventually, she decides to contact her supervisor, Emma, and they arrange a meeting.

'OK' says Emma, 'I can see you have done a lot of work here, but it does need a bit more focus.' Katrina sighs, 'But what should I be focusing on?' Emma discusses a few strategies for generating good research topics and questions, such as scanning the 'further research' sections of recent journal articles, looking for topical issues raised in specialist media, or talking to practitioners. Katrina then remembers something her sister mentioned about a women's enterprise network she had joined the previous year, which was providing her with support and encouragement. Emma asks if any of the journal articles covered this topic, since this could help provide useful concepts, frameworks and questions that would give the dissertation a real focus. Katrina recalls a popular but fairly old article by Aldrich et al. (1989) called, 'Women on the verge of a breakthrough: networking among entrepreneurs in the United States and Italy.' Emma agrees that this could be a good starting point and suggests looking for more recent studies that have cited that article, such as Bogren et al. (2013) 'Networking women entrepreneurs: fruitful for business growth?'

(Continued)

(Continued)

Next, the discussion turns to collecting suitable evidence for the study. Katerina tells Emma a bit about her sister's business, and her network connections. Pernille's network looks like an ideal basis for an empirical study. However, given the distances involved it isn't going to be possible for her to conduct any interviews in person. Another option is to contact members of the network by email and ask them to complete a survey questionnaire. Emma agrees that this could work, though response rates can be fairly low and Katerina only has a few weeks to complete the research. 'Can you think of any other sources of evidence that might give you an insight into this network?' asks Emma. 'Well, there is a discussion thread on the website but I'm not sure it's proper evidence – I mean, it's just a lot of people asking questions and exchanging advice.' Katerina finds the discussion thread on her table and shows it to her supervisor. After scanning through some recent entries, Emma sits back in her chair and smiles. 'This discussion thread could be exactly what you need. We'd need to consider whether there are any ethical issues involved, but if you treated the text of the discussions as anonymised qualitative evidence, it could be very useful indeed.'

QUESTIONS

1. In what ways might you make use of academic research when you are developing a new venture proposal?

2. What do you see as 'top three' advantages and disadvantages of e-journal collections for someone trying to decide on a research topic?

3. Conduct your own e-journal search, selecting suitable key words, and find at least three articles that Katerina might find helpful when she is drafting her project.

Having considered the principal sources of information about entrepreneurship, the most important lesson is to be *selective* – taking time to search for the most appropriate sources – and remaining *critical* when you are making use of the information they contain. For example, certain types of information are likely to be more useful for *practical* tasks (e.g. preparing a financial forecast as part of a business plan, or developing relationships with key stakeholders), while other types are more relevant when we are 'taking a step back', and looking at the more *theoretical* aspects of entrepreneurship (e.g. trying to understand why there is more entrepreneurial activity in a particular team of people, organisation, or geographical location). Table 10.2 summarises these differences by identifying four broad types of knowledge about entrepreneurship, which range from 'more concrete' to 'more abstract' knowledge.

The important point here is that all four types are potentially valuable, and that the real issue is in selecting the appropriate type for particular purposed. The four types shown in Table 10.2 build on the work of a twentieth-century political economist, Friedrich von Hayek, who first used the term 'practical knowledge' to refer to the kind of specialised local knowledge that an entrepreneur might use from day to day in order to secure a profit (Hayek [1945] 1972: 80) (Section 11.4). In Table 10.2, we can see the founders of the biotech start-up and the social enterprise both making use of this kind of knowledge in order to establish their new ventures. Hayek contrasted this with 'scientific knowledge', of the kind used by economists. The examples in Table 10.2 are the correlation between

TABLE 10.2 Four broad types of knowledge

Type of knowledge		Practical examples
More concrete ↑	Practical knowledge of the entrepreneur	The founders of a biotech start-up know about the technical performance of a new pharmaceutical drug. The founders of a new social enterprise know about the needs of young disabled people in their city.
	Practical knowledge about entrepreneurship	The owner-manager of an established Internet service provider knows which providers of venture finance to approach in order to grow her business. The directors of a local food retailing co-operative know that it is important build strong relationships with their suppliers.
	Social science knowledge with practical implications for entrepreneurship	Organisational researchers show how web-based entrepreneurs can use social networks more effectively when operating internationally. Entrepreneurial finance researchers uncover new evidence of how limited access to credit affects the number of new ventures being created in a post-conflict economy.
↓ More abstract	Social science knowledge with no [direct] implications for practical entrepreneurship	Economists identify a correlation between R&D (research and development) 'spillovers' and economic growth in two countries. Historians provide a new explanation for the success of manufacturing firms in a nineteenth century industrial district.

Source: Swedberg (2000): 38; by permission of Oxford University Press; examples added.

R&D spillovers and economic growth, and the findings from the historical study, both of which have no *immediate* practical implications for entrepreneurial practice. However, while all these forms of knowledge have their uses, entrepreneurship research needs to draw on both the more 'practical' and the more 'scientific' ends of the continuum:

> *One conclusion that can be drawn from Hayek's argument is that economics, as well as the other social sciences, need to incorporate some of this 'practical knowledge' into their analyses. By this is not meant that the social sciences should become a depository for all the empirical facts that have ever played a role in successful business ventures – this would clearly be absurd and also make it impossible to produce any science. What it does mean, however, is that **if the social sciences are ever to get a better handle on entrepreneurship, they will have to learn to pay more attention to the concrete ways in which entrepreneurs locate and exploit opportunities**. This type of knowledge has a certain degree of generality to it; and it is precisely this generality which makes it relevant to the social sciences. (Swedberg 2000: 10 – emphasis in original)*

In other words, entrepreneurship researchers need to combine the theoretically informed, research-based evidence generated by academics and the more concrete 'practical' insights of entrepreneurs. Otherwise, our understanding of entrepreneurship can easily 'fall between two stools', becoming either too abstract and divorced from reality, or too anecdotal and context-specific. The two-part structure of *Exploring Entrepreneurship* can help you to bridge this gap, with Part One emphasising the 'practice' issues involved in creating a new venture and Part Two providing the necessary social scientific 'perspective'. The next case (Case 10.3) illustrates how researchers have attempted to make this kind of link between the worlds of academic investigation and entrepreneurial practice.

CASE 10.3

Research in action: CIRCLE at Lund University

CIRCLE (the Centre for Innovation, Research and Competence in the Learning Economy) is an interdisciplinary research centre, established in 2004, which operates across several faculties at Lund University in the province of Scania, southern Sweden. CIRCLE's activities are funded from a number of sources including research councils, government agencies and charitable foundations. It comprises a team of around 35 academic researchers, research students, administrative and support staff, plus visiting faculty. The centre describes its overall ambitions in the following terms:

> Our aim is to understand and explain how innovation can contribute to a good society and tackle societal challenges like economic crises, climate change or increased globalisation of economic activities. This aim requires advanced insights into how knowledge is created and diffused in organisations, networks, regions, countries, and globally; how knowledge is turned into innovations; and which societal conditions promote the creation and diffusion of innovation.

The centre has five interconnected research themes: (1) Innovation and Entrepreneurship, (2) Globalisation of Innovation, (3) Innovation and Sustainability, (4) Innovations Skills, Strategies and Industry Renewal, and (5) Innovation Systems and Policy. Each of these hosts its own research projects; researchers are often involved in several themes. Examples of the types of research questions tackled by the CIRCLE team include:

- How can we measure the strength of entrepreneurial systems, including the mapping of actors, networks, and institutions?

- What are the main drivers of innovative entrepreneurship in entrepreneurial systems?

- How do incumbent firms and new entrants cooperate, compete and network in eco-innovation and sustainable transitions?

The centre has a working papers series, which provides for early dissemination of their findings prior to publication of the final versions in international academic journals. It also publishes reports for a wider audience, including academics, funding organisations, policy-makers and members of the public. These cover a variety of themes such as start-up ventures, regional development, smart specialisation, academic entrepreneurship, university–industry cooperation, and environmental sustainability challenges. CIRCLE is also involved in developing research students, working in close cooperation with the Social Science Faculty, the School of Economics and Management, and the Faculty of Engineering, and in contributing to Master's programmes at the university.

Source: CIRCLE 2016.

QUESTIONS

1. What are the researchers at CIRCLE doing in order to engage directly with the worlds of policy and practice?

2. Review a few recent CIRCLE publications and find out how they are making connections between innovation and entrepreneurship.

3. Search online for a similar entrepreneurship research centre in your own country or region and compare their: (a) specialist interests; (b) research approaches with those of CIRCLE.

10.3 RESEARCH APPROACHES AND METHODS

10.3.1 Five disciplinary perspectives

In this section, we introduce the broad disciplinary perspectives, which form the basis for the next five chapters:

- Psychology and behavioural studies (Chapter 11).
- Sociology, human geography and anthropology (Chapter 12).
- Economics (Chapter 13).
- Historical studies, including business history (Chapter 14).
- Political science and policy studies (Chapter 15).

Researchers have used these perspectives to generate important new insights into entrepreneurship, which have subsequently been published in peer-reviewed journals, research-based books and reports. Some of this research evidence and new theoretical insight has influenced public policy and practice (Chapter 15). It has also helped to shape wider public understanding of entrepreneurship via educational courses, books, and mass media coverage. Our introductory comments cover three aspects of each perspective: (a) What kinds of questions does it address? (b) What kinds of research methods does it tend to employ? (c) What kinds of findings does it generate?

Psychology and behavioural studies: The common theme in psychological and behavioural research is that the focus is on *individual* human beings. People are often attracted to these perspectives on entrepreneurship because it relates directly to their own personal experience. Again, there are two broad strands: (a) the first tries to identify what makes people entrepreneurial; (b) the second examines the behaviours associated with being entrepreneurial. The first strand is perhaps most strongly associated with the efforts of psychologists to isolate specific personality 'traits' and 'characteristics'. Though these approaches are now largely dismissed, they remain remarkably influential. Other, more significant work in the first strand includes the work of developmental psychologists on the influence of childhood experiences, and of social psychologists on peer groups and role models. The second strand, which developed in response to critiques of some of the earlier studies, looks at the actual behaviours of people identified as entrepreneurial. One of the more compelling questions raised by such research is whether it is possible to 'teach' someone to behave entrepreneurially – and furthermore, how far is entrepreneurial behaviour a predictor of becoming a successful entrepreneur? Assuming that you were not 'born' an entrepreneur, can you still be 'made' into one – and, if so, how? We address these questions in Chapter 11.

Sociology, human geography, and anthropology: while individual-level research has produced interesting findings, entrepreneurship is a phenomenon that extends well beyond the minds and behaviours of individual entrepreneurs. The major contribution of sociology, human geography, and anthropology is to examine how entrepreneurship is shaped by larger social forces. For example, a sociologist might examine gender differences in entrepreneurship, including the tendency to underplay the role of women in many accounts of entrepreneurial activity. The geography of enterprise is another important research field, with themes such as **spatial variation** (i.e. why are more new ventures being created in this area?) and clustering (i.e. why do similar enterprises tend to locate close to one another?). Anthropologists may seem an unlikely breed of entrepreneurship researcher but their studies of other cultures, including pre-industrial ones, have revealed interesting insights into the different forms that entrepreneurial activity can take. Social research of this kind adopts a very wide range of approaches, and is often conducted at multiple levels of analysis (e.g. individual, group, organisation, local community, or region). The use of qualitative data is probably more common, particularly in anthropology, but researchers may also make use of quantitative data in some cases (e.g. industry statistics and social survey data). In much of the work adopting a social perspective, there is a largely uncritical approach to entrepreneurship – the assumption is that we are simply interested in encouraging more of the same. However, there is also some more critical work, which examines its more negative forms and more destructive impacts (e.g. organised crime, environmentally harmful businesses), as well as possible alternatives. We consider these, and other related issues in Chapter 12.

Economics: Of all the disciplines, economics probably has the best claim to having 'invented' entrepreneurship. Or, more strictly speaking, the pioneers of what we now know as economics were responsible for introducing the term, 'entrepreneur', firstly into the French language in the early eighteenth century, and subsequently into English. At the same time, they provided us with the first definition of the entrepreneurial function (Section 13.1). Over the years, economists have developed two broad strands of entrepreneurship research: (1) a more theoretical and inward-looking strand that tries to specify the function of the entrepreneurial actor within conventional economic frameworks (i.e. how to reconcile the active role of the entrepreneur with the 'invisible hand' of the market); (2) a more policy-oriented and outward-looking strand that examines the relationship between entrepreneurial activity and achieving greater economic growth (e.g. researchers might examine the impact of policies such as deregulation, tax breaks, and support for new ventures). In empirical research, economists often make use of large data sets (e.g. macro-economic measures such as rates of growth, employment, unemployment, interest, etc.), which are then subjected to quantitative analysis and modelling. Economics-based research on entrepreneurship has also tended to emphasise the collection and analysis of quantitative data. In addition to macro-economic data of the kind already mentioned, researchers have often relied on individual-level data derived from questionnaire surveys (e.g. a telephone-based survey of a large representative sample of owner-managers). However, economists do also make some use of qualitative data (e.g. from in-depth interviews). The findings generated by economists have, for obvious reasons, tended to focus on the economic aspects of entrepreneurship. If non-economic factors are considered (e.g. the role of culture), it is usually in order to evaluate the impact of such factors on economic outcomes. So how should you organise an economy in order to get the most from entrepreneurship? We begin our search for an answer in Chapter 13.

Business history: In one of the opening quotations, William Bygrave suggests that entrepreneurship is fundamentally about a 'change of state'. The implication of this is that 'history matters'. In other words, we can only understand entrepreneurship as a process that unfolds over time, and where current activity is influenced, to some degree, by what has happened in the past. In order to grasp the importance of historical perspectives, just think of another process unfolding over time, such as a football match. A 'snapshot' image taken at some point during the game might be interesting, but it would tell us very little about how the game was being played, or where it was going. However, it would also be true to say that reviewing the whole match once it is over is an entirely different experience from that of the players (or the spectators), who are involved in real time, and where the outcome is unknown. In practice, many researchers take some account of the time dimension. Some make limited use of historical methods, while others at least introduce some kind of longitudinal element into their research. However, there is also a distinct tradition of business history research, with strong links to entrepreneurship. Business historians have addressed a variety of questions across the full range of the other perspectives. Their methods are also distinctive, with a particular focus on archive-based research (e.g. investigating early company documents, personal diaries, trade publications, etc.). In Chapter 14 we see how the use of such methods, coupled with the longer-time horizons of the historian, can enhance our understanding.

Political science and policy studies Having started this review of the main disciplinary perspectives with the pioneers of economics, our final chapter comes full circle, with a discussion of politics – or what is sometimes termed 'political economy' – and policy studies. In an echo of the period when Adam Smith, John Stuart Mill, and Karl Marx were writing, there has been a recent trend to examine the connections between the political and the economic aspects of contemporary society. In the late twentieth century, a powerful coalition of economists and political scientists, sometimes referred to as the 'New Right', developed a series of policy initiatives to create more entrepreneurial economies based on a liberalised market model. Today, we are in a rather different environment, in which alternatives to the 'free' market have largely disappeared, yet where the world is faced with enormous social, environmental, and economic challenges (e.g. international terrorism, climate change, the global financial crisis). Policy studies provide us with insights into the sort of intervention that governments have adopted to promote entrepreneurial activity of various kinds. For example, there is a strong strand of research on policies to promote new venture creation in difficult environments, including marginalised communities and post-conflict situations. Political scientists have contributed to research on the role of government in relation to entrepreneurship. This includes a more critical research tradition that challenges aspects of the 'enterprise culture' project, including its negative impacts on certain individuals and communities. In Chapter 15, we examine previous policy initiatives and evaluate their impact on both the 'quantity' and the 'quality' of enterprise in various parts of the world. Building on insights from policy, political science and the other perspectives, we will also raise some questions about the ways that entrepreneurship might develop in the twenty-first century.

10.3.2 Multi- and interdisciplinary research

We have now reviewed the five main disciplinary perspectives on entrepreneurship, noted the approaches they have adopted, and indicated what kinds of findings each has contributed. Each perspective has something to contribute to our understanding of entrepreneurship. Of course, these are broad categories, comprising a rich variety of research approaches and insights, but our grouping is based on some common ground between the academic researchers involved. However, it is also important to recognise that many of the most interesting studies of recent years have been **_multi_disciplinary**, meaning that they involve collaborations by researchers from two or more disciplines (e.g. economics and psychology), or **_inter_disciplinary**, meaning that insights from different disciplines are combined to create new models, approaches and methods. Furthermore, there are many overlaps and 'grey areas' within and between disciplines, contributing to occasional 'turf wars' (i.e. intellectual disputes) concerning issues such as the most appropriate methods, theoretical frameworks, and terminology in use. Our approach to these problems is to build each Part Two chapter around a distinctive perspective on entrepreneurship, while also indicating how different disciplines and levels of analysis can be combined to pursue specific research questions.

10.3.3 The current state of entrepreneurship research

So what is the current state of entrepreneurship research? The answer is likely to vary, depending on who you speak to and what you choose to read. Some researchers argue that we already know a great deal about our subject, while others are more cautious. Two decades ago, William Bygrave, a former physicist, argued that the field was still in its infancy. As a consequence, he thought researchers should be spending less time on theoretical modelling and sophisticated statistical analysis, and more on basic field research:

> _Unlike physics, which has been central to intellectual thought for more than two millennia, entrepreneurship has barely begun to be noticed. This has important implications for the theory and methods that we use. [...] It is rather like biology before Darwin's natural selection theory, or nuclear physics before Rutherford's model. At that stage, the emphasis should be on painstaking observations rather than theory building. (Bygrave 1989: 12–19)_

Since that time, entrepreneurship research has continued to blossom, extending into new academic disciplines and yielding a rich harvest of empirical and conceptual material. One of the major challenges for today's researchers is in making sense of the many different kinds of evidence that are now available. With a few notable exceptions, most studies have been conducted at a single level of analysis (e.g. individuals, firms, **industries**), often reflecting the disciplinary backgrounds of the researchers (e.g. psychology, organisation studies, economics). This tendency was noted in an earlier review of the entrepreneurship research field (Low and MacMillan 1988). The authors argued that **multi-level** studies, though limited in number, had demonstrated their potential to provide a richer understanding of the subject, and that more work was needed in this area:

> _The challenge for entrepreneurship research is to increase the incorporation of multiple levels of analysis into future research designs. (Low and MacMillan 1988: 152)_

More than a decade later, a survey of articles published in the leading US and European entrepreneurship journals revealed that research was still dominated by micro-level analysis, and that integrated approaches still represented a small proportion of published work (Davidsson and Wiklund 2001). While there has been a lot of debate over the relative importance of different research approaches, relatively little progress has been made in integrating them, either empirically or conceptually. Low and MacMillan (1988: 153) also drew attention to the need for 'wide time frame studies' that would allow researchers to pursue causal linkages (e.g. demonstrating how a particular combination of factors contributed to a change in the level of entrepreneurial activity). Since that time, there *has* been something of a shift towards studies that address the process of entrepreneurship. This has proved particularly useful when examining questions such as the relationship between **entrepreneurial learning** and the **growth** of ventures (e.g. Macpherson and Holt 2007; Rae and Wang 2015) (Chapter 16). Process-based research can be distinguished from variance-based research by its emphasis on the complex interactions that generate particular outcomes:

> *Whereas variance theories provide explanations for phenomena in terms of relationships among dependent and independent variables (e.g. more of X and more of Y produced more of Z), process theories provide explanations in terms of the sequence of events leading to an outcome (e.g. do A and then B to get C).'* (Langley 1999: 691)

Researchers have employed various strategies to build or refine process theories (Hjorth et al. 2015). Each has sought to understand 'patterns in events', but their methodologies differ in the extent to which they can probe beyond observed events (i.e. surface-level effects), to explore the underlying causal sequences and mechanisms. For example, **population ecology** is a well-established approach to studying entrepreneurial activity (e.g. Swaminathan 1995: Staber 1997). It uses a single-level methodology, exploring macro-level processes with aggregated quantitative data (e.g. official statistical data sets recording firm entries and exits) (Section 13.2). There are also approaches that examine entrepreneurship at a more detailed level. These include **ethnographic** studies (e.g. Fletcher 2006; Ram 1999), who reveal micro-level processes by collecting mainly qualitative evidence through fieldwork (e.g. observing and engaging with a particular group of entrepreneurs) (Section 13.2). There is also a long tradition of **historical research** in entrepreneurship, which has used a variety of approaches, sometimes combining multiple levels of analysis (e.g. studying how an interplay between entrepreneurs, organisations, and institutions has shaped the growth of industrial districts) (Section 14.3). Multi-level studies can provide us with more sophisticated explanations of entrepreneurial activity that take account of interaction between individual-level processes and those identified at higher levels (i.e. the firm, industry sector, and region). Examples of studies include Best's (2001) analysis of the resurgence of entrepreneurial firms and inter-firm networks in the USA, and Jones's (2001) examination of divergent strategies of technology- and content-driven entrepreneurs in the early years of the US film industry. However, this kind of research is difficult to undertake, and there is still plenty of scope for researchers to develop new multi-level research approaches:

> *Despite our advances in understanding the process and context of entrepreneurial activities, we still have a long way to go before achieving Low and MacMillan's [1988: 14–16] vision. They not only suggested a need to study process*

*and context, but also to integrate them into a coherent theoretical framework.
We would like to go a step beyond their statement and suggest that we also need
to* empirically *integrate process and context. (Aldrich and Martinez 2001: 51;
emphasis in original)*

In summary, we can argue that the entrepreneurship research field is healthy and
active, with considerable progress being made in addressing its limitations and
extending its scope. The subject is also of central importance, both in terms of
economic performance and social well-being.

The remaining Part Two chapters feature many examples of research studies that are
providing us with fresh insights into entrepreneurship, in all its variety. The potential contribution of research is illustrated in an extended case study 'Deconstructing
Dyson' (Case 10.4). It shows how two researchers applied the concepts of social
networks and **entrepreneurial networking** in order to reinterpret a well-known
entrepreneur's account of his efforts to build a technology-based enterprise. In
doing so, they revealed the previously hidden roles played by other key actors, and
highlighted important features of the institutional context in which this entrepreneur
was operating.

CASE 10.4

Deconstructing Dyson: applying a network perspective

This case study re-examines a story of entrepreneurial success using insights from social
networks research, an approach that we will examine in greater detail in Chapter 12.

James Dyson is a successful British industrial designer, innovator, and entrepreneur,
best known for his 'Dual-Cyclone' vacuum cleaner. His autobiography, *Against the Odds*, is

very readable and inspiring, showing how creative thinkers can succeed, even in very mature markets dominated
by large incumbent corporations (Dyson 2003). Dyson's
personal journey was far from easy, and his lively writing
style emphasises the importance of self-belief, courage,
persistence, and sheer hard work in creating a new venture. But is this the full story? Steve Conway and Oswald
Jones decided to examine the role played by other people located on the margins of Dyson's narrative. In their
re-reading of the autobiography, the two researchers
focused on the role played by the entrepreneur's informal
or 'social' network (Conway and Jones 2012). The following
extracts indicate a few of the ways that network connections contributed important resources, including support,
information, and knowledge.

FROM SEA TRUCKS TO VACUUM CLEANERS: THE BASIC STORY

While studying for a Master's degree course in design at the Royal College of Art (RCA),
London, James Dyson began to work for an entrepreneur named Jeremy Fry who

manufactured motorised valve actuators for pipelines. Fry encouraged him to adopt a 'hands-on' (i.e. practical) approach to design rather than one based on theory. Dyson was soon working on one of his innovative ideas, the 'Sea Truck', and over the following months went on to build a prototype. He patented his idea and Fry set up a subsidiary of his company, 'Rotork', to manufacture the product. While working for Rotork, Dyson and his family moved from London to a 300-year-old farmhouse in the Cotswolds. Undertaking most of the rebuilding work himself, he became familiar with the failings of the traditional wheelbarrow: unstable when fully laden, tyres prone to puncture, liable to sink into soft ground, and with a steel body that damaged door frames and human limbs. Having considered the problem for around a year, he hit upon the idea of reinventing the wheelbarrow by constructing it in plastic and replacing the wheel with a ball. At this point, Dyson decided to set up his own manufacturing company. He launched the 'Ballbarrow', which soon became a commercial success. However, the idea was then stolen by a US company and Dyson's company lost the subsequent legal case. This failure led to tension between board members and Dyson was voted out by his business associates. Undeterred, he decided to investigate another problem encountered during the refurbishment of his old farmhouse: why did the performance of his vacuum cleaner decline so rapidly after fitting a new dust bag? Dyson found that it needed only a thin layer of dust inside the bag to clog the pores and reduce the suction. Experience with industrial cyclone technology, which is widely used in sawmills and to handle other powdery materials, gave him the idea for a cyclone vacuum cleaner. Using an old vacuum cleaner, cardboard, and industrial tape, he spent one evening constructing a fully working model of the world's first bagless cleaner – the prototype for the 'Dual-Cyclone'. After two years of trying to convince British and European companies of the Dual-Cyclone's potential, Dyson decided to try the USA. Despite the optimism and the 'can-do' spirit of the USA, which he found refreshing after the negativity he experienced in the UK, no company was willing to manufacture the Dual-Cyclone. In November 1984, after five years of trying to gain interest in the Dual-Cyclone among European and US manufacturers, Dyson received an informal approach from a Japanese company, who agreed to produce the Dual-Cyclone for the Japanese market under the 'G-Force' brand name. He then managed to set up a deal with a Canadian company, who agreed to produce the Dual-Cyclone for the US market under the 'Drytech' brand name. However, just before the product launch, Dyson discovered that Amway, a US company that had rejected the Dual-Cyclone concept several years before, had now launched their own version. Reluctantly, Dyson found himself involved in another long-running and extremely expensive legal battle. In 1991, after almost five years of litigation, Amway agreed to a deal over their patent infringement and the haemorrhage of legal fees stopped. Finally, in July 1993, 15 years after his original idea, the first 'DC01' Dual-Cyclone vacuum cleaner rolled off Dyson's own assembly line, and the innovation was successfully launched in the UK.

FRIENDS AND CONTACTS: THE STORY FROM A SOCIAL NETWORK PERSPECTIVE

While studying at the RCA Dyson met theatrical and film impresario Joan Littlewood, who invited him to design a new theatre. Dyson created a 'mushroom-shaped auditorium built of aluminium rods'. He sought financial support for the project from British Aluminium. During his first meeting, a manager suggested that he contact Jeremy Fry; this was to be the start of a long relationship:

(Continued)

(Continued)

> I had shown Fry my model of the proposed theatre, and I think he rather liked it, if not enough to cover me with gold. What he did offer me, however, was to prove far more useful in the long run: work [at Rotork], and the first of many collaborations. (Dyson 2003: 47)

Dyson eventually left Fry's company, to establish his 'Ballbarrow' venture. This is one of several occasions where the entrepreneur acknowledges the considerable emotional and practical support provided by his wife, Deirdre:

> I still marvel at Deirdre's encouragement of me at that time. It could have meant losing everything. But she was always philosophical, and insisted that if everything failed she could paint pictures for money and I could make furniture. (Dyson 2003: 78)

Although he had made money from the Sea Truck, Dyson needed financial support to establish his company. As with many entrepreneurs, he turned to his family. These direct and indirect network ties were fundamental to the start-up, providing legal advice on company formation, plus funding to develop the Ballbarrow and to invest in production equipment:

> I went to see a lawyer friend of my brother-in-law ... Andrew Phillips not only helped with the formation of the company, but fell in love with the Ballbarrow and persuaded said brother-in-law (Stuart Kirkwood) to invest in it. Stuart was the son of one Lord Kirkwood, former chairman of the mining company RTZ. He and his brother ... as a result, inherited some family money. Which is always nice. (Dyson 2003: 79–80)

Following his departure from the Ballbarrow venture, Dyson decided to concentrate his efforts on developing the 'Dual-Cyclone' vacuum cleaner. However, he needed finance to proceed, and thus sought a partner to invest in the setting up of the 'Air Power Vacuum Cleaner Company'. Dyson generated some capital from his own resources, but for the balance, he turned again to Jeremy Fry:

> Fry ... was always likely to be my best hope. And so it proved. With £25,000 from Jeremy, and £25,000 from me, £18,000 of which I raised by selling the vegetable garden at Sycamore House and the rest borrowed with my home as security ... I was in the vacuum cleaner business. (Dyson 2003: 120)

Dyson eventually built around 5,000 prototypes over a three-year period, and by 1982 he had a Dual-Cyclone that was 100% efficient, but he also had debts of more than £80,000. Dyson's connection with Jeremy Fry and Rotork again proved invaluable in providing essential funding (Dyson 2003: 138). However, a key element in the ultimate success of the Dual-Cyclone was the deal he established with the Canadian company run by Jeffery Pike, a fellow British national:

> [W]ith whom I had become friendly quite by chance after we sat next to each other on an aeroplane in May 1986, and both turned out to be reading the same novel by Fay Weldon. Having flunked English A-level [school examination] all those years before, my fortune looked as if it was about to be made by a novel. (Dyson 2003: 175; emphasis added)

As plans for the manufacture of the Dual-Cyclone in the UK progressed, Dyson used his connections to hire talented young design engineers direct from the RCA, just as Jeremy Fry had done previously (Dyson 2003: 192). Dyson's continuing involvement with the RCA illustrates his ability to maintain and to utilise long-standing social networks:

> Round about the time I was planning the DC-02, I was at the RCA degree show – for I had since become an internal examiner on their product design course – and I went around offering one or two of the graduates jobs, as is my habitual wont. (Dyson 2003: 239)

By 1996 Dyson was considering ways in which he could extend into the increasingly global market for consumer products. After considering the attractions of Germany and France as the first step in his expansion, he eventually settled on Australia:

> I got a call from a man called Ross Cameron. Cameron was an Australian who had seen a presentation of mine at Johnson-Wax in Racine, Wisconsin. 'Why not start up in Australia?' I asked. A couple of days later Ross rang back to say 'OK'. He was that sort of man, not one to mess about. (Dyson 2003: 252–3)

Yet again, Dyson's social network proved to have a major impact on the direction and fortunes of his entrepreneurial venture.

QUESTIONS

1. Select three examples of entrepreneurial networking and in each case, identify: (a) the main actors, (b) the kinds of things that are flowing through the network (e.g. finance, information and influence), (c) the outcome for Dyson and his business ventures.

2. Choose another example of entrepreneurial activity, either from your own personal experience or from a secondary source (e.g. a biography, website or novel), and try to identify evidence of entrepreneurial networks and networking.

3. What does a network perspective add to your understanding of entrepreneurial activity?

Sources: Conway and Jones 2012; Dyson 2003; Johannisson 2000 – original case material adapted with permission and acknowledgements.

10.4 PRACTICAL IMPLICATIONS

The theories, concepts and findings generated by entrepreneurship researchers can be useful to various audiences, including policy-makers, practitioners, and citizens. The organisational psychologist, Kurt Lewin once famously argued that 'Nothing is as useful as a good theory' (Lewin 1945: 142). However, as the management scholar Sumantra Ghoshal has also pointed out, 'Nothing is as dangerous as a bad theory' (Ghoshal 2005: 96). In other words, while theories can benefit society if they are well developed and based on sound research evidence, poorly developed theories can do a lot of damage if they are used to guide our policy and practice. Ghoshal was particularly concerned that management research was generating what he described as 'ideologically inspired amoral theories' (ibid., 76), that applied *natural* science research approaches to the *social* world of management and organisations. Researchers need to recognise that morality and ethics are an integral part of human activity and need to be incorporated into their theorising.

With these warnings in mind, the concluding section highlights the implications of applying the different research perspectives discussed in the chapter, including their impact on policy and practice. You will find a similar section on the practical implications of research at the end of each Part Two chapter.

10.4.1 Improving policies

In the opening case we discussed how governments had adopted the enterprise culture 'project' in an attempt to achieve various economic and social goals by encouraging new waves of entrepreneurial activity (Case 10.1). During its first three decades (i.e. from the mid-1970s to the mid-2000s), the main policy goals were economic growth, reduced unemployment, and increased competitiveness. It is clear that major changes have taken place in countries that have engaged in this project, including some improvements in economic performance. However, in recent years there has been an increasing concern over the effectiveness of policy. At this point, we can indicate three reasons why research is needed in order to make better policy; each of these will be taken up in more detail in Chapter 15. Firstly, analysis of the recent historical evidence suggests that some of the economic achievements of the last 30 years may not be directly attributable to **entrepreneurship policies**, but rather to cyclical trends, and there is also evidence that some of the least 'enterprising' regions have failed to respond to successive policy initiatives (e.g. Audretsch et al. 2007; Greene et al. 2008). Secondly, we are not well informed about many areas of entrepreneurial activity, making it difficult to know what policies are required in particular circumstances (Huggins and Thompson 2015). Thirdly, there is considerable evidence to suggest that some policies are having extremely damaging effects, however unintended, on the social and natural world. These include increased inequality, the destruction of wilderness areas, and environmental pollution (e.g. Della-Guista and King 2008; Porritt 2006). Fourthly, with the increasing interest in social entrepreneurship in the early twenty-first century, some people are beginning to recognise that entrepreneurial activity has the potential to contribute towards a much broader range of positive outcomes, beyond conventional economic measures of profitability and growth. To some degree, this may simply be a matter of changing the 'hearts and minds' of those engaged in entrepreneurship. However, policy tools, including regulations, incentives, and penalties, will also play an important part in efforts to redirect entrepreneurial energy away from destructive, unsustainable activity and towards more constructive and benign alternatives (Baumol 1990; Blundel et al. 2013; Parrish and Foxon 2009).

10.4.2 Informing practice

Throughout history, entrepreneurs seem to have managed quite well without the benefit of researchers, and the seemingly endless supply of books, journal articles, and conference papers that they produce. So what does a practitioner stand to gain by engaging with academics? Though some areas of entrepreneurship research have no obvious practical application, there are other areas where research could influence entrepreneurial activity:

[I]t is totally uninteresting, from the perspective of practical entrepreneurship, whether the activities of the entrepreneur should be understood as restoring an equilibrium (Kirzner) or as disturbing an equilibrium (Schumpeter). To conceptualise entrepreneurial profit as rent on ability, as Mangoldt and Marshall do, is also of minimal interest from a practical perspective. What is much more relevant is to figure out what this 'ability' consists of, how to develop it, and how to spot it. (Swedberg 2000: 21)

In the next five chapters, there are many specific cases where research findings are making a contribution to everyday practice. To take one example, recent research on the financing of entrepreneurial start-ups has been used to inform the work of **venture capitalists** and other finance providers. It also feeds back into practice through education and training programmes, which provided guidance for entrepreneurs seeking to raise capital (Section 13.2 and Case 13.3). Another example is where people are making use of results obtained from studies of entrepreneurial learning and networking to design new kinds of peer support programme for entrepreneurs and owner-managers (Section 12.4 and Case 13.2). The other major contribution is made by entrepreneurship research as a whole, rather than by particular studies. In combination, this large body of research is broadening our horizons. It can provide new insights into people and places we would not otherwise come into contact with, suggest new ways of thinking about the subject, and open up different ways of acting entrepreneurially. But how does all of this knowledge convert into *practical* guidance for an existing or an aspiring entrepreneur? Here are three ways that research can improve your chances of establishing a successful venture:

1. By learning from the research that reports on the experiences of other people, and from other sources such as statistical evidence on firm performance, you can identify common pitfalls and consider alternative approaches to creating an entrepreneurial venture.

2. By making use of research findings and analytical techniques, you can be more selective when bombarded by a mass of information and guidance, including 'recipe book' advice and anecdotes from successful entrepreneurs, which may not be relevant to your situation.

3. By reflecting on the research evidence, you can think more deeply about the kind of venture you really want to establish, what is going to be involved in acting entrepreneurially, and how best to prepare yourself in order to achieve your ambition.

A common theme here is that people need to act in different ways depending on the kind of venture they are trying to establish, the context in which they are operating, as well as their personal vision and values. So, for example, an entrepreneurial art and design student setting up a new craft-based venture needs to develop practices that are relevant to her profession, rather than simply following a standardised approach (HEA/NESTA 2007). In the same way, the founders of a new social enterprise need to decide on its legal form, the markets it should serve, and the balance they want to strike between social, economic, and environmental goals as the venture develops over time (Spear et al. 2009; Blundel and Lyon 2015). Research is useful because it can broaden your horizons, helping you to make these important practical choices in more open-minded, creative, and thoughtful ways.

10.5 SUMMARY

- There are various sources of evidence about entrepreneurship. It is important to be clear about the potential strengths and limitations of different sources in order to make intelligent use of such knowledge to address particular problems and research questions. 'Practical' knowledge is often passed on through direct contact between 'apprentices' and their entrepreneurial mentors, or through some form of experiential learning; it is sometimes highly context-specific, so may not always be applicable to other situations. The knowledge produced by academic researchers is often (but not always) of more general relevance, but can be seen as serving a complementary role.

- Entrepreneurship has attracted the interest of researchers from a number of academic disciplines, including psychology, behavioural studies, economics, sociology, anthropology, human geography, business and management studies, and history. While each of these disciplines has brought its own preferred research methods, some of the most interesting research has been interdisciplinary in nature, examining entrepreneurship at multiple levels of analysis. These approaches are examined in more detail in Chapters 11–15.

- Entrepreneurship research is relevant to several different audiences, including students, academics, policy-makers, practitioners, and citizens. These audiences will have different views and priorities, regarding the kinds of questions that they want answered, and also the types of knowledge they find most useful.

- Everyone comes to this subject with some previous experiences, views, and assumptions about entrepreneurship, which are likely to influence the way they respond to new ideas. To be an effective entrepreneurship researcher, it is important to keep an open mind about your subject, while also treating new sources of evidence critically. Before proceeding with the rest of Part Two, you may find it helpful to spend a few minutes time reviewing your current understanding of the subject and what you would like to gain from reading the remaining Part Two chapters.

Practical activities

1. **Comparing entrepreneurial ventures:** Using sources listed in Section 10.2 as a guide, search for a two contrasting examples of an entrepreneurial venture. Try to include one example that you consider to be a fairly 'extreme' or 'marginal' case, but that you could still argue for as illustrating entrepreneurship in some meaningful way. Summarise your examples as either a two-page comparative case study, or as a four-slide presentation, using visual material as appropriate. In the accompanying text, highlight what you consider to be the distinctively 'entrepreneurial' aspects of each example, and also their major differences. If you are working with other students, presentations can be followed by a discussion with the following themes: (a) what makes these examples entrepreneurial?; (b) are the extreme/marginal cases really 'entrepreneurial', or do they represent something different?; (c) which, if any, of these types of entrepreneurship appeals to you as a potential career path?

2. **Linking research to policy and practice:** Re-read Cases 10.1 and 10.2, focusing on the ways that the researchers have engaged with policy-makers and practitioners. Locate and download a policy-related entrepreneurship research published by Per Davidsson, members of CIRCLE. Using the report

as a starting-point, summarise the key findings and identify what you see as the main implications for policy and/or practice.

3. **First steps in entrepreneurship research:** One of the best ways to get started is through a personal connection. For this activity, you need to find someone with a direct involvement in some kind of entrepreneurial venture. This person could be a relative, friend, neighbour, or even someone you do business with (e.g. the owner of a local shop or restaurant). Ask your interviewee the following questions (or devise your own versions), and draft a summary report. Keep this for future reference and compare the responses you obtained with the research findings discussed in Chapters 11 and 12:

    *   Why did you set up this venture?
    *   How did you identify the opportunity?
    *   Who else is involved in the venture?
    *   What are your ambitions for the venture?
    *   Do you consider yourself to be an entrepreneur?
    *   What makes someone 'entrepreneurial'?
    *   Have other members of your family set up new ventures?
    *   What lessons have you learned about setting up a new venture?

Discussion topics

1. Refer back to Section 10.2, which discusses different sources and types of knowledge about entrepreneurship. Which sources and types of knowledge do you find: (a) most interesting; (b) least interesting? What are your reasons? If you are working in a group, compare your responses with those of other students. Why are particular sources and types of knowledge more or less appealing? Retain your notes and re-read them when you have completed Part Two.

2. Re-read the discussion about different academic research approaches to entrepreneurship (Section 10.4). Which approaches do you find: (a) most interesting; (b) least interesting? What are your reasons? If you are working in a group, compare your responses with those of other students. Why are particular academic disciplines more or less appealing? Retain your notes and re-read them when you have completed the other Part Two chapters.

3. Richard Swedberg suggests that social science researchers could get a better understanding of entrepreneurship by paying more attention to the 'practical knowledge' of entrepreneurs (Section 10.3). How might you achieve this in practice? To focus your discussion, you might consider one of the following: (a) researching gender differences in high-technology entrepreneurship; (b) researching the impact of entrepreneurial role models on young people; (c) researching the motivations of social entrepreneurs.

Recommended readings

These readings address two important topics in entrepreneurship research and are recommended for anyone wanting to build on the material covered in this chapter. Recommended readings have been selected from leading Sage journals and are freely available for readers of this textbook to download via the Online Resources.

Zahra, S. A., Wright, M., and Abdelgawad, S. G. (2015) 'Contextualization and the advancement of entrepreneurship research'. *International Small Business Journal*, 32, 5: 479–500.

This article analyses the role of context in entrepreneurship research. The authors examine different dimensions of entrepreneurial context, focusing in particular on temporal (i.e. time), industry, spatial, social and organisational, ownership and governance. They discuss why it is important to take these different contexts into account and identify some of the challenges of undertaking contextualised entrepreneurship research.

Henry, C., Foss, L., and Ahl, H. (2016) 'Gender and entrepreneurship research: a review of methodological approaches'. *International Small Business Journal*, 34, 3: 217–41.

This article presents the findings of a systematic literature review (SLR) of the gender and entrepreneurship literature over the last 30 years. It examines methodological trends in the field of gender and entrepreneurship. The authors find that there are many large-scale empirical studies focused on male/female comparisons, but that little detail is provided on industry sector or sampling methods and that the feminist critique is often missing. They recommend new approaches to address these issues in the future

References

Aldrich, H., Reese, P. R., and Dubini, P. (1989) 'Women on the verge of a breakthrough: networking among entrepreneurs in the United States and Italy'. *Entrepreneurship and Regional Development*, 1, 4: 339–56.

Aldrich, H. E. and Martinez, M. A. (2001) 'Many are called, but few are chosen: an evolutionary perspective for the study of entrepreneurship'. *Entrepreneurship Theory and Development*, 25, 4: 41–56.

Audretsch, D. B., Grilo, I., and Thurik, A. R. (eds) (2007) *Handbook of Research in Entrepreneurship Policy*. Cheltenham: Edward Elgar.

Baumol, W. (1990) 'Entrepreneurship: productive, unproductive, and destructive'. *Journal of Political Economy*, 98: 893–921.

Best, M. (2001) *The New Competitive Advantage*. Oxford: Oxford University Press.

Blundel, R. K. and Tregear, A. (2006) 'Artisans and factories: the interpenetration of craft and industry in English cheese-making, c1650–1950'. *Enterprise and Society*, 7, 4: 1–35.

Blundel, R. K., Monaghan, A., and Thomas, C. (2013) 'SMEs and environmental responsibility: a policy perspective'. *Business Ethics: A European Review*, 22, 3: 246–62.

Blundel, R. K. and Lyon, F. (2015) 'Towards a "long view": historical perspectives on the scaling and replication of social ventures'. *Journal of Social Entrepreneurship*, 6, 1: 80–102.

Bogren, M., von Friedrichs, Y., Rennemo, Ø., and Widding, Ø. (2013) 'Networking women entrepreneurs: fruitful for business growth?' *International Journal of Gender and Entrepreneurship*, 5, 1: 60–77.

Bryman, A. and Bell, E. (2015) *Business Research Methods* (4th edn). Oxford: Oxford University Press.

Bygrave, W. D. (1989) 'The entrepreneurship paradigm (I): a philosophical look at its research methodologies'. *Entrepreneurship Theory and Practice*, 14, 1: 7–26.

Carter, S. and Jones-Evans, D. (2012) *Enterprise and Small Business: Principles, Practice and policy* (2rd edn). Harlow: Pearson.

Casson, M., Yeung, B., Basu, A., and Wadeson, N. (2006) *The Oxford Handbook of Entrepreneurship*. Oxford: Oxford University Press.

Choi, N. and Majumdar, S. (2014) 'Social entrepreneurship as an essentially contested concept: opening a new avenue for systematic future research'. *Journal of Business Venturing*, 29, 3: 363–76.

Chowdhury, F., Terjesen, S., and Audretsch, D. (2015) 'Varieties of entrepreneurship: institutional drivers across entrepreneurial activity and country'. *European Journal of Law and Economics*, 40, 1: 121–48.

CIRCLE (2016) *CIRCLE Annual Report 2015*. Lund: Lund University / Centre for Innovation, Research and Competence in the Learning Economy.

Clarke, J., Holt, R., and Blundel, R. K. (2014) 'Re-imagining the growth process: (co)-evolving metaphorical representations of entrepreneurial growth'. *Entrepreneurship and Regional Development*, 26, 3–4: 234–56.

Conway, S. and Jones, O. (2012) 'Networking and the small business'. In S. Carter and D. Jones-Evans (eds) op. cit. (338–61).

Davidsson, P. (2016) *Researching Entrepreneurship: Conceptualization and Design* (2nd edn). Heidelberg: Springer.

Davidsson, P. and Wiklund, J. (2001) 'Levels of analysis in entrepreneurship research: current research practice and suggestions for the future'. *Entrepreneurship Theory and Development*, 25, 4: 81–99.

Della-Guista, M. and King, Z. (2008) 'Enterprise culture'. In M. Casson et al. (eds) op. cit. (629–47).

Dodd, S. D. and Anderson, A. R. (2007) 'Mumpsimus and the mything of the individualistic entrepreneur'. *International Small Business Journal*, 25, 4: 341–60.

Dyson, J. (2003) *Against the Odds: An Autobiography (new edition)*. London: Texere Thomson.

Easterby-Smith, M., Thorpe, R. and Jackson, P. R. (2016) *Management and Business Research* (5th edn). London: Sage.

Fayolle, A. (ed.) (2015) *Handbook of Research on Entrepreneurship: What We Know and What We Need to Know*. Cheltenham: Edward Elgar.

Fletcher, D. E. (2006) 'Entrepreneurial processes and the social construction of opportunity'. *Entrepreneurship and Regional Development*, 18, 5: 421–40.

Ghoshal, S. (2005) 'Bad management theories are destroying good management practices'. *Academy of Management Learning and Education*, 4, 1: 75–91.

Greene, F. J., Mole, K. F., and Storey, D. J. (2008) *Three Decades of the Enterprise Culture: Entrepreneurship, Economic Regeneration and Public Policy*. Basingstoke: Palgrave.

Hayek, F. von ([1945] 1972) 'The use of knowledge in society'. In *Individualism and Economic Order*. Chicago: Henry Regnery Company (77–91).

HEA/NESTA (2007) *Creating Entrepreneurship: Entrepreneurship Education for the Creative Industries*. London: Higher Education Academy, Art Design Media Subject Centre and NESTA.

Henry, C., Foss, L., and Ahl, H. (2015) 'Gender and entrepreneurship research: a review of methodological approaches'. *International Small Business Journal*, 34, 3: 217–41.

Hjorth, D., Holt, R., and Steyaert, C. (2015) 'Entrepreneurship and process studies'. *International Small Business Journal*, 33, 6: 599–611.

Huggins, R. and Thompson, P. (2015) 'Culture and place-based development: a socio-economic analysis'. *Regional Studies*, 49, 1: 130–59.

Johannisson, B. (2000) 'Networking and venture growth'. In D. L. Sexton and H. Landström (eds), *The Blackwell Handbook of Entrepreneurship*. Oxford: Blackwell (368–86).

Jones, C. (2001) 'Co-evolution of entrepreneurial careers, institutional rules and competitive dynamics in American film, 1895–1920'. *Organization Studies*, 22, 6: 911–44.

Langley, A. (1999) 'Strategies for theorising from process data'. *Academy of Management Review*, 24, 4: 691–717.

Lewin, K. (1945) 'The Research Center for Group Dynamics at Massachusetts Institute of Technology'. *Sociometry*, 8, 2: 126–35.

Low, M. B. and MacMillan, I. C. (1988) 'Entrepreneurship: past research and future challenges'. *Journal of Management*, 14, 2: 139–61.

Macpherson, A. and Holt, R. (2007) 'Knowledge, learning and small firm growth: a systematic review of the evidence'. *Research Policy*, 36, 2: 172–92.

McNeill, D. (2008) 'The hotel and the city'. *Progress in Human Geography*, 32, 3: 383–98.

Melin, L., Nordqvist, M., and Sharma, P. (eds) (2014) *The Sage Handbook of Family Business*. London: Sage.

Minniti, M. (2008) 'The role of government policy on entrepreneurial activity: productive, unproductive, or destructive?' *Entrepreneurship Theory and Practice*, 32, 5: 779–90.

Neergaard, H. and Ulhøi, J. P. (eds) (2007) *Handbook of Qualitative Research in Entrepreneurship*. Cheltenham: Edward Elgar.

Parrish, B. D. and Foxon, T. J. (2009) 'Sustainability entrepreneurship and equitable transitions to a low-carbon economy'. *Greener Management International*, 55: 47–62.

Porritt, J. (2006) *Capitalism as if the World Matters*. London: Earthscan.

Rae, D. and Wang, C. L. (eds) (2015) *Entrepreneurial Learning: New Perspectives in Research, Education and Practice*. London: Routledge.

Ram, M. (1999) 'Trading places: the ethnographic process in small firms' research'. *Entrepreneurship and Regional Development*, 11, 2: 95–108.

Ram, M., Barrett, G., and Jones, T. (2006) 'Ethnicity and entrepreneurship'. In S. Carter and D. Jones-Evans (eds) op. cit. (192–208).

Ridley-Duff, R. and Bull, M. (2015) *Understanding Social Enterprise* (2nd edn). London: Sage.

Spear, R. G., Cornforth, C. J., and Aiken, M. (2009). 'The governance challenges of social enterprises: evidence from a UK empirical study'. *Annals of Public and Cooperative Economics*, 80, 2: 247–73.

Staber, U. (1997) 'An ecological perspective on entrepreneurship in industrial districts'. *Entrepreneurship and Regional Development*, 9, 1: 45–64.

Swaminathan, A. (1995) 'The proliferation of specialist organizations in the American wine industry, 1941–1990'. *Administrative Science Quarterly*, 40: 653–80.

Swedberg, R. (ed.) (2000) *Entrepreneurship: the Social Science View.* Oxford: Oxford University Press.

Williams, C. C. and Nadin, S. J. (2013) 'Beyond the entrepreneur as a heroic figurehead of capitalism: re-representing the lived practices of entrepreneurs'. *Entrepreneurship and Regional Development*, 25, 7–8: 552–68.

Wilson, J. (2013) *Essentials of Business Research: A Guide to Doing your Research Project.* London: Sage.

Zahra, S. A., Wright, M., and Abdelgawad, S. G. (2015) 'Contextualization and the advancement of entrepreneurship research'. *International Small Business Journal*, 32, 5: 479–500.

11

INDIVIDUAL PERSPECTIVES: BEYOND THE 'HEROIC' ENTREPRENEUR

I try to explain to young people about entrepreneurial spirit. It's something you either have or you don't. You cannot become an entrepreneur, just like you cannot become a concert pianist.

Alan Sugar, entrepreneur

The quality of entrepreneurial judgement is only partly a question of the personal characteristics or temperament of the individual.

Edith Penrose, economist

LEARNING OUTCOMES

After reading this chapter you should be able to:

- Examine individual-level approaches to entrepreneurship research, making particular reference to psychology and behavioural studies.
- Evaluate key research areas in psychology and behavioural studies, including: entrepreneurial personality; cognition; creativity; mindset; skills; values; and learning.
- Identify some initial connections between research conducted at the level of the individual and other entrepreneurship research approaches.
- Recognise how psychological and behavioural research influences policy and practice.
- Apply these insights to your own experiences of entrepreneurship.

11.1 INTRODUCTION

Many people regard 'entrepreneurship' as equivalent to the activities of individual entrepreneurs. Entrepreneurship researchers have long recognised that 'the entrepreneur' is part of a much more complex set of processes, operating at multiple levels of analysis (Section 10.3). However, it is also true to say that particular individuals can, and do, play a decisive roles in many situations, ranging from the creating a new venture start-up to reviving a long-established public or private sector organisation. So what do we know about the entrepreneurial individual? Magazine profiles, biographies and autobiographies present us with compelling stories but can often raise more questions than answers – for example:

- Do these individuals share a distinctive set of 'entrepreneurial' characteristics?
- Were they 'pre-programmed' to act entrepreneurially, or was it a personal choice?
- Do their minds work in different ways to those of other people?
- How important are personal values in shaping their entrepreneurial careers?
- Is it possible to learn to be like them?

In this chapter we aim to provide a concise overview the more prominent research approaches that focus on the entrepreneurial individual, and to critically evaluate the insights that they have generated. The individual-level focus of this chapter opens up many opportunities to compare the research evidence with your own personal experiences (Case 11.1): you will find plenty of suggestions about making these connections in the Practical Activities and Discussion Topics at the end of the chapter. Section 11.2 provides a critical review of the extensive body of research that has attempted to identify entrepreneurial personality characteristics. Section 11.3 is concerned with research on entrepreneurial cognition, or ways of thinking, with a particular focus on cognitive biases, opportunity recognition, and creativity. Section 11.4 provides a short introduction to entrepreneurial learning, a core theme that runs throughout Part Two, before being brought together in Chapter 16. In Section 11.5, we conclude by drawing out some practical implications. Given the individual focus of the chapter, there is also an opportunity for you to reflect on the ideas discussed, and the implications for your own entrepreneurial journey.

CASE 11.1   STUDENT FOCUS

Making sense of 'Entrepreneurial Intentions'

These short fictionalised accounts, based on real world examples, illustrate two ways that students have made good use of entrepreneurship research to achieve successful outcomes in their studies.

Alison is completing a joint honours degree in Business Studies and Psychology. She's trying to think of an interesting topic for her final year dissertation, which is meant to include some empirical work. After reading the dissertation guide and spending some time online, Alison decides that she wants to include some psychological research in her study, but she's also keen to tackle a topic related to entrepreneurship. She quickly realises that it's going to be difficult to recruit a sample of 'real life' entrepreneurs to take part in her study – even though she knows a few older people who have set up their own businesses, a few phone calls confirm that they're either far too busy or live too far away to take part.

Feeling a little disheartened, Alison takes another look at the library's e-journals collection, but gets distracted by an archived news article about graduates being forced to set up their own businesses as an alternative to unemployment (Allen 2014). Perhaps she could do something on young people and the reasons why they might end up becoming entrepreneurs? She goes back to the e-journals database and enters

(Continued)

(Continued)

the search terms: 'psychology', 'entrepreneur', and 'student'. The search produces hundreds of articles, but she decides to focus on fairly recent ones that seem to be attracting citations. Her shortlist includes a study of entrepreneurial intentions and actions based on semi-structured interviews with students (Geldhof et al. 2014), and an earlier one that tests the effect of entrepreneurship programmes on the entrepreneurial attitudes and intentions of science and engineering students (Souitaris et al. 2007). Alison also spots a 'meta-analytic' review of the research literature (Bae et al. 2014), which sounds useful as a way of putting the more recent research into some kind of perspective, and another article looking at future directions (Fayolle and Liñán 2014), which will help her focus her research questions.

After downloading the articles, she starts reading and highlights a number of paragraphs that spark her interest – in addition to narrowing her search and identifying a suitable research topic, she's on the look-out for key concepts related to students' attitudes and intentions, research methods that she could use in her own study, and mentions of other research articles that could be relevant to her chosen subject. While she is analysing one of the papers, Alison spots a reference to Schoon and Duckworth's (2012) article, which uses longitudinal data to look at the impact of early life experiences on people's subsequent career choices. This reminds her that several of the students she has spoken to informally about their intentions to become an entrepreneur have referred to episodes in their childhood, including the influence of parents and other members of the family. Having made this connection, she decides that it's worth following up in her own study. After a few hours of searching, reading and note taking, Alison packs her bag and heads for home. There's still lots of work to do, but she's pleased to have made so much progress today and is now feeling a lot more confident about her dissertation.

QUESTIONS

1.   List the five distinct ways in which Alison is using these journal articles?

2.   Conduct your own e-journal search, find one additional article related to entrepreneurial intentions, and analyse it using these three approaches.

3.   Try to identify at least one alternative research topic that you might select, based on these articles, and note why you think it could be interesting.

11.2 IN SEARCH OF THE ENTREPRENEURIAL INDIVIDUAL

11.2.1 Isolating personality 'traits' or characteristics

There is a long history of psychological studies that have attempted to isolate the personality 'traits' or characteristics of entrepreneurs. This work forms part of a much larger tradition of personality research, which developed from the mid-twentieth century. In entrepreneurship, it developed around the observation that certain personality characteristics, such as risk-taking and need for achievement, might influence entrepreneurial performance (e.g. McClelland 1961; Brockhaus 1980). Table 11.1

TABLE 11.1 Five 'classic' individual-level entrepreneurial characteristics

Characteristic	Background and commentary	Sample references
Need for achievement	McClelland (1961) argued that people with high need for achievement (NAch) scores are attracted to open-ended entrepreneurial situations because they provided an opportunity to satisfy this need. It has become one of the best-known personality characteristics. It suggests intrinsic motivations for engaging in entrepreneurial activity. For example, people are motivated by the prospect of making a difference, or having a tangible impact of some kind. Modified versions of the NAch concept have been supported in subsequent empirical studies.	McClelland (1961), Miner et al. (1994)
Over-optimism	Another popular image of the entrepreneur is of someone who generally 'looks on the bright side', or makes positive evaluations of the future. As with locus of control and risk-taking propensity, much depends on the context in which an individual is asked to make an assessment. Empirical studies have detected evidence of entrepreneurs being over-optimistic about the prospects of their own ventures, but this does not demonstrate that over-optimism is a settled personality characteristic. More recent work on entrepreneurial cognition has provided useful insights into the relationship between a person's perceptions and the assessments they make.	Cooper et al. (1988), Hmieleski and Baron (2009)
Risk-taking propensity	Frank Knight distinguished between risk and uncertainty, the latter characterising many entrepreneurial decision-making situations (Section 11.3). In popular imagery, entrepreneurs are big 'risk-takers', but the belief in this personality characteristic is not supported by the research evidence. Studies have revealed a much more complex picture, in which the degree of risk-taking (or tolerance of uncertainty) depends on a variety of factors, relating to the individual (e.g. age, educational level, prior experience, cognitive biases) and to the situation in which the decision is being made.	Knight (1921), Kirzner (1979), Brockhaus (1980)
Desire for autonomy	There is some evidence that entrepreneurs, defined in occupational terms as owner-managers, value their autonomy and are resistant to external forms of control in comparison to other occupational groups. However, there is a paradoxical element to the desire for autonomy. For both owner-managers and social entrepreneurs, wanting to retain personal control becomes a barrier to the further growth of the organisation. Prospective entrepreneurs may be motivated by a desire for autonomy, but this desire may also develop as a product of the experience of setting up a new venture, or of taking control of an existing organisation.	Caird (1991), Cromie (2000)
Locus of control	This concept described a person's perception of whether achieving outcomes or goals, was under their own control, or subject to external factors. In other words, 'do you make things happen in the world?' (i.e. internal locus of control), or, 'do things happen to you?' (i.e. external locus of control). Empirical testing of the concept produced inconclusive results, with some studies showing no significant differences between populations of entrepreneurs and managers. Locus of control has largely been superseded by more sophisticated concepts, notably 'self-efficacy' (Section 11.3).	Rotter (1966), Sexton and Bowman-Upton (1985), Furnham and Steele (1993)

summarises five of the characteristics that have been most commonly associated with entrepreneurship. Can you identify examples of 'real-world' entrepreneurs who display one or more of these characteristics? It would be very useful if you could identify the ingredients of a successful entrepreneur. As one of our opening quotations suggests, investors are often as interested in the people as they are in their venture. The 'entrepreneurial personality' is a compelling idea that is also supported by anecdotal evidence. For example, most of us can think of an individual who stands out as being particularly 'entrepreneurial', and we could probably point to several ways in which this person is distinctive.

Characteristics-based approaches are still widely used by practitioners, teachers, and researchers. One of the commonest applications is online tests designed to diagnose or evaluate entrepreneurial potential (Practical activity 1). There is also an interesting series of studies that have examined how the psychological characteristics of entrepreneurs may be related to the performance of their ventures (e.g. Begley and Boyd 1987; Miner 1997; Rauch and Frese 2007). However, despite their considerable popularity, these approaches have become controversial, with methodologies and findings being challenged. In the next section, we review the current state of play.

11.2.2 Entrepreneurial characteristics: limitations and applications

Arguments over the uses and limitations of characteristics-based approaches date back over more than two decades. Critics have challenged a number of assumptions, including the notion that these 'entrepreneurial' characteristics are relatively stable (over time), and consistent (across different contexts). The main criticisms are summarised in the following quotes:

> Definitional and methodological problems associated with these past psychological studies, such as non-comparable samples, bias toward successful entrepreneurs, and the possibility that observed entrepreneurial traits are the product of entrepreneurial experience, make it difficult to interpret the results. Furthermore, at a more fundamental level, it can be argued that the wide variations among entrepreneurs make any attempt to develop a standard psychological profile futile. (Low and Macmillan 1988: 148)

> It is not possible to profile the typical entrepreneur. No psychological or sociological characteristics have been found which predict with high accuracy that someone will become an entrepreneur or excel at entrepreneurship. (Davidsson 2006: 1)

However, despite these criticisms, interest in the concept of the 'entrepreneurial personality', exists both amongst researchers and the wider public. It is therefore worth considering the key issues in a little more detail. Firstly, there are problems in defining and operationalising the concept of personality characteristics. As we have seen, researchers have identified a large number of characteristics that *might* be associated with entrepreneurial behaviour but the causal relationships remain unclear. Taking 'desire for autonomy' as an example, a person may be content to take orders at one point in time (e.g. while learning a new trade), but require more autonomy at another point (e.g. once they are qualified, or have experienced a more independent way of life). In addition, it is difficult to establish a causal link between individual-level characteristics and outcomes at an organisational level. At an anecdotal level, it is easy to identify examples of successful social and commercial ventures founded by individuals who lack one (or more) of the entrepreneurial characteristics summarised in Table 11.1. There are also plenty of people who possess many entrepreneurial characteristics, yet prove to be either unsuccessful entrepreneurs, or who pursue different careers. Secondly, it is not clear how the outcome, 'entrepreneurship' can be measured reliably, whether your focus is on future intentions or actual behaviours. The act of founding a new venture, is generally the result of a complex series of interactions, involving a number of people in a particular context. Research has shown that possessing entrepreneurial attitudes at one point in time is not, in isolation, a good predictor of a person subsequently engaging in entrepreneurial behaviours such as starting or growing a business. Lastly, much of the characteristics literature has adopted what we have termed a 'narrow' definition of entrepreneurship (Section 1.2), as the act of founding and controlling an independent, commercial business venture.

Following recent advances in psychology, there have been calls for entrepreneurship scholars to update the way they interpret personality. These developments are summarised in the next case (Case Study 11.2):

CASE 11.2

Introducing the Five Factor Model (FFM)

Many psychologists now agree that there are five fundamental personality dimensions, commonly referred to as the 'Five-Factor Model' (FFM) (Goldberg 1993; Wiggins 1996). Taking each of these factors in turn, you might expect a person who is at the 'higher' end of the scale to display the following typical dispositions, and someone who is at the 'lower' end to display the opposite:

1. **Extraversion** tends to be outgoing, sociable, and optimistic.
2. **Neuroticism** tends to be anxious, emotionally unstable, prone to depression.
3. **Agreeableness** is easy to get on with, widely liked by other people.
4. **Conscientiousness** is hard-working, reliable, conformist.
5. **Openness to experience** adopts liberal, innovative approaches to problems.

Psychologists suggest that each of these broad dimensions of personality is made up of a number of narrower traits (e.g. anxiety or gregariousness), although their exact number and nature is still hotly debated. In another important refinement of the theory, personality traits are now generally seen as 'potentialities' or 'basic tendencies' which may (or may not) be realised in the lives of particular individuals (McCrae and Costa 1996: 69). Though you might expect to inherit certain tendencies, these remain open to a variety of other influences during the course of your life. For example, aspects of your personality may be modified as a result of early childhood experiences. As a result, the FFM can only provide part of the explanation for human behaviour:

(Continued)

(Continued)

In itself FFM does not explain how social roles are forged in to a personal identity, or how the flow of behaviour is organised, or how attitudes are formed and changed. (McCrae and Costa 1996: 65)

In other words, while 'the big five' factors may be influential, they are only one component in a more complex relationship between individuals and the societies in which they live. For example, there are continuing arguments, between those who claim to have identified common 'entrepreneurial' personality characteristics across different cultural settings, and those who argue that some of these characteristics are country-specific, or the product of cultural conditioning in the countries where the original studies were conducted (e.g. Stimpson et al. 1990, Gupta and Fernandez 2009). McCrae and Costa (1996: 66–9) identify a number of categories and sub-categories, that are reproduced below. It is not necessary to explore these in detail to realise just how complex the picture has become! Take a look at these bullet points and consider how each factor might be interacting with others in the list to shape your own personality:

BASIC TENDENCIES

- Physical characteristics (e.g. height, weight, health)
- Cognitive capacities (e.g. general intelligence, verbal ability)
- Personality traits (i.e. the 'five factors')
- Physiological drives (e.g. appetite)

CHARACTERISTIC ADAPTATIONS

- Acquired competencies (e.g. language, social and technical skills)
- Attitudes, beliefs and goals (e.g. moral values, personal projects)
- Learned behaviours (e.g. habits, hobbies)
- Interpersonal adaptations (e.g. social roles, relationships, perceptions of others)

OBJECTIVE BIOGRAPHY

- Overt behaviour (e.g. as observed by researchers)
- Life course (e.g. career path, historical accidents)

SELF-CONCEPT

- Self-esteem
- Self-identity
- Life story, personal myth

EXTERNAL INFLUENCES

- Developmental influences (e.g. parent–child relationships, traumatic events)
- Macro-environment (e.g. culture, sub-culture, vocational group)
- Micro-environment (e.g. situational constraints, social cues)

The authors also emphasise the importance of distinguishing between traits, which they regard as underlying potentialities (i.e. tendencies), and the process by which these rather abstract concepts become concrete in the lives of particular individuals (McCrae and Costa 2000: 69). More generally, while individuals may inherit some 'basic tendencies', they also remain open to external influence; personality characteristics may be modified as a result of early childhood experiences, while cognitive capacities can be affected by life events (e.g. illness or injury).

QUESTIONS

1. Search online for the 'typical dispositions' of individuals at the low end of the FFM scale, and compare them to those at the 'high end' (listed above).

2. Why does the FFM only provide part of the explanation of a person's behaviour?

3. How might some of the key entrepreneurial traits: (a) become concrete; (b) remain dormant in the lives of particular individuals?

So what are the implications of these developments for our understanding of the entrepreneurial individual? The personality debate remains unresolved: are an individual's personality characteristics really 'set in plaster' by the age of 30, or can they continue to change into adulthood (e.g. Srivastava et al. 2003)? The long-running search for a stable, universal, and defining set of entrepreneurial traits is looking increasingly like a 'dead end' (Davidsson et al. 2001: 12). However, there is still a great deal to discover about the way an individual's entrepreneurial potential develops over time and the how particular entrepreneurial behaviours operate in practice. Studying these processes requires alternative approaches, such as cognitive science research (Section 11.3).

11.3 ENTREPRENEURIAL COGNITION

11.3.1 Introduction and four key themes

Research on human cognition is concerned with the way individuals *think* (i.e. their perceptions, memory and mental processes), and how this influences their *behaviour*. As Mitchell et al. (2002: 96) explain, 'cognitive psychology emerged to help explain the mental processes that occur within individuals as they interact with other people and the environment around them'. So, while the focus remains at the individual level, there is also a social dimension. This research theme has become very popular in the last decade, and now comprises several sub-fields, including social cognition theory. The research is important to entrepreneurship researchers because it fills some of the gaps we have already identified between individual-level factors and entrepreneurial activity:

> *Research in entrepreneurial cognition has investigated a very broad range of issues and topics and has generally found that cognitive factors play an important role in key aspects of the entrepreneurial process. (Baron and Ward 2004: 557)*

Table 11.2 summarises a number of key themes in cognitive research on entrepreneurship. This is a very broad field, so we have selected four of these themes for more detailed discussion: opportunity perception (Section 11.3.2), cognitive

TABLE 11.2 Entrepreneurial cognition: summary of key themes

Research theme	Commentary
Differences in cognition	Are there measurable differences between the cognition of entrepreneurial individuals and others, both in terms of content (i.e. what they think about) and process (i.e. how they think)?
Opportunity perception	How does the distinctive cognition of entrepreneurial individuals help them to be more alert to opportunities and/or more capable of exploiting them?
Cognitive biases	What kinds of cognitive biases (i.e. misinterpretations of evidence) are associated with entrepreneurial decision-making?
Entrepreneurial mindset	How can individuals adapt their cognitions in order to deal more effectively with the dynamic and uncertain conditions that are associated with entrepreneurial ventures?
Creativity	How does the cognition of entrepreneurial individuals help them to be more creative, both in terms of 'creating opportunities' and in addressing entrepreneurial challenges (e.g. raising finance, gaining legitimacy)?
Perceived self-efficacy	How does a person's belief in their capacity to achieve a specific performance (e.g. setting up a new venture) influence their behaviour?
Developmental cognition	How does a person's cognition affect the way that they learn, and how can formal approaches to learning take these factors into account?

biases (Section 11.3.3), entrepreneurial mindset (Section 11.3.4), and creativity (Section 11.3.5). In each case, we will focus on how they are relevant to the practical task of creating new entrepreneurial ventures.

Sources: Bandura 1995; Baron and Ward 2004; Chia 2008; Gudmundsson and Lechner 2013; Haynie et al. 2010; Mitchell et al. 2002; Simon and Houghton 2002.

11.3.2 Opportunity perception

When students are considering options for a new venture creation assignment, there are often a few individuals who quickly identify several brilliant ideas, while many others struggle to find an interesting opportunity. There is a continuing, sometimes heated debate over the concept of 'entrepreneurial opportunity', which we will revisit in other Part Two chapters (Suddaby et al. 2015; Kitching and Rouse 2016). Among the most influential ideas is that some individuals may be more 'alert' to potential opportunities than the rest of us (Kirzner 1979). This raises the question of how their perception might differ from those of other people. Kirzner suggested that it was not yet clear how how entrepreneurs obtained their superior foresight (ibid., 8). However, the following factors may help to explain these differences:

- **Special (or local) knowledge:** Frederick Hayek, one of the early contributors to this field made the fairly obvious, but often-overlooked, point that the kind of knowledge needed to exploit entrepreneurial opportunities is often 'special' in the sense of only being available to a limited number of people in a particular place (Hayek 1945: 522). For example, people living in the same town might hear that the local library had been damaged in a storm, while those living in other areas would remain unaware (see also Section 13.3).

- **Relevant resources and capabilities:** Another pioneering scholar pointed out that people tend to recognise opportunities that are able to exploit using their firms' existing 'bundle' of resources and capabilities (Penrose [1959] 2009: 31–3). For example, you're more likely to identify an opportunity to repair the damaged building if your firm has the necessary equipment and skills.

- **Learning and self-efficacy**: There is evidence that people learn in different ways from their experiences, and that these differences can influence how future opportunities are identified and exploited (Corbett 2005). Here, the concept of 'self-efficacy' (Bandura 1995), meaning a person's subjective perception that they are able to achieve a particular task, will influence their decision (Wadeson 2008: 99). We will discuss the relationship between learning and self-efficacy in more detail in Chapter 16.

There is a clear connection between perceived self-efficacy and the likelihood of succeeding in a task. However, a very high level of perceived self-efficacy can be problematic since it, 'carries the risk of over-optimism, and of escalating commitments to failing courses of action' (Wadeson 2008: 99). As we shall see in the next section, people can get carried away by their great ideas, ignore the warning signs, and eventually find themselves with a failed venture.

11.3.3 Cognitive biases

Entrepreneurs' cognitive biases have emerged as central themes in understanding the performance of entrepreneurial firms (Gudmundsson and Lechner 2013). The concept of cognitive bias challenges conventional views of entrepreneurs as deliberate risk-takers. Rather than being predisposed to take bigger risks, it may be that there are systematic differences in the cognitive processes of entrepreneurs, as compared to other people (Palich and Bagby 1995: 428). In other words, even though two individuals might have a similar propensity to take risks, the entrepreneurial individual might make different decisions because they process information differently. The most widely reported cognitive biases are:

- **Over-confidence**: entrepreneurs often display a degree of personal over-confidence, meaning that they over-estimate their own ability to deal with particular issues. For example, you are so confident in your powers of persuasion that you fail to do the necessary background research before pitching to a sceptical financier; or you ignore the advice of specialists, because you are sure that your ideas are better. Over-confidence can result in an illusion of control (Bandura 1995). In individualistic cultures it is often presented as a positive characteristic – self-confident people are dynamic, exciting and willing to take the initiative, while their less confident counterparts 'sit on the fence', looking hesitant and uncertain. However, research evidence suggests that *over*-confidence can lead to serious mistakes, such as introducing riskier products, underestimating the competition and failing to build support networks (Gudmundsson and Lechner 2013: 279–80).

- **Unrealistic optimism:** this is where a person faced with an uncertain situation tends to over-estimate the likelihood of a positive outcome, or under-estimate the likelihood of a negative one (Weinstein and Klein 1996). It has been defined as, 'the difference between an individual's subjective estimate of the probability of a good/bad event occurring and the "true" value of that probability'. (Coelho 2010: 399). This differs from conventional optimism, in that the individual is not For example, you might assume that demand for your new product will be much higher than is suggested by the available evidence at that point in time, or underrate the threat posed by competitors, regulators or other potential challengers. This bias, which is closely related to personal over-confidence, might occasionally produce successful outcomes – you are the person who took the risk and grabbed the opportunity, while your competitors hesitated. However unrealistic optimism can also lead to failures that can be both harmful at a personal level, and contribute to a loss of efficiency in the wider economic system (ibid.: 406).

Other common cognitive biases, which can reinforce over-confidence and unrealistic optimism biases in entrepreneurial decision-making, include:

- **The 'law of small numbers'**: this is the tendency of individuals to place too much reliance on a very limited amount of information, and to use this evidence when making assumptions about much larger populations. For example, if you are developing a new venture, it would be very dangerous to assume that there is a wider demand for your product or service because your close friends and family have told you that it is a great idea!

- **Reasoning by analogy**: when people are confronted by a new and unfamiliar situation, they often attempt to make sense of it by thinking back to a seemingly similar example from their existing body of knowledge (i.e. an analogy). This kind of reasoning can be effective, but it is important to recognise that there may be critical differences between the new situation and their previous experience (Schwenck 1984: 118). For example, you are likely to encounter problems if you try to enter an entirely new market sector using an approach that just happened to work with your previous customers.

- **Distrust of others**: the risk of failure can be greatly increased when this cognitive bias, which has been defined as, 'having confident negative expectations about the behaviour and abilities of others' (Lewicki, et al. 1998), is combined with over-confidence. It is sensible to be cautious when entering into relationships with business partners, and to take a realistic view of the balance of risks and opportunities. However, most entrepreneurs need to build social networks in order to operate successfully so high levels of distrust of others, combined with excessive over-confidence in your own abilities, looks to be a dangerous combination (Gudmundsson and Lechner 2013: 288–9).

By identifying the more common cognitive biases, entrepreneurs (and those who work with them) can be better prepared, and take the necessary actions to avoid making costly mistakes. For example, they might guard against the 'law of small numbers' by undertaking some additional market research or statistical analysis (Simon and Houghton 2002: 118), and be particularly wary of the reinforcing effects when over-confidence is combined with either unrealistic optimism or excessive distrust of others.

11.3.4 Entrepreneurial mindset

The concept of an 'entrepreneurial' mindset was popularised by McGrath and MacMillan (2000) to describe what they saw as a distinctive set of behaviours that were well-suited to individuals leading organisations under conditions of uncertainty. The work was based on their observations of successful habitual (or serial) entrepreneurs. Rather than treating such situations as a problem, the authors argued that people with an entrepreneurial mindset would passionately seek out new opportunities, pursue these opportunities in a highly disciplined and selective way, and engage the energies of other people in order to exploit them. Haynie et al. (2010) developed the concept, arguing that it was primarily about cognitive adaptability, which they defined as, 'the ability to be dynamic, flexible, and self-regulating in one's cognitions given dynamic and uncertain task environments.' (ibid.: 218). Their 'situated metacognitive model' of the entrepreneurial mindset examines what are termed 'higher-order' cognitive processes (i.e. how individual entrepreneurs select particular cognitive strategies in response to uncertain and rapidly-changing conditions).

The American psychologist, Carol Dweck's has also been influential in shaping the concept of the 'mindset' and particularly in the way it has been applied in educational settings such as primary schools. Dweck examined the implicit (i.e. unconscious) way that individuals perceive their own intelligence and abilities, and the effect that this has on their self-esteem, motivation and behaviour. This stream of ideas, based around a distinction between 'fixed' and 'growth' mindsets, became more widely known following the publication of her (2006) work, *Mindset: The New Psychology of Success*. Dweck has argued that individuals with 'fixed' mindsets view their abilities as essentially unchangeable. As a consequence, they tend to respond negatively to failure because they see it as evidence that they lack these abilities. By contrast, those who develop 'growth' mindsets recognise that their abilities can be enhanced over time. As a result, these individuals tend to see failures and setbacks as sources of new learning and self-improvement. We discuss how entrepreneurs can learn from failures in the concluding Chapter 16 (Section 16.5).

11.3.5 Entrepreneurial creativity

You can be creative without being in any way entrepreneurial – think of a poem, or a child's painting. However, it is difficult for an entrepreneur to survive for long without displaying some creative thinking along the way. Successful entrepreneurs are often seen as having a distinctively creative approach to problem-solving, sometimes described informally as 'lateral thinking', or 'thinking outside the box'. Entrepreneurial creativity has been defined as, 'the generation and implementation of novel, appropriate ideas to establish a new venture' (Amabile 1997: 18), whether that initiative takes place in a new or a more established organisation. Cognitive science is enhancing our understanding of creativity and its role in entrepreneurial activity (Ward 2004), but many questions remain. For example: how can entrepreneurs be encouraged to develop new, and more productive ideas?; how do you guard against the potential dangers of creativity?; and, more broadly, what can be done to promote the truly creative and innovative approaches that are needed to address today's economic, social, and environmental challenges? As one of the leading thinkers in this field has noted, one of the main tasks is to promote a greater openness to new ideas and ways of thinking:

> *Clearly, humans have the capacity to move beyond what currently exists to generate and implement new ideas. It is also clear, however, that people's attempts at creativity often reveal unnecessarily limited thinking. (Ward 2004: 175)*

Researchers have examined several cognitive processes that enable creativity, including:

- **Combining concepts**: this is perhaps the most obvious mechanism for creating new ideas, and it is well-known to entrepreneurship researchers from the early work of Joseph Schumpeter and his concept of 'new combinations' (Gibb 2002) (Section 13.3); by bringing two (or more) previously separate concepts together you can create something with 'emergent features' (i.e. properties that go beyond what was previously available from its component parts). For example, the combining of skateboards and skis generated an entirely new sport, snowboarding, with its own culture and fashions.

- **Analogical reasoning**: analogies can be as a source of creativity, often generating dramatic results. For example, Gordon Roddick, John Bird, and colleagues also took a familiar concept (selling magazines on street corners), and re-applied it to an entirely different context, to address the challenge of homelessness in an innovative way. The Big Issue Foundation is the concrete outcome their creative thinking. Chia (2008) argues that entrepreneurial creativity is often the result of this kind of 'peripheral vision', where individuals look beyond the immediate and obvious, avoid jumping to conclusions, and allow themselves to attend to less obvious ideas.

- **Play and interaction**: The pioneering developmental psychologist Vygotsky examined the way that the creative imagination was fostered over time, beginning with a child's playful substitution of one object (e.g. a stick) for another (e.g. a horse) and progressing though internal conversations (i.e. your 'inner voice') and the more complex interactions that take place over time, both with other people and with the culture in which you grow up (Smolucha 1992). This approach recognises that creativity is something that everyone possesses to some degree (i.e. it is not the sole preserve of a few 'creative' individuals), and that 'being creative' depends, in large part, on human beings actively engaging with one another in particular places:

- Much human creativity is *social*, arising from *activities* that take place in a *context* in which interaction with other people and the artifacts that embody collective knowledge are essential contributors (Fischer et al. 2005: 482 – emphasis added).

The following case, a profile of the furniture designer-maker Philip Koomen, provides a vivid example of creative entrepreneurship, which enables us to examine many of these issues (Case 11.3).

CASE 11.3

Philip Koomen: furniture designer-maker

Philip Koomen is a master craftsman who has developed a distinctive approach to design and creative practice. In the process he has founded a successful business that has produced many fine pieces of furniture over the last 40 years, while also promoting more sustainable approaches to sourcing timber and helping to foster a new generation of designer-makers (www.philipkoomen.co.uk). In this case study, we examine the key influences on Philip's career, with a particular focus on the roles played by creativity and entrepreneurship.

Philip sees his upbringing as having had a major influence on his choice of career. His parents had been inspired by the radical educational ideas of A. S. Neill, founder of the Summerhill School, which emphasise the importance of play, self-managed learning and democratic, community living (www.summerhillschool.co.uk). As Philip recalls, both he and his brother were always encouraged to, 'do their own thing' throughout their childhood. Though his parents' career paths were fairly conventional (his father worked in sales and his mother was a legal secretary), there was a history of entrepreneurship in the family. Philip's paternal grandfather had established a successful horticultural business in Somerset, while his maternal grandfather was a retailer with outfitting and grocery stores around Reading.

Another important factor in Philip's life has been the Bahá'í Faith (www.bahai.org), a world religion that recognises the unity of all religions and the oneness of humanity. Bahá'í teachings also celebrate the arts, crafts, and sciences as applied spiritual practices that should serve humanity. Inspired by the vision that artists and craftspeople can contribute to the advancement of civilisation, Philip set about the lengthy process of pursuing excellence in furniture making. Philip describes himself as having been a, 'pretty average' school pupil. His mother saw him as something of a 'dreamer', and he decided to leave university after completing the first year of a social science degree, having realised it was not for him: 'By the time I got to college, I thought, actually I don't really want to do this! ... it was just preparing me to become a teacher or social worker, and that's not where I wanted to go.' Having left university, he teamed up with another young Bahá'í to work as a self-employed jobbing builder for a few years. He wanted to make a living doing something creative, and was attracted to furniture-making, which also seemed to offer the kind of autonomy that he was looking for. In the mid-1970s he enrolled on courses in Furniture Design and Technology and Wood Science and Technology at a local college, before embarking on a self-directed apprenticeship that lasted almost a decade. In the early years he restored and copied antique furniture, then began to develop his own distinctive designs, which were inspired by the Arts & Crafts movement, American Shaker furniture and the work of twentieth-century Scandinavian designers. In the mid-1980s Philip relocated his workshop to an old farm building in Checkendon, a small Oxfordshire village, which continues to be the home for his business and a showcase for his work (Figure 11.1 and Figure 11.2).

Philip recalls that his career as a furniture maker coincided with a revival of interest in traditional craft skills, both in Britain and internationally. The craft revival can be seen as a reaction against mass-produced industrial products and the associated production processes. It has fuelled a demand for handmade, and often locally-sourced, alternatives in sectors that range from brewing and cheesemaking to furniture making and pottery. In each of these fields, new gen-

FIGURE 11.1   Philip Koomen, furniture designer-maker

Source: Philip Koomen Furniture

(Continued)

(Continued)

FIGURE 11.2 Sculpted chair and 'Pondlife' table

Source: Philip Koomen Furniture

erations of makers (or artisans) have rediscovered and, in some cases, reinvented earlier practices. While some people have found it difficult to make a living from their craft, others have established successful small enterprises, marketing their products through specialist retailers or via their own websites.

Philip's personal values are central to the way he has developed his own enterprise (Schwartz 2012, Williams and Schaefer 2013). Inspired by the 1992 United Nations' Earth Summit in Rio de Janeiro, he decided to research sustainable forestry practices, tracing the links through global supply chains from foresters to the market for finished products. He found that certain types of wood were underutilised, resulting in dangerous species' imbalances that threaten the quality and biodiversity of forests. Over a 15-year period, he developed furniture ranges that highlighted these lesser-known species. In the late 1990s his attention turned to sustainability issues closer to home. In 2007 he completed a PhD at Brunel University, London, examining the principles and practice of sustainable furniture-making in the Chilterns, a once thriving furniture-making district in this part of England, which saw a period of decline from the mid-1950s as a result of global competitive pressures. Philip currently collaborates with the Sylva Foundation, an Oxfordshire-based organisation with a national strategy to encourage a more integrated approach to forestry and wood culture with the aim of reviving local woodlands while also providing new economic opportunities.

For Philip, a craft workshop offers practical ways to balance reverence for nature, creativity and sustainable livelihoods. He sees it primarily as a community rather than as a business. As a master craftsman, he has aimed to create a viable and resilient practice that provides a decent living for all of its members without compromising craft excellence. Philip's workshop has produced the equivalent of over 130 years of furniture making over a

40-year period. This includes work for private clients and public commissions that include choir stalls for the historic Dorchester Abbey and furniture for the new Blavatnik School of Government at the University of Oxford. He sees its success as the result of a combination of factors, including the support received from loyal clients, the expertise and dedication of his team, careful financial management and a coherence between his Bahá'í-inspired values and vision of the importance of craft to our economic, cultural and spiritual development.

Sources: author interview with Philip Koomen (29 April 2016); Lisle, N. (2015) 'Profile: Philip Koomen – the professional dreamer'. *Oxford Times* (30 April); 'Forest to furniture: ideas in the making – the work of Philip Koomen'. Available at: www.philipkoomen.co.uk.

QUESTIONS

1. What do you see as the main influences on Philip Koomen's creativity?

2. In what ways can Philip be seen as an entrepreneur as well as a craftsman?

3. Find another example of a small, values-based enterprise and make a comparison of: (a) the key values that guide its activities; (b) the source(s) of these values; (c) their impact on the way the enterprise operates.

This section has illustrated how entrepreneurial creativity can generate positive economic, social and environmental outcomes. Case 11.3 has also highlighted the way that personal values can guide entrepreneurial creativity, influencing an individual's career choices, the type of venture they create and its impact on the wider world. However, there is a potential downside to creativity, particularly when it is coupled with less benign personal (or corporate) values. For example, many new ventures have failed because they were based on creative ideas that have proved to be impractical or simply too far ahead of their time. Creative thinking has also resulted in damaging, and occasionally disastrous, consequences. For example, it provided the foundations for a series of clever yet reckless technical innovations in the world's financial markets, which sparked a global financial crisis in the first decade of the century (Tett 2009) (Section 13.4).

11.4 ENTREPRENEURIAL LEARNING: A SHORT INTRODUCTION

11.4.1 Nature and nurture – are entrepreneurs 'born' or 'made'?

This short section introduces the theme of entrepreneurial learning, which is developed further in Chapter 16. We begin with the longstanding question of whether entrepreneurs are 'born' or 'made'. Perhaps surprisingly, it is still the subject of fierce debate. Some researchers argue that inherited factors have a decisive impact on an individual's entrepreneurial potential. For example, Shane and Nicolaou (2015) examine the evidence on genetic factors. Others place much greater emphasis on life experience. For example, Cope's (2005) 'dynamic learning perspective' challenges the static nature of conventional entrepreneurial personality approaches. As we have already seen, the psychological and behavioural issues are complex and much depends on questions such as how you define the core terms, 'born', 'made' and 'entrepreneur'. This is illustrated by when practitioners make their case. For example, in the quotation at the start of this chapter, the British entrepreneur and TV presenter, Alan

Sugar makes a strong claim for 'entrepreneurial spirit' (or 'juice') being an inherited characteristic. This means that, 'You cannot go into Boots [the retail chemist] and buy a bottle of entrepreneur juice. It's either there or it's not.' (Sugar 2010). By contrast, another leading serial entrepreneur, having recalled his own upbringing with a self-employed father, argues that childhood exposure to entrepreneurial role-models plays a vital role:

> *'I have found over the years, having worked with many entrepreneurs, and having met hundreds of them, that they all have, in their backgrounds, a close family member or friend who is a role model, a self-employed person or boss running their own company.' (Luke Johnson, quoted in Treanor 2013)*

Alan Sugar's reference to concert pianists raises another set of questions about the importance of *practice* in shaping and nurturing entrepreneurial talent. For Christiane Lemieux, founder of the design and lifestyle company Dwell Studios, the very act of founding a venture means that you are thrown into all kinds of situations you cannot anticipate – and that dealing with unfamiliar practical tasks is in itself a valuable source of learning. Though there is no explicit reference to an inherited 'entrepreneurial spirit', she also recognises that it is important to be 'extremely passionate' about your venture if it is to be a success. In addition, Christiane highlights the inspiration gained from people she works with, and the key role played by her mentors. Indeed, this process of 'constant learning' is her 'absolute favorite part of being an entrepreneur' (Dunn 2014). These insights echo the work of researchers such as Jayawarna et al. (2014) who argue that entrepreneurial careers are shaped by life-long learning, starting from childhood. There are also links with a growing body of research evidence that a key aspect of entrepreneurial learning is about how people respond to the inevitable setbacks and failures that they will encounter along the way (e.g. Cope 2011; Ucbasaran et al. 2013).

11.4.2 'Learning the ropes': so how can you learn to be an entrepreneur?

Philippe Petit, the French high-wire artist, became famous – or perhaps infamous – for walking between the bell towers of Notre Dame, and subsequently between the Twin Towers of the World Trade Center. Petit says that he began by teaching himself the standard techniques, but then abandoned most of them in order to develop his own distinctive technique. There is a similar paradox in entrepreneurship. You might be able to learn many of the set of practices that we associate with successful entrepreneurship, but how do you convert this learning into practical action? Do you need to follow Philippe Petit's example and throw most of them away in favour of your own distinctive approach?

As a starting point, it is important to recognise that learning is particularly difficult when you are actually engaged in an entrepreneurial venture. The authors of a study of technological entrepreneurship highlighted three powerful reasons as to why this is the case (Ravasi and Turati 2005: 138):

- **Ambiguity:** entrepreneurs may be seeking solutions to ill-defined problems, using prototype technologies, or trying to guess which opportunities prove fruitful.
- **Multiple actors:** entrepreneurs need to secure contributions (e.g. of knowledge, skills, resources) from many different people, within and beyond their immediate team.

- **Constraints:** entrepreneurial ventures are often short of money, the entrepreneur's time is limited, and it is not possible to pay sufficient attention to all areas, including critical reflection and learning.

So how can people overcome obstacles and 'learn' to act entrepreneurially? And if each situation has its own unique, open-ended challenges, how can entrepreneurial learning be transferred from one setting to another? The rapidly expanding literatures on entrepreneurial learning and entrepreneurship education are generating many interesting insights into these questions (e.g. Neary and Parker 2004; Kuratko 2005; Pittaway and Cope 2007). In Chapter 16, 'Entrepreneurial Learning', we will revisit our earlier discussion of the entrepreneurial learning cycle (Section 1.3), and discuss different ways of learning in much greater detail.

In the final case study, our profiled researcher, **Ute Stephan**, discusses her research on the psychology of culture and entrepreneurship (Case 11.4):

CASE 11.4   RESEARCHER PROFILE

UTE STEPHAN, ON THE PSYCHOLOGY OF CULTURE AND ENTREPRENEURSHIP

Ute Stephan is a Professor at Aston Business School and the Director of the Aston Centre for Research into International Entrepreneurship and Business. She is also the Editor-in-Chief of *Applied Psychology: An International Review*. Previously Ute was at the University of Sheffield, the London School of Economics, the Catholic University Leuven, Belgium. She holds a PhD in Psychology from the University of Marburg (Germany).

Ute's two main research interests are (1) the relationships between culture, institutions, and entrepreneurship and (2) social entrepreneurship. Related work explores entrepreneurial motivations and well-being. Her work is published in leading journals such as the *Journal of Management*, *Journal of International Business Studies*, *Management Science*, *Journal of Business Venturing*, *Journal of Occupational and Organisational Psychology* among others.

In this interview, Ute discusses how as a psychologist working on entrepreneurship she came to appreciate the role that context and culture play for entrepreneurial actions.

Why did you want to research in this area?

I have always been fascinated by cultural differences. When I began researching entrepreneurship for my PhD, the Global Entrepreneurship Monitor (GEM) project had started to accumulate evidence that entrepreneurship rates tended to be stable over time and differed considerable across countries. These patterns suggested that culture may be an important influence on entrepreneurship.

(Continued)

(Continued)

HOW DID YOU DECIDE ON YOUR MAIN RESEARCH QUESTIONS?

Early research on culture and entrepreneurship approached the topic by taking a values lens. It seemed intuitive that if we think about entrepreneurs as proactive and risk-taking innovators then a culture in which people value individualism should support such entrepreneurs. Yet it is also true that entrepreneurs rarely launch businesses in a vacuum and often rely on the support of many others around them. The GEM data also showed us that we also see high rates of entrepreneurship in more collectivist countries. So it is perhaps no surprise that research on culture and entrepreneurship seemed plagued by conflicting findings. Fortunately, at the time I first started thinking about these issues, new cross-cultural research was emerging that offered a view of culture as typical patterns of behaviour, so-called cultural practices or norms (e.g. House et al. 2004). I thought this perspective may be key to making sense of culture and entrepreneurship.

What methods did you use?

I use regression based techniques and combine data from multiple sources and databases. I typically focus on relating country-culture to entrepreneurship mea-sured at a later point in time. Such time-lags and the consideration of the interplay of culture with formal institutions are important to isolate distinct effects of culture on entrepreneurship.

What are your key findings?

I find that cultures which can be described as 'socially supportive' facilitate entrepre-neurship as they reflect weak-tie social capital and enable entrepreneurs to access important resources and support. While not the same as collectivism, socially sup-portive culture is related to aspects of collectivism. It describes culture in which people are friendly, helpful and cooperative. Conversely, the influence of individualistic and performance-based cultures on entrepreneurship appears to be more indirect and related to the strength of formal institutions. The beneficial effects of socially sup-portive cultures seem rather universal. They hold for different types of commercial entrepreneurship (independence-motivated and innovative start-ups, Stephan and Uhlaner 2010) and social entrepreneurship (Stephan et al. 2015). Others have replicated these findings. My research shows that these effects also hold at the level of *community* cultures (Hopp and Stephan 2012).

So one answer as to why there are conflicting findings in research on culture and entrepreneurship lies in the way we understand culture. If we measure cultural practices instead of values, there is a consistent pattern of socially supportive culture relating to entrepreneurship. More recently, my research also offers a second answer: Cultural values indeed influence entrepreneurship but they do so only indirectly and via a pathway that is independent from how cultural practices influence entrepreneurship (Stephan and Pathak 2016). Extant research on values tells us that whether or not we act on what we find important is subject to intervening variables. We found that the way cultures view leaders (so-called culturally shared leadership prototypes) medi-ates the influence of cultural values on entrepreneurship.

Do they have practical implications?

There are two types of practical implications. Firstly implications for policy-makers who wish to support entrepreneurship. The consistent effect of socially supportive cultures suggests that entrepreneurship can be supported by fostering norms of cooperation and helpfulness in society (e.g. through education, the media and in the workplace). One small example is to depict entrepreneurship not as a 'lone hero' cut-throat approach to business in the media but instead to promote cooperative and diverse role models of entrepreneurs.

Secondly, there are implications for entrepreneurs operating across borders especially for entrepreneurs moving between high and low socially supportive and performance based cultures or who work with others in these cultures. Knowledge of the different behavioural expectations in these cultures can help avoid disappointments and conflicts.

Where do you think research in this area needs to develop in future?

There are at least three areas for future development. Firstly, research on culture and entrepreneurship has primarily focused on country cultures. Less research is devoted to how variations in culture across regions and local communities effect entrepreneurship. Secondly, some research including my own has started to unpack the individual-level mechanisms through which culture influences entrepreneurial behaviour, but our understanding is patchy at best. Are the impacts of culture on individuals and organisations homogenous; or could it be that culture effects different individuals and organisation differently? Third, we need more research to understand how and when culture may be changed. Research on social entrepreneurship suggests one interesting avenue depicting organisations as social change agents (Stephan et al. 2016).

11.5 PRACTICAL IMPLICATIONS

In the following paragraphs, we draw out some other practical implications of the research evidence presented in this chapter.

Entrepreneurial characteristics: The research evidence suggests that there is no definitive list of traits or characteristics that are essential – so you could act entrepreneurially even though you did not display a particular trait. However, the essential truth behind the 'characteristics' debate is that, though there may not be a universal set of entrepreneurial characteristics, personal qualities can and *do* make a difference. For example, the venture capitalist Arthur Rock, who played a key role in launching some of the most successful Silicon Valley start-ups, once observed that entrepreneurs needed intellectual honesty to attract investors:

> *I'm not enough of a technologist to be able to understand what most of these entrepreneurs are about technically. The way I went about it was to spend a lot of time with these would-be entrepreneurs. The main thing is, 'are they honest?' By honest I don't mean taking money out of your pocket, but intellectually honest. Do they see things the way they are and not the way they want them to be? (Arthur Rock, quoted in Krause 2009: A3)*

As Case 11.3 illustrates, personal values can be a key influence on the life of an entrepreneur, and on the types of venture that they create (Schwartz 2012, Williams and Schaefer 2013). By combining findings from more recent personality research with insights from cognitive science and entrepreneurial learning, you could become more aware of your current personal strengths and weaknesses, and better able to achieve your entrepreneurial potential and set the kind of goals that are right for you.

Entrepreneurial cognition: We have seen how paying attention to the ways that people think, and to the content of their thoughts, can help to overcome potential biases, most notably overconfidence, that might lead to poor decision-making. We also saw how cognitive science research is helping to open up the ways in which entrepreneurs identify opportunities. Finally, we discussed how creative thinking operates, and how it relates to entrepreneurial activities, both in terms of creating new opportunities and in dealing with challenges and obstacles more effectively. These insights can be applied in practical contexts, including by entrepreneurs engaged in new venture creation activities and by those concerned with entrepreneurial learning.

Entrepreneurial learning: This is a rapidly developing field, which builds on many of the ideas developed by psychologists and cognitive scientists, as well as more sociological approaches. By discovering more about the way people learn, and the effectiveness of different methods, it should be possible to develop more effective approaches. At a more personal level, entrepreneurs can gain from a better understanding how they learn, and the kind of support they need to develop their capabilities. Another important lesson is that learning to be a more effective entrepreneur often involves collaborating with other people; we revisit this topic in the next chapter (Section 12.3) and in Chapter 16.

So despite the popular stereotypes, it seems that all kinds of people can become entrepreneurs, and (by implication) that there are many different ways of acting entrepreneurially. The management writer, Peter Drucker reflected on this point in typically strong language:

> In 30 years I have seen people of most diverse personalities and temperaments perform well in entrepreneurial challenges. Some entrepreneurs are ego-centric and others are painfully correct conformists. Some are fat and some are lean. Some entrepreneurs are worriers and some are relaxed, some have great charm ... and some have no more personality than a frozen mackerel! (Drucker [1985] 2007: 243)

11.6 SUMMARY

- Individual-level perspectives using a variety of psychological and behavioural approaches have enhanced our understanding of entrepreneurship.

- Earlier research focused on the search for distinctive entrepreneurial traits or personality characteristics. These ideas remain popular and influential, but it is important to be aware of their limitations and of subsequent advances in psychological and behavioural research.

- Recent research on entrepreneurial cognition provides some interesting insights in areas such as opportunity recognition. Researchers have also helped to explain cognitive biases can contribute to mistakes and the failure of some entrepreneurial ventures.

- There are three main vehicles for entrepreneurial learning: formal education; informal sources; and learning from direct experiences. People can acquire entrepreneurial skills and understanding from each of these sources; it is also possible, though arguably more difficult, to develop entrepreneurial attitudes and values in this way.

- The relationship between social interactions and individual behaviour is attracting increasing attention. Research in this area has challenged traditional assumptions in areas such as the creation of entrepreneurial self-identity and gender roles.

- Individual-level research findings from sub-fields, such as entrepreneurial cognition and entrepreneurial learning, have practical implications for individual entrepreneurs, entrepreneurial ventures and for policy-makers.

Practical activities

1. **My entrepreneurial personality:** Re-read the arguments in Section 11.2, and try at least one of the entrepreneurial assessment tests detailed there or on the Online Resources. What is your impression of the results? Do they reflect your own assessment? Were there any surprises? If possible, compare the findings with those of a close colleague or friend. (NB: If these results suggest a lack of enterprising attributes do not assume that your entrepreneurial journey is over. Instead, review the various limitations of characteristics-based approaches and refer to the discussion on entrepreneurial learning, and how it can transform skills, knowledge, and attitudes.)

2. **Exploring other entrepreneurial lives:** Using Case 11.3 as a guide, find three examples of people talking about the factors that prompted them to act entrepreneurially. This may be establishing a social or commercial enterprise, or becoming an 'intrapreneur' in an existing organisation. Compare the accounts, highlighting examples of each of the following: (a) early signs of entrepreneurial potential; (b) informal learning; (c) formal learning; (c) other influences on their behaviour. Write a short commentary (800 words), reviewing your findings with reference to concepts discussed in this chapter. To find your source material, conduct a web search and try searching in biographies, autobiographies, and magazine profiles.

3. **Entrepreneurial learning – a student's perspective:** Parts One and Two of this textbook, and the Online Resources, have been designed to encourage entrepreneurial learning. What techniques have the authors used? To consider this question, take a look through the textbook and the Online Resources, noting the kinds of resources available and how they have helped you to explore various aspects of entrepreneurship. Write a short commentary (800 words) on your thoughts and experiences in using these resources.

Discussion topics

1. The entrepreneurial personality debate: Form two teams and prepare a set of arguments 'for' and 'against' the motion: 'This House believes that there is such a thing as an entrepreneurial personality.' Allow five minutes for each side, followed by a further five minutes to respond to the arguments presented. Then move to a vote. To make the debate more interesting, allocate team members so

that those who disagree with the motion have to defend it, and vice-versa. The debates can also be adapted for use in a virtual learning environment.

2. The entrepreneurial learning debate: Following the guidance for Discussion topic 1, organise a debate based on the motion, 'This House believes that you can teach successful social and/or commercial entrepreneurship.' Entrepreneurship tutors could take on the role of challenging the motion.

3. Encouraging 'better' kinds of entrepreneurship: Many governments and governmental agencies have the aim of promoting what might loosely be termed 'better' kinds of entrepreneurial activity (e.g. more innovative, more competitive, and more socially and environmentally responsible) (Section 15.4.2). But how would you change the behaviour of an individual entrepreneur? Apply the ideas discussed in this chapter to address *one* of the following practical challenges at an individual level: (a) encouraging the founder of a struggling social enterprise, or the owner-manager of a struggling small firm, to become a more effective leader; (b) encouraging a young woman, currently studying at secondary school (i.e. high school), to develop her entrepreneurial potential in a responsible way; (c) persuading a criminal entrepreneur to move into a legitimate form of entrepreneurial activity. Identify at least three actions that you would take in order to achieve your goal. Do you think your strategy would succeed? What other kinds of intervention might help?

Recommended reading

These readings address two important topics in entrepreneurship research and are recommended for anyone wanting to build on the material covered in this chapter. Recommended readings have been selected from leading Sage journals and are freely available for readers of this textbook to download via the Online Resources.

Ucbasaran, D., Shepherd, D. A., Lockett, A., and Lyon, S. J. (2013) 'Life after business failure the process and consequences of business failure for entrepreneurs'. *Journal of Management*, **39, 1: 163–202.**

This article reviews research evidence on entrepreneurs' experience of business failure, from the immediate aftermath through to recovery and re-emergence. The authors examine the financial, social, and psychological costs of failure. They also look at research about the way that entrepreneurs make sense of, and learn from, business failure. The concluding section considers cognitive and behavioural outcomes of failure and the process of recovery.

Zou, H., Chen, X., Lam, L. W. R., and Liu, X. (2016) 'Psychological capital and conflict management in the entrepreneur–venture capitalist relationship in China: the entrepreneur perspective'. *International Small Business Journal*, **34, 4: 446–67.**

This article explores the divergent interests and goals that have led to inherent conflicts in the dyadic relationship between entrepreneurs and venture capitalists (VCs). The authors propose that an entrepreneur's psychological capital (as opposed to economic, human and social capital) can help shed light on how they manage conflicts in their relationships with VCs. The article is an interesting application of psychological concepts such as self-efficacy, which also integrates socio-cultural factors.

References

Ajzen, I. (1991) 'The theory of planned behavior'. *Organizational Behavior and Human Decision Processes*, 50: 179–211.

Allen, K. (2014) 'Youth unemployment pushes graduates to start up own businesses'. The Guardian. Available at: https://www.theguardian.com/business/2014/may/12/youth-unemployment-graduates-start-up-own-businesses (accessed 25 May 2017).

Amabile, T. M. (1997) 'Entrepreneurial creativity through motivational synergy'. *Journal of Creative Behaviour*, 31, 1: 18–26.

Bae, T. J., Qian, S., Miao, C., and Fiet, J. O. (2014) 'The relationship between entrepreneurship education and entrepreneurial intentions: a meta-analytic review'. *Entrepreneurship Theory and Practice*, 38, 2: 217–54.

Bandura, A. (1995) 'Exercise of personal and collective efficacy in changing societies'. In A. Bandura (ed.), *Self-efficacy in Changing Societies*. Cambridge: Cambridge University Press (1–45).

Baron, R. A. (2000) 'Psychological perspectives on entrepreneurship: cognitive and social factors in entrepreneurs' success'. *Current Directions in Psychological Science*, 9, 1: 15–18.

Baron, R. A. and Ward, T. B. (2004) 'Expanding entrepreneurial cognition's toolbox: potential contributions from the field of cognitive science'. *Entrepreneurship Theory and Practice*, 28, 6: 553–74.

Begley, T. M. and Boyd, D. B. (1987) 'Psychological characteristics associated with performance in entrepreneurial firms and small businesses'. *Journal of Business Venturing*, 2: 79–93.

Binks, M. (2005) *Entrepreneurship Education and Integrative Learning*. Birmingham: National Council for Graduate Entrepreneurship.

Blundel, R. K., Ippolito, K., and Donnarumma, D. (2013) *Effective Organisational Communication: Perspectives, Principles and Practices* (4th edn). Harlow: Pearson.

Brockhaus, R. (1980) 'Risk-taking propensity of entrepreneurs'. *Academy of Management Journal*, 23, 3: 509–20.

Caird, S. P. (1993) 'What do psychological tests suggest about entrepreneurs'. *Journal of Psychology*, 8, 6: 11–20.

Carland, J. C., Boulton, F. H., and Carland, J. A. C. (1984) 'Differentiating entrepreneurs from small business owners: a conceptualization'. *Academy of Management Review*, 9, 2: 354–9.

Casson, M., Yeung, B., Basu, A., and Wadeson, N. (2008) *The Oxford Handbook of Entrepreneurship*. Oxford: Oxford University Press.

Chell, E. (2008) *The Entrepreneurial Personality: a Social Construction* (2nd edn). London: Routledge.

Chen, C., Greene, P., and Crick, A. (1998) 'Does entrepreneurial self-efficacy distinguish entrepreneurs from managers?' *Journal of Business Venturing*, 13, 4: 295–316.

Chia, R. (2008) 'Enhancing entrepreneurial learning through peripheral vision'. In R. T. Harrison and C. Leitch (eds) op. cit. (27–43).

Ciavarella, M. A., Buchholtz, A. K., and Riordan, C. M. (2004) 'The Big Five and venture survival: is there a linkage?' *Journal of Business Venturing*, 19, 4: 465–83.

Coelho, M. P. (2010) 'Unrealistic optimism: still a neglected trait'. *Journal of Business and Psychology*, 25, 3: 397–408.

Colli, A., Fernandez Perez, P., and Rose, M. B. (2003) 'National determinants of family firm development?: family firms in Britain, Spain, and Italy in the nineteenth and twentieth centuries'. *Enterprise and Society*, 4, 2: 28–64.

Cooper, A. C., Woo, C. A., and Dunkelberg, W. (1988) 'Entrepreneurs perceived chances for success'. *Journal of Business Venturing*, 3, 2: 97–108.

Cope, J. (2005) 'Towards a dynamic learning perspective of entrepreneurship'. *Entrepreneurship Theory and Practice*, 29, 4: 373–98.

Cope, J. (2011) 'Entrepreneurial learning from failure: an interpretative phenomenological analysis'. *Journal of Business Venturing*, 26, 6: 604–23.

Corbett, A. C. (2005) 'Experiential learning within the process of opportunity identification and exploitation'. *Entrepreneurship Theory and Practice*, 29, 4: 473–91.

Cromie, S. (2000) 'Asessing entrepreneurial inclinations: some approaches and empirical evidence'. *European Journal of Work and Organisational Psychology*, 9, 1: 7–30.

Davidsson, P. (2006) 'The types and contextual fit of entrepreneurial processes'. In A. E. Burke (ed.), *Modern Perspectives on Entrepreneurship*. Dublin: Senate Hall, 1–22.

Davidsson, P., Low, M. B., and Wright, M. (2001) 'Editor's introduction: Low and MacMillan ten years on: achievements and future directions for entrepreneurship research'. *Entrepreneurship Theory and Development*, 25, 4: 5–15.

Down, S. and Reveley, J. (2004) 'Generational encounters and the social formation of entrepreneurial identity: "Young Guns" and "Old Farts"'. *Organization*, 11, 2: 233–50.

Drucker, P. F. ([1985] 2007) *Innovation and Entrepreneurship* (new edn). Oxford: Butterworth-Heinemann.

Dunn, L. (2014) Women in business: Q&A with Christiane Lemieux, founder of DwellStudio. *The Huffington Post*, 23 January. http://www.huffingtonpost.com/laura-dunn/women-in-business-qa-with_6_b_4055979.html (accessed 25 May 2017).

Dweck, C. S. (1999) *Self-theories: Their Role in Motivation, Personality and Development*. Philadelphia: Psychology Press.

Dweck, C. S. (2006) *Mindset: The New Psychology of Success*. New York: Random House.

Essers, C. and Benschop, Y. (2009) 'Muslim businesswomen doing boundary work: the negotiation of Islam, gender and ethnicity within entrepreneurial contexts'. *Human Relations*, 62, 3: 403–23.

Fayolle, A. and Liñán, F. (2014) 'The future of research on entrepreneurial intentions'. *Journal of Business Research*, 67, 5: 663–6.

Fischer, G., Giaccardi, E., Eden, H., Sugimoto, M., and Ye, Y. (2005) 'Beyond binary choices: integrating individual and social creativity'. *International Journal of Human-Computer Studies*, 63, 482–512.

Flannery, P. (2008) *Grabbing the Oyster!: Anecdotes and Advice from Icons of Irish Business*. Cork: Oak Tree Press.

Foss, N. J., Klein, P. G., Kor, Y. Y., and Mahoney, J. T. (2008) 'Entrepreneurship, subjectivism, and the resource-based view: toward a new synthesis'. *Strategic Entrepreneurship Journal*, 2: 73–94.

Frese, M., Chell, E., and Klandt, H. (eds) (2000) 'Psychological approaches to entrepreneurship'. *European Journal of Work and Organizational Psychology*, 9, 1, 3–102 (Special Issue).

Gartner, W. B. (1989a) '"Who is an entrepreneur?" is the wrong question'. *Entrepreneurship Theory and Practice*, 13, 4: 47–67.

Gartner, W. B. (1989b) 'Some suggestions for research on entrepreneurial traits and characteristics'. *Entrepreneurship Theory and Practice*, 14, 1: 27–38.

Geldhof, G. J., Malin, H., Johnson, S. K., Porter, T., Bronk, K. C., Weiner, M. B., Agans, J. P., Mueller, M. K., Hunt, D., Colby, A., and Lerner, R. M. (2014) 'Entrepreneurship in young adults: initial findings from the young entrepreneurs study'. *Journal of Applied Developmental Psychology*, 35, 5: 410–21.

Gibb, A. (2002), 'In pursuit of a new "enterprise" and "entrepreneurship" paradigm for learning: creative destruction, new values, new ways of doing things and new combinations of knowledge'. *International Journal of Management Reviews*, 4, 3: 233–69.

Goldberg, L. R. (1993) 'The structure of phenotypic personality traits'. *American Psychologist*, 48, 1: 26–34.

Gudmundsson, S. V. and Lechner, C. (2013) 'Cognitive biases, organization, and entrepreneurial firm survival'. *European Management Journal*, 31, 3: 278–94.

Gupta, U. (2000) *Done Deals: Venture Capitalists Tell Their Story*. Cambridge MA: Harvard Business School Press.

Gupta, V. and Fernandez, C. (2009) 'Cross-cultural similarities and differences in characteristics attributed to entrepreneurs: a three-nation study'. *Journal of Leadership & Organizational Studies*, 15, 3: 304–18.

Hamilton, E. E. (2006) 'Whose story is it anyway?: narrative accounts of the role of women in founding and establishing family businesses'. *International Small Business Journal*, 24, 3: 253–71.

Harrison, R. T. and Leitch, C. (eds) (2008) *Entrepreneurial Learning: Conceptual Frameworks and Applications*. Abingdon: Routledge.

Hayek, F. A. (1945) 'The use of knowledge in society'. *The American Economic Review*, 35, 4: 519–30.

Haynie, J. M., Shepherd, D., Mosakowski, E., and Earley, P. C. (2010) 'A situated metacognitive model of the entrepreneurial mindset'. *Journal of Business Venturing*, 25, 2: 217–29.

Henley, A., (2016) 'Does religion influence entrepreneurial behaviour?' *International Small Business Journal* [Online First].

Hmieleski, K. M. and Baron, R. A. (2009) 'Entrepreneurs' optimism and new venture performance: a social cognitive perspective'. *Academy of Management Journal*, 52, 3: 473–88.

Hobbs, D. (1988) *Doing the Business: Entrepreneurship, the Working Class, and Detectives in the East End of London.* Oxford: Clarendon Press.

Hopp, C. and Stephan, U. (2012) 'The influence of socio-cultural environments on the performance of nascent entrepreneurs: community culture, motivation, self-efficacy and start-up success'. *Entrepreneurship and Regional Development*, 29 : 1–29.

House, R. J., Hanges, P. J., Javidan, M., Dorfman, P., and Gupta, V. (2004) *Culture, Leadership, and Organizations: The GLOBE Study of 62 Societies.* Thousand Oaks, CA: Sage.

Howorth C. A., Rose M. B., and Hamilton E. E. (2008) 'Definitions, diversity and development: key debates in family business research'. In M. Casson et al. (eds) op. cit. (225–47).

Jayawarna, D., Jones, O., and Macpherson, A. (2014) 'Entrepreneurial potential: the role of childhood human capital'. *International Small Business Journal*, 32, 8: 918–43.

Kets de Vries, M. F. R. (1985) 'The dark side of entrepreneurship'. *Harvard Business Review*, 63, 6: 160–7.

Kets de Vries, M. F. R. (1996) 'The anatomy of the entrepreneur: clinical observations'. *Human Relations*, 49, 7: 853–83.

Kirzner, I. M. (1979) *Perception, Opportunity and Profit: Studies in the Theory of Entrepreneurship.* Chicago: University of Chicago Press.

Kitching, J. and Rouse, J. (2016) 'Opportunity or dead end?: rethinking the study of entrepreneurial action without a concept of opportunity'. *International Small Business Journal* [Online First].

Knight, F. H. (1921) *Risk, Uncertainty, and Profit.* Boston MA: Houghton Mifflin.

Kondo, D. K. (1990) *Crafting Selves: Power, Gender and Discourses of Identity in a Japanese Workplace.* Chicago: University of Chicago Press.

Krause, R. (2009) 'A gem among venture capitalists. Get out front: Arthur Rock saw early that Intel and Apple were winners'. *Investors Business Daily*, 23 April, A3.

Krueger, N. (2000) 'The cognitive infrastructure of opportunity emergence'. *Entrepreneurship Theory and Practice*, 24, 3: 5–23.

Kuratko, D. F. (2005) 'The emergence of entrepreneurship education: development, trends, and challenges'. *Entrepreneurship, Theory and Practice*, 29, 5: 577–98.

Lewicki, R. J., McAllister, D. J., and Bies, R. J. (1998) 'Trust and distrust: New relationships and realities'. *Academy of Management Review*, 23, 3: 438–58.

Licht, A. N. and Siegel, J. I. (2008) 'The social dimensions of entrepreneurship'. In Casson et al. (eds), op. cit. (511–39).

Low, M. B. and MacMillan, I. C. (1988) 'Entrepreneurship: past research and future challenges'. *Journal of Management*, 14, 2: 139–61.

McClelland, D. C. (1961) *The Achieving Society.* New Jersey: Van Nostrand.

McCrae, R. R. and Costa P. T. (1996) 'Toward a new generation of personality theories: theoretical context for the five-factor model'. In J. S. Wiggins (ed.), *The Five-Factor Model of Personality: Theoretical Perspectives.* New York NY: Guilford Press (51–87).

McGrath, R. G. and MacMillan, I. C. (2000) *The Entrepreneurial Mindset: Strategies for Continuously Creating Opportunity in an Age of Uncertainty.* Cambridge MA: Harvard Business Press.

Miner, J. B. (1997) 'A psychological typology and its relationship to entrepreneurial success'. *Entrepreneurship and Regional Development*, 9, 4: 319–34.

Mitchell, R. K., Busenitz, L., Lant, T., McDougall, P. P., Morse, E. A. and Brock Smith, J. (2002) 'Toward a theory of entrepreneurial cognition: rethinking the people side of entrepreneurship research'. *Entrepreneurship Theory and Practice*, 27, 2: 93–104.

Neary, M. and Parker, A. (2004) *Enterprise, Social Enterprise and Critical Pedagogy: Reinventing the HE Curriculum.* Birmingham: National Council for Graduate Entrepreneurship.

Neergaard, H. and Leitch, C. (2015) *Handbook of Qualitative Research Techniques and Analysis in Entrepreneurship.* Cheltenham: Edward Elgar.

Neergaard, H. and Ulhoi, J. P. (2007) *Handbook of Qualitative Research Methods in Entrepreneurship.* Cheltenham: Edward Elgar.

NIRAS (2008) *Survey of Entrepreneurship in Higher Education in Europe.* Brussels: European Commission, Directorate General for Enterprise and Industry.

Palich, L. E. and Bagby, D. R. (1995) 'Using cognitive theory to explain entrepreneurial risk taking: challenging conventional wisdom'. *Journal of Business Venturing*, 10, 6: 425–38.

Penrose, E. T. ([1959] 2009) *The Theory of the Growth of the Firm* (4th edn). Oxford: Oxford University Press.

Pittaway, L. and Cope, J. (2007) 'Entrepreneurship education: a systematic review of the evidence'. *International Small Business Journal*, 25: 479–510.

Rae, D. and Wang, C. L. (eds) (2015) *Entrepreneurial Learning: New Perspectives in Research, Education and Practice.* London: Routledge.

Rauch, A., and Frese, M. (2007) 'Let's put the person back into entrepreneurship research: a meta-analysis on the relationship between business owners, personality traits, business creation, and success'. *European Journal of Work and Organizational Psychology*, 16, 4: 353–85.

Ravasi, D. and Turati, C. (2005) 'Exploring entrepreneurial learning: a comparative study of technology development projects'. *Journal of Business Venturing*, 20, 1: 137–64.

Rotter, J. B. (1966) 'Generalized expectancies for internal versus external control of reinforcement'. *Psychological Monographs.* 609, 80: 1–28.

Sarasvathy, S. D. (2001) 'Causation and effectuation: toward a theoretical shift from economic inevitability to entrepreneurial contingency'. *Academy of Management Review*, 26, 2: 243–63.

Sarasvathy, S., Kumar, K., York, J. G., and Bhagavatula, S. (2014) 'An effectual approach to international entrepreneurship: overlaps, challenges, and provocative possibilities'. *Entrepreneurship Theory and Practice*, 38, 1: 71–93.

Schoon, I. and Duckworth, K. (2012) 'Who becomes an entrepreneur?: early life experiences as predictors of entrepreneurship'. *Developmental Psychology*, 48, 6: 1719–26.

Schwartz, S. H. (2012) 'An overview of the Schwartz theory of basic values'. *Online Readings in Psychology and Culture*, 2, 1: 1–20. Available at: http://dx.doi.org/10.9707/2307-0919.1116 (accessed 5 January 2017).

Schwenk, C. R. (1984) 'Cognitive simplification processes in strategic decision-making'. *Strategic Management Journal*, 5, 2: 111–28.

Sexton, D. L. and Bowman-Upton, N. (1985) 'The entrepreneur: a capable executive and more'. *Journal of Business Venturing*, 1, 1: 129–40.

Shane, S. and Nicolaou, N. (2015) 'Creative personality, opportunity recognition and the tendency to start businesses: a study of their genetic predispositions'. *Journal of Business Venturing*, 30, 3: 407–19.

Simon, M. and Houghton, S. M. (2002) 'The relationship among biases, misconceptions, and the introduction of pioneering products: examining differences in venture decision contexts'. *Entrepreneurship Theory and Practice*, 27, 2: 105–24.

Smolucha, F. (1992) 'The relevance of Vygotsky's theory of creative imagination for contemporary research on play.' *Creativity Research Journal*, 5, 1: 69–76.

Souitaris V. Zerbinati, S., and Al-Laham, A. (2007) 'Do entrepreneurship programmes raise entrepreneurial intentions of science and engineering students?: the effects of learning, inspiration and resources'. *Journal of Business Venturing*, 22, 4: 566–91.

Srivastava, S., John, O. P., Gosling, S. D., and Potter, J. (2003) 'Development of personality in early and middle adulthood: set like plaster or persistent change?' *Journal of Personality and Social Psychology*, 84: 1041–53.

Stephan, U. and Pathak, S. (2016) 'Beyond cultural values?: cultural leadership ideals and entrepreneurship'. *Journal of Business Venturing*, 31, 5: 505–23.

Stephan, U. and Uhlaner, L. M. (2010) 'Performance-based vs: socially supportive culture: a cross-national study of descriptive norms and entrepreneurship'. *Journal of International Business Studies*, 41, 8: 1347–64.

Stephan, U., Uhlaner, L. M., and Stride, C. (2015) 'Institutions and social entrepreneurship: the role of institutional voids, institutional support, and institutional configurations'. *Journal of International Business Studies*, 46, 3: 308–31.

Stephan, U., Patterson, M., Kelly, C., and Mair, J. (2016) 'Organizations driving positive social change: a review and an integrative framework of change processes'. *Journal of Management*, 42, 5: 1250–81.

Stimpson, D. V., Robinson, P. B., Waranusuntikule, S., and Zheng, R. (1990) 'Attitudinal characterisitics of entrepreneurs and non-entrepreneurs in the United States, Korea, Thailand, and the People's Republic of China'. *Entrepreneurship & Regional Development*, 2, 1: 49–56.

Suddaby, R., Bruton, G. D. and Si, S. X. (2015) 'Entrepreneurship through a qualitative lens: insights on the construction and/or discovery of entrepreneurial opportunity'. *Journal of Business Venturing*, 30, 1: 1–10.

Sugar, A. (2010) 'Lord Alan Sugar on entrepreneurship, The Apprentice, and being rich'. Growing Business, 27 October. http://startups.co.uk/lord-alan-sugar-on-entrepreneurship-the-apprentice-and-being-rich/ (accessed 25 May 2017).

Tett, G. (2009) *Fool's Gold: How Unrestrained Greed Corrupted a Dream, Shattered Global Markets and Unleashed a Catastrophe.* London: Little, Brown.

Treanor, S. (2013) 'Are entrepreneurs born or can they be taught?' BBC News, 3 July. http://www.bbc.co.uk/news/business-23157638 (accessed 25 May 2017).

Ucbasaran, D., Shepherd, D. A., Lockett, A., and Lyon, S. J. (2013) 'Life after business failure: the process and consequences of business failure for entrepreneurs'. *Journal of Management*, 39, 1: 163–202.

Valliere, D. (2008) 'Exploring Buddhist influence on the entrepreneurial decision'. *International Journal of Entrepreneurial Behaviour and Research*, 14, 3: 172–91.

Wadeson, N. (2008) 'Cognitive aspects of entrepreneurship: decision-making and attitudes to risk'. In Casson et al. (eds), op. cit. (91–113).

Ward, T. B. (2004) 'Cognition, creativity and entrepreneurship'. *Journal of Business Venturing*, 19, 2: 173–88.

Weinstein, N. D. and Klein, W. M. (1996) 'Unrealistic optimism: present and future. *Journal of Social and Clinical Psychology*, 15, 1: 1–8.

White, R. E., Thornhill, S., and Hampson, E. (2006) 'Entrepreneurs and evolutionary biology: the relationship between testosterone and new venture creation'. *Organizational Behavior and Human Decision Processes*, 100, 1: 21–34.

Whyley, C. (1998) *Risky Business: the Personal and Financial Costs of Small Business Failure*. London: Policy Studies Institute.

Wiggins, J. S. (ed.) (1996) *The Five-Factor Model of Personality: Theoretical Perspectives*. New York: Guilford Press.

Wiklund, J., Davidsson, P., and Delmar, F. (2003) 'What do they think and feel about growth?: an expectancy-value approach to small business managers' attitudes toward growth'. *Entrepreneurship Theory and Practice*, 27, 3: 247–70.

Williams, S. and Schaefer, A. (2013) 'Small and medium-sized enterprises and sustainability: managers' values and engagement with environmental and climate change issues'. *Business Strategy and the Environment*, 22, 3: 173–86.

12

SOCIAL PERSPECTIVES: UNDERSTANDING PEOPLE AND PLACES

To understand how any society functions you must understand the relationship between the men and the women.

Angela Davies. civil rights campaigner and academic

Without persons, no society; without society, no persons.

Thomas Hill Green, nineteenth-century philosopher

LEARNING OUTCOMES

After reading this chapter you should be able to:

- Explore social-level perspectives on entrepreneurship, with a focus on sociological, anthropological, and geographical approaches.
- Recognise the contribution of these approaches to our understanding of entrepreneurship, in terms of empirical findings, research methods, and theoretical frameworks.
- Consider the kinds of knowledge generated by these approaches, and begin to relate it to that obtained from other research perspectives.
- Appreciate the practical relevance of this research for policy-makers and practitioners.
- Apply these insights to your own experiences of entrepreneurship.

12.1 ENTREPRENEURSHIP IN A SOCIAL CONTEXT

In this chapter, we are concerned with the ways in which **entrepreneurial activity** is influenced by the societies in which it takes place. As we saw in the previous chapter, studying **entrepreneurship** at an individual level of analysis is far from straightforward. However, in moving to a social level, researchers find themselves in an even more complicated and varied landscape. It may be tempting to avoid all this complexity and simply assume that your research is picking up some universal features of entrepreneurship. Some earlier research has since been criticised for making this kind of assumption, and as a consequence failing to grasp the sheer variety of entrepreneurship practices around the world. Zafirovski (1999: 351) points out that, 'Entrepreneurship possesses an eminently social character and is subject to the operation of definite societal processes.' As the author goes on to argue, many aspects of entrepreneurship have a culture-specific dimension. The lesson for researchers is that we should not simply assume that the motives, preferences, and values of other people are going to be similar, irrespective of their social background, or of the culture and institutions in which they operate (Case 12.1).

In the last century, this literature was dominated by empirical studies located in a fairly narrow range of societies and cultures, notably those of North America and Europe, and almost exclusively on commercial ventures. The situation has changed over the last two decades due to the increase in entrepreneurship research focusing on other parts of the world and on social ventures. This proliferation of activity has produced a lot of rich and interesting material, but the literature can be difficult to navigate due to the complex web of research themes, research settings, theoretical frameworks, and methodologies that have emerged. The main aims of this chapter are to find a way through the web, and to indicate how the various strands can be combined.

The remainder of the chapter is structured as follows. In Section 12.2, we take a broad overview of how researchers explore the social dimensions of entrepreneurship then look more closely at three contrasting approaches: analysing large data sets, conducting ethnographic studies, and mapping **entrepreneurial networks**. Section 12.3 introduces some of the main social research themes, indicating the scope and the variety of studies that have been conducted. The remaining sections provide a more detailed insight into two of these research areas, gender (Section 12.4) and geography (Section 12.5). Finally, in Section 12.6, we consider the practical implications for **entrepreneurs**, entrepreneurial organisations, and those involved in policy-making.

CASE 12.1   STUDENT FOCUS

Unlikely subjects?

These short fictionalised accounts, based on real world examples, illustrate how students have made good use of entrepreneurship research to achieve successful outcomes in their studies.

Joel was struggling to find an interesting angle to pursue. His dissertation proposal deadline was just a few days away and, despite a lot of background reading, he was unable to find a topic that looked sufficiently relevant, novel – and interesting enough to keep him motivated. Like many students on his course, Joel was particularly keen on social entrepreneurship; he had waded through dozens of research papers, news features and websites that featured inspiring projects, often started by people just a few years older than himself – having just celebrated his 21st birthday he was half way through the final year of his undergraduate degree. Social entrepreneurship was fashionable on campus, particularly among students in his faculty, where many saw it as a potential alternative to a more conventional 'corporate' career. However, one of the slight concerns Joel felt in relation to social entrepreneurship – and the media coverage in particular – was the tendency to focus almost exclusively on aspirational 'good

(Continued)

(Continued)

news' stories, often featuring equally attractive and exciting people. Having grown up in a relatively deprived industrial city, he could sense a disconnection between some of this coverage and the everyday challenges faced by the social ventures operating in his own part of the world. Perhaps he could develop something around this idea? Still lacking inspiration, Joel decided to set off for a much-needed cup of coffee.

The café was busy, but he spotted his classmate Pernille, who was seated in a quiet corner reading – perhaps she could help? Pernille was a mature student with a background in health and social care. She listened patiently to Joel's account and after a few moments' thought, asked him:

'So, if you really think youngsters are getting all the airtime, have you considered searching for some *older* social entrepreneurs?

Joel admitted that the thought had not crossed his mind – in fact, he rather doubted that there were any. Pernille continued:

'I happen to know a couple of people around my age who've set up social ventures; in fact, I'm thinking of joining one myself – it's what they call a "co-housing" project, where older folk become property developers!'

'So how does that work?' Joel asked.

'Well, the basic idea is that we invest our life savings – or a large part of it anyway – and form a kind of cooperative. We buy the land and commission someone to build us a new, eco-housing development that, if all goes well, also includes communal facilities – so we're less isolated – and some social housing for younger families.'

Joel went back to the library with lots of new ideas for his dissertation. A quick web search and a scan through the e-journals collection unearthed several useful sources. For example, interview findings from one North American study found that, 'older-adult social entrepreneurs have an almost irrepressible drive to make the world better' (Pitt-Catsouphes et al. (2014: 8)), while research conducted in the UK identified a tendency for older social entrepreneurs to focus more on creating social rather than economic value, and to have a different approach to growing their ventures (i.e. preferring a micro-franchising model of growth to expanding it themselves) (Stumbitz et al. (2012: 3)). He was also struck by the finding that ventures founded by older people often addressed issues related to aging (ibid.: 3). Thinking back to the earlier conversation with Pernille, he searched for articles about co-housing and saw how social entrepreneurial and cooperative principles were being used to address the accommodation and social care needs of older people. For example, some co-housing ventures brought different generations together as part of a shared project (Labit 2015).

Joel was feeling much happier; he now had a great research topic – and a potential interviewee!

QUESTIONS

1. Why do you think Joel is finding it difficult to identify a suitable dissertation topic?

2. How does his understanding of social entrepreneurship change as a result of meeting Pernille?

3. What practical lessons might you take from Joel's experience when you are conducting social research?

12.2 SOCIAL RESEARCH APPROACHES: A BRIEF OVERVIEW

12.2.1 Introduction and three contrasting examples

As we have already seen, entrepreneurship researchers have adopted a variety of perspectives and research approaches in order to explore their subject (Section 10.2). Research at the individual level has been dominated by a few disciplines, most notably psychology, but with increasing contributions from other fields such as learning (Section 12.1). By contrast, research at a social level has always drawn on a much wider range of social science disciplines, including sociology, anthropology, geography, and many cross-cutting fields such as cultural studies and policy studies (NB economics-based approaches are addressed in more detail in Chapter 11; **historical research** is discussed in Chapter 14). In some cases, research designs may be based around a single approach, such as a piece of ethnographic fieldwork or analysis of questionnaire data. In others, researchers may draw on multiple sources of evidence. For example, an analysis of the start-up process may take the form of a number of detailed case studies of new ventures. This reflects a broader call for entrepreneurship researchers to examine their subject using **multi-level** approaches (Low and MacMillan 1988; Davidsson and Wiklund 2001). This means making connections between entrepreneurial behaviour at various levels, including the individual, the organisation, and the social context (Zafirovski 1999: 353). Social scientists use a variety of research methods and sources of evidence to probe these different levels (Table 12.1):

TABLE 12.1 Some common research methods

Ethnography and participant observation
Action research
Semi-structured in-depth interviews
Recording verbal histories
Focus groups
Documentary sources (e.g. minutes, accounts)
E-research (e.g. analysing social media)
Structured interviews
Self-completion questionnaire surveys
Secondary analysis of official data sets (e.g. VAT registration data)

In practice, researchers often develop research designs that combine more than one method, and draw on multiple sources of evidence. To illustrate this process, we have selected three contrasting research approaches for more detailed consideration:

- Analysing and modelling of entrepreneurial activity using statistical data from surveys and official data sets (Section 12.2.2).

- Interpreting the entrepreneurial experience through ethnographic fieldwork (Section 12.2.3).

- Revealing patterns and changes in entrepreneurial relationships through social network mapping (Section 12.2.4).

We compare the different sources of evidence obtained from each of these approaches and profile some recent research studies to illustrate the kinds of questions they are able to address. Further coverage of the issues discussed, and other relevant methodological questions, can be found in business research methods texts such as Bryman and Bell (2015) or Easterby-Smith et al. (2015), or in specialist entrepreneurship methods books such as Davidsson (2016).

12.2.2 Statistical analysis and modelling: surveys and official data sets

A great deal of the entrepreneurship research conducted at a social level makes use of quantitative data of various kinds. One of the most widely used sources of data is official data sets, which are generally compiled by international agencies (e.g. International Monetary Fund, World Bank), and from regional, national, and local governments. Census data, which records the 'births' and 'deaths' of businesses, is often available for researchers in the form of downloadable spreadsheets. These data sets typically include several kinds of categorical and variable data, including location, industry sector, legal form (e.g. limited company), sales turnover, and number of employees. Industry surveys are another common source of published data; these are often compiled by specialist research companies and cover particular industrial sectors (e.g. food retailing, tourism, consumer electronics) and markets (e.g. the growing markets in organic and fair trade certified clothing). Researchers also obtain primary data, typically by conducting or commissioning their own questionnaire surveys. Some of these surveys have been run over extended periods. For example, the *Quarterly Survey of Small Business in Britain* was established by Graham Bannock, author of the influential Bolton Report on small firms, and operated for three decades (Blundel et al. 2014). These approaches have been influential in areas such as economic geography, where researchers have attempted to explain the relationship between entrepreneurial activity and regional economic development (Section 12.5). Looking back over two decades of research in that field, Acs and Storey (2004: 872) noted a significant improvement in the quality of data being used and in the sophistication of the statistical analysis. For example, whereas earlier comparative studies tended to compare regional cross-section data using ordinary least squares regressions, more recent work had access to both cross-section and time-series data. The following example indicates the kinds of research question that can be addressed using these approaches. Van Stel and Storey (2004) conducted an examination of the relationship between firm births and job creation in 60 British regions, covering the period 1980–98. The study drew on a number of sources of published data, including the VAT registration data (used as a proxy for start-ups) from the Small Business Service, population density data from the Office of National Statistics (ONS), and data on regional wage rates from the ONS's New Earnings Survey Panel Data-set. A number of technical issues were addressed to test the validity of the regression results, including efforts to test for both short- and long-run effects. For the 1980s, the researchers discovered no significant relationship for Great Britain as a whole, but a negative relationship for the north-east of England, an area which had been dominated by large industrial firms, contributing to low levels of independent entrepreneurial activity: this is the so-called 'Upas tree effect', previously identified in a study of entrepreneurial activity in Glasgow (Checkland 1976) (Section 14.3). By contrast, for the 1990s they found a significant positive relationship for Great Britain as a whole, but a negative relationship for Scotland, a country that had focused its enterprise policies on start-ups. The authors concluded by questioning current UK enterprise policies, which appeared to be returning to an earlier emphasis on promoting start-ups in order to promote economic development: 'The lessons from the present paper are that public policies to raise the formation of new firms, particularly in unenterprising areas, are likely to be unproductive at best and counterproductive at worst.' (Van Stel and Storey 2004: 903). Other recent examples of studies adopting this kind of approach include, Allen et al. 2008 (international comparisons of female entrepreneurship), and Blumberg and Letterie (2008) (credit rationing and business start-ups), and Wang (2008) (entrepreneurial orientation, learning orientation, and firm performance). Case 12.2 illustrates how survey methods can be to gather data in a previously under-researched area.

CASE 12.2

Examining barriers to growth: a Ghanaian perspective

This case study is based on a large research project conducted by Dr Bernard Acquah Obeng, which examined barriers to growth among small businesses and the role of enterprise support services in Ghana, West Africa. This extract focuses on the survey work conducted in order to examine possible barriers to growth in small and medium-sized firms. Additional details on the research methods and findings can be found in Obeng (2007), Robson and Obeng (2008) and Obeng and Blundel (2015). For background information on the informal sector in Ghana, see Debrah (2007) and Obeng et al. (2012).

INTRODUCTION: A GAP IN RESEARCH AND POLICY

Previous research into barriers to growth has focused on developed nations such as Canada, Hong Kong, and the UK (e.g. Orser et al. 2000; Moy and Luk 2003), and transition countries, such as Lithuania (Aidis 2005). There have been few studies examining the barriers and problems encountered by entrepreneurs in Africa; exceptions include Wolf (2004), Tagoe et al. (2005), and Mambula (2002). Entrepreneurs have a vital role to play in promoting economic development, but much depends on the institutional structures established to foster and regulate enterprise. In order to support the development process, governments need a better understanding of micro, small, and medium-sized businesses, and of the challenges faced by their owner-managers. Many initiatives have been launched in order to investigate the underlying problems in Ghana and to provide institutional support for enterprise development. However, there have been few large-scale research studies that would enable the government to respond more effectively to the needs of entrepreneurs.

(Continued)

(Continued)

RESEARCH APPROACH

The research evidence presented in this case study is drawn from a survey of 500 entre-preneurs in the six regions of Ghana where approximately 91% of all businesses are located. The survey covered the manufacturing (193), services (217), and agriculture (90) sectors, the numbers in parentheses representing the number of respondents in each sector. The main criteria for selection were that the entrepreneur employed between 4 and 50 full-time workers. This range of employment was selected because they are the focus of the Ghanaian government policy and are also the businesses served by the main support organisations. In each case the entrepreneurs completed the written questionnaire, which was given to them in person by the researcher, over the period of January to June 2005. The 37 factors which could be barriers to entrepreneurs' firms achieving their objectives in the three previous years, 2002–05, covered a broad range of factors and these were categorised into the following seven groups: (i) finance, (ii) market, (iii) managerial and technical, (iv) inputs, (v) economic and regulatory, (vi) socio-cultural, and (vii) other. The piloting of the survey minimised the number of factors which fell within the other group of factors. The project involved a detailed investiga-tion of each area. The overall findings are summarised below (Figure 12.1). This case concentrates on two social themes: family and geographic location. However, before turning to these themes, we summarise the main findings of the study.

SUMMARY OF THE OVERALL FINDINGS

The component bar chart summarises the owner-managers' responses, ranking the factors from the greatest to the least important in limiting their ability to meet their business objectives in the last three years. The research indicated that economic *factors* were perceived as the most important barriers to growth. Firstly, a *high rate of inflation* was seen by 71.4% of the respondents as an 'important' or 'crucial' factor. This result confirmed the findings of an earlier survey of 100 businesses in the Greater Accra and the Northern regions of Ghana (Wolf 2004). Although it has been the Ghanaian govern-ment's policy to reduce the rate of inflation to a single-digit level since the beginning of the Economic Recovery Programme (ERP) in 1983, this objective has been difficult to achieve in practice. Information provided by the Bank of Ghana revealed that the rate of inflation had declined from 23.6% in December 2003 to 11.6% in January 2005. However, in March 2005, the rate jumped to 16.7%. The resulting impact on the prices of general goods could explain the importance of this factor. Secondly, high interest rates were identified by 68.5% of respondents as an 'important' or 'critical' factor. As one person noted, 'Even [though] I went to a financial institution the previous day, the interest rates put me off to take the loan.' Thirdly, the high depreciation rate was mentioned by 63.5% of the respondents as an 'important' or 'crucial' factor. In the last five years to 2005 the Cedi (the currency of Ghana) was more stable than in the 1980s and the 1990s against the major international currencies. However, the high rate of depreciation of the Cedi in the recent past has had an adverse effect upon businesses in Ghana.

Having established that economic factors were perceived as the most important barriers, we now turn to social factors, and consider how two of these – family and location – influence the growth of Ghanaian firms.

THE INFLUENCE OF FAMILY RELATIONSHIPS

A family business is defined here as any business which employs one or more family members who are related to the person running the business, and it is owned by that person and their family. In other words, an entrepreneur and their family control the business and there is at least one other member of the family working in the business. The contribution of family business in income generation, job creation, and the development of the economy cannot be underestimated. Even in developed countries family business contributes more than a half of the total national income and a similar proportion of the labour force (Kets de Vries 1996, Morris et al. 1997). Despite their social and economic importance, there are few quantitative studies of family businesses in Ghana (Wolf 2004). In this study, 72.4% of the businesses were family businesses. In Ghana, as with many other African countries, the entrepreneurs are put under pressure to provide employment and resources for their immediate and extended family. This suggests that the people recruited on the basis of being a member of a family may not necessarily have the skills, experience, and expertise that the entrepreneur was seeking; or the entrepreneur may not have been looking to recruit, but family ties resulted in the family member being employed. The employing of a potentially less desirable, and possibly unwanted, group of workers may result in the business being less able to deal with day-to-day problems than those businesses which recruit on the basis of ability. Kotey (2005) and Sharma (2004) have also demonstrated that family businesses are more likely to face financial and managerial problems compared with the non-family businesses. Thus, it was hypothesised that family businesses were more likely to face financial problems than non-family businesses. This proved to be the case, with obligations to family members being an important constraint on growth. Growing firms were more likely to have the problem of the use of business resources to support families. This finding is consistent with the previous research of Buame (1996), Takyi-Asiedu (1993), and Kiggundu (2002) although none of these studies utilised regression techniques. The communal nature of African society and the nature of inheritance of some tribes mean that if a person becomes successful in the family he has the social obligation to cater for the other siblings who are not successful in life. Buame (1996: 197) noted that, '[n]o Ghanaian can easily do away with his or her relatives. Our traditional life is centred on kinship, I mean our relatives.'

THE ROLE OF BUSINESS LOCATION

Various studies in Europe have found that small businesses which were located in more 'accessible' rural areas performed better than their counterparts in the urban areas (e.g. Keeble 2003). However, similar research on urban micro and small businesses in East Africa revealed evidence to the contrary (Liedholm 2002). Thus, the role of location of the business and its impact on the performance of businesses has divided researchers. In this study, the location of the businesses has been related to three classifications: 'conurbations' (i.e. the capital, Accra, Tema and the surrounding area), 'large towns' (i.e. settlements with populations of 150,000 to 1,500,000), and small towns (i.e. settlements with populations of less than 150,000): 55.4% of the respondents were

(Continued)

(Continued)

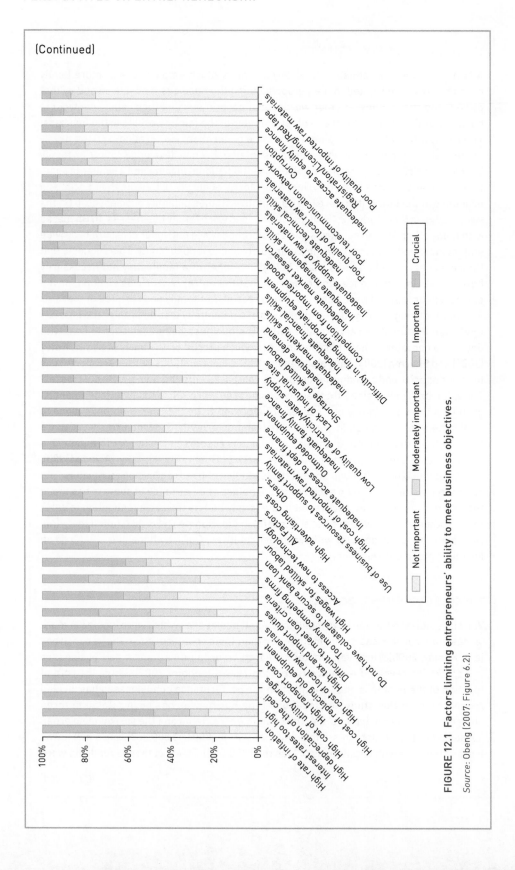

FIGURE 12.1 Factors limiting entrepreneurs' ability to meet business objectives.

Source: Obeng (2007: Figure 6.2).

from conurbations, 21.6% from large towns, and 23.0% from small towns. There are virtually no businesses with five or more employees in the small towns. The definition of the settlements was adapted from the work of Keeble (2003), which also examined the performance and growth of small businesses by location. Closeness between firms and their customers can provide impetus for development due to the ease with which the firms can identify customer needs. Thus, it was expected that firms in conurbations would encounter fewer barriers than those in other locations. This was supported by the findings, though the picture is more complicated than it might first appear. For example, the use of business resources to support family members was identified by 42% of respondents as limiting their ability to meet their business objectives. This particular factor needs special attention because most small businesses in Africa which have collapsed or failed to grow have been due to the use of business resources to support social causes (Takyi-Asiedu 1993, Kiggundu 2002). For instance, Kiggundu (2002: 242) noted that although the African social set-up has a positive impact in the development of small business in terms of the social status of owner-managers, the overall impact has been negative. Buame (1996: 166) found in Ghana that entrepreneurs often had to relocate their businesses away from their hometowns because of the fear of the businesses becoming encumbered with family members. Location influenced the likelihood of firms encountering barriers, and the types of barriers that they faced. For example, firms in conurbations and large towns were more likely than those in small towns to experience a lack of collateral to secure bank loans, too many competing firms, and competition from imported goods. However, compared to their small town counterparts, businesses in conurbations were less likely to encounter managerial and technical constraints. This may be due to a lack of external support services in small towns, contributing to a lower capacity to absorb external knowledge (Barringer et al. 2005). By contrast, firms in conurbations, with their closer proximity to national and local government, were more likely to encounter stereotypical problems associated with Africa, including low-quality electricity and water supplies, higher utility charges, higher taxation, and more bureaucratic 'red tape', though these relationships were not statistically significant. In summary, though firms in conurbations may benefit from the closer presence of a larger customer base, they can also experience overcrowding problems due to the number of firms, size of population, and an infrastructure that is struggling to cope.

CONCLUSION

This research study examined the problems that are encountered by firms in meeting their business objectives. We have discussed three factors in some detail. However, it is important to note that the three problems perceived as most important by the entrepreneurs surveyed were economic ones: (1) the high rate of inflation; (2) high interest rates; and (3) the high depreciation rate of the Cedi. Turning to other factors, the study also found that businesses that employed family members were more likely to face problems than the non-family businesses. This particularly applied to financial problems. These results are consistent with previous research in Africa, which has highlighted the importance of the extended family, although in the case of Ghana there was a lack of empirical research. The findings also revealed that in general firms in conurbations were more likely to encounter barriers than their small town counterparts.

(Continued)

(Continued)

This underlines the need for further infrastructural improvements in Ghana if future growth and development are not to be jeopardised.

QUESTIONS

1. Why do you think these entrepreneurs perceived economic factors as the most important constraint on the growth of their ventures?

2. What do these findings suggest may be distinct about the Ghanaian context, and what factors are more likely to be found elsewhere in Africa and beyond?

3. What research approaches might you adopt in order to explore some of the issues raised by this research, including (a) family relationships in Ghanaian businesses; (b) location decisions of entrepreneurs?

Source: Obeng (2007) – adapted with permission.

12.2.3 Conducting ethnographic studies 'in the field'

If you were looking for a polar opposite to researching entrepreneurship by analysing data sets, ethnography would seem a good choice. Ethnographic researchers cannot study at a distance; they get out into the field and engage directly with their research subjects. In the case of entrepreneurship, this is likely to involve periods of time spent with entrepreneurs, observing their activities and recording what takes place in real time. The approach originates in cultural anthropology, and some of the pioneering studies were conducted by researchers who travelled to unfamiliar, and often pre-industrial, societies with the aim of gaining a better understanding of their cultures and practices. For example, in the early 1960s, the Norwegian anthropologist Frederik Barth produced a classic study of entrepreneurial activity among the agricultural communities of the Jebel Marra mountain massif in Darfur (Barth [1967] 2000). The following definition provides a useful summary of the approach:

> *Ethnography is the study of people in naturally occurring settings or 'fields' by methods of data collection which capture their social meanings and ordinary activities, involving the researcher participating directly in the setting, if not also in the activities, in order to collect data in a systematic manner but without meaning being imposed on them externally. (Brewer 2000: 6)*

In writing ethnographies, researchers are always caught up in a tension between subjectivity and objectivity (Johnstone 2007: 105). In other words, they need to position themselves somewhere between the 'authenticity' derived from getting very close to subjects in the field, and the 'distance' seen as necessary in order to address questions in an academic research community (Pearson 1993: xi). Based on his own experience of researching small firms using an ethnographic approach, one experienced researcher concluded, 'It could almost be argued that researchers operating in such contexts have to act in very similar ways to small business owners: both have to exploit opportunities, manage relationships and engage in a variety of negotiations with different actors.' (Ram 1999: 106) In recent years, entrepreneurship researchers have made increasing use of ethnographic approaches in order to study the cultures and practices of entrepreneurs in industrialised countries. In the introduction to her detailed study of 'Freddy the Strawberry man', an entrepreneurial strawberry dealer based in the Venezuelan Andes, the anthropologist Monica Lindh de Montoya makes a very good case for the distinctive contribution that can be made by ethnographies; her comments are worth quoting at length:

> *While economists have theorized about growth and progress and the nature of entrepreneurship within the larger economic system, they more seldom undertake concrete case studies of entrepreneurial action. And despite prevailing ideas about cold, rationality and the cutthroat world of business, this world is an intensely social one the functioning of which requires shared cultural understandings and the constant cooperation of a myriad of actors. The kinds of 'bright ideas' and nascent entrepreneurial ventures that become established depend to a great extent on what is socially possible within a particular society, and issues such as trust, risk, and the relationship between individual gains and social responsibility are inherent in the process of developing a business. (Lindh de Montoya 2000: 335)*

12.2.4 Investigating entrepreneurial networks and networking

Social networks play an important role in the creation of new entrepreneurial ventures (Section 4.4). Networking is now seen as a key area of entrepreneurial activity, and has been the subject of many research studies (e.g. Johannisson 1998; Blundel 2002; Shaw 2006). One of the early findings was that entrepreneurs rely largely on *informal* sources in their personal contact network (PCN) to mobilise resources before the formation of a venture (Birley 1985: 113). The unique connections between people in the PCN play an important communication role, enabling the entrepreneur to identify opportunities that are not evident to others. At the heart of this network, there are normally a small number of 'strong' ties that provide the entrepreneur with a shelter from the opportunism and uncertainty of the market. For example, one study found that most business owners report between three and ten strong ties, primarily business associates plus a few close friends and family members (Aldrich et al. 1989). The time and energy that entrepreneurs invest in these 'pre-organisational' networks appears to be converted into future benefits for their emerging firms. This includes 'human capital', in the form of relevant experiences, skills, and knowledge, and 'social capital' (i.e. being known and trusted by others). Trust facilitates access to resources, through collaboration, and helps to overcome institutional barriers to entrepreneurial activity (e.g. local political resistance to a proposed development). However, the extensive personal ties used by entrepreneurs often lead a blurring of business and social life, with mixed consequences. For example, reliance on particular individuals can sometimes lead to sudden, unpredictable, and potentially disruptive, structural changes. Furthermore, while all start-up businesses make some 'entrepreneurial' use of their personal networks, most small firms settle down into an established and fairly limited pattern of interactions. By contrast, entrepreneurs continuously develop their networks, with the more or less explicit aim of expanding existing ventures or establishing new ones. To achieve this, they maintain a broader 'latent network', parts of which are activated when required (Ramachandran and Ramnarayan 1993). Episodes of entrepreneurial networking can also be triggered by external events, such as the liberalisation of a market or the entry of new organisations into an industry (Blundel 2002). What happens to the entrepreneurial network as the venture develops? Researchers have found that entrepreneurs are active in managing the complex pattern relationships that make up their network. Despite a significant growth in research interest in networks over the last two decades, there are still gaps in our understanding of networking behaviour and its relationship to venture performance (Shaw 2006). What appears to happen is that the actions of solo entrepreneurs and **entrepreneurial teams** create a favourable 'organising context' around the venture, in which it becomes relatively easier to deal with uncertainties and to exploit emerging opportunities (Johannisson 2000: 379).

Our next case (Case 12.3) builds on the topic of **entrepreneurial learning**, which was introduced in the previous chapter (Section 11.4), but with a particular focus on the way learning is a product of the relationships that entrepreneurs form with other actors. Founders of small entrepreneurial ventures face considerable leadership challenges, which are quite different from those working in larger firms (Davies et al. 2002; Gray and Mabey 2005; Kempster and Cope 2010). They have to take on many responsibilities (or 'wear many hats'), leaving little time to deal with their own personal development. They also have to deal with many new and unfamiliar demands, as the venture develops. At the same time, they can be quite isolated, with nobody to support them from within the organisation, and often limited access to help from outside. The case discusses an innovative approach to this problem, in which leadership skills training and support is provided by bringing small groups of small business owner-managers together to share their experiences.

CASE 12.3

Entrepreneurial leadership: a relational learning approach

This case study reviews some of the experiences gained during 'Leading Enterprise and Development' (LEAD) programme, a project based at the Institute for Entrepreneurship and Enterprise Development (IEED), Lancaster University, and sponsored in its initial phases by the UK's North West Development Agency. LEAD was designed to support the business and personal development of small firm owner-managers (i.e. between 4 and 20 employees). The intended outcomes were: *improved leadership skills; personal and professional development; a motivated workforce; increased productivity; greater competitiveness and genuine business growth.* Seventy-two participants were divided into four cohorts (of 18). One of the selection criteria was that people could demonstrate a desire to grow and develop their businesses. The following summary is based on research conducted a member of the LEAD programme team, Dr Sarah Robinson. More detailed commentary on the programme can be found in Robinson (2006, 2007), Smith and Robinson (2007), and Kempster and Cope (2010).

DESIGNING THE LEAD PROGRAMME

In designing the programme, the team drew on research evidence and on their previous experience of delivering support programmes. They identified three essential requirements: (1) formal learning (i.e. informing); (2) guided reflexive learning (i.e. applying knowledge and thinking to own context); (3) peer interaction (i.e. enhancing and supporting learning by comparing, contrasting and affirming). These three elements were integrated into a holistic design that centred on the business and the owner-manager. The three learning processes were through several different kinds of activity:

- Masterclasses (formal learning).
- Action learning (reflexive learning/peer interaction).
- Coaching and mentoring (reflexive learning).
- Business exchanges (reflexive learning/peer interaction).
- Business support (formal learning).
- Experiential learning events (reflexive learning/peer interaction).
- Mentoring (formal learning/reflexive learning).
- Participants also had access to an online forum where they could discuss and reflect on issues emerging from the different course components. The course was delivered by a mixture of academics from Lancaster University, external facilitators and professional coaches.

WHAT DID THE PROGRAMME ACHIEVE?

As the course proceeded, the LEAD team monitored its progress. In this section, we summarise briefly the findings on two aspects of the programme: (1) the training and development needs of the owner-managers as they joined; (2) how far their needs were addressed at the end of the course.

(1) **Initial learning needs** Based on their pre-course and exit interviews, it seems that participants were often facing quite serious emotional problems, lacking confidence, feeling alone and isolated, frustrated, and missing or having lost passion and direction. This is reflected in the following interview extracts: 'I need some vision for the future, I am looking for a bit of inspiration I suppose really and a bit of direction – vision, inspiration, direction'; 'I felt very alone at the start of the course lacking in confidence, running the business to survive.' There was also a feeling of personally not being of a high enough standard as a leader, or of having the knowledge and skills required to develop the business: '[I] knew that I was missing some attributes to bring the business forward.'; 'I lack confidence in the overall finance business side of things.' There were also concerns about being too preoccupied with the day-to-day running of the business, and finding it difficult to stand back and see the bigger picture. Based on these initial findings, four main types of leadership challenge were identified, relating to: 'people'; 'task'; '[strategic] thinking'; and 'implementation'.

(2) **Leadership learning at the end of the course** As the course progressed, participants began to share their experiences with their peers. In their subsequent review of the programme, the original leadership challenges were re-conceptualised in terms of the new relationships that were being developed. This 'relational learning' became particularly apparent in the exit interviews where participants described the learning processes they had actually experienced on the course. Many of the learning processes described during the course can be categorised as four sets of relationships. The impact on each participant is bound to vary but the programme seems to have supported and strengthened these relationships:

(Continued)

(Continued)

- **Relationship with the self:** This involves participants in accepting and in developing themselves as an entrepreneurial leader: '[Participating in the course has] boosted my confidence. [It] has made me recognise my own skills and ability. You are a bit isolated in your own business. You have no measure; you don't realise how good you are.'

- **Relationship with staff:** This means gaining respect and leading people in a more effective way: 'I feel that I am closer and more aware of other people's feelings and this has proved effective in helping them to achieve their goals.'

- **Relationship with the business:** This is where the owner-manager is able to step back from the business, in order to gain a strategic perspective and to create a vision: '[Participating in the course] gave me the tools to look at my business and find my own answers.'

- **Relationship with the wider SME community:** This is where entrepreneurs start to build up a network of people in a similar situation, as a source of support and ideas: 'Since meeting my fellow [course participants], and listening to their everyday workplace problems and sharing experiences, I have returned to my company more confident and determined to make it successful, and question my own ability as the business owner and my leadership style.'

The importance and ongoing development of these relationships, and the interplay between them, was reinforced by the follow-up questionnaires, which were completed one year after the formal end of the course. This questionnaire focused specifically on the interplay between the 'relationship with self' and 'relationship with staff'. In particular, the owner-managers reported a growing confidence in themselves and in others compared with their situation before the LEAD programme. They also reported other constructive outcomes, including: being more proactive; being less interventionist/stepping back; having more patience / finding it easier to listen to others; having more communication with staff; identifying and making time for training; recognising the link between training and the growth of the business; delegating, empowering, and generally having more trust in staff.

It appears that the LEAD programme helped the owner-managers in a number of ways. It enabled them to gain and to practise certain techniques. Coaching, for example, helped with moving thinking and processes forward, and with forward planning. Action learning was seen as important in the discussion with peers and learning from others. The masterclasses gave new ideas, but also served an affirmation purpose, leading to confidence in existing practice and giving people the courage to try out new ideas and to move forward. Learning from the experience of others, and from their 'real life case studies', was highlighted as being an especially important part of the programme. Interacting with other people in a similar situation helped to build up trust and support among the course participants. This seems to have translated itself into their businesses, with the owner-managers gaining more confidence both in their own abilities and in those of their staff. Though these entrepreneurial leaders are bound to face continuing challenges, they should now be much better placed to tackle them.

The LEAD programme illustrates how individual owner-managers can learn to become more effective entrepreneurial leaders through building more effective relationships with their peers and with other actors. Joe Hall's experience illustrates its potential. Joe's family bakery business was founded by his grandfather in 1933. The company went into liquidation in 2006 but Joe bought it back and began a major reorganisation. In 2009 he joined Lancaster University's LEAD programme, and later described it as a 'transformational' moment in his business career. The course helped him to work through difficult issues and an opportunity to share business problems with other members of his cohort. With the company experiencing growth after the long post-2008 downturn, Joe concludes that the programme, 'has been critical to our survival as well as our success' (Small Business Charter 2016).

QUESTIONS

1. What are the main obstacles faced by small firm owners in leading their businesses?

2. What can entrepreneurial leadership programmes do to address these problems?

3. How could you adapt or extend the ideas developed in this programme in order to encourage one of the following: (a) more effective leadership in a social enterprise; (b) more innovative activity in an existing corporation (i.e. 'intrapreneurship'); (c) more socially and environmentally responsible approaches to business.

12.3 SOCIAL RESEARCH THEMES: AN OVERVIEW

Having reviewed some of the more widely adopted research approaches, we now turn our attention to the main research themes that fall under our broad umbrella term, 'social perspectives'. Table 12.2 lists some of the more significant research themes and topics. For example, the 'family' theme includes performance (i.e. do family firms out-perform other types of business?), competing goals and values (i.e. how do you balance business ambitions with family loyalties?) and succession (i.e. what happens when families transfer businesses to the next generation?). Researchers also connect different themes. For example, there are studies investigating the relationship between ethnicity, gender, and firm-level growth rates, and others looking at policies to encourage entrepreneurial activity in post-conflict situations or to promote social inclusion in deprived communities.

We have selected two contrasting research themes from this list for more detailed consideration. Section 12.4 introduces the theme of gender and how it may relate to the ways in which people engage in entrepreneurial activity. Section 12.5 considers the themes of geography and location.

12.4 RESEARCH ON GENDER AND ENTREPRENEURSHIP

12.4.1 Exploring gender difference

Over the last 30 years, gender has moved from the margins to become one of the central themes in entrepreneurship research. It has created a dynamic research community, and has made many connections into the worlds of policy and practice. In parallel with these developments, there has been an equally dramatic growth in female entrepreneurial activity rates, including commercial and social enterprise. Though recorded rates remain lower than for men, the differences have narrowed in many

TABLE 12.2 'Social' perspectives on entrepreneurship – some popular themes and topics

Competitiveness – of firms, sectors, regions and nations
Culture – its influence at organisational, local, sectoral, regional level
Economic development – including in deprived areas and post-conflict situations
Education and training – most effective approaches
Entrepreneurial learning – formal and informal modes, learning from failure
Environmental sustainability – impacts, barriers and measures to promote improvements
Ethics and ethical practices – differences and underlying influences
Ethnicity – relationship with entrepreneurial activity, barriers, types of venture
Failure – reasons for, impact on individuals, families and communities, learning
Family – performance of family firms, competing values, succession planning
Gender – differences in businesses and approaches, barriers, performance
Geography and location – spatial variations in enterprise, urban-rural differences, clusters
Growth – causal factors and processes, impacts
Identity – impact on entrepreneurial activity, relationship to culture
Information and communication technologies – impact on performance, types of venture
Migration – influence on economic development, barriers, relationship to other factors
Networks and networking – structure and dynamics, impact on venture creation and performance
Performance – economic, social and environmental
Politics and policy – effectiveness in promoting entrepreneurial activity
Religion – influence at organisational, local, sectoral, regional level
Resilience – how it is created at (individual), firm, sectoral and community level
Social capital – how it is created, relationship with networks, impact on performance
Social ventures – distinctive features, growth, performance and impact
Social sustainability – including social inclusion and community resilience
Technological and social innovations – role of entrepreneurs, as sources of new opportunities

countries (e.g. Allen et al. 2008). However, it is also important to be cautious about the results of survey evidence. Women are often 'hidden' entrepreneurs, particularly when their contribution is made as a member of a family business (Hamilton 2006). The historical development of this research theme is well documented (e.g. Brush 2008; Henry et al. 2016). As in other areas of entrepreneurship research, much of the early work was based on North American and European experience. The focus of this work was often on making comparisons between male and female entrepreneurs, including their personality characteristics, age and social background, and motivation for starting a business. Other studies investigated barriers faced by female owner-managers, including access to finance. Another strand examined the characteristics of female-owned businesses, including their sectoral distribution, size, and growth rates. There is still a need for descriptive studies, particularly in previously under-researched countries and sectors. However, there has also been an effort to move the field forward, with studies addressing the nature of female entrepreneurial activity, including the ways that women manage various aspects of the business (e.g. raising finance, marketing). There have also been studies investigating the performance characteristics of female-owned businesses (e.g. profitability, long-term survival prospects, social responsibility). Gender-related research has been conducted with a full range of methods, from the analysis of questionnaire surveys and financial data sets to ethnographies, and has been framed by a variety of theoretical frameworks. This can be seen by comparing recent studies, such as Di Domenico (2008) and Madsen et al. (2008).

12.4.2 Different ways of acting entrepreneurially?

People often assume that entrepreneurs always plan their ventures in advance. However, there is also evidence that entrepreneurs sometimes act in less formal ways (e.g. Garud and Karnøe 2003; Di Domenico et al. 2010). In this sub-section, we focus on a new theoretical perspective called **effectuation** theory, which has developed in order to explore this kind of behaviour (Sarasvathy 2001). Effectuation theory provides a fresh perspective on the ways that entrepreneurs behave as they attempt to create something new, whether it be a product, an organisation, or a market. In one of her initial articles, Saras Sarasvathy distinguishes between the ways that entrepreneurs make decisions using effectuation processes with a more planned 'causation' approach:

> Causation processes take a particular effect as given and focus on selecting between means to create that effect. Effectuation processes take a set of means as given and focus on selecting between possible effects that can be created with that set of means. (Sarasvathy 2001: 245)

This distinction can be made clearer with a concrete example. Imagine being asked to make someone a meal from scratch. If you adopted a causation approach, the process would begin with a recipe. You would use the recipe to identify a list of the ingredients, go out and buy them (or perhaps collect them from your garden), return to the kitchen, and follow the instructions in order to prepare the meal. By contrast, an effectuation process would begin with a search around the kitchen, and possibly the garden, to see what you could find by way of ingredients and utensils. In Sarasvathy's (2001: 245) words, you would then, 'imagine possible menus' and create your meal, making use of what was available. A similar thought experiment can be applied to the task of creating a new business venture. In a causation process, the entrepreneur would engage in a formal planning, starting with an analysis of potential market opportunities, with further rounds of analytical efforts to segment, target, position, and ultimately to implement the plan. By contrast, in an effectuation process the starting point for the entrepreneur would be to imagine possible ventures, building on the resources at their disposal, and adjusting their approach in response to what they discover along the way. So how do these ideas relate to practical entrepreneurship? The point is not that one process is inherently superior to the other; people often make use of both processes in their decision-making. However, Sarasvathy argues that entrepreneurial behaviour often follows effectuation logic, rather than the causation logic that is assumed in many economics-based explanations. Her concluding remarks combine striking images with some sound practical advice about creating new ventures:

> *Human imagination and human aspirations influence each other and reshape one another continually, both directly and through economic artefacts. The swirls and eddies these interactions engender often change the shoreline and make the waters treacherous for economic shipbuilders and navigators. That is why destinations as well as paths are often unclear in economic decision-making. And when destinations are unclear and there are no pre-existent goals, causal road maps are less useful than effectual exchanges of information between all stakeholders involved in the journey. Bold expeditions and even one-eyed pirates rule such seas, and voyages to India effectually end up in the Americas. (Sarasvathy 2001: 262; emphasis added).*

In the last 15 years, the effectuation approach has been examined in a wide variety of contexts. This work has generated new insights though more recently it has stimulated a fierce methodological debate, which is still being fought out in a leading management journal (e.g. Arend et al. 2016, Read et al. 2016). There has also been considerable interest in the closely-related concept of 'bricolage'. This sociological term has been adopted by entrepreneurship researchers to describe an approach to venture creation that is based around improvisation and making the most of available resources, and is particularly relevant in situations where resources are tightly constrained, including developing economies (Garud and Karnøe 2003; Di Domenico et al. 2010; Stinchfield et al. 2013).

In the following Researcher Profile (Case 12.4), we return to the theme of gender and see how effectuation theory is being used by a Danish researcher in order to study the behaviour of female entrepreneurs.

CASE 12.4   RESEARCHER PROFILE

HELLE NEERGAARD, APPLYING EFFECTUATION THEORY TO GENDER

Helle Neergaard is Professor of Entrepreneurship at Aarhus University, Denmark. She was awarded an MSc in International Business Administration and Modern Languages in 1995 and completed her doctorate in International Business in 1999. Her doctoral thesis was titled 'Networks as Vehicles of Internationalization'. Helle's present research interests include: entrepreneurship education, existential learning, effectuation, entrepreneurial identity, gender and narratives. Among other major journals, she sits on the editorial review board of the *Entrepreneurship: Theory and Practice; International Small Business Journal* and *International Journal of Gender and Entrepreneurship*. She has been a special issue editor for *Entrepreneurship Theory and Practice* (2010). She has received several awards for her work on female entrepreneurs and entrepreneurship education. Helle is also the lead editor of two *Handbooks in Qualitative Research*, both published by Edward Elgar (Neergaard and Ulhøi 2007 and Neergaard and Leitch 2015). Since 2008, Helle has been a board member of the European Council for Small Business (ECSB), responsible for the Doctorial Programme and she was president of the organisation from 2013 to 2015. She has organised numerous PhD courses on qualitative methodology and successful publication.

In this interview, Helle discusses her research on effectuation theory and its role in entrepreneurship, with particular reference to gender and education. In doing so, she raises a number of important questions about the ways that women act entrepreneurially and how students learn to think entrepreneurially:

Why did you want to research in this area? How did you decide on your main research questions?

Sarasvathy's theory of effectuation is one of the most interesting new areas of research in recent years (Sarasvathy 2001, Sarasvathy et al. 2014). Her work shows that many, if not most, entrepreneurial businesses are based on principles of effectuation rather than causation, which means that instead of looking for a hole in the market to be filled,

successful entrepreneurs base their businesses on who they are, what they are competent at and their existing knowledge as well on whom they know. Sarasvathy based her study on expert entrepreneurs, which she defined as individuals who had started several ventures. 'My work with female entrepreneurs in Denmark showed that these very often followed the five principles of effectuation even in their first attempt at founding a business. So I was intrigued: How come that female entrepreneurs act as expert entrepreneurs?' Sarasvathy identified five principles of successful venture start-ups – 'and we want to investigate how female entrepreneurs apply these principles in practice. Our research agenda also includes an investigation of various principles of venture growth.

The issue here is that women do not grow their businesses, at least not in ways that are readily measurable statistically. The result is that their contribution to economic growth is not recognised by the Danish government. Instead they use various growth principles: for example, the small steps principle and the "layer-cake" principle of growth. If they choose organic growth, women tend to grow their businesses more slowly and they want to see black figures on the bottom line before they take the next step. However, instead of growing their business organically, thus enlarging the cake, they tend to split the cake into smaller bites and share them with other female entrepreneurs in their network. This means that they do not hire new employees and hence do not grow on this dimension. It also means that profits have to be shared between many different one-woman businesses. Consequentially, even though the total is the same, each business grows only a little. Since the usual measures of growth are number of employees and turnover, what do you think happens? So our agenda is to develop a typology of growth. This might also assist women in choosing the right way of growing for their particular business. In my view, there is no one right recipe. However, women also effectuate in many other instances. For example, in a small pilot study, together with a colleague I investigated the impact of the Danish welfare system on female entrepreneurs and found that this is actually detrimental to female entrepreneurs (Neergaard and Thrane 2009). But they use a strategy we call "babystrapping" (*). This strategy is also a way of effectuating because women adapt to government regulations so that they can still run their business while

(Continued)

(Continued)

being on maternity leave and receiving benefits, which in essence they are not allowed to do according to the Danish legislation.'

What methods are you going to use?

The research described above has actually been dormant for some years, although we are currently reviving it now. We still intend to access these women's stories about how and why they started a business, so naturally a major part will be narratives. It is impossible to address the 'why?' question underlying female entrepreneurs' actions purely with quantitative methods. Sarasvathy used what she called, 'think-aloud protocol analysis' in her study, and some form of this technique would probably be useful.

The reason my research on female entrepreneurs has been dormant is that together with my research group I received a €3 million grant from the Danish Council for Strategic Research (now part of Innovation Fund Denmark) to research what works and what does not work in entrepreneurship education (the PACE® project). This is probably the biggest grant awarded in Europe to conduct research on entrepreneurship education. In this study we have used both qualitative and quantitative methods including ethnographic methods, interviews and observation as well as think-aloud protocol techniques (to tap into students' effectual thinking patterns) and self-efficacy questionnaires. We have collected data across three countries: Denmark, Finland, and the USA since one of the premises of our research was that in Europe we tend to borrow many frameworks and models from the USA but what if 'one size does not fit all', so what we need to teach is culturally dependent?

What are your key findings? Do they have practical implications for entrepreneurs?

We are reaching the end of the PACE® project, and I have to say that we have such an abundance of data that it will be years before we get to the bottom of it. However, there are still some interesting observations from the study. We have not asked the students to actually start a business, which is what many programmes do. Instead we have mimicked what entrepreneurs do through a set of interventions to assist the students in learning to think like an entrepreneur. By nudging students in this way they adapt gradually to believing that they can actually become entrepreneurs, if not today then at some time in the future. This also has implications for the way that we train female entrepreneurs particularly because what keeps many women back is a lack of confidence in their own ability to pull it off. So I plan to use the learning from the PACE® project to inform the research project on female entrepreneurs and growth.

Are there any particular challenges in conducting these studies?

The biggest challenge will probably be in identifying female entrepreneurs and get sufficient numbers to participate in the research, so that we can draw solid conclusions. In the last couple of years the number of female networks has mushroomed, so it is much easier today to identify potential participants for research than it was five years ago. However, it will probably still be difficult to identify companies with different growth trajectories; it is the sort of thing you can only see afterwards not a priori.

Where do you think research in this area needs to develop in future?

I think that there is a vast amount of work to be done to understand the challenges of growth for small businesses better. In times of crisis, such as those we are experiencing now, businesses, which have not used external capital to support fast growth, may actually be better off. A lot of the conceptual work on growth was done in the 1970s, but times have changed so significantly in the last four decades that we need to re-conceptualise the phenomenon.

  * 'babystrapping' is a variation on the term, 'bootstrapping', where entrepreneurs get a venture started using their own financial resources (i.e. 'pulling yourself up by your bootstraps').

12.5 THE GEOGRAPHY OF ENTERPRISE

12.5.1 Exploring spatial variations in enterprise

Why is entrepreneurial activity distributed so unevenly? Some places are hives of activity, while others are much quieter, and some are growing while others are in decline. Looking back to history, we can see how physical geography influenced the location of industry. For example, metalworking firms were established close to mineral deposits, furniture-making grew up new areas of suitable woodland and leatherworking where plentiful supplies of pasture encouraged cattle farming. These geographic factors also provided the foundations for traditional 'industrial districts', localised networks of small businesses and support institutions that worked together to produce specialist products and services – examples include footwear manufacturing in the Emilia-Romagna region of Italy and silk weaving around the French city of Lyons (Section 14.3). Economic geographers have also examined spatial variations in enterprise between countries and regions, using measures such as new firm formation rates (e.g. Greene et al. 2007; Díaz-Foncea and Marcuello 2015).

While location has been a key theme in research on the geographic dimensions of entrepreneurship, there are also several important sub-themes. For example, researchers have identified some distinctive features of entrepreneurial activity taking place in rural areas, which distinguish it from that taking place in larger towns and cities. These include:

- **'Pluriactivity'**: this is where rural entrepreneurs engage in several different enterprises at the same time (i.e. a form of 'portfolio working'), or in some cases combine employment with self-employment (Rønning and Kolvereid 2006). These distinctive patterns have been explained as a way of maintaining secure income streams, which can be particularly difficult for farmers and others based in remoter places due to the uncertainties associated with extreme weather, poor transport links and changing market conditions.

- **'Rural returners'**: this type of rural entrepreneur is someone who grew up in a rural location, moved away to an urban centre for work or study, but subsequently returned to the countryside, either to raise a family or because they simply prefer a rural lifestyle. The evidence on this kind of mobility is contested but some studies suggest that rural returners can play an important role in reinvigorating rural economies as they often bring financial capital, new forms of knowledge, capabilities, and connections, which they can use to establish a new venture (Démurger and Xu 2011).

- **'Community resilience'**: another strand of research examines the role of small businesses in making localities more resilient in the face of economic, social, and environmental turbulence (Steiner and Atterton 2015). For example, rural areas can struggle following the departure of a single large employer. However, the effect can be offset when there is a more varied ecosystem including many smaller firms. Large rural firms can also help to promote new venture creation, attracting skilled employees who subsequently decide to set up their own business in the area.

In the next section, we examine another prominent strand of locational research, which looks at the structure and dynamics of today's clusters, technology hubs and incubators.

12.5.2 Examining contemporary clusters, 'smart cities', and incubators

Clusters are localised networks of businesses and other institutions, including universities and research institutes. Research into their structure and dynamics has become a key theme over the last two decades (Boari et al. 2016). Unlike most traditional industrial districts, modern clusters are created for a specific purpose. For example, biotech clusters and science parks are designed to promote high-technology innovation and entrepreneurship (Kim 2015). There has also been a growth in 'smart city' initiatives, which aim to harness the information and communication technology (ICT) systems, along with the innovative and entrepreneurial capacities of urban areas in order to promote sustainable economic development. However, while such initiatives may create opportunities for entrepreneurs, questions have been raised over their effectiveness and longer-term impacts (Buck and While 2015, Kraus et al. 2015). Researchers have also been examining the role played by technology incubators, smaller-scale interventions that are often linked to local universities and research institutes (McAdam et al. 2016; Rubin et al. 2015).

This increase in localised networking seems to operate against the homogenising effects of globalisation. Researchers have identified several fairly straightforward explanations for the formation of clusters. For example, despite modern technologies, population mobility is limited, as people tend to become attached to particular locations. However, there are also some more general explanations of clustering. Amin and Thrift (1995: 92) suggest that the performance of a local economy is closely linked to its capacity to 'capture' global economic flows. Rapid circulation of people between organisations has been identified as an important mechanism for exchanging and developing the kinds of tacit knowledge that are required in these innovative, high-technology sectors (e.g. Hendry and Brown 2006; Henry and Pinch 2000). However, this is not to suggest that clusters are *easily* formed, nor that they are insensitive to location. The dynamism of the Minneapolis medical equipment cluster and the technology parks around Cambridge is partly explained by the presence of long-established, elite universities, though the distinctive structure of the firm population is also a factor (Lawson and Lorenz 1999: 314).

Contemporary clusters are fragile creatures. High-technology clusters are driven by the production, exchange, and fruitful recombination of knowledge. This requires a fine balance between cooperation and competition, which can easily be jeopardised by institutional changes. In the case of the high-technology clusters, one of the main dangers is the desire to 'protect' intellectual property. More specifically, the free flow of knowledge is likely to be constrained as universities become more 'commercial', internalising research activity and resorting to the threat of litigation (Lawson and Lorenz 1999: 314). Ultimately, high-technology clusters remain exposed to global economic forces. This means that a previously successful cluster can still be undermined by changes in international supply chain relationships or changes in institutional arrangements (e.g. a country's status in relation to international trade agreements or transnational bodies such as the European Union).

12.6 PRACTICAL IMPLICATIONS

There is a rich and varied literature addressing social dimensions of entrepreneurship. Some of this research, though it might be interesting and important in other ways, is unlikely to have direct implications for entrepreneurs. However, though it is not always possible to draw simple lessons directly from the social research literature, but there are ways that entrepreneurs can benefit from this knowledge (Swedberg 2000). Perhaps the most important of these is in helping people to become more 'reflective practitioners', for example:

Gender differences: by learning about the experiences of other female-owned businesses, you may draw useful lessons that can be applied to your own venture.

Entrepreneurial networks: by gaining a better understanding of the way that social networks operate, you may realise the importance of making new connections and become more skilled in managing your own personal contact network.

There are also practical implications for policy-makers, and for others concerned with broader questions about the kinds of entrepreneurial activity that take place, and their impact in terms of the economy, society, and the natural environment:

Encouraging economic development: In many countries, policy-makers are unsure how best to make their economies more competitive, innovative and capable of surviving in a globalised world. They are often lacking a detailed understanding of the entrepreneurial activity already taking place, or of what could be done to enhance its potential in the future. By making use of the full range of research approaches outlined in this chapter, governments could gain insights into both the 'big picture' (i.e. the broad patterns of activity, which can be mapped using large-scale data sets) and the fine detail (i.e. the more complex interactions between people, which can be investigated using qualitative research approaches).

Examining social and environmental impacts Entrepreneurship research has tended to concentrate on the ways in which social factors exert an influence on entrepreneurial activity, rather than the other way round. Exceptions include Blackburn and Ram's (2006) study on enterprise policies and social exclusion and the growing body of research on social and sustainable entrepreneurship (e.g. Kibler et al. 2015;

Pinske and Groot 2015). There are signs that things are changing. Sarasvathy (2002: 95) has called for entrepreneurship researchers to tackle what she describes as 'the central task of imagination in economics, i.e. to create from the society we have to live in, the society we *want* to live in'. As the world confronts an increasingly difficult set of environmental and social challenges over the next few decades, these research strands are likely to become increasingly active and influential.

SUMMARY

- There is a rich variety of social-level perspectives on entrepreneurship, drawing on many disciplines, theories and research methods. It can be challenging to navigate a way through the research literature but review articles and book chapters can provide useful signposts.

- The scope of the research is vast, ranging from micro-level interpretive studies of entrepreneurial behaviour to macro-level economic development studies using national and regional data sets. Each of these approaches can increase our understanding of different aspects of the subject.

- It is important to select theories and methods that are appropriate both to the research area, and the specific research questions addressed. It is also essential to apply the selected methods correctly, referring to relevant texts and seeking guidance where necessary.

- Researchers may need to draw on several approaches in order to meet the needs of policy-makers and practitioners. For example, statistical analysis of survey evidence and official data sets can detect broad patterns and associations between variables, while more detailed qualitative methods can provide insights into subjective perceptions and underlying causal mechanisms.

Practical activities

1. **Comparing research approaches** Complete an online search for peer reviewed journal articles that tackle *one* of the following research themes: (a) gender; (b) ethnicity; (c) family; (d) spatial variations; (e) clusters; (f) national or organisational culture. For your chosen theme, select *two* articles that have adopted different approaches. Prepare a table, comparing their research questions, research methods, theoretical frameworks used, and findings.

2. **Effectuation in practice** Re-read the profile of Helle Neergaard (Case 12.4) and take a look at a recent article on effectuation. Compare the main features of effectuation with a real-world example, using either the biography of an entrepreneur, one of the case studies in this book, or your own personal experience. Does your practical example match up with Sarasvathy's 'effectuation logic'?

3. **Learning the lessons?** Imagine that you were making *one* of the following decisions: (a) where to locate your new high-technology start-up venture; (b) how to organise the supply chain for your new manufacturing venture; (c) how to encourage more entrepreneurial and innovative activity in your existing public, private or social sector organisation. What research would you undertake (or commission) in order to ensure that you made a well-informed decision? Support your argument with examples.

Discussion topics

1. **What's your topic?** What would you like to know about entrepreneurship? Refer back to the opening discussion about potential social research themes (Section 12.1), and compare the themes identified (Table 12.2) with your own favourite research topics. If you are working in a group, turn this into a 'brainstorming' exercise. Start by calling out whatever topics come to mind. Then, discuss the list you have produced and identify the three most interesting ideas. To extend the exercise, try to convert your chosen topics into potential research questions (n.b. this is a useful exercise to complete if you need to prepare an extended essay or dissertation as part of your course).

2. **Methods, methods, methods:** Discuss the three following questions: (a) What research method would you prefer to use to explore entrepreneurship from a social perspective? (b) Why might some researchers prefer to use particular methods? (c) What reasons should guide you in selecting research methods?

3. **Entrepreneurial societies:** Entrepreneurship researchers have tended to concentrate on the ways in which social factors exert an influence on entrepreneurial activity, rather than the other way round (Section 12.1). What kinds of questions might you ask about the influence of entrepreneurial activity on the societies in which it takes place? What methods might you adopt to research these questions?

Recommended reading

These readings address two important topics in entrepreneurship research and are recommended for anyone wanting to build on the material covered in this chapter. Recommended readings have been selected from leading Sage journals and are freely available for readers of this textbook to download via the Online Resources.

Henry, C., Foss, L. and Ahl, H. (2016) 'Gender and entrepreneurship research: a review of methodological approaches'. *International Small Business Journal*, 34, 3: 217–41.

This article presents the findings of a systematic literature review (SLR) of the gender and entrepreneurship literature published in 18 journals over a 30-year period. It identifies methodological trends and identifies the changes needed in order for this field to move forward. The authors argue that future scholars need to engage with post-structural feminist approaches and make use of more innovative, in-depth qualitative methodologies such as life histories, case studies, and discourse analysis.

Ahlstrom, D. and Ding, Z. (2014) 'Entrepreneurship in China: an overview'. *International Small Business Journal*, 32, 6: 610–18.

This article offers an overview of entrepreneurship in China and introduces a special issue of the journal covering this subject. The authors summarise the range of entrepreneurship research being conducted and highlight important topics that are relevant to the Chinese context including entrepreneurial firms in China and the distinctive challenges faced by Chinese entrepreneurs. The article also discusses a potential research agenda in this area.

References

Achtenagen, L. and Welter, F. (2007) 'Media discourse in entrepreneurship research'. In H. Neergaard and J. P. Ulhøi (eds) op. cit. (193–215).

Acs, A.J. and Storey, D.J. (2004) 'Introduction: entrepreneurship and economic "development."' *Regional Studies*, 38, 8: 871–8.

Ahlstrom, D. and Ding, Z. (2014) 'Entrepreneurship in China: an overview'. *International Small Business Journal*, 32, 6: 610–18.

Aidis, R. (2005) 'Institutional barriers to small- and medium-sized enterprise operations in transition countries'. *Small Business Economics*, 25, 4: 305–17.

Aldrich, H. E., Reese, P. R., and Dubini, P. (1989) 'Women on the verge of a breakthrough: networking in the United States and Italy'. *Entrepreneurship and Regional Development*, 1, 339–56.

Allen, E., Elam, A., Langowitz, N., and Dean, M. (2008) *Global Entrepreneurship Monitor 2007 Report on Women and Entrepreneurship*. Wellesley MA: Babson College/Global Entrepreneurship Research Association.

Amin, A. and Thrift, N. (1995) 'Globalisation, institutional "thickness" and the local economy'. In P. Healey, S. Cameron, S. Davoudi, S. Graham, and A. Madani-Pour (eds), *Managing Cities: The New Urban Context*. Chichester: John Wiley (91–108).

Arend, R. J., Sarooghi, H. and Burkemper, A. C. (2016) 'Effectuation, not being pragmatic or process theorizing, remains ineffectual: responding to the commentaries'. *Academy of Management Review*, 41, 3: 549–56.

Barringer, B. R., Jones, F. F., and Neubaum, D. O. (2005) 'A quantitative content analysis of the characteristics of rapid growth firms and their founders'. *Journal of Business Venturing*, 20, 5: 663–87.

Barth, F. ([1967] 2000) 'Economic spheres in Darfur'. [Extract] in R. Swedberg (ed.), op. cit. (139–60).

Basu, A. (2008) 'Ethnic minority entrepreneurship'. In M. Casson et al. (eds) op. cit. (580–600).

Birley, S. (1985) 'The role of networks in the entrepreneurial process'. *Journal of Business Venturing*, 1, 1: 107–17.

Blackburn, R. and Ram, M. (2006) 'Fix or fixation?: the contributions and limitations of entrepreneurship and small firms to combating social exclusion'. *Entrepreneurship and Regional Development*, 18, 1: 73–89.

Blumberg, B. F. and Letterie, W. (2008) 'Business starters and credit rationing'. *Small Business Economics*, 30, 2: 187–200.

Blundel, R. K. (2002) 'Network evolution and the growth of artisanal firms: a tale of two regional cheesemakers'. *Entrepreneurship and Regional Development*, 14, 1: 1–30.

Blundel, R. K. and Thatcher, M. (2005) 'Explaining cluster responses to globalization: the case of volume yacht manufacturing in Europe'. *Entrepreneurship and Regional Development*, 17, 6: 405–29.

Blundel, R. K., Baldock, R. and Dadd, D. (2014) *The Quarterly Survey of Small Business in Britain* 30th Anniversary Issue (with invited contributions from: G. Bannock, R. Blackburn, C. Gray, J. Stanworth, R. Roberts, J. Sullivan, and A. Thomson). Milton Keynes, The Open University.

Boari, C., Elfring, T., and Molina-Morales, X. F. (eds) (2016) *Entrepreneurship and Cluster Dynamics* [Routledge Studies in Entrepreneurship]. London: Routledge.

Brewer, J. D. (2000) *Ethnography: Understanding Social Research*. Milton Keynes: Open University Press.

Brown, B. and Butler, J. E. (1995) 'Competitors as allies: a study of entrepreneurial networks in the US wine industry'. *Journal of Small Business Management*, 33, 3: 57–66.

Brush, C. G. (2008) 'Women entrepreneurs: a research overview'. In M. Casson et al. (eds), op. cit. (611–28).

Bryman, A. and Bell, E. (2015) *Business Research Methods* (4th edn). Oxford: Oxford University Press.

Buame, S. K. (1996) *Entrepreneurship: A Contextual Perspective – Discourses and Praxis of Entrepreneurial Activities within the Institutional Context of Ghana*. Lund: Lund University Press.

Buck, N. T. and While, A. (2015) 'Competitive urbanism and the limits to smart city innovation: the UK Future Cities initiative'. *Urban Studies*, [Online First].

Casson, M., Yeung, B., Basu, A., and Wadeson, N. (eds) (2008) *The Oxford Handbook of Entrepreneurship*. Oxford: Oxford University Press.

Checkland, S. G. (1976) *The Upas Tree: Glasgow 1875–1975: A Study in Growth and Contraction*. Glasgow: University of Glasgow Press.

Cope, J., Jack, S., and Rose, M. B. (2007) 'Social capital and entrepreneurship: an introduction'. *International Small Business Journal*, 25, 3: 213–19.

Davidsson, P. (2016) *Researching Entrepreneurship: Conceptualization and Design* (2nd edn). Heidelberg: Springer.

Davidsson, P. and Wiklund, J. (2001) 'Levels of analysis in entrepreneurship research: current research practice and suggestions for the future'. *Entrepreneurship Theory and Practice*, 25, 4: 81–100.

Davies, J., Hides, M., and Powell, J. (2002) 'Defining the development needs of entrepreneurs in SMEs'. *Education and Training*, 44, 8/9: 406–12.

Debrah, Y. (2007) 'Promoting the informal sector as a source of gainful employment in developing countries: insights from Ghana'. *International Journal of Human Resource Management*, 18, 6: 1063–84.

Démurger, S. and Xu, H. (2011) 'Return migrants: the rise of new entrepreneurs in rural China'. *World Development*, 39, 10: 1847–61.

Dhaliwal, S. and Adcroft, A. (2007) 'Accurate portrayal or lazy stereotype?: the changing nature of the Asian business sector in the UK'. In M. Dowling and J. Schmude (eds), op. cit. (31–44).

Díaz-Foncea, M. and Marcuello, C. (2015) 'Spatial patterns in new firm formation: are cooperatives different?' *Small Business Economics*, 44. 1: 171–87.

Di Domenico, M. (2008) '"I'm not just a housewife": gendered roles and identities in the home-based hospitality enterprise'. *Gender, Work and Organization*, 15, 4: 313–422.

Di Domenico, M., Tracey, P., and Haugh, H. (2010) 'Social bricolage: theorizing social value creation in social enterprises'. *Entrepreneurship Theory and Practice*. 34, 4: 681–703.

Dubini, P. and Aldrich, H. (1991) 'Personal and extended networks are central to the entrepreneurial process'. *Journal of Business Venturing*, 6: 305–13.

Easterby-Smith, M., Thorpe, R., and Jackson, P. R. (2015) *Management and Business Research* (5th edn). London: Sage.

Essers, C. and Benschop, Y. (2009) 'Muslim businesswomen doing boundary work: the negotiation of Islam, gender and ethnicity within entrepreneurial contexts'. *Human Relations*, 62, 3: 403–23.

Fadahunsi, A. and Rosa, P. (2002) 'Entrepreneurship and illegality: insights from the Nigerian cross-border trade'. *Journal of Business Venturing*, 17, 5: 397–429.

Fletcher, D. (2006) 'Family and entrepreneurship'. In S. Carter and D. Jones-Evans (eds), op. cit. (209–19).

Garud, R. and Karnøe, P. (2003) 'Bricolage versus breakthrough: distributed and embedded agency in technology entrepreneurship'. *Research Policy*, 32: 277–300.

Godley, A. (2008) 'Migration of entrepreneurs'. In M. Casson et al. (eds), op. cit. (601–10).

Gray, C. W. J. and Mabey, C. L. (2005) 'Management development: key differences between small and large businesses in Europe'. *International Small Business Journal*, 23, 5: 467–85.

Greene, F. J., Mole, K. F., and Storey, D. J. (2007) *Three Decades of the Enterprise Culture: Entrepreneurship, Economic Regeneration and Public Policy*. Basingstoke: Palgrave.

Greene, P., Brush, C. G., Carter, N. M., Gatewood, E., and Hart, M. M. (eds) (2006) *Growth Oriented Women Entrepreneurs and Their Business: A Global Perspective*. Cheltenham: Edward Elgar.

Hamilton, E. E. (2006) 'Whose story is it anyway?: narrative accounts of the role of women in founding and establishing family businesses'. *International Small Business Journal*, 24, 3: 253–71.

Hansen, E. L. (1995) 'Entrepreneurial networks and new organization growth'. *Entrepreneurship Theory and Practice*, 19, 4 (Summer): 7–29.

Hendry, C. and Brown, J. (2006) 'Dynamics of clustering and performance in the UK opto-electronics industry'. *Regional Studies*, 40, 7: 707–25.

Hendry, C., Brown, J., and DeFillipi, R. (2000) 'Regional clustering of high technology-based firms: opto-electronics in three countries'. *Regional Studies*, 34, 2: 129–44.

Henry, C., Foss, L., and Ahl, H. (2016) 'Gender and entrepreneurship research: a review of methodological approaches'. *International Small Business Journal*, 34, 3: 217–41.

Henry, N. and Pinch, S. (2000) 'Spatialising knowledge: placing the knowledge community of Motor Sport Valley'. *Geoforum*, 31, 2: 191–208.

Howorth, C., Rose, M., and Hamilton, E. (2008) 'Definitions, diversity and development: key debates in family business research'. In M. Casson et al. (eds), op. cit. (225–47).

Janjuha-Jivraj, S. and Spence, L. J. (2009) 'The nature of reciprocity in family firm succession'. *International Small Business Journal*, 27(6): 702–19.

Johannisson, B. (1998) 'Personal networks in emerging knowledge-based firms: spatial and functional patterns'. *Entrepreneurship and Regional Development*, 10, 4: 297–312.

Johannisson, B. (2000) 'Networking and entrepreneurial growth'. In D. L. Sexton and H. Landström (eds), *The Blackwell Handbook of Entrepreneurship*. Oxford: Blackwell.

Johannisson, B. and Monsted, M. (1997) 'Contextualizing entrepreneurial networking'. *International Studies of Management and Organization*, 27, 3: 109–36.

Johnstone, B. A. (2007) 'Ethnographic methods in entrepreneurship research'. In H. Neergaard and J. P. Ulhøi (eds), op. cit. (97–121).

Jones, C. (2001) 'Co-evolution of entrepreneurial careers, institutional rules and competitive dynamics in American film, 1895–1920'. *Organization Studies*, 22, 6: 911–44 (Special Issue on: Multi-level Analysis and Co-evolution).

Keeble, D. (2003) 'British SMEs in the 21st century: north–south and urban–rural variations in performance and growth'. In A. Cosh and A. Hughes (eds), *Enterprise Challenged: Policy and Performance in the British SME sector, 1999–2002*. Cambridge: ESRC Centre for Business Research, University of Cambridge (87–102).

Kempster, S. and Cope, J. (2010) 'Learning to lead in the entrepreneurial context'. *International Journal of Entrepreneurial Behaviour and Research*, 16, 1: 5–34.

Kets de Vries, M. F. R. (1996) *Family Business: Human Dilemmas in the Family Firm*. London: Thomson.

Kibler, E., Fink, M., Lang, R., and Muñoz, P. (2015) 'Place attachment and social legitimacy: revisiting the sustainable entrepreneurship journey'. *Journal of Business Venturing Insights*, 3: 24–9.

Kiggundu, M. N. (2002) 'Entrepreneurs and entrepreneurship in Africa: what is known and what needs to be done'. *Journal of Developmental Entrepreneurship*, 7, 3: 239–58.

Kim, S. T. (2015) 'Regional advantage of cluster development: a case study of the San Diego biotechnology cluster'. *European Planning Studies*, 23, 2: 238–61.

Kotey, B. (2005) 'Goals, management practices, and performance of family SMEs'. *International Journal of Entrepreneurial Behaviour and Research*, 11, 1: 3–24.

Kraus, S., Richter, C., Papagiannidis, S., and Durst, S. (2015) 'Innovating and exploiting entrepreneurial opportunities in smart cities: evidence from Germany'. *Creativity and Innovation Management*, 24, 4: 601–16.

Labit, A. (2015) 'Self-managed co-housing in the context of an ageing population in Europe'. *Urban Research & Practice*, 8, 1: 32–45.

Lawson, C. and Lorenz, E. (1999) 'Collective learning, tacit knowledge and regional innovative capacity'. *Regional Studies*, 33, 4: 305–17.

Leitch, C. (2007) 'An action research approach to entrepreneurship'. In H. Neergaard and J. P. Ulhøi (eds), op. cit. (144–68).

Liedholm, C. (2002) 'Small firm dynamics: evidence from Africa and Latin America'. *Small Business Economics*, 18. 1–3: 225–40.

Lindh de Montoya, M. (2000) 'Entrepreneurship and culture: the case of Freddy the strawberry man'. In R. Swedberg (ed.), op. cit. (332–55).

Lockett, N. and Brown, D. H. (2007) 'Aggregation and the role of trusted third parties in SME e-business engagement: a regional policy issue'. *International Small Business Journal*, 24, 4: 379–404.

Low, M. B. and MacMillan, I. C. (1988) 'Entrepreneurship: past research and future challenges'. *Journal of Management*, 14, 2: 139–61.

Madsen, M., Neergaard, H., and Ulhøi, J. P. (2008) 'The influence of roles and identity on female entrepreneurial agency'. *International Journal of Entrepreneurship and Small Business*, 5, 3/4: 358–72.

Mambula, C. (2002) 'Perceptions of SME growth constraints in Nigeria'. *Journal of Small Business Management*, 40, 1: 58–65.

McAdam, M., Miller, K. and McAdam, R. (2016) 'Situated regional university incubation: a multi-level stakeholder perspective'. *Technovation*, 50–51: 69–78.

McKenzie, B. (2007) 'Techniques for collecting verbal histories'. In H. Neergaard and J.P. Ulhøi (eds), op. cit. (308–30).

Morris, M. H., Williams, R. O., Allen, J. A., and Avila, R. A. (1997) 'Correlates of success in family business transitions'. *Journal of Business Venturing*, 12, 5: 385–401.

Moy, J. W., and Luk, V. W. M. (2003) 'The life cycle model as a framework for understanding barriers to SME growth in Hong Kong'. *Asia Pacific Business Review*, 10, 2: 199–220.

Neergaard, H. and Leitch, C. (2015) *Handbook of Qualitative Research Techniques and Analysis in Entrepreneurship*. Cheltenham: Edward Elgar.

Neergaard, H. and Thrane, C. (2009) 'The Nordic welfare model: barrier or facilitator of women's entrepreneurship in Denmark'. Paper presented at ISBE 32nd Annual Conference (4–7 November) Liverpool, UK.

Neergaard, H. and Ulhøi, J. P. (eds) (2007) *Handbook of Qualitative Research Methods in Entrepreneurship*. Cheltenham: Edward Elgar.

Neergaard, H., Nielsen, K., and Kjeldsen, J. (2006) 'State of the art of women's entrepreneurship, access to financing and financing strategies in Denmark'. In P. Greene et al. (eds), op. cit. (88–111).

Obeng, B. A. (2007) 'Business development services and small business growth in Ghana'. Unpublished PhD thesis. Durham: University of Durham.

Obeng, B. A., Blundel, R. K., and Agyapong, A. (2012) 'Developing informal sector enterprises: the case of Sokoban Wood Village, Ghana'. In: M. Thai and E. Turkina (eds), *Entrepreneurship in the Informal Economy: Models, Approaches and Prospects for Economic Development*. London: Routledge (192–207).

Obeng, B. A. and Blundel, R. K. (2015) 'Evaluating enterprise policy interventions in Africa: a critical review of Ghanaian small business support services'. *Journal of Small Business Management*, 53, 2: 416–35.

Orser, B. J., Hogarth-Scott, S., and Riding, A. L. (2000) 'Performance, firm size, and management problem solving'. *Journal of Small Business Management*, 38, 4: 42–58.

Parker, S. C. (2009) *The Economics of Entrepreneurship*. Cambridge: Cambridge University Press.

Pearson, G. (1993) 'Talking a good fight: authenticity and distance in the ethnographer's craft'. In D. Hobbs and T. May (eds), *Interpreting the Field: Accounts of Ethnography*. Oxford: Oxford University Press (vii–xviii).

Pinkse, J. and Groot, K. (2015) 'Sustainable entrepreneurship and corporate political activity: overcoming market barriers in the clean energy sector'. *Entrepreneurship Theory and Practice*, 39, 3: 633–54.

Pitt-Catsouphes, M., Birzin, S., and Halvorsen, C. J. (2014) *Been a Long Time Coming: Social Entrepreneurship in Later Life*. The Sloan Centre on Aging and Work Issue Brief 20 (January). Boston MA: Boston College.

Ram, M. (1999) 'Trading places: the ethnographic process in small firms' research'. *Entrepreneurship and Regional Development*, 11, 2: 95–108.

Ramachandran, K. and Ramnarayan, S. (1993) 'Entrepreneurial orientation and networking: some Indian evidence'. *Journal of Business Venturing*, 8, 6: 513–24.

Read, S., Sarasvathy, S. D., Dew, N., and Wiltbank, R. (2016) 'Response to Arend, Sarooghi, and Burkemper (2015): co-creating effectual entrepreneurship research'. *Academy of Management Review*, 41, 3: 528–36.

Robinson, S. (2006) 'Learning to lead: developing SME leadership support for business development'. *Proceedings of the 27th ISBE National Small Firms Policy and Research Conference*, Cardiff (November).

Robinson, S. (2007) 'Relational learning: towards a model of owner-manager development'. *Proceedings of the HRD conference*, London (April).

Robson, P. J. A. and Obeng, B. A. (2008) 'The barriers to growth in Ghana'. *Small Business Economics*, 30, 4: 385–403.

Rønning, L. and Kolvereid, L. (2006) 'Income diversification in Norwegian farm households: reassessing pluriactivity'. *International Small Business Journal*, 24, 4: 405–20.

Rubin, T. H., Aas, T. H., and Stead, A. (2015) 'Knowledge flow in technological business incubators: evidence from Australia and Israel'. *Technovation*, 41–42: 11–24.

Sarasvathy, S. D. (2001) 'Causation and effectuation: toward a theoretical shift from economic inevitability to entrepreneurial contingency'. *Academy of Management Review*, 26, 2: 243–63.

Sarasvathy, S. D. (2002) 'Entrepreneurship as economics with imagination'. *Ethics and Entrepreneurship*. The Ruffin Series 3, Charlottesville, VA: Society for Business Ethics.

Sarasvathy, S. D. (2008) *Effectuation: Elements of Entrepreneurial Expertise*. Cheltenham: Edward Elgar.

Sarasvathy, S., Kumar, K., York, J. G., and Bhagavatula, S. (2014) 'An effectual approach to international entrepreneurship: overlaps, challenges, and provocative possibilities'. *Entrepreneurship Theory and Practice*, 38, 1: 71–93.

Saxenian, A. (1991) 'The origins and dynamics of production networks in Silicon Valley'. *Research Policy*, 20, 5: 423–37.

Sharma, P. (2004) 'An overview of the field of family business studies: current status and directions for the future'. *Family Business Review*, 17, 1: 1–36.

Shaw, E. (2006) 'Small firm networking: an insight into contents and motivating factors'. *International Small Business Journal*, 24, 1: 5–29.

Small Business Charter (2016) 'The small business owner's story – Hall's Food Group'. London: Small Business Charter. Available at: http://smallbusinesscharter.org/the-small-business-owners-story-halls-food-group (accessed 6 October 2016).

Smith, L. and Robinson, S. (2007) 'Leading enterprise and development: report on the design and delivery of a programme to engage and motivate small businesses in leadership and management development'. Lancaster: IEED, Lancaster University Management School.

Spence, L. J. and Rutherfoord, R. (2001) 'Social responsibility, profit maximisation and the small firm owner-manager'. *Small Business and Enterprise Development*, 8, 2: 126–39.

Steiner, A. and Atterton, J. (2015) 'Exploring the contribution of rural enterprises to local resilience'. *Journal of Rural Studies*, 40: 30–45.

Stinchfield, B. T., Nelson, R. E., and Wood, M. S. (2013) 'Learning from Levi-Strauss' legacy: art, craft, engineering, bricolage, and brokerage in entrepreneurship'. *Entrepreneurship Theory and Practice*, 37, 4: 889–921.

Stumbitz, B. (2013) 'Social entrepreneurship shaped by the life course: a case study of older social entrepreneurs in the UK'. Unpublished doctoral dissertation, London: Middlesex University.

Stumbitz, B., McDowall, H., and Gabriel, M. (2012) *Golden Opportunities: Social Entrepreneurs in an Ageing Society*. London: UnLtd Research.

Storper, M. J. (1997) *The Regional World: Territorial Development in a Global Economy*. London: Guilford Press.

Swedberg, R. (ed.) (2000) *Entrepreneurship: The Social Science View*. Oxford: Oxford University Press.

Tagoe, N., Nyarko, E., and Anuwa-Amarh, E. (2005) 'Financial challenges facing urban SMEs under financial sector liberalization in Ghana'. *Journal of Small Business Management*, 43, 3: 331–43.

Takyi-Asiedu, S. (1993) 'Some socio-cultural factors retarding entrepreneurial activity in sub-Saharan Africa'. *Journal of Business Venturing* 8, 2: 91–8.

Terjesen, S. A. and O'Gorman, C. (2007) 'Informal investment and venture financing in Ireland'. In H. Landström, M. Raffa, and L. Iandoli (eds), *Entrepreneurship, Competitiveness and Local Development Frontiers in European Research*. Cheltenham: Edward Elgar (145–69).

Valliere, D. (2008) 'Exploring Buddhist influence on the entrepreneurial decision'. *International Journal of Entrepreneurial Behaviour and Research*, 14, 3: 172–91.

Van Stel, A. J. and Storey, D. J. (2004) 'The link between firm births and job creation: is there an Upas tree effect?' *Regional Studies*, 38, 8: 893–909.

Volkov, V. (1999) 'Violent entrepreneurship in post-communist Russia'. *Europe-Asia Studies*, 51, 5: 741–54.

Wakkee, I, Englis, P., and During, W. (2007) 'Using e-mails as a source of qualitative data'. In H. Neergaard and J. P. Ulhøi (eds), op. cit. (331–58).

Wang, C. L. (2008) 'Entrepreneurial orientation, learning orientation, and firm performance'. *Entrepreneurship Theory and Practice*, 32, 4: 635–56.

Wolf, S. (2004) 'Performance and problems of enterprises in Ghana'. Department of Agricultural Economics and Agribusiness Working Paper. Accra: University of Ghana.

Zafirovski, M. (1999) 'Probing into the social layers of entrepreneurship: outlines of the sociology of enterprise'. *Entrepreneurship and Regional Development*, 11, 4: 351–71.

13

ECONOMIC PERSPECTIVES: INFLUENCES AND IMPACTS

An entrepreneur is someone who specialises in taking judgemental decisions about the coordination of scarce resources.

Mark Casson, economist

By pursuing opportunities that otherwise would not have been pursued by the incumbent organizations, entrepreneurship plants the seeds for entire new industries and is, thus, a driving force of industrial restructuring.

David Audretsch and Max Keilbach, entrepreneurship researchers

LEARNING OUTCOMES

After reading this chapter you should be able to:

- Explore entrepreneurial activity from an economic perspective.
- Identify the contribution made by the main economic research approaches, and related research evidence, to our understanding of entrepreneurship.
- Understand the relationship between entrepreneurial activity and performance outcomes, including economic growth, innovation, and competitiveness.
- Recognise how entrepreneurship can become unproductive or destructive.
- Evaluate economics-based evidence and relate it to findings obtained from other research perspectives.
- Apply these insights to your own experiences of entrepreneurship.

13.1 INTRODUCTION

This chapter is concerned with the economic perspectives on **entrepreneurship.** There are competing views on what economics is, or should be, concerned about. For our purposes, economics can be described, in general terms, as a branch of social science that examines how societies allocate and manage scarce resources between alternative uses. In the past, these activities have taken place under different economic systems, with varying degrees of control being exercised by political leaders (e.g. feudalism in the medieval era and state socialism in the twentieth century). Today, most of the world's resources are allocated and managed under various forms of industrial capitalism (Thurik et al. 2013). In this chapter, we investigate the entrepreneurial function in these modern economies, including its capacity to generate wealth, employment, and economic development. The opening case illustrates how even the most modest enterprises can transform the livelihoods of individuals, families, and local communities. Over the last few decades, entrepreneurial activity has also been transforming the prospects of people in transition countries and creating new economic superpowers (e.g. Sauka and Welter 2006; Khanna 2008). The economic transformation is particularly dramatic in some of today's high-technology 'hot spots' (e.g. Shanghai, Bangalore, Dubai), with massive new construction projects, vast inflows of human and natural resources, and flamboyant displays of personal wealth – the luxury yachts, private aircraft, and exclusive fashion stores (Case 10.1). The economic outcomes of entrepreneurship are often obvious. But what is going on beneath the surface? Simon Parker, an economist with a specialist interest in entrepreneurship, provides us with a concise definition of the scope of the field:

> *In essence, the economics of entrepreneurship analyses how economic incentives influence entrepreneurial behaviour, and how entrepreneurial behaviour in turn affects the broader economy. (Parker 2009: 4)*

As the chapter title suggests, we are paying particular attention to the second of these questions, exploring the economic impact of entrepreneurship on individuals, organisations, and geographic regions. However, we also touch on the first theme, identifying the economic pre-conditions for entrepreneurship. In particular, we consider how resource constraints influence entrepreneurial activity, and the practical ways in which entrepreneurs overcome these limitations. Economics-based research has a strong influence on our understanding of entrepreneurship, which can be seen in many areas of life. For example, when analysts describe the performance, including the 'success' or 'failure', of an entrepreneurial venture, they often define the outcome in purely economic terms. The same thing happens when politicians and policy-makers talk about the outcomes of entrepreneurial activity on a larger scale. Economists can rightly claim to have originated the term, 'entrepreneur', and over the years they have built up a strong body of economic theory and research evidence. We can draw on these valuable sources to make sense of what entrepreneurial activity is, and how it works. However, economics does not have all the answers. There are still many unresolved questions within the discipline of economics, and many aspects of entrepreneurship that require the perspectives and insights of other academic disciplines.

Economists have identified many different roles for the entrepreneur. These include: identifying or creating opportunities, making innovations, taking risks, bearing uncertainty, acting as an intermediary, allocating resources between different uses, coordinating resources, and leading organisations. One common theme in this varied list is a capacity to exercise judgements under conditions of risk and uncertainty (Casson [1982] 2003). Entrepreneurs have to make (and to implement) all kinds of decisions. The quality of these judgements can have a profound impact on both the performance of the venture and its capacity to generate economic value. Case 13.1 provides a practical illustration of these entrepreneurial judgements in a start-up venture.

The chapter proceeds as follows. In Section 13.2, we review some of key insights that have been provided by economists, concentrating on the positive contribution that entrepreneurial activity can make to the economy, and on the economic factors that either promote or constrain such activity. Section 13.3 is concerned with the different ways in which the entrepreneurial function has been explained by economists, from the early pioneers to present-day researchers. Section 13.4 examines how entrepreneurial activity can become economically unproductive or destructive, and opens up a debate about how these negative outcomes might be avoided. In Section 13.5, we conclude by considering the practical implications of economics-based research for individual entrepreneurs, entrepreneurial organisations, and those involved in policy-making.

CASE 13.1 STUDENT FOCUS

Creating economic value in a start-up venture

These short fictionalised accounts, based on real world examples, illustrate how students have made good use of entrepreneurship research to achieve successful outcomes in their studies.

Three engineering students, Julie, Sam and Michael, have been developing their final year design project, 'EcoDry', into a new venture that has the potential to seize a growing market for more environmentally friendly products and services. They have teamed up with a friend, Silvia, who is studying for a combined degree in Economics and Management. She provides them with some useful advice on how to convert a novel technology into a living and breathing business. In return, the team let her use their idea to illustrate her dissertation, 'Economic approaches to entrepreneurship: a case study of a technology-based start up venture.' Silva analyses the main activities involved in a start-up, using her friends' venture as an example and adding a brief commentary (her notes are reproduced in Table 13.1 below). When the dissertation is submitted, the markers are particularly pleased with the way she has managed to integrate theory and practice. Meanwhile Julie, Sam and Michael are preparing for their first pitch to prospective investors. Are they making the right decisions about EcoDry? Have they got the foundations of a viable business? Silvia's advice was certainly helpful but they are beginning to realise that lots of uncertainty remains and that (alongside all the hard work) launching a new venture is largely a matter of judgement.

QUESTIONS

1. Compare the activities of this student team with either: (a) your own experiences in a student new venture competition, or; (b) an example of a student new venture team that you have located online.

2. Present your findings as a table, similar to the one produced by Silvia.

3. Locate at least one research article on each of the four activities listed in Silvia's table, read the abstracts (or ideally the whole article), and note any insights they provide into the new venture creation process.

(Continued)

(Continued)

TABLE 13.1 Silvia's notes: opportunities, resources and value

Activity	Practical illustration – 'EcoDry'	Commentary
Identifying or creating new opportunities	The three engineering students have combined several existing technologies in their 'EcoDry' product, which offers a new, more environmentally friendly technique for dry cleaning textiles, and which could secure a premium price in the market.	Entrepreneurs identify and/or create new opportunities to generate value. Economic value is typically measured as sales, profits, and cash flow that would not otherwise have existed but can also include social and environmental value.
Mobilising and leveraging resources	The team secures financial resources from a number of sources, including their own family and friends. They also decide to recruit an experienced technology entrepreneur to increase their credibility with potential investors and business partners.	Entrepreneurs mobilise economic resources, often overcoming resource constraints through a combination of creativity and initiative – including financial 'bootstrapping' to minimise start-up finance requirements, and using personal contact networks to access vital resources.
Appropriating and accumulating value	The founders set up franchise-based business model with a holding company; they considered adopting a social enterprise model, but decided that this had the greater growth potential. The founders accumulate wealth from the franchisees and from their own equity stake.	Entrepreneurs create suitable organisational forms to coordinate financial, human, intellectual, and technological resources. These decisions are likely to affect the longer-term economic performance and impact of the venture. Social enterprises also need to balance social and economic goals.
Redistributing and redirecting value	Once trading, 'Eco-Dry' pays wages to employees, reimburses suppliers, distributes dividends to investors and pays taxes to local and national governments. The founders also decide to re-invest a percentage of their profits in a local environmental charity.	Entrepreneurs also decide how to make use of the value they have secured. For example, is the capital re-circulated within the local economy, or taken abroad? Is it re-invested in the venture or in personal consumption (e.g. sports cars and art collections)?

13.2 ECONOMIC INSIGHTS INTO ENTREPRENEURSHIP

13.2.1 Applying economic methods

The economics of entrepreneurship can be something of an obstacle course. Economic theory is often rather abstract and inaccessible to those without the necessary technical background. As a consequence, theoretical debates in economics can appear far removed from the everyday realities of creating a new entrepreneurial venture. In addition, economists tend to have distinctive ways of viewing the world, which are not always clear to non-specialists. For these reasons, the next two sections of this chapter review some of the more interesting *questions* that economists have addressed, coupled with examples of *contributions* that economics has made to our understanding of entrepreneurship. It is not possible to offer a comprehensive picture of such a large and diverse research field in a single chapter. However, to give a flavour of the work that is being done, we have selected three contrasting themes, each highlighting a different set of insights that can be gained by applying economic research techniques:

- Patterns in the number of enterprises.
- Entrepreneurship, economic growth, and regional development.
- Access to finance as a barrier to entrepreneurship.

In addition, each of these research areas has a high profile in government circles. As a consequence, there is an opportunity to follow up on some of the issues raised in Chapter 15, when we examine the world of policy-making.

13.2.2 Patterns in the number of enterprises

There are no simple measures of entrepreneurial activity, but researchers often use data that are based on the number of enterprises. Perhaps the simplest indicator is how the numbers are distributed between enterprises of different sizes. The differences between countries can be quite striking. For example, Table 13.2 compares SMEs in three European Union countries as a percentage of all enterprises, Gross Value Added (GVA) and employment, expressed as Full Time Equivalents (FTE). The table also distinguishes between 'independent' SMEs and those that are 'dependent', meaning that they are part of a larger group of companies.

Size distributions provide a basic picture of the current 'stock' of enterprises but they do not reveal anything about their 'flow' (i.e. the numbers of new firms being created and of existing firms that cease to exist). These flows can be substantial, as indicated by the authors of an annual survey of EU enterprises:

> *Each year about 1.5 million new enterprises are established, corresponding to 9% of the total enterprise population. At the same time 1.3 million enterprises annually cease to exist, corresponding to a death rate of 8% of the stock of enterprises. (Audretsch et al. 2009: 9)*

New firm formation data are often used as an indicator of entrepreneurial activity in different geographic locations (e.g. comparing the rates between countries, regions, cities, urban and rural areas) (Section 13.5), and over time (e.g. identifying historical trends in industries) (Section 14.3). These patterns are often used as a starting-point for enquiry. For example, they have prompted researchers to look at factors that might either promote or inhibit new firm formation rates, such as the number of creative people living in a particular area (Lee et al. 2004), or to scrutinise claims that new firm formations have a positive impact on economic goals such as job creation (e.g. Van Stel and Storey 2004).

13.2.3 Entrepreneurship, economic growth, and regional development

Economists have always been interested in growth, and how it is created. In one of the earliest and most influential works in English, Adam Smith launched *An Inquiry into the Nature and Causes of the Wealth of Nations* (Smith [1776] 2008). Smith identified a number of reasons why some economies grew more, and hence became wealthier, than others. One of the main strands in his explanation was concerned with the

TABLE 13.2 Sample SME statistics for three European Union countries

Country	Type	Size	Enterprises total	Enterprises %	GVA (million €) total	GVA (million €) %	FTE total	FTE %
Denmark	Independent	Micro	152835	72.1	16301	22.9	121075	17.0
		Small	8247	3.9	9533	13.4	111979	15.8
		Medium	1091	0.5	6949	9.8	77170	10.9
		All SME	**162173**	**76.5**	**32783**	**46.1**	**310225**	**43.6**
	Dependent	Micro	37101	17.5	7394	10.4	64925	9.1
		Small	10383	4.9	15421	21.7	162296	22.8
		Medium	2310	1.1	15521	21.8	173319	24.4
		All SME	**49794**	**23.5**	**38336**	**53.9**	**400539**	**56.4**
Germany	Independent	Micro	1732568	79.3	172249	22.4	2222556	18.8
		Small	269061	12.3	176222	22.9	3652745	30.9
		Medium	26865	1.2	92283	12.0	1922349	16.3
		All SME	**2028493**	**92.9**	**440753**	**57.2**	**7797650**	**65.9**
	Dependent	Micro	71321	3.3	44783	5.8	152222	1.3
		Small	53955	2.5	82821	10.8	1077104	9.1
		Medium	29957	1.4	201602	26.2	2802352	23.7
		All SME	**155233**	**7.1**	**329206**	**42.8**	**4031678**	**34.1**
Latvia	Independent	Micro	71699	88.2	1114	19.7	87191	34.0
		Small	3172	3.9	890	15.8	46450	18.1
		Medium	743	0.9	844	15.0	49322	19.2
		All SME	**75614**	**93.0**	**2849**	**50.5**	**182963**	**71.3**
	Dependent	Micro	4020	4.9	466	8.3	6914	2.7
		Small	1097	1.3	793	14.1	19050	7.4
		Medium	584	0.7	1535	27.2	47839	18.6
		All SME	**5701**	**7.0**	**2794**	**49.5**	**73803**	**28.7**

Source: Eurostat (2015) – Table 3 (extract, based on 2012 data).

ways that individual enterprises could increase productivity through the division of labour (i.e. giving workers more specialised tasks) and other economies of scale – as illustrated by Smith's well-known example of the pin factory. Another strand concentrated on the way that economic activity was coordinated, and here Smith argued that the 'invisible hand' of the market, or the combined effect of individuals making their own self-interested choices, was likely to be more effective than coordination by political leaders and other bodies, such as the medieval craft guilds. Over the years, economists developed a number of theories about the growth process, focusing to varying degrees on issues related to industrial production, technological innovation, and the role of market mechanisms. In the last two decades, a new approach known as 'endogenous growth theory' (or '**new growth theory**') has become particularly influential (cf. Romer 1994; Solow 1994). New growth theory recognises the role of played by technological innovation and associated 'knowledge spillovers' (Arrow [1959] 2010) (Case 13.3). For economists, **knowledge spillovers** are a type of positive externality, in which knowledge created by scientists and other technical specialists becomes more widely available, creating new opportunities for others to exploit it:

> *[A]ny original, valuable knowledge generated somewhere that becomes accessible to external agents, whether it be knowledge fully characterizing an innovation or knowledge of a more intermediate sort. This knowledge is absorbed by an individual or group other than the originator. (Foray 2004: 91)*

What function do entrepreneurs perform in this process? Economists and economic geographers have examined a variety of ways in which entrepreneurial activity influences economic development (Section 13.5). However, one of the central findings is that commercially driven entrepreneurs keep economies moving forward by recognising (and exploiting) opportunities to shift resources into functions that yield a higher return:

> *Entrepreneurs seek out these opportunities for personal gain and, in so doing, ensure that resources are constantly being reallocated in a manner that improves efficiency. In the absence of entrepreneurs, resources continue to be devoted to functions where the returns are low, leading to an ossified [i.e. fixed and unchanging] economy in which resources are under-used. (Acs and Storey 2004: 872–3)*

> *Of course, entrepreneurs have always pursued opportunities. However, research suggests that entrepreneurs in today's innovative, technology-based industries need appropriate institutions and infrastructures, including well-established systems of intellectual property rights and networks of university-based researchers and spin-off firms, if they are to compete effectively (e.g. Van de Ven 1993; Best 2001).*

13.2.4 Access to finance as a barrier to entrepreneurship

It is possible to identify a number of economic factors that can influence the level of entrepreneurial activity in different countries, regions or industries. These include broad 'macro-economic' (i.e. economy-wide) factors, such as interest rates, gross domestic product (GDP), inflation rates, taxation, and public spending, as well as narrower 'micro-economic' (i.e. market-specific) factors such as access to finance. From an economist's perspective, these financing constraints are evidence of 'market imperfections', which in turn are produced by 'information asymmetries'. In practical terms, this means that entrepreneurs are facing excessive financing costs because finance providers do not have sufficient access to information about their ventures. There are two kinds of information asymmetry:

> *First, one party to a transaction is in possession of relevant information that is not known by the other party. Specifically, entrepreneurs possess more information about their own abilities and the prospects of their firm than the provider of finance and may misrepresent this information. This creates the risk of adverse selection by the funder, which can only be mitigated by incurring the expense*

of a lengthy due diligence process to obtain relevant information about the entrepreneur and the business (which because of its private nature may not be available) and interpret it. This is particularly problematic in technology sectors, where it is difficult to value the firm's scientific knowledge and intellectual property, the products are likely to be new and untested in the market, and the management may lack commercial skills. Second, one party to a transaction cannot observe relevant actions taken by the other party that might influence the outcome of the investment. Dealing with this problem – moral hazard – is also costly to the investor, requiring complicated contracts that are time consuming to design and negotiate, and labour-intensive monitoring systems. Because the costs involved in investment appraisal and monitoring are fixed regardless of the size of investment, this makes small investments uneconomic for funders. (Mason 2009: 537)

These market failures have created funding gaps for new ventures, particularly in technology-based sectors. As Colin Mason's study indicates, governments have responded to this situation by intervening in various ways, including:

- **Introducing fiscal incentives**, including tax relief for new start-up ventures.
- **Promoting networks of 'business angel' investors**, and helping them locate new ventures.
- **Reforming securities (i.e. stock market) legislation** to reduce the burden on entrepreneurs.
- **Building the capacity of entrepreneurs**, including training delivered by business angels.
- **Building the capacity of investors**, by training and learning within their networks.
- **Co-investing with business angels** through government-financed venture capital funds.

There has also been a growth in alternative finance approaches, such as crowdfunding (Mollick 2014). This work on access to finance illustrates how economics-based research can inform public policy-making (Section 15.1). It also suggests why the relationship between entrepreneurial activity and economic growth is complex and difficult to untangle. As a result, researchers need to use a combination of methods, including economics and other social science disciplines (Section 15.5).

The following Researcher Profile (Case 13.2) continues this theme, illustrating how qualitative methods can be used to study the emerging practice of crowdfunding, and the valuable insights that can be obtained from this kind of approach.

CASE 13.2 RESEARCHER PROFILE

OTHMAR M. LEHNER, INVESTIGATING CROWDFUNDING FOR SOCIAL VENTURES

Othmar M. Lehner is the Vice Dean for Research and a fully tenured professor at the University of Applied Sciences Upper Austria, a professorial fellow at the Smith School of Enterprise and the Environment at the University of Oxford, and a long-term academic visitor at the SAID Business School of the University of Oxford.

After graduation in the field of finance and computer science he went into a professional career working as chartered accountant and bank manager for more than ten years and starting two successfully exited ventures before he continued his academic calling at the University of Jyväskylä in Finland with research time spent abroad in New York, Boston and Amsterdam. He completed his research-based Doctorate of Science in Business and Economics with a major in Social and Sustainable Entrepreneurship (one of the world's first at that time).

Othmar's research interests are social and sustainable entrepreneurship, related venture finance and impact investing, looking specifically at the motivations and the complex interplay of institutions, the participants and new instruments such as crowdfunding in the field. His latest project is the editorship of the *Routledge Handbook of Social and Sustainable Finance*.

In this interview, Othmar discusses his research in social finance and crowdfunding for social ventures.

Why did you want to research in this area? How did you decide on your main research questions?

I have been an entrepreneur myself and found it increasingly difficult to communicate and translate the ideas and opportunities at hand to banks and traditional investors. Yet, friends and people in general seemed to be very enthusiastic and supportive concerning my ideas. This discrepancy made me rethink the funding process (Lehner 2013) and I thought when and how can people with brilliant ideas use alternative funding sources for their ventures, what makes an idea "legitimate" in the eyes of the public (Lehner and Nicholls 2014) and how is this legitimacy communicated and transported in times of social media and information overload (Lehner 2014).

What methods did you use?

I am keenly interested in receiving a holistic picture, in understanding the rich and detailed background of a phenomenon. So, true to the approach suggested by Edmondson and McManus (2007), my co-researchers and I chose to work inductively through learning from the field and carefully conceptualising our findings into models and propositions. Especially in young and dynamic fields such as social entrepreneurship as a whole, with a variety of new instruments and players such as crowdfunding or crowdfunding platforms, case studies with a multi-perspective approach seem to be the method of choice. We found that the quantitative studies in this area often lack face validity because their models are not really robust when it comes to identifying and including mediating and moderating variables. We prefer to talk to people, look at cases from a longitudinal perspective and understand the dynamical change of the configurations that we see. So, overall we collected around 1800 documents, ranging from web-snapshots to various internal memos and interview transcripts and we used the methodological approach described in Eisenhardt's (1989) article on building theory from case study research inductively.

(Continued)

(Continued)

What were your key findings?

In our article 'Crowdfunding for Social Ventures', that turned out to have quite an impact, we look specifically on the necessary antecedents and the chain of logic – how social ventures can showcase opportunities and offer social and financial rewards to the public via crowdfunding in order to convince investors. The model was a first and we tried in addition to provide a well-crafted research agenda to help structure the field (Lehner 2013).

Based on this first article, Professor Alex Nicholls and I worked together with members of the UK Cabinet to examine how policy-makers can enhance and support the crowdfunding market for social ventures. We came up with a scheme for public–private partnerships that was later (April 2015) implemented in parts as law in the UK. It supports the CIC (Community Interest Company) as a legal form and helps build the crowdfunding market for social ventures in the UK through public intervention, taxes, and collateralisation (Lehner and Nicholls 2014).

In parallel, I was working on a long-term multiple-case study using networking theory to identify the role of the four types of capital (Bourdieu and Wacquant 1992) in transforming social capital into economic capital. It was particularly interesting how the roles of cultural capital and symbolic capital had to be redefined in the sphere of crowdfunding. Whereas in traditional finance, auditing and cash flow statements have a strong symbolic character, this was not the case at all in crowdfunding campaigns, rather the opposite – traditional business-oriented symbols such as suits and ties and even management talk were identified as being detrimental to the conversion of social capital (people you know and those you can reach by campaigning) to economic capital (actual financial contributions). What was seen as most important was the alignment of the diverse cultural capital through storytelling and the co-creation of opportunities with a strong stakeholder inclusion (Lehner 2014).

A final work I would like to mention was the recently published article on entrepreneurial implications of crowdfunding (Lehner et al. 2015). In this, two of my colleagues and I were looking at 'the Good, the Bad and the Ugly' of crowdfunding and what engaging with a crowd for funding purposes means for the entrepreneurs themselves. The spectrum of unforeseen consequences of this seemingly innocent choice of a funding source ranged from receiving unexpected help through crowd-sourcing via problems in scaling the venture to a global witch-hunt for the entrepreneurs of an allegedly fraudulent CF campaign.

Were there any particular challenges in conducting these studies?

Longitudinal case studies are always time consuming and involve a lot of costly on-site presence. In addition, and as probably with all qualitative methods, the hermeneutic interpretation of the material is challenging. Making sense of all the observations and colloquial talks in a structured way and not to let your own ideas and presumptions distort the picture is difficult and needs lots of experience and personal reflection. I would also mention that the right choice of a sample is of uttermost importance. Too often cases are selected based on convenience but unfortunately the hard ones to tackle, for example the stories of those who failed and are embarrassed to talk to researchers, are the ones we can learn the most from.

Where do you think research in this area needs to develop in future?

In the near future we will see many more changes in entrepreneurial finance. Crowdfunding as a phenomenon can be understood as a result of broader societal changes. Through the use of modern technologies, CF enables a much wider range of people to participate and control economic activities, often described as the advent of 'Capitalism 2.0'. Besides the orthodox focus on financial risk and return, more and more of these new investors will additionally look for a social return along the ESG (Environmental, Social, and Governance) criteria. In order to understand what is happening, research needs to be of an interdisciplinary nature, including traditional business and management scholars, researchers from, for example, Sociology and even the Humanities. We need to embrace neo-institutionalist as well as critical discursive perspectives in the entrepreneurship literature and reconcile these with finance theory. Overall, there's plenty of work to do in a very rewarding field.

13.3 ECONOMIC PERSPECTIVES ON ENTREPRENEURSHIP

13.3.1 Introduction: contrasting approaches and contributions

Entrepreneurial activity comes in all shapes and sizes. At one extreme, there are the small group of highly innovative 'system builders', who are responsible for leading major structural transformations. Examples can be found in the railway, steel, and oil industries of the nineteenth century, the car manufacturing, electricity generation, and computing industries of the twentieth century. At the other extreme, there are a multitude of 'low-level' entrepreneurs trading on a relatively small scale in local markets. Is it possible to identify a common 'entrepreneurial function' shared by such a diverse group? Economists have always recognised that entrepreneurs are significant economic actors, but it has proved difficult to integrate the entrepreneur into economic theory. Over the last century, economists have continued to explore, and to argue about, the entrepreneurial function. There have been important contributions from a number of leading economists, including Frank Knight, George Shackle, Joseph Schumpeter, Edith Penrose, Mark Casson, David Audretsch, and many others. In the following paragraphs, we review some of these contributions, and consider their practical implications. The section is written in non-technical language; economists and others with a more specialist interest in this subject will find relevant sources in the Further reading guide. We begin by looking back to some of the earliest attempts at identifying the economic function of the entrepreneur. The section concludes with some examples of the current state of play in economics-based research.

13.3.2 Pioneering contributions: Cantillon and Mill

In his *Essai sur la nature du Commerce en Generale*, the economist Richard Cantillon (1697–1734), depicts the entrepreneur as a risk-taker who acquires labour and raw materials when the price of the end-product was still uncertain. Cantillon was writing in a pre-industrial economy and many of his examples were based on agriculture. In this English translation, his 'undertaker' (i.e. entrepreneur) is a farmer, who has to make decisions about allocating resources under conditions of uncertainty:

The farmer is an undertaker who promises to pay to the landowner, for his farm or land, a fixed sum of money (generally supposed to be equal in value to the third of the produce) without assurance of the profit he will derive from this enterprise. He employs part of the land to feed flocks, produce corn, wine, hay, etc. according to his judgement without being able to foresee which of these will pay best. The price of these products will depend partly on the weather, partly on the demand; if corn is abundant relatively to consumption it will be dirt cheap, if there is scarcity it will be dear. Who can foresee the increase or reduction of expense which may come about in the families? And yet the price of the farmer's produce depends naturally upon these unforeseen circumstances, and consequently he conducts the enterprise of his farm at an uncertainty. (Cantillon [1755] 1959: Part I, Chapter XIII.1)

Cantillon identifies three distinct types of economic actor: landowners, entrepreneurs, and what the original English translation describes as 'hirelings' (i.e. employees). Though his contemporaries still saw landowning as a more prestigious occupation, Cantillon recognised that entrepreneurs played a more decisive role, and one that influenced many different aspects of economic life:

Cantillon's entrepreneur is someone who engages in exchanges for profit; specifically, he exercises business judgements in the face of uncertainty. This uncertainty (of future sales prices for goods on their way to final consumption) is rather carefully circumscribed. As Cantillon describes it, entrepreneurs buy at a certain price to sell again at an uncertain price, with the difference being their profit or loss. Cantillon stressed the function, not the personality of the entrepreneur. He generalized the function of the entrepreneur so that it embraced many different occupations and cut across production, distribution, and exchange. (Hébert and Link 1989: 42; emphasis added)

The political economist, John Stuart Mill introduced the term 'entrepreneur' into the English language in the mid-nineteenth century, noting that the, 'exertions of entrepreneurship demanded no ordinary skill' (i.e. it required special abilities). Though a person might combine it with other tasks, such as financing or managing, Mill recognised that this *entrepreneurial* function was different, and required its own place in economic theory:

It is to be regretted that this word, in this sense, is not familiar to an English ear. French political economists enjoy a great advantage in being able to speak currently of 'les profits de l'entrepreneur'. (Mill [1848] 1909: Chapter 15, note 93)

13.3.3 The disappearing entrepreneur: classical and neoclassical economics

In the late eighteenth and early nineteenth centuries, the first industrial revolution saw a new generation of entrepreneurs taking an increasingly powerful role in the economy, transforming industrial sectors such as manufacturing (e.g. cotton), transport (e.g. canals), and services (e.g. banking):

As rulers gradually submitted to constitutional constraints on their power, and property rights became more secure within the nation states, entrepreneurial energy was released at an unprecedented rate. (Ricketts 2008: 37)

Paradoxically, it was during this period that economists lost track of the distinctive entrepreneurial function that had been identified by pioneering figures such as Richard Cantillon. As one leading economist has noted, 'the strange disappearance of the entrepreneur from the centre of the stage of economic debate has a long history' (Blaug [1986] 2000: 77). The story is complicated, but we can isolate two of the more important developments:

- **Classical political economy:** The most influential figures of this school, notably Adam Smith, David Ricardo, and Karl Marx, did not separate the entrepreneurial function from that of providing finance. For example, Marx examined the relationship between suppliers of capital and labour (i.e. the 'labour process'), but did not extend his analysis to consider providers of entrepreneurial services. Important exceptions include J. S. Mill, discussed in the previous section, and the French economist, Jean-Baptiste Say (1767–1832), who attempted to reintroduce the entrepreneur into economic theory as a fourth factor of production. Say also put his ideas into practice, setting up a cotton mill in Northern France, which proved to be very profitable.

- **Neoclassical economics:** From the late nineteenth century, economics became dominated by the marginal or 'neoclassical' theories of William S. Jevons, Carl Menger, and Leon Walras. Neoclassical thinkers developed a static general equilibrium model of the economy, and attempted to model economic relationships using the formal language of mathematics. The main problem of economics became that of allocating resources in an optimum way:

    Given, a certain population, with various needs and powers of production, in possession of certain lands and other sources of material: required, the mode of employing their labour which will maximize the utility of the produce. (Jevons 1911: 267)

Neoclassical theory proved to be an effective tool for analysing micro-economic phenomena such as price movements and their relationship with changes in supply and demand. It has also been successfully applied within entrepreneurship. For example, Baumol (1990) used it to examine how a fixed supply of entrepreneurial talent is allocated between 'productive', 'unproductive', and 'destructive' activities (Section 15.4). However, as economists began to explore dynamic problems, such as the processes that generate technological innovation (Schumpeter [1934] 2004) and the growth process inside the 'black box' of the firm (Penrose [1959] 1995), it became clear that neoclassical theory did not deal adequately with role played by entrepreneurial individuals:

[T]he entrepreneur was gradually extruded from economic analysis when economists attempted more and more to emulate the physical sciences by incorporating the mathematical method. Mathematics introduced greater precision to economics, and thereby promised to increase the power of economics to predict. Yet it was a two-edged sword. Its sharp edge cut through the tangled confusion of real-world complexity, making economics more tractable and accelerating its theoretic advance. But its blunt edge hacked away one of the fundamental forces of economic life – the entrepreneur. Because there was not and is not a satisfactory mathematics to deal with the dynamics of economic life, economic analysis evolved by concentrating on comparative statics, and the entrepreneur took on a purely passive, even useless, role. (Hébert and Link 1989: 48)

In the next section, we consider two alternative theoretical perspectives that have attempted to address this problem and shed new light on the entrepreneurial function.

13.3.4 The entrepreneur returns: neo-Austrian and evolutionary economics

During the twentieth century, the entrepreneur returned to mainstream economics by a number of different routes, the most significant influences being **neo-Austrian** and **evolutionary economics.** Though they are often treated as alternative perspectives on the entrepreneurial function, they can be seen as complementary:

- **Neo-Austrian economics:** This approach derives its name from the home country of its most well-known founding figures, Ludwig von Mises and Frederick Hayek. The tradition remains influential in economics, and is also having an increasing impact on entrepreneurship research (Chiles et al. 2010). Neo-Austrians challenged neoclassical assumptions about resource allocation. They drew attention to the many forms of economic activity that are based on 'local' knowledge, and argued that these seemingly ordinary activities should have a more prominent place in economic theory:

  > [T]he shipper who earns his living from using otherwise empty or half-filled journeys of tramp steamers, or the estate agent whose whole knowledge is almost exclusively one of temporary opportunities, or the arbitrageur [i.e. intermediary] who gains from local differences of commodity prices, all are performing eminently useful functions based on special knowledge of circumstances of the fleeting moment not known to others. (Hayek 1945: 522)

  Building on the ideas of Cantillon and Say, neo-Austrians argued that exploiting 'special knowledge' represents a distinctive entrepreneurial function. Entrepreneurial profits are earned when people make use of their knowledge (NB: this argument contrasts with another influential research strand in economics, in which entrepreneurial profits are a reward for bearing uncertainty (Knight 1921)). Israel Kirzner has refined earlier neo-Austrian ideas, arguing that profits could be attributed to entrepreneurial 'alertness' to previously unidentified opportunities (Kirzner 1979). The typical 'Kirznerian' entrepreneur identifies opportunities to exploit price differentials, typically due to over-supply of products in one location or unsatisfied customer demand in another. By pursuing these opportunities, entrepreneurs bring markets to life, and in the process help to restore equilibrium. As von Mises recognised, these entrepreneurs were also free to make errors, which could have an impact on the economy as well as creating further opportunities for others (Swedberg 2000: 21).

- **Evolutionary economics:** This term covers a great variety of contributions but is primarily concerned with the changes that take place over time in economic systems, and in their component parts (i.e. it has been applied at various levels including individual firms, industry sectors and national economies) (Witt 2008). As the name suggests, this approach to economics addresses the three fundamental mechanisms of selection, retention, and variation (or creativity). Evolution in the natural world operates through biological mechanisms that are essentially 'blind' (Dawkins 2006), meaning that they are not based on any plan or purpose. By contrast, in economics these terms describe social mechanisms that are driven by *conscious* human actions, and where entrepreneurs can play a central role. One of the leading influences on this approach, Joseph Schumpeter, admired neoclassical theory but developed an early ambition to replace it with a more dynamic alternative. Schumpeter identifies five ways in which innovative entrepreneurial activity creates variety by introducing 'new combinations' of productive means, including the introduction of a new good or a new method of production, opening a new market, 'conquest' of new sources of raw materials or 'half-manufactured goods', and creating a new way of organising an industry (ibid., 51–2). These new combinations are important from an evolutionary perspective, because they transform the economic conditions for other entrepreneurs, disrupting existing patterns and creating new opportunities for investment, growth and employment. Researchers working in this evolutionary tradition have since discovered a great deal about the process of economic development, including the ways in which industries tend to rise and fall (Section 14.3). In his book, *Capitalism, Socialism and Democracy*, Schumpeter describes a characteristic evolutionary pattern of innovation, boom, and recession that has been repeated many times, and which he termed 'creative destruction':

> *The opening up of new markets, foreign or domestic, and the organizational development from the craft shop to such concerns as U.S. Steel illustrate the same process of industrial mutation – if I may use that biological term – that incessantly revolutionizes the economic structure from within, incessantly destroying the old one, incessantly creating a new one. This process of Creative Destruction is the essential fact about capitalism. (Schumpeter [1942] 2010: 83)*

Schumpeter's most famous statements about entrepreneurship are taken from Chapter 2 of his earlier work, *The Theory of Economic Development*, which was first published in English in 1934. For Schumpeter, the entrepreneurial function is about 'innovation' (i.e. carrying the new combination into practice). Though it can involve the same people, this task requires an entirely different set of capabilities to 'invention' (e.g. creating a new technology). Innovation is also much more demanding than managing existing activities, where you can rely on established routines and experiences:

> *Carrying out a new plan and acting according to a customary one are things as different as making a road and walking along it. (Schumpeter [1934] 2004: 64)*

These two contrasting perspectives have helped to reinstate entrepreneurship as a key element in economic research and policy-making. The entrepreneurial functions depicted by these researchers are often treated as opposites, with Kirzner's entrepreneur making a profit while moving the market towards equilibrium and Schumpeter's entrepreneur doing the same while creating a new *dis*equilibrium. Technical distinctions of this kind remain important to economists, even though they may be of little interest to the practising entrepreneur (Swedberg 2000: 21). In this particular case, there are signs of a move towards integration (e.g. Kirzner 2008).

Case 13.3 builds on this discussion with an example of economics-based research, which examines knowledge spillover theory (Section 13.2.3) and how entrepreneurial activity influences the development of today's globalised and knowledge-based economies.

CASE 13.3

Entrepreneurship in the knowledge economy

This case is based on extracts from a study by three leading entrepreneurship scholars, David Audretsch, Max Keilbach, and Erik Lehmann (Audretsch et al. 2006). The case focuses on three themes that are addressed in the book: the role played by entrepreneurship in a modern knowledge-based economy; the sources of entrepreneurial opportunity in such an economy; and the idea of entrepreneurial activity as 'creative construction'.

KNOWLEDGE, VALUE CREATION, AND GROWTH

'The role of entrepreneurship in the economy and, in particular, the impact of entrepreneurship on economic growth and employment has evolved considerably since World War II. In the post-war economy, investments in physical capital were the driver of economic

growth. Economic activity based on physical capital was most efficiently organized in large-scale operations. In the physical capital economy, there was little room for entrepreneurship and small business, at least not as an engine of economic growth. At best, small firms were tolerated for social and political values, and the ensuing inefficiency associated with small-scale production was endured as the cost of such non-economic

goals. As recognition grew, both among scholars and policy-makers that knowledge was also a key factor shaping economic growth, a new set of public policy instruments for generating economic growth became prominent, with a focus on research, intellectual property, and human capital. If anything, the inclusion of knowledge as a factor of production served only to reinforce the view that small firms were anathema to economic growth. Recognition of the model of the knowledge production function seemed to mandate economic organisation in large-scale enterprises in the knowledge economy, just as it had in the capital economy. In fact, small firms and entrepreneurship emerged as essential to economic growth in the 1990s. Part of this recognition came from the empirical or policy experience emanating from investments in new knowledge in the absence of entrepreneurship. Much has been made about the so-called European Paradox, wherein high levels of investment in new knowledge exist from private firms as well as public research institutes and universities. Countries such as Sweden rank among the highest in terms of investment in research, at least as measured by the ratio of R&D [i.e. investment in research and development] to GDP. Similarly, levels of human capital and education in Sweden as well as throughout many parts of Europe rank among the highest in the world. Yet growth rates remained stagnant and employment creation sluggish throughout the 1990s and into the new century. [...] [A] growing consensus has emerged that investment in new economic knowledge alone will not guarantee economic growth and employment creation. Rather, key institutional mechanisms are a prerequisite for such knowledge investments to become transmitted and transformed into economic knowledge, through the process of spillovers and commercialization. Entrepreneurship has emerged as a driving force of economic growth because it is an important conduit of knowledge spillovers and commercialization. Thus, as knowledge has become more important as a factor of production, knowledge spillovers have also become more important as a source of economic growth. Entrepreneurship takes on new importance in a knowledge economy because it serves as a key mechanism by which knowledge created in one organization becomes commercialized in a new enterprise, thereby contributing to the economic growth, employment, and vitality of the overall economy.' (Audretsch et al. 2006: 33)

THE SOURCES OF ENTREPRENEURIAL OPPORTUNITIES

'While much has been made about the key role played by the recognition of opportunities in the cognitive process underlying the decision to become an entrepreneur, relatively little has been written about the actual source of such entrepreneurial opportunities. The Knowledge Spillover Theory of Entrepreneurship identifies one source of entrepreneurial opportunities: new knowledge and ideas. In particular, this theory posits that new knowledge and ideas created in one context, such as a research laboratory in a large corporation or a university, but left uncommercialized or not vigorously pursued by the source, generates entrepreneurial opportunities. Thus, in this view, one mechanism for recognizing new opportunities and actually implementing them by starting a new firm involves knowledge spillovers. This implies that the source of knowledge and ideas, and the organization actually making (at least some of) the investments to produce these, is not the same as the organization actually attempting to commercialize and appropriate the value of that knowledge – the new firm. If the use of that knowledge by the entrepreneur does not involve full payment to the firm making the investment that originally produced that knowledge, such as a licence or royalty, then the entrepreneurial act of starting a new firm serves as a mechanism for knowledge spillovers.' (Audretsch et al. 2006: 39)

ENTREPRENEURSHIP AS 'CREATIVE CONSTRUCTION'

'We would not want to argue that the view of the youthful Schumpeter ([1934] 2004: xxvii) was wrong about "a perennial gale of creative destruction is going through capitalism." However, it does seem that twenty-first century entrepreneurship has more to do with creative construction than with creative destruction. By facilitating the spillover of knowledge investments that might otherwise remain uncommercialized, entrepreneurship takes little away from the incumbent enterprises, but instead creates alternative opportunities for employment. Rather, as we suggested [in Chapter 2], the destruction comes from the side of globalization that presents competitive alternatives to standardized production in high-cost *Standort* [i.e. a specific geographical location]. This destructive element, emanating from globalization, comes with or without entrepreneurship. The exposure of a *Standort* to global competition has less to do with its endowment of entrepreneurship capital and more to do with its traditional source for economic activity. By contrast, the construction comes from an entirely different source: the entrepreneurship capital of that *Standort*. Perhaps because he dealt with a singular closed and unglobalized economy in both his early (1911) and later (1942) writings, Schumpeter did not consider that the destructive force would actually come from opportunities coming from outside of the domestic economy. In contrast, the entrepreneurial opportunities that might not otherwise have been pursued

(Continued)

(Continued)

come from within the *Standort*. Thus, rather than serving as a force for destruction of the status quo, entrepreneurship serves as a constructive force for a new economic alternative from knowledge and ideas that otherwise might have not been commercialized. To the individual, the knowledge accessed to reach the entrepreneurial decision is virtually a free good. To the firm or non-profit organization, the knowledge has no *a priori* economic value. Whereas Schumpeter's ([1942] 2010) pronouncement that innovation is becoming routinized may have been correct, the generation of entrepreneurial opportunities and their concomitant assessment by economic agents are anything but routine. Thus, entrepreneurship is a constructive force because it increases the value of knowledge and ideas that might otherwise not be pursued and commercialized.' (Audretsch et al. 2006: 191–2)

QUESTIONS

1.   How has entrepreneurship changed since the mid-twentieth century?

2.   How can knowledge spillovers lead to new entrepreneurial opportunities?

3.   What are the practical implications of these arguments for: (a) governments seeking to defend their economies against global competition; (b) entrepreneurs seeking to make use of new knowledge?

Source: Audretsch et al. (2006): extracts reproduced by permission of Oxford University Press.

13.4 ENTREPRENEURSHIP AS DYSFUNCTIONAL

13.4.1 Economically 'unproductive' and 'destructive' enterprise

Much of the economics literature assumes that entrepreneurship is, by definition 'a good thing'. Research has indicated that increased levels of entrepreneurial activity are associated with positive economic outcomes, including more employment opportunities, less unemployment, lower prices, more rapid technological innovation, and increased rates of economic growth. While there are good reasons for this emphasis, it is also important to consider how entrepreneurial activity can become dysfunctional and inflict damage on the world's economic systems. The global financial crisis of 2007–10 was a recent dramatic example, with serious repercussions for individuals, businesses, and communities around the world (Stiglitz 2010). In a widely cited paper, the US economist and entrepreneurship researcher, William Baumol distinguished between economically 'productive', 'unproductive', and 'destructive' forms of entrepreneurship (Baumol 1990). Productive entrepreneurship has a beneficial impact (e.g. increasing incomes and employment). By contrast, unproductive entrepreneurship (e.g. 'rent-seeking' activities, such as tax avoidance) has negative effects, while destructive entrepreneurship (e.g. organised crime) can undermine an entire economy.

Baumol's historical study explores how entrepreneurial resources have been reallocated between these three roles over the centuries. This is an important, yet relatively under-researched area, which is now attracting the attention of researchers (e.g. Sobel 2009; Minniti 2008) and policy-makers (Section 15.3). For example, Douhan and Henrekson (2008) take a political economy approach to the subject, arguing that entrepreneurs can influence formal economic institutions in at least two ways: through direct involvement in politics, by using their entrepreneurial talent to wield de facto political power and by altering the effect of formal institutions. These influences are evident in the context of the recent financial and economic crises, which have been attributed, at least in part, to unproductive and destructive types of entrepreneurial activity. The authors offer a typology of different kinds of entrepreneurship, sub-divided into activity that either 'abides with' (i.e. follows) existing institutions or attempts to 'evade' (i.e. break the rules) (ibid., 5). For example, entrepreneurial business owners who pursue new opportunities to generate wealth and employment while also complying with current rules and regulations would fit into the 'Productive/abide' category, but if they decided to use their entrepreneurial abilities to avoid some costly health and safety regulations, their activity might be described as 'Productive/evade'. At the other extreme, the activities of illegal syndicates, mafia groupings, and others engaged in sophisticated frauds and economic crimes could fit into the 'Destructive or predatory' category, with either 'evade' (where there are still rules, regulations, and enforcement agencies in place to challenge them) or 'abide' (in failed states, where such activity has become the institutional norm).

You might like to identify some examples of kinds of activity that would fit into each category. In some cases it may be difficult to weigh up the economic and non-economic impacts of entrepreneurial activity. For example, a few years ago there were plans to open a number of 'mega-casinos' in the UK. Arguments about economic benefits such as job creation, economic development and urban regeneration, were countered by concerns about negative social impacts, including potential increases in problem gambling, which could also be presented as externalities in economic terms. Chapter 15 considers the policy implications.

13.5 PRACTICAL IMPLICATIONS

Economic approaches are important in examining many aspects of entrepreneurship. But what is the practical value of economic research for prospective or practising entrepreneurs, and for others interested in entrepreneurship? Having reviewed a number of sub-fields, we have seen how economics provides insights into both the impacts of entrepreneurial activity and the factors that encourage or constrain it, such as credit rationing (Blumberg and Letterie 2008). The following examples illustrate how you might apply this knowledge to a new venture:

- **Evidence and patterns:** Entrepreneurs can use economic data, such as new firm formation rates and firm survival rates, to guide their decisions in setting up or growing a venture. For example, you might decide to reconsider your ambitions found a new technology-based empire having seen recent data on the failure rate of new firms in that industry sector. If the economic data are more positive, you may also make use of them to support a new venture proposal, demonstrating the attractiveness of your target market or showing how your new organisation is responding to recent industry trends.

- **Entrepreneurial finance:** Research on the financing of entrepreneurial ventures, including the phenomenon of crowdfunding (Case 13.2), is particularly relevant to new start-ups. The findings summarised in this chapter provide an important warning to new entrepreneurs, particularly those who are seeking finance in unfamiliar industry sectors, or who are attempting to fund unproven technologies, product concepts, and business models. On a more positive note, recent research in this area has also highlighted a number of practical techniques that entrepreneurs can use to deal with financial constraints.

- **Economic development:** This might seem a rather low-priority area for entrepreneurs preoccupied with the practical demands of creating a successful venture. However, it may be worth considering how your venture is contributing to the development of your local town, city, or region. Politicians and public officials can be important gatekeepers and in some situations, demonstrating the broader economic value of your venture (e.g. its capacity to generate local employment and income), could prove worthwhile.

- **Economics and policy-making:** Economic perspectives have been particularly influential in policy terms, so it is obvious that the policy-makers need to have a good grounding in economic methods and in the research evidence that it produces. We return to this theme in other Part Two chapters, and Chapter 15 in particular.

Economics has made a major contribution to our understanding of entrepreneurship, but we have also seen some of its limitations. Some of the most influential economic thinkers, including Joseph Schumpeter, have recognised the need for multidisciplinary approaches. Economists can refine their theories, improve their methods, and make more sense of their evidence by interacting with researchers from other disciplines:

> *[E]conomists who study entrepreneurship should in the future begin to borrow a little more freely from other disciplines where appropriate. For example, sociologists can tell us a lot about trust, and the basis for social relationships within teams. While the study of trust is beginning to make itself felt in economics, the economics of entrepreneurship is yet to incorporate it in any serious way. Other examples abound. The key point here is that the economics of entrepreneurship has nothing to lose and much to gain from occasionally looking over the fence to learn from other disciplines. (Parker 2005: 43–4)*

The Part Two chapters encourage this kind of exchange, by examining entrepreneurship from other disciplinary perspectives, including psychology, sociology, geography, history, and policy studies. This is also one of the themes of Case 13.4, which considers how entrepreneurship can be theorised.

CASE 13.4

Entrepreneurship: theory, networks, history

This case is based on the economist Professor Mark Casson's book, *Entrepreneurship: Theory, Networks, History* (Casson 2010). It builds on ideas introduced in his classic work, *The Entrepreneur: An Economic Theory* (Casson [1982] 2003). Though grounded in economics, the book explores the relationship between entrepreneurship studies and other disciplines, including sociology, social psychology, international relations, management, and business history. As Professor Casson explains, the theory of entrepreneurship set out in the book was originally developed to 'plug a gap' in economic theory, including its capacity to explain how firms and markets are created:

> *Conventional economics, it is often pointed out, is inherently static; even growth is often analysed as a steady-state process. By recognizing the importance of a specific class of people dedicated to the pursuit of change, the study of entrepreneurship transforms static analysis into dynamic analysis. (Casson 2010: 372)*

Entrepreneurship research can also address another fundamental problem in economics. Because it lacks a satisfactory theory of success, conventional theory, 'does not explain fully why certain people are able to derive so much profit from the market process, nor why some small firms grow into successful large firms whilst many others fail' (Casson 2010: 372). In the following extract, Professor Casson introduces the concept of entrepreneurial judgement, and explains how it helps us to address these issues. He begins with a review of the leading traditional (or 'canonical') theories of entrepreneurship.

THE THEORY OF ENTREPRENEURSHIP: FROM CANTILLON TO KIRZNER

It is the function of the entrepreneur that is important – 'an entrepreneur is what an entrepreneur does'. But what does an entrepreneur do? The canonical literature suggests a variety of tasks, including 'high-level' activities like innovation and risk taking, and also 'low level' activities such as spotting opportunities for arbitrage. The theory presented in this book is based on a synthesis of the principal insights set out by the canonical authors on the subject.

- **Cantillon and risk:** The term 'entrepreneur' appears to have been introduced into economic theory by Richard Cantillon (1759), an Irish economist of French descent. According to Cantillon, the entrepreneur is a specialist in taking on risk. He 'insures' workers by buying their output for resale before consumers have indicated how much they are willing to pay for it. The workers receive an assured income (in the short run, at least), while the entrepreneur bears the risk caused by price fluctuations in consumer markets.

- **Knight and uncertainty:** This idea was refined by the US economist Frank Knight (1921), who distinguished between risk, which is insurable, and uncertainty, which is not. Risk refers to recurrent events whose relative frequency is known from past experience, whilst uncertainty relates to unique events whose probability can only be subjectively estimated. Knight thought that most of the risks relating to production and marketing fall into the latter category. Since business owners cannot insure against these risks, they are left to bear them by themselves. Profit is a reward for bearing this uninsurable risk: it is the reward of the pure entrepreneur. With freedom of entry into industries, profits in one industry can exceed profits in another industry in the long run only if the uncertainties are greater in the more profitable industry – in other words, if the demands on entrepreneurship are greater in that industry.

- **Schumpeter and the Entrepreneur-Hero:** Popular notions of entrepreneurship are based on the heroic vision put forward by Joseph A. Schumpeter ([1934] 2004). The entrepreneur is visualised as someone who creates new industries and thereby precipitates major structural changes in the economy. The entrepreneur innovates by carrying out new combinations; he is not a pure inventor, because he adopts the inventions made by others, nor is he a financier, because he relies on bankers to fund his investments. The entrepreneur takes the crucial decision to commit resources to the exploitation of new ideas. An element of calculation is involved, but it is not pure calculation, because not all of the relevant factors can be accurately measured. He is motivated by profit, but not purely by profit: the other motivators include the 'dream and the will to found a private kingdom'; the 'will to conquer: the impulse to fight, to prove oneself superior to others'; and the 'joy of creating'.

(Continued)

(Continued)

- **Marshall and low-level entrepreneurship:** Schumpeter was concerned with the heroic or 'high-level' kind of entrepreneurship that, historically, has led to the creation of railways, the development of the chemical industry, and the growth of integrated oil companies. A weakness of his analysis is that it leaves little room for the much more common, but no less important, 'low-level' entrepreneurship carried on by small firms. Few economic histories nowadays would ignore the important role of small firms in economic development. Alfred Marshall (1919) emphasised their importance and described the role of these firms in some detail, but critically omitted them from his formal analysis of supply and demand. Given the techniques that were available to him, Marshall could only model equilibrium situations, and so could not fit entrepreneurship into his analysis. But he explicitly recognised the importance of low-level entrepreneurship.

- **The Austrian School and arbitrage:** The essence of low-level entrepreneurship can be explained by the Austrian approach of Friedrich A. von Hayek (1937) and Israel M. Kirzner (1973). Entrepreneurs are middlemen who provide price quotations as an invitation to trade. While bureaucrats in a socialist economy have little incentive to discover prices for themselves, entrepreneurs in a market economy are motivated to do so by profit opportunities. They hope to profit by buying cheap and selling dear. In the long run, such differentials, once discovered, generate a profit for the entrepreneur. The difficulty with the Austrian approach is, however, that it isolates the entrepreneur from the organisation of routine activities, which is so character-istic of a firm. It fits an individual dealer or speculator far better than it fits a small manufacturer, say, because the latter has to oversee an organisation whereas the former does not. For a fuller understanding of entrepreneurship we need to clarify the link between the entrepreneur and the firm.

JUDGEMENTAL DECISION-MAKING

The insights of these economists can be synthesised by identifying an entrepreneurial func-tion that is common to all approaches. This is the exercise of judgement in decision-making (Casson [1982] 2003). Judgement is the ability to come to a sound, defensible decision in the absence of complete information. A middleman who buys before he knows the price at which he can resell must make a judgement about what the future price will be, for instance. Or an arbitrager must make a judgement about where price differentials are most likely to be found, in order to focus his price discovery effort on a suitable segment of the market. An innovator must assess whether a new product will prove attractive to consum-ers, or whether a new technology will really cut costs by as much as its inventor claims.

Examples of judgemental decisions include the following:

- An opportunity to exploit a new technology has been identified and a quick decision is required in order to pre-empt a rival. The investment is irreversible – i.e. the costs are sunk – so that a mistake cannot be corrected afterwards. The revenue stream is uncertain, and cannot be guaranteed by forward sales of output. Should the investment be undertaken right away?

- A new source of competition has just emerged from a firm in a newly-industrialising country. Should the dominant firm in the industry cut its price, or can it rely upon its existing customers not to switch to the rival firm? Is the rival firm producing more cheaply because of low-cost labour and/or subsidies, about which nothing can be done, or is it using more efficient techniques which ought to be imitated?

Judgemental decisions normally require the synthesis of different types of information. The high-level entrepreneur of the Schumpeterian type, for example, needs to synthesise information about new inventions with information about trends in product demand, and in the prices of raw materials, in order to determine whether an innovation is worthwhile. If the entrepreneur does not possess this information himself then he must know where to acquire it. If some of the information is confidential then it will have to be acquired through personal contact rather than from published sources. The entrepreneur therefore needs to create a network of contacts that can feed him the information that he requires.

A synthesis of information has commercial value only if it relates to a profit opportunity. If everyone recognises the same opportunity at the same time then profits will be competed away. As rival entrepreneurs bid for up the price of inputs, and the prospect of increased supplies drives output prices down, everyone's profits will disappear. The only beneficiaries will be the customers and the suppliers. Profit opportunities arise on a regular basis when economic conditions are volatile, because the allocation of resources continually needs to be adjusted. In addition, long-term trends such as the accumulation of knowledge, the growth of population, and the depletion of non-renewable resources also create a need for change. When incentives work well, profit is the reward that the entrepreneur obtains for expediting economic adjustments and, in some cases, for making adjustments that might otherwise never occur.

If information were freely available, and could be costlessly processed, then there would be no need for judgement. Every decision would be correctly taken and no mistakes would ever be made. But in practice information is costly. It is time-consuming to make and record observations. Human memory capacity is limited. Interpretative skills are scarce. Above all, communication is an expensive process. It follows that people do not have all the information they need when taking a decision. When decision-makers cannot afford to collect all the information they need, they have to act under uncertainty. But the uncertainty faced by one person may be different from the uncertainty faced by another person. Sources of primary information are highly localised; for example, only people 'on the spot' can directly observe an event. Different people in different places will therefore have different perceptions of any given situation. They may therefore make different decisions. The nature of the decision therefore depends on the identity of the person who makes it. The entrepreneur matters because their judgement of a situation is potentially unique.

Not all information is reliable. The senses may be confused, but the biggest risk relates to information obtained from other people. The other person may be unreliable, or their message may be misunderstood. Alternatively, they may set out deliberately to mislead, so that they can extract more profit from their information for themselves. One person may check their information sources more carefully than another, and therefore stand less chance of being misled. The interpretation of information may differ too. Different people may hold different theories about the way the environment works. As any social scientist knows, it is difficult to test conclusively between rival theories because of data limitations. Thus different theories coexist because of data limitations, leading to different interpretations of similar evidence. In a business context, entrepreneurs may act differently on the basis of similar information because they interpret the situation in different ways (Harper 1996).

(Continued)

(Continued)

If a situation recurs frequently, it is worthwhile investigating it carefully in order to find the theory that fits it best. This theory identifies which information is required to make the correct decision. Arrangements can be made to collect the information on a regular basis, so that it is always to hand when required. Whenever a decision needs to be made, this information is processed using an appropriate decision rule in order to arrive at a correct decision. If some information is very costly to collect, then its costs have to be traded off against its benefits to arrive at the correct decision rule. This rule does not guarantee the correct decision; but it is optimal in economic terms, in the sense that it trades off the risk of a mistake against the saving in information cost.

Once this optimal decision rule is known there is no further need for the entrepreneur. Everyone knows how the decision rule has been specified, and so no reward can be earned by those who take the decision properly. Now consider the opposite case in which no such rule is available. This is likely to involve a novel situation. It either has no precedent, or is so unusual that it never pays to investigate it fully. Nobody knows the correct decision rule, and nobody systematically collects information on the situation. The more complex the situation, the more inadequate the theory is likely to be. There may be no theory at all, or there may be a range of rival theories which it is difficult to choose between. There may be no information, or a surfeit of information, because no one is quite sure what information is relevant and what is not. Matters are even worse if the decision has to be arrived at quickly – for example, because the situation is unstable, and will continue to deteriorate until something is done. This is the kind of situation that calls for the most intensive judgement. To improvise a decision quickly, people have to rely on the theories with which they are already familiar, and the information that they can retrieve from their memory. Differences in theories, combined with differences in memories, lead to differences in decisions. In the intermediate case, the situations are less complex, more relevant information may be available and situations less volatile. But once again, the people with the most relevant theories and the most comprehensive memories will tend to make the best decisions. These are the entrepreneurs – they possess the quality of judgement required to improvise a decision successfully when no agreed decision rule is available. Entrepreneurs – whether at a high or low level – are therefore those who exercise entrepreneurial judgement.

QUESTIONS

1. Why it is important for economists to develop a better theory of entrepreneurship?

2. What practical steps can entrepreneurs take to ensure they are capable of: (a) synthesising different kinds of information effectively; (b) obtaining the most accurate and reliable information; (c) improvising important decisions under intensive time pressure?

3. In what ways (if any) would you expect entrepreneurial judgement to operate differently in social and commercial enterprises?

4. Search business news websites (or other case studies in this book) and identify one example of an entrepreneurial judgement that proved to be correct and one that turned out to be incorrect. How do the explanations given for the different outcomes compare to the arguments presented in this case?

Source: Casson (2010): extract reproduced by permission of Edward Elgar Publishing.

13.6 SUMMARY

- Economists have explored entrepreneurial activity from within several distinct traditions. Neoclassical theory has provided limited insights, but there have also been contributions from mainstream economics, neo-Austrians, and evolutionary theorists.

- Empirical studies have provided evidence on the relationship between entrepreneurial activity and specific economic indicators, notably employment creation, economic growth, technological innovation, and competitiveness.

- Economic theory has helped to clarify our understanding of the entrepreneurial function, but there are many unresolved issues, some of which require the application of non-economic concepts, theories, and evidence.

- Researchers have also examined how entrepreneurial activity can generate economically unproductive and destructive outcomes; this research field remains under-developed, but is attracting increasingly interest.

- Economic theory and research evidence can have practical value for prospective and practising entrepreneurs, and for policy-makers, particularly when combined with insights from other disciplines.

Practical activities

1. Neo-Austrian school researchers have investigated how entrepreneurs identify opportunities arising from disequilibrium in a product or factor market (i.e. a temporary difference in supply and demand of raw materials, intermediate or finished goods and services). Using the illustrations in Section 13.3 as a starting-point, identify three real-world examples. How might you exploit these differences? What practical obstacles do you envisage?

2. Re-read Schumpeter's five cases of 'new combinations' (Section 13.3.4). Identify *one* real-world example of an entrepreneurial venture that is based on each of the types listed, and present as a simple table. If you are unable to identify an example, try to imagine ventures that would fit each description.

3. As an extension of Activity 2, try to identify *one* entrepreneurial venture in each of the following categories: (a) commercial manufacturing businesses; (b) social enterprises involved in manufacturing; (c) commercial service-based businesses; (d) social enterprises providing services.

Discussion topics

1. There is a continuing debate among economists over the role of entrepreneurial activity in generating employment and economic growth. Sometimes there seems to be a tension between what is good for the local economy, and what is in the national interest. Join the debate by arguing either for or against one of the following:

   (a) Small firms are better for the economy than large corporations.

   (b) Start-up ventures are better for the economy than established firms.

   (c) Competition between social enterprises generates more social value than cooperation.

2. Re-read the discussion about 'productive, unproductive and destructive forms of entrepreneurship' (Section 11.4). Are governments justified in taking action to encourage

economically productive forms of entrepreneurial activity, and to discourage those that are economically destructive? Do your arguments extend beyond the economic sphere to cover the social and environmental impacts of entrepreneurial activity?

3. Which of the following *economic* functions of entrepreneurs do you consider to be the most important? Select your 'top five' and give the reasons for your choice:

    • To create new firms.
    • To 'grow' existing firms.
    • To make industries more competitive.
    • To create new employment.
    • To stimulate innovation
    • To promote economic regeneration.
    • To generate taxable profits.
    • Any other *economic* functions you have identified.

Recommended reading

These readings address two important topics in entrepreneurship research and are recommended for anyone wanting to build on the material covered in this chapter. Recommended readings have been selected from leading Sage journals and are freely available for readers of this textbook to download via the Online Resources.

Nel, E. and Stevenson, T. (2014) 'The catalysts of small town economic development in a free market economy: a case study of New Zealand'. *Local Economy*, 29, 4–5: 486–502.

This article examines the impact of neoliberal policy changes on smaller and more marginal urban communities in New Zealand. The authors drawn on statistical indicators of change and a study of 68 small towns to identify common catalysts and barriers to economic development and diversification. They find that local entrepreneurs can play a key role in improving economic wellbeing, in particular by encouraging others relocate to their town.

Wilson, N., Wright, M. and Altanlar, A. (2013) 'The survival of newly-incorporated companies and founding director characteristics'. *International Small Business Journal*, 32, 7: 733–58.

This article applies econometric techniques to examine the success or failure of newly-incorporated companies. It makes use of a unique dataset of more than 5.8 million observations to test hypotheses regarding director characteristics, while also controlling for macro-economic conditions, recursive relationships and non-insolvency exits.

References

Acs, Z. J. and Audretsch, D. B. (eds) (2003) *Handbook of Entrepreneurship Research: An Interdisciplinary Survey and Introduction*. Dordrecht: Kluwer.

Acs, Z. J. and Storey, D. J. (2004) 'Introduction: entrepreneurship and economic development'. *Regional Studies*, 38, 8: 871–7.

Arrow, K. ([1959] 2010) 'Economic welfare and the allocation of resources for invention in the rate and direction of inventive activity'. Santa Monica CA: Rand Corporation.

Audretsch, D. B., Keilbach, M., and Lehmann, E. (2006) *Entrepreneurship and Economic Growth*. Oxford: Oxford University Press.

Audretsch, D. B., van der Horst, R., Kwaak, T., and Thurik, R. (2009) 'First section of the annual report on EU small and medium-sized enterprises'. Zoetermeer: EIM Business and Policy Research. Available at http://ec.europa.eu/enterprise/ (accessed 21 April 2010).

Baumol, W. (1990) 'Entrepreneurship: productive, unproductive, and destructive'. *Journal of Political Economy*, 98: 893–921.

Baumol, W. (2002) *Free Market Innovation Machine: Analyzing the Growth Miracle of Capitalism*. Princeton: Princeton University Press.

Best, M. H. (2001) *The New Competitive Advantage: The Renewal of American Industry*. Oxford: Oxford University Press.

Birley, S. (ed.) (1998) *Entrepreneurship*. Aldershot: Dartmouth.

Blaug, M. (2000) 'Entrepreneurship before and after Schumpeter'. In R. Swedberg (ed.), op. cit. (76–88).

Blumberg, B. F. and Letterie, W. (2008) 'Business starters and credit rationing'. *Small Business economics*, 30, 2: 187–200.

Bourdieu, P. and Wacquant, L. J. (1992) *An Invitation to Reflexive Sociology*. Chicago and London: University of Chicago Press.

Cantillon, R. E. ([1755] 1959) *Essai sur la nature du commerce in général* [Essay on the nature of trade in general] (tr. H. Higgs). London: Frank Cass. http://www.econlib.org/library (accessed 21 April 2010).

Casson, M. C. (ed.) (1990) *Entrepreneurship*. Aldershot: Edward Elgar.

Casson, M. C. (1995) *Entrepreneurship and Business Culture*. Cheltenham: Edward Elgar.

Casson, M. C. ([1982] 2003) *The Entrepreneur: An Economic Theory* (2nd edn). Cheltenham: Edward Elgar.

Casson, M. C. (2010) *Entrepreneurship – Theory, Networks, History*. Cheltenham: Edward Elgar.

Casson, M., Yeung, B., Basu, A., and Wadeson, N. (2008) *The Oxford Handbook of Entrepreneurship*. Oxford: Oxford University Press.

Chiles, T. H., Tuggle, C. S., McMullen, J. S., Greening, D. W., and Bierman, L. (2010) 'Dynamic creation: extending the radical Austrian approach to entrepreneurship'. *Organization Studies*, 31, 1: 7–46.

Dawkins, R. (2006) *The Blind Watchmaker* (new edition). London: Penguin.

Douhan, R. and Henrekson, M. (2008) 'The political economy of entrepreneurship: an introduction. In: Henrekson, M. and Douhan, R. (eds) *The Political Economy of Entrepreneurship, Vols. I and II*. Cheltenham: Edward Elgar.

Edmondson, A. C. and McManus, S. E. (2007) 'Methodological fit in management field research'. *Academy of Management Review*, 32, 4: 1246–64.

Eisenhardt, K. M. (1989) 'Building theories from case study research'. *Academy of Management Review*, 14, 4: 532–50.

Eurostat (2015) Statistics on small and medium-sized enterprises: dependent and independent SMEs and large enterprises. http://ec.europa.eu/eurostat/statistics-explained/ (accessed 7 March 2017).

Foray, D. (2004) *The Economics of Knowledge*. Cambridge MA: MIT Press.

Foss, N. J. (ed.) (1997) *Resources, Firms and Strategies: A Reader in the Resource-Based Theory of the Firm*. Oxford: Oxford University Press.

Foss, N.J. and Klein, P.G. (eds) (2002) *Entrepreneurship and the Firm: Austrian Perspectives on Economic Organization*. Cheltenham: Edward Elgar.

Greene, F. J. and Storey, D. J. (2010) *Small Business and Entrepreneurship*. Harlow: Pearson.

Harper, D. A. (1996) *Entrepreneurship and the Market Process: An Inquiry into the Growth of Knowledge*, London: Routledge.

Hayek, F. A. (1937) 'Economics and knowledge'. *Economica*, n.s. 4: 33–54.

Hayek, F. A. (1945) 'The use of knowledge in society'. *American Economic Review*, 35: 519–30.

Hébert, R. F. and Link, A. N. (1989) 'In search of the meaning of entrepreneurship'. *Small Business Economics*, 1, 39–49.

Hébert, R. F. and Link, A. N. (2006) 'Historical perspectives on the entrepreneur'. *Foundations and Trends in Entrepreneurship*, 2, 4: 261–408.

Jevons, W. S. ([1911] 1965) *The Theory of Political Economy* (4th edn). New York: Sentry Press.

Khanna, T. (2008) *Billions of Entrepreneurs: How China and India Are Reshaping Their Futures – and Yours*. Cambridge MA: Harvard Business School Press.

Kirzner, I. M. (1973) *Competition and Entrepreneurship*. Chicago: University of Chicago Press.

Kirzner, I. M. (1979) *Perception, Opportunity and Profit*. Chicago: University of Chicago Press.

Kirzner, I. M. (2008) 'The alert and creative entrepreneur; a clarification'. (IFN Working Paper No. 760.) Stockholm: Research Institute of Industrial Economics.

Knight, F. H. (1921) *Risk, Uncertainty and Profit*. Boston, MA: Houghton Mifflin.

Lee, S. L., Florida, R., and Acs, Z. J. (2004) 'Creativity and entrepreneurship: a regional analysis of new firm formation'. *Regional Studies*, 38, 8: 879–91.

Lehner, O. M. (2013) 'Crowdfunding social ventures: a model and research agenda'. *Venture Capital*, 15, 4: 289–311.

Lehner, O. M. (2014) 'The formation and interplay of social capital in crowdfunded social ventures'. *Entrepreneurship & Regional Development*, 26, 5–6: 478–99.

Lehner, O. M. and Nicholls, A. (2014) 'Social finance and crowdfunding for social enterprises: a public–private case study providing legitimacy and leverage'. *Venture Capital*, 16, 3: 271–86.

Lehner, O. M., Grabmann, E., and Ennsgraber, C. (2015) 'Entrepreneurial implications of crowdfunding as alternative funding source for innovations'. *Venture Capital*, 17, 1–2: 171–89.

Loasby, B. (1976) *Choice, Complexity and Ignorance*. Cambridge: Cambridge University Press.

Marshall, A. M. (1919) *Industry and Trade*. London: Macmillan.

Mason, C. M. (2009) 'Public policy support for the informal venture capital market in Europe'. *International Small Business Journal*, 27, 5: 536–56.

McCraw, T. (2007) *Prophet of Innovation: Joseph Schumpeter and Creative Destruction*. Cambridge MA: Harvard University Press.

Mehlum, H., Moene, K, and Torvik, R. (2003) 'Predator or prey?: Parasitic enterprises in economic development'. *European Economic Review*, 47, 2: 275–94.

Milgrom, P. R. and Roberts, J. (1992) *Economics of Organisation and Management*. Englewood Cliffs NJ: Prentice-Hall.

Mill, J. S. ([1848] 1909) *Principles of Political Economy with Some of Their Applications to Social Philosophy* (7th edn). London: Longmans (note: an electronic version is available at http://www.econlib.org).

Minniti, M. (2008) 'The role of government policy on entrepreneurial activity: productive, unproductive, or destructive?' *Entrepreneurship Theory and Practice*, 32, 5: 779–90.

Mollick, E. (2014) 'The dynamics of crowdfunding: an exploratory study'. *Journal of Business Venturing*, 29, 1: 1–16.

Nelson, R. R. and Winter, S. G. (1982) *An Evolutionary Theory of Economic Change*. Cambridge MA: Harvard University Press.

North, D. C. (2005) *Understanding the Process of Economic Change*. Princeton NJ: Princeton University Press.

OECD (2016) *Entrepreneurship at a Glance 2016*. Paris: OECD Publishing. http://dx.doi.org/10.1787/entrepreneur_aag-2016-en (accessed 11 October 2016).

Parker, S. C. (2005) 'The economics of entrepreneurship: what we know and what we don't'. *Foundations and Trends in Entrepreneurship*. 1, 1: 1–54.

Parker, S. C. (2008) 'Entrepreneurship, self-employment and the labour market'. In Casson, M. et al. (eds), op. cit. (435–60).

Parker, S. C. (2009) *The Economics of Entrepreneurship*. Cambridge: Cambridge University Press.

Penrose, E. T. ([1959] 1995) *The Theory of the Growth of the Firm* (3rd edn with new Foreword). Oxford: Oxford University Press.

Rehn, A. and Taalas, S. (2004) 'Crime and assumptions in entrepreneurship'. In D. Hjorth and C. Steyaert (eds), *Narrative and Discursive Approaches in Entrepreneurship*. Cheltenham: Edward Elgar (144–59).

Romer, P. (1994) 'The origins of endogenous growth'. *Journal of Economic Perspectives*, 8, 1: 3–22.

Ricketts, M. (2008) 'Theories of entrepreneurship: historical development and critical assessment'. In M. Casson et al. (eds), op. cit. (33–58).

Sauka, A. and Welter, F. (2006) 'Productive, unproductive and destructive entrepreneurship in an advanced transition setting: the example of Latvian small enterprises'. In M. Dowling and J. Schumde (eds), *Empirical Entrepreneurship in Europe: New Perspectives*. Cheltenham: Edward Elgar (87–111).

Sautet, F. E. (2000) *An Entrepreneurial Theory of the Firm*. London: Routledge.

Schumpeter, J. A. (1939) *Business Cycles: A Theoretical, Historical and Statistical Analysis of the Capitalist Process*. New York: McGraw-Hill.

Schumpeter, J. A. ([1934] 2004) *The Theory of Economic Development: An Enquiry into Profits* (2nd edn, translated by R. Opie). New Brunswick NJ: Transaction.

Schumpeter, J. A. ([1942] 2010) *Capitalism, Socialism and Democracy*. London: Routledge.

Shackle, G. L. S. (1979) *Imagination and the Nature of Choice*. Edinburgh: Edinburgh University Press.

Shane, S. (ed.) (2002) *The Foundations of Entrepreneurship*. Cheltenham: Edward Elgar.

Smith, A. ([1776] 2008) *Wealth of Nations: A Selected Edition*. Oxford: Oxford University Press.

Sobel, R. S. (2009) 'Testing Baumol: institutional quality and the productivity of entrepreneurship'. *Journal of Business Venturing*, 23, 6: 641–55.

Solow, R. M. (1994) 'Perspectives on growth theory'. *Journal of Economic Perspectives*, 8, 1: 45–54.

Stiglitz, J. (2010) *Freefall: Free Markets and the Sinking of the Global Economy*. London: Allen Lane.

Swedberg, R. (1991) *Joseph A. Schumpeter: His Life and Work*. Cambridge: Polity.

Swedberg, R. (ed.) (2000) *Entrepreneurship: The Social Science View*. Oxford: Oxford University Press.

Thurik, A. R., Stam, E., and Audretsch, D. B. (2013) 'The rise of the entrepreneurial economy and the future of dynamic capitalism'. *Technovation*, 33, 8: 302–10.

Van de Ven, A. H. (1993) 'The development of an infrastructure for entrepreneurship'. *Journal of Business Venturing*, 8, 3: 211–30.

Van Stel, A. J. and Storey, D. J. (2004) 'The link between firm births and job creation: is there an Upas tree effect?' *Regional Studies*, 38, 8: 893–909.

Volkov, V. (1999) 'Violent entrepreneurship in post-communist Russia'. *Europe-Asia Studies*, 51, 5: 741–54.

Westhead, P. and Wright, M. (eds) (2000) *Advances in Entrepreneurship*. Cheltenham: Edward Elgar.

Witt, U. (2008) 'What is specific about evolutionary economics?' *Journal of Evolutionary Economics*, 18, 5: 547–75.

14

HISTORICAL PERSPECTIVES: THE 'LONG VIEW'

Life can only be understood backwards; but it must be lived forwards.

Søren Kierkegaard, Danish philosopher (1843)

I would like to call on young people to commit themselves to activities that contribute toward achieving their long-term dreams. They have the energy and creativity to shape a sustainable future.

Wangari Maathai, Kenyan social entrepreneur and environmentalist

LEARNING OUTCOMES

After reading this chapter you should be able to:

- Identify the main types of historical research and the ways that they can be used to study entrepreneurship.

- Explain the distinctive insights that historical approaches can provide into the nature of entrepreneurs and entrepreneurship.

- Recognise that entrepreneurs often create their own historical narratives, and how these stories can be used to support and develop their ventures.

- Explain how entrepreneurial activity influences the development of organisations, communities, industries, and regions over time.

- Apply these insights to your own experiences of entrepreneurship and when considering your own options for the future.

14.1 INTRODUCTION

Does history really 'matter' to our understanding of entrepreneurship? Though other disciplines, such as psychology and economics, might make a more obvious contribution to our field of study, we argue that historical research needs to be taken just as seriously. For example, as we have seen in several of the previous chapters, there is a longstanding argument around the concept of 'entrepreneurial opportunity'. Do opportunities exist 'out there' in the environment, just waiting to be discovered, or are they more subjective in nature, created in the minds – and through the actions – of entrepreneurial individuals? This issue was examined in a recent Special Issue of the journal *Business History*, with several research-ers providing fresh insights. As the editors indicated, the articles demonstrate how historical studies shed new light on a core concepts like 'entrepreneurial opportunity', and more generally:

> '[E]mphasise that entrepreneurship is a rooted phenomenon *that can only be fully understood with reference to context, conditions and historical processes, with the impact of history being both enabling and constraining'. (Mason and Harvey 2013: 3 – emphasis added)*

Historians examine both the *causes* and the *consequences* of entrepreneurial activity over extended periods. As a result, historical studies span different levels of analysis, including: detailed biographies of individual entrepreneurs and company histories; accounts of the growth and decline of particular industries, industry sectors, and industrial regions; and broader accounts of industrialisation and economic develop-ment (Table 14.1). We will examine each of these areas in turn, illustrating our review with relevant examples. Furthermore, entrepreneurs are going to be better placed to take decisions for the future, if they have a better understanding of what has happened in the past.

The chapter proceeds as follows. In Section 14.2, we review historical studies of entrepreneurial individuals and their organisations; this section builds on some of the themes introduced in Chapter 12 ('individual perspectives'). Section 14.3 examines entrepreneurial activity at the level of industries, industry sectors, and the regions in which they are located. This section is developing theories and concepts from Chapter 13 ('social perspectives'), including the network perspective. Section 14.4 is concerned with the role played by entrepreneurial activity in broader historical pro-cesses. In this section we ask why the world industrialised in the way that it did and examine the variety of 'alternatives' that have been pursued. Finally, in Section 14.5, we consider how you might apply insights from history to your own experiences. This section also looks forward to the final chapter on policy-making.

TABLE 14.1 Historical research on entrepreneurship – sample topics and studies

Focus of study	Sample studies
Entrepreneurial individuals and organisations (Section 14.2)	Pierre Dupont (Chandler and Salsbury 1971), Alfred Nobel (Fant 2007), ICI (Pettigrew 1985), John Shaw (Popp 2007, Popp and Holt 2013), IBM (Black 2005), Starbucks (Clark 2008)
Industries, sectors, and regions (Section 14.3)	Oil (Yergin [1991] 2009), Jewellery (Carnevali 2003), Motorsport (Henry and Pinch 2001), Wind energy (Asmus 2001), Engineering (Scranton 1997), Motorcycles (Wezel 2005), Shipping containers (Levinson 2007), Hollywood (Jones 2001)
Industrialisation and economic development (Section 14.4)	Schumpeter ([1942] 2010), Landes ([1969] 2003), Sabel and Zeitlin (1997)

14.2 ENTREPRENEURIAL INDIVIDUALS AND ORGANISATIONS

14.2.1 Introduction

People like to read about the lives of successful entrepreneurs. You will find a variety of entrepreneurial autobiographies, some written directly by the person concerned, others with the help of a 'ghost' writer. There are also many biographies, ranging from popular books about current media celebrities to more scholarly studies of historical figures. A common feature of all these accounts is that the life of the entrepreneurial individual is usually intertwined with the history of the organisation, or organisations, that they helped to create. These accounts also follow a characteristic structure, with a chronological account of the person's achievements, preceded by a look back at their early years. Autobiographies tend to be interspersed with the author's reflections on what they have achieved, often linked to more general thoughts about the nature of entrepreneurship. It is important to be cautious when using biographies and autobiographies; there is a strong incentive for people to present themselves in the best possible light, so the account that you read may give a false impression of the subject. For example, authors can exaggerate their achievements and either down-play or avoid more controversial episodes (i.e. 'hagiography'). By contrast, a well-researched biography or autobiography can be very useful, providing unique insights into entrepreneurial worlds that might otherwise be difficult or impossible to access. For example, Lewis (2001) depicts life in Silicon Valley in the late twentieth century through an entertaining account of its more colourful figures, while Berlin's (2005) scholarly biography of Robert Noyce, the co-founder of Fairchild Semiconductor and Intel, provides an interesting contrast. Through a combination of interviews, direct observation, and use of documentary evidence, a good author can reveal both personal worlds (e.g. how people perceived and created opportunities in an era of rapid technological innovation), and the relationship between individuals and their broader context (e.g. how Robert Noyce and other Silicon Valley entrepreneurs made use of their social and business networks).

In the following sub-sections, we first consider how historians have written biographies of individuals, before turning to a distinct tradition of writing company histories.

14.2.2 Historical biographies

Most people's lives remain unwritten; though they may be remembered by relatives and friends, there is no published record to tell us how they lived or what they achieved. Most historical biographies tend to be written about famous, and sometimes infamous, individuals (e.g. leading politicians, artists, military leaders, social reformers, and entrepreneurs). This leaves considerable scope for writing about other entrepreneurial lives. If you have entrepreneurial ancestors, there may be an opportunity to discover more about their place in history (see Practical Activity 3). Early in his career, the business historian Alfred H. Chandler wrote a biography of his great-grandfather, Henry Varnum Poor, a journalist who provided business information to the newly emerging railway industry (Chandler 1956). In common with other historical researchers (e.g. Popp and Holt 2013), Chandler found personal letters to be a useful source of evidence, which could be combined with business correspondence and published materials. He found that Henry's wife Mary, 'like many nineteenth-century New England ladies, saved nearly all the correspondence she received from her family and close friends and also collected a large number of letters that she had written to the various members of the family' (Chandler 1956: 285). Letters exchanged between Mary and her husband between 1838 and the late 1890s shed light on the couple's business and social activities. Henry was an entrepreneurial individual, and the biography shows how he developed his business, providing comment, information, and advice. The biography also provides insights into the activities of the railway entrepreneurs. For example, as the industry began to develop in the 1850s, his editorials in the *American Railroad Journal* addressed what he saw as the most pressing problems of the day, including the problem of 'over-construction' (i.e. building too many railway lines), and the need for financial and administrative reforms. Chandler discusses his ancestor's achievements, but also emphasises his weaknesses, often referring to errors of judgement, such as placing too much confidence, 'in leading railroad and financial entrepreneurs' (Chandler 1956: 121).

Published biographies and autobiographies can be a useful source of information in a historical study, but can be very long and complicated accounts. So how can you avoid getting lost in the details of the narrative? One answer is to focus your attention on particular research themes. For example, if you are particularly interested in individual-level factors (e.g. personality characteristics, educational background), or social factors (e.g. ethnicity, social networks), you can search the biography for evidence; you may also find that the authors of biographies have addressed your theme as part of their discussion. To illustrate this process, we can make a very brief comparison between the lives of two historical figures: (a) George Cadbury, the British entrepreneur who helped build a successful and innovative confectionery business; and (b) Alfred Nobel, the Swedish technology entrepreneur who developed a new generation of explosives, and later provided funding for the Nobel Peace Prize (Table 14.2).

There is a long and continuing tradition of writing biographies of entrepreneurs (Corley 2008). The best historical biographies place the lives of individuals in a wider context, enabling readers to see how their subjects interact with other people and with the technologies, cultures, institutions, and economic conditions in which they lived. Biographical studies can also be more useful to researchers if they are informed by relevant theoretical frameworks (Jones and Wadhwani 2008). The theoretical framing enables researchers to make comparisons between different historical studies, and even between the past and the present. By applying suitable theories and concepts, you could explore a variety of issues, based on evidence from the lives of historical figures, such as George Cadbury and Alfred Nobel. For example, with reference to the previous three chapters, we might consider the following questions:

- How did economic conditions and other factors influence their activities?
- What were the economic and social impacts of the businesses they created?
- How did their family upbringing influence their behaviour?
- Why were they able to perceive these entrepreneurial opportunities?
- How did ethical considerations influence their behaviour?
- What role did social networks play in the success of their ventures?
- What kinds of entrepreneurial learning did they undertake?

TABLE 14.2 Comparing the lives of historical figures: possible starting points

Research theme	George Cadbury (1839–1922)	Alfred Nobel (1833–96)
Role of family business	Company founded by his father; worked with his brother Richard, initially including tea and coffee before focusing on chocolate and seeing more rapid growth.	Family of engineers and business people; family moved with father to St. Petersburg (1842) to set up armaments business for Tsar's army.
Religious and ethical influences	Quaker religious practice influenced entrepreneurial motivation (e.g. marketing chocolate as alternative to alcohol consumption), and practice (e.g. improving working and living conditions).	His younger brother Emil was killed in an explosion; is also thought to have been influenced by anti-war views of long-time friend, Bertha von Suttner and by contemporary depictions of him as a 'merchant of death'.
Socio-economic conditions	Cocoa could be sourced through British colonies; opportunities opened up by Gladstone's free trade budget (1860), growth in urban mass markets.	Fall in demand at end of Crimean War (1856) contributed to failure of company. Alfred and two brothers given an opportunity to restore the business.
Technological and social innovation	Company was the first to use Van Houten's new cocoa-making machine (1860s); quality product fitted new food regulations; built new factory with workers' welfare in mind (e.g. sports fields, parks), but also competitive (created French-style 'Bourneville' branding).	After many experiments, he patented a more stable form of nitroglycerine, originally invented by the Italian scientist, Ascanio Sobrero; he subsequently patented dynamite (1867). Late in life, he was responsible for several lasting social innovations, including the Nobel Peace Prize.

Sources: Bradley (2007); Fant (2007); Cadbury (2010); Nobel (2016)

Well-researched biographies, and some of the more reflective autobiographies, provide their readers with insights into areas of entrepreneurial activity that might otherwise remain inaccessible. However, some of the more popular biographies and autobiographies can paint a rather incomplete and distorted picture of their subject. This kind of distortion is more likely in biographies of living subjects, who may still have an opportunity to influence what is written. It can be identified by comparing biographical writing with other information sources (e.g. industry data, newspaper articles, other biographies), and by reading book reviews. This kind of material can still be a useful source of evidence if you read it *critically*. For example, it could reveal how an entrepreneur wants to be perceived, or how stories are used to mould entrepreneurial self-identities (Section 12.4).

The opening case illustrates the different ways that a group of students managed to make good use of historical evidence (Case 14.1).

CASE 14.1   STUDENT FOCUS

History matters ... to me!

These short fictionalised accounts, based on real world examples, illustrate how students have made good use of entrepreneurship research to achieve successful outcomes in their studies.

(Continued)

(Continued)

Katherine's class has been set a project on examining entrepreneurship using research techniques from a number of different academic disciplines. The tutor is looking for case studies, based on real entrepreneurial examples. Unfortunately, she has drawn the short straw and is wondering what on earth she can do with the topic 'historical approaches'. At school, Katherine had abandoned history as soon as she possibly could. She recalls the intense boredom and weariness of learning dates, or trailing around museums with endless cabinets of dusty artefacts. After all, she's studying entrepreneurship in order to develop her *future* career – and how could looking back at the past possibly help with that?

Having leafed through a few journal articles, Katherine's still feeling uninspired. She decides to look online to see if there are any videos that might be worth watching. Remembering that her own family once ran a small tailoring business, she tries searching for 'family businesses'. One of the search results is a series of television programmes called 'Hidden Histories: Britain's Oldest Family Businesses'. The first episode features Richard Balson, whose family have been running a retail butchers in the small market town of Bridport, Dorset since the time of King Henry VIII: with an unbroken line dating back to 1515, Richard is running Britain's oldest family business (www.rjbalson.co.uk). There is also an episode that features a family building company. While she finds the historical accounts quite interesting, Katherine is particularly struck by the human story. For example; the current owner talks about the Kent-based building company, R. Durtnell and Sons (www.durtnell.co.uk), who have been in operation for more than 400 years. Alex Durtnell, who has recently taken over from his father, is able to visit one of their first buildings, constructed by his ancestors during the reign of Queen Elizabeth I. During the programme, he discovers how the family failed to capitalise on the building boom that followed the Great Fire of London in 1666 – while many of their rivals moved into brick construction, Durnell's continued to build timber frame houses. The business went into a long decline, which was only reversed in the late nineteenth century, when a particularly entrepreneurial predecessor responded to market trends by reconfiguring the business as a 'general builder'.

Katherine becomes quite interested in these entrepreneurial stories, but she's particularly taken by the episode that features Fiona Toye of the medals and regalia company Toye and Co. (www.toye.com). Fiona Toye tracks the history of her family's business from its eighteenth-century origins – when the family first arrived in Britain as illiterate, artisan silk weavers working in London's East End. They experience many ups and downs over the years. For example, by the late nineteenth century the company was making traditional, brightly coloured uniforms for the British military. The colours and gold braid, which played an important role in the days of gunpowder, became a liability when the military switched to smokeless powders. This technological innovation undermined one of the core products and the owners responded by moving into new markets, such as banners for the trades union movement and the uniforms worn by campaigners for women's voting rights.

Katherine finds Fiona's story especially powerful. Having joined the family by marriage, she became much more directly involved in the business when her husband suffered a near fatal heart attack. As Chief Executive, she describes the heavy responsibility she feels for a business with such a long, proud history and for the welfare of its current staff. As with Alex Durtnell and Richard Balson, there is also the important question of succession, and of how the business can best continue into the future. Now it's time to start to thinking about her own project, and Katherine has a number of new ideas. She decides to talk to her grandmother, who's talked about how her own family tailoring business closed down in the mid-1960s. Katherine would like to know why it closed. Could it be something to do with the kinds of products it was selling at the time? Was it the result of growing international competition or changes consumer behaviour? Or perhaps there was some kind of crisis in the family that she's not heard about? In any event, there seems to be scope for an interesting historical case study.

Note: 'Hidden Histories: Britain's Oldest Family Businesses' is a series of three television programmes, co-produced by the BBC and The Open University (2014). You will find video extracts online and look for a 'further insights' feature at the OpenLearn website: www.open.edu by searching on the tag 'family business'.

QUESTIONS

1. Why does Katherine think that, as an entrepreneurship student, she has little or nothing to learn from history?

2. What kinds of historical insights does she identify as a result of viewing the videos?

3. Are there any examples from your own family history, that could help you to make this kind of personal connection?

14.2.3 Company and other organisational histories

The lifetime of an organisation is not limited in the same way as that of its human founders. While most organisations 'die young', others manage to survive for extended periods. In 2007, *Business Week* reported the failure of Kongo Gumi, a Japanese Buddhist temple builder, its assets being acquired by a larger construction company. Kongo Gumi had been founded in 578 CE and was in independent existence for more than 1,400 years (Hutcheson 2007). Other organisations, including the Scandinavian packaging and wood products company Stora Enso, have extended lifespans, but few can compete with Kongo Gumi. The histories of such organisations, including public bodies and charities, can provide a good insight into the ways that entrepreneurial activity plays out over time. Alfred Chandler drew on his family history a second time, to write an account of Pierre S. DuPont, and the industrial enterprise that bears his name (Chandler and Salsbury 1971). Historical accounts may be commissioned by the organisation, often to mark a significant anniversary. For example, Castronovo's (1999) history of Fiat was published in the Italian car maker's centenary year.

Histories can address many aspects of organisational life, from operations management to marketing, but they usually include examples of entrepreneurial activity. The most obvious place to look is in the early years of the organisation's life, but entrepreneurial activity can also be found in later periods, such as following succession in a family firm, when the younger generation gets an opportunity to introduce new ideas; both George Cadbury and Alfred Nobel illustrated this phenomenon (Table 14.2). Larger and longer-established organisations often engage in corporate entrepreneurship (or 'intrapreneurship') during major strategic realignments, such as acquisitions, mergers, and diversifications, though they often find it difficult to reconcile the different organisational arrangements needed to 'explore' new opportunities while also continuing to 'exploit' existing ones (March 1991).

Organisational histories can be useful sources in addressing research questions related to many aspects of entrepreneurial activity. As with historical biographies, these questions can be linked to relevant theoretical frameworks and concepts, for example:

- How did people within an organisation identify or create entrepreneurial opportunities?
- How were the resources and capabilities of the organisation reconfigured in order to exploit these opportunities?
- What were the longer-term outcomes of a particular episode of corporate entrepreneurial (or 'intrapreneurial') activity?

They can also provide important sources of evidence about entrepreneurial growth and resilience, both in commercial and social ventures (e.g. Smith and Blundel 2014; Blundel and Lyon 2015).

The critics of organisational histories often raise similar issues to those discussed in relation to biographies. For example, when an organisation commissions such a study, the main concern is that the authors might downplay or ignore unsuccessful or controversial episodes. It is important to be aware of that some historical accounts may lack objectivity. However, there are also many historical studies that have addressed negative aspects of entrepreneurial activity. These range from Ida Tarbell's ([1904] 2010) pioneering 'muckraking' investigation into the early history of Standard Oil, to more recent accounts in this tradition, which have criticised the behaviour of large corporations such as Starbucks and IBM (Black 2001; Clark 2008). As with biographies, the better company histories do not depict their subject as though it existed in isolation. Instead, the scope of the study moves beyond the administrative boundaries of the organisation, and the researchers also examine its interactions with other actors including its suppliers, customers, competitors, government agencies, and local communities (e.g. Pettigrew 1985; Casson and Godley 2007).

In the next section, we move from the level of individual organisations to consider the histories of the industries, sectors, and regions in which they are operating (Section 14.3). By way of introduction, the next case study illustrates how researchers have used historical approaches to study technology-based entrepreneurship, showing how it can be influenced by factors such as previous policies and underlying economic, social, and cultural influences (Case 14.2).

CASE 14.2

Wind energy: charting the creation of an industry

Wind energy is now a major growth industry, with an estimated global capacity of 433 GW (Gigawatts) by the end of 2015, a cumulative increase of 17% on the previous year (GWEC 2016: 4). Growth is concentrated in Asia, North America, and Europe. China, the world's largest market, invested more than $100 billion in renewables in 2015 (ibid., 4). The Danish company Vestas Wind Systems A/S is the world's leading turbine manufacturer

with 74 GW installed to date, comprising 56,860 wind turbines on six continents (Vestas 2016). Having delivered its first turbine in 1979, the company – which merged with another Danish manufacturer in 2004 – now employs more than 20,000 people (Vestas 2016). But how do particular companies, and countries, become technology leaders? In practice, success in technology entrepreneurship depends on a large cast of actors, including manufacturers, designers, technology users, evaluators, and regulators. In the case of wind energy, countries have adopted different approaches to technology entrepreneurship, and we are now able to see some of the longer-term consequences. For example, the Danish approach was distinctly low-tech and 'bottom-up', with a great deal of interaction between different groups of actors and steady improvements in the technology. By contrast, the United States took a high-tech, 'top-down' engineering-led route, in search of a more sophisticated technological breakthrough. So why were the Danes more successful, despite what appeared to be far more modest resources (Garud and Karnøe 2003: 278)?

THE DANISH TURBINE STORY

With its large coastline, strong prevailing winds and lack of alternative sources of energy, Denmark seemed well-positioned to develop wind energy. Simple wind turbines had been used in Denmark in the early twentieth century, but today's three-blade turbine originates from a design by Johannes Juul, which operated between 1956 and 1967. Juul's ideas were revived in the early 1970s, when the global oil crisis led politicians and others to seek alternative sources of energy. Wind turbine pioneers included a number of self-builders, including amateur enthusiasts and grassroots opponents of nuclear power. Their work was promoted by the magazine *Naturlig Energie* and by the Danish Windmill Owners Association, both of which were founded in the late 1970s (Gipe 1995: 59). Other developments in this period included the founding of a small wind turbine testing station at Roskilde and government interventions to subsidise and regulate the emerging industry. At this point Vestas, a small manufacturer of farm equipment and cranes, decided to develop wind turbines. In 1979, the firm signed a licensing agreement with the self-builder, Karl Erik Jørgensen, to produce one of his new designs. Meanwhile, policy-makers in the United States identified the aerospace industry as the obvious source of expertise on turbine design (Gipe 1995: 56, 83–6). US engineers concentrated on perfecting the aerodynamic qualities of their designs, whereas their Danish counterparts focused on reliability. Danish designers were in much more regular contact with the user community, which comprised mainly small independents and cooperatives, sharing their ideas through regular 'wind meetings'. Geographic proximity, varied site conditions, and a spirit of open experimentation

(Continued)

(Continued)

helped generate a rapid pace of learning, based on practical experience in the field. Danish designers were responsible for several key innovations, including brakes to slow the turbines and fibreglass blades, which had their origins in boat building. However, the overall approach was of rapid cycle incremental innovation, rather than sudden radical breakthroughs. Despite changes of government, the political coalition around wind energy was sufficient to 'steer' the industry towards maturity, with a gradual reduction in subsidies in the decade to 1989 (Garud and Karnøe 2003: 293). By contrast, government intervention in the United States, including tax credits, tended to promote building rather than operating turbines. This helped stimulate a speculative boom in California, with some installations being pursued for tax breaks rather than for power generation (Asmus 2000: 116). This was followed by a dramatic collapse in the mid-1980s when the tax credits were withdrawn; the speculative boom ended in financial failures and lawsuits, with many turbines left rusting and unused (Gipe 1995; Asmus 2000: 122).

MEANWHILE IN GERMANY ...

Researchers studying wind energy in the German state of North Rhine-Westphalia (NRW) and the Netherlands also found a strong historical influence, with initial differences in public policies influencing subsequent entrepreneurship patterns. In the Netherlands, policies related to wind energy had favoured the large energy companies over independent entrepreneurs. Though these policies were revised in the second half of the 1990s, the German wind energy industry expanded at a faster rate. The researchers concluded that public policies had played a decisive role in this outcome: 'While in the Netherlands, the dominance of [existing energy companies] impeded the implementation capacities of other entrepreneurs, in NRW a diversity of entrepreneurs was encouraged from early on' (Agterbosch and Breukers 2008: 645). As in Denmark, both federal and state-level policies encouraged grassroots initiatives in the early years, with farmers and small, community-owned projects being given access to the electricity grid via preferential 'feed-in' tariffs (Agterbosch and Breukers 2008: 639). After the mid-1990s, many of these locally owned initiatives were displaced by larger organisations. However, these earlier developments played an important role in helping wind energy to gain social acceptance, so accelerating the growth of the industry in this region.

QUESTIONS

1. Why did the 'low-tech' approach of the Danish wind turbine industry prove more successful than the 'high-tech' approach adopted in the United States?

2. What challenges would wind energy entrepreneurs in: (a) the United States; (b) the Netherlands, have faced in comparison with their Danish and German counterparts?

3. Given the current spread of wind and solar energy around the world, what practical lessons might you draw from these historical cases?

14.3 INDUSTRIES, INDUSTRY SECTORS, AND REGIONS

14.3.1 The rise and fall of industries

In the previous chapter, we discussed 'spatial' variations: how rates of entrepreneurship, and the nature of the activity undertaken, vary between geographical locations (Section 13.5). Here, we are looking at 'temporal' variations: how entrepreneurial activity also varies in intensity and form when it is tracked across time. There are many cases of this kind of variation in our recent history. New industries have been born, sometimes during fairly dramatic bursts of entrepreneurial activity (e.g. the 'dot com' boom of the 1990s), while long-established industries have failed because they have got 'locked-in' to particular ways of operating (e.g. Schreyögg et al. 2011), and either collapsed entirely or relocated to other parts of the world. So what can historical research tell us about these longer-term changes, and how they connect with our exploration of entrepreneurship? We address these questions in two stages. We begin by reviewing evidence of trends or patterns in the way that entrepreneurial activity fluctuates over time and ask how they relate to the rise and fall of industries (Section 14.3.2). Then we examine the underlying mechanisms, making particular reference to creation and growth of geographic clusters (Section 14.3.3).

14.3.2 Looking for patterns: tracking variations over time

Historical studies are often written up as narratives. However, there is a contrasting approach, in which researchers assemble historical data sets in order to explain patterns in entrepreneurial activity over extended periods. This is one of the aims of the Global Entrepreneurship Monitor (GEM) study, which is now collecting data on a regular basis in more than 60 countries around the world (Kelley et al. 2016: 12–13). Researchers adopting this approach face several challenges, including that of identifying suitable measures. For example, Shane (1996) used a measure of entrepreneurship as the number of registered organisations per head of population to study changes in rates in the United States between 1899 and 1988. Though this measure might appear unproblematic at first sight, it has several limitations. As the author notes, it can result in the under-counting of smaller firms, which do not appear on official lists. Increases in the average size of firms can also introduce distortions (Shane 1996: 748, 777). Researchers are now beginning to address these technical issues, and extending the scope of their data collection and analysis. As a result, we have access to new evidence about changes in entrepreneurial attitudes, perceptions, and activity rates over time.

Other researchers have identified patterns and trends in data collected at an industry level, with measures such as the birth and death rates of firms fluctuating over time. The typical pattern is for an initial rush of new entrants in the early years of a new industry to be followed at some point by a 'shake-out', with some firms failing and others consolidating; though new firms may continue to be added, the population stabilises around a smaller number of large, established firms. This strand of research, known as 'population ecology' or 'organisational ecology', can provide evidence that can be combined with the more in-depth qualitative studies discussed earlier in this chapter. For example, Figure 14.1 shows some of the data used in a study contrasting the performance of the world's leading motorcycle

Italian motorcycle industry: new firms and population density

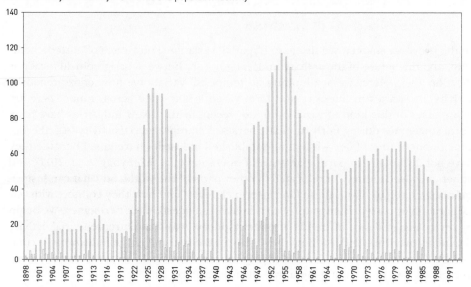

Japanese motorcycle industry: new firms and population density

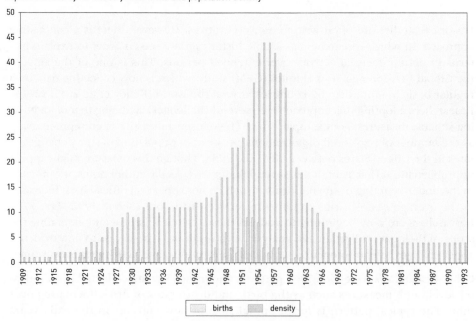

births   density

FIGURE 14.1 Motorcycle industries: two contrasting growth patterns.

Source: Wezel and Lomi (2003: 373–4, Figures 2 and 3).

producer, Japan, with that of another leading country, Italy (n.b. the full study includes a comparison with a third country, Belgium).

The dramatic contrast in the patterns indicated by these graphs was just a starting point for the researchers, who used a range of data in as part of a multivariate modelling exercise. The aim of their analysis was to identify how the competitive advantage of a nation might be related to the dynamics of its organisational populations (Wezel and Lomi 2003: 379). Their findings suggest that one of the factors contributing to the competitive advantage of nations was the ability of organisational populations to learn from the experience of their unsuccessful members. The researchers also found 'mixed evidence' on the influence of geographical location and clustering in the countries studied and joined the call for more comparative and longitudinal studies of this factor (Wezel and Lomi 2003: 385–6). Similar approaches have been adopted to study the factors underpinning the evolution of this industry in other countries (e.g. Wezel 2005).

14.3.3 Identifying causal mechanisms: the case of industrial districts and clusters

A wide variety of mechanisms can be drawn upon to explain the contrasting patterns in entrepreneurial activity discussed in the previous section, including:

- **Individual level mechanisms**, such as education and training (i.e. are we producing young people with skills, energy and ideas?).

- **Organisational-level mechanisms**, such as (i.e. do we have organisations of an appropriate size, with the right capabilities?).

- **Institutional level mechanisms**, such as rules, regulations and social norms (i.e. does our country or region have the kind of taxation system, intellectual property rights or cultural values?).

While each of these levels of analysis is important, there has been a particular focus on the role played by inter-organisational networks (Sections 4.4 and 13.5). In this section we have concentrated on a type of inter-organisational networking that occurs in particular geographic locations.

The idea of geographic concentrations of economic activity was outlined by the economist Alfred Marshall in his work on 'industrial districts' ([1920] 2010: 222–31), and was subsequently rediscovered and refined in the late twentieth century (Beccatini et al. 2014). Researchers studying Italian regions such as Emilia-Romagna identified a link between prosperous local economies and the dense networks of independent, specialised enterprises. Many researchers investigated what Bagnasco (1977) called *Tre Italia* (i.e. the 'Third Italy'), and the idea that economic activity based on geographic clusters of smaller firms could be more competitive and flexible than either conventional **markets** or large vertically integrated corporations (e.g. Piore and Sabel 1984). We will consider two research questions from this literature, which have strong historical dimensions. Firstly, how are clusters created? Secondly, how do they survive and develop over time?

How are clusters created? From the earliest times, economic activity had a strong local flavour, with communities developing distinctive products and services which could trade with people from other areas. Perhaps the most important *initial* impetus for geographic specialisation was the uneven distribution of natural resources. As Alfred Marshall observed, geological formations, soil types, plant varieties, and microclimates provided the basis for many of the traditional industrial districts:

> *Straw plaiting has its chief home in Bedfordshire, where straw has just the right proportion of silex to give it strength without brittleness; and Buckinghamshire beeches have afforded the material for the Wycombe chair-making. The Sheffield cutlery trade is due chiefly to the excellent grit of which its grindstones are made. (Marshall [1920] 2010: 223)*

Today, the landscape or 'amenity' value of a particular location can be a significant natural resource, providing a 'quality of life' that can attract and retain 'footloose' entrepreneurs and knowledge workers. The combined effects of an attractive environment and existing institutional resources (e.g. leading research universities) can be a strong incentive for people to relocate around new clusters of high technology and knowledge-intensive enterprises (e.g. Keeble and Wilkinson 1999; Lawson and Lorenz 2000; Best 2015). Clusters can also be created, or encouraged to develop, through public policy interventions. Governments may seek to divert external resources to a location (e.g. by providing incentives for inward investment or in-migration), to enhance local resources (e.g. by investing in education, training, political institutions, and infrastructure), or to achieve a combination of the two. Marshall provides us with a very early example of policy-based clustering; he claimed that the 'mechanical faculty' (i.e. engineering skills) of nineteenth century Lancashire, in the north-west of England, could be traced to an eleventh-century decision by the Norman duke, Hugo de Lupus, to relocate skilled metalworkers to that area. Though Marshall's claim might be open to challenge, there are many examples of long-standing local specialisms, particularly in areas such as agriculture, traditional crafts, and food production. Today's policy initiatives tend to have a rather shorter time-horizon; recent examples include the Finnish nanotechnology cluster, the biotechnologies clusters in Belgium's Brussels-Capital Region and the distinctive ecosystem in the Greater Boston area (Table 14.3).

TABLE 14.3 Variations in entrepreneurial activity over time

Period	Industry trends	Changes in entrepreneurial activity
1970s to 1990s	Decline of large manufacturing industries in the UK, other European countries, and the United States (e.g. steel-making, shipbuilding, vehicle manufacturing, consumer electronics), due to cost competition in an increasingly globalised market.	Transfer of manufacturing to Indian sub-continent and South East Asian countries created new opportunities for local manufacturers and suppliers. Some former industrial regions experienced long-term decline in activity; others have been regenerated, creating new opportunities.
1980s to date	Emerging technology-based sectors such as nanotechnologies and bio-pharmaceuticals, with geographic concentrations of activity in particular locations around the world (e.g. Silicon Valley, USA; Bangalore, India; Cambridge, England; Piedmont, Italy; Cork, Ireland). Clusters are also influenced by policy initiatives such as Finland's Nanotechnology Cluster Programme (www.nanocluster.fi), and the Biopharma initiative in Belgium's Brussels-Capital Region (www.biotechinbrussels.be).	High levels of new firm formation, including 'spin-out' ventures linked to research centres in leading universities and regional outposts of major multinational corporations. Has also created many opportunities for specialist service providers (e.g. venture finance, intellectual property law, recruitment of scientists and technicians).

How do clusters survive and develop? Whatever the initial impetus for creating a cluster, it requires other mechanisms if it is to continue to prosper. Marshall described this process as creating an 'industrial atmosphere':

> *When an industry has chosen a locality for itself, it is likely to stay there long: so great are the advantages which people following the same skilled trade get*

*from the near neighbourhood of one another. The mysteries of the trade become
no mysteries; but are as it were in the air, and children learn many of them
unconsciously. Good work is rightly appreciated, inventions and improvements
in machinery, in processes and the general organisation of the business have
their merits promptly discussed: if one man starts a new idea, it is taken up by
others and combined with suggestions of their own; and thus becomes the source
of further good ideas. (Marshall [1920] 2010: 225)*

Subsequent research has greatly refined and extended Marshall's original ideas,
while retaining the key insight that economic activity is often socially 'embedded'
(Granovetter 1985) (Section 13.5). To see how this works, we can look in more detail
at the widely adopted concept of 'institutional thickness', which has been defined
as a measure of the degree to which a geographic location is capable of supporting
productive economic activity (Amin and Thrift 1995: 14–16). Perhaps the easiest way
to grasp its meaning and significance is to picture the opposite: imagine yourself in
a country in the aftermath of civil war or a major natural disaster. Think how difficult it would be to establish a new venture in a place where there were no support
institutions (enterprise agencies, chambers of commerce, universities) and nobody
exercising control over rule-breakers and 'rogue traders'. Without these sources of
'institutional thickness' it would be difficult to operate a venture, let alone to compete
with businesses located in established locations. Institutional thickness can fluctu-
ate over time. For example, an assessment of the high-technology cluster around
Cambridge, in the East of England, concluded that until the mid-1990s, the University
of Cambridge played an important yet isolated role in creating a supportive culture
and initiating spin-offs. Institutional thickness has since increased with the introduction of new organisations, including an innovation centre, specialist services firms,
and science parks (Keeble et al. 1999: 327–9). By contrast, a study of remote rural
communities in Ireland illustrated how institutions can be undermined by socio-
economic changes. During the 1980s, increased personal mobility, coupled with an
urban shift in employment, retailing, and other services, contributed to a weakening
of local economic and social institutions (Keane 1990).

Institutional thickness is not necessarily a guarantee of survival. Geographic clusters
with strong, long-established institutional frameworks, cultures, and practices can
find it very difficult to identify external threats, or to make the changes required in
order to tackle them. The rapid decline of the Swiss watch industry in the late twentieth century is a widely cited example, where socially embedded craft traditions and
institutions (i.e. a form of 'institutional thickness') were seen as playing a negative role
(Glasmeier 1994). Similarly, a number of British manufacturing regions, districts, and
clusters have experienced fluctuating fortunes over time, often leading to catastrophic
decline. Historians, with their long-term perspectives, are well-placed to study these
dynamics (e.g. Wilson and Popp 2009, Schreyögg et al 2011). A key insight from this
research is that while individual firms, or groups of firms, can make heroic efforts
to resist industrial decline, they can be overwhelmed by more powerful forces. For
example, between 1960 and 2002, the UK-based shoemaking firm R. Griggs created a
successful international brand, *Dr Martens*, against a backdrop of widespread factory
closures in a declining traditional industrial district. Despite this, in 2003, the owners
found it necessary to relocate the bulk of their production to China and Thailand,
though they did later recommence production of a premium hand-crafted range in
the original Northampton factory.

In the next case study we profile a business historian who collaborate with an experienced entrepreneur to chart the growth of the mountaineering and outdoor equipment industries from the mid-nineteenth century to the present day (Case 14.3).

CASE 14.3   RESEARCHER PROFILE

MARY ROSE, ON COMBINING INNOVATION, ENTREPRENEURSHIP, AND THE 'CALL OF THE MOUNTAINS'

Mary Rose is Emeritus Professor of Entrepreneurship at Lancaster University, UK. She specialises in evolutionary approaches to innovation and the relationships between innovation, entrepreneurship, and communities of practice. Mary has published widely on the evolution of business values, networking behaviour by family firms, and the problem of leadership succession, including books, edited books, and articles in refereed journals. A former president of the Association of Business Historians and European Business History Association, Mary was also research director of the Institute of Entrepreneurship and Innovation at Lancaster (2003–13) and director of the Pasold Research Fund, a charitable trust working in the field of textile history (1997–2006). Mary's books include, *Firms, Networks and Business Values: The British and American Cotton Industries since 1750* (Rose 2000). She has also collaborated Dr Andrea Colli (Bocconi University, Milan) and Dr Paloma Fernadez Perez (University of Barcelona), in research on family firms in Britain, Italy, and Spain. In

this interview, she talks about her collaborative research with Mike Parsons, former MD of the outdoor equipment company, Karrimor. The company was founded by Mike's parents in 1946, initially to make bags for bicycles; Mike joined the family firm at 18 and was instrumental in growing the company into a leading manufacturer of outdoor clothing and equipment. Their findings were published as, *Invisible on Everest: Innovation and the Gear Makers* (Parsons and Rose 2003), and in journal articles (Rose and Parsons 2004; Parsons and Rose 2005). Mary and Mike traced the evolution of clothing and equipment for outdoor activities, from the middle of the nineteenth century to the present day. In doing so, they gained new insights into the ways that entrepreneurial actors respond to social, cultural, and technological developments, and the long-term impact of their activities. The project also led to specialist courses and conferences serving today's dynamic global outdoor products industry.

Why did you want to research in this area?

The outdoor industries – including design, manufacturing, and retailing of clothing and equipment for mountaineering, skiing, polar exploration, cycling, and hill walking – form an important economic sector, but in 2000, when the research began, they were under-researched. As a keen mountain walker, with an academic background in business history, this was an opportunity to carry out serious research on my hobby. I can remember vividly when I first had the idea for the book: it was in the Lake District, on a wet, windy spring weekend in 1995, having just bought some new gear, when it struck me that no one had written a history of how mountaineering clothing and equipment had developed. At the time I was struggling to finish Anglo-American book, and so the idea stayed just that for some years. Writing history is a complex process and research questions emerge and are often shaped by the research process. From the start I was interested in how the evolution of innovations in clothing and equipment shaped or were shaped by sports' users.

What methods did you use?

This research began with a conventional historical methodology which places innovation in its long-term context by critically appraising archives, interviews, and secondary material. In January 2000 I made a phone call to Mike Parsons, the past owner of the outdoor brand Karrimor, asking him for an interview. Within six months that phone call had transformed the book from a conventional history to an innovative methodology. An email exchange developed as I travelled round carrying out the research which convinced me that combining Mike's technical, business, and sporting knowledge with my academic experience could contribute to an unusual book. Mike's position as one of the key innovators of his generation obviously raised methodological issues relating to how to be both researcher and researched. We resolved this by adopting a holistic approach to evaluating innovations by interviewing designers, suppliers, manufacturers, outdoor journalists, and users and setting alongside a range of archival materials, including correspondence, expedition reports, and published materials.

Do your findings have any practical implications for entrepreneurs?

Invisible on Everest highlights the importance of understanding user needs for successful innovation. Innovation is a social process based on combinations of knowledge often built at the boundaries of communities of practice. This is especially clear in outdoor sports and was exemplified in Mike's experience at Karrimor where his own multi-sport activity placed him in a position to devise a 'Think Tank' of lead users, including mountain photographers, polar explorers, as well as climbers and mountain guides. He met with them quarterly to brainstorm on product innovation. Throughout the book we focused on the needs of lead users, and it is worth remembering that while they may seem to be an elite niche, their needs are typically around five years ahead of the normal user. Companies developing meaningful engagement with lead users are in a better position to anticipate market needs than those relying only on conventional market research.

Are there any particular challenges in conducting historical studies?

The challenges of historical research are what attract me to it. It involves applying theory to the analysis of a combination of archives, secondary material, and in the case of modern studies, interviews. One of the biggest challenges may come as a surprise in an era of easy access to digitised information: there is no guarantee of the availability

(Continued)

(Continued)

of archives for a particular company or organisation. It was my concern that there were significant gaps in archival material for outdoor industries. As a result of numerous mergers and takeovers from the 1990s onwards, few outdoor companies have archives. Even when one is available, it is often no more than a jumble of public relations materials and catalogues. Part of the imagination of the historian is identifying alternative sources which help fill the gaps. While I travelled and assessed whether the project was viable I emailed Mike about the materials. The interactions helped build the trust and shared understanding which inspired our collaboration. One of the challenges of working with a business person to co-write research is the scepticism of colleagues that this can create rigorous research. The gains were new research questions around the social processes underpinning innovation, and the opportunities for developing innovative practices in teaching and engagement with business.

Where do you think research in this area needs to develop in future?

There has been a tendency for historical approaches to innovation and entrepreneurship to develop in entirely different silos from management studies, where much work is uninformed by history. Setting innovation and entrepreneurship in historical context helps to develop a more rounded understanding of innovation processes. This is about much more than looking at how companies or regions become 'locked in' to technologies, products, or processes. History is about change as well as continuity and this can provide the basis for combining new knowledge and skills with the traditional and develop something radically new and often unforeseen. Think about Facebook – developed for social networking for college students and now helping transform business marketing; old and new leading to a radical process change that can only be understood in the historical context of the twenty-first century.

In the final part of this section, we turn to industrialisation and economic development, considering the role that entrepreneurial activity might play in shaping these large-scale processes.

14.4 INDUSTRIALISATION AND ECONOMIC DEVELOPMENT: THE ENTREPRENEURIAL ROLE

In the last two decades, some historical researchers have begun to challenge earlier views of economic development and industrialisation, including those of Landes ([1969] 2003) and Chandler (1990). Proponents of the 'historical alternatives' approach argue that economic development takes place along different paths. Though the process may be influenced by economic drivers (e.g. resource costs, transaction costs, economies of scale and scope), and by new technologies, there is still scope for people to make strategic choices about the way forward. Recent contributions in this tradition include Sabel and Zeitlin (1997), Scranton (2000), and Carnevali (2003, 2004). The following list summarises arguments presented by Zeitlin (2008a):

- It is wrong to assume that different countries, regions and industries are all following a 'narrow track' towards a similar model of industrialisation.
- The large vertically integrated corporations and mass-production models that developed in the twentieth century are not the only ways to organise production.

- Economic actors can act strategically, adjusting to their context, considering alternative courses of action and – to varying degrees – shaping the world around them.

- One of the results of the interplay between these actors and their contexts is many 'hybrid' (i.e. mixed and combined) forms of economic organisation, with their own distinctive practices.

- Much depends on the way that economic activity is organised beyond the boundaries of any individual organisation; as we saw in the case of geographic clusters, inter-organisational networks and support institutions play an important role.

Following a different path into the future can have serious consequences for the people and organisations concerned. Consider, for example, the silk manufacturers of London and Lyons, who adopted radically different approaches, with equally dramatic effects. The British pursued an aggressive modernisation strategy. When trade was deregulated in the mid-1820s, they opted for large-scale vertically integrated manufacturing, a model that they borrowed from the country's successful cotton industry. Their French rivals organised themselves in a different way, with dispersed, localised networks of smaller firms. By mid-century, silk manufacturing in Lyons was highly successful, with a strong export trade. By contrast, London went into a steep decline and by 1900, 90% of British consumption was imported (Cottereau 1997: 81). However, as the Dr Martens story (Section 14.3.3) illustrates, entrepreneurial actors can act strategically, anticipating and adapting in order to compete more effectively.

The historical alternatives approach suggests how entrepreneurial activity can shape economic development, helping to create different paths into the future. This process is illustrated in the following case study, which charts a transformation in food production methods from traditional craft-based approaches to industrial scale manufacturing (Case 14.4).

CASE 14.4

Big cheese: charting an industrialisation process

In the first half of the nineteenth century, English cheese-makers devised a standardised production system that became a template for industrial-scale food manufacturing and helped to create an international market in cheese. However, their own path to industrialisation proved to be rather long and winding. This case study looks at how a combination of entrepreneurial initiative and broader geo-political and economic factors shaped this technological innovation.

As they approached the 1850s, English cheese-makers appeared to be on the brink of a transition to full-scale industrial development. The early commercialisation of the country's agricultural and food manufacturing sectors had provided the essential

(Continued)

(Continued)

infrastructure, while its increasingly urbanised population created a growing demand for industrial products. Furthermore, by the mid-nineteenth century, many of the commercial English cheese-makers were engaged in scientific experimentation, their aim being to deliver increased consistency to satisfy the needs of the wholesalers and retailers. Although each of the main English regional varieties was subject to experimentation, Cheddar was the focus of attention. This can be attributed to a combination of the intrinsic characteristics of the cheese, its increasing economic significance – Cheddar was now overtaking Cheshire as the leading commercial variety on the London market – and the pioneering efforts of several leading Somerset cheese-makers. The most prominent of these was Joseph Harding (1805–76), a successful dairy farmer. Harding and his contemporaries conducted many experiments involving the precise and systematic control and monitoring of key variables such as temperature and acidity. They also invested in human capital, promoting educational programmes for cheese-makers and dairy maids, and calling for improvements in the physical condition of dairies in order to tackle quality problems. The results of these experiments were published in specialist agricultural and dairy journals, the free flow of information reflecting the new spirit of scientific enquiry. This cycle of experiment and publication contributed to the formalising of cheese-making practices into distinctive 'systems', in effect, sets of standardised instructions or 'recipes' for the more efficient production of specific English regional varieties. The efforts of Joseph Harding and others to improve English cheese-making were motivated, to some degree, by the awareness that cheese-makers faced a potential threat from imported products. However, the nature of the knowledge being developed, and the enthusiasm with which it was disseminated, had the paradoxical effect of intensifying the competitive threat. Once formalised, Harding's Cheddar system was readily reproducible in other locations. The process of imitation was actively encouraged by leading figures in English cheese-making. Harding's own family illustrate this phenomenon, his son Henry Harding being instrumental in exporting the Cheddar system to Australia.

As experiments continued on England's commercial cheese-making farms, developments in North America were about to provide a springboard for industrial scale production. As in England, one of the primary aims was to produce a more uniform cheese for the volume market. The first cheese factory was constructed in Oneida County, New York State, in 1851, but the innovation did not catch on immediately. Furthermore, though the term 'factory' was used from the outset, production processes were essentially unchanged from those used on the farm, the main differences being that the building was purpose-built for volume production, cheese-making equipment was larger, and milk supplies were drawn from several contributing farms (McMurry 1995: 3 n6, 129). The American Civil War (1861–65) triggered a surge in factory-building and an equally dramatic increase in the export trade. The war removed men and women from the dairy farms, blocked lucrative Southern markets, and contributed to a doubling of market prices, as English importers paid for cheese in gold, which was converted into inflated paper money. In 1864, it is estimated that 205 factories were responsible for about a third of the cheese produced in New York State; by 1870 there were over 900 factories, and by 1875 one observer estimated that over 90% of the state's cheese was factory made. Given this context, it is perhaps unsurprising that visitors to Harding's cheese dairy included Xerxes A. Willard, a representative of the American Dairyman's Association, who toured England in the summer of 1866. Though modest quantities of American Cheddar had been sold in England shortly before the emergence of the first factories, Willard's visit marked a turning point for cheese-making in both countries. On his return to the United States, Willard set about promoting the essential principles of Harding's Cheddar system at dairy conventions, on factory visits, and in technical papers. These ideas were duly applied and further developed by the new generation of cheese factory managers, in conjunction with innovative mass-production technologies, such as the steam boiler and the 'gang-press', which is illustrated below.

In addition to the potential scale economies associated with the factory system, the American factories benefited from access to extensive, high-quality grazing land and large, productive dairy herds. It was also unencumbered by traditional production practices and local market preferences. Exports to the United Kingdom increased tenfold, from around 5 million pounds (2,300 tonnes) in 1859 to more than 50 million pounds (22,700 tonnes) in 1863. They continued to increase over the following decade, doubling in volume by 1874. By this time, factory cheese from the United States represented more than half of total imports and, based on contemporary estimates, more than a quarter of the English market (see Figure 14.2 and Table 14.4).

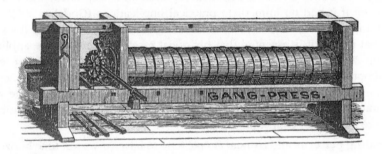

FIGURE 14.2 The gang-press: moving towards mass-production.

Source: Willard (1877: 369). The gang-press was one of several innovations in this period that enabled factories to process increasing volumes of cheese.

TABLE 14.4 Global traders: cheese imports into United Kingdom, 1874

Country of origin	Quantity (Tonnes)	% share by volume
USA	49,296	57.2%
Netherlands	23,136	26.9%
Canada	12,820	14.9%
France	318	0.4%
Germany	254	0.3%
Sweden	182	0.2%
Other	139	0.2%
Total	86,145	

Source: Evans (1878: 156).

(Continued)

(Continued)

QUESTIONS

1.   Why were entrepreneurs in the United States better positioned to develop this technological innovation, compared to their English counterparts?

2.   What other social, cultural, and technological innovations would have influenced the growth of an international trade in perishable food products?

3.   How would you contrast the sharing of ideas by nineteenth-century dairy farmers like Joseph Harding and the actions of twenty-first century 'open source' pioneers such as Linus Torvalds (www.linux.org) and Liam Mulhall (brewtopia.com.au)?

Note: This case is based on research conducted by Angela Tregear and Richard Blundel. For an extended version, see Blundel and Tregear (2006).

14.5 PRACTICAL IMPLICATIONS

There would be a strong case for historical research on entrepreneurship and organisations, even if it had no immediate practical implications (Godelier 2009; Kobrak 2009; Tiffany 2009). In this chapter we have argued that history really does matter, and for that reason it is essential that historical research methods are applied with care (Popp 2009; Rowlinson et al. 2014; Pittaway and Tunstall 2016). If researchers can avoid potential pitfalls, such as over-emphasising the role of individual actors and failing to interpret evidence in a critical way, these approaches can provide valuable insights into present-day entrepreneurial activity. We conclude by highlighting some of the more significant contributions:

- **Revealing patterns and trends:** People tend to have very short time horizons, and pay insufficient attention to longer-term trends. One way of addressing this limitation is to collect and analyse quantitative data (e.g. entrepreneurial activity rates, firm birth and death rates) over extended periods of time. Analysis of this kind can reveal interesting patterns, such as the characteristic 'boom and bust' cycle seen in many new growth industries – such as occurred in automobile manufacturing at the dawn of the twentieth century, or web-based commerce at its end. Though history never repeats itself, it may be possible to identify broadly similar patterns in events, or in underlying processes. For example, you could examine the challenges faced by entrepreneurs who attempted to introduce a product too early, and struggled to gain legitimacy, or others who entered the market too late and were unable to catch up with the knowledge and experience gained by incumbent firms. More historically aware entrepreneurs and investors are therefore likely to make better informed judgements by learning from these earlier experiences.

- **Doing justice to entrepreneurial lives:** One of the biggest challenges is to reconstruct past events in ways that take account of the thoughts, feelings, and strategic judgements of the people concerned. While this is true of all areas of activity, this is a particular problem when you begin to examine the perceptions and judgements of historical entrepreneurs (Sabel and Zeitlin (1997: 29). It can be easy to forget that everyone's life is 'lived forwards'. Historical entrepreneurs did not have a crystal ball; like us, they had to rely on whatever 'local knowledge'

(Section 11.3.4) was available in order to form their judgements about the future. Good historical research helps us to address this issue. By recovering archive evidence (e.g. from personal correspondence, diaries, and minutes of meetings), and in some cases through careful retrospective interviewing, researchers can find out more about the ways that people came to particular decisions. The resulting accounts are useful in two related ways. Firstly, they show us how difficult it can be to act entrepreneurially, something that is easily lost in a typical chronological summary of events (i.e. the kind of thing you find on many organisational websites). Secondly, we can learn some important lessons from previous generations by following them through time as they tackle the uncertainties, complexities, and the inevitable pitfalls of their entrepreneurial lives.

- **Uncovering hidden stories and providing fresh perspectives:** By revealing previously hidden stories, and by reinterpreting what people assumed to be the case, historical research can also alter ideas in the present day. Contemporary views about the nature of entrepreneurship are based on a set of social and economic perspectives, which are themselves the product of a particular history. Until the late twentieth century, most of the scientific research on entrepreneurship was conducted by researchers based in Europe and North America, and much of the work was conducted by people who shared similar social and ethnic backgrounds. More recent historical research is bringing to our attention stories and perspectives that were not previously addressed. For example, Walker's (1986) article examines black entrepreneurship in the United States before the Civil War, while Osirim (2008) looks at the recent history of women entrepreneurs in the African diaspora.

- **Creating more informed and effective enterprise policies:** Through each of these contributions, historical research can help us obtain a better understanding of entrepreneurial activity, including the different ways that it operates and its potential to contribute economically, socially and environmentally. It would also be nice to think that we could learn from past mistakes, or at least to recognise the scale of the challenge faced by people attempting to act entrepreneurially. The 'historical alternatives' approach (Section 14.5), highlights a number of practical implications for policy-makers and others who might want to influence the kind of world that we hand on to our children and grandchildren. These issues are taken up again in Chapter 15 (Section 15.1).

14.6 SUMMARY

- There is a wide variety of historical approaches and themes, from biographies addressing the lives of particular individuals to broad historical studies concerned with industrialisation processes; each of these themes provides interesting and sometimes unexpected insights into different aspects of entrepreneurship.

- Entrepreneurial biographies and company histories are traditional approaches, each of which remains relevant today. It is essential that studies of this kind extend beyond the boundaries of the immediate subject, in order to see how people and organisations interact with their surrounding context.

- The analysis of historical data sets has revealed patterns of growth and decline of industries and industrial sectors. By drawing selectively on social science concepts, historians have also examined in detail how entrepreneurial activity has developed over an extended period of time, providing many useful insights.

- Entrepreneurs and entrepreneurial activity feature in large-scale theoretical explanations of industrialisation and economic development, but there is continuing debate over their role in these processes. The historical alternatives approach challenges deterministic accounts and highlights the capacity of entrepreneurial actors to influence social and technological innovations.

- Historically informed research can help to show how entrepreneurial actors 'make their own history' in a life lived forward. It can also help to shed new light on hidden and misunderstood aspects of the past, and to show how entrepreneurial activity is capable of creating alternative pathways into the future.

Practical activities

1. **Comparing entrepreneurial lives:** Using references identified in Section 14.2 and the Further reading guide as a starting point, locate the historical biographies of two entrepreneurs. Read their life stories and summarise under suitable headings (NB: the following categories are suggestions, but you may want to adjust or add to them): (a) 'family background and early childhood'; (b) 'education'; (c) 'location and travel'; (d) 'networking activity'; (e) 'venture type(s)'; (f) 'major challenges'; (g) 'how it all ended'. Write a short (500 word) commentary, comparing and contrasting these individuals.

2. **Comparing organisational histories:** Using references identified in Section 14.2 and the Recommended reading suggestions as a starting point, locate the histories of two commercial companies or social enterprises. Read the histories and summarise using the following questions (NB: these are suggested questions; you may want to adjust or add to them): (a) When, where, and by whom was the organisation founded? (b) Why was it founded (i.e. what internal and external factors)? (c) What were its original aims? (d) How has it developed over time? (e) What factors have influenced its development? Write a short (500 word) commentary, comparing and contrasting these organisations.

3. **Uncovering my entrepreneurial history:** Re-read Section 14.2 and the Student focus case (Case 14.1), then contact members of your wider family and try to discover whether one of your ancestors was involved in entrepreneurial activity, broadly defined. If so, write an account of their life, based on whatever information you are able to collect and using the categories from Practical activity 1 as a guide. If your story includes the founding of an organisation, you could also use the questions from Practical activity 2 to help organise your thoughts. If you are unable to identify an entrepreneurial ancestor, you can work with friends and acquaintances in order develop an historical narrative based on their family histories, or more recent experiences.

Discussion topics

1. **What 'use' is history?** There is a continuing debate regarding the role and the relevance of historical research in 'practical' subjects like management and entrepreneurship; see, for example, the exchange between Godelier (2009), Tiffany (2009), Kobrak (2009), and Popp (2009). To debate this issue, form two teams and prepare a set of arguments 'for' and 'against' the motion: 'This House believes that

entrepreneurs have nothing to learn from history.' Allow five minutes for each side, followed by a further five minutes to respond to the arguments presented. Then move to a vote. To make the debate more interesting, allocate team members so that those who disagree with the motion have to defend it, and vice-versa (note: the debate format can be adapted for use in a virtual learning environment, or as an individual essay topic).

2.   **Adopting historical methods** In Section 14.1, we considered some of the methods available to researchers who want to examine entrepreneurial activity from an historical perspective. Imagine that you were researching entrepreneurial activity in the early days of the Internet (i.e. the period 1985–2000). What methods would you select in order to discover more about this subject? What challenges would you expect to face in conducting your research?

3.   **Whose history?** There is often a great deal of argument between historians (and others) over the factual accuracy of an account, or of how the evidence should be interpreted. For example, an entrepreneurial autobiography may give one account – perhaps emphasising the individual's own abilities and impact – while others might argue that it was all down to luck, or to external factors. Who should you believe, and how can you be sure that the narrative you are reading is a fair representation of what actually happened?

Recommended reading

These readings address two important topics in entrepreneurship research and are recommended for anyone wanting to build on the material covered in this chapter. Recommended readings have been selected from leading Sage journals and are freely available for readers of this textbook to download via the Online Resources.

Haveman, H.A., Habinek, J., and Goodman, L.A. (2012) 'How entrepreneurship evolves: the founders of new magazines in America, 1741–1860'. *Administrative Science Quarterly*, 57, 4: 585–624.

This article examines how individual actors navigate social structures in order to acquire resources and launch their new ventures. The researchers test the argument that, as industries develop, it becomes increasingly difficult for newcomers to become established. This historical study is based on evidence about the American magazine industry in the eighteenth and nineteenth centuries. Though initially restricted to an elite group of publishing-industry insiders, they found later founders were mostly newcomers, of more modest social status, but that their success was uneven and that insiders retained their dominance at the centre of the industry.

Jones, C. (2001) 'Co-evolution of entrepreneurial careers, institutional rules and competitive dynamics in American film, 1895–1920'. *Organization Studies*, 22, 6: 911–44.

This article presents an historical case analysis of the early American film industry, tracing the careers of two distinct groups of pioneering entrepreneurs – one group were developing the new technologies of film-making while the other group, which emerged from the existing entertainment industry, was focused on the content. The researcher uses archival data and historical analysis to show how these different elements co-evolved, and how changes in the institutional 'rules' affected the fortunes of each group of entrepreneurs.

References

Agterbosch, S. and Breukers, S. (2008) 'Sociopolitical embedding of onshore wind power in the Netherlands and North Rhine-Westphalia'. *Technology Analysis and Strategic Management*, 20, 5: 633–48.

Amin, A. and Thrift, N. (1995) *Globalization, Institutions, and Regional Development in Europe*. Oxford: Oxford University Press.

Asmus, P. (2000) *Reaping the Wind: How Mechanical Wizards, Visionaries, and Profiteers Helped Shape Our Energy Future*. Washington DC: Island Press.

Bagnasco, A. (1977) *Tre Italia. La Problematica Territoriale Dello Sviluppo Economico Italiano*. Bologna: II Mulino.

Becattini, G., Bellandi, M., and De Propris, L. (eds) (2014) *A Handbook of Industrial Districts*. Cheltenham: Edward Elgar.

Berlin, L. (2005) *The Man Behind the Microchip. Robert Noyce and the Invention of Silicon Valley*. Oxford: Oxford University Press.

Best, M. H. (2001) *The New Competitive Advantage: The Renewal of American Industry*. Oxford: Oxford University Press.

Best, M. H. (2015) 'Greater Boston's industrial ecosystem: a manufactory of sectors'. *Technovation*, 39–40: 4–13.

Black, E. (2001) *IBM and the Holocaust: The Strategic Alliance Between Nazi Germany and America's Most Powerful Corporation*. London: Little, Brown.

Blundel, R. K. and Lyon, F. (2015) 'Towards a "long view": historical perspectives on the scaling and replication of social ventures'. *Journal of Social Entrepreneurship*, 6, 1: 80–102.

Blundel, R. K. and Tregear, A. (2006) 'Artisans and "factories": the interpenetration of craft and industry in English cheese-making, c1650–1950'. *Enterprise and Society*, 7, 4: 1–35.

Bornstein, D. (2004) *How to Change the World: Social Entrepreneurs and the Power of New Ideas*. Oxford: Oxford University Press.

Bradley, I. C. (2007) *Enlightened Entrepreneurs: Business Ethics in Victorian Britain*. Oxford: Lion Hudson.

Cadbury (2010) 'Cadbury: our story'. Bourneville: Cadbury. Available at: http://www.cadbury.co.uk (accessed 18 February 2010).

Carnevali, F. (2003) 'Golden opportunities: jewellery making in Birmingham between mass production and speciality'. *Enterprise and Society*, 4, 2: 272–98.

Carnevali, F. (2004) '"Crooks, thieves and receivers": transaction costs in nineteenth century industrial Birmingham'. *Economic History Review*, 57, 3: 533–50.

Cassis, Y. and Minoglou, I. P. (2005) *Entrepreneurship in Theory and History*. Basingstoke: Palgrave.

Casson, M. and Godley, A. (2007) 'Revisiting the emergence of the modern business enterprise: entrepreneurship and the Singer global distribution system'. *Journal of Management Studies*, 44, 7: 1064–77.

Casson, M., Yeung, B., Basu, A., and Wadeson, N. (2008) *The Oxford Handbook of Entrepreneurship*. Oxford: Oxford University Press.

Castronovo, V. (1999) *Fiat 1899–1999: Un Decolo di Storia Italiana*. Milan: Rizzoli.

Chandler, A. D. (1956) *Henry Varnum Poor: Business Editor, Analyst and Reformer*. Cambridge MA: Harvard University Press.

Chandler, A. D. (1990) *Scale and Scope: the Dynamics of Industrial Capitalism*. Cambridge MA: Belknap Press.

Chandler, A. D. and Salsbury, P. (1971) *Pierre S. Du Pont and the Making of the Modern Corporation*. New York: Harper and Row.

Clark, T. (2008) *Starbucked: a Double Tall Tale of Caffeine, Commerce and Culture*. London: Sceptre.

Colli, A. and Rose, M. (2008) 'Family business'. In G. Jones and J. Zeitlin (eds), op. cit. (194–218).

Connell, C. M. (2003) 'Jardine Matheson & Company: the role of external organization in a nineteenth-century trading firm'. *Enterprise and Society*, 4, 1: 99–138.

Corley, T. A. B. (2008) 'Historical biographies of entrepreneurs'. In M. Casson et al. (eds), op. cit. (138–75).

Cottereau, A. (1997) 'The fate of collective manufacturers in the industrial world: the silk industries of Lyons and London, 1800–1850'. In C. F. Sabel and J. Zeitlin (eds), op. cit. (75–152).

Evans, M. (1878) 'Butter and cheese'. In G. Phillips (ed.), *British Manufacturing Industries*. London: Edward Stanforth.

Fant, K. (2007) *Alfred Nobel: A Biography* (Tr. Ruuth, M.), New York: Arcade.

Garud, R. and Karnøe, P. (2003) 'Bricolage versus breakthrough: distributed and embedded agency in technology entrepreneurship'. *Research Policy*, 32: 277–300.

Gilbar, G. G. (2003) 'The Muslim big merchant-entrepreneurs of the Middle East, 1860–1914'. *Die Welt des Islams*, 43, 1: 1–36.

Gipe, P. (1995) *Wind Energy Comes of Age*. New York: Wiley.

Glasmeier, A. (1994) 'Technological discontinuities and flexible production networks: the case of Switzerland and the world watch industry'. *Research Policy*, 20, 5: 469–85.

Godelier, E. (2009) 'History, a useful "science" for management?: from polemics to controversies'. *Enterprise and Society*, 10, 4: 791–807.

Graham, B.W. (2008) 'Technology and innovation'. In G. Jones and J. Zeitlin (eds), op. cit. (120–40).

Granovetter, M. (1985) 'Economic action and social structure: the problem of embeddedness'. *American Journal of Sociology*, 91: 481–510.

GWEC (2016) *Global Wind Energy Report 2015*. Brussels: Global Wind Energy Council.

Haggerty, S. (2006) *The British-Atlantic Trading Community, 1760–1810: Men, Women, and the Distribution of Goods*. Leiden and Boston, MA: Brill.

Henry, N. and Pinch, S. (2001) 'Neo-Marshallian nodes, institutional thickness, and Britain's "Motor Sport Valley": thick or thin?' *Environment and Planning A*, 33, 7: 1169–83.

Hutcheson, J. O. (2007) 'The end of a 1,400-year-old business'. *Business Week* (16 April). http://www.bloomberg.com/news/articles/2007-04-16/the-end-of-a-1-400-year-old-businessbusinessweek-business-news-stock-market-and-financial-advice (accessed 16 October 2016).

Jones, C. (2001) 'Co-evolution of entrepreneurial careers, institutional rules and competitive dynamics in American film, 1895–1920'. *Organization Studies*, 22, 6: 911–44.

Jones, G. and Wadhwani, R. D. (2008) 'Entrepreneurship'. In G. Jones and J. Zeitlin (eds), op. cit. (501–28).

Jones, G. and Zeitlin, J. (eds) (2008) *The Oxford Handbook of Business History*. Oxford: Oxford University Press.

Keane, M. J. (1990) 'Economic development capacity amongst small rural communities'. *Journal of Rural Studies*, 6, 3: 291–301.

Keeble, D. and Wilkinson, F. (1999) 'Collective learning and knowledge development in the evolution of regional clusters of high technology SMEs in Europe'. *Regional Studies*, 33, 4, 295–303.

Keeble, D., Lawson, C., Moore, B., and Wilkinson, F. (1999) 'Collective learning processes, networking and "institutional thickness" in the Cambridge Region'. *Regional Studies*, 33, 4: 319–32.

Kelley, D., Singer, S., and Herrington, M. (2016) *Global Entrepreneurship Monitor 2015 Global Report*. London: Global Entrepreneurship Research Association. http://www.gemconsortium.org (accessed 16 October 2016).

Kirby, M. (1993) 'Quakerism, entrepreneurship and the family firm in north-east England, 1780–1860'. In J. Brown and M.B. Rose (eds), *Entrepreneurship, Networks and Modern Business*. Manchester: Manchester University Press (105–43).

Kobrak, C. (2009) 'The use and abuse of history as a management tool: comments on Eric Gordelier's view of the French connection'. *Enterprise and Society*, 10, 4: 808–15.

Landes, D. S. ([1969] 2003) *The Unbound Prometheus: Technological Change and Industrial Development in Western Europe from 1750 to the Present* (2nd edn). Cambridge: Cambridge University Press.

Lawson, C. and Lorenz, E. (2000) 'Collective learning, tacit knowledge and regional innovative capacity'. *Regional Studies*, 33, 4: 305–17.

Levinson, M. (2006) *The Box: How The Shipping Container Made the World Smaller and the World Economy Bigger*. Princeton NJ: Princeton University Press.

Lewis, M. (2001) *The New New Thing: a Silicon Valley Story*. London: Penguin.

Mallett, O. and Wapshott, R. (2015) 'Contesting the history and politics of enterprise and entrepreneurship'. *Work, Employment & Society*, 29, 1: 177–82.

March, J. G. (1991) 'Exploration and exploitation in organization learning'. *Organization Science*, 2, 1: 71–87.

Marshall, A. M. ([1920] 2010) *Principles of Economics* (8th edn; abridged). New York: Cosimo.

Mason, C. and Harvey, C. (2013) 'Entrepreneurship: contexts, opportunities and processes'. *Business History*, 55, 1: 1–8.

McCabe, I. B., Harlaftis, G., and Minoglou, I. P. (2005) *Diaspora Entrepreneurial Networks: Four Centuries of History* (2nd edn). New York: Berg.

McMurry, S. A. (1995) *Transforming Rural Life: Rural Dairying Families and Agricultural Change 1820–1885*. Baltimore, MD, Baltimore: Johns Hopkins University Press.

Nobel (2016) 'Nobel Peace Prize'. Oslo: Norwegian Nobel Institute. Available at: http://nobelpeaceprize.org (accessed 11 November 2016).

Osirim, M. J. (2008) 'African women in the new diaspora: transnationalism and the (re) creation of home'. *African and Asian Studies*, 7, 4: 367–94.

Parsons, M. C. and Rose, M. B. (2003) *Invisible on Everest: Innovation and the Gear Makers*. Philadelphia PA: Old City Publishing.

Parsons, M. C. and Rose, M. B. (2005) 'The neglected legacy of Lancashire cotton: industrial clusters and the UK outdoor trade 1960–1990'. Enterprise and Society, 6, 4: 682–709.

Pettigrew, A. (1985) *The Awakening Giant: Continuity and Change in Imperial Chemical Industries*. Oxford: Blackwell.

Piore, M. and Sabel, C. (1984) *The Second Industrial Divide*. New York: Basic.

Pittaway, L. and Tunstall, R. (2016) 'Is there still a Heffalump in the room?: examining paradigms in historical entrepreneurship research'. In H. Landstrom, A. Parhankangas, A. Fayolle, and P. Riot (eds), *Challenging Entrepreneurship Research*. Abingdon: Routledge (173–209).

Popp, A. (2007) 'Building the market: John Shaw of Wolverhampton and commercial travelling in early nineteenth-century England'. *Business History*, 49, 3: 321–47.

Popp, A. (2009) 'History, a useful "science" for management?: a response'. *Enterprise and Society*, 10, 4: 831–6.

Popp, A. and Holt, R. (2013) 'Entrepreneurship and being: the case of the Shaws'. *Entrepreneurship & Regional Development,* 25 (1–2): 52–68.

Popp, A. and Wilson, J. F. (2007) 'Life-cycles, contingency and agency: growth, development and change in English industrial districts and clusters'. *Environment and Planning A*, 39, 12: 2975–92.

Rose, M. B. (2000) *Firms, Networks and Business Values: The British and American Cotton Industries Since 1750*. Cambridge: Cambridge University Press.

Rose, M. B. and Parsons, M. C. (2004) 'Communities of knowledge: entrepreneurship, innovation and networks in the British outdoor trade 1960–1990'. *Business History*, 46, 4: 606–37.

Rose, M. B., Love, T., and Parsons, M. C. (2007) 'Path dependent foundation of global design-driven outdoor trade in the North West of England'. *International Journal of Design*, 1, 3: 57–68.

Rowlinson, M., Hassard, J., and Decker, S. (2014) 'Research strategies for organizational history: a dialogue between historical theory and organization theory. *Academy of Management Review*, 39, 3: 250–74.

Sabel, C. F. and Zeitlin, J. (eds) (1997) *World of Possibilities: Flexibility and Mass Production in Western Industrialization*. Cambridge: Cambridge University Press.

Schreyögg, G., Sydow, J. and Holtmann, P. (2011) 'How history matters in organisations: the case of path dependence'. *Management & Organizational History*, 6, 1: 81–100.

Schumpeter, Joseph ([1942] 2010). *Capitalism, Socialism, and Democracy.* London: Routledge.

Scranton, P. (2000) *Endless Novelty: Specialty Production and American Industrialization, 1865–1925.* Princeton NJ: Princeton University Press.

Shane, S. (1996) 'Explaining variation in rates of entrepreneurship in the United States 1899–1988'. *Journal of Management*, 22, 5: 747–81.

Smith, D. J. and Blundel, R. K. (2014) 'Improvisation and entrepreneurial bricolage versus rationalisation: a case-based analysis of contrasting responses to economic instability in the UK brass musical instruments industry'. *Journal of General Management*, 40, 1: 53–78.

Tarbell, I. M. ([1904] 2010) *History of the Standard Oil Company.* New York: McClure & Phillips. http://www.history.rochester.edu/fuels/tarbell (accessed 8 March 2010).

Tiffany, P. (2009) 'Does history matter in business?' *Enterprise and Society*, 10, 4: 816–30.

Vestas (2016) *Annual Report 2015*. Hedeager: Vestas Wind Systems A/S. http://www.vestas.com/en/investor/financial_reports#!financialreports2015 (accessed 16 October 2016).

Walker, J. (1986) 'Racism, slavery, free enterprise: black entrepreneurship in the United States before the Civil War'. *Business History Review* 60, 3: 343–82.

Wezel, F. C. (2005) 'Location dependence and industry evolution: founding rates in the United Kingdom motorcycle industry, 1895–1993'. *Organization Studies*, 26, 5: 729–54.

Wezel, F. C. and Lomi, A. (2003) 'The organizational advantage of nations: an ecological perspective on the evolution of the motorcycle industry in Belgium, Italy and Japan, 1898–1993'. *Geography and Strategy: Advances in Strategic Management*, 20: 359–92.

Willard, X. A. (1877) *Practical Dairy Husbandry.* New York: Excelsior.

Wilson, J. F. and Popp, A. (2009) 'Business in the regions: from "old" industrial districts to "new" clusters'. In R. Coopey and P. Lyth (eds), *Business in Britain in the Twentieth Century: Decline and Renaissance?* Oxford: Oxford University Press (65–81).

Yergin, D. ([1991] 2009) *The Prize: The Epic Quest for Oil, Money and Power* (with new epilogue). New York: Simon and Schuster.

Zeitlin, J. (2008a) 'The historical alternatives approach'. In G. Jones and J. Zeitlin (eds), op. cit. (120–40).

Zeitlin, J. (2008b) 'Industrial districts and regional clusters'. In G. Jones and J. Zeitlin (eds), op. cit. (219–43).

15

POLITICAL PERSPECTIVES: FROM POLICY TO PRACTICE

A State which dwarfs its men [sic] in order that they be more docile instruments in its hands, even for beneficial purposes – will find that with small men no great thing can really be accomplished.

John Stuart Mill, nineteenth-century philosopher and political writer (1869)

Indigenous businesses and entrepreneurs are a vital part of the ideas boom. This is the new boom. This is the inexhaustible ever renewable boom. It is limited only by our imagination and our enterprise and I think we have as Australians unlimited imagination and unlimited enterprise.Günter

Malcolm Turnbull, Australian prime minister's speech to young Indigenous businesses and entrepreneurs (2016)

LEARNING OUTCOMES

After reading this chapter you should be able to:

- Explore entrepreneurship from a political perspective, with a particular focus on public policy, economic development, and innovation.

- Understand why governments and non-governmental organisations intervene in the entrepreneurship process, and what they seek to achieve.

- Appreciate the wide range of strategies and techniques used to encourage and to guide enterprise in particular directions.

- Critically evaluate the impact of enterprise policies, and consider how they might be adapted or developed in order to respond to contemporary issues.

- Make connections between policy-making and the current state of knowledge about entrepreneurship, as reviewed in the other Part Two chapters.

- Recognise how policies can be related to your own entrepreneurial experiences, and how they may influence your future activities.

15.1 INTRODUCTION

The environments in which entrepreneurs operate are, to a large extent, shaped by public policies, both those currently in place and earlier policies whose influence is still felt today. It is important to understand these policies and their impact on entrepreneurial activity. Looking to the future, it is also worth considering how changes in policy might create new challenges and opportunities for entrepreneurs. Entrepreneurial activity is a powerful force in the world. It has enormous potential to contribute to our general well-being, but it can also do widespread and long-lasting damage to our societies and to the natural world on which we all depend. Politics is also about the exercise of power, and has a similar potential for making things better or worse. This chapter concludes our exploration of entrepreneurship by looking at its relationship with politics and policy-making. As the editors of a special issue point out, entrepreneurship policy is still an area where we have a great deal to learn:

> *While the benefits of entrepreneurship are becoming near universally acknowledged, our understanding of how and when governments intervene to assist entrepreneurs, and indeed which, if any, specific entrepreneurs should receive assistance in some shape or form, still has substantial knowledge gaps, and remains controversial. (Robson et al. 2009: 533)*

We address a number of policy-related questions in this chapter. For example: Should governments be attempting either to encourage or to guide enterprise in the first place? Do policy-makers have the capacity to influence something as diffuse and 'slippery' as entrepreneurship? And what are the practical implications for entrepreneurs? The following case study can be used as a starting point for thinking through these issues (Case 15.1).

CASE 15.1   STUDENT FOCUS

Ruling the world for a day

These short fictionalised accounts, based on real world examples, illustrate how students have made good use of entrepreneurship research to achieve successful outcomes in their studies.

   A small group of entrepreneurship students has just been to hear a panel of national politicians speak at a pre-election event. On the way home, they start arguing about the

 politician's contrasting approaches to economic and social development. The arguments continue for several hours but nobody can agree on the best course of action. There is a fairly clear political divide in the group, but nobody is willing to compromise. They decide to raise the issue with their tutor in class the following morning. Perhaps unsurprisingly, the tutor is not willing to

support either side of the argument. Instead, she challenges them with the following 'thought experiment':

Congratulations! Following a bloodless coup, you have just taken control of the government. You have widespread support in the general population, at least for the time being. The legal officers have ensured that all existing enterprise policies are to be cancelled, effective from tomorrow. In other words, you have been given a 'blank sheet', and are free to decide on an entirely new set of policies that will be effective both in promoting more entrepreneurial activity in your country, while also controlling for potential negative impacts. As you sit at your impressive new desk, two thoughts come to mind. Firstly, leading a coup against a very unpopular regime is relatively easy. Secondly, now *you* are in charge, things are beginning to look a bit more complicated.

Having outlined the scenario, the tutor divides the students into teams and sets them the three questions below, asking for a short presentation at next week's class. With a deep sigh, they head off in search of some inspiration – and a strong cup of coffee.

QUESTIONS

1.   What are our 'top three' policy objectives?
2.   How are we going to achieve them?
3.   How will we know if they have worked?

Note: you might find it useful to try this thought experiment before completing the rest of this chapter, then revisit your answers later and see whether you would make any changes.

This scenario may seem unrealistic and extreme, but there are some strong parallels with real-world policy-making. Firstly, as you probably realised, there is really no such thing as a 'blank sheet'. Even with unlimited budgets and public support, your incoming government faces many challenges and constraints. For example, there may be large regional variations in the level of entrepreneurial activity, reinforced by geography (e.g. remote rural locations, low population densities, hostile natural environments) and historical factors (e.g. the 'Upas tree' effect of declining heavy **industries**) (Sections 13.5 and 14.3). Secondly, in order to make any decisions on policy objectives, priorities, design, and implementation, you will need to have views about what entrepreneurship is and how it works in practice. These views may be based on research evidence, anecdotal evidence, your personal opinion, or political expediency (i.e. what best fits the short-term agenda of the people in power). In reality, policy-making is often driven by a combination of these four factors. Some policy studies specialists have argued strongly for what is known as 'evidence-based' policy (e.g. Pawson 2006), coupled with a rigorous system to evaluate its outputs, impact, and longer-term outcomes. In our case, this means making better use of the research approaches discussed in previous Part Two chapters, in order to ensure that enterprise policies are well-designed and effective in achieving their objectives.

The chapter is organised as follows. In Section 15.2, we consider the political context in which recent policies have been developed, identify key features of today's policy landscape, and clarify some widely used terms. Section 15.3 asks why governments consider it necessary to become involved in the activities of entrepreneurs, distinguishing between economic and non-economic arguments for intervention. In Section 15.4, we consider the wide range of approaches that governments have adopted, and the combinations of techniques they have employed in order to pursue their chosen policy goals. Section 15.5 looks at how existing enterprise policies are evaluated and ways in which they could be enhanced in the future.

15.2 THE POLITICAL CONTEXT

15.2.1 Shaping the entrepreneurial economy

During the last quarter of the twentieth century, many industrialised countries pursued a programme of reforms designed to create an 'entrepreneurial' economy (Audretsch and Thurik 2000) (Sections 1.1, 10.1, and 13.1). This transition is now widely recognised as being, at least in part, a political project. In other words, national and regional governments have been engaged in a conscious attempt to change existing economic and social institutions in order to encourage entrepreneurial activity. This project, and the policies adopted to pursue it, can be explained in a number of ways. From an economic perspective, they can be seen as part of a move from interventionist policies based on Keynesian economics to a 'neo-liberal' economics, which placed an increased reliance on market mechanisms. Secondly, they responded to a perceived need to reverse a decline in the population of smaller firms, and to recognise their contribution to the economy. Thirdly, they reflected a concern that big business corporations lacked entrepreneurial energy, and that large organisations of all kinds needed to recover the virtues of their smaller counterparts in order to remain innovative and to compete effectively in the future.

15.2.2 The policy landscape: scope and terminology

So far, we have been using the umbrella term 'enterprise policy' to refer to any attempt to encourage or guide entrepreneurial activity. In this section, we outline the scope of enterprise policy and clarify some of the language used in policy debates:

- **SME policies and entrepreneurship policies:** These two strands of policy are at the centre of the enterprise policy landscape (Figure 15.1). Though there is considerable overlap, and the terms are often used quite loosely, researchers have noted some important differences of emphasis (e.g. Stevenson and Lundström 2002; Huggins and Williams 2009). SME policies are usually concerned with improving the short- to medium-term economic performance of existing firms. Entrepreneurship policies tend to have a wider scope and a longer-term orientation (Audretsch and Beckmann 2007), and are designed to promote entrepreneurial vitality, including the encouragement of potential entrepreneurs and of new start-up ventures. This difference is also reflected in the methods adopted to drive the policy forwards. For example, in order to help existing small firms in the house-building sector, you might decide to simplify regulations, reduce the tax burden, provide access to information, or subsidise current training schemes. By contrast, if your priority was to encourage more innovative entrepreneurial activity in the sector, you might decide to launch pre-start and start-up support schemes (e.g. linking university-based building technologists with external sources of venture finance and business advice), and promote networking activity among the most dynamic and technologically advanced materials, design and construction firms.

FIGURE 15.1 Small Business Saturday: SME policy or entrepreneurship policy?

Source: https://creativecommons.org/licenses/by-nd/2.0/

- **Other policies that influence entrepreneurship:** The level and quality of entrepreneurial activity can be influenced, both directly and indirectly, by many other areas of public policy that operate alongside the policies we are discussing in this chapter. Examples might include taxation, industry regulation, international trade, and education. The influence of these related policies is bound to vary: an arts-based social enterprise, for example, would be affected by a different combination of policies to a biotechnology start-up venture. In some cases, their effect may be to support, or reinforce entrepreneurship and SME policies (e.g. investing in the education system could help to promote new venture creation), but there may also be tensions and conflicting objectives (e.g. groups representing small firms often complain that new government regulations increase their costs, making them less competitive against international competitors). Science and innovation policy, which is probably the most closely connected of these 'related' policy areas, makes an appearance later in the chapter (Sections 15.2 and 15.4).

- **Other dimensions of policy – scale and scope:** We have already seen that the policy landscape contains a variety of types of policy, which can combine in different ways to influence entrepreneurial activity. Enterprise policies also operate at different geographic scales, from international policies coordinated by cross-national bodies (e.g. the European Union's 'Enable' Programme) to small-scale initiatives, developed at a local level (e.g. creating a farmers' market or promoting social enterprises in a small town). Policies can also vary in scope: they may be economy-wide (e.g. income tax reforms); sector-specific (e.g. industry de-regulation); or targeted at particular groups (e.g. supporting young entrepreneurs) (Section 15.4.2).

It is not possible to do justice to such a complex policy landscape in a single chapter. Rather than attempt a comprehensive review, we consider a more limited range of policies, looking at the arguments used to support them, how they were implemented, and what they have achieved.

15.3 ARGUMENTS FOR INTERVENTION

15.3.1 How (and why) do governments intervene?

When politicians talk about entrepreneurship and enterprise, they often refer to things like 'deregulation', 'liberalisation', and reducing the role of government. Yet in practice policy-makers are often tempted to intervene in the entrepreneurship process. These interventions can range from new laws and regulations to financial incentives and support programmes. The aims and objectives vary widely but are likely to fall into one or more of the following broad categories: (1) encouraging people to engage in entrepreneurial activity; (2) increasing the overall scale and impact of that activity; (3) guiding it in particular directions. In the next sub-section (Section 15.3.2), we examine the main *economic* arguments for intervention, which tend to be based on the pursuit of increases in growth, employment and competitiveness. The *non-economic* arguments, which tend to revolve around the social and environmental impacts of enterprise, are discussed in Section 15.3.3.

15.3.2 Economic arguments: growth, employment, and competitiveness

The economic case for intervention has been built on the idea that governments can generate employment and stimulate economic growth, either by supporting SMEs or by promoting various forms of entrepreneurial activity. The primary objectives of **SME policies** have typically been to strengthen an existing population of small firms, ensuring that they are able to compete effectively against larger firms. These interventions have often addressed specific 'market failures' that create disadvantages for small firms in relation to their larger counterparts (Audretsch et al. 2007; Huggins and Williams 2009). SME policies have also attempted to increase the population of smaller firms in order to address issues such as under-development and economic decline in particular regions (e.g. remote rural communities or post-industrial cities).

In summary, the economic case for intervention could include one or more the following objectives:

- to provide employment, particularly important for communities in some locations (e.g. inner cities, remote rural areas);
- to create new economic activity, particularly important at regional and local level, where a decline in the population of firms can increase income disparities;
- to contribute to economic competitiveness at a regional and sectoral level (e.g. networks of small firms are needed to supply large manufacturing firms); despite globalisation, this can also have a regional competitiveness dimension;
- because smaller firms can pursue entrepreneurial opportunities that cannot readily be taken up by larger firms;
- to increase industry competition and act as a countervailing force against powerful groups of larger firms.

A common theme is that intervention is justified because SMEs are economically disadvantaged, leading to inefficiencies that cannot be corrected solely through free market mechanisms. The following examples illustrate the disadvantages you might face as the owner-manager of a small firm based in a remote rural location. How might these factors impact on your competitiveness?

- Your costs of financing the venture are higher because banks lack information on small rural firms and charge premium rates to reflect this uncertainty. You are also finding it more difficult to get information on, or access to, attractive public procurement contracts.

- Your delivery costs are higher and there is limited access to higher speed broadband due to your remote location. Administrative costs in complying with industry regulations are also proportionately higher due to the size of your organisation.

- You are having difficulties in protecting intellectual property and costs are higher, in comparison to a larger firm, because you do not have access to specialist legal advice.

Underlying these 'market failure' arguments is the suggestion that there may be unequal power relationships between organisations of a different size (e.g. small shops or small food producers and large multiple retailers). One of the best ways to see these power relationships in operation is to look at the policy and campaigning activities of small business lobbying organisations, such as the UK's Federation of Small Businesses or Sweden's Federation of Private Enterprises (*Företagarna*).

The economic case for **entrepreneurship policies** is often built on similar arguments to those already discussed, the orientation is different. While there are many overlaps, entrepreneurship policies tend to focus less on the fortunes of smaller firms, and more on the long-term development of new entrepreneurs. Policies of this kind have been introduced by many market economies to promote goals such as innovation and international competitiveness. They were also implemented in the so-called 'transition countries' during the post-Soviet era as a way of promoting their reorientation from state control towards a more market-based system (Smallbone and Welter 2010). Instead of making the case for a particular category of organisation (i.e. small and medium-sized enterprises), the argument for entrepreneurship policy is based around the need to respond to major changes in the world economy, such as globalisation. Policies have also been influenced by the emergence of post-industrial, knowledge-based economies, where entrepreneurial start-ups are seen as playing a pivotal role in promoting technological innovation through 'knowledge spillovers':

> *Entrepreneurship takes on new importance in the knowledge economy because it serves as a key mechanism by means of which knowledge created in one organization becomes commercialized in a new enterprise. (Audretsch and Beckmann 2007: 41)*

Economic arguments for intervention are usually discussed in isolation, with economists often going to considerable effort to express them in rigorous, quantifiable terms. For example, governments might seek to discourage economically 'destructive' outcomes and promote those that are more economically 'productive' (Baumol 1990) (Section 13.4). However, in practice it is difficult to separate the economic, social, and environmental dimensions of policy-making. This is because even the most rigorous economic argument is underpinned by ideas about the kind of world that we want to live in. For example, a government introduces SME policies to defend small specialist shops against the power of large multiple retailers. These policies could be defended in purely *economic* terms, with reference to market imperfections (e.g. by measuring the impact of anti-competitive, rent-seeking behaviour on consumer prices). However, the policy could be also defended on *social* and *environmental* grounds (e.g. reviving local food varieties, reducing 'food miles' by local sourcing), which reflects the fact that entrepreneurial activity is capable of generating different kinds of 'value' (Sections 13.1 and 13.3).

15.3.3 Non-economic arguments: social and environmental impacts

Consider the major global challenges of the early twenty-first century: climate change, international migration, financial instability, international terrorism and populist uprisings, and the 'bottom billion' of the world's population who continue to live in poverty. It is clear that governments are not capable of addressing these issues by themselves, and that entrepreneurial actors have the potential to make significant contributions in many areas. For example, technology entrepreneurs are already involved in creating new, low-carbon technologies and industry sectors, and social entrepreneurs are helping to increase incomes in the poorest countries. However, as critics have pointed out, in some cases the activity of entrepreneurs is making things much worse. The problem arises when people decide to pursue economically attractive opportunities that have socially or environmentally destructive consequences. For example, the continuing boom in low-cost aviation is increasing global greenhouse gas emissions, while the exploitation of global demand for timber and palm oil is leading to the disappearance of irreplaceable rainforests. Should entrepreneurial activity be controlled, in order to minimise its more destructive effects, or guided towards more productive directions? So is it possible to extend Baumol's (1990) distinction between productive, unproductive and destructive entrepreneurship beyond the economic sphere (Section 13.4)?

Social arguments – combating exclusion and other problems: The world of enterprise is open to anyone, at least in principle. However, as we have seen in previous chapters, there are significant variations in the amount of entrepreneurial activity to be found in different locations and among certain social groups. If we assume, for a moment, that participation in entrepreneurial activity is a 'good thing', and capable of increasing the life chances of individuals and communities, there is a strong case for intervening to ensure that such opportunities are more widely available. This line of argument has led to a range of enterprise policies that are designed to encourage increased participation by excluded groups, including the young, older people, people with a disability, and members of some ethnic minority communities (LDA 2005; Blackburn and Ram 2006; Carter et al. 2015). As Blackburn and Ram (2006: 75) have noted, current thinking – at least in the United Kingdom context – is that there is an 'inextricable link' between enterprise policy and efforts to tackle social exclusion. Across Europe, social enterprises of various kinds are often seen as an effective vehicle for integrating marginalised groups into society (Spear and Bidet 2005). Other examples of socially oriented enterprise policies can be found in rural areas, where the objective is not simply to generate wealth, but to maintain – and in some cases to revive – local communities and cultures. Rural enterprise initiatives raise complex issues, reflecting the distinctive characteristics of rural businesses and of remoter rural areas in particular (Smallbone et al. 2002). For example, it has long been recognised that in-migrants can become a potent source of new entrepreneurial ventures, generating income and employment. On the other hand, wealthy in-migrants can distort local housing markets, forcing younger people to relocate to urban centres. The flow of in-migrants is also uneven, with more scenic and accessible locations (so-called 'honey-pots') drawing much larger numbers than their less attractive and more remote counterparts. There can also be tensions between encouraging the growth of new businesses and preserving heritage sites (e.g. ancient monuments) and natural resources (e.g. unique wildlife habitats). Efforts to attract inward investment can also create problems for rural areas. Large companies may be attracted to an area in response to a combination of government grants, subsidies, tax exemptions, and infrastructure investments. However, these new arrivals can prove to be 'foot-loose', relocating to other areas in response to changes in their own strategic priorities. The sudden loss of a large employer can wreak havoc on any community, but the effects can be particularly severe in rural regions, where alternative sources of employment (for local people), and of customers (for local business supplying the corporation) are few and far between (Section 13.5).

Environmental arguments – 'greening' business: In recent years, governments have made increasing use of SME policy interventions in order to control against environ-mentally damaging activity, and to encourage more environmentally benign ways of operating (Parker et al. 2009; Mazur 2012; Blundel et al. 2013). The arguments for intervening are based on evidence that SMEs have been slow to adopt environmental improvements, with research evidence suggesting that this is due to a combination of internal and external barriers. The case for intervention echoes previously discussed economic arguments (e.g. limited resources and information), but requires a sound understanding of the drivers of improved environmental performance (Parry 2012; Muñoz and Dimov 2015). In some cases, there is also a lack of clear market signals and an inadequate 'business case' for making the necessary changes. Given the short-term pressures facing many small business owners, why should they invest time, effort, and resources to improve their performance? Since SMEs represent such a high percentage of businesses, intervention is seen as necessary for a number of reasons, including: (1) helping to address governmental targets (e.g. reducing greenhouse gas emissions); (2) enabling larger firms and the public sector to source from environmentally sustain-able suppliers; and (3) ensuring that SMEs are able to take up the new opportunities of a low-carbon economy (e.g. Parry 2012). Entrepreneurship policies in the envi-ronmental area are often linked to more conventional economic aims. Encouraging environmental technology start-ups, for example, could form part of an innovation strategy, in which traditional industries are transformed to help countries and regions remain internationally competitive (e.g. UNEP 2009; McDowall and Ekins 2014).

These economic, social and environmental arguments can sometimes be combined. For example, Cultivate (Figure 15.2), a co-operative social enterprise that supplies locally-grown produce to people living in Oxford, delivers a range of benefits:

- Strengthens the local economy: money spent local stays local – supporting local organic and ecological producers.

- Food tastes better: local fruit and vegetables are fresh and ripe – they can go from the field to your hands in hours.

- Cuts down on food miles: buying food produced 20 miles away, rather than 2,000 miles, emits less CO_2 from transport.

- Builds community: local people get to know each other better by becoming involved in the project.
- Creates shared culture: people develop a closer bond with their city and natural environment.

As a result, entrepreneurial initiatives of this kind can generate social and environmental value in addition to promoting economic activity in a particular locality.

FIGURE 15.2 Cultivate – a community-based enterprise

Source: Cultivate (www.cultivate.org.uk)

In the following case study (Case 15.2), Friederike Welter talks about her research on entrepreneurship and policy-making in different contexts.

CASE 15.2   RESEARCHER PROFILE

FRIEDERIKE WELTER: ON EXAMINING ENTREPRENEURSHIP IN
DIFFERENT CONTEXTS

Friederike Welter is head of the Institut für Mittelstandsforschung (IfM) Bonn, Germany's oldest research institute focusing on small business and entrepreneurship policy, and professor at the University of Siegen, since 2013. She received her degree ('Diplom') in economics and business administration from the University of Bochum in 1989. Her doctoral thesis was on SMEs, their strategic behaviour and SME support in Nigeria. From 1993 to 2006, she worked in the Rhine-Westphalia Institute for Economic Research (RWI), becoming deputy head of the research division, Entrepreneurship and Enterprise Performance. From 2005 to 2008, she worked at the University of Siegen and from 2008 to 2012, as a professor at Jönköping International Business School, Sweden. In 2011, she was elected Fellow of the European Council for Small Business and Entrepreneurship (ESCB) and in 2014, Wilford White Fellow of the International Council for Small Business (ICSB). In 2015, she received the DIANA International Legacy Award for her research on women's entrepreneurship.

Friederike's main research interests are in entrepreneurship and small business development across different contexts, entrepreneurial behaviour, and entrepreneurship policies. She has edited and (co-)authored several books on topics such as entrepreneurship policies in the new Europe (Welter and Smallbone, 2011), the *Routledge Companion to Entrepreneurship* (Baker and Welter, 2015) and a research agenda for entrepreneurship and contexts (Welter and Gartner, 2016). She has also been co-editor for special issues, for example, on women's entrepreneurship in *Entrepreneurship Theory & Practice* (2006, 2007, 2012). She is also co-editor for a special issue of the *Strategic Entrepreneurship Journal* on the role of contexts, history and time for entrepreneurship.

In this interview, Friederike discusses her research on entrepreneurship in different contexts.

Why did you want to research in this area?

Initially, this was not a decision I made, but in the RWI we had acquired a large project, commissioned by the German Federal Ministry of Economics, to analyse the emergence and development of new and small ventures in Poland, Hungary, and the Czech and Slovak Republics. The topic was fascinating, in particular as little was known about SMEs and entrepreneurship in formerly planned economies at that time (1993). And I could continue my research interest from my doctoral thesis. Some of the research projects coming along after this initial project was finished were financed by national governments or international organisations such as the International Labour Office or USAID.

How did you decide on your main research questions?

I had little to say in determining the research questions but most of these studies tackled applied, policy-related issues of SME development, which have been core to my research since then. I also participated in, and later coordinated, several research projects financed by the European Union. In these cases our group could determine our own research questions which were driven by what we ('we' being a network of Western and East European researchers which had developed over time) felt were knowledge gaps in SME and entrepreneurship research. For example, one project researched women's entrepreneurship in Ukraine, Moldova, and Uzbekistan (Welter et al. 2006), another looked at trust in a Western and Eastern European context. Looking back, I see that from early projects onwards I developed a strong interest in the role of contexts for entrepreneurial behaviour and in the possible implications for entrepreneurship theory and policy (Welter, 2011, 2016).

(Continued)

(Continued)

What methods did you use?

All projects used a method mix: that started with desk research (especially where projects were government financed as in those cases we often could not fund empirical studies), secondary analysis of statistical data, and, where possible own data collection. The first project I participated in concentrated on a survey of SMEs, key expert interviews and profiles of business organisations in order to analyse the support needs of SMEs in the Ukraine, Belarus, and Moldova from different perspectives and to develop policy recommendations. In later projects, we added case studies (in-depth interviews, which were semi-structured) to our method box as those provided deep insights into the 'why' of entrepreneurial behaviour. And in the latest two projects, on cross-border cooperation and cross-border entrepreneurship, we relied on case studies only which provided very rich material.

What were your key findings?

That's a huge question, asking to summarise 20 years of research! One of my key findings sounds quite simple, namely that contexts matter – but this has become central to my policy-related research. For example, what constitutes, at first glance, 'irrational' behaviour from an economic point of view, such as unrelated diversification or portfolio entrepreneurship by entrepreneurs who had but very few resources, emerged as rational behaviour in an environment where banks did not finance new businesses, so that entrepreneurs were using these methods to self-finance their main business. Or take 'shuttle trading' (i.e. individuals crossing borders, exporting and importing all types of goods, often illegally). At first glance, you could debate whether this constitutes genuine entrepreneurship, but in some of the institutional contexts we had surveyed, small business owners progressed from shuttle trading, which provided them with financing, to more substantial businesses.

Were there any particular challenges in conducting these studies?

Definitely! Firstly, how to make our samples representative in those projects where we conducted surveys? There were no statistics of businesses, only outdated lists, etc. We used, again, a mix of sampling methods. Secondly, in the last projects on cross-border entrepreneurship we faced additional challenges, as we included petty traders in our samples. Most of those operate (partly) illegally, so interviews were conducted at border crossings, sometimes on trains or buses or at open air markets. Interviews could not be recorded, but had to be written up afterwards; and it took time to build up trust with our interviewees. Another challenge concerns data interpretation – we as researchers are also a product of our own contexts. Luckily, the close cooperation with Eastern European colleagues since the mid-1990s helped me to gain a really deep understanding of their environments – and also to question our 'Western' research concepts. We had long discussions when we started working together on seemingly simple concepts such as 'entrepreneur', 'profit', and 'management'.

Where do you think research in this area needs to develop in future?

At the moment, I am particularly interested in what our research results mean for the theories and concepts we apply in entrepreneurship research. For example, how do we incorporate different contexts into our theories, and also into empirical research? Are theories and concepts developed for a mature market economy appropriate to explain phenomena in different contexts? I don't think that we need new theories but it is important to consider the implications of contextualising: Theories of entrepreneurship need to be robust enough to accommodate the various forms of entrepreneurship that emerge in a variety of circumstances. And, contextualising makes your research so much more interesting – it basically is about looking for the variations and differences in entrepreneurial behaviour which can explain a lot more about entrepreneurship than our search for common patterns.

15.4 HOW DO GOVERNMENTS INTERVENE?

15.4.1 Intervening to encourage entrepreneurial activity

In this section, we focus our attention on entrepreneurship policies, and the methods used to pursue them. As we have already seen, policy-makers are operating in environments that are complex, variable, and often uncertain. Given these contingencies, how can they intervene to encourage entrepreneurial activity? There are three basic policy options:

> *They can try to increase the supply of potential entrepreneurs. Efforts can be made to increase the ratio of active to potential entrepreneurs. Assistance can be provided during the birth and early life of the business to increase the chances that the firm can survive. (Mokry 1988: 23)*

All three options have a role to play in entrepreneurship policy, but as the author noted, increasing the supply of potential (or nascent) entrepreneurs is likely to be the most difficult, particularly in the short to medium term, while supporting existing firms is more straightforward. Since this time, governments have conducted many different experiments in pursuit of greater entrepreneurial vitality. However, in an influential series of entrepreneurship policy studies, researchers have identified four basic levels of engagement (Stevenson and Lundström 2002, 2007). These range from what the authors term 'E-extension' policies, 'added-on' to traditional SME support measures, to more wide-ranging 'Holistic' entrepreneurship policies:

- **E-extension policy** Measures to support new firm creation and encourage other forms of entrepreneurial activity tend to be embedded within existing SME policy frameworks and implemented through existing SME programmes and services.

- **Target group policy** Measures focus on increasing the number of new firm start-ups in particular population segments. In one version, they may seek to tackle specific barriers faced by under-represented groups (i.e. unemployment, access to labour market, social inclusion). Alternatively, as part of a 'techno-entrepreneurship policy', they may encourage graduates, research scientists, and technologists to create high-growth potential ventures.

- **New firm creation policy** Measures focus on reducing barriers to business entry and exit in order to encourage new business creation. For example, they might simplify or enhance business registration, incorporation, bankruptcy, competition, and labour market policies. They might also introduce 'one-stop shops', offering easier access advice and information for entrepreneurial start-ups.

- **'Holistic' entrepreneurship policy** Measures are typically much broader and longer-term, and designed to strengthen the entrepreneurial culture and capacity of a country. The approach is more cohesive and comprehensive than other policy types. For example, they are likely to involve changes to the education system, as well as regulatory reform, better access to start-up support and financing, and strategies tailored to meet the needs of specific target groups.

As the authors emphasise, the policies adopted by national governments did not fall neatly into any one of the four categories, but there were dominant approaches, sometimes complemented by a secondary approach. For example, governments that 'added-on' an entrepreneurship focus to their existing SME support structure might offer special programmes and services to identified target groups. Though there may not be a universal model for entrepreneurship policy, Stevenson and Lundström (2007: 107–13) have argued convincingly that governments need to adopt an integrated framework comprising the following core components:

1. **Entrepreneurship promotion:** This group of policies is designed to enhance the perceived value of entrepreneurial activity in society and more generally, to create greater awareness of entrepreneurs and entrepreneurship. It can be achieved in a variety of ways. For example, government departments and agencies can engage with high-profile entrepreneurs, using them to publicise and endorse their initiatives. They can also organise events, such as the European Commission's 'SME week', and awards programmes. Other organisations also have a role to play, including television broadcasters, who have been responsible for profile-raising programmes such as the reality television format, *Money Tigers*, which originated in Japan and can be found in different variants including: *Al Aareen* ('The Den'), *Dragons' Den* and *Shark Tank* (Australia).

2. **Entrepreneurship education:** Governments have pursued a number of policies to promote and to integrate entrepreneurship skills, knowledge and motivation into the curricula of schools, colleges, and universities. Policy measures include teacher and researcher training courses, new curriculum guidelines, sponsored business plan competitions, and support for student entrepreneurship organisations. Policies in this area are often delivered by third sector bodies, such as the Danish Foundation for Entrepreneurship, Australian Business Week, and the UK's Princes Trust.

3. **Barriers to entry and exit:** The aim of these policies is to make it less time-consuming and more attractive to pursue an entrepreneurial career. They require governments to systematically review the impact of their administrative, legal, and regulatory systems on existing SMEs and new ventures, which are often disproportionately affected by these structures. Some governments have also simplified reporting requirements (e.g. for tax or employment purposes). One of

the biggest challenges for policy-makers is to ensure that the potential impact of new laws and regulations is evaluated before they are introduced. In recent years, many countries have set up 'better regulation' task forces and similar initiatives in order to assess and, where possible, to reduce negative impacts on businesses. In the field of social enterprise, new legal entities, such as the UK's 'Community Interest Company' (CIC), have been introduced in order to provide a more straightforward legal structure (Section 2.5)

4. **Start-up business support:** Policies in this area aim to deliver information, advice and specialist support and networking for entrepreneurs as they move through the start-up phase. Typical measures include personalised mentoring and training, financial support for incubators (i.e. low-cost accommodation with related support services) and science parks, and supporting networks that provide an opportunity to interact with other entrepreneurs. In recent years, governments have also invested in electronic resources, such as the European Small Business Portal, which provides a single online point of access to specialist advice, information, and services in multiple European language versions (http://ec.europa.eu/small-business).

5. **Start-up and seed financing:** Policies in this area are specifically directed at market failures (Section 11.3.2) and funding gaps that are experienced by some new and early-stage ventures, including those caused by lack of relevant information. Measures to address these deficiencies include the provision of microfinance (see Case 11.1), loan guarantees, and specialist 'seed capital' funds, which are designed to enable technology entrepreneurs to move beyond the prototype stage. Governments may also seek to encourage networks of **business angels, venture capitalists,** and venture philanthropists, the latter specialising in finance for social enterprises.

6. **Target groups:** This group of policies comprises two sub-sets. The first is designed to reduce systematic barriers to an entrepreneurial career for members of under-represented groups in the population, while the second is concerned with encouraging the creation of high-growth potential, technology-based start-ups. The measures required to deliver these objectives are essentially specialised versions of those identified in the previous two headings (e.g. providing specialist peer-support networks and sources of funding).

Though written some time ago, the following remarks are still equally relevant today. They summarise the continuing challenge faced by policy-makers attempting to encourage more entrepreneurial activity in a particular location:

> *The easiest solution for a policy maker who wants to promote entrepreneurship is to get elected in a place where natural entrepreneurial activity is already well established. The start-up process is complex and policy tools available to influence it are few and frustratingly crude. Physical buildings, financing, information, and supportive attitudes are things that governments can offer, but these fail to reach the fundamental forces that cause entrepreneurship to come about. Policy to assist entrepreneurship will need to be flexible, targeted to gaps in market processes, proactive, and imbued with a long-term perspective that patiently waits for results. Unfortunately, the environment in which economic development policy operates rarely shares these characteristics. (Mokry 1988: 29)*

Perhaps the most important lesson learned in the intervening years is that, though there are many challenges, carefully integrated, and well-targeted enterprise policies can deliver results. This was illustrated recently in the field of technological entrepreneurship, where researchers demonstrated that the combination of innovation and entrepreneurship policy can have a measurable impact on new venture creation. The study compared policies adopted by different US states in relation to nanotechnology start-ups. The researchers found that states that adopted *both* economic and innovation policies saw six times as many new firms created, compared to those that lacked this combination. While economic initiatives had a stronger effect than innovation initiatives, states with the earliest innovation policies also had relatively higher rates of new firm formation (Woolley and Rotner 2008).

15.4.2 Intervening to control and guide entrepreneurial activity

Having reviewed a number of techniques for encouraging entrepreneurial activity, we now turn to interventions that seek to control or to guide the kind of activity that takes place, revisiting the two examples discussed previously (Section 15.3.3):

- **Promoting enterprise in order to tackle social exclusion:** Blackburn and Ram's (2006) review of UK polices to address social exclusion provides a good illustration of why enterprise policies need to be well thought out, with clear objectives that are grounded in a deep understanding of their subject matter. The authors conclude that social exclusion is a complex, multifaceted concept (i.e. to understand it, you need to consider both individual-level behaviours and broader social structures), and one that is contested (i.e. there is no consensus over its causes or how it can be 'cured'). In the light of this analysis, they argue that policies to encourage more commercial start-up ventures in socially excluded communities need to be reviewed:

  > *Our analysis tends to run against the latest policy 'fad' of uncritically advocating that small firms and entrepreneurship are a key route for individual and societal economic and social salvation. [...] Small firms are the crucible of an economic system which both generates inequalities as well as provides a source of employment and economic well-being for individuals. From this we argue that entrepreneurship, as manifested in business ownership, provides opportunities for inclusion for some people in some contexts but little scope for others. (Blackburn and Ram 2006: 85; emphasis added)*

  The authors also suggest that the implementation of policies needs to take more account of the needs of those they are attempting to support:

  > *The excluded groups that we have discussed have often been sceptical of mainstream business support agencies and by their relatively non-inclusive nature are often difficult to reach. In relation to ethnic minority businesses, we have witnessed a burgeoning of ethnic-specific support agencies and groups. Young people often gravitate to more informal and fluid networks for their sources of economic and social capital. We need to explore whether these, perhaps more organic, vehicles of support are more efficacious in realizing the social inclusion agenda. (Blackburn and Ram 2006: 86)*

- **Promoting sustainable entrepreneurship:** Policies to promote sustainability entrepreneurship take a variety of forms. Measures designed to promote technological innovation often have the highest profile. For example, policy-makers have also supported a variety of 'socio-technical' transitions, which aim to reduce environmental impact through the development of new technological systems such as electric vehicles (Geels 2012; Steinhilber et al. 2013). The example of electric vehicles illustrates how environmental sustainability is often about longer-term changes that involve many different kinds of actors, including governments, entrepreneurs, universities, research institutes, and the wider public. As a consequence, one of the most important lessons from research in this area is that policy-makers need to design measures that take into account existing industrial structures and social institutions. For example, in the case of entrepreneurship and innovation in the Danish and US wind turbine industries, the policies adopted in each country produced radically different outcomes (Case 14.2).

We have now reviewed a range of public policies to promote SMEs and entrepreneurship. Though far from comprehensive, the illustrations indicate that policy-makers have made use of a wide variety of measures in order to achieve their chosen objectives. While some of these interventions are having a real impact on entrepreneurial activity, others have proved much less effective. Should poor outcomes be blamed on the policies themselves, the design of specific interventions, their implementation, or perhaps wider contextual factors? We seek to answer this question in the final section, which looks at the difficult task of evaluating enterprise policies.

15.5 EVALUATING ENTERPRISE POLICIES

15.5.1 Why is policy evaluation needed?

There is still considerable debate over the effectiveness of enterprise policies, and the measures they employ. In some cases, the evidence points to unintended and even counter-productive outcomes (e.g. displacement effects and increased bureaucratic hurdles), leading some critics to question whether interventions are justified (e.g. Curran 2000; Parker 2007). Governments and other organisations spend substantial amounts of money on programmes to encourage entrepreneurship. There is increasing evidence that implementation plays a key role in the process (Arshed et al. 2016), but there is still a relatively limited evidence base in key areas such as growth policy (Wright et al. 2015). We develop this theme with two contrasting examples of researchers responding to the evaluation challenge (Case 15.3).

CASE 15.3

Evaluating enterprise policies: two illustrations

This case looks at research studies that have investigated the effectiveness of two contrasting enterprise policies. The first study examines policies adopted over three decades, and in three different English regions, that attempted to increase the number of new start-up ventures. The second looks at the World Bank's approach to measuring entrepreneurial activity in fragile, post-conflict states. Though the issues are different, both studies raise important questions about the kinds of enterprise policies that are being implemented, the ways they are being measured, and whether these interventions can really make a difference to what actually happens on the ground.

(Continued)

(Continued)

ENTERPRISE POLICIES IN THREE ENGLISH REGIONS

This research study, by Francis Greene, Kevin Mole, and David Storey of Warwick University is an important contribution to the debate on enterprise policies, and in particular those that have attempted to promote the creation and growth of new businesses in geographic regions (Greene et al. 2007). The empirical core of the study is a large dataset, drawn from interviews with more than 900 'entrepreneurs', defined as owner-managers of new businesses. The study is comparative, in that it contrasts three English regions and three time periods. The regions have been selected as examples of different levels of 'enterprise performance', using the proxy measure of per capita VAT registrations. In a striking early figure, the authors indicate how relative positions of the three regions: Buckinghamshire ('high'), Shropshire ('middling'), and Teesside ('low') have remained remarkably consistent over the period 1980–2005. Teesside provides perhaps the most important and interesting theme in the study – the extent to which enterprise culture policies have influenced outcomes over an extended period. As the authors indicate, Teesside was effectively an 'experimental region' in this regard, and was subjected to successive initiatives designed to boost its economic prospects. In the Teesside data, the researchers find that businesses started by individuals who have been business owners previously are more likely to have slower sales growth than those of individuals starting a business for the first time. The authors interpret this finding as suggesting that 'most new entrepreneurs do not learn significantly from their previous business experiences and, even if they do, they are unable or unwilling to apply it to their current business venture' (Greene et al. 2007: 199). With regard to entrepreneurial finance in Teesside, the authors find that, '27.3 per cent of new businesses made use of public support in Teesside, compared to 2.3 per cent in Buckinghamshire' (Greene et al. 2007: 166). However, the authors note that it was not possible to reach clear conclusions about the impact of such funding. One of the most telling graphs compares population growth in the three regions between 1981 and 2003. While growth rates have increased consistently in Shropshire and Buckinghamshire, the Tees Valley has seen a steady decline of around 2% per annum over the study period. In their concluding remarks, the authors draw our attention back to the limits of policy interventions in the face of complex and deep-seated structural constraints:

> *What is clear is that more of the same is unlikely to enhance economic welfare of the residents of Teesside. By this we mean that efforts to raise new business formation will, if they have any effect at all, merely lead to more businesses established by individuals with low human capital, who are starting businesses in easy-to-enter industries because of a lack of alternative employment opportunities in the locality. We are also unpersuaded that the provision of public funds either to provide advisory services to such businesses, or to provide them with grants of one form or another, is likely to enhance their economic performance. The businesses themselves clearly appreciate the support, and an 'enterprise industry' has emerged to provide this support, but our evidence is that its impact is small. Whilst there have been no recent other studies of new entrepreneurs on Teesside, our view is that it is of questionable benefit for individuals to be enticed into enterprise without being made aware of the potentially considerable expected downside losses. (Greene et al. 2007: 246)*

MEASURING THE ENVIRONMENT FOR ENTREPRENEURSHIP IN FRAGILE STATES

This research, conducted by Chiara Guglielmetti of the University of Trento, examines entrepreneurship support policies for 'fragile states' that are recovering from periods of conflict and civil upheaval. The primary focus of this study is the role of performance indicators, in particular the World Bank's 'Doing Business' (DB) measures. The researcher questions whether these indicators are capable of capturing entrepreneurial dynamics and of informing policy-making in an effective way. The author begins by setting out the nature and scale of the problem:

> More than a billion people live in around 50 developing countries which have been described as 'fragile states' (Naudé et al. 2008). In fragile states, governments lack the authority, legitimacy and often the willingness to promote economic development. According to Binzel and Brück (2007: 5) fragility refers to 'the existence of persistent, systematic, significant and interrelated social, political and economic uncertainties'. Increasingly, donors and international development agencies are turning to private sector development where state capacity is lacking. Promoting entrepreneurship in fragile states, and in conflict and post-conflict situations, has therefore assumed high importance in strategies dealing with fragile states. (Guglielmetti 2010: 1)

She also notes that fragile states face a number of distinctive challenges. For example, resources need to be reallocated away from military purposes, people need to be reintegrated into economic activities, the quality of entrepreneurship needs to be considered, and the role of women needs to be addressed. In addition, it is likely that new economic networks will have to be created, and existing ones strengthened, in order to generate flows of economic resources that can reinforce the transition towards a peacetime economy. Having conducted a detailed review of current practices, she concludes that the 'Doing Business' (DB) measures do not take such context-specific issues sufficiently into account:

> DB therefore fails to stress the variety and the complexity of ways through which governments can influence the productive allocation of entrepreneurship, and does not detect fundamental inputs of entrepreneurial development. (Guglielmetti 2010: 12)

QUESTIONS

1. How do these policy issues compare with those discussed in this chapter?

2. What are the main lessons for policy-makers attempting to encourage entrepreneurial activity in: (a) regions with low levels of enterprise; (b) fragile, post-conflict states?

3. What research methods would you use to answer one of the following questions: (a) why firms started by previous business owners were more likely to have *slower* sales growth than those of first timers; (b) why a higher percentage of new businesses made use of public support in Teesside, compared to Buckinghamshire; (c) whether new networks are being created in a fragile state; (d) the potential for female entrepreneurship in a post-conflict state.

15.5.2 Policy evaluation: approaches and implications

Traditionally, public policies have been evaluated using economic criteria, such as job creation and economic growth. Though it might be difficult to isolate the impact of particular policies, suitable statistical measures and data sets (e.g. for unemployment and GDP) were generally available, at least in industrialised countries. Today, policy-makers have a much more ambitious agenda for entrepreneurship. Policy interventions are being directed at economic, social, and environmental goals. They are also being used in a much wider range of contexts, including newly industrialised and developing economies (Obeng and Blundel 2015). So what measures should we use to evaluate this new generation of entrepreneurship policy? And, at a more general level, what is the 'value' generated by entrepreneurial activity and how can we know whether it is being delivered (Section 13.1)? In an effort to develop internationally comparable measures of entrepreneurial activity, the OECD created an Entrepreneurship Indicators Programme (EIP). In their discussion of value, the OECD's researchers emphasise that the policy objectives and measures are likely to vary, depending on political considerations about the kinds of value that are being sought:

> Therefore 'value' covers both monetary and non-monetary returns. These values are, naturally, identified as objectives or targets by policy makers, who will then develop policies designed to achieve these targets although clearly they are carried out by entrepreneurs and entrepreneurial firms. Some countries for example will focus on entrepreneurship's contribution to economic growth. Other countries however might focus on entrepreneurship's contribution to solving environmental problems or its contribution to social inclusion. (Ahmad and Hoffman 2007: 5).

The policy evaluation literature is still in its infancy, but many policy researchers would agree with the following conclusions about the current state of play in entre-preneurship policy. Building on the work of several leading researchers:

> One of the main policy implications of the previous analysis is that 'one size does not fit all'. In other words, if entrepreneurial efforts are to be allocated to produc-tive activities, policy strategies, with respect to entrepreneurship, need to be tailored to the specific institutional context of each economic region [...] For example, the environments required for the emergence of productive entrepreneurship are likely to differ significantly between a rural area, a high-technology cluster, and a met-ropolitan area. Therefore, policy design needs to take account of local differences, and to adapt to the different scale and nature of existing resources, networks, and market capabilities. In spite of this need for diversity, entrepreneurship policies tend to be based on a handful of policy tools. (Minniti 2008: 708–81; emphasis added)

Evaluating enterprise policy will remain an important and challenging field. The social world is complex and dynamic, and it is often difficult to obtain the necessary evidence, and to analyse in ways that reveal the underlying causes (Pawson 2006). Enterprise policies can make a difference, and the closing case provides a striking example of this, by tracing the way that policy-making has shaped the economic development of Bavaria over the last 30 years. However, as we saw in Case 15.3, it is not always entirely clear what has happened, or whether any of the observed changes can be attributed to a particular policy intervention. What remains certain is that entrepreneurs will go on pursuing their personal visions, more or less successfully, and that the outcomes of their collective efforts will continue to shape our economies, societies and the natural world upon which we all depend.

SUMMARY

- Entrepreneurial activity is a powerful phenomenon, and public policy has been used both as a vehicle for fostering more activity and for regulating its impact on society.

- SME policies and entrepreneurship policies overlap to some degree, but there are important differences of emphasis, and in associated policy measures.

- Government intervention in pursuit of SME and entrepreneurship policies has traditionally been justified on economic grounds, but the scope of policy is increasingly being extended to address broader social and environmental goals.

- Governments have adopted different approaches and measures in order to pursue their policy objectives. The most effective appear to be integrated policies that are also sensitive to the context in which they are implemented.

- Entrepreneurship policies have been criticised by some as representing an ineffective or economically inefficient use of resources and by others as reinforcing socially and environmentally unsustainable systems of production and consumption.

- Policies must be informed by research evidence and subject to rigorous evaluation if they are to respond effectively to today's economic, social, and environmental challenges.

- Existing and nascent entrepreneurs need to be aware of policies that are likely to impact on their ventures. Unexpected policy changes can create serious problems for commercial and social ventures but also new sources of opportunity.

Practical activities

1. **Spot the policy:** Using the case illustrations and web links in this chapter as a starting point, search for the websites of three national or regional governments and download examples of their enterprise policies. Categorise and compare the policies using the frameworks introduced in Sections 15.3 and 15.4 of this chapter. What do your findings suggest about the way governments intervene to foster or regulate enterprise?

2. **What works?** Select *two* examples of policies that are being evaluated. You can begin with the case illustrations in Section 15.5 or search any of the following sources: (a) media coverage (e.g. newspaper articles, television programmes, journalists' blogs); (b) official reports (e.g. by governments and external assessors); (c) academic studies reported in books, conference papers, or journal articles. Prepare a one-page summary, addressing the following questions: (a) What policy is being evaluated? (b) What were the policy objectives? (c) How were the policy outcomes and impacts evaluated? (d) How successful has the policy been? (e) What lessons (if any) are being drawn for the future?

3. **On the receiving end:** Find out what real-life entrepreneurs think about government attempts to foster and regulate enterprise. Search the biographies, autobiographies, public speeches, media profiles, and blogs of some well-known entrepreneurs; you can start with the people featured in case studies throughout this book. Alternatively, arrange an interview with an entrepreneur

that you can contact through your friends or family. Use the discussion in Section 15.5 as a starting point. Summarise your findings as either a one-page report or as five presentation slides (NB: this activity can be linked to Discussion topic 3).

Discussion topics

1. **Promoting technological innovation:** The research evidence suggests a number of different views on how best to promote technological innovation. Compare, for example, Hendry and Brown's (2006) research on opto-electronics technology firms and Henry and Pinch's (2000) findings on motor-sport technology clusters. Select one of the following technological fields and discuss what combination of policy initiatives would be most likely to support innovation.

2. **The challenges of enterprise policy:** The articles by Blackburn and Ram (2006) and Carter et al. (2015) highlight a number of challenges for policy-makers who are seeking to use enterprise policies to combat social exclusion and promote diversity (Section 15.5): (a) Summarise the challenges identified in one (or both) of these articles; (b) How would you go about tackling the issues you have identified?

3. **What policy means to me:** Take one of the following roles and discuss how the policies discussed in this chapter might apply to you: (a) an existing entrepreneur, considering how best to develop her/his business; (b) a prospective entrepreneur, deciding whether to move out of regular employment and start up a new venture; (c) a small business advisor, designing courses to support existing or prospective entrepreneurs. To illustrate the discussion, you can draw on your own experiences of entrepreneurship, a new venture creation activity (i.e. Part One of this textbook), and/or material collected for Practical activity 3 (above).

Recommended reading

These readings address important topics in entrepreneurship research and are recommended for anyone wanting to build on the material covered in this chapter. Recommended readings have been selected from leading Sage journals and are freely available for readers of this textbook to download via the Online Resources.

Wright, M., Roper, S., Hart, M., and Carter, S., (2015) 'Joining the dots: building the evidence base for SME growth policy'. *International Small Business Journal*, 33, 1: 3–11.

This short article introduces a special issue on building the evidence base for small and medium-sized enterprise (SME) growth policy. The authors review the themes covered by other contributions to the special issue, including the article below. They also identify a number of directions for future research and policy.

Carter, S., Mwaura, S., Ram, M., Trehan, K., and Jones, T. (2015) 'Barriers to ethnic minority and women's enterprise: existing evidence, policy tensions and unsettled questions'. *International Small Business Journal*, 33, 1: 49–69.

This article reviews the field of diversity with particular reference to ethnic minorities and women engaging in enterprise. The authors examine research evidence on their access to finance, market selection and management skills. They identify a number of tensions and unresolved questions, draw out the implications for policy and practice and identify possible directions for future research.

Arshed, N., Mason, C., and Carter, S. (2016) 'Exploring the disconnect in policy implementation: a case of enterprise policy in England'. *Environment and Planning C: Government and Policy,* **[Online before print – p.0263774X16628181].**

This article examines how far the ineffectiveness of enterprise policy can be attributed to the way it has been implemented. The researchers, who interviewed central government policy-makers, Regional Development Agency staff and business development managers in local enterprise agencies over an extended period, discovered the implementation process was complex and confusing, with fragmented relationships between the actors involved. Contributing factors included the absence of clearly defined objectives and of measurement and evaluation processes

References

Ahmad, N. and Hoffman, A. (2007) 'A framework for addressing and measuring entrepreneurship'. Paris: Organisation for Economic Cooperation and Development (OECD).

Arshed, N., Mason, C., and Carter, S. (2016) 'Exploring the disconnect in policy implementation: a case of enterprise policy in England'. *Environment and Planning C: Government and Policy,* [Online before print – p.0263774X16628181].

Audretsch, D. B. and Beckmann, I. A. M. (2007) 'From small business to entrepreneurship policy'. In D. B. Audretsch et al. (eds), op. cit. (36–53).

Audretsch, D. B. and Thurik, A. R. (2000) 'Capitalism and democracy in the 21st century: from the managed to the entrepreneurial economy'. *Journal of Evolutionary Economics,* 10: 17–34.

Audretsch, D. B., Grilo, I., and Thurik, A. R. (eds) (2007) *Handbook of Research in Entrepreneurship Policy.* Cheltenham: Edward Elgar.

Baker, T. and Welter, F. (eds) (2015) *The Routledge Companion to Entrepreneurship.* Abingdon: Routledge.

Baumol, W. (1990) 'Entrepreneurship: productive, unproductive, and destructive'. *Journal of Political Economy,* 98: 893–921.

Binzel, C. and Brück, T. (2007). 'Analyzing conflict and fragility at the micro-level'. *UNU-WIDER Conference on Fragile States-Fragile Groups,* Helsinki, 15–16 June.

Blackburn, R. and Ram, M. (2006) 'Fix or fixation?: the contributions and limitations of entrepreneurship and small firms to combating social exclusion'. *Entrepreneurship and Regional Development,* 18, 1: 73–89.

Blundel, R. K., Monaghan, A. and Thomas, C. (2013) 'SMEs and environmental responsibility: a policy perspective'. *Business Ethics: A European Review,* 22, 3: 246–62.

Carter, S., Mwaura, S., Ram, M., Trehan, K., and Jones, T. (2015) 'Barriers to ethnic minority and women's enterprise: existing evidence, policy tensions and unsettled questions'. *International Small Business Journal,* 33, 1: 49–69.

Casson, M., Yeung, B., Basu, A., and Wadeson, N. (2008) *The Oxford Handbook of Entrepreneurship*. Oxford: Oxford University Press.

Curran, J. (2000) 'What is small business policy in the UK for?: evaluation and assessing small business policies'. *International Small Business Journal*, 18, 3: 36–50.

De, D. (1999) 'SME policy in Europe'. In D. L. Sexton and H. Landström (eds), op. cit. (87–106).

Defra (2009) 'About the Greener Living Fund'. London: Department for the Environment, Food and Rural Affairs. http://www.greenerlivingfund.org.uk/about/ (accessed 10 November 2009).

Della-Guista, M. and King, Z. (2008) 'Enterprise culture'. In M. Casson et al. (eds), op. cit. (629–47).

Dowling, M. and Schmüde, J. (eds) (2007) *Empirical Entrepreneurship in Europe*. Cheltenham: Edward Elgar.

European Commission (2008) *Putting Small Business First: Europe is Good for SMEs, SMEs are Good for Europe* (2008 edition). Brussels: European Commission, Enterprise and Industry.

European Commission (2009) *The Small Business Act for Europe*. Brussels: European Commission, Enterprise and Industry.

Eurostat (2008) *Enterprises by Size Class – Overview of SMEs in the EU* (31/2008). Luxembourg: Eurostat.

Fagenberg, J., Mowery, D. C., and Nelson, R. R. (2005) *The Oxford Handbook of Innovation*. Oxford: Oxford University Press.

Fritsch, M. (2005) 'Regionalization of innovation policy – introduction of the Special Issue'. *Research Policy*, 34, 8: 1123–7.

Geels, F. W. (2012) 'A socio-technical analysis of low-carbon transitions: Introducing the multi-level perspective into transport studies'. *Journal of Transport Geography*, 24: 471–82.

Greene, F. J., Mole, K. F., and Storey, D. J. (2007) *Three Decades of the Enterprise Culture: Entrepreneurship, Economic Regeneration and Public Policy*. Basingstoke: Palgrave.

Guglielmetti, C. (2010) 'Measuring the business environment for entrepreneurship in fragile states (Working Paper 2010/14)'. Helsinki: United Nations University/World Institute for Economic Development Research.

Hendry, C. and Brown, J. (2006) 'Dynamics of clustering and performance in the UK opto-electronics industry'. *Regional Studies*, 40, 7: 707–25.

Henry, N. and Pinch, S. (2000) 'Spatialising knowledge: placing the knowledge community of Motor Sport Valley'. *Geoforum*, 31, 2: 191–208.

Huggins, R. and Williams, N. (2009) 'Enterprise and public policy: a review of Labour government intervention in the United Kingdom'. *Environment and Planning C: Government and Policy*, 27, 1: 19–41.

Hülsbeck, M. and Lehmann, E. E. (2007) 'Entrepreneurship policy in Bavaria: between laptop and Lederhosen'. In Audretsch, D. B., et al. (eds), op. cit. (200–12).

LDA (2005) *Re-defining London's BME-owned businesses*. London: London Development Agency/Mayor of London.

Lyon, F. and Ramsden, M. (2006). 'Developing fledgling social enterprises? A study of the support required and means of delivering it'. *Social Enterprise Journal*, 2, 1: 27–41.

Mason, C. M. (2009) 'Public policy support for the informal venture capital market in Europe: a critical review'. *International Small Business Journal*, 25, 5: 536–56.

Mazur, E. (2012) *Green Transformation of Small Businesses: Achieving and Going Beyond Environmental Requirements. OECD Environment Working Papers, No. 47*, Paris: OECD.

McDowall, W. A. S. and Ekins, P. (2014) *Green Innovation: Industrial Policy for a Low Carbon Future*. London: UCL / Trades Union Congress.

Mill, J. S. ([1869] 2015) 'On Liberty'. In M. Philp and F. Rosen (eds), *On Liberty, Utilitarianism and Other Essays* (2nd edn). Oxford: Oxford University Press (5–114).

Minniti, M. (2008) 'The role of government policy on entrepreneurial activity: productive, unproductive, or destructive?' *Entrepreneurship Theory and Practice*, 32, 5: 779–90.

Mokry, B. W. (1988) *Entrepreneurship and Public Policy: Can Government Stimulate Business Start-Ups?* New York: Quorum.

Mole, K. F. and Bramley, G. (2006) 'Making choices in nonfinancial business support: an international comparison'. *Environment and Planning C: Government and Policy*, 24, 6: 885–908.

Muñoz, P. and Dimov, D. (2015) 'The call of the whole in understanding the development of sustainable ventures'. *Journal of Business Venturing*, 30, 4: 632–54.

Naudé, W., Santos-Paulino, A. U., and McGillivray, M. (2008) *Fragile States – Research Brief 3*. Helsinki: United Nations University/World Institute for Economic Development Research.

Obeng, B. A. and Blundel, R. K. (2015) 'Evaluating enterprise policy interventions in Africa: a critical review of Ghanaian small business support services'. *Journal of Small Business Management*, 53, 2: 416–35.

Parker, C. M., Redmond, J., and Simpson, M. (2009) 'A review of interventions to encourage SMEs to make environmental improvements'. *Environment and Planning C: Government and Policy*, 27, 2: 279–301.

Parker, S. C. (2007) 'Policymakers beware!' in D. B. Audretsch et al. (eds), op. cit. (54–63).

Parrish, B. D. and Foxon, T. J. (2009) 'Sustainability entrepreneurship and equitable transitions to a low-carbon economy'. *Greener Management International*, 55, 47–62.

Parry, S. (2012) 'Going green: The evolution of micro-business environmental practices'. *Business Ethics: A European Review*, 21, 2: 220–37.

Pawson, R. (2006) *Evidence-Based Policy: A Realist Perspective*. London: Sage.

Robson, P. J. A., Wijbenga, F., and Parker, S. C. (2009) 'Entrepreneurship and policy: challenges and directions for future research'. *International Small Business Journal*, 25, 5: 531–5.

Sexton, D. L. and Landström, H. (2000) *The Blackwell Handbook of Entrepreneurship*. Oxford: Blackwell.

Smallbone, D. and Welter, F. (2010). 'Entrepreneurship and government policy in former Soviet republics: Belarus and Estonia compared'. *Environment and Planning. C: Government and Policy*, 28, 2: 195–210.

Smallbone, D., North, D., Baldock, R., and Ekanem, I. (2002) *Encouraging and Supporting Enterprise in Rural Areas (Research Report RR009/02)*. Sheffield: Small Business Service.

Spear, R. and Bidet, E. (2005) 'Social enterprise for work integration in 12 European countries: a descriptive analysis'. *Annals of Public and Co-operative Economics*, 76, 2: 195–231.

Spear, R. G., Cornforth, C. J., and Aiken, M. (2009). 'The governance challenges of social enterprises: evidence from a UK empirical study'. *Annals of Public and Cooperative Economics*, 80, 2: 247–73.

Steinhilber, S., Wells, P. and Thankappan, S. (2013) 'Socio-technical inertia: understanding the barriers to electric vehicles'. *Energy Policy*, 60: 531–9.

Stevenson, L. and Lundström, A. (2002) *Beyond the Rhetoric: Defining Entrepreneurship Policy and its Best Practice Components*. Stockholm: Swedish Foundation for Small Business Research.

Stevenson, L. and Lundström, A. (2007) 'Dressing the emperor: the fabric of entrepreneurship policy'. In D. B. Audretsch et al. (eds), op. cit. (94–129).

Storey, D. J. (2008) 'Evaluating SME policies and programmes: technical and political dimensions'. In M. Casson et al. (eds), op. cit. (248–78).

Turnbull, M. (2016) Speech to young Indigenous businesses and entrepreneurs (6 February). https://www.pm.gov.au/media/2016-02-09/speech-young-indigenous-businesses-and-entrepreneurs (accessed 28 October 2016).

UNEP (2009) 'An introduction to the Green Economy report'. Geneva: United Nations Environment Programme/Green Economy Initiative.

Welter, F. (2011) 'Contextualizing entrepreneurship – conceptual challenges and ways forward'. *Entrepreneurship Theory and Practice*, 35, 1: 165–84.

Welter, F. (2016) 'Wandering between contexts'. In D. Audretsch and E. Lehmann (eds), *The Routledge Companion to Makers of Modern Entrepreneurship*. London: Routledge.

Welter, F. and Gartner, W. B. (eds) (2016) *A Research Agenda for Entrepreneurship and Context*. Cheltenham: Edward Elgar.

Welter, F. and Smallbone, D. (eds) (2011) *Handbook of Research on Entrepreneurship Policies in Central and Eastern Europe*. Cheltenham: Edward Elgar.

Welter, F., Slonimski, A., and Smallbone, D. (2006). 'Small enterprise internationalization: national and regional aspects'. *Economic Bulletin*, 6, 33–50.

Woolley, J. L. and Rottner, R. M. (2008) 'Innovation policy and nanotechnology entrepreneurship'. *Entrepreneurship Theory and Practice*, 32, 5: 791–811.

Wright, M., Roper, S., Hart, M., and Carter, S. (2015) 'Joining the dots: building the evidence base for SME growth policy'. *International Small Business Journal*, 33, 1: 3–11.

16

REFLECTIONS: ENTREPRENEURIAL LEARNING

Chance favours only the prepared mind.

Louis Pasteur

If you really look closely, most overnight successes took a long time.

Steve Jobs

The only real mistake is the one from which we learn nothing.

Henry Ford

LEARNING OUTCOMES

After reading this chapter you should be able to:

- Understand the concept of entrepreneurial learning.
- Recognise the different approaches to learning in the entrepreneurial process.
- Appreciate the role of entrepreneurial learning in discovering and pursuing an entrepreneurial opportunity.
- Understand the concepts of entrepreneurial alertness and preparedness.
- Critically evaluate the importance of entrepreneurial learning from success and failure.
- Apply these insights to your own entrepreneurial experience and reflect on your own learning styles.

16.1 INTRODUCTION

This chapter provides an overview on the entrepreneurial learning research and practice. Entrepreneurial learning has drawn a great deal of insights from individual and organisational learning literature, but emphasises the application and adaptation of learning theories in different entrepreneurial contexts. These entrepreneurial contexts include new venture creation or business start-ups as well as entrepreneurial learning to reinvigorate large corporations. Our examples focus on entrepreneurial learning in starting up new ventures but the lessons have a wider relevance. Entrepreneurs and would-be entrepreneurs will gain a better understanding of the different approaches to entrepreneurial learning, and can better assess their own learning. In particular, they will be able to appreciate the need to reflect on learning not only from success but also from failure on their entrepreneurial journeys.

This chapter proceeds as follows. In Section 16.2, we define what entrepreneurial learning is. In Section 16.3, we discuss four types of learning that are most relevant to new venture creation and business start-ups: learning from experience, learning from others, learning by doing, and formal learning in schools, colleges and universities. In Section 16.4, we discuss the role of learning in entrepreneurial opportunities, by focusing on two contrasting but complementary approaches to discovering entrepreneurial opportunities: being alert to entrepreneurial opportunities and being prepared for entrepreneurial opportunities. Finally, in Section 16.5, we take a closer look at why success and failure are like a double-edged sword in one's learning journey. We discuss how entrepreneurs and would-be entrepreneurs can learn from success and failure experience, and avoid being complacent about their own past experience and competences.

CASE 16.1

Jonathan Hick: birth of a serial entrepreneur

With such a long history of entrepreneurs in his family, perhaps it shouldn't be surprising that Jonathan should become a successful serial entrepreneur. But is his past a help or hindrance? Are entrepreneurs born or bred? The roots to Jonathan's success may lie in the past but his business interests increasingly include international companies in diverse sectors. But this journey has not been easy and he is open about both the pressures and rewards of entrepreneurship in the twenty-first century.

GRANDFATHERS – THE GREAT AND THE GOOD

'I suppose the entrepreneurial side of me started 150 years ago when my great, great grandfather set up a timber traders business in Bradford called Beacroft and Whiteman. ... I think somehow some genes have come through from the family. Actually the entrepreneur was probably his son, my great grandfather Charles John Whiteman, who built the business into quite a significant enterprise importing timber from large saw mills.' In fact Jonathan's great grandfather also had an eye for emerging technologies and innovation. 'He backed a man who had got certain patents on the cooling tower. Modern cooling towers are concrete shells full of timber; the hot water cools as the steam rides over that timber.' The family timber business passed down the generations through his grandfather, Ben – who won a Military Cross in WWII and sadly died near the end of the war – and finally to his father, Peter. 'My father found himself in the timber trade after national service and was sent to learn the business at Hull.' Jonathan recalled the effect this had on him, 'So Dad became managing director of the whole business in the 60s and I grew up with a father who went to work on a Saturday. I remember the timber coming on railway lines from the docks, going to Bradford on the railway lines from the sawmills.' He also recalled the intense pressure on his father, 'When people talk about recession, I've seen three of them. The biggest recession ever was in 1973/74 when we had a three-day week. The dockers' strike nearly killed us as a business and I remember my father in tears saying we have been in business 120 years and I think this is going to finish us.'

What did Jonathan pick up from watching his father running a group of businesses that, at its peak, employed over 1,000 people? He recalled, 'I am very much a people person and "prince and pauper" [see Mark Twain's novel, of the same name, about two boys, one a prince and one a pauper, who trade places] person. Everybody called my father Peter not Mr Hick and he knew the names of every single employee. He knew their wives' names and their children's names. Dad always involved me with "we are thinking of buying this company" and "we are thinking of selling this company" and in all the sort of deals that they were doing. You just don't realise what an incredible effect that has on you in terms of firing your interest in business.'

SIGNIFICANT EARLY INFLUENCES

Jonathan was also influenced by his mother and recalled, 'My mum had come from a fairly poor background. She had grown up in a council house, her father had been a bit of a gambler and Granny didn't know whether there would be any money this week. So that was very difficult and she [Jonathan's mother] bettered herself through education and became a teacher. Education and hard work were very important to her.' He also recalled, 'I have seen that insecurity, as well as some terrible losses. My grandfather dying, and also losing some friends in my late teens and early 20s – suicide, a friend with a terrible illness that came from nowhere turned out to be pneumonia and another friend who had a very bad car accident.'

Jonathan remembers some early entrepreneurial experiences, 'As a kid I remember at five designing membership cards for a club and bringing people together in a little bit of leadership in classrooms. By eight I would design all the letterheads and we were into transport and shipping and then by the age of 12, I was actually forming companies and doing things.' He recalled one particular enterprise. 'I was selling union jack socks for the Queen's Silver Jubilee. I bought a thousand pairs [but] they all turned out to be laddered and we got agents in five schools and all wanting their money back. I think I went off sick from school for a couple of weeks!'

But, Jonathan was not easily deterred as he recalls, 'I started a mobile disco when I was 13. That was my first business with Barclays Bank and not only did they lend me the money to buy equipment but they gave me three staff parties. By the time I was leaving school I was selling sweatshirts for the local rugby league clubs – I was the first person to bring huge cut-out foam hands in from American football ... I bought 5,000 of these from a foam manufacturer. We borrowed some walkie-talkies and there were four entrances and eight of us went down to the stadium. One lot started selling at £1.50 at one gate, another £2.50 at another gate. We all walkie-talkied as to how sales were going and within ten minutes found out the best selling price was £1.75.'

Not all of Jonathan's new ventures were successful, he remembers, 'In 1992 I had quite a costly mistake but it was one of the big lessons in life. I had a friend who was big in the fish industry. I was in the marketing and advertising business and we bought in a third friend who was in fish and chip retail. We bought x tons of fish, filleted it and sold it in regular sizes – we called it the Hudson Bay Clipper Company and sold 8,000 portions a week at the peak. But it just became too corporate and we were not listening

(Continued)

(Continued)

to what was going on the ground. A national newspaper mounted a campaign against us, for supposedly selling cod in a haddock area, and we had a really hard time of it. Local chippies were saying this big company has come over from Canada and it is going to kill us all and we must all fight together to see them off.'

BUILDING A CAREER IN ADVERTISING

Initially, at the insistence of his mother, Jonathan went to study Law at university but he did not enjoy it, 'I hated it from day one. It was a massive mistake and I only did two of the three years and failed.' But, he knew what he was going to do, 'I had worked in advertising in my holidays for a wonderful man called Richard Milner who had quite a big agency and some international interests.' He was 'a glamorous man, fired me with enthusiasm for advertising and I worked many school holidays thanks to him ... I knew I was going back into advertising'.

In fact, Jonathan got his first job, after leaving university, in Barrington Advertising, the second biggest outside London. He enjoyed his work and made some key contacts in the industry. Within two years Jonathan and two others bought, 'a 50 year old advertising agency in Sheffield ... we thought we could take on the world and I had a young, aggressive take on the world. By the time I was 25, I was Managing Director.' But after financial difficulties Jonathan brought in, 'two other guys [investors] who put some cash in and helped stabilise us ... and then began a very stable period in my life'. However, Jonathan recalled the financial pressure of running a business, 'I did get quite frightened actually ... a terrible knotting up inside, a general nervousness, an unsettledness, sickness all the time where I really did think I was up against it. I felt it was a terrible failure to owe people money and yet when I look back it was one of the proudest moments.'

The advertising agency worked out really well and Jonathan recalled, 'The father [of the investors] was a great influence on me in terms of discipline, money, board meetings ... he was totally self-taught in business but he was a very disciplined man, a tough cookie ... he ran sophisticated board meetings.' By his early thirties Jonathan was running a 'very successful business, making good money, employing about 50 people and by this time everything was fantastic'.

MONEY IN DIRECTORBANK

Jonathan began to see the opportunity of working with other enterprises and started to work one-day a week for an International Business Convention organiser. Jonathan recalled, 'I started getting involved with some people in the City ... I read a story about 3i [private investment company] which had a register of non-executive and executive directors who were looking to invest. I was aware that there was an increase in corporate people wanting to get into management buy-ins because they kept banging on my door and saying "You did one, Jonathan, how do I get it?" So I set up a register of people willing to do these management buy-ins. I put an advertisement in the *Financial Times* ... fortunately there were 267 replies and I never looked back – I think that is probably my proudest achievement.'

In 1998, Jonathan started to build MBi Register, the business that was to become The Directorbank Group. He recalled, 'I recruited a couple of guys from the City – one as chairman and one as a non-exec director to help me. They made lots of introductions into London where I had very few contacts and I just pounded the streets. We created the framework, the base of what became Directorbank, an online database of chairmen, chief execs, finance directors who are immediately available to do private equity deals. The immediate availability is the key thing to look at deals in the private equity space.'

QUESTIONS

1. What role did Jonathan's family play in firing Jonathan's interest in business in the early days?

2. What did Jonathan learn from his own success and failure?

3. To what extent do you think Jonathan was born with entrepreneurial traits or made an entrepreneur through learning?

This case was written by Professor Nigel Lockett. The author does not intend to illustrate either effective or ineffective handling of a management situation. The author may have disguised certain names, locations, dates and other identifying information to protect confidentiality. It is mainly based on primary data from interviews.

16.2 WHAT IS ENTREPRENEURIAL LEARNING?

Nascent entrepreneurs often describe their new ventures as a sharp learning curve. Reid Hoffman, the founder of LinkedIn, compares entrepreneurship to jumping off a cliff and building an airplane on the way down. Even seasoned entrepreneurs, such as Richard Branson, learn to build their business empires: 'Nothing can fully prepare you for life as an entrepreneur. However many times you have built a successful company, however many times you have failed and fallen flat on your face, there are always new things to learn.' (Virgin 2016).

There's no doubt that learning is crucial to entrepreneurs, but where does entrepreneurial learning stand in the entrepreneurship literature? Let's go back to Chapter 11, where we discussed the personality 'traits' or characteristics of entrepreneurs. Such characteristics help us understand the mental, physical, and psychological profiles of successful entrepreneurs. In other words, the characteristic-based approaches help us identify who an entrepreneur is. They also help would-be or nascent entrepreneurs to assess and reflect on their own personality traits or characteristics.

We also discussed the limitations of characteristic-based approaches. They overlook the developmental process of individuals in their entrepreneurial journeys. In Chapter 14, we briefly discussed the debate on whether entrepreneurs are born or bred. There are many examples of entrepreneurs, such as Jonathan Hick, who learned from an early age through their experiences and those of others. Jonathan learned from his parents to become who he is today – a people person, hard working and able to cope with adversity and learn from failure. These are indeed personality traits of successful entrepreneurs, which are shaped by learning in the case of Jonathan and many other entrepreneurs. In William Gartner's (1988) words, 'who is an entrepreneur' is the wrong question. Instead, we should be asking questions such as: how are these entrepreneurial characteristics developed over time? How can individuals adapt themselves and learn new skills to pursue their entrepreneurial careers? This is what we will discuss in this chapter.

Entrepreneurial learning is broadly defined as 'learning in the entrepreneurial process' (Ravasi and Turati 2005; Politis 2005; Holcomb et al. 2009). As discussed in Chapter 1, the entrepreneurial process entails a wide range of activities where individuals on their own or inside organisations pursue opportunities regardless of resources they currently control (Stevenson and Jarillo 1990). The entrepreneurial learning literature provides a great deal of insight on not only what entrepreneurs learn, but also how they learn, and what conditions help them learn (Wang and Chugh 2014). Entrepreneurial learning is fundamental to our understanding of how entrepreneurs discover and pursue opportunities. In fact, Minniti and Bygrave (2001) argue that entrepreneurship is essentially a process of learning.

16.3 APPROACHES TO ENTREPRENEURIAL LEARNING

It is worth noting that individuals learn differently. They can learn informally through day-to-day living and observation, or in a formal setting such as in schools, colleges and universities. There is no right or wrong way of learning. Jeff Haden, an Inc.com columnist, once said:

> In business for every rule there's an entrepreneur who proves the exception to that rule. My way is not your way, and neither is the right way ... until we prove it works for us, as individuals. (Haden 2012)

The different approaches to learning are known as learning styles. Individual and organisational learning literature has a long-standing body of knowledge on a variety of learning styles that individuals may be drawn to. Some individuals may even vary their learning styles in different contexts, or combine different learning styles. Entrepreneurial learning research has built on this body of literature on learning styles. Below, we discuss four key approaches to learning that are very relevant to entrepreneurs and their new ventures.

16.3.1 Learning from experience

Entrepreneurs learn from their experience. Would-be and nascent entrepreneurs need to develop entrepreneurial and business skills to enable them to set up and grow new ventures. As illustrated in Case Study 16.2, Geetie Singh gained experience by working in pubs and restaurants around London before setting up her own organic and environmentally sustainable gastro pub – The Duke of Cambridge.

'Experience is the best teacher, but only if one learns from it,' according to Robert Sternberg (2004). How do individuals learn from their experience – not only gain and reflect on experience, but also transform that experience into action? The Experiential Learning theory developed by David Kolb (1984) sheds some light on the experiential learning process (see Figure 16.1). He recognises that 'learning is best conceived as a process, not in terms of outcomes' (Kolb 1984: 26). The learning process consists of four key stages: concrete experience – reflective observation – abstract conceptualisation – active experimentation (Kolb 1984).

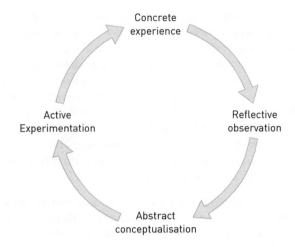

FIGURE 16.1 Kolb's experiential learning cycle

Source: adapted from Kolb (1984: 33)

- **Concrete experience** comes from active involvement by doing something. One can watch or read about something, but it is the actual 'doing' that provides the concrete experience for individuals to learn and develop.
- **Reflective observation** refers to consciously reflecting on the concrete experience. Individuals need to step back and reflect on what has happened, and reflect on the root causes of success and failure.
- **Abstract conceptualisation** is the process where individuals make sense of what has happened, make comparison between actual outcomes and desired goals, question what they have already known, and form new knowledge or theory to explain their observation.
- **Active experimentation** involves planning on how to test the knowledge or theory developed through abstract conceptualisation in a forthcoming experience. This starts another cycle of concrete experience.

The majority of entrepreneurship students want to gain some experience before setting up their own businesses, as opposed to doing so straightaway after graduation. Many of them prefer to work for large companies to gain experience, and a much smaller number of them may choose to work for small firms. Compared with small firms, large companies have more resources for staff training and individual development. In Case 16.3, Gregor Lawson, and Fraser and Ali Smeaton all worked for large companies, and their business skills accumulated through their corporate experience have proved invaluable to their own business. However, the skills developed in large companies are not always suited for start-ups. Dave Lavinsky, the founder of Growthink, a US-based business specialising in business planning, consulting, and investment banking, has some advice for entrepreneurs. Since it started in 1999, Growthink has helped over half a million entrepreneurs start and grow their businesses.

> *Sure, you can learn some things from big companies – mainly how to run a big company. You'll learn the type of corporate structures that are needed and the key departments, etc. But most of that doesn't help you when you first start a*

company. For that, you need to think very differently. You need to think and act like an entrepreneur, which is the art and science of accomplishing more with less (less money, less human resources, less time, etc.). Big companies are not great at accomplishing more with less, nor are they great innovators. So it's very easy to pick up bad habits that actually make it harder to start your own business. I, too, started my career at a big company. The main lesson I learned? Do things very differently than they did. And if you do work for the larger company for too long you will probably develop too comfortable a lifestyle. You start bringing in money. You get married. You buy a house. You have kids. And now your risk profile has changed dramatically, and starting your own company may not be a viable option. (Dave Lavinsky, cited in Haden 2012)

Dave Lavinsky also advises entrepreneurship students to learn from the best start-ups. He reckons that start-ups backed by venture capital (VC) provide a fertile environment for graduate entrepreneurs to learn. He emphasises that all three of YouTube's founders, Chad Hurley, Steve Chen, and Jawed Karim, worked for PayPal when it was a start-up.

In that regard, I would strongly support a young or first-time entrepreneur working for a VC-funded start-up. Most VCs are very good about only investing in start-ups with great founders and solid management teams. Clearly bigger companies generally have better managers than start-ups, but the VC-backed start-up is unique, so I like that option a lot: You learn from great people, wear many hats, and learn about the start-up environment. (Dave Lavinsky, cited in Haden 2012)

16.3.2 Learning from others: peers, role models and mentors

'Example is not the main thing in influencing other people; it's the only thing' (Abraham Lincoln). People do not exist in a vacuum. Our beliefs, ideas, and ways of thinking are influenced by those around us, through various forms of persuasive communication and argument (Ajzen 1991; Blundel et al. 2013). In the case of entrepreneurship, this kind of interaction is likely to affect people's attitudes towards the kinds of ventures they want to create, the way they approach the task and their expectations about how much it should grow (e.g. Wiklund et al. 2003). One of the most powerful influences is that exerted, often over extended periods of time, by the members of an entrepreneurial family firm:

[A]t the level of the individual firm, shared family experience leads to shared understandings and perceptions which shape the evolution of the firm. This is not the same as saying that the development of family firms is in some way pre-determined. Instead history matters in the change and innovation process as it affects choices and informs development. (Howorth et al. 2008: 230)

In a family firm, learning occurs among family members involved in the family business, but also across generations of the family. In Case 16.1, Jonathan Hick was inspired by his grandfathers' entrepreneurial spirits, and observed how his father ran multiple businesses. At times, he was even involved in important business discussions with his father at a very young age. Such experiences had a considerable effect on how Jonathan thinks and the successful entrepreneur he has become. Learning across generations is particularly important in the case of family business succession when the older generation plans to pass the baton on to the younger generation.

The theory behind learning from others dates back to Albert Bandura's social learning theory or observational learning: people learn through observing others and imitating their behaviour. Bandura (1977) believes that individuals do not automatically observe the behaviour of others and imitate it. Instead, individuals learn from others only when certain cognitive processes take place. These cognitive processes mediate or intervene in the learning process to determine whether the learner will retain and imitate the behaviour of others. Bandura (1977) proposes four cognitive processes (see Figure 16.2):

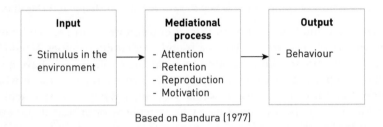

Based on Bandura (1977)

FIGURE 16.2 Bandura's Cognitive Model.

Attention: the extent to which individuals are exposed to the behaviour and actively observe the behaviour. The behaviour to be imitated by the learner has to grab the learner's attention in the first place, and the learner has to recognise its significance.

Retention: the extent to which individuals remember the behaviour of others. For the behaviour to be imitated, the learner has to form a memory of it and internalise it through comprehension. Retention is important because much of observational learning is not immediate, and the imitation of the behaviour may take place some time later.

Reproduction: the extent to which the learner has the ability to imitate the desired behaviour. More importantly, it is the learner's self-beliefs about his or her ability to produce desired performance. Such self-beliefs are also called self-efficacy (Bandura 1994). Self-efficacy influences individuals' decisions on whether to try and imitate the behaviour of others or not.

Motivation: the extent to which individuals have the will to imitate the desired behaviour. Motivation is likely to be stronger when the rewards that follow a behaviour outweigh the punishment. Bandura (1994) stresses that self-regulation, in terms of exercising influence over one's own motivation, thought processes, emotional states, and patterns of behaviour is instrumental to learning.

Entrepreneurs can learn from different people, such as peers, role models and mentors. It is good to learn from the best, as Dave Lavinsky said (Haden 2012). However, it is also good to learn from someone who is just like them – not a genius or a superstar; someone who has made a good go at it, according to Bev Hurley, a serial entrepreneur who set up Enterprising Women to help women into business (Howard 2016).

Nascent entrepreneurs may find it hard to judge what and who is the best to learn from. Haden (2012) observes that some of the reasonably successful entrepreneurs can be bad examples of how to run a business. Their businesses may succeed in spite of themselves, but people who work for them think that is how a business should be run, because they have not much experience to judge whether it is a good business practice or not. Here are a few tips on how to learn from peers, role models, and mentors.

Peers: effective peer learning is built on trust relations among peers (Zhang and Hamilton 2010). Entrepreneurs are more likely to help others when they can also get something out of it. Therefore, shared learning is appealing to entrepreneurs (Stokes 2001). Avoiding issues of competition is key to peer learning (Zhang and Hamilton 2010).

Role models: role models can be successful entrepreneurs in the public eye, but often they are people just around you – a friend or a family member. Would-be and nascent entrepreneurs are often inspired by what their role models have achieved, but it is more important that they learn how their role models achieve what they have achieved and how they develop skills over time. What they have achieved in life and in business can be aspiring, but maybe unrealistic or unsuitable for everyone to achieve. It is also important not only to learn from role models' success, but also from their failure – not to make the same mistakes. Both successful and unsuccessful role models help improve entrepreneurs' self-efficacy and entrepreneurial intention (Laviolette et al. 2012).

Mentors: What Richard Branson, Steve Jobs, and Larry Page have in common is that they had guidance from their mentors when they started up. According to Richard Branson (2014), the very first step to finding a good mentor is 'coming to terms with the fact that you actually can benefit from having one'. Entrepreneurs are motivated by independence, but this could mean a lot of ego and cocoon-like state of mind, as Richard Branson points out. His advice for entrepreneurs is:

> *No matter how incredibly smart you think you are, or how brilliant, disruptive or plain off-the-wall your new concept might be, every start-up team needs at least one good mentor. Someone, somewhere, has already been through what you are convinced nobody else has ever confronted! (Branson 2014).*

In summary, it is clear that an individual's entrepreneurial self-identity, attitudes, and ways of thinking are not set in stone. To varying degrees, they remain open to the influence of other people, and can be modified by circumstances. An entrepreneur's ethical practices can be learned from peers, mentors, and role models, including family members and others in their social circle.

16.3.3 Learning by doing

Learning by doing is a form of experiential learning. It involves learning from experiences resulting directly from one's own actions, as opposed to learning from watching others perform, reading or listening to others' instructions or descriptions (Reese 2011). It is often considered as the starting point of learning, as described in Kolb's experiential learning theory. We discuss it further here, given its prominent and relevance to entrepreneurs, as entrepreneurs are action-orientated individuals (Pittaway et al. 2015). Successful entrepreneurs are good at 'learning as they go' (Gartner 1988). As Richard Branson says, *'You don't learn to walk by following rules. You learn by doing, and by falling over.'*

The theory of learning by doing goes back to Kurt Lewin's (1951) field theory of learning that emphasises 'here-and-now' concrete experience to test and validate abstract concepts, as well as the importance of the feedback process in generating information to assess deviations of actions and outcomes from desired goals (Kolb, 1984). On the developmental nature of learning, John Dewey (1938) articulates how individuals learn to transform concrete experience into purposeful action:

> *The formation of purposes is, then, a rather complex intellectual operations. It involves (1) observation of surrounding conditions; (2) knowledge of what has happened in similar situations in the past, a knowledge obtained partly by recollection and partly from the information, advice, and warning of those who have had a wider experience; and (3) judgment which puts together what is observed and what is recalled to see what they signify. A purpose differs from an original impulse and desire through its translation into a plan and method of action based upon foresight of the consequences of acting under given observed conditions in a certain way... More foresight, even if it takes the form of accurate prediction, is not, of course, enough. The intellectual anticipation, the idea of consequences, must blend with desire and impulse to acquire moving force. It then gives direction to what otherwise is blind, while desire gives ideas impetus and momentum. (Dewey 1938: 69).*

Entrepreneurship scholars have built on the work of Kurt Lewin, John Dewey, David Kolb and many others to understand how entrepreneurs learn from their own experiences. For example, David Rae (2013) develops a momentary perspective to entrepreneurial learning and creativity. He emphasises the awareness of time because it connects past experience with anticipation of future opportunities. Especially, time consists of a qualitative and narrative aspect in terms of significant events that we subjectively and selectively perceive (i.e. Kairotic time), and a quantitative and objective aspect of chronological time (i.e. Chronos). David Rae focuses on the 'aha moment' or the 'eureka' moment of entrepreneurial activity to understand how entrepreneurial learning takes place, taking into account entrepreneurs' mental processes and the situations in which entrepreneurial events unfold (see Figure 16.3).

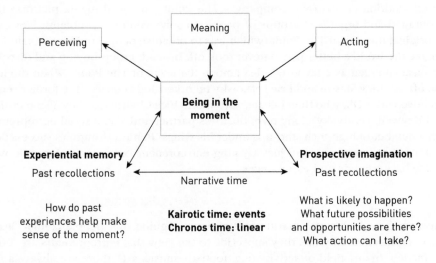

FIGURE 16.3 Rae's 'momentary perspectives' in entrepreneurial learning.

Source: Rae (2013: 417)

In each momentary experience, we are constantly perceiving, generating mean-ing, both consciously and unconsciously, and acting in response, through speech and behaviour, in interconnected ways. This occurs both consciously, with selec-tive attention being paid to a small proportion of the sensory data being perceived in the mental 'foreground'; and unconsciously, with awareness of a much wider range of experiential data taking place as 'background'. The subconscious is 'in control' of human behaviours to a far greater extent than we might think; the subconscious governs most momentary behaviours, whilst the conscious mind selects 'special' moments from memory in retrospect. This conceptualises, in a simplistic way, the complex interactions which occur constantly in our experi-ence of every moment (Rae 2013: 416).

In a similar sentiment, Cope (2005) warns that, although entrepreneurs are action-oriented, they are not just doers but 'reflective practitioners' as Cope and Watts (2000) and Schön (1983) refer to. It is through reflection and making sense of experience and its feedback that entrepreneurs learn (Cope 2005). Learning by doing focuses on learning through experimentation and discovery. In the processes of experimen-tation and discovery, entrepreneurs identify problems and solve problems through trial-and-error.

For nascent entrepreneurs who do not have much prior entrepreneurial experience but intend to learn by doing, the advice is to complement learning by doing with learning from others. Once again, Dave Lavinsky has some suggestions for young entrepreneurs: identifying a co-founder that has more managerial and/or investment experience; forming a Board of Advisers consisting of experienced entrepreneurs and others with a strong track record of managing and growing entrepreneurial firms; and raising funding to hire seasoned managers to work with you (Haden 2012).

The start-up process of Groupon is a good example of how young entrepreneurs can learn by doing, with the support of more experienced entrepreneurs. According to Carlson (2011), Andrew Mason was a student in 2006, working part-time for Eric Lefkofsky, a serial entrepreneur. In January 2007, supported by Eric Lefkofsky, Mason started working on his own company – The Point – a social media platform that encouraged and organised groups of people to solve common problems. However, the original mission of The Point (which was to organise people to identify solutions to make the world a better place) never took off. Instead, group-buying and discount purchase emerged as a favoured idea among the users of The Point. When the idea took off, Andrew Mason and Eric Lefkofsky recruited Ted Leonsis – the former senior executive with AOL, who then became Groupon's Vice Chairman. They also recruited Brad Keywell, Lefkofsky's long-term business partner and also a serial entrepreneur with a number of high-tech start-ups under his wings. Behind Groupon's success (and its many controversies) is not just a young entrepreneur but a team of people with diverse backgrounds and experiences.

16.3.4 Formal learning in schools, colleges, and universities

You often hear highly successful entrepreneurs arguing that people cannot 'learn' to act entrepreneurially (i.e. they subscribe to the view that entrepreneurs are 'born' not 'made'). In any field of activity (e.g. football, music, art), there are always a few exceptionally talented individuals, and it is clearly not possible for the rest of us to match their levels of performance, however many lessons we take. But even superstars can benefit from formal education. Returning to our previous examples, a few really great footballers, musicians, and artists are largely self-taught, but most achieved their greatness after a long apprenticeship and coaching. While it is unlikely that many of today's most successful entrepreneurs took a formal course in entrepreneurship, most acknowledge that they benefited from informal learning, often obtained through influential figures encountered during their upbringing.

More importantly, if we look away from the exceptional few, there is a much larger group of people that can benefit from entrepreneurship education, as shown in Case 16.3. Nathaniel Ru, Jonathan Neman, and Nicolas Jammet benefited directly from formal entrepreneurship education at the Georgetown University. On the other hand, Ehab Sayed combined his design engineering expertise obtained through formal education with his entrepreneurial spirit. He also actively participated in a wide range of formal and semi-formal entrepreneurship bootcamps and competitions to sharpen his business planning and pitching skills, as well as learning from mentors and peers at the Brunel Innovation Hub.

There is evidence that educational courses, if properly structured, can help to develop and enhance entrepreneurial skills and attitudes (e.g. Binks 2005; NIRAS 2008). Formal education can, in effect, 'fill the gap' for those whose lives have not provided more informal entrepreneurial learning experiences. Structured courses of study can provide the practical skills, knowledge, and understanding that people need in order to become more effective, and possibly more reflective, as they embark on an entrepreneurial career. For example, the School for Social Entrepreneurs (2016) works with people wanting to set up social enterprises. Education can also help others who do not see themselves as 'entrepreneurs' to gain a better understanding. These include: scientists, engineers, or artists who may find themselves part of an entrepreneurial team (Chapter 5); marketing, operations, or finance professionals providing services to entrepreneurial ventures (Chapters 6, 7, 8 and 9); and policy-makers seeking to encourage new enterprises (Chapter 15). There is still a great deal of ignorance and misunderstanding surrounding entrepreneurship in its various forms. Tackling this is vital if societies are to realise their entrepreneurial potential fully, and to find ways of guiding it towards more socially and environmentally productive ends.

There is now considerable interest in entrepreneurship education, extending from school to university level. Recent publications have highlighted the fact that entrepreneurship courses are already well established in some institutions (e.g. business schools), though under-represented in others (NIRAS 2008). Formal educational initiatives need to take account of students' motivations and learning styles (e.g. Gibb 2002; Souitaris et al. 2007), such as those discussed in this section.

CASE 16.2

Geetie Singh

Geetie Singh opened her organic and environmentally sustainable gastro pub, the Duke of Cambridge in north London, in 1998. It was and still is Britain's first and only certified organic pub. To Geetie Singh, the business means Good Business. Her business ethos is 'a fair deal for all: suppliers, staff, customers and the planet' (The Duke of Cambridge 2016).

(Continued)

(Continued)

They minimise the environmental impact in every possible way, from using grade-out vegetables and 100% certified organic ingredients, to upcycled furniture, to renewable energy using food waste. In the meantime, they forge strong links with the local community, from using locally sourced seasonal produce, to community events, to charitable activities at home and abroad (The Duke of Cambridge 2016). Geetie's business principle is to remain an independent, ethical, and sustainable business, as well as a successful business. Over the years, The Duke of Cambridge has won multiple organic, ethical and sustainable business awards. Geetie herself was awarded an MBE for services to the Organic Pub Trade in 2009. The experience of dining at The Duke of Cambridge is described as 'perhaps best understood as a temple rather than a pub, and eating there as a rite of belonging and respect rather than hoggish gratification' (Sexton 2014).

EARLY LIFE IN A COMMUNE

Where did Geetie Singh's idea of an organic and sustainable gastro pub come from? It goes back to Geetie's upbringing, growing up on a commune in the Midlands. Geetie was born to an English mother and a Sikh father originally from the Punjab. Growing up as a child of mixed race, she had a very hard time in her early life, including being threatened in the streets and teased by pupils in the school (Weale 2010). When her parents' marriage broke down in the 1970s, at the age of two, Geetie and her mum moved into a commune at the Birchwood Hall, a Victorian mansion with 40 rooms and eight acres of land in the shadow of the Malvern hills (Weale 2010). The place is still a commune called Diggers & Dreamers (2016), a not-for-profit collective promoting communal living. Communal living gave her a sense of freedom from conventional family life, and she soon learned to appreciate the order among the chaos. She learned to manage relationships, resolve conflicts, and appreciate the natural world in which we are living in. The commune was self-sufficient in their own food, and if they could not grow any food themselves, they bought produce from local shops. They also set up their food cooperative with the local community to promote organic and sustainable food (BIPC 2009).

> That's where my real education was at home – in this fabulously alternative way of living. We grew our own food; we went to every demo; we wrote letters and took politics very seriously. It was the best education I could have had. (Weale 2010)

FORMAL EDUCATION

According to Weale (2010), despite the fantastic informal education, Geetie felt that communal living let her down in formal academic education. Some parents living in the commune were sceptical about formal education; they had dropped out schools, and encouraged their children to drop out too. Geetie did go to a local primary school, but she stood out for the wrong reasons – her colour and her living in a commune. She did move on to get a place at the Birmingham Conservatoire to study to be an opera singer, but she quit after a year. Years later, she recalled that:

> I was a punk, I had a mohican, I was pretty and thin and I arrived with completely the wrong attitude. I couldn't read or write music. I found myself in this incredibly competitive atmosphere. I dropped out after a year, and I've never sung since. (Weale 2010)

ENTREPRENEURIAL CAREER

Geetie moved to London to live with her father, while working as a waitress. Life in London was a complete contrast to her early life. In her talk at the British Library's Inspiring Entrepreneurs (BIPC 2009), Geetie recalled that she was shocked to see the lack of sustainability in the food industry – lamb shipped from New Zealand and chemicals poured down the drain. It was at that point that she found her passion for organic and sustainable food and decided to set up her own restaurant. She then worked in different restaurants in London, learning various aspects of the restaurant trade, from wine lists to profit margins. She then found a business partner; she was very clear at that stage that she needed someone to set up the restaurant together. They wrote a 60-page business plan, which was then tailored to whoever the audience was. For example, they brought the ethics and sustainability forward if the audience was like-minded entrepreneurs, but highlighted the financial aspect if they were talking with banks.

Sometimes entrepreneurs have to make a conscious choice to run their businesses ethically and sustainably, even if at a higher cost of sourcing materials resulting in reduced profits. However, since the start of The Duke of Cambridge, Geetie Singh has stayed true to her core values as an ethical and environmentally minded entrepreneur, whilst running a successful business.

> Am I an environmentalist or a restaurateur? Well I don't think you can do what I do without being bloody good at your job, but I would say both are equally important to me. Food is my love – but food at any cost? Not on your life! (The Duke of Cambridge 2016).

> Undoubtedly I take less profit because of the way I run my business, from my choice of electricity supplier to how much I pay my staff. But who knows how much my turnover has increased as a result of the loyalty of my staff and all the people who spend money with me because of the positive effect the pub has on society and the environment? (The Startup Team 2013).

In June 2014, Geetie Singh married Guy Watson, an organic farmer at Riverford in South Devon, and an entrepreneur. He is known as an organic 'veg nerd who thinks outside the box', and has built a multi-million pounds business of home-delivered vegetable boxes and a farm restaurant (Lambert 2015). Naturally, Geetie and Guy's businesses followed suit – Riverford at the Duke of Cambridge offers a unique field-to-plate dining experience.

QUESTIONS

1. How did Geetie's early life in a commune shape her views on ethical and sustainable businesses?
2. How would you describe Geetie's learning styles?
3. What can you learn from Geetie's entrepreneurial experience?

This case was written by Catherine Wang. The author does not intend to illustrate either effective or ineffective entrepreneurial learning. The information included was drawn from the website of The Duke of Cambridge and a variety of publications cited in the text.

16.4 LEARNING AND ENTREPRENEURIAL OPPORTUNITY

Entrepreneurial opportunities are 'those situations in which new goods, services, raw materials, and organizing methods can be introduced and sold at greater than their cost of production' (Shane and Venkataraman 2000: 220). This definition implies that entrepreneurial opportunities are objective phenomena, though their existence is not recognised by everyone. There is a wide debate among entrepreneurs and entrepreneurship scholars on where opportunities come from.

There are two main schools of thoughts on entrepreneurial opportunities (Gartner et al. 2003): one school of thought argues that opportunities exist independently in the environment, waiting to be discovered; the other school of thought posits that entrepreneurial opportunities are enacted through entrepreneurs' perception and interpretation of the situations in the environment. An individual's ability to discover and pursue business opportunities is one of the most important qualities of successful entrepreneurs (Politis 2005).

Why are some people more likely to discover and pursue entrepreneurial opportunities than others? Research has identified at least two factors that influence individuals' ability to discover entrepreneurial opportunities: individuals possess the prior information required to identify an opportunity, and individuals possess the cognitive properties required to identify new means-ends relationships in response to a change in the environment (Shane and Venkataraman 2000; Ardichvili et al. 2003; Politis 2005). Below, we discuss two concepts – entrepreneurial alertness and entrepreneurial preparedness to help us understand how these two factors influence individuals' ability to discover opportunities, and what role learning plays.

16.4.1 Being alert to entrepreneurial opportunities

Sir Alan Sugar, a British entrepreneur and the star of *The Apprentice*, started at a school age to make extra money by making and selling his own ginger beer, boiling beetroots for a local greengrocer, and selling car antennas and cigarette lighters out of a van (Sugar 2011). Sir Alan Sugar's early entrepreneurial career is a good example of an entrepreneur who has an eye for opportunities – the ability to spot the opportunity of buying something at a lower price in the market, and selling them at a higher price. These activities of buying and selling to profit from price discrepancies in the market are called arbitrage (von Mises 1949). Spotting opportunities to engage in arbitrage are essentially what Israel Kirzner (1973) describes as 'entrepreneurial alertness'.

Entrepreneurial alertness refers to 'an attitude of receptiveness to available (but hitherto overlooked) opportunities' (Kirzner 1997: 72). What sets entrepreneurs apart from the crowd is their natural alertness to possible opportunities, often unnoticed by other people, in an uncertain environment (Kirzner 1973). In the eyes of Kirzner, entrepreneurs are gifted individuals, with 'flashes of superior insights' to recognise the potential value of an opportunity (Kirzner 1997). They often discover an opportunity with 'a sense of surprise', as the opportunity might have been previously overlooked by themselves and others. Kirzner's concept of entrepreneurial alertness is considered one of the most significant contributions to the theory of entrepreneurship (Gunning, 1997). It helps us understand where entrepreneurial opportunities are from.

On the other hand, Kirzner's entrepreneurial alertness has also attracted a great deal of criticism, as it aligns with the idea of natural-born entrepreneurs. Scholars such as Starr and Fondas (1992) and Harvey and Evans (1995) argue that alertness, as an attitude, is often formed over time; it is shaped cumulatively by prior knowledge, skills, and experience. Entrepreneurs' level of alertness changes over time through a learning process. When it comes to opportunities, we cannot neglect the role of entrepreneurs' prior knowledge and their personal motivation and willingness to bear uncertainty (McMullen and Shepherd 2006). In Case 16.2, it was through her early life in a commune that Geetie Singh developed a strong value in ethical and sustainable living. This prompted her to spot the lack of ethical and sustainable restaurants when she worked in restaurants in London.

There is also abundant evidence on the role of prior knowledge on opportunity identification in the literature. For example, experienced entrepreneurs are more likely than novice entrepreneurs to spot entrepreneurial opportunities, because they have acquired valuable and relevant knowledge about potential customers, suppliers, competitors, market viability, and product availability (Hudson and McArthur 1994; Shepherd et al. 2000). This echoes some scholars' views (e.g. Ardichvili et al. 2003; Shane and Venkataraman 2000; Politis 2005) that individuals need to possess prior knowledge required to identify an opportunity – this is the first factor as mentioned above that influences entrepreneurs' ability to discover opportunities.

On the other hand, experienced entrepreneurs are also more likely than nascent entrepreneurs to have developed an entrepreneurial mindset that helps them focus their mind on entrepreneurial opportunities with both creativity and discipline (McGrath and MacMillan 2000; Politis 2005). This echoes the second factor – individuals must possess the cognitive properties required to value opportunities (Ardichvili et al. 2003; Shane and Venkataraman 2000; Politis 2005). In summary, it is clear that lessons learned and skills accumulated from prior entrepreneurial experience improve entrepreneurs' ability to discover and pursue entrepreneurial opportunities (Ronstadt 1988). This is why many entrepreneurship scholars question Kirzner's concept of gifted individuals; instead, it is through learning and development that individuals become entrepreneurs (Cope 2005).

16.4.2 Being prepared for entrepreneurial opportunities

Recognising the importance of learning, scholars have drawn attention to how entrepreneurs can prepare themselves for entrepreneurial careers. Entrepreneurial preparedness (Cope 2005; Wang et al. 2014), a key concept within the entrepreneurial learning literature, addresses this issue. The concept can be traced back to Scherer et al.'s (1989) work on how students can prepare themselves for their entrepreneurial careers: they need to develop confidence in undertaking entrepreneurial tasks, and identify and fulfil their needs for entrepreneurial education and training. Later on, Festervand and Forrest (1993) develop a multi-stage model of entrepreneurial preparedness to highlight the developmental process of knowledge, skills and business planning required to prepare entrepreneurs for their new ventures.

Since then, while a handful of studies have touched on the concept (e.g. Harvey and Evans 1995; Jones and Tullous 2002; Johnsen and McMahon 2005; Dimov 2007; Lee and Jones 2008; Cooper and Park 2008), it is Cope (2005) who brings it to the forefront of the entrepreneurial learning literature. Building on Cope (2005), Wang et al. (2014) articulate three key features of entrepreneurial preparedness:

- **Cumulative learning**. Entrepreneurial preparedness relies on experiential learning, and in particular emphasises the cumulative process of experiential learning. Prior accumulated knowledge and experience forms a 'knowledge corridor' that allows the entrepreneur to immediately get interested in certain kind of information (Busenitz 1996), and to recognise certain opportunities (Venkataraman 1997). Prior knowledge of markets, of ways to serve markets, and of customer problems is especially useful for entrepreneurs (Shane 2000). Jon Beekman, the founder and CEO of Man Crates, a company that sells gifts for men, recounts how he learned from failing to pay attention to customers first in his previous failed venture. They had a great idea and a smart technical team, but they fell in love with their own technology and their concept of what customers wanted, instead of listening to what customers really wanted (Honigman 2014).

- **Social learning**. Entrepreneurial preparedness stresses the social nature of entrepreneurial learning. Learning takes place when entrepreneurs are in close contact with others and can observe and imitate behaviour of others (Bandura 1977), as we have discussed in the above section of learning from others. It is through socialisation that entrepreneurs improve their self-efficacy, managerial experience, business skills and education (Jones and Tullous 2002). Would-be and nascent entrepreneurs would benefit from socialising with other entrepreneurs – novice or experienced, and being immersed in an environmental where entrepreneurship is encouraged. Entrepreneurial learning is a lived experience involving a series of events (Cope 2003; Morris et al. 2012; Rae 2013).

- **Purposeful or goal-oriented learning**. Entrepreneurial preparedness emphasises the role of an entrepreneurial goal or aspiration in the learning process (Scherer et al. 1989). Entrepreneurial activity by nature involves a high degree of uncertainty and risk-taking for individuals taking on entrepreneurial endeavours. Under such conditions, establishing learning goals would help individuals to identify needs for knowledge and skills development, as well as develop strategies to implement learning. The knowledge accumulation process is directed by an entrepreneurial goal, and the cumulative learning process builds up to the point of entrepreneurial readiness to realise the goal (Festervand and Forrest 1993).

CASE 16.3   STUDENT FOCUS

Graduate entrepreneurs

David Pickernell and his colleagues at the University of Glamorgan conducted a large-scale study on graduate entrepreneurs. Based on 8,000 responses collected for the 2008 UK Federation of Small Business Survey, they identify a number of factors that differentiate graduate entrepreneurs from non-graduate entrepreneurs:

> Graduate entrepreneur-owned firms were statistically significantly more likely (than non-graduate-owned firms) to have younger owners, be younger and more export-oriented businesses, in high-knowledge services, to have intellectual property, make more use of web sites and be of high-growth potential. In terms of external resources,

graduate-owned businesses were more likely to have received beneficial business advice from informal networks/trade associations, government business services, friends and family, customers and suppliers, and to have public procurement customers at the national/international level. (Pickernell et al. 2011: 183)

Here are some inspiring stories of successful graduate entrepreneurs around the world.

SWEETGREEN

Nathaniel Ru, Jonathan Neman, and Nicolas Jammet were students at Georgetown University in the USA. They were frustrated because it was not easy for students to find a place to eat healthy food in a casual setting. Shortly after graduation in 2007, they raised $375,000 from family and friends to set up their own restaurant, Sweetgreen, near  the university campus (Frieswick, 2015). Sweetgreen was profitable in the first year, and expanded to two more restaurants in Washington DC within 18 months. By 2016, Sweetgreen has dozens of stores nationwide (Sweetgreen, 2016).

Nathaniel, Jonathan, and Nicolas are very proud of their business, because they believe that Sweetgreen aligns the business value with their personal value (Sweetgreen, 2016). It is 'value-aligned' dining, as Kris Frieswick (2015) calls it, which creates a unique selling proposition of their business. Nathaniel, Jonathan and Nicolas attribute their business idea and ethos to the entrepreneurship class that they attended with Professor William Finnerty at Georgetown, and the key lesson they learned is: 'it's possible to build successful business that meshes with your personal values' (Frieswick 2015). Together with Joe Bastianich, a restaurateur, Professor Finnerty became a mentor to Nathaniel, Jonathan, and Nicolas. Sweetgreen's $57.5 million business development funding also included an early investment by Professor Finnerty.

MORPHCOSTUMES

Gregor Lawson, and Fraser and Ali Smeaton (who are brothers), were all Edinburgh University graduates. According to their own account (MorphCostumes, 2016), their business idea started one night after an 'athletics competition' (fuelled by drinking) where they had to 'wear one colour'. Their best mate in a 'dodgy fetish suit' stole the limelight and became king of the party. That became their lightbulb moment – they wanted to make and sell fancy dress costumes. They started in 2009 with six plain colour costumes, invested in a website for about £450, used Facebook to advertise their business, and within two weeks, they sold out 2,500 suits (Griffiths, 2015; MorphCostumes). In the first year, they reached sales of £1.2m (Griffiths, 2015). In 2016, they have 30 team members, hundreds of costumes including over 100 of their own costumes, and nearly 1.7 million Facebook followers (MorphCostumes, 2016). The business has won numerous awards including Golden Hedgehog Awards 2014, Disney Toys and Stationery Product Awards 2014 (MorphCostumes, 2016).

(Continued)

(Continued)

When Gregor, Fraser, and Ali set up MorphCostumes in 2009, they already had established careers alongside the new business. Fraser was Head of Marketing for BT Broadband, Gregor a brand manager for Procter and Gamble, and Ali an accountant working at Barclays (Griffiths, 2015). Working full-time in corporate jobs plus running the business at night proved unsustainable. In 2010, Gregor, Fraser, and Ali decided to leave behind their 'normal jobs' (in their own words), to concentrate on their business (MorphCostumes, 2016). Fraser is the Chief Executive, Gregor the Marketing Director, and Ali the Operations Director.

BIOHM

Ehab Sayed was an international student from Egypt and studied MSc Integrated Product Design student at Brunel University London. He builds on his expertise in design engineering to set up his business – Biohm, the Future of Home. Biohm is a research and development-led company that creates architecture and construction with zero-waste systems that benefit both the human and the environment (Biohm, 2016).

In the early stage of the start-up, Ehab Sayed was supported by Brunel Innovation Hub that supports student and graduate entrepreneurs. Brunel Innovation Hub (2016) has a detailed account of Ehab's entrepreneurial journey: when Ehab came up with his business idea, he had 1-to-1 business consultations with advisers at the Hub to help him develop his business model and business plan. He then attended Venture Bootcamp where he learned more about business models and their applications in his business, as well as pitching skills. His business plan was highly praised by a professional panel, which boosted his confidence in business planning and pitching. He further improved these skills through attending the Entrepreneur Training Week, Santander Universities Entrepreneurship Competition, and eventually successfully pitched for a space on the Graduate Entrepreneur Scheme (for which he was endorsed for a Tier 1 Graduate Entrepreneur visa). Ehab then joined StartUP Lab within Brunel Innovation Hub and won a £1,000 at the StartUP Lab Pitch.

QUESTIONS

1. In the above mini-cases, how did the entrepreneurs discover business opportunities?

2. Comparing the three mini-cases, can you describe how formal education help prepare the entrepreneurs for their new ventures?

3. What can you learn from these entrepreneurs?

The case was written by Catherine Wang, based on information from a variety of sources cited in the text.

16.5 LEARNING FROM SUCCESS AND FAILURE

Entrepreneurs often describe their ventures as a rollercoaster with many ups and downs. The ability to pick yourself up after failing and learn from failures is as important as the ability to avoid being complacent and see what is coming next beyond current success. It is the ability to learn from both success and failure that really makes or breaks entrepreneurs.

16.5.1 Learning from success

Learning from success can pose greater challenges for entrepreneurs and their firms, than learning from failure (Gino and Pisano 2011). This is because a success tells people exactly what to do, whereas information about a failure only excludes one of many possible courses of actions (Lee and Van den Steen 2010). Driven by performance and rewards, people are motivated to learn from success and take the tested and proven actions that they associate with good performance, instead of experimenting to find even better solutions. This self-reinforcing effect of success can create a comfortable position in which entrepreneurs and their firms are trapped in (Wang et al. 2015). This powerful effect of success explains why firms want to share best practices and replicate success and why success has more prominence than failures (Lee and Van den Steen 2010).

History is replete with cases of entrepreneurs and their ventures failing to learn from success. Why are people wary of learning from success? Gino and Pisano (2011) summarise three key inter-related impediments to learning:

- **Fundamental attribution errors**: people are inclined to attribute success to their own talents, and overlook the role of those factors that are beyond their control, such as environmental factors and critical events leading up to the success. It is quite possible that the success is simply a stroke of luck or the result of competitors' failure.

- **Overconfidence bias:** entrepreneurs tend to have a higher level of independence and self-efficacy. Such self-confidence allows them to make decisions and take risks. However, nothing inflates confidence like success does, and over confidence and too much faith in oneself can cause complacency.

- **Failure-to-ask-why syndrome:** unlike failure, success is celebrated, and very rarely investigated. As a result, there is no systematic understanding of the cause of success. If not handled properly, success can cause delusion that everything is going well, and create blind spots where threats are just around the corner.

We often believe that 'if it ain't broke, don't fix it'. It is exactly this mentality that prevents us from learning from success and to overcome success traps. Gino and Pisano (2011) invite us to change the way of thinking to 'if it ain't broke, experiment it'. Success should be celebrated to boost morale, but there is a huge difference between merely enjoying success and actually learning from success (Sagarin 2014). We should always cast a critical eye on our own success to examine exactly what has contributed to the success and what could have been improved.

16.5.2 Learning from adversity: challenges, mistakes, setbacks, and failures

Entrepreneurial learning can also occur as people deal with challenges, mistakes, setbacks, and failures. All of us encounter adversity during our lifetimes. It can range in intensity from the superficial (e.g. losing your car keys), to the profound (e.g. dealing with the loss of a close relative or friend). Entrepreneurial activity is characterised by a whole series of challenges, which can begin to seem insurmountable. Some of these are inevitable. For example, it is always going to be difficult to convince people about a new technology, particularly when your team lacks a 'track record'. Even when things are going well, entrepreneurs often face hostility from vested interests, along with usual competitive pressures. Other challenges arise as a result of making judgements under conditions of uncertainty, and sometimes getting it wrong. So is there a distinctively 'entrepreneurial' approach to the problems that are bound to come your way? When it comes to making mistakes, many successful entrepreneurs would echo this insightful comment:

> *With respect to mistakes made in business, my only advice is that you've just got to learn from them and move on quickly. Anyone who wants to run their own business has to get comfortable with the reality that they are going to make mistakes and even, at times, to experience failure. I learn as much from failure as success. (Anne Heraty, quoted in Flannery 2008: 74–5)*

Entrepreneurs often talk about learning from failure (Honigman 2014; Cooper 2013). Many companies have established a culture of learning from failure (Sagarin 2014). Yet those who do it very well are extremely rare. Several things are in the way that prevent us from learning from failure:

- **The blame game**: people instantly attribute success to their own abilities, but when it comes to failure, it is others to blame (Gino and Pisano 2011). This is easy to understand as we are brought up to believe failure is bad and only success is recognised and rewarded in business and in life. Taking a biopsy of one's own failure can be painful or very uncomfortable at least. Failure often brings punishment, which is hard to face. This is why in new venture teams or established firms, the culture needs to shift to provide some psychological safety in which failure is not penalised, and learning from failure is encouraged (Edmondson 2011).

- **Uncertainty associated with failure:** success is easier to dissect, because it is something that has already been accomplished. Failure is much harder to reflect on, as by its very own nature, entrepreneurs fail something because they did not know how to do it in the first place. The lack of relevant information, knowledge, skills, and abilities to perform tasks in the first place may well be the reason why many entrepreneurs don't or cannot learn from failure.

- **Not all failures are equal:** Edmondson (2011) argues that an infinite number of things can go wrong, but mistakes largely fall into three categories: (a) preventable failures that occur which, in hindsight, can be easily fixed and shouldn't be repeated in the future; (b) unavoidable failures that happen due to complex systems or unpredictable environment; and (c) intelligent failures that generate valuable new knowledge charting new territories way ahead of competition. Finally, we add a fourth type of failure – strategic failure as a result of deliberate deviation from known and well-tested solution in order to experiment and generate new knowledge. Entrepreneurs need to carefully analyse failures and use relevant strategies to learn from different types of failures.

There are plenty of examples of entrepreneurs coping with adversity and learning from failures. Meridith Valiando Rojas, prior to setting up DigiTour Media, failed to successfully manage artists on Capital Records. She learned from this 'devastating failure' and came to understand the role of social media in breaking talent in the digital world, which led to the creation of DigiTour (Honigman 2014). In time of difficulty, it may be hard for entrepreneurs to see light at the end of the tunnel. However, we should always remember:

when one door closes, another one opens. Many experienced entrepreneurs would tell you that some of their most dreaded moments at the time turn out to be their most proud moments years later. In Case 16.1, Jonathan Hick brought in two investors due to his company's financial difficulty. At the time, he felt it was a terrible failure, but years later, when looking back, he realised that it was one of the proudest moments.

Learning from success and failure goes hand in hand. Success can breed failure if entrepreneurs fail to learn from success. Gino and Pisano (2011) call this a 'success-breeds-failure trap'. We want to point out that failing to learn from failure can set you in a failure-breeds-failure trap. Only effective learning from failure can turn failure into success. Learning from success and failure not only requires knowledge and skills for entrepreneurs to understand the causes of success and failure, but also discipline and courage to face up to the challenge in the first place. Finally, it is not just learning from one's own success and failure but those of others, as we discussed in the Section 16.3.2 learning from others. As Brandon Mull, the author of *Fablehaven* (a best-selling children's fantasy novel) says, 'Smart people learn from their mistakes. But the real sharp ones learn from the mistakes of others.'

CASE 16.4 RESEARCHER PROFILE

DAVID RAE ON THE MOMENTARY PERSPECTIVES TO
ENTREPRENEURIAL LEARNING

David Rae is a leading innovator and researcher in the human and social dynamics of entrepreneurship, learning and small business management. He holds a PhD in Entrepreneurial Learning, and his innovative work has been recognised internationally for its contributions to research, policy, and practice in entrepreneurial learning and education. He aims to engage people across business, professional, community, and academic groups in proactive innovation, learning, and change.

He was Professor of Business & Enterprise at the University of Lincoln, then became Dean of the Shannon School of Business, Cape Breton University, Canada, before returning to the UK as the first Executive Dean for Research & Knowledge Exchange at Bishop Grosseteste University. David is currently Professor of Enterprise at Leicester Business School, De Montfort University.

What interests you most about research in entrepreneurial learning?

I have been intrigued by entrepreneurial learning since getting started in the mid-1990s in the UK, when it was a very niche topic. The combination of human creativity applied to real situations, with the dynamic of learning, as a means of people achieving personal and social transformation continues to fascinate me. Entrepreneurship then was dominated by economic theories, and now we rightly consider entrepreneurship to be as much a humanistic and sociological as an economic area of study.

(Continued)

(Continued)

Entrepreneurial learning is still quite an elusive topic, continually changing as a practice and academic discipline, and being shaped by developments in the social, economic, technological and cultural contexts. And we as researchers and educators are creating new understandings in our interactions with entrepreneurial people.

What are the key findings of your research, and have you even been surprised by a particular set of research findings?

My research has explored the interactions between entrepreneurial people, the context they experience, their responses, behaviours and learning narratives. At the beginning I interviewed experienced business people and was amazed by the richness and depth of their learning experiences. My involvement in researching entrepreneurial learning and teaching entrepreneurship helped produce the 'Opportunity-Centred Entrepreneurship' approach which has been influential. The concept of learning at points and periods of time emerged as significant, both in my own and Jason Cope's work, and that has developed to inform later work on significant 'moments' in learning.

More recently I researched business owner-managers we'd worked with during the 2008–10 recession and how they had learned to adapt to uncertainty. The economic and external issues were there, but it was surprising how much the social relationships, peer learning, and reassurance people gained in their strategic and decision-making from being part of a group mattered. This informed a piece of work on 'momentary perspectives' in entrepreneurship, which explores how the realisations in 'the moment' can be formative in recognising opportunities, finding partners and investors, making strategic decisions, and many other ways.

What do you see as the main challenges for entrepreneurial learning research over the next decade?

I think entrepreneurship will remain a contested arena, between the 'free-enterprise/profit maximisation' and the 'sustainable/ethical/responsible' schools. Entrepreneurship is global, and is working across most societies, and political and belief systems, in different ways. This diversity increases the scope for learning hugely, but also represents challenges, especially if the aim is to create generalisable theories, because the contexts vary so much.

How do you make a connection between the worlds of entrepreneurial learning research, teaching/education, and practice?

Making these connections, and others – including with policy, community, and social development – is essential. The way I make these connections is by acting across boundaries, with others. So I'm involved in leading entrepreneurial projects which connect making new futures with research, innovation, business creation, community development, and education. I work with people working within and across these domains and we're continually making exchanges and connections that enrich the knowledge, practice, and opportunities they offer.

What advice would you offer to an entrepreneurship student who is navigating the entrepreneurial learning literature for the first time?

I have a PhD student who is doing just that. I encourage a stance which is reflective, appreciative, and then critical, but never to neglect or suppress her own experiences and responses. The emotional dynamics of entrepreneurship were neglected for too long when the field was dominated by economic and then logical cognitive perspectives, before neuroscience demonstrated how hugely important unconscious processes, feelings and emotions are in the ways people perceive, behave, and interact.

So follow what is interesting and speaks to you because you can't read everything. But be ready to go back to the roots of seminal works in philosophy, sociology, psychology, and education, let's say, back in Europe and the US in the 1920s. These are just examples, but they're important. So when a student talks about John Dewey, Jerome Bruner, or Edmund Husserl, for example, and has actually read the original source, that's important. And there are people doing great work right now, so find and follow them. I think each student needs to find the writers who are significant and meaningful for them.

16.6 SUMMARY

- Entrepreneurial learning refers to learning in the entrepreneurial process. It is fundamental to the understanding of how entrepreneurs discover and pursue entrepreneurial opportunities.

- Entrepreneurial learning focuses on the developmental process of entrepreneurs – the becoming of entrepreneurs, instead of personality traits of entrepreneurs. Indeed, personality traits are often shaped by the learning process, sometimes lifelong learning of entrepreneurs.

- There is no one right or wrong way of learning. Individuals learn differently and may also vary or combine learning styles in different contexts. Entrepreneurs can benefit from at least four types of learning: learning from experience, learning from others, learning by doing, and formal learning.

- Discovery and pursuit of entrepreneurial opportunities requires entrepreneurs to possess superior insights to spot opportunities that are often neglected by others or even themselves previously (i.e. entrepreneurial alertness). On the other hands, entrepreneurs need to prepare themselves through learning and development, and acquire knowledge needed to generate superior insights on emerging entrepreneurial opportunities (i.e. entrepreneurial preparedness).

- Entrepreneurial learning from success and failure goes hand in hand. Success can breed failure, and failure may lead to further failure, if entrepreneurs fail to learn from success and failure. Entrepreneurs must learn from their own success and failure, and that of others.

Practical activities

1. Entrepreneurial learning in practice: Review each of the cases in the chapter and each of the video cases on the website to identify the key learning styles and processes as discussed in this chapter. What did the entrepreneurs learn? How did they learn: similarly or differently?

2. Reflection on your own learning styles: Evaluate your own learning styles, relating to the different learning styles discussed in this chapter. How do you learn effectively? What have you learned from the entrepreneurs mentioned in this chapter? Who is your entrepreneurial role model? How does this entrepreneur inspire you?

Discussion topics

1. What are the key challenges for entrepreneurs and their new ventures to cope with the demand of multiple learning processes and styles? How easy or difficult is it to learn from success and failure? Can you discuss a few strategies to learn from success and failure?

2. How is entrepreneurial learning different in a classroom compared to in a real-life business venture? What have you learned in your entrepreneurial education? What can you do to accelerate your own personal development, and prepare yourself for an entrepreneurial career?

3. Which particular topic within entrepreneurial learning do you think is worthwhile to pursue as a dissertation topic? How can you approach the topic? What methodology do you plan to use? What would be the implications of this dissertation topic for entrepreneurs?

Recommended reading

The first two books below contain a collection of articles on entrepreneurial learning theory, practice, and education. The paper by Wang and Chugh (2014) provides an overview of the development of entrepreneurial learning and a list of key references on entrepreneurial learning.

Harrison, R. T. and Leitch, C. M. (eds) (2008) *Entrepreneurial Learning: Conceptual Frameworks and Applications*. London: Routledge.

Rae, D. and Wang, C. L. (eds) (2015) *Entrepreneurial Learning: New Perspectives in Research, Education and Practice*. London: Routledge.

Wang, C. L. and Chugh, H. (2014) 'Entrepreneurial learning: past research and future challenges'. *International Journal of Management Reviews*, 16, 1: 24–61.

These readings below address important topics in entrepreneurship research and are recommended for anyone wanting to build on the material covered in this chapter. Recommended readings have been selected from leading Sage journals and are freely available for readers of this textbook to download via the Online Resources.

Amankwah-Amoah, J., Boso, N., and Antwi-Agyei, I. (2016) 'The effects of business failure experience on successive entrepreneurial engagements: An evolutionary phase model'. *Group and Organization Management*, DOI: https://doi.org/10.1177/1059601116643447.

This study draws insights from the literatures on entrepreneurial learning from failure and organisational imprinting to develop an evolutionary phase model to explain how prior business failure experience influences successive newly started businesses. Using multiple case studies of entrepreneurs located in an institutionally developing society in sub-Saharan Africa, we uncover four distinctive phases of post-entrepreneurial business failure: grief and despair, transition, formation, and legacy phases. We find that while the grieving and transition phases entailed processes of reflecting and learning lessons from the business failure experiences, the formation and legacy phases involve processes of imprinting entrepreneurs' experiential knowledge on their successive new start-up firms. We conclude by outlining a number of fruitful avenues for future research.

Cope, J. (2003) 'Entrepreneurial learning and critical reflection: Discontinuous events as triggers for "higher-level" learning'. *Management Learning*, 34, 4: 429–50.

The importance of 'learning events' has become an emergent theme within theorising on how entrepreneurs learn. This article builds a deeper understanding of the learning outcomes triggered by significant, discontinuous events during the entrepreneurial process. It suggests that the domain of entrepreneurship represents a special and unique context in which to study management learning. It is argued that there is more to learning from discontinuous events than the incremental accumulation of more routinised, habitual, 'lower-level' learning. This article illustrates that these events have the capacity to stimulate distinctive forms of 'higher-level' learning – learning that is fundamental to the entrepreneur in both personal and business terms. It goes on to explore the concept of critical reflection and suggests that these learning outcomes are the result of what can be described most precisely as 'inward' critical self-reflection.

Pittaway, L. and Cope, J. (2007) 'Simulating entrepreneurial learning: integrating experiential and collaborative approaches to learning'. *Management Learning*, 38, 2: 211–33.

Theorising about entrepreneurial learning is examined in this article to determine key learning processes within this body of research. It explores how these processes might be simulated in a student-learning environment and highlights the role of emotional exposure, situated learning, action-orientation and discontinuity. An argument is made for experiential, work-based learning when seeking to simulate contexts similar to those in which entrepreneurs learn. A conceptual framework is introduced that highlights a course design based on the factors identified. In the analysis, formal course assessments are reviewed and narrative coding based on student reflections is evaluated. The article illustrates that it is possible to simulate aspects of entrepreneurial learning, such as emotional exposure and situated learning, but not others. It also demonstrates a range of learning benefits linked to experiential learning. In conclusion, the article explains why entrepreneurship education can play an important role in encouraging management learning.

References

Ajzen, I. (1991) 'The theory of planned behavior'. *Organizational Behavior and Human Decision Processes*, 50: 179–211.

Ardichvili, A., Cardozo, R., and Ray, S. (2003) 'A theory of entrepreneurial opportunity identification and development'. *Journal of Business Venturing*, 18, 1: 105–23

Bandura, A. (1977) *Social Learning Theory*. Englewood Cliffs, NJ: Prentice Hall.

Bandura, A. (1994) 'Self-efficacy'. In V. S. Ramachaudran (ed.), *Encyclopedia of Human Behavior*, 4, New York: Academic Press (71–81).

Binks, M. (2005) *Entrepreneurship Education and Integrative Learning*. Birmingham: National Council for Graduate Entrepreneurship.

Biohm (2016) 'Our philosophy'. http://www.biohm.co.uk/ (accessed 12 November 2016).

BIPC (2009) *Geetie Singh, The Duke of Cambridge* (Inspiring Entrepreneurs – Ethical Entrepreneurs), British Library Business & IP Centre in partnership with HSBC. https://www.youtube.com/watch?v=OeeUtUOyh0I (accessed 4 November 2016).

Blundel, R. K., Ippolito, K., and Donnarumma, D. (2013) *Effective Organisational Communication: Perspectives, Principles and Practices* (4th edn). Harlow: Pearson.

Branson, R. (2014) *The Virgin Way: Everything I Know about Leadership*. Portfolio.

Brunel Innovation Hub (2016) 'Student journey: Ehab Sayed'. https://brunelinnovationhub.com/student-journey-ehab-sayed/ (accessed 12 November 2016).

Busenitz, L. W. (1996) 'Research on entrepreneurial alertness: sampling, measurement, and theoretical issues'. *Journal of Small Business Management*, 34, 4: 35–44.

Carlson, N. (2011) *Inside Groupon: the truth about the world's most controversial company. Business Insider*. http://www.businessinsider.com/inside-groupon-the-truth-about-the-worlds-most-controversial-company-2011-10?IR=T (accessed 4 November 2016).

Cooper, B. B. (2013) *The 13 Biggest Failures from Successful Entrepreneurs and What They've Learned from Them*. https://blog.bufferapp.com/failure-entrepreneur-12-successful-entrepreneurs-tell-us-the-biggest-lessons-theyve-learned (accessed 4 November 2016).

Cooper, S. Y. and Park, J. S. (2008) 'The impact of "incubator" organizations on opportunity recognition and technology innovation in new, entrepreneurial high-technology ventures'. *International Small Business Journal*, 26, 1: 27–56.

Cope, J. (2003) 'Entrepreneurial learning and critical reflection: discontinuous events as triggers for "higher-level" learning'. *Management Learning*, 34, 4: 429–50.

Cope, J. (2005) 'Toward a dynamic learning perspective of entrepreneurship'. *Entrepreneurship Theory and Practice*, 29, 4: 373–97.

Cope, J. and Watts, G. (2000) 'Learning by doing: an exploration of experience, critical incidents and reflection in entrepreneurial learning'. *International Journal of Entrepreneurial Behaviour and Research*, 6, 3: 104–24.

Dewey, J. (1938) *Experience and Education*. New York, NY: Kappa Delta Pi.

Diggers & Dreamers (2016) Diggers & Dreamers website. http://www.diggersanddreamers.org.uk/index.php?fld=initial&val=B&one=dat&two=det&sel=brchwood (accessed 4 November 2016).

Dimov, D. (2007) 'From opportunity insight to opportunity intention: the importance of person-situation learning match'. *Entrepreneurship Theory and Practice*, 31, 4: 561–83.

Edmondson, A. C. (2011) 'Strategies for learning from failure'. *Harvard Business Review*, April. https://hbr.org/2011/04/strategies-for-learning-from-failure (accessed 4 November 2016).

Festervand, T. A. and Forrest, J. E. (1993) 'Entrepreneurial preparedness: a multi-stage model'. *Journal of Business and Entrepreneurship*, 5, 3: 65–77.

Flannery, P. (2008) *Grabbing the Oyster!: Anecdotes and Advice from Icons of Irish Business*. Cork: Oak Tree Press.

Frieswick, K. (2015) 'Turning a passion for healthy food into a fast-casual juggernaut'. *Inc.com*. http://www.inc.com/kris-frieswick/2015-30-under-30-sweetgreen.html (accessed 12 November 2016).

Gartner, W. B. (1988) 'Who is an entrepreneur? is the wrong question'. *American Journal of Small Business*, 13, 1: 11–32.

Gartner, W. B., Carter, N. M., and Hills, G. E. (2003) 'The language of opportunity'. In C. Steyaert and D. Hjorth (eds), *New Movements in Entrepreneurship*. Cheltenham, UK: Edward Elgar (103–24).

Gibb, A. (2002), 'In pursuit of a new "enterprise" and "entrepreneurship" paradigm for learning: creative destruction, new values, new ways of doing things and new combinations of knowledge'. *International Journal of Management Reviews*, 4, 3: 233–69.

Gino, F, and Pisano, G. P. (2011) 'Why leaders don't learn from success'. *Harvard Business Review*, April. https://hbr.org/2011/04/why-leaders-dont-learn-from-success (accessed 4 November 2016).

Griffiths, J. (2015) 'The multi-million pound business started as a laugh'. BBC News. http://www.bbc.co.uk/news/business-34504174 (accessed 12 November 2016).

Gunning, J. P. (1997) 'The theory of entrepreneurship in Austrian economics'. In W. Keizer, B. Tieben, and R. van Zijp (eds), *Austrian Economics in Debate* (Routledge Studies in the History of Economics). London: Routledge (172–90).

Haden, J. (2012) *Best Way to Learn to Be an Entrepreneur?* http://www.inc.com/jeff-haden/debate-best-work-experience-for-aspiring-entrepreneurs.html (accessed 4 November 2016).

Harrison, R. T. and Leitch, C. M. (2008) *Entrepreneurial Learning: Conceptual Frameworks and Applications*. London: Routledge.

Harvey, M. and Evans, R. (1995) 'Strategic windows in the entrepreneurial process'. *Journal of Business Venturing*, 10, 331–47.

Holcomb, T. R., Ireland, R. D., Holmes Jr., R. M., and Hitt, M. A. (2009) 'Architecture of entrepreneurial learning: exploring the link among heuristics, knowledge, and action'. *Entrepreneurship Theory and Practice*, 33, 1: 167–92.

Honigman, B. (2014) *33 Entrepreneurs Share Their Biggest Lessons Learned from Failure*. http://www.huffingtonpost.com/brian-honigman/35-tech-entrepreneurs-failure_b_5529254.html (accessed 4 November 2016).

Howard, E. (2016) 'One of the barriers for women entrepreneurs is a lack of role models'. *The Guardian*, 8 March. https://www.theguardian.com/small-business-network/2016/

mar/08/one-of-the-barriers-for-women-entrepreneurs-is-a-lack-of-role-models (accessed 4 November 2016).

Howorth, C. A., Rose, M. B., and Hamilton, E. E. (2008) 'Definitions, diversity and development: key debates in family business research'. In M. Casson, B. Yeung, A. Basu, and N. Wadeson (eds), *The Oxford Handbook of Entrepreneurship*. Oxford University Press (225–47).

Huang, Y. (2010). 'Entrepreneurship in China'. *The World Financial Review*. http://www.worldfinancialreview.com/?p=2782 (accessed 4 November 2016).

Hudson, R. L. and McArthur, A. (1994) 'Contracting strategies in entrepreneurial and established firms'. *Entrepreneurship Theory and Practice*, 18, 4: 43–59.

Johnsen, G. J. and McMahon, R. G. P. (2005) 'Owner-manager gender, financial performance and business growth amongst SMEs from Australia's business longitudinal survey'. *International Small Business Journal*, 23, 2: 115–42.

Jones, K. and Tullous, R. (2002) 'Behaviors of pre-venture entrepreneurs and perceptions of their financial needs'. *Journal of Small Business Management*, 40, 3: 233–49.

Kelley, D., Singer, S., and Herrington, M. (2016) *Global Entrepreneurship Monitor, 2015/2016 Global Report*. http://gemconsortium.org/report/49480 (accessed 4 November 2016).

Kirzner, I. M. (1973) *Competition and Entrepreneurship*. Chicago: University of Chicago Press.

Kirzner, I. M. (1997) 'Entrepreneurial discovery and the competitive market process: an Austrian approach'. *Journal of Economic Literature*, 35: 60–85.

Kolb, D. A. (1984) *The Experiential Learning: Experience as the Source of Learning and Development*. Englewood Cliffs, NJ: Prentice-Hall, Inc.

Lambert, V. (2015) 'Guy Watson interview: veg nerd who thinks outside the box'. *The Telegraph*. http://www.telegraph.co.uk/lifestyle/11484925/Guy-Watson-interview-Veg-nerd-who-thinks-outside-the-box.html (accessed 4 November 2016).

Lans, T., Biemans, H., Verstegen, J., and Mulder, M. (2008) 'The influence of the work environment on entrepreneurial learning of small-business owners'. *Management Learning*, 39, 5: 597–613.

Laviolette, E. M., Lefebvre, M. R., and Brunel, O. (2012) 'The impact of story bound entrepreneurial role models on self-efficacy and entrepreneurial intention'. *International Journal of Entrepreneurial Behavior & Research*, 18, 6: 720–42.

Lee, D. and Van den Steen, E. (2010) 'Managing know-how'. *Management Science*, 56: 270–85.

Lee, R. and Jones, O. (2008) 'Networks, communication and learning during business start-up: the creation of cognitive social capital'. *International Small Business Journal*, 26, 5: 559–91.

Lewin, K. (1951) *Field Theory in Social Science: Selected Theoretical Papers*. New York: Harper & Row.

McGrath, R. G. and MacMillan, I. C. (2000) *The Entrepreneurial Mindset*. Boston, MA: Harvard Business School Press.

McMullen, J. S. and Shepherd, D. A. (2006) 'Entrepreneurial action and the role of uncertainty in the theory of the entrepreneur'. *Academy of Management Review*, 31, 1: 132–52.

Minniti, M. and Bygrave, W. (2001) 'A dynamic model of entrepreneurial learning'. *Entrepreneurship Theory and Practice*, 25, 3: 5–16.

MorphCostumes (2016) 'Our story'. http://www.morphsuits.co.uk/story (accessed 12 November 2016).

Morris, M. H., Kuratko, D. F., Schindehutte, M., and Spivack, A. J. (2012) 'Framing the entrepreneurial experience'. *Entrepreneurship: Theory and Practice*, 36, 1: 11–40.

NIRAS (2008) *Survey of Entrepreneurship in Higher Education in Europe.* Brussels: European Commission, Directorate General for Enterprise and Industry.

Pickernell, D., Packham, G., Jones, P., Miller, C., and Thomas, B. (2011) 'Graduate entrepreneurs are different: they access more resources?' *International Journal of Entrepreneurial Behavior & Research*, 17, 2: 183–202.

Pittaway, L. A. and Cope, J. (2007) 'Simulating entrepreneurial learning: integrating experiential and collaborative approaches to learning'. *Management Learning*, 38, 2: 211–33.

Pittaway, L. A., Gazzard, J., Shore, A., and Williamson, T. (2015) 'Student clubs: experiences in entrepreneurial learning'. *Entrepreneurship & Regional Development*, 27, 3–4: 127–53.

Pittaway, L. A., Rodriguez-Falcon, E., Aiyegbayo, O., and King, A. (2010) 'The role of entrepreneurship clubs and societies in entrepreneurial learning'. *International Small Business Journal*, 29, 1: 37–57.

Politis, D. (2005) 'The process of entrepreneurial learning: a conceptual framework'. *Entrepreneurship Theory and Practice*, 29, 4: 399–424.

Rae, D. (2013) 'The contribution of momentary perspectives to entrepreneurial learning and creativity'. *Industry & Higher Education*, 27, 6: 407–20.

Rae, D. and Wang, C. L. (eds) (2015) *Entrepreneurial Learning: New Perspectives in Research, Education and Practice.* Abingdon: Routledge.

Rae, D., Gee, S. and Moon, R. (2009) 'Creating an enterprise culture in a university: the role of an entrepreneurial learning team'. *Industry and Higher Education*, 23, 3: 183–97.

Ravasi, D. and Turati, C. (2005) 'Exploring entrepreneurial learning: a comparative study of technology development projects'. *Journal of Business Venturing*, 20, 1: 137–64.

Reese, H. W. (2011) 'The learning-by-doing principle'. *Behavioral Development Bulletin*, 11: 1–19.

Ronstadt, R. (1988) 'The corridor principle'. *Journal of Business Venturing*, 3, 1: 31–40

Sagarin, R. (2014) 'Why we learn more from success than failure'. *Business Insider*, 30 June. http://www.businessinsider.com/we-learn-more-from-success-than-failure-2014-6?IR=T (accessed 4 November 2016).

Scherer, R. F., Adams, J. S., Carley, S. S., and Wiebe, F. A. (1989) 'Role model performance effects on development of entrepreneurial career preference'. *Entrepreneurship Theory and Practice*, 13, 3: 53–71.

Schön, D. A. (1983) *The Reflective Practitioner: How Professionals Think in Action*. New York: Basic Books.

School for Social Entrepreneurs (2016) *Company website*. https://www.the-sse.org (accessed 4 November 2016).

Schwab, K. (2016) *The Global Competitiveness Report 2015–2016*. World Economic Forum. http://reports.weforum.org/global-competitiveness-report-2015-2016/ (accessed 4 November 2016).

Sexton, D. (2014) 'Riverford at the Duke of Cambridge – restaurant review'. *Evening Standard*. http://www.standard.co.uk/goingout/restaurants/riverford-at-the-duke-of-cambridge-restaurant-review-9899759.html (accessed 4 November 2016).

Shane, S. (2000) 'Prior knowledge and the discovery of entrepreneurial opportunity'. *Organization Science*, 11: 448–69.

Shane, S. and Venkataraman, S. (2000) 'The promise of entrepreneurship as a field of research'. *Academy of Management Review*, 25, 1: 217–26.

Shepherd, D. A., Douglas, E. J., and Shanley, M. (2000) 'New venture survival: ignorance, external shocks, and risk reduction strategies'. *Journal of Business Venturing*, 15, 5/6, 393–410.

Souitaris V., Zerbinati, S., and Al-Laham, A. (2007) 'Do entrepreneurship programmes raise entrepreneurial intentions of science and engineering students?: the effects of learning, inspiration and resources'. *Journal of Business Venturing*, 22, 4: 566–91.

Starr, J. A. and Fondas, N. (1992) 'A model of entrepreneurial socialization and organization formation'. *Entrepreneurship Theory and Practice*, 17, 1: 67–76.

Sternberg, R. J. (2004). 'Successful intelligence as a basis for entrepreneurship'. *Journal of Business Venturing*, 19, 2: 189–201.

Stevenson, H. H. and Jarillo, J. C. (1990) 'A paradigm of entrepreneurship: entrepreneurial management'. *Strategic Management Journal*, 11 (Summer Special Issue), 17–27.

Stokes, A. (2001) 'Using telementoring to deliver training to SMEs: a pilot study'. *Education and Training*, 43, 6: 317–24.

Sugar, A. (2011) *What You See Is What You Get: My Autobiography*. Pan Macmillian, UK.

Sweetgreen (2016) 'Core values'. http://www.sweetgreen.com/our-story/ (accessed 12 November 2016).

The Duke of Cambridge (2016). *Company website*. http://dukeorganic.co.uk/ethical-business/ (accessed 4 November 2016).

The Startup Team (2013) *Duke of Cambridge: Geetie Singh*. http://startups.co.uk/duke-of-cambridge-geetie-singh/ (accessed 4 November 2016).

Thompson, C. (2016) *China Is No Longer a Nation of Tech Copycats*. Wired.co.uk, 20 March, http://www.wired.co.uk/magazine/archive/2016/04/features/china-tech-copycat-yy-meituan-xinchejian-zepp-labs (accessed 4 November 2016).

Venkataraman, S. (1997) 'The distinctive domain of entrepreneurship research'. In J. Katz and R. Brockhaus (eds), *Advances in Entrepreneurship, Firm Emergence, and Growth*. JAI Press, Greenwich, CT (119–38).

Virgin (2016) 'Entrepreneur: someone who jumps off a cliff and builds a plane on the way down'. https://www.virgin.com/richard-branson/entrepreneur-someone-who-jumps-off-a-cliff-and-builds-a-plane-on-the-way-down (accessed 4 November 2016).

von Mises, L. (1949) *Human Action: A Treatise on Economics*. New Haven: Yale University Press.

Voudouris, I., Dimitratos, P., and Salavou, H. (2011) 'Entrepreneurial learning in the international new high-technology venture'. *International Small Business Journal*, 29, 3: 238–58.

Wang, C. L. and Chugh, H. (2014) 'Entrepreneurial learning: past research and future challenges'. *International Journal of Management Reviews*, 16, 1: 24–61.

Wang, C. L., Rafiq, M., Li, X., and Zheng, Y. (2014) 'Entrepreneurial preparedness: an exploratory case study of Chinese private enterprises'. *International Journal of Entrepreneurial Behavior & Research*, 20, 4: 351–74.

Wang, C. L., Senaratne, C. and Rafiq, M. (2015) 'Success traps, dynamic capabilities and firm performance'. *British Journal of Management*, 26, 1: 26–44.

Weale, S. (2010). 'It was an amazing way to grow up'. *The Guardian*, 17 July. https://www.theguardian.com/lifeandstyle/2010/jul/17/geetie-singh-organic-pub-commune (accessed 4 November 2016).

Wiklund, J., Davidsson, P., and Delmar, F. (2003) 'What do they think and feel about growth?: an expectancy-value approach to small business managers' attitudes toward growth'. *Entrepreneurship Theory and Practice*, 27, 3: 247–70.

Yueh, L. (2008) 'China's entrepreneurs'. University of Oxford, Department of Economics, Discussion Paper No. 324. http://www.economics.ox.ac.uk/Research/wp/pdf/paper324.pdf (accessed 4 November 2016).

Zhang, J. and Hamilton, E. (2010) 'Entrepreneurship education for owner-managers: the process of trust building for an effective learning community'. *Journal of Small Business and Entrepreneurship*, 23, 2: 249–70.

GLOSSARY OF KEY CONCEPTS

Balance sheet statement a summary of the financial position of the business at a specific date, such as at a month end or the year end. It shows the balance between the assets, liabilities and ownership equity. The difference between assets and liabilities is net worth or net assets or, simply, equity. The net worth must equal assets minus liabilities and ownership equity.

Bootstrapping an informal term describing the way that entrepreneurs get a venture started by making the most of their own financial resources. It derives from the expression, 'pulling yourself up by your bootstraps'. See also: 'Bricolage' and 'Effectuation'.

Bricolage a sociological term that has been adopted by entrepreneurship researchers to describe an approach to venture creation that is based around improvisation and making the most of available resources, and is particularly relevant in situations where resources are tightly-constrained, including developing economies. See also: 'Effectuation'.

Business angels tend to be wealthy individuals who want to invest in high-growth businesses. They may also be part of a syndicate with other business angels. In addition to money, they often bring with them experience, skills and contacts. They will tend to look for opportunities in industries and sectors where they feel they have relevant experience.

Business models emerged during the 1990s as a way of understanding and comparing the plethora of new business ideas that developed around the Internet. They identify the key components, underlying assumptions and their relationships in order to make comparisons and to identify ideas that were unique or particularly robust. In essence, business models show how a venture is going to be able to generate revenues and to make a profit from its operations.

Cash flow forecast a financial statement that predicts the movement of cash into and out of an enterprise over a specified period such as weekly, monthly, or quarterly. In the early phases of most new ventures, there is usually a negative cash flow. It is calculated by using the balance sheet and profit and loss statements, together with predictions regarding significant variables such as interest rates, creditor and debtor days, stock holding, planned purchases and sales forecasts.

Clusters are geographic concentrations of firms and other organisations in particular locations. For example, the technology clusters in and around cities such as Minneapolis, Cambridge, and Munich. New clusters can often be a focus for intensive entrepreneurial activity, including a mixture of competition and collaboration. See also: 'Spatial variations' and 'Temporal variations'.

Creative construction a more recent variant on the term, 'creative destruction', which describes the way that entrepreneurial activity can facilitate knowledge spillovers that open up new opportunities for existing (or 'incumbent') businesses. See also: 'Creative destruction', 'Knowledge spillovers'.

Creative destruction a term coined by the twentieth-century scholar, Joseph Schumpeter, to refer to the way that entrepreneurial activity can lead to innovation and new business opportunities by undermining and subsequently displacing earlier business models, organisations and institutional structures. See also: 'Creative construction'.

Credit rationing this refers to the imbalance between demand for finance by start-up ventures and what is made available by banks and other finance providers. It has been seen as an example of a market failure, and may constrain entrepreneurial activity.

Customer relationship management (CRM) has emerged as a set of activities supported by technologies, which facilitate relationship marketing. CRM technologies support this important business process.

Effectuation theory is a perspective on the way that entrepreneurs may behave as they attempt to create a new venture, or engage in other forms of entrepreneurial activity. It suggests that rather than conducting an initial detailed analysis of the situation and select the best option, some entrepreneurs adopt more informal and improvised approaches. See also: 'Bricolage' and 'Bootstrapping'.

Electronic communication platforms support interactions between individuals and enterprises. New technologies, such as the Internet and 3G mobile networks, are constantly emerging and having an impact on markets and industries by creating opportunities.

Enterprise culture this refers to a late-twentieth-century political project or initiative designed to encourage an increase in independent entrepreneurial activity and a corresponding decrease in the role of the state in regulating and intervening in the economy. Initially associated with neo-liberal governments in the UK and USA, the enterprise culture has since developed in many other countries around the world.

Enterprise is an alternative term for an organisation or firm, which is engaged in economic activities for financial or social gain. See also: 'Enterprise culture', 'Social enterprise' and 'Small and medium-sized enterprise (SME)'.

Enterprise policies this is a general term that describes a wide range of initiatives to promote and guide entrepreneurial activity. These initiatives have been implemented by governments and public agencies at a local, national and international level. They may be reinforce (or undermined) by other public policy initiatives. Examples include: investments in higher education spending or changes to international trade regulations. See also: 'SME policies' and 'Entrepreneurship policies'.

Entrepreneurial activity is enterprising human action in pursuit of the generation of economic and social value through the creation or expansion of economic activity, by identifying and exploiting new opportunities for new products, processes or markets, and by meeting outstanding social and environmental needs.

Entrepreneurial characteristics or 'traits' comprise a number of psychological concepts that have been associated with a person's entrepreneurial capabilities or potential, such as need for achievement, over-optimism, risk-taking propensity, desire for autonomy. Though still popular and widely used, the idea of defining characteristics has been challenged by more recent psychological and behavioural research. See also: 'Entrepreneurial cognition' and 'Entrepreneurial creativity'.

Entrepreneurial cognition is a research field that examines how people think, and the role that ways of thinking might play in entrepreneurial processes. For example, one major theme asks why entrepreneurs appear to be more 'alert' to opportunities than other people. See also: 'Entrepreneurial creativity' and 'self-efficacy'.

Entrepreneurial creativity is largely associated with the capacity of entrepreneurs and others to generate or invent new business ideas, involving new products, processes, services or markets. For many reasons the vast majority of these ideas are not developed beyond a conceptual stage. The attrition rate is very high but without creativity there is no innovation and without innovation there are no entrepreneurial opportunities. See also: 'Entrepreneurial cognition'.

Entrepreneurial economy is a term used to refer to a market-based economic system in which there is less reliance on the public sector and greater emphasis placed on entrepreneurial activity, which may involve both commercial and social enterprises. The term is also used to refer to an economy with a thriving population of smaller entrepreneurial firms (i.e. the economy is not dominated by large corporations). See also: 'Enterprise culture'.

Entrepreneurial learning is a type of learning that takes place as individuals participate in the entrepreneurial process. Entrepreneurs can often learn from their direct experience, including their active roles in creating and developing ventures. However, they can also learn from others, including their peers, role models, and mentors, and through formal learning in schools, colleges, and universities.

Entrepreneurial opportunities are a particular type of opportunity, which could lead to the creation of self-sustaining ventures. The process is complex, and is closely related to creativity and innovation. They often arise because some people have access to potentially valuable concrete knowledge, which is not available to others.

Entrepreneurial process describes a sequence of activities from idea generation and opportunity recognition up to the point where an opportunity is exploited, or converted into a real venture. It is possible to distinguish the generation of new business ideas (i.e. creativity and innovation) from the recognition of opportunities with the potential for exploitation (i.e. evaluation and selection). However, in practice, there is usually a lot of interplay and iteration between these activities.

Entrepreneurial teams are people who come together to engage in some form of entrepreneurial activity, such as creating a new venture. Entrepreneurs rarely work in isolation, so if a new venture is to be successful, it is essential to consider both the composition of the founding entrepreneurial team, the role(s) that each team member is going to play, and how the team needs to develop once the venture begins to grow.

Entrepreneurial thinking is a mindset that is opportunity focused and draws on creative and innovative ideas to recognise and develop solutions as well as obtain the resources required to exploit or implement them. It is increasingly seen as a desirable skill in a wide range of organisations.

Entrepreneurs are people who seek to generate economic and social value through the creation or expansion of economic activity, by identifying and exploiting opportunities for new products, processes, markets, and for meeting outstanding social and environmental needs.

Entrepreneurship is the phenomenon associated with entrepreneurial activity. It involves a complex pattern of social interactions that extends beyond individual entrepreneurs to incorporate teams, organisations, networks and institutions. It is often associated with new venture creation but can occur throughout the life of an organisation. See also: 'Intrapreneurship'.

Entrepreneurship policies are usually concerned with promoting entrepreneurial activity over the longer term. They may include initiatives designed to promote new start-up ventures in particular high-tech sectors, such as biosciences or low-carbon industries, and others designed to enhance the growth and economic performance of existing organisations. See also: 'Enterprise policies' and 'SME policies'.

Equity or owner's equity is the difference between the total assets and total liabilities. The ownership equity includes the share capital and retained profit or loss. In a new commercial venture, the founding directors are normally shareholders. For potential investors, this shareholding may be seen as indicating the founders' level of commitment to the venture.

Evolutionary economics is primarily concerned with the ways that economic systems change over time through the processes of selection, retention and variation (or creativity). Entrepreneurs influence the process in various ways, creating what Joseph Schumpeter termed, 'new combinations'. See also: 'Neo-classical economics', 'Neo-Austrian economics'.

Extended enterprise recognises that for many new ventures interaction with external organisations is at the core of their activities. The ability to develop, facilitate, and manage these interactions is a critical ability. These entrepreneurial and commercial networks are often enabled by electronic communications platforms.

Flotation is the offering of shares on a public trading platform, such as the Alternative Investment Market (AIM) or NASDAQ. It involves an initial public listing (IPO), which results in increase investment and a subsequent opportunity for shareholders to trade shares for personal gain.

Founders, family, and friends (3Fs) are the initial funders of new ventures who typically play a vital, though often unrecognised, part in new venture creation. This initial investment is often supported by burrowing, which might be secure on a property or by a personal guarantee. 3Fs can also refer to 'family, friends and fools'!

Historical research on entrepreneurship examines the causes and consequences of entrepreneurial activity over extended periods. It ranges from biographies and organisational histories to studies that examine the rise and fall of particular industries and regions. See also: 'Temporal variations'.

Industries (or industrial sectors) are made up of individual organisations and inter-organisational networks that supply particular categories of products or services to customers, usually in competition with others. The terminology of industries and industry sectors normally refers to commercial enterprises, but can also be applied to social enterprises. Many of these organisations also operate in competition, and sometimes in collaboration, with public and private sector counterparts.

Innovation is a process that takes various forms. For example, it may involve the introduction of new products, services, processes, markets, ways of working, or wider social practices (i.e. 'social innovation'). There is a close connection between innovation and entrepreneurial activity. For example, entrepreneurs may be involved in promoting a technological innovation and in exploiting new opportunities that the technology creates.

Interdisciplinary research combines specialist knowledge, methods and theoretical frameworks or two or more disciplines. Related terms include 'neo-disciplinary' and 'trans-disciplinary' research. Researchers from different disciplinary backgrounds often find it useful to collaborate in order to tackle complex social phenomena such as entrepreneurship.

Intrapreneurship is a term used to refer to entrepreneurial initiatives that take place within larger and more established organisations in the private, public and voluntary sectors. These activities are also described as, 'corporate entrepreneurship'.

Key performance indicators (KPIs) are produced in addition to the normal financial statements. They are based on critical information and can give an indication of how well (or not) an organisation is performing in particular areas of its activities. Typically these indicators have been identified by the organisation as playing a vital role in achieving specific short- or medium-term organisational goals.

Knowledge spillover is an economic term describing the way that new ideas and innovations created by scientists and other technical specialists becomes more widely available, creating new opportunities for entrepreneurs. Economists also use the broader term 'positive externality' to describe this kind of outcome.

Market segmentation is a technique of grouping customers that are sufficiently similar yet different to be characterised homogeneously. These segments need to be accessible and large enough to be profitable. Entrepreneurial marketing tends to recognise the importance of customer needs rather than simply their characteristics.

Marketing mix is a traditional and popular framework that can be used to consider the market positioning of products and services. Originally consisting of four elements (4Ps): (1) Product; (2) Price; (3) Place; (4) Promotion, it has expended into 7Ps to include: (5) People, (6) Processes; (7) Physical evidence.

Markets are made up of customers and potential customers, which are sometimes divided up into segments, comprising product and customers that share common characteristics. Marketers often distinguish between 'business to consumer' (B2C) and 'business to business' (B2B) markets.

Multidisciplinary research draws on two or more academic disciplines such as economics, geography, and sociology. It is sometimes distinguished from 'interdisciplinary' research, where specialist knowledge, methods, and theoretical frameworks are actively combined.

Multi-level research studies involve more than one level of analysis, such as entrepreneurial individuals, teams, organisations, and networks. Entrepreneurship researchers are frequently encouraged to adopt more multi-level approaches though it can prove difficult to achieve in practice.

Neo-Austrian economics challenged the assumptions of earlier neo-classical economists and emphasised the distinctive economic function performed by entrepreneurs.

In doing so, they also drew attention to the 'practical knowledge' of entrepreneurs. See also: 'Evolutionary economics', 'Neo-classical economics'.

Neo-classical economics became highly influential from the late nineteenth century and tended to exclude the entrepreneur from economic analysis, despite some important exceptions. See also: 'Evolutionary economics', 'Neo-Austrian economics'..

New growth theory is an economic theory developed in the late twentieth century. It recognises the important role played by technological innovation and associated 'knowledge spillovers' in promoting economic growth. It is sometimes described as 'endogenous growth theory'. See also: 'Knowledge spillovers'.

Opportunity business models is a technique adopted in this book to help readers to understand the dimensions and drivers for a business idea in order to decide whether there is a genuine entrepreneurial opportunity that can be exploited. It is also a way of shaping a vision, and can be compared to entrepreneurs drafting a traditional business plan or expressing their 'gut feeling'. It describes both the key dimensions (Proposition, People, Place, Process, Profit) and the key drivers (Societal, Commercial, Legal, Technological) that enable and underpin new entrepreneurial opportunities. See also: 'Business models'.

Practical knowledge, refers to the kind of specialised local knowledge that an entrepreneur might use on a day-to-day basis. Other closely related terms include 'local knowledge' and 'concrete knowledge'. It can be contrasted with the 'scientific knowledge' created and used by researchers. See also: 'Scientific knowledge'.

Profit and loss statement (P&L) indicates the relationship between sales (revenue or turnover), cost of sales, gross profit, operating expenses, interest, tax and net profit for a specific period (i.e. per month, quarter or year). This is vital management information for directors, shareholders, and staff and needs to be produced in a timely nature. In other words, quickly enough after a period end so that decisions can be taken to maintain or improve the trading position.

Scientific knowledge refers to the kind of knowledge used by academic researchers, including economists, sociologists, and historians, when they are examining particular aspects of entrepreneurship. It can be contrasted with the 'practical knowledge' created and used by individual entrepreneurs. See also: 'Practical knowledge'.

Self-efficacy refers to a person's belief in their own capacity to achieve a specific outcome, such as setting up a new venture, and is thought to be an important influence on behaviour. An entrepreneur's perception of self-efficacy may differ depending on circumstances, and can also vary over time. See also: 'Entrepreneurial characteristics' and 'Entrepreneurial cognition'.

Small and medium-sized enterprises (SMEs) are categorised in various ways. In the European Union they are defined as firms with fewer than 250 employees, annual turnover of less than €50 million or total assets less than €43 million, and not more than 25% owned by a corporation. Simpler definitions refer to firms employing less than 250 people. In the EU, small enterprises have less than 50 employees and micro-enterprises less than 10. These definitions vary around the world. For example, in the United States, small to medium-sized businesses (SMBs) employ less than 500 people and small businesses less than 100.

SME policies are usually concerned with improving the short- to medium-term performance of existing firms in this size category. They may focus on particular sectors such as tourism or house building, or particular geographic regions. The policies may be enacted using a variety of initiatives, including: simplifying regulations, reducing taxes, providing information or offering training schemes. See also: 'Enterprise policies' and 'Entrepreneurship policies'.

Social enterprises (or 'social ventures') are trading organisations that primarily serve a social purpose, which may be expressed formally in a mission statement. They can take a variety of legal forms, including cooperative, a limited company and a community interest company (CIC). 'For profit' enterprises and entrepreneurs may also deliver social benefits but this is normally a secondary purpose.

Spatial variations in enterprise refer to differences in the quantity and type of entrepreneurial activity found in different geographical locations. These differences can be identified at various levels, such as between regions within a country and between different countries. See also: 'Clusters' and 'Temporal variations'.

Temporal variations in enterprise refer to changes in the quantity and type of entrepreneurial activity taking place over time. For example, researchers have shown similar patterns in the birth of new industries, with many new entrants in the early years, followed by consolidation. It is also possible to identify variations in the life of a particular organisation or individual. See also: 'Spatial variations'.

Venture capitalists are a source of private equity capital but they usually manage larger funds than syndicates of business angels. They are also more likely to look for an exit through an initial public listing (IPO) or trade sale to a larger company.

INDEX